human development
and learning

human development
and learning

HUGH V. PERKINS

Institute for Child Study
University of Maryland

Wadsworth Publishing Company, Inc.
Belmont, California

Third printing: October 1969

HUMAN DEVELOPMENT AND LEARNING
BY HUGH V. PERKINS

L. C. Cat. Card No.: 69–14212

Printed in the United States of America
by American Book–Stratford Press, Inc.

To Cynthia

preface

This book brings together material that usually appears in separate books on child development, child psychology, adolescent psychology, educational psychology, and psychology of learning. It is designed to be used as a text in teacher-education courses which focus upon the psychological foundations of education. It also speaks to the needs and interests of parents, counselors, community workers, and others who seek a deeper understanding of the growth, development, learning, and becoming of children and youth.

Unlike many books on child or adolescent psychology, which are organized according to stages of development, this book focuses upon the processes of development and learning—physical, affectional, cultural, peer group, self-developmental, and self-adjustive—and the interrelationships among these processes. This integration of the concepts of human development and learning is a major feature of the book; for although these two areas of knowledge have, in the past, been taught as separate subjects, the successful teacher continuously interrelates his knowledge of human development with principles of learning. The extensive use of case-record materials in this book further clarifies this interrelationship.

The book is organized into five parts. Part One describes the needs, analyzes the procedures, and discusses the principles of motivation. Procedures for collecting and analyzing case-record information on individual students are described and illustrated.

Part Two presents in separate chapters each of the processes that shape development and learning. These process areas identify the range of concepts and principles of human growth and development that one must understand in order to achieve a valid understanding of another human being.

Part Three examines the outcomes of human development and learning as these are manifested in the emerging individual. This emerging individual is described in relation to the developmental tasks he encounters at successive stages of childhood and adolescence.

Part Four focuses on learning and the educative process. The nature of learning and the representative theories of learning are examined briefly, and each of the major outcomes of learning—cognitive, psychomotor, and affective—are described and illustrated. In a discussion of the factors (maturation, intellectual development, and experience) which facilitate or impede readiness for learning, particular emphasis is given to the problems of development and learning for culturally disadvantaged children and youth.

Part Five analyzes the task of the teacher in organizing and applying his knowledge of human behavior so as to facilitate the development and learning of students. Organization of the classroom for learning, selection of instructional methods and patterns of organization, and evaluation of development and learning are discussed. Two types of students who need special help, the emotionally disturbed and the underachiever, are identified and described.

The book concludes with the presentation of a model of effective teaching which emphasizes the need for the teacher to know, to understand, and to accept himself as well as his students.

I wish to express a special note of appreciation to Dr. Daniel A. Prescott, Director Emeritus of the Institute for Child Study, University of Maryland, for introducing me to the study of children and youth and for providing his understanding, support, and encouragement over a period of more than two decades. I am indebted also to Dr. H. Gerthon Morgan, Director of the Institute for Child Study, and to my colleagues, the staff of the Institute, for the contributions each has made to my knowledge of human development and learning. Special thanks, too, is extended to Dr. Walter B. Waetjen, who made many valuable suggestions regarding the organization and content of the book. The responsibility for the specific content of the book is, of course, my own.

Finally, I wish to express my appreciation to Dr. Herman D. Behrens of Ohio Northern University, Dr. Meryl E. Englander of Indiana University, and Dr. William W. Wattenberg of Wayne State University, for their many helpful suggestions in their critiques of the manuscript, and to Dorothy Ohliger and Jon Emerson of Wadsworth Publishing Company, for their care and diligence in the final editing of the manuscript.

I gratefully acknowledge the permission granted by the following persons to reproduce material from unpublished case records: Virginia Creed, Dorothy H. Denick, Mollie Joyce, Orva Leta Ledbetter, Madelaine Mershon, Lucile S. Mooney, Dorothy V. Nichols, Evelyn P. Reed, Hannah Sessions, Herbert R. Stolz, Martha E. Thompson, and L. Idella Watts.

The poem "Outwitted," by Edwin Markham, is quoted by permission of Virgil Markham.

HUGH V. PERKINS

contents

*understanding human
behavior*

1

the need to understand human behavior

Human history becomes more and more a race between education and catastrophe.

≡   H. G. WELLS

The greatest resources of any nation or society are its human resources. A nation is rich or poor to the degree that its freedoms and its institutions enable each individual to become all that he is capable of being. This book describes the forces that contribute to the growth, development, learning, and becoming of people. With an understanding of these forces, parents, educators, and other concerned adults can better understand human behavior and thus can make decisions that will facilitate the development and learning of the child and the adolescent.

Traditionally, parents have been almost solely responsible for the development of the child in his critical early years—the period when important steps in physical development are taken and the bases for future emotional health and mental development are established. However, the family has become a declining influence in the promotion of mental health and development. Although its members may live under the same roof, today's family is becoming dispersed—its members drawn out of the home by little

3

league, scouts, teen-age clubs, cars belonging to youth, job opportunities for the wife, and demands on the time of the father. The consequent lack of communication within the family, as well as the stresses produced when the family is poor or when the parents themselves have emotional problems, often contributes to breakdowns in human understanding and consequent separations or divorces. About one fourth of the marriages recorded each year end in divorce,[1] and this rate is going up. Even more disturbing in its implications for human understanding and human development is the rising incidence of offenses by family members against each other. In the total population these crimes are small in number, but they are symptoms of a lack of human understanding within family life.

The schools too are losing sight of the individual's needs and problems. Despite their expanding counseling, special education, and pupil personnel services, their increasingly cumbersome administrative techniques and procedures often inhibit human understanding between and among administrators, teachers, and pupils. With the development of elaborate procedures for grouping, grading, and passing or failing students, the individual is often neglected and sometimes even demeaned. A student's experiences in school are valued only if they lead him to a passing grade—not for what they contribute to broadening his development and clarifying his purposes.[2] This larger purpose of education is particularly well expressed by Peck and Prescott :[3]

> In the competition between the democratic and totalitarian powers for the minds and hearts of men, it is undeniably true that the scientific and material accomplishments of the two societies will be compared. Therefore, we must stress competition and achievement. But there is more to the image of America that we want to project into the world. It is the image of a society where the individual values himself and other people, is generous, spontaneous, loving, autonomous, who, in a sentence, is in the process of realizing his human potential in creative and compassionate interaction with his fellow beings in the world culture. This is the image of America which will win the world, and it is the task of American education, in conjunction with other institutions such as home, church, and including our factories, offices, etc., to create the conditions under which such individuals may emerge.

In addition to the family and the schools, human understanding often is lacking in the community as a whole. Personal frustration and social unrest

---

[1] *The World Almanac and Book of Facts, 1968* (Cleveland: Newspaper Enterprise Association, 1968), pp. 893–894.

[2] Oscar Handlin, "Are the Colleges Killing Education?" *Atlantic*, 209 (May 1962), 41–45.

[3] Bernard Peck and Daniel A. Prescott, "The Program at the Institute for Child Study, The University of Maryland," *Personnel and Guidance Journal*, 37 (October 1958), 115–122. Quoted by permission.

within communities are reflected in rising crime rates and numbers of juvenile offenders, in increases in alcoholism, and in the high incidence of mental illness. This deficiency in human understanding is also revealed in our numerous labor-management disputes—strikes involving more than a million workers, hundreds of millions of dollars in lost wages, and even greater losses to corporations in lost production.

Finally, if peace is to be secure, human understanding must permeate deeply into the largest community of all—the world community. Here too, although the United Nations provides a forum for increasing human understanding between nations through discussions and debate, complete understanding among nations has not yet been achieved.

The preceding discussion strongly supports the conclusion that human understanding, undergirded by acceptance of and compassion for others, is a need second only to the physical needs of life itself. Indeed, without this understanding the physical processes themselves have been known to fail.[4]

The Teacher's Need to Understand

The public's conception of the role of the teacher has changed greatly in recent years. Few thoughtful persons today subscribe to the once popular stereotype that a teacher does little more than assign work, listen to recitations, and give and grade a few tests; and it is no longer assumed that anyone who knows his subject well can teach it. If telling or showing were all there is to education, we wouldn't need teachers. We could simply give students some books and equipment and let them learn things by themselves.

But in some very important respects students cannot make satisfactory progress by themselves. Each child and each adolescent needs help if he is to realize his potential in all aspects of his development. Specific subject matter and skills are important to the degree that they contribute to the overall integrated development of the individual. The task of the teacher, then, is to help each student realize his optimum development, thus enabling him to help others and to enrich the world in which he lives.

What kinds of teachers do we need to perform this task? When we discuss the nature and processes of learning in later chapters, we will find that *teaching is primarily a matter of relating to people.* Teaching is most effective when the teacher offers resources and understanding in a helping relationship with each student. Though the teacher is called upon to be many persons and to do many kinds of things, the essence of teaching is the ability to relate to the learner and his problems. The effectiveness of the teacher's helping relationship with his students depends in great measure upon his knowledge of the general characteristics of growth and development at his students' maturity level. It depends further upon his understanding each

[4] Margaret A. Ribble, *The Rights of Infants* (New York: Columbia University Press, 1943).

student *as an individual*. This kind of understanding is especially difficult to achieve when enrollments are climbing and when more and more is being expected of teachers.

How does the student reveal his need for help, and how can the teacher use these cues to increase his general knowledge of human behavior and development and his understanding of this particular individual? The following summaries of case records on three students provide partial answers to the first part of the question. Materials in later chapters provide help with the second part of the question.

DICKY

Dicky—a shy, small, round-faced, roly-poly youngster in first grade— had had his sixth birthday just prior to the opening of school in September. Dicky's father is a successful lawyer and prominent in civic affairs. The family, which includes four children, lives in a large ranch-style home in a new community with large yards and many trees and shrubs. Mrs. Agar, the first-grade teacher, greeted Dicky warmly on the first day of school and recalled what fine students the other Lawrence children had been during previous years in her classroom.

Many weeks were spent in reading-readiness activities and with experience charts before more formal reading was begun. It was soon evident that Dicky was not learning to recognize words as quickly and as easily as his sisters had. Mrs. Agar started him in the middle group, but even there the pace was too fast and he was moved to a lower group. She tried to help and to encourage Dicky in his reading but was met by a lack of response and by vacant stares into space. Mrs. Agar did not understand how a child whose parents are college graduates and prominent in the community could be having so much difficulty in reading. She was deeply troubled and wondered how she could possibly recommend him for promotion at the end of the year. Perhaps, she thought, it would help if the school and home would bear down a little harder.

An interview with the mother revealed that Dicky had been slow in learning to walk and talk. He had no boys his age at home to play with, and during much of his early life he had been left with a maid or baby sitter.

HANK

Hank was the despair of his ninth-grade teachers. Since the third grade his scores on intelligence tests consistently resulted in intelligence quotients of between 130 and 140. Yet, except for shop and physical education, his school marks were all *C*'s and *D*'s. Hank was a ham radio operator. His teachers reported that he would sit in class drawing circuits for a radio transmitter, receiver, or amplifier. At other times, he and two other boys would discuss plans for "souping up" the second-hand Ford which the three had jointly purchased. At still other times, Hank stared into space, did not participate in class discussions, and failed to complete any of his assignments. Once during a unit on communication he gave an outstanding report complete with drawings and models showing how radio and television receivers work; but then, when the class moved on to a study of government, he slipped back into the previous behavior pattern.

Hank had had numerous conferences with his teachers, principal, and guidance counselor. A statement frequently made by one of these to Hank was "Hank, you have the ability to be an excellent student. All you have to do is apply yourself. You'll never get into college unless you pull those grades up." Hank shrugged his shoulders and mumbled, "I am doing the best I can."

A conference with the father was requested by the guidance counselor. Mr. Harding, Hank's father, was a very successful businessman who owned the most lucrative auto dealership in town. He reported that he had been forced to quit school at the end of the eighth grade. Although he did not believe his limited education had handicapped him at all, he recognized that "a fellow needs more education today if he really wants to get ahead." However, Mr. Harding felt that the schools were not providing the "right kind" of education—the "right kind" being an education in practical and useful skills. He said, "Why, I hired a young college graduate to run my office, and I have had to train him from scratch."

MARY ELLEN

All of her teachers held sixteen-year-old Mary Ellen in high esteem. She was quiet and reserved and did not talk and giggle as did most of the girls in the class. Her work was done neatly and on time, and she consistently made high grades on tests. A frequent comment made by her teachers was "I wish I had a whole class of Mary Ellens."

Mrs. Rodgers, Mary Ellen's chemistry teacher, noted that she seemed eager to please. She would offer to stay after school to help the teacher set up and take down lab equipment used for demonstrations. Mrs. Rodgers also noted that Mary Ellen came and left class alone. Other students seemed to respect her ability, but they had little to say to her. Mary Ellen was frequently seen at the edge of a group of students but never as a part of the group. Even Mrs. Rodgers was unable to get very close to her.

During her senior year Mary Ellen earned further academic honors, including a coveted four-year scholarship to a nearby university. At the same time, she became even further withdrawn. Although her written work continued to be excellent, she communicated less and less with fellow students and also less with teachers with whom she had been quite friendly.

The climax came in the spring of her senior year in high school, about the time that the divorce of Mary Ellen's parents was announced in the papers. A week later Mary Ellen disappeared and could not be located by her parents or the police. Six weeks later she was found in Arizona, working but suffering from amnesia. By the following September, when her classmates were preparing to enter college, Mary Ellen was still hospitalized.

In each of the preceding case examples the teachers, in spite of considerable formal training and experience, were unable to provide the help that Dicky, Hank, and Mary Ellen needed. Dicky revealed a serious lack of readiness for the kinds of tasks expected of first graders. Hank's underachievement in school subjects baffled his teachers, and they increased the pressures on him by giving him poor grades and exhorting him to greater efforts. Mrs. Rodgers apparently had an inkling that all was not well with Mary Ellen, but even she was unprepared for Mary Ellen's eventual disappearance.

These teachers perhaps were unable to help Dicky, Hank, and Mary Ellen for two reasons. (1) Somehow their education and experience had not given them sufficient *sensitivity* to and *understanding* of human behavior. They were unable to interpret certain acts as flashing signals of the need for help and action. They were not even aware that additional information was urgently needed before they could make an adequate diagnosis of each problem. (2) Because of their lack of understanding, these teachers could not *take appropriate action* and therefore took inappropriate action or no action at all.

The Nature of Human Nature

Before one can learn to understand and help others in their development and learning, he must have a conception of what human beings are like. And, he will soon discover, there is no single generally accepted concept of human nature but instead a great many different conceptions. Some compare the newborn infant to a blank slate; his growth and development, his learning and becoming, is a life story recorded on this slate. Human development, in this view of human nature, is a process of unfolding. Freud's dynamic psychology, however, presents quite a different conception of human nature: Man is a composite of sometimes conflicting internal and external forces, which he seeks to reconcile as he adjusts to his environment. Still others conceive of the human being as a series of relatively discrete age or maturity levels, with specific norms and behavior associated with each age or maturity level.

Any conception of human nature we choose will determine what we expect from children and the approaches we employ in helping them to develop and to learn. In this book we view the human being as a dynamic, evolving complex of three interrelated and interacting forces: *organism, culture,* and *self*. Only the most fundamental aspects of this conception of human nature are discussed here, since subsequent chapters examine each of these forces in greater detail. Although we will consider these three aspects separately, they do not, of course, function separately; *the human being functions and responds as a whole.*

The Human Being as a Physical Organism

Man as a physical being has a particular place in the biological ordering of animal life. As a member of the Chordata phylum he shares with other animals of that group a highly complex tissue and organ differentiation and highly developed bilateral symmetry. As a vertebrate he possesses a jointed backbone. As a mammal he provides special care of his young before birth, maintains a high level of activity, maintains stability and flexibility of the skeleton during growth, and utilizes food efficiently. His differentiated brain, large in relation to body size, marks him as a primate. Finally, his advanced brain and nervous system enable him to develop qualities of intelligence, flexibility, and sociableness to a much higher degree than other animal forms can. These characteristics identify man as the only member of the classification *Homo sapiens*.

Man is highly sensitive to changes in his environment. This sensitivity is manifested in tissue irritability, which increases when the organism is stimulated by internal or external changes. The body seems to require and to seek stimulation of various kinds in order to reduce its irritability and disequilibrium. A child can hardly be expected to sit still in school for any extended period of time, since maintaining arms, legs, and trunk in the same position creates tensions which soon become painful. On the other hand, the child whose arms and legs ache from the fatigue of hard play seeks a change of stimulation that is provided in reading, resting, listening to a story, listening to music or working on a puzzle. This tendency to seek stimulation seems to relate to another human quality, curiosity—the curiosity of boys exploring caves or wading in creeks, of girls trying on a new dress or a new hat, and of men going big-game hunting and traveling into space.

The organism, then, seeks change—imbalance and discontentment; at the same time, it seeks stability—balance and contentment. This condition is a fundamental paradox of organic life. The child seeks contentment and rest after an exciting game or movie. Too much contentment or inactivity produces discontentment, which activates a drive for new or added stimulation. Stimulation, change, and some imbalance are needed if the individual is to reach out and to achieve progressive steps in development. As a new development level is reached, adjustment processes serve to return the individual to equilibrium; but, soon, further stimulation and change signal a movement toward further development. The alternating contentments and discontentments are the reflection of the alternating tides of human activity: development and adjustment. In short, the human being can gain satisfaction only if he has previously experienced dissatisfaction.

Tissue irritability and the tendencies to seek stimulation and at the same time to achieve a degree of internal stability are physical characteristics that have far-reaching implications for human development and learning. These processes provide us with a partial understanding of the physical basis for *motivation*—why people behave as they do.

The Human Being as a Social Organism

Man's existence has no meaning apart from his interactions and relationships with other men. The human infant is more helpless and matures more slowly than any other animal. The young child is dependent on other persons for love, care, and nurturance. In maturing, the child not only grows and develops physically in response to his genetic endowment; he also comes to behave and to develop like those human beings with whom he lives and associates. These significant other persons serve as models for the child's patterning of his own feeling, thinking, and behaving.

Man has a lifelong need to belong—to be loved, wanted, and accepted. When these needs are in large measure satisfied, the individual has a secure underpinning that enables him to move toward development and greater independence. Maturing is accompanied by growth away from dependency on others toward greater independence. A maturing adolescent becomes less dependent when his parents refrain from telling him what he should wear, whom he should have as friends, and what time he should be home. In this sense he is less dependent on his family, but he will never be completely independent of the need for people who will care for and love him. Every human being needs the love and support of family and friends, especially in times of stress.

The Human Being as a Psychological Organism

Man's large, well-differentiated brain provides him with the possibilities for developing an intelligence far exceeding that of any other living thing. Man is extremely complex at all levels, physical and psychological; but the complexity is most startling and impressive on the psychological level. Man's brain and nervous system have frequently been compared to electronic computers; and, indeed, computer models have been developed for the study of the functioning of the brain and nervous system. When we learn that in a matter of seconds high-speed computers compute answers to complex mathematical problems which would take a human mathematician months or years to compute, we may be tempted to conclude that a large computer is more complex than the human brain. Admittedly, the computer can transmit information more rapidly and does have a larger memory-storage capacity; but it lacks the capacities for growth, self-repair, and reproduction that are characteristic of man. Therefore, in spite of the computer's superiority over man in the computation of difficult problems, it remains a very crude mechanism when compared with the human brain.

The brain and the nervous system, consisting of roughly ten billion neurons, form a fantastically complicated system. As many as ten thousand neurons connect with a single nerve cell, and the branches of one neuron may connect with thousands of others. The total number of nerve circuits that could be activated in the human nervous system is vastly greater than the number of particles in the universe. Even the smallest elements of the nervous system are so complex that something like an eighth-order differential equation would be needed to describe one neuron's behavior.

The marvelous coordination of this system makes possible an almost limitless number and variety of human responses. Because of this potentiality for variation of response, the human organism is better equipped than other organisms to adjust both to its present environment and to the unknown and unpredictable environment of the future. That is, man is endowed with flexibility—which enables him, more than any other living thing, not only to survive but also to develop and flourish in a wide variety of environments.

The complex psychological qualities of human behavior are most dramatically revealed in the human being's potentialities for symbolizing the meanings of his experience through the use of language. With this symbolization of meanings, the possibilities for variability of response are enormously increased. Symbols may be stored in memory, they may be used to communicate meanings to others, and they may be manipulated so as to capture higher-level meanings through the cognitive processes of thinking, reasoning, and problem solving.

Basic Assumptions Underlying the Study of Human Behavior

The preceding discussion makes it abundantly clear that the task of understanding human behavior is awesome. However, it is certainly not hopeless. Understanding human behavior is not something we need to leave completely to the "head shrinkers." In fact, for more than twenty-five years teachers have been gaining increased insights into human behavior, development, and learning by participating in in-service child-study programs.[5]

Each of us has both the need and the ability to understand better those with whom he lives and works. Before we begin this task, let us examine some basic assumptions underlying our study of human behavior.[6]

1. *Every human being is inherently valuable.* The assumption that every human being has worth and dignity is of first importance. Without it, there is the very real danger that skills in human understanding might be used to exploit or even to destroy human beings. The sophistication of the Communists' brainwashing techniques suggests that they are well advanced in their understanding of human behavior. In benign but exploitative ways,

---

[5] Richard M. Brandt and Hugh V. Perkins, "Research Evaluating a Child Study Program," *Monographs of the Society for Research in Child Development*, 21 (1956), 62.

[6] These assumptions are adapted from Daniel A. Prescott, *The Child in the Educative Process* (New York: McGraw-Hill Book Co., 1957), pp. 26–50. Used by permission.

some advertisers also use a shrewd understanding of human behavior to entice the unwary consumer into purchasing products that he does not need and cannot use, and that may even be harmful. Thus, this assumption of human worth cannot be naïvely taken for granted. It must be continuously reiterated, in word and deed, by those who seek to understand and to help others.

Accepting every human being as valuable is a very high ideal that most persons find difficult to live up to completely. We find it especially difficult to accept those whom we do not like or trust or those who reject us. But this assumption of human worth does not deny us the right to choose our friends or to hold some persons in higher esteem than others. It simply means that we grant everyone the right and the opportunity for human realization.

Our task in living up to this assumption is to strive genuinely and consciously to be more accepting in all of our human associations. The parent or teacher has taken great strides toward human acceptance when his acceptance and value of Freddy as a person remains unchanged even though Freddy's behavior is very unacceptable. This distinction between the person and his behavior is a crucial one. The person has value and is worthy of acceptance because of his potentialities for fulfillment as a human being. His antisocial behavior is merely a symptom and a reaction to the stresses involved in growing up. If this were not so, how would we explain the many despaired-of boys and unlovely girls who grow up into fine human beings?

2. *Every individual is unique.* The assumption that each person is unique is well documented by scientific evidence. Geneticists have demonstrated each individual's unique genetic inheritance; in addition, each individual has developed his own pattern of thinking and behaving as a result of his own unique experiences. However, although this assumption of the uniqueness of each individual is generally accepted intellectually, a great many people still act as if everyone were pretty much alike. Parents expect their child to be just as athletic, just as popular, or just as smart as the kid down the street. Teachers seem to expect all students to be much the same in intelligence, readiness, and motivation for learning and are unable to deal with the student who deviates from the norm—in either direction. Our commitment to mass education has made it difficult for teachers to be truly responsive to human differences or to treat students as unique individuals.

Failure to realize the uniqueness of the human individual frequently leads to grave errors in interpretations of behavior. A person may or may not play golf just because others of his group play; he may play because he is challenged by the demands and pleasures of the game itself. Moreover, we make a serious mistake when we automatically assume that two persons with the same behavioral symptoms behave that way for the same reason. Because each person is different, we must seek to understand each individual by analyzing what we know about him (from case records or other data), using those principles of human behavior, development, and learning which apply to his case or situation.

If we are to facilitate the optimum development and learning of each person, we must respond to him as a unique individual. Too often, uniqueness and creativity are crushed by demands for conformity. School programs which encourage growth, openness, and expression of individuality must be developed and expanded if our needs for imaginative, divergent, and creative individuals are to be met.

3. *Behavior is caused. The causes are multiple, complex, and interrelated.* This assumption, an application of the principle of causal relationships to the behavioral and social sciences, has strong scientific support in the physical and biological sciences from which it is taken. Just as there is a cause-effect relationship between heating a liquid and producing a gas, so there is a causal relationship between the stimuli people receive and their responses to those stimuli. The task of the behavioral scientist in achieving an understanding of human behavior is more difficult than the natural scientist's search for an understanding of physical phenomena because the causes of human behavior are infinitely more complex.

Once the individual fully accepts and acts upon the assumption that behavior is caused, life will never be quite the same. A teacher who accepts and acts on this premise will see the student and his behavior quite differently than before, and will be in a better position to help the child. When Sam speaks disrespectfully to Miss Brown, instead of meting out automatic, swift punishment, she is more likely to pause and ask herself, "I wonder what has gotten into Sam? He doesn't usually respond this way." Furthermore, this assumption enables us to approach with optimism the task of understanding human behavior. As we strive to understand another person, we cannot help gaining increased respect and awe for the order, intricate design, flexibility, and marvelous complexity of the human being which this process reveals.

4. *The human being is an indivisible unity. He can be understood only as each part is related to the other parts and to the total person.* The tendency to divide the human being into parts so that he may be better understood has a long history. The ancient Greeks thought of man as possessing several faculties: a rational faculty, a spiritual faculty, and an appetite faculty. More recently, it has been popular to view man as a body-mind dualism or as the product of a heredity-environment dualism. It is often useful and even necessary to examine separate aspects of the human being. Misinterpretations arise, however, if we think of the two parts of these dualisms as separate entities rather than as parts of an interrelated, integrated whole person. Kelly emphasizes this concept of the whole person when he says, "If we want to produce whole men, we will have to abandon our efforts to train or educate them in parts. . . . When a man meets a problem he meets it with all he has—foot, ear, fist, purpose, value."[7]

5. *The scientific method provides the most valid basis for interpreting human behavior.* Because man is complex and his behavior often seems

[7] Earl C. Kelley, *Education for What Is Real* (New York: Harper & Row, 1947), p. 65.

mysterious, over the period of several thousands of years, sorcery, the workings of supernatural beings, mythology, folklore, qualities and characteristics presumably within man himself, and empirical observations have all been used by persons to explain the behavior of other human beings.

The scientific method—that is, the search for knowledge through the testing of alternative explanations or solutions by empirical, objective evidence—has been the keystone of research in the physical and biological sciences since the Renaissance. Only during the present century, however, has the scientific method of experimentation been applied to social and behavioral phenomena.

The application of the scientific method to problems of understanding human behavior and development requires that one develop both a self-discipline in collecting and analyzing objective data and a healthy skepticism for the conclusions which emerge from these analyses. Valid interpretations of behavior depend on (1) a broad range of objective data and (2) initial assumptions that are tentative and subject to modification in the light of additional evidence.

The use of the scientific method is no less important in the human sphere than it has been in the physical world, where scientists on many frontiers are probing the universe. Though our instruments and methodologies are still quite crude for studying the most complex of systems, the scientific method of experimentation has enabled us to make progress in human understanding and to anticipate even greater progress from its use and refinement in the future.

What It Means to Understand

Understanding implies more than knowledge and comprehension of what has been observed. In seeking to understand another person, one looks for pertinent data in present and past situations; he also searches for relationships between seemingly isolated facts. More specifically, if one is to acquire something more than a superficial understanding of another person, he must have the following information and skills:

1. *Functional knowledge of human development and learning principles.* Man's seeking to understand his fellow man is hardly a new goal or aspiration. Historians, poets, storytellers, philosophers, and religious leaders have for centuries recorded and interpreted men's motives and actions. However, not until the latter part of the nineteenth century, with the work of Wilhelm Wundt in Germany, did there emerge a separate scientific discipline focusing on the study of behavior—the science of psychology. During the twentieth century a great many other disciplines have contributed to increased human understanding. These disciplines (*anatomy, physiology, endocrinology, genetics, pediatrics, morphology, anthropology, sociology, child* and *adolescent psychology, educational psychology, learning theory, psychology of personality, psychoanalysis and psychiatry*) are referred to collectively as *the behavioral sciences.*

An interdisciplinary field of knowledge called *human development* brings together and synthesizes data and principles of human behavior from the several behavioral sciences, and organizes these principles into a coherent body of knowledge about human behavior, development, learning, and adjustment.

2. *Valid and complete information about the person whom one seeks to understand.* When one lacks information that is needed to answer a question or to solve a problem, he is likely to look for a good book on the subject. Books, lectures, and talks with experts frequently provide one with useful clues and insights into a youngster's behavior. Valuable though these resources are in building a synthesis of scientific knowledge of human development and learning, books and lectures alone will seldom explain why a particular student, Joey Harrison, does not do his homework. Something more than general principles and descriptions are needed if we are to understand and help a particular Joey Harrison.

In addition to the principles of human development and learning which may be gained from books and lectures, one needs a factual descriptive picture (a case record) of the child in various situations. What is he like? What does he do and say? How does he seem to feel about his various experiences? How do others respond to him? In short, one must discover and record a broad range of data about the child, his environment, and the significant people in his life.

3. *Acceptance and application of the scientific method.* The steps and general method which scientists use in seeking a cure for cancer or in studying the behavior of high-energy particles are also those used by behavioral scientists. Since the steps of the scientific method are in general the same as those used in the solution of any problem, they can be understood and applied by the teacher, parent, and nonscientist as well as by the scientist. The scientific method consists of a series of steps or operations which begin with an identification, clarification, and statement of the problem. This is followed by data gathering, suggesting hypotheses, hypothesis testing, drawing conclusions, and application of the new concept or principle.

Acceptance and use of the scientific method as a tool in the study of human behavior necessarily implies a commitment to specific values and standards, especially with respect to the kinds of evidence which the scientist accepts as valid and the steps and safeguards which he uses in drawing inferences or conclusions from evidence. The specific steps which implement these values and standards have been established by convention and custom. In the next chapter, we will consider their application to the study of human behavior.

Summary

A nation's greatest resources are its people and their potentialities for development and self-realization. The efforts of parents, teachers, and others in helping children and youth to develop and to realize their full potentialities are greatly influenced by two kinds of understandings: (1) a general understanding of growth, development, and learning at successive maturity levels and throughout the life span; and (2) an understanding of the specific individual whose development one seeks to promote.

The need for human understanding is widespread at all levels and in all areas of human living: within the family, in the schools, in the community, and among the nations of the world.

One's understanding of people is based upon his conception of what human beings are like. The human being is a dynamic, evolving complex of three interrelated and interacting processes: physical, social, and psychological. Physically, man is a highly organized and dynamic energy system. His greater differentiation and complexity mark him as distinct from all other living things. Tissue irritability produced by physiological imbalance is characteristic of the human organism at its many levels of activity. At times this tissue irritability signals a need for stimulation; at other times it signals a need for release from stimulation. These alternating contentments and discontentments are a reflection of the alternating tides of human activity: development and adjustment. Man becomes a social being through inter-action and association with other human beings. Through these relationships he seeks to fulfill his need to belong—to be loved, wanted, and accepted. Man's uniqueness is demonstrated most clearly in his psychological develop-ment—his highly differentiated brain and nervous system, which promote flexibility, adaptability, and symbolization of meaning.

Our study of the human being is guided by the following assumptions:

1. Every human being is inherently valuable.

2. Every individual is unique.

3. Behavior is caused. The causes are multiple, complex, and interrelated.

4. The individual is an indivisible unity.

5. The scientific method provides the most valid basis for interpreting human behavior.

Finally, if we are to increase our understanding of another person, we must acquire (1) a knowledge of the important concepts and principles which assist in explaining behavior, (2) as much information as possible about the person whom we wish to understand, and (3) the ability to use the steps and safeguards that the scientific method offers for checking and rechecking our facts, interpretations, and conclusions.

Study Questions

1. What, in your opinion, are the purposes of education? What role does human understanding play in the achievement of these purposes?

2. Fritz Redl has suggested that children are at least as complex as cars. Are we more concerned with technological development than with human under-standing and development? If so, why?

3. What do you feel are the greatest blocks or deterrents to human understanding? Which of these are most amenable to change?

4. Can one understand others if he does not fully understand himself? Explain.

5. Does acceptance of another person necessarily imply approval of his behavior? Discuss.

Suggested Readings

Howard Lane and Mary Beauchamp. *Understanding Human Development.* Englewood Cliffs, New Jersey: Prentice-Hall, 1959. Emphasizes that youth can be helped to achieve optimum development if teachers and others who work with young people will acquire and apply understanding of human development.

Daniel A. Prescott. *The Child in the Educative Process.* New York: McGraw-Hill Book Co., 1957. Chapter 1 stresses the importance of teachers' having an adequate understanding of children and youth if they are to make wise decisions in guiding their development and learning. Chapter 2 discusses the religious, philosophical, and ethical assumptions; the social values; and the scientific axioms that are fundamental to a study of human behavior and development.

Fritz Redl. *Understanding Children's Behavior.* New York: Bureau of Publications, Teachers College, Columbia University, 1949. Clear, nontechnical guide to the understanding of children's behavior.

Carl R. Rogers. *On Becoming a Person.* Boston: Houghton Mifflin Co., 1961. Chapter 1 presents a brief autobiographical sketch followed by a candid and lucid analysis of the experiences that contributed to the development of Rogers' own personal beliefs and values. The reader is afforded considerable insight into Rogers' development as a person, psychotherapist, and teacher.

Films

Incident on Wilson Street, 16 mm, sound, black and white. Part 1, 24 min.; Part 2, 27 min. Syracuse, New York: Film Library, Syracuse University, 1455 E. Colvin Street. This film shows individual and group reactions to an in-school "incident" when a young student suddenly strikes out at her teacher. A ten-year-old child is revealed as a person frustrated by her surroundings, a father is enraged by what he believes classmates are doing to his child, and a young teacher feels she cannot keep the child in her class. Classmates express a surprising amount of concern and understanding. As it reveals the responses of teachers, pupils, and parent, *Incident on Wilson Street* points to the need for human understanding by all persons concerned.

2

the scientific study
of human behavior

*We now know, from the scientific point of view, that we cannot neglect
little children and expect them to grow into fine adults.*

≡   HOWARD A. LANE

Scientists in all disciplines use the same general method in their search for and application of knowledge. Essentially, this method involves a series of seven steps[1] toward the solution of a problem. (These steps are summarized in Table 2.1, pp. 22–23.)

1. *Location and definition of a problem.* The first step in the solution of any problem is to recognize that a problem exists. Often, the existence of a problem will be experienced as a perplexity, a felt need, or a recognized difficulty. The problem that requires a solution may be as mundane as getting a car started or deciding which brand of toothpaste is the best buy. On the other hand, the problem may be one of profound importance, such as the large-scale desalinization of sea water or a cure for cancer. One has located and defined his problem when he can state it in a way that clearly communicates what he wishes to find out.

---

[1] These steps are adapted from statements found in C. V. Good, A. S. Barr, and D. E. Scates, *The Methodology of Educational Research* (New York: Appleton-Century-Crofts, 1941), pp. 15–25. They also follow in general the steps of reflective thinking presented in John Dewey, *How We Think* (New York: D. C. Heath & Co., 1910), pp. 68–78.

Educators who seek to facilitate their pupils' development and learning face one general problem: to discover how and why children and youth behave and develop as they do. Since each individual is different, this general problem becomes further defined and limited to discovering the causes for the behavior of a specific student. Scotty's teacher has noticed that on several occasions Scotty does not complete his art picture. An example of this behavior is shown in the teacher's case-record entry for November 6.

> In art class today Scotty sketched a fantastic but lovely imaginative bird. He started to paint it with water colors and when he was about half finished brought it up to show me. I complimented him on his work, and he smiled and said, "I think it looks nice, too. I'll go finish it."
>
> About five minutes later I noticed him sitting idly, his arm resting on the back of his seat, his head propped on his hand. I strolled back to his desk to see if there was any reason for the apparent change in attitude.
>
> He had made a small blot on the body of the bird and had decided the picture was ruined. I showed him how to remove the blot, but he seemed uninterested. Later, I saw the picture in the wastebasket.

This recurring behavior pattern intrigues Scotty's teacher, so that in this instance the general problem is limited to the specific question "Why does Scotty not complete his art work?"

2. *Collecting and organizing pertinent data.* After one has identified and defined the problem, he surveys what is already known about this problem. This step is essentially one of gathering data on the problem being investigated.

In a study of human behavior the educator's information about a particular child can be drawn from a variety of sources. The teacher who wants to find out why Scotty did not finish his picture would need to secure a great deal of data about Scotty, including those from the school records, from other persons at school and at home, and from his own direct observations of Scotty in a variety of situations. (A further elaboration of these sources of information appears on pp. 25–39.)

3. *Formulation of hypotheses as tentative solutions to the problem.* The preliminary survey of data in step 2 frequently points to one or more possible solutions to the problem. After the data have been collected, the step of formulating hypotheses begins in earnest. A hypothesis is simply a tentative statement regarding events or relationships which is provisionally accepted as valid for the purposes of reasoning, experiment, or investigation. The medical researcher hypothesizes about a particular drug or some other type of therapy which he suspects may prove effective in combating a disease or which has already proved effective in tests with animals but must yet be fully tested with human beings.

In the study of human behavior, hypotheses explaining why a person behaves as he does may be of three types: (1) hypotheses suggested by the particular circumstances wherein the behavior occurred, (2) hypotheses suggested by other case-record information on the person, and (3) hypotheses suggested by scientific concepts and principles of human development and learning. The following hypotheses were suggested by Scotty's teacher as tentative explanations for Scotty's failure to finish his picture of the bird. Other equally plausible explanations for Scotty's behavior might also be added to this list.

1. Scotty is in competition with another student in the class. (Hence he does not want his work to appear in comparison.)
2. Scotty is ambivalent in his attitude toward art.
3. Scotty believes that art is sissyish and feminine.
4. Other children laugh at and make fun of Scotty's pictures.
5. Scotty expresses an interest in sports and games. (This he views as incompatible with an interest in art.)
6. Scotty expects high standards of performance from himself.
7. Scotty has aspirations inconsistent with his abilities.
8. His parents place high expectations on Scotty for achievement and proper deportment.
9. Scotty is in rivalry with a sibling.
10. Scotty adjusts to unpleasant situations by withdrawing or giving up.
11. Scotty's parents believe that art is a waste of time.
12. Scotty talks about and identifies with his father and masculine interests.
13. Scotty is asserting his independence of adult authority. (He showed this by not finishing the picture that the teacher liked.)
14. Scotty has a warm, friendly, permissive relationship with the teacher. (He feared his completed picture might not fulfill her expectations.)
15. Scotty lacks confidence in his own abilities.
16. Scotty has a short attention span.
17. Scotty's interest is in working with art materials but not in completing a project.
18. Scotty has a preference for realism rather than for things imaginary.
19. Scotty's family has not trained him in completing things that have been started.
20. Scotty gains emotional support by depending on others.

4. *Testing the hypotheses.* The researcher cannot know which of his hypotheses are valid until he tests them in the light of the data he has

collected. His data therefore become the basis for his confirming or refuting each of the hypotheses he has advanced as tentative solutions to his problem. In an analysis of Scotty's failure to finish his picture, Scotty's teacher found that the evidence in her case record seemed to confirm four of her hypotheses:

13. Scotty asserts his independence of adult authority.
14. Scotty has a warm, friendly, permissive relationship with the teacher.
18. Scotty has a preference for realism over things imaginary.
20. Scotty gains emotional support by depending on others.

Hypothesis 9 (rivalry with a sibling) and hypothesis 19 (lack of training at home for taking responsibility) were clearly refuted.

5. *Collection of additional data.*   Sometimes the initial testing of hypotheses fails to confirm or to refute some of the hypotheses. In analyzing the case of Scotty, his teacher found that additional information would be needed before she could adequately test hypothesis 11 (attitude of parents that art is a waste of time) and hypothesis 12 (Scotty identifies with his father).

The collection of additional data permits new hypotheses to be tested and existing hypotheses to be rechecked or verified. This step of gathering additional data is similar to step 2, except that here the researcher's or educator's discrimination in the kinds of data needed has become sharper and more precise as a result of what he has learned in the preceding steps of making and testing hypotheses.

6. *Summary of data and drawing of conclusions.*   After all the hypotheses in a particular study have been tested and the various analyses have been completed and reported, the data are summarized and conclusions are drawn. That is, in a brief statement or series of statements the researcher reports the essence of what he has learned from the particular scientific problem-solving activity. In the study of human behavior, the conclusions or summary may take one of two forms: (1) validated explanations (hypotheses) of why the person behaved as he did in the specific situation chosen for analysis, or (2) a series of tentative generalizations or conclusions about the person's state of physical health, growth, and energy; the qualities of his interpersonal relationships; his culture; the peer group and his relationships to it; his self-development and self-adjustment; his perceptions and goals, as revealed in the developmental tasks he is working on; and his concept of self.

7. *Formulation of new generalizations, principles, or laws from what has been learned in the study.*   A final step in the scientific method of problem solving is the formulation of new generalizations, principles, or laws which make a further contribution to man's understanding of the problem

being studied. The uniqueness of the individual, the continuous change in events, and the complexity of human behavior make the generalizations emerging from scientific problem solving in the behavioral sciences highly tentative. Each passing day, we are learning more and more about human beings, but much of human behavior is still unexplained. Even the tentative conclusions we make about a single individual are tenuous, for the events of the next moment may alter them completely.

The scientific method of problem solving does not end with the completion of these seven steps; problem solving is a never-ending process. New data being fed into the process at each step may change the initial problem or permit the formulation of a more complex problem. Hence, this never-ending cycle of investigation enables man continuously to extend his field of knowledge and understanding.

Table 2.1. Steps in the scientific method and their adaptation for studying human behavior.

STEP	SCIENTIFIC METHOD	STUDYING HUMAN BEHAVIOR
1.	Location and definition of a problem	General Problem: How can I achieve a deeper understanding of human behavior and development? Specific Problem: How can I gain a more complete understanding of this particular student? Why does this student behave this way?
2.	a. Survey of what is already known about the problem—gather data b. Organizing the data	Building an objective, descriptive, complete case record of information on a specific student, using the seven sources of information listed. (1) Identifying and listing recurring patterns *or* (2) Grouping data according to an organizing framework.
3.	Formulating hypotheses or tentative solutions to the problem	(1) Listing tentative multiple hypotheses which may explain a particular behavior *or* (2) Formulating tentative generalizations suggested by the data collected in each process area *or* (3) Making inferences about the child's self-concept.

STEP	SCIENTIFIC METHOD	STUDYING HUMAN BEHAVIOR
4. Testing the hypotheses		Testing the hypotheses, generalizations, or inferences by checking them against the evidence to determine whether case-record data support or refute them.
5. Collection of additional data		Obtaining additional case-record data, particularly in areas where information about this student is meager.
6. Summarizing findings and drawing conclusions		Final analysis and summary of case record may be completed in relation to (1) Developmental tasks and adjustment problems *and/or* (2) Child's concept of self vs. world's (e.g., teacher, parent) concept of child.
7. Formulation of new principles or laws and the application of these to the solution of new problems		Application of increased knowledge and understanding of this student and of human behavior in facilitating this and other students' development and learning. (1) In view of what I have learned about this student, what have I done to help him? (2) In view of my increased understanding of this student, what would I recommend for further helping this student to develop and to learn more effectively?

Selecting a Student for Study

We noted earlier that depth of understanding is best achieved through an intensive case study of one individual. The initial step in applying the scientific method to the study of human behavior is to select a student to study. Which student of a classroom of thirty or forty should the in-service teacher or the student teacher choose to study? What guidelines should one follow in making a choice? Since the educator will be focusing on the dynamics of human behavior common to all persons at that maturity level, the selection of a student from the broad normal range of behavior and development would probably best satisfy the professional objectives of the study experience. The educator is urged to select from that range a student in whom he is really interested. When the teacher selects a student who interests him, he is much more likely to become absorbed in finding out what makes the youngster tick and thus will find the task of collecting information less burdensome. Finally, since the teacher's success and satisfaction depend upon the amount and variety of information he can obtain about this student, he should select a fairly active student with whom he has frequent contacts.

The following are brief statements which teachers or observers wrote in stating why they selected a particular student for study.

> I'm not sure whether it's lack of inhibition, unpredictable sense of humor, or something more subtle which attracts me to Heidi.

> I chose [Pedro] because my observations, his records, his activities, and the responsibilities that he shares at home all point to greater potentialities in both mental and physical abilities than he usually displays in his classroom learning activities.

> My decision in choosing V. Jones, a twelve-year-old seventh grader, is based on the conversation which I had with her mother during the summer. She remarked, "I do hope you are her teacher. I believe you can make her happy. She is broken-hearted because she has to go to Edison. She wants to go to Lee where all her little friends will be going."

> I have chosen Teena as my object for study because I was much attracted by her large brown eyes set in a small dark face.

Frequently a teacher will want to choose a so-called problem student for his initial case study. Understandably, the teacher wants especially to understand this kind of student so that he can help him to adjust and thus perhaps can alleviate some difficult classroom situations. However, such a choice has often proved unwise. First, studying a student who deviates considerably from the norm makes it more difficult for the teacher to understand the dynamics of normal behavior. Second, the causes of deviant behavior may be so imbedded in the student's past that the educator cannot gain the information necessary for understanding the case. An outcome of the teacher's growing understanding of human behavior is his increased skill in discriminating between normal but *disturbing* behavior (such as occasional poking, pushing, talking, or failing to follow directions) and deviant, *disturbed* behavior (such as chronic lying, fighting, stealing, or daydreaming). As the teacher learns to discriminate between these two types of behavior, he is able to make appropriate referrals to pupil personnel or psychological services. Early identification of these students needing such services makes it possible for them to receive specialized help sooner.

One final point: Neither the student nor anyone else except professional personnel involved in the study experience should be informed that the student is being studied. A person who knows he is being observed is unlikely to act spontaneously and naturally.

Gathering Information

Ethics of Information Gathering

From our discussion thus far, it is apparent that an educator's understanding of human behavior depends to a considerable degree upon the depth and amount of information about the student he is able to obtain. The numerous sources and broad scope of information about a student indicate clearly the need for a professional attitude and code of ethics for guiding educators and others in their study of human behavior. Consistent with our belief in the value of every human being is the need to protect the student and his family by keeping all information about them completely confidential. Safeguarding information which one obtains and uses in serving patients, clients, or students is a fundamental principle in the ethical codes of all professions that serve people.

The general ethical principle of safeguarding information about a student and protecting his identity has been translated by educators who study behavior into the following specific codes of conduct :

1. One does not reveal the identity of the student or his family to anyone not involved in studying students. Giving the pupil a fictitious name in writing the case record helps to protect his identity.

2. The educator keeps the information he acquires about a child in strict confidence. He does not gossip about what he has learned, and he especially refrains from discussing his case study where he may be overheard by others.

3. Information about a student should be written in a hard bound stitched notebook. This case record should be safeguarded at all times.

4. The educator keeps his information as objective as possible. Differences in points of view should not alter his fundamental acceptance of the student as an individual.

Seven Sources of Information

The educator begins his study of human behavior by collecting and writing up in a case record as much information as he can obtain about the particular student he has selected for study. Since interpretation and understanding of human behavior depend upon the validity and completeness of the information, the teacher should utilize a variety of sources of information. Seven sources of information can be used in developing a case-study record. Information from these seven sources enables the educator to view the student from different perspectives and in relation to different areas of his life; it also enables him to verify information obtained from different sources. In the following pages, each of the seven sources will be discussed and illustrated by excerpts from the case of Scotty.

1. *Direct observation and objective description.* The first source of information, the teacher's own observation and description of the student, is immediately and continuously available to the teacher. Each situation that the teacher describes is called an *anecdote.* A case record contains a great many anecdotes about the child's behavior, his interactions with others, and the specific details of a wide variety of situations that the teacher has observed. Anecdotes may include descriptions of the child in class, in the hallway or the cafeteria or on the playground, after school in the shopping center, or in almost any other conceivable place.

At the beginning, teachers often wonder, "What shall I write about?" and "How shall I begin?" The absence of a set pattern permits teachers to begin their records in a variety of ways. Some begin by describing what they already know about the student. Others begin by watching a student and writing a description of the behavior and events which first brought him to their attention. Scotty's teacher began her record by writing a physical description of her student.

> Scotty is a tall, slender boy, thirteen years old. He is freckle-faced and brown-eyed and has two dimples when he smiles. His teeth are white and even. He is cleanly dressed, but his hands are usually dirty.

As the teacher observes and records what he sees and hears day after day, he learns to select events that illuminate important characteristics of the student and events that present a new or different side of his life or his behavior. However, although the teacher cannot help being *selective,* he must always be *objective.* Some teachers find it difficult to refrain from including opinions, generalizations, and interpretations in their descriptions, since they have habitually used generalized interpretative words in communicating ideas to others. Teachers become increasingly objective when they describe as completely as possible exactly what took place, what each person did or said, what reactions of others were noted, what facial expressions and gestures were used, and any other details observed. The goal is to describe behavior and situation vividly, objectively, and completely, so that the people and the situation come alive to the person reading or listening to the anecdote.

Anecdotes that are not objective reflect the evaluations, interpretations, or generalizations of the observer. The teacher's entry for October 5 is an example of an *evaluative anecdote:*

> Scotty is reading, and reading well, on the fifth-grade level. His arithmetic work is very good, and he is an average speller. He seems

uninterested in social studies but is very interested in art, in which he does beautiful work.

This anecdote could have been written more objectively if data on learning performance, test scores, and projects were included in place of the subjective evaluations. What reader or outside reading books is he reading? What kinds of arithmetic problems can he solve? What contributions does he make in science and social studies?

The teacher's background description of Scotty is an example of an *interpretative description:*

Scotty is quiet-spoken and seems to have a sulky look on his face. He becomes glum and resentful when corrected, but if the correction is made with a smile, one is rewarded with a quick grin and a flash of dimples.

Again, this statement would have been more objective if the teacher had included a specific description of Scotty's face (knitted brows, turned-down mouth, drooping jaw) in a specific situation. What did Scotty actually do that gave rise to the interpretation "sulky"? If specific details are included, they provide us with a far clearer, more precise picture than interpretations do.

An example of a *generalized description* has also been taken from the background statement:

His hair is nicely combed [evaluation] when he arrives at both morning and afternoon sessions [generalization], but as soon as it dries from the combing it receives, it hangs down in his eyes [generalization]. He tosses his head back frequently to try to clear his view, but the hair continues to hang in front of his eyes [generalization].

The writer of this record could have avoided generalizations and achieved objectivity if she had described completely what occurred on each of several different occasions. If "hair hanging down in front of his eyes" is included in several anecdotes, we have what later will be called a "recurring pattern."

Finally, we include an anecdote which is predominantly specific and objective:

NOVEMBER I

Scotty punched Dick today and Dick told me about it. I hadn't seen Scotty do it but Dick said, "Every time he goes by my desk he punches me." I called Scotty up to the desk and asked him about it.

"Sure, I punched him," said Scotty. "Every time he goes by my desk he says, 'wise guy!' under his breath, so I just let him have it. If he stops calling me a wise guy I'll stop punching him, but he's not going to call me names and get away with it!"

I looked at Dick. Dick said, "Yeah, I call him 'wise guy' because he thinks he is one. He acts like a big shot."

Scotty said, "Who acts like a big shot? Me or you? What did I ever do to you?"

Dick hung his head and mumbled, "Nothing, but I think you act like a big shot."

Scotty looked at me and smiled. "See? I don't know why he calls me a wise guy and I don't think he knows either, but every time he says it I'm going to punch him."

I talked to them both and then told them to return to their seats. As Dick sat down he looked at Scotty and said, "Wise guy!" Scotty punched him.

Dick looked at me and I said, "You asked for it." He said no more.

While there is no one correct way of describing an incident, we have noted several criteria which characterize good anecdotal recording:

1. The description begins with the date, time, and place and includes a statement or explanation of the background situation or setting in which the event occurred.

2. The *action*—what happened, who did what or said what, and how it was done—is described as objectively and completely as possible.

3. *Interactions* of the student with classmates and teacher are included in the description, together with *reactions* of each of these persons during each phase of the episode.

4. Verbal interaction is reported as much as possible in *direct quotes*. With practice the observer will markedly increase his ability to recall the words and phrases used in conversations.

5. Posture, facial expressions, gestures, and voice qualities are described without interpretation: "His eyes flashed, he frowned, his body became rigid, and his fist was clenched" instead of the interpretative "He became angry."

6. The recording of the anecdote continues until all aspects, interactions, and reactions of the episode have been fully described; until the scene or activity shifts or terminates. The teacher avoids leaving the description "up in the air" like a continued magazine serial. Instead, he includes final or follow-up actions and conversations to give a sense of closure and completeness.

2. *School records.* A second source of information, school records contain a wide variety of data about the student's development and learning:

Family data: parents' names and education; father's occupation; home address; number and ages of siblings.

Health data: records of physical examinations, diseases, immunizations, physical defects, physical-growth measurements, school attendance.

Results of standardized tests: intelligence, achievement in academic skill areas, aptitude and interest inventories.

Records of academic progress: school marks, promotions, reports of teacher-parent conferences, teacher evaluations.

Teachers' evaluations of the child: brief generalized evaluations or impressions of the child by teachers at successive grade levels; teacher ratings of the child's relationships with his peers, his interests, his hobbies, and his characteristic adjustment patterns.

Written communications: between the home and school.

Data from the school records should be recorded verbatim in the case-record book. No attempt should be made at this point to interpret these data. Interpretations of them may be made later, when they are shared with a psychologist, a guidance worker, or a professional group studying behavior. Material from Scotty's school cumulative record, copied by Scotty's teacher into her case-record book, is reproduced in Figure 2.1.

3. *Information from other people.* Facts and anecdotes about a student or the family are frequently obtainable from the student's teachers and friends and acquaintances and from the school's principal and guidance counselor. As much as possible, the teacher should try to secure facts as well as opinions. If another teacher reports, "Scotty was sneaky and deceitful," the teacher studying Scotty might ask, "Can you describe what Scotty did in one or two specific situations last year in which he revealed this type of behavior?" Thus, one may record many specific, objective facts describing Scotty's behavior in these situations, as well as other people's feelings and opinions about Scotty. However, any material based upon opinion, hearsay, or general impressions should be verified with other data.

Miss Sawyer, Scotty's teacher, learned things about Scotty from another teacher and also from a neighbor, as the following entries reveal.

DECEMBER II

I was talking to Scotty's fifth-grade teacher today and she commented on how Scotty has grown in the past two years. Among other remarks passed in a desultory conversation was this made by her: "You know, don't you, that Mr. Martin isn't Scotty's real father?"

I blinked and said, "No, how do you know?" I received the following story.

During Scotty's year in the fifth grade we had been asked to check vital information preparatory to the adopting of a new type of cumulative record card. All children were asked to bring in their birth certificates. Scotty's didn't appear and the teacher kept after him about it. His excuse

Figure 2.1. A cumulative record.

Name: Walter Scott Martin
Date of birth: July 23, 1950
Place of birth: Orion, Michigan

Three previous addresses
are shown on the
cumulative record card.
The fourth and latest
is: 316 Beechwood
Avenue.

Father's name: Edward
Father's education:12th grade h.s.
Father's occupation: cab driver,
            Yellow Cab Co.

Mother's name: Helen
Mother's education: 11th grade h.s.
Mother's occupation: housewife

Siblings: Frank, age 7 (attending 2nd grade in this school)
          Eddie, age 17 months

The following standardized test scores have been recorded:

ACHIEVEMENT TESTS

Date	Grade	Test	CA	Total Grade Equiv.	Expected Grade Equiv.
5-6-57	1	Metropolitan	6-10	1.2	1.8
5-8-59	3	Metropolitan	7-10	2.5	3.8
10-2-59	3	Iowa Test of Basic Skills	8-2	2.7	3.2
4-10-62	5	Stanford Achievement Total	11-9	4.8(composite)	5.7
		Reading Vocab. 4.5			
		Reading Compr. 4.2			
		Arith Reasoning 5.6			
		Arith Fund. 5.8			
		English Mechanics 4.9			
		English Spelling 4.0			

INTELLIGENCE TESTS

Date	Grade	Test	CA	Verbal	Nonverbal	Total IQ
10-2-60	4	Lorge Thorndike	10-2	81	92	86
4-5-62	5	Calif. Test of Mental Mat.	11-9	87	96	92

HEALTH RECORD

Height and Weight

Date	Age	Grade	Height	Weight
11-56	6-4	1	47	48
5-57	6-10	1	48½	50
11-57	7-4	2	49½	55
5-58	7-10	2	51	60
11-58	8-4	3	52¼	65
5-59	8-10	3	53	69½
11-59	9-4	3 (Re-tained)	55¼	75
5-60	9-10	3	57	82
10-60	10-3	4	58	82
4-61	10-9	4	59¼	88½
10-61	11-3	5	60	100
5-62	11-10	5	61½	101½
10-62	12-3	6	62	107

TEACHERS' COMMENTS

First Grade (1956-57)
    Scotty is a large boy, active, and well coordinated. Progress in reading was very slow. Was still in a pre-primer at the end of the year. Showed interest in our social studies and science projects.
                                    F. Schultz
Second Grade (1957-58)
    Scotty is still very slow in his reading. Likes science. Mother very cooperative. Enjoys games and people. Takes active part in group discussions.
                                    C. Brown
Third Grade (1958-59)
    No interest, a poor student, needs motivation. Retained.
                                    T. Bowles
Third Grade (1959-60)
    Scotty is a large, active boy. Became a leader among boys on playground. Seems to dislike reading and spelling.
                                    H. Fairfax
Fourth Grade (1960-61)
    Not willing to work hard enough to achieve. Mother attended spring conference. She is interested in Scotty's progress, but said she is unable to help him at home.
                                    E. Abel

Fifth Grade (1961-62)

Scotty was new to our school this year. He is a large, well-coordinated boy, and quickly became a leader among boys, especially in games. Has shown an interest in art, but many times will not finish a picture. Scotty spent two days a week with a remedial-reading teacher, and he made considerable progress in his reading. Conference with mother revealed Scotty is very helpful at home. Scotty seems to have real potential, if we could onlv help him to improve his skills in reading and language.

E. Downing

READING BOOKS COMPLETED

First Grade (56-57)
Ride Away
Tip and Mitten
The Big Show
Come with Us

Second Grade (57-58)
Guess Who
Fun with Dick and Jane
Up and Away
Our New Friends
Open the Gate

Third Grade (58-59)
Come Along
On We Go
Around the Corner

Third Grade (59-60)
Over a City Bridge.
Just for Fun
Neighbors on the Hill
Looking Ahead

Fourth Grade (60-61)
Neighbors Far and
Near
If I Were Going

Fifth Grade (61-62)
High Road
Times and Places

was that his mother wouldn't let him have it. Finally, the teacher sent a note home and Scotty's mother brought it to school herself.

She explained to the teacher that Scotty didn't know Mr. Martin wasn't his father and she never wanted him to find out.

The secret was so well guarded that the fact is not on the record card.

FEBRUARY 5

I gathered a bit of news from a neighbor over the weekend about Mr. Martin, Scotty's stepfather.

Said the neighbor, "I know that guy. He and I were in high school together and a nicer fellow you'd never meet. He was one of our football stars and was very popular and well liked. What's he call himself Martin for? That's not his name. He's 'Lefty' Logan."

I tried to take this knowledge unblinkingly and assured the neighbor I didn't know why the change in name, but when he mentioned "Logan" it certainly rang a bell!

About two years ago there was a lurid divorce court trial described in the paper with "Lefty" as the defendant and the grounds as adultery. The then Mrs. Logan accused her husband of living with another woman and having a son by her. The divorce was granted.

The above information, furnished by another teacher and a person outside the school, provides clues helpful in understanding Scotty's home situation. It emphasizes, too, the extreme care which those who study children must take in keeping confidential the information they have about a student. Adherence to a professional code of ethics is essential.

Studies of students made by persons training to become teachers will in most cases be limited to the three sources of information already described: (1) direct observation and objective description, (2) school records, and (3) information from other people. Limitations imposed by their unofficial status as observers and their brief visits to the classroom preclude their utilizing four additional sources of information available to the child's teacher and other professional personnel in the school.

4. Home visits and parent conferences. Unfortunately, many parents initially feel apprehensive when a teacher asks to visit the home. Their previous experiences with a representative of the school coming to the house may have been with a truant officer or someone who has complained about the student's behavior. However, teachers who have studied children say that home visits, when they are carefully planned in advance and when the primary purpose is that of establishing friendly relationships between the school and home, result in greater teacher-parent rapport and communication.

From the first the teacher seeks to establish warm, friendly relationships by placing the parent at ease and by being gracious and accepting. To accomplish this, the teacher refrains from making notes of any kind during the visit. He is alert and pays full attention to objects, people, and events in the home. Later, he will write up in narrative form what was observed and what he and the parents talked about.

The teacher's description of a home visit includes what he observes while driving through the neighborhood—the street, the houses, the yards, the general appearance and state of upkeep, and other details. The teacher may also wish to include a description of the student's home—furnishings, magazines, books, TV, appliances, and number and size of rooms. He will also include descriptions of the family—their speech and gestures and facial expressions. Asking the mother to describe Jimmy when he was a baby or inquiring about his interests and hobbies outside of school is often effective in putting the mother at ease and encouraging her to talk. The teacher can describe the projects the class is working on at school and Jimmy's role and participation in these projects. The ideal home visit is characterized by a free-flowing, easy interchange of ideas and information by persons who have a mutual interest in and concern for the student. In such a climate, the major purpose of the home visit, the establishment of rapport and friendly relations between home and school, has in large measure been fulfilled.

Parent-teacher conferences also provide opportunities for teachers and parents to share information about the child. Conferences are more frequent than are home visits and often are more formal, since they are usually held at school and are often used in the elementary grades as a method of reporting the student's progress. Although parent-teacher conferences are held for the specific purpose of obtaining or communicating information about the child, the suggestions made for home visits apply also to parent-teacher conferences.

Miss Sawyer had many opportunities to become acquainted with Scotty and his family in their home, as the following excerpts from the record reveal.

NOVEMBER 13

The house in which I live has an apartment on the first floor (one step above street level) which was recently vacated.

Today, Scotty and his family moved into it. The apartment has a living room, two bedrooms, a kitchen, and a bath. One bedroom is very small, just large enough for a single bed. This is to be Cotton's room. The parents have the large bedroom with a crib in it for Wally, the seventeen-month-old boy. Scotty is to sleep on the studio couch in the living room.

The puppy, too, is still a member of the family.

NOVEMBER 27

Saturday we experienced a severe storm with the ocean moving into our street. The water began rising shortly before seven A.M. and by nine

A.M. had reached a depth of eleven inches in the Martins' apartment. They were forced to make a hasty exit through the rear window, and Mrs. Martin and Cotton (the seven-year-old child) came up to my quarters. She wanted to know if we would take the children in with us. . . .

Scotty was in the front room watching the rising water; and when he saw that it apparently wasn't going to recede, he began to move the furniture about and roll up the rug. He then went to the kitchen to get his mother's help. Mrs. Martin says Scotty said, "Which is more important, for you to get your coffee or help me get things off the floor so the water won't hurt them?". . .

When we had them all corralled, Scotty announced that he was hungry. None of them had had breakfast. The electricity had failed, so we fed them by the light of an oil lamp, which Scotty examined carefully. After the table was cleared, Scotty started to wash the dishes. I tried to chase him from the job, but he said he always did them. . . . When the dishes were done, Scotty was told to mind his brothers. Mr. Martin went for several more walks, and Mrs. Martin went down to their apartment to try to salvage some of their food from low cupboard shelves.

Scotty rocked Wally until he went to sleep. Then he carefully placed him on the couch and covered him up. He played with Cotton for a while and then gave him some magazines to look at.

The pup was next on his list of chores. He went downstairs and got the jar containing the pup's formula, brought it upstairs, heated it, and tried to feed the squirming and very hungry dog. I volunteered my services as puppy-holder and Scotty held the bottle. In the excitement the puppy's breakfast had been forgotten and she was ravenous, gulping her food much too fast.

As soon as the bottle was empty, what had been in the dog was out of the dog all over my slacks. Scotty let out a horrified "Oh!" and his face turned crimson. I couldn't move but told him to get me a rag. He got a rag and began to mop me off. I said I'd do it but he said no, that his dog had done it and he'd clean me up. He kept apologizing as he wiped me off and said he'd get my slacks cleaned for me. After much talking he got over his embarrassment and was able to laugh about it. . . .

When Scotty came to school this morning, he looked at me and grinned and said, "Wasn't Saturday some day? But we had fun, didn't we?"

DECEMBER 25

Mrs. Martin visited us today to see our gifts and seemed embarrassed at Scotty's contribution of soap. It seems that Scotty had asked her to get me something nice for him to give me, so Mrs. Martin bought a very pretty pair of nylon panties. She showed them to Scotty, and he agreed that they were nice but, he said, "Mom, I can't give my teacher pants!"

There ensued a discussion, and Scotty reluctantly agreed to present me with the panties. Mrs. Martin wrapped them up and gave Scotty the package to deliver. She said he walked slowly to the door, stopped, looked at the package, and said, "Mom, I just can't! I'll run downtown and buy something else for Miss Sawyer." He went, but all the stores were closed except the Sun Ray Drug Store. So Scotty bought soap. Mrs. Martin said that Scotty said, "When we go back to school after vacation the kids are going to ask me what I gave Miss Sawyer. I can't tell them I gave her pants!" "So," said Mrs. Martin, "I have a pair of fancy nylon panties now!"

Through these home contacts, Miss Sawyer learned things about Scotty and his family that she could not have obtained in any other way: the quality of the relationships between Scotty and other members of the family, including the puppy; his taking on responsibilities at home—in sharp contrast to his failure to take responsibility for his work at school.

5. *Life space.* The environment in which the child lives is another important source of information because it contains clues to the kinds of experiences he may be having. Since the school environment is described in other sources of information, the term *life space* generally refers to the student's out-of-school environment. Life space is that part of the world with which the child comes into direct contact. It includes the child's physical environment: the houses, yards, stores, factories, churches, railroad yards, wharves, woods, open fields, and streams; the people with whom he interacts; the attitudes, feelings, and folkways of the region.

The teacher may obtain important life-space data by driving or walking through the neighborhood around the child's home and by writing up fully what he sees, hears, smells, and feels. Many teachers ask the child to write about what he sees as he plays in his neighborhood or on his way to school, and they include the child's impressions in the record. A teacher then can contrast the child's perceptions to his own perceptions of the child's life space.

Life-space information helps to complete the descriptive picture of the child and his world; in addition, it reveals the kinds and qualities of the child's sensory experience (which, as we will note in a later chapter, is of crucial importance in a child's learning). Since the child at birth knows nothing of the world, what he learns and knows depends upon what he has experienced—everything he sees, smells, hears, touches, manipulates, explores, reads about, and talks about. Life space, then, is the setting for all experiences, and experiencing is fundamental to all learning.

The following is a description of Scotty's life space prior to his family's moving into the apartment in the same building where Miss Sawyer lived.

OCTOBER 10

This afternoon after school I decided I would drive through the community where Scotty lives. The street where Scotty lives is about three blocks from school in Southtown, an area of small one-story homes which adjoins an industrial area. Most of the fathers of children who attend our school are employed as semiskilled workers in the nearby plants. I approached Southtown by way of Fulton Avenue, which is a busy street with stores, service stations, and a variety of business establishments including a real estate office, beauty parlor, bar, dry cleaning, launderette, and pool hall.

Two blocks beyond Madison I turned right, went one block, and turned left on Beechwood, the street on which Scotty lives. This street is in a development of small two-bedroom clapboard homes built by a developer fifteen years ago to sell for $8,500. All homes have the same floor plan. Homes are mainly distinguishable from one another by the color of the exterior paint. Scotty's house is white and occupies a good part of the 60-by-90-foot lot. Paint is peeling off the house, there are several bare spots in the front lawn, and only in the living room did I see curtains. I noticed a baseball bat and glove on the steps, a '56 Chevrolet sedan in the driveway, and an old bicycle in the front yard.

As I passed down the street, I saw many mothers outdoors with small children, sitting with neighbors on their steps or pushing small children in strollers. The street seemed to be crawling with children. I spotted Scotty and some of the older boys playing football in the street. I smiled and waved to them as I drove by. On the next corner I saw a small Christian Church and a nearby gas station. Two blocks to the west there is a small electronics plant and a warehouse. Three blocks east is a three-acre wooded area and ravine which Scotty has often mentioned.

I noticed in my drive back that several houses were vacant. I then recalled that the new freeway is to be built through here, and several houses have been condemned to make way for the freeway. I expect Scotty and his family will be looking for another home before long.

DECEMBER 3

Scotty took a Sunday morning stroll to the local dump and returned with the skull of a dog. When my doorbell rang, there stood Scotty with a hand full of teeth.

"Look at these, Miss Sawyer," he said. "I found them on the dump."

"Ye gods, Scotty," I exclaimed, "how did you find so many teeth? Weren't they fastened to some kind of bone? They look like dog's teeth to me."

He laughed heartily and said, "They are dog's teeth. I found the whole skull and brought it home. Then I pulled the teeth out. The skull's downstairs. It don't smell, though; there's nothing but bone left of it. I thought the Science Club might like to see it."

So I told him to bring it to Science Club next Thursday!

6. *Samples of work and evidences of creativity.* Samples of a student's work and products of his creative expression are a sixth source of information. This information is helpful in two ways. First, a child's drawings, paintings, models, stories, and autobiographical sketches provide important information about the child himself—his feelings, fears, concerns, interests,

goals, and values. These are not revealed directly in the student's products but may be inferred when these data appear to be consistent with other facts in the record. The teacher must take care not to project his own ideas and feelings into the creative product he is interpreting. It is best to include the picture, painting, or essay in the case record, together with the student's comments about it and the teacher's and other children's comments and evaluations of it.

Second, samples of work and creative products are evidences of a student's development and learning. An arithmetic paper may reveal evidence of the student's computation and reasoning skills. A language paper may show the level of the student's physical maturation and development of motor coordination as reflected in his handwriting, his mastery of spelling and punctuation skills, and his mastery of skills for organizing ideas and expressing himself in writing. Drawings and paintings provide evidence of the student's development of artistic skills, motor coordination, and aesthetic sense. Samples of work and creative products arc included in the case record, and these may be accompanied by evaluative comments of the student, the teacher, the art consultant, and other teachers and children.

Further evidence of Scotty's creativity and his feelings about his creative products are described in the following anecdote.

NOVEMBER 20

In art class we designed Thanksgiving cards. Scotty worked carefully and painstakingly on a pencil sketch of a Pilgrim man, gun on shoulder and a wild turkey lying at his feet.

The other children were doing theirs in water color. Scotty asked if he had to paint his, saying he always made a mess with paint. I told him I thought with his type of drawing that it would look well if it were done in India ink. "India ink?" said Scotty, "What's that?" "I'll show you," I replied, and got the ink and a pen for him, showing him how to use it. He returned to his seat and worked very carefully, finishing the card. He came up to the desk with the finished product, laid it down in front of me, and queried, "How does it look?" "Scotty," I exclaimed, "that's lovely. You did a beautiful job. Aren't you pleased with it?" "Yeah," he replied, "I think it looks nice. Would it be all right if I made another one like it? Then I'd have one for both my mother and father." "By all means," I replied. "Go ahead." The second card lacked the exactness and precision of the first, but it too was nicely done.

7. *Teacher-student conversations.* It the teacher has been successful in establishing a warm, friendly relationship with the student and has his confidence, conversations which take place between them (before school, on the playground, at noon, after school, or at any other appropriate time) will constitute yet another valuable source of information. If there is good rapport between teacher and pupil, these conversations often take place spon-

taneously and are almost always informal. The teacher avoids probing for information but appears interested in listening to whatever the student wants to talk about.

If a warm, friendly, trusting relationship is established, significant information can emerge from these conversations. Again, as with descriptions of behavioral episodes in anecdotes, these conversations are most vivid and meaningful when they are reported in direct quotes and when they include descriptions of posture, facial expressions, gestures, and other evidences of feeling and emotion.

The warm, friendly, valuing relationship which developed between Scotty and his teacher enabled Miss Sawyer to make effective use of informal conversations as a source of information. This is shown in the following entries.

NOVEMBER 7

Scotty came up to me today and told me he had acquired a two-day-old boxer puppy. I said, "Two days old? That puppy's too young to leave its mother. How do you care for it?" Scotty replied, "Its mother died so the man had to get rid of all the puppies. There were seven of them so he gave me one. I make a formula for it like you do for a baby and I feed it with a medicine dropper. I keep it in a box wrapped in a woolen blanket. It'll be all right if I take care of it."

FEBRUARY 8

Scotty has developed the habit of punching the girls in the muscles of their upper arms whenever he passes them. He is indiscriminate in his choice of arms, showing no particular preference for the arm of any one girl.

That's a painful wallop to receive and I've spoken to him about it. His reply was, "Aw, they just like to complain. It really doesn't hurt."

I said, "It does hurt. I've had it happen to me and I want you to stop it." Scotty replied, "Girls are just a lot of sissies, anyway."

I laughed and said, "But you think some of them are pretty nice sissies, don't you?" Scotty shrugged and answered, "They're all right, I guess."

MARCH 15

Scotty told me that his dog, Chubby, is sick. He looked worried when he talked to me about it and said that she doesn't eat. He said, "I went over to the store and bought some liver for her. I cooked it and mashed some vegetables in it but she wouldn't even eat it."

I suggested that he give Chubby some mineral oil and he said he'd get some for her.

Analyzing the Case Record

The case record that the teacher or observer compiles will, hopefully, utilize extensively the sources of information that have been described. The purpose of writing this case record has been to collect information about the student's life story, so that accurate, objective analyses of his behavior, development, and learning may be made from these data. The teacher may acquire some hunches and a partial understanding of a student in the process of gathering information and building a case record, but a more complete understanding follows the observer's utilization of the final steps in the scientific method of problem solving described earlier in the chapter.

Although some insights are gained from observing and from building a case record, a formal analysis of the record should be delayed until a considerable body of data has been gathered and recorded. This delay reduces the likelihood that incorrect interpretations will be made because of insufficient information. Also essential to the observer's understanding of a student are the knowledge and application of principles of development and learning. Thus, although steps and processes in analyzing a case record are briefly described here, analyses of the case record should be deferred until a considerable body of facts about the student has been collected and some understanding of important principles and concepts in the later chapters has been acquired.

Analysis with Multiple Hypotheses

Whenever the case-record information yields a fairly complete and valid picture of this student and his life situation, a *multiple-hypothesis analysis* can be made—that is, an analysis in which a number of tentative hypotheses are advanced to explain a subject's recurring behavior patterns.

The multiple-hypothesis analysis follows explicitly the steps of the scientific method of problem solving described earlier in the chapter. The reader will recall that the recurring behavior of Scotty which Miss Sawyer selected was "Why does Scotty not complete his art work?" She had collected a great deal of information about Scotty over a two-month period before beginning her multiple-hypothesis analysis. In our earlier discussion, twenty tentative hypotheses were suggested as possible explanations of this behavior. Miss Sawyer found that the facts of her case record strongly supported four of her hypotheses, refuted two others, and neither confirmed nor refuted the remaining fourteen (suggesting the need for collecting additional data).

Final Analysis and Summary of Case Record

A further opportunity for enlarging one's understanding of behavior and development is afforded by the completion of a final analysis and summary of the case record near the end of the period of studying a student. The final analysis and summary of a case record could take any one of several forms.

One approach involves organizing the data into a list of *recurring patterns*. A recurring pattern is any behavior, event, or situation which has occurred two or more times. The following are illustrative of the recurring patterns to be found in the complete case of Scotty:

1. Scotty fails to complete his picture.
2. Scotty argues or fights with another boy.
3. Scotty punches girls on the arm.
4. Scotty talks to the teacher about his dog.
5. Scotty helps his mother, teacher, and others in the community.

In studying the list of recurring patterns that emerged from the case of Scotty, Miss Sawyer noted that the patterns could be grouped according to the forces or critical activities or events of Scotty's life. She found clusters of recurring patterns which related to Scotty's physical coordination and abilities, his relationships with others, his acceptance of responsibility, his progress in specific school subjects, his aesthetic sense, and his values. Miss Sawyer's final analysis and summary of Scotty's case record consisted of tentative answers to the following guide questions:

1. What developmental tasks is this student working on?
2. What adjustment problems does he face?
3. What assets does he have?
4. What have the school and the teacher done to help this student develop and learn more effectively?
5. What more can the teacher and the school do to help this student develop and learn more effectively?

By reexamining the case-record data presented in this chapter, the reader may wish to test his skill and understanding by developing tentative answers to these summarizing questions, either now or after he has gained an understanding of the principles presented in later chapters.

Summary

The steps in the scientific method of problem solving are (1) location and definition of a problem; (2) collection and organization of data; (3) formulation of hypotheses or possible solutions; (4) testing of the hypotheses; (5) collection of additional data; (6) drawing of conclusions and summarizing of findings; and (7) formulation of new generalizations, principles, or laws and the applications of these in the solution of further problems.

In his study of a student, the teacher is guided by an explicit code of professional ethics, which ensures the safeguarding of information about a student and which protects the student's identity.

In studying a student, the educator builds a case record by utilizing seven sources of information: (1) direct observation and objective anecdotal description, (2) school records, (3) information from other people, (4) home visits and parent conferences, (5) life space, (6) samples of work and evidences of creativity, and (7) teacher-student conversations.

The attainment of a depth of understanding of human behavior depends upon analyses of case-record data, using the steps of the scientific method of problem solving. A tentative *multiple-hypothesis analysis* is available to teachers or observers during their initial experiences in studying behavior. Later, in final analysis and case-record summary, the teacher or observer interprets the recurring patterns and total case-record data and forms tentative answers to guide questions.

Study Questions

1. This chapter describes the procedures that may be used in the teacher's intensive study of one student. How would you respond to the teacher who says, "I have thirty students in my class, and it isn't fair for me to give most of my time and attention to one student and neglect the other twenty-nine"?

2. What differences do you see in the application of a scientific method in the study of human behavior and its application in the solution of problems in the natural sciences?

3. Objectivity of data is a fundamental requirement of research activity in a science. Since much of the data which a teacher gathers about a student consists of statements made by him or by others talking about him, how can the teacher ascertain that what is said is factual and objective?

4. Apply the steps in the scientific method to your own major field of interest. What problems in your own field are amenable to scientific investigation? How might the steps of the scientific method be employed in the solution of these problems?

Suggested Readings

Helen Bieker. "Using Anecdotal Records to Know the Child," in Caroline Tryon (Chairman), *Fostering Mental Health in Our Schools*. Washington: Association for Supervision and Curriculum Development, 1950. Describes and illustrates characteristics, uses, and advantages of complete and objective anecdotal records in teachers' studies of pupils' behavior and development.

Commission on Teacher Education. *Helping Teachers Understand Children.* Washington: American Council on Education, 1945. Describes and illustrates the steps and procedures utilized by teachers in a child-study program in observing and studying a student through time. Chapter 2 contains examples of adequate and inadequate anecdotes; other chapters describe the analysis and interpretation of case records through the use of actual case illustrations.

Ira J. Gordon. *Studying the Child in the School.* New York: John Wiley, 1966. Emphasizes the teacher's need to understand the transactional nature of learning. Describes techniques and tools which the teacher may use in assessing children's intellectual, cognitive, personality, and social development.

Howard Lane and Mary Beauchamp. *Understanding Human Development.* Englewood Cliffs, New Jersey: Prentice-Hall, 1959. Chapter 15 describes sources of information and procedures that teachers may use in child and adolescent study. Included are discussions of school and anecdotal records, home visits, parent conferences, free play, creativity, role playing, and sociometric techniques.

Daniel A. Prescott. *The Child in the Educative Process.* New York: McGraw-Hill Book Co., 1957. Describes with numerous case illustrations the steps and procedures by which a teacher obtains, organizes, and analyzes case-record data on a student.

Films

Helping Teachers Understand Children, 16 mm, sound, black and white. Part 1, 21 min; Part 2, 25 min. Bloomington, Indiana: Audio-Visual Center, Indiana University. Part 1 presents a case study of one child and illustrates sources of information a teacher may use in writing a case record. Part 2 shows a summer workshop in child study, wherein educators and others study the processes which influence and shape the child's behavior, development, and learning.

Learning to Understand Children, (part 1—*A Diagnostic Approach;* Part 2—*A Remedial Program*), 16 mm, sound, black and white. Part 1, 22 min., Part 2, 25 min. Bloomington, Indiana: Audio-Visual Center, Indiana University. Part 1 presents the case of Ada Adams, an emotionally and socially maladjusted girl of fifteen. Her teacher diagnoses her difficulties by observation of her behavior, study of her previous record, personal interviews, and home visits, and formulates a hypothesis for remedial measures. Part 2 continues the case study. An interest in art improves her self-confidence and interest in schoolwork, although some of her problems remain unsolved.

3

the direction of human behavior

Childhood may do without a grand purpose, but manhood cannot.

≡   J. G. HOLLAND

Probably no problem is more puzzling, intriguing, and crucial in the study of human development and learning than the one posed in the question *What is this person trying to accomplish and why?* Before we can enlarge our understanding of behavior, development, and learning, we must extend our understanding of what is meant by the term *motivation*.

The need to discover and to understand what makes people behave as they do is shared by all human beings, young and old, in all cultures at all ages; for an individual can respond appropriately and effectively in life's varying situations only if he assesses accurately other people's motives. The district attorney, in developing a case for the prosecution, seeks to establish the defendant's motives for committing the crime. The advertiser promotes a product most successfully when he discovers, responds to, and influences the desires and preferences of millions of consumers. The parent must understand his children's motives if he is to guide and socialize them in accordance with their own expressed needs and goals. The teacher must understand his students' interests and needs if he is to plan effectively for their learning.

Psychologically unsophisticated persons explain behavior in terms of simple motives. One may overhear a parent or a teacher say, "Freddie does not do his homework because he is lazy." Behavior, however, is never a simple, separate, or isolated phenomenon. Rather, it is related to the conditions, forces, and events which precede and accompany it. Perhaps this is just another way of stating that behavior has many interrelated causes.

If behavior does not occur as an isolated, spontaneous response, it must be instigated by something. This something, a bodily state or condition which impels one to respond, is called *motivation*. Motivation, then, is an internal state that mobilizes and directs an individual's energy toward some object or part of the environment. After the individual achieves the goal toward which he is motivated, his energy expenditure decreases and his effectiveness in coping with his environment increases.

Motivation, as it may be inferred from observations of animal and human behavior, involves three interrelated processes. McDonald has included in his definition of motivation all three processes: "Motivation, an energy change within the person, is characterized by affective arousal and anticipatory goal reactions."[1]

The first of these processes is an internal *energy change*—usually the result of some kind of imbalance. The individual gets hungry, or too warm or too cold, or his best friend doesn't speak to him, or he faces an arithmetic test on material he does not understand, or the coach urges him to try out for the varsity football team. In each case the student undergoes a change from a more or less quiescent state to an activated state. Such a change, impelling him to restore balance, is sometimes called a *drive*.

As a result of this internal energy change the motivated individual usually experiences some emotional arousal (or, in McDonald's words, "affective arousal"). For most persons, the physical discomfort of hunger, heat, or cold, or the experience of being misunderstood by friends, or the prospect of a test for which one is not prepared is unpleasant. Being asked by the coach to try out for the team may be pleasant if the student considers himself a pretty good player. If, however, he loathes football, or fears contact sports, or feels he is a poor player, his placidity prior to the coach's invitation may give way afterward to apprehension and anxiety—evidence of strong affective arousal.

Affective arousal prepares one for the third aspect of motivation: appropriate action in dealing with the situation ("anticipatory goal reactions"). Appropriate action in the examples cited above may be buying and eating a candy bar (if hungry), turning off the radiator or opening a window (if one is too hot), turning up the thermostat (if one is too cold), writing a conciliatory note to the estranged friend, and asking the teacher or a classmate for help with difficult arithmetic problems. Appropriate action by the student invited to try out for the team may involve performing enthusiastically the exercises needed to get in top physical condition and putting forth maximum effort in blocking and tackling (if the coach's invitation reinforces

[1] Frederick J. McDonald, *Educational Psychology*, 2nd ed. (Belmont, California: Wadsworth Publishing Co., 1965), p. 112.

his own aspirations and feelings of competence in playing football). If the student dislikes football or believes he is a mediocre or poor player, appropriate action in response to the coach's invitation may be getting an after-school job, becoming involved in other extracurricular activities, or pleading to be excused from trying out for the team because of the pressure of studies. In each case the appropriate action is directed toward reducing the imbalance created by the initial energy change. In the process, affective arousal diminishes and a state of relative quiescence is restored.

One's internal basis for responding in a learning situation is greatly influenced by present and past events and future aspirations, as the following anecdote reveals.

As Hazel Brown watched her eleventh-grade English class taking a test, she observed a wide variety of behaviors among her students. Some were busily at work—reading, thinking about the questions, jotting down the answers. Others were biting their pencils, erasing, and staring at the ceiling in hopes that correct answers would somehow come to them. A few were staring out the window, looking around, playing with objects on their desks—apparently making no effort to complete the examination.

That some students were strongly motivated toward academic achievement while others were much less motivated in this direction was quickly discernible to Hazel. She did not expect to find, however, a variety of motivations among her top students. She had assumed that her best students were motivated by a desire for personal achievement and for remaining in the college-prep section, but her conferences with students revealed an astonishing variety of individual motives. Ronnie Wilson wanted most of all to beat out his arch rival, Bill James. Shirley Weston sought to maintain her parents' approval, which high grades earned for her. Ted Jenkins frankly admitted he had to make the grades to be admitted to engineering school. It seemed clear that Bob Hammond was compensating in academic areas for his lack of skill in sports. Barbara, Jean, and Tim were mainly interested in staying on the honor roll no matter what, while quiet Margaret Hanson, seemingly oblivious to grades, was more interested in analyzing the plot and characters of *Macbeth*. The statements of several students revealed not one but two or three such motives.

This anecdote illustrates several principles which are important to our understanding of motivation. First of all, each student's behavior during the test was in response to some internal state or bodily condition. *Motivation is a process within the individual.* It is not something that the teacher does or gives to the student.

Second, we cannot observe motives directly. Behavior may be observed directly, but *motives may only be inferred.* When his group is called to the reading circle, Andy frequently reports that he has misplaced his book. After test papers have been handed back, Evie brings her paper to the teacher to complain that the teacher's scoring of her paper has not been fair.

In each case, we observe the situation and the child's response in that situation, but we have no direct evidence of the coordinated activities of receptors, nervous system, muscles, and glands which presumably intervened and influenced the observed behavior. Since motives are inferred, they are tentative and must be checked and revised in the light of additional evidence. Hazel Brown's initial inferences about her top students, based on her observations of them as they took the test, proved to be oversimplified and only partially correct. As Hazel observes these and other students over a period of several months in a variety of situations, the consistencies she observes in their behavior will enable her to make successively more accurate inferences of their motives.

Finally, an individual's behavior is not the result of just one motive or one need but *is influenced by many different and complex motives, some of which may be unconscious.* Hazel Brown was surprised to learn not only that she had to cope with different levels and kinds of motivation within a single classroom but also that students who behave in a similar manner often respond in this way for quite different reasons. How can a teacher organize a learning environment which will be meaningful to persons with such widely varying motive patterns? It is on this problem that the present chapter focuses.

Motivation in Historical Perspective

Free Will

Philosophers from the time of Plato and Aristotle have conceived of man as a rational being who uses his human capacities to achieve his conscious desires. According to this view, man's behavior is explained by what he has willed; and through the faculty of will, man can control the base and evil side of his nature in the interests of virtue and salvation.

Psychologists have not found free will satisfactory for explaining why a person has acquired his particular set of wants and desires—why one man, for instance, steals money while another gives it away in philanthropic enterprises. One must perforce look beyond each man's will for a more adequate explanation of his behavior.

Hedonism

Everyday experience suggests that individuals respond to stimuli or events in ways that bring pleasure and avoid pain. This "seeking-pleasure-avoiding-pain" conception of motivation is called *hedonism*. Hedonism as a theory of motivation has had a long history, extending back to the ancient Greek philosophers; but it gained its greatest prominence in the eighteenth and nineteenth centuries—probably achieving its fullest development and advocacy in the words of Jeremy Bentham (1748–1832), who argued that man's conduct of practical affairs must be in accord with what is good, *good* being defined as pleasure or happiness.

Psychologists have criticized hedonism as a theory of motivation because of its dependence on the subject's self-reports of his own internal, private affective state. How can we really know the degree of pleasure or pain that another person feels, and does the presence of unconscious factors permit the person to give an objective account of his own feelings? The problem is further complicated by evidence that some persons do things and seek out experiences that bring pain, while others avoid doing things that would bring pleasure. Climbing mountains, hunting wild animals, and fighting in wars are activities in which pain, discomfort, and the possibilities of death are very great. Yet men and women choose dangerous occupations or volunteer for dangerous missions in preference to the comforts and pleasures they would have at home in a more sedentary occupation. To explain this apparent paradox by suggesting that some people gain pleasure from the rigors and dangers of mountain climbing is circular.

A second limitation of hedonistic theories of motivation is that they explain a person's motivation only after the behavior has occurred. Florence worked uninterruptedly at her desk until she completed the assignment. When she handed in her paper, the teacher smiled and said, "Well done!" Frank refused to join his friends who skipped school yesterday and were sent to the office this morning. If the observer must wait until after the behavior occurred to infer that Florence in completing her work sought pleasure and that Frank in refusing his peers wished to avoid punishment, it is evident that hedonistic theories of motivation offer little help for predicting a subject's future behavior. The limitations of hedonism in explaining motivation are succinctly summarized by Allport: "Happiness is at best a byproduct of otherwise-motivated activity. One who aims at happiness has no aim at all."[2]

In spite of its limitations as an overall theory, many current psychological theories incorporate elements of hedonism. Freud's pleasure principle, for example, hypothesizes that the id functions to discharge tension and to restore balance. In learning theory, Thorndike's initial statement of his law of effect proposed that stimulus-response (S-R) connections are strengthened or weakened if they are followed, respectively, by a satisfying or annoying state of affairs. More recently, two researchers have suggested that the arousal, maintenance, and direction of behavior depend upon the degree of positive or negative feelings associated with the activity or goal. Young,[3] for example, found that well-fed, healthy animals responded more vigorously in running a maze when sugar was the reward than when casein (protein in milk), a less palatable food, was the reward. McClelland[4] suggests that when a variety of

[2] Gordon W. Allport, *Pattern and Growth in Personality* (New York: Holt, Rinehart and Winston, 1961), p. 200.

[3] P. T. Young, "Food-Seeking Drive, Affective Process and Learning," *Psychological Review,* 56 (March 1949), 98–121. See also P. T. Young, *Motivation and Emotion* (New York: John Wiley, 1961).

[4] David C. McClelland, *Personality* (New York: William Sloane Associates, 1951).

stimuli or cues are associated with a pleasant situation, any one or several of these stimuli or cues, on subsequent occasions, may reactivate the pleasant feeling. Thus, if the pleasures of a very special date are linked with a particular food, song, or perfume, the individual on subsequent occasions is likely to prepare the food, select the song, or use the perfume in seeking to reexperience the pleasures initially associated with these stimuli.

Instincts

Darwin's theory of evolution provided an impetus for the development of more objective and scientific theories of motivation. Darwin observed that many responses of lower animals to specific environmental stimuli are apparently unlearned. The homing tendencies of pigeons and salmon are examples of such innate behavior patterns, called instincts. An *instinct* has been defined as an inherited and specific stereotyped pattern of behavior elicited by particular environmental stimuli. Higher animals possess fewer of these innate behavior patterns. Most of their behaviors are learned and reflect the advantage of a highly developed brain and nervous system.

During the latter half of the nineteenth century, considerable progress was made in identifying specific innate behavioral tendencies of birds, ants, wasps, spiders, and various mammals. In the early part of the twentieth century, McDougall[5] developed a theory that instincts and their associated emotions are the most important determiners of conduct. According to McDougall, instincts are not mere reflexes or mechanical blind strivings; rather, they are purposive, inherited, goal-seeking tendencies which serve as mainsprings for action. The major instincts postulated by McDougall were those for flight, repulsion, curiosity, pugnacity, self-abasement, self-assertion, and parenthood. Freud gives a prominent place to instincts in his theory of psychoanalysis, but since his instincts of sex, self-preservation, and death are more like drives, they are discussed in the section on drive theories.

By 1920, instinct theories, when used to explain human motivation, had come under increasing attack. The list of instincts grew so large that little difference remained between the naming of an instinct and the listing of the behavior it was trying to explain. This loss of meaning of the term was shown by Bernard, who listed nearly 6,000 instincts—including "the instinct to avoid eating apples that grow in one's own orchard."[6]

The term *instinct* by this time had become barren in meaning and of little use in explaining human motivation. However, the concept is still used in studies of animal motivation—most notably in studies of *imprinting*. Imprinting is the process whereby an animal such as a baby duck becomes attached to and follows any stimulus object that appears during a critical period of a few days after it has hatched from the egg. Although the attach-

[5] William McDougall, *An Introduction to Social Psychology* (London: Methuen, 1908), pp. 39–76.
[6] Luther L. Bernard, *Instinct: A Study in Social Psychology* (New York: Holt, Rinehart and Winston, 1924), p. 212.

ment is usually made to the mother duck, it may be made to a hen, a decoy, or a quacking human experimenter. Once this attachment is made, the duckling will thenceforth continue to follow that object. The response pattern to the "imprinted" stimulus becomes fixed. After the critical period, the duckling does not change to follow a different object.

Through imprinting, animals acquire unlearned, fixed motivation and behavior patterns, each of which is peculiar to a given species. Imprinting and the older, more general term *instinct* now refer to the specific, built-in, automatic motives and responses of lower animals, who possess limited capacities for learning. Learning, on the other hand, plays a central role in the development of human motives. Drives and needs, most of which are learned, have proved more useful for understanding human motivation.

Drives

About 1925, the term *drive* gained prominence as an explanatory concept in motivation and learning theory. Woodworth introduced the concept of drive in 1918 to describe energy which impels the organism to action in response to tissue needs arising from hunger, thirst, sex, or bodily inactivity. Soon the term *drive* became associated with specific drives instead of the general supply of energy to which Woodworth had initially referred. In this manner the term gradually supplanted the term *instinct*.

Psychologists generally have preferred a theory of motivation based on drives, because the concept of drive has proved more amenable to scientific investigation. In a typical experimental study, a single drive is selected and defined operationally in measurable terms. The effects of drive, expressed in terms of a specific number of hours of food or water deprivation or level of intensity of an electric shock, can then be studied in relation to various behavior and learning outcomes. These experiments have used animals as subjects and thus appear to have few implications for classroom learning; however, they have made important contributions to the development of a general theory of behavior.

Drive, as a motivational concept, had a central role in Hull's reinforcement learning theory. Hull[7] described two kinds of drive, primary and secondary. A *primary drive* is an arousal state produced by deprivation of food, water, or other physiological requirement. A *secondary drive* (also called an acquired drive) is a stimulus present at the time a primary drive is activated. When a child touches a hot stove, the pain (primary drive) is followed by a withdrawal of the hand, while fear of being burned (secondary drive) leads to an avoidance of stoves. In Hull's theory, responses which are associated with a reduction of drive (primary or secondary) are said to be reinforced; reinforced behaviors tend to be repeated and to become habits, and indicate that learning has occurred.

Further support for a drive theory of motivation was provided by

[7] Clark E. Hull, *Principles of Behavior* (New York: Appleton-Century-Crofts, 1943).

Cannon's[8] concept of *homeostasis*—numerous complex physiological processes which maintain most of the steady states in the organism. Any physiological imbalance arising from extremes in temperature or from changes in the water, salt, sugar, protein, fat, or calcium content of the blood triggers certain physiological mechanisms; these mechanisms effect a return of the organism to a stable state. For example, loss of body fluids in hot weather activates compensatory neural and chemical changes (involving principally the sympathetic portion of the autonomic nervous system) which divert fluid from the lymph system and tissues into the blood stream. Increasing one's salt intake during hot weather assists the organism's homeostatic response of effecting a retention of water in the body.

Cannon points out that hunger and thirst produce instabilities which require behavioral intervention to restore homeostatic balance. When an organic imbalance (such as hunger, thirst, or pain) requires behavioral intervention to restore equilibrium, the state of arousal, manifested in heightened sensitivity and tense muscles, is called *drive*.

Some psychologists[9] have extended the concept of homeostasis and have used it to explain psychological phenomena. One's perceptions, habits, beliefs, and values thus are regarded as higher-level (psychological) responses which function to maintain personality organization. Critics of this position,[10] however, object to the use of a physiological concept to explain a psychological problem. Furthermore, the critics contend, this position fails to account for spontaneous, altruistic, creative behaviors—unique characteristics of human beings.

Needs

The term *needs* refers to general and specific conditions of lack or deficiency within the organism. In seeking to explain motivation by a concept of needs, psychologists and educators suggest that it is more meaningful and useful to identify the specific deficiencies and their causes than to focus upon the drive state which these deficiencies arouse. The existence of a need provides an impetus for goal-seeking behavior directed toward reducing the lack or deficiency. Subjectively, the reduction of the lack or deficiency is often associated with satisfaction. Thus, needs describe the general sources of people's motives. By observing an individual over a period of time, we may make inferences about his motives and the needs he is attempting to satisfy. If we observe that a particular student, Virginia, makes frequent contributions to class discussions, carefully prepares assignments and gets high test marks, tries out for the school's academic quiz team, and expresses concern

---

[8] Walter B. Cannon, *Wisdom of the Body* (New York: W. W. Norton & Co., 1939).

[9] J. M. Fletcher, "Homeostasis as an Explanatory Principle in Psychology," *Psychological Review*, 49 (1942), 80–87; R. Stagner, "Homeostasis as a Unifying Concept in Personality Theory," *Psychological Review*, 58 (1951), 5–17.

[10] See H. H. Toch and A. H. Hastorf, "Homeostasis in Psychology," *Psychiatry*, 18 (1955), 81–92.

over maintaining a high scholastic average and getting into a good college, we may infer that she has needs for achievement and self-esteem.

The term *needs* is popular with educators because it points to the goals toward which students are striving and thus can lead to effective curriculum planning. In inferring needs from observations of a student's behavior, however, some teachers unfortunately use the term normatively—that is, they use the term to refer to what the student *should* need, do, or accomplish. In contrast to *normative needs, psychological needs* are the actual states of deficiency or tension in a particular individual—states that are inferred from his goal-directed behaviors. A chief distinction between the two kinds of needs is that psychological needs are linked to motives and specific behavior, whereas normative needs represent what ought to occur. The two meanings reflect a confusion as to whose needs and goals are being described—the adult's or the child's.

A number of schemes for classifying psychological needs have been developed. Three of these systems (Murray's, Maslow's, and Raths and Burrell's) are presented in Tables 3.1, 3.2, and 3.3.

Murray,[11] through a series of individual interviews, tests, and experiments with fifty men of college age, sought to discover some of the principles that govern human behavior. He attempted to correlate observed directions of behavior with subjective reports of intention (wish, desire, aim, or purpose) and to infer the operation of one or more drives or needs. By analyzing the responses of his subjects to certain contrived situations, he identified twelve viscerogenic (physical) needs and twenty-eight psychogenic needs. Later these were reduced in number to the list of twenty needs shown in Table 3.1. Murray's system of needs has been widely used in personality and motivation research. Both the Thematic Apperception Test (TAT) and McClelland's need-for-achievement research (discussed later in the chapter) are based on Murray's need theory.

Maslow[12] proposed a hierarchical set of five basic needs: physiological, safety, love and belongingness, self-esteem, and self-actualization. The highest of these needs (self-actualization) can, according to Maslow, be satisfied only after the lower-level needs have been satisfied. Thus, only after man's physical need for water and food is satisfied is he free to pursue higher-level goals. The satisfying of needs at one level is followed by restlessness and discontent, symptoms which mark the presence of other needs at yet higher levels.

Raths and Burrell[13] have identified eight needs (emotional needs for belonging, for achievement, for economic security, for freedom from fear, for love and affection, for freedom from intense feelings of guilt, for self-respect, and for understanding). Raths and Burrell provide suggestions designed to

[11] Henry A. Murray, *Explorations in Personality* (New York: Oxford University Press, 1938), pp. 152–226. Table 3.1 is adapted from this work by permission.

[12] Abraham H. Maslow, *Motivation and Personality* (New York: Harper & Row, 1954), pp. 80–106. Table 3.2 is drawn from this work by permission.

[13] Louis E. Raths and Anna P. Burrell, *Understanding the Problem Child* (West Orange, New Jersey: The Economics Press, 1963), pp. 7–20. Table 3.3 is condensed from this work by permission.

Table 3.1.   Murray's list of needs.

Abasement. To submit passively to external force. To accept injury, blame, criticism. To admit inferiority.

Achievement. To accomplish something difficult. To master or manipulate. To excel oneself. To rival and surpass others.

Affiliation. To please and win affection of a valued object. To adhere and remain loyal to a friend.

Aggression. To overcome opposition forcefully. To fight. To revenge an injury. To attack, injure, or kill.

Autonomy. To get free. To resist coercion and restriction. To be independent and free to act according to impulse. To defy conventions.

Counteraction. To master or make up for failure by restriving. To overcome weakness, to repress fear.

Defendance. To defend the self against assault, criticism, and blame. To vindicate the ego.

Deference. To admire and support a superior. To praise, honor, or eulogize. To conform to custom.

Dominance. To control one's human environment. To influence or direct the behavior of others.

Exhibition. To make an impression. To be seen and heard. To excite, amaze, fascinate, entertain, shock, amuse, or entice others.

Harmavoidance. To avoid pain, physical injury, illness, and death. To escape from a dangerous situation. To take precautionary measures.

Infavoidance. To avoid humiliation. To refrain from action because of the fear of failure.

Nurturance. To give sympathy and gratify needs of a helpless other. To feed, help, support, console, protect, nurse, heal.

Order. To put things in order. To achieve cleanliness, arrangement, organization, balance, neatness, and precision.

Play. To act for "fun" without further purpose. To laugh and make jokes. To participate in games, sports, dancing, parties.

Rejection. To separate oneself from a negatively cathected other. To exclude, abandon, expel, or remain indifferent to someone who is inferior.

Sentience. To seek and enjoy sensuous impressions.

Sex. To form and further an erotic relationship.

Succorance. To have one's needs gratified by the sympathetic aid of an allied other. To be nursed, supported, sustained, protected, loved, guided, forgiven, consoled.

Understanding. To ask or answer general questions. To speculate, formulate, analyze, and generalize.

Table 3.2.   Maslow's list of needs.

Physiological needs
Safety needs
Love and belongingness needs
Self-esteem needs
Need for self-actualization

Table 3.3. Raths' and Burrell's list of needs.

Belonging is manifested by a child who feels unwanted or neglected. He may ask why he is not desired by group, club, or agemates.

Achievement is shown when a child expresses a desire for more attention and praise. He may wish to "do more" or "do something better."

Economic security is seen when a child worries about his father's job, the cost of things, or why he cannot have some of the things he wants.

Freedom from fear is shown when child evidences anxiety concerning persons in authority, sickness, death, or certain animals. Fear of being in a minority group.

Love and affection is shown when child asks teacher if he can sit beside her, and if she likes him. May shower affection on others.

Freedom from intense feelings of guilt is revealed when child expresses guilt concerning relationships with people. May blame self and internalize guilt.

Sharing and self-respect is shown when child indicates he wishes people had more faith in his judgment or that he might have more of a part in group activities.

Understanding is evidenced when child seems bewildered by his surroundings and the demands upon him. May ask questions, insist on answers to his questions, or express doubt about things he is told.

---

help teachers identify these needs as they are expressed in students' behavior. In addition, they discuss approaches which teachers can use in helping school children to gain increased satisfaction of these needs.

Essentially, a classification of needs provides a framework for the study of human behavior. Although they will not be identified as such, human needs which emerge from the interplay of physical, cultural, and psychological forces will be a central focus of the next six chapters.

Innate versus Acquired Motives

Some of the motives we have discussed (such as those arising from hunger, thirst, and nonactivity) have a direct bearing on man's existence as a physical organism. These motives are said to be basic because they relate to the satisfaction of needs that are essential to the preservation of life and health of the individual. Motives which relate to the social and psychological development of man, however, seem to be of a different order. They are acquired and appear to bear little relationship to physiological needs. An *acquired motive* is an arousal state within the organism which has been learned.

Evidence that much of human motivation is acquired comes from anthropologists' studies of other cultures. Some societies (such as the Zuñi and Hopi Indian cultures of Arizona and New Mexico and the Arapesh of New Guinea) attach little importance to acquisitiveness and competitiveness— motives that are prominent in many parts of Western culture. Studies of social-class differences, reported in Chapter 6, show that motives for academic achievement and self-esteem are more strongly manifested among middle-class persons, whereas motives reflecting strong loyalty to and support of family, friends, and community are commonly observed among lower-class persons and groups.

A frequently observed example of an acquired motive is fear—a learned response to stimuli associated with pain or discomfort (stimuli such as a hot stove or being left alone). Fears may be specific, objective, and real; or they may be imaginary, irrational, and generalized. A persistent fear of the latter type is often called *anxiety*. The anxieties people reveal concerning an examination, their job, their families, or their sense of adequacy indicate that anxiety, too, is a powerful motive for shaping human behavior.

Several theories have been advanced to explain how acquired motives are derived from physiological motives. One such theory is Freud's explanation of sublimation. According to Freud, the instincts, impulses, and energies of the id become redirected by the ego away from socially disapproved objects and toward socially approved ones by a process called *displacement*. When the substitute object represents a higher or more socially approved cultural goal, the displacement is called *sublimation*. In the process of sublimation, new motives are acquired as energies are rechanneled into intellectual, humanitarian, cultural, or artistic pursuits. Boys may sublimate their aggressive impulses by participating in contact sports such as football, boxing, and hockey. Adolescent girls may channel and sublimate their sex and nurturing drives by serving as a nurse's aid or by caring for young children. In this manner new motives (in the form of arousals toward substitute goals and activities) are formed as energies are expended and tensions are reduced through sublimation.

Allport,[14] in his theory of the functional autonomy of motives, offers another explanation for the emergence of acquired motives. He contends that a motivation based solely on instincts (as suggested by McDougall) or on sublimation of sexual and aggressive impulses (as put forth by Freud) is inadequate for explaining the uniqueness, the spontaneity, and the forward-looking, concrete character of adult motivation. *Functional autonomy* describes the process through which the child's early physiological and social

[14] Allport, pp. 226–253.

drives, expressed in his dependence on parents, are replaced by self-sustaining contemporary goals, which often bear little relationship to earlier antecedents. A successful businessman in a large city may purchase a farm so that he may savor on weekends some of the experiences he had as a boy growing up on a farm. He no longer has the need to identify with his father, to prove himself able to do a man's work, or to feel needed by his family. His desire to reexperience the joys of country living is functionally autonomous. Similarly, the desire to attend school persists in a few "perpetual students" long after they have earned the academic degrees for entrance into their vocation or profession. They long to remain students even though this role no longer earns them parental approval or social recognition. Do some people become teachers to satisfy curiosity and learning motives, experienced initially as a student, which have since become functionally autonomous?

It is frequently difficult to discern whether certain motives are innate or acquired. Since the needs for affiliation with and love of another human being do not appear to be expressed in the newborn infant's behavior, one might conclude that motives reflecting these needs are acquired. However, human infants who have been denied tactual experience and "mothering" by a human mother or her substitute suffer disabling effects—which seems to suggest that there is an innate component in the motives for affiliation and love.

A strong desire on the part of human beings for environmental stimulation is shown by Heron's[15] studies of *sensory deprivation,* wherein male college students were paid twenty dollars a day to be enclosed in a lighted cubicle and do nothing. They wore translucent plastic visors which transmitted diffuse light but prevented patterned vision. Cotton gloves and cardboard cuffs extending beyond the fingertips prevented feeling by touch. Auditory perception was limited by a U-shaped foam-rubber pillow and the continuous hum of an air conditioner. Most of the subjects had planned to use their time in the sensation-free cubicle reviewing their studies, planning a term paper, or organizing a lecture. During perceptual isolation their thoughts changed from thinking about studies to reminiscing about past incidents and friends. Eventually it took too much effort to concentrate, and they let their minds drift. The most striking effects were the subjects' reports of hallucinations over which they felt they had little control. One subject could not stop "seeing" dogs, while another could see nothing but eyeglasses. The childish emotional responses, disturbed visual perception, and hallucinations suggest that the human being requires continuous sensory stimulation; for, without it, the brain ceases to function adequately, and behavioral abnormalities appear.

Organic motives for food, water, and activity are dominant when the life of the organism is threatened. For most human beings, however, learned (acquired) motives, such as those expressed in needs for affiliation, achieve-

15 Woodburn Heron, "The Pathology of Boredom," *Scientific American,* 196 (January 1957), 52–56.

ment, and self-esteem, exert the greatest influence on behavior. The origin of these motives is not certain. They might be derived from basic physiological motives (such as a child's learning to love the person who feeds him), or they may be functionally autonomous (an achievement drive becoming autonomous as it replaces an earlier need for love or self-esteem), or they may be evidences of intrinsically motivated behavior (a boy takes apart an old clock to learn how it works).

Intrinsic Motives

Intrinsic motives are energy arousals with no known antecedents. The intrinsic motives discussed in this section cannot be traced to a specific homeostatic imbalance nor are they derived from a physiological drive.

Exploratory and Curiosity Drives

Organisms appear to seek not just any kind of environmental stimulation but some degree of novelty and change in what they see, hear, feel, and touch. Novel stimuli arouse curiosity in animals, children, and adults. An individual manifests curiosity when he avoids familiar aspects of the environment; seeks new experiences; approaches and investigates new, ambiguous, or incongruous aspects of the environment; or asks for information from other people.[16] Children show curiosity when they examine and manipulate toys, puzzles, or mechanical gadgets, when they explore woods, dumps, caves, or beaches, or when they ask questions about events or ideas that appear to be incomplete or incongruous.

The observation that young children appear to be curious is supported by a number of researches. Mendel[17] showed 60 nursery school children, ages three to five, first one array of eight small toys (either 0 or 100 percent in novelty) and then four other arrays. The five arrays of toys were graduated in degree of novelty as follows: 0, 25, 50, 75, and 100 percent. Most of the children chose the novel arrays of toys in preference to more familiar toys.

Other studies have investigated the motivational basis of curiosity. Smock and Holt[18] sought to ascertain children's responses to a series of quite different pictures—some of them ambiguous and incongruous, others relatively familiar. The subjects, 44 first-grade children (22 boys and 22 girls), were shown pictures projected on the screen of a mock TV set. Each child sat in front of the mock TV set and was instructed to press a "repeat"

[16] Daniel E. Berlyne, *Conflict, Arousal, and Curiosity* (New York: McGraw-Hill Book Co., 1960), pp. 79–162.
[17] Gisela Mendel, "Children's Preferences for Differing Degrees of Novelty," *Child Development*, 36 (June 1965), 453–465.
[18] Charles D. Smock and Bess G. Holt, "Children's Reactions to Novelty: An Experimental Study of 'Curiosity Motivation,'" *Child Development*, 3? (September 1962), 631–642.

button to request a repetition of the same picture. He was also shown a lever which he could press to signal a "change" to a different picture. Results of the study showed that novel stimuli (ambiguous and incongruous pictures) elicited significantly more "repetition" responses than did non-novel pictures. Smock and Holt also found that children who were perceptually rigid (reluctant to change their interpretations of a picture in response to change in cues) were less responsive to the incongruous pictures. In general, however, the results of this study suggest that curiosity is aroused in response to a mismatch between one's mental set and his perception of environmental events.

In a study involving fifth-grade children, Maw and Maw[19] found that children with high curiosity (those so identified by teachers, peers, and themselves) chose unbalanced and unusual pictures, in preference to balanced and usual ones, more frequently than did children identified as having low curiosity. Maw and Maw conclude that curiosity level may be more important than IQ for determining the teaching materials and procedures that should be used with a given classroom group. Children with similar IQ's may desire different degrees of uncertainty in a learning situation.

Activity and Manipulatory Motives

Children may be observed to persist in physical movements and manipulatory activities over fairly extended periods of time. Swinging, running, climbing the jungle gym, riding a tricycle, punching the keys on a toy cash register or typewriter are activities which children appear to continue for their own sake. Few studies have investigated manipulatory drives in children; but Piaget's[20] observations of his infant son, Laurent, tell us something about how these drives develop. Piaget observed that Laurent accidentally shook the rattle that was placed in his hand and then continued shaking it for fifteen minutes, during which time he emitted peals of laughter. Later, giving Laurent a notebook, a beaded purse, and a wooden parrot, Piaget noted four stages of response: (1) visual exploration, passing the object from hand to hand; (2) tactile exploration, passing his hand over the object; (3) moving the object slowly in space; and (4) shaking the object, then striking it, then rubbing it against his bassinet, then sucking it. In each instance, Laurent seemed to study the effect of his activity.

Cognitive Motives

Other intrinsic motives are those wherein the individual utilizes mental processes and cognitive functioning. Children become fascinated with making up limericks and solving puzzles and riddles; adults read murder stories, play chess, or work crossword puzzles—apparently for the intrinsic satisfac-

19 Wallace H. Maw and Ethel W. Maw, "Selection of Unbalanced and Unusual Designs by Children High in Curiosity," *Child Development*, 33 (December 1962), 917–922.
20 Jean Piaget, *The Origins of Intelligence in Children*, trans. by M. Cook (New York: International University Press, 1952), pp. 162, 255.

tions that these cognitive activities provide. Indeed the doctor who tries to save the life of a patient, the businessman who works to stay ahead of the competition, and the teacher who helps a nonreader learn to read are motivated by something beyond the remuneration they receive. In each case, the use of cognitive processes and intellectual abilities is intrinsically satisfying, even though these processes and abilities are directed toward external goals.

Another aspect of cognitive motivation is one's motivation to make his behavior consistent with his ways of viewing, evaluating, and thinking about this behavior. Inconsistency between one's behavior and his cognitive responses toward the behavior creates what Festinger[21] calls *cognitive dissonance*. According to Festinger, if a discrepancy exists between one's behavior and his evaluation of that behavior, the individual will justify and rationalize his behavior so as to reduce the discrepancy. The motive to reduce dissonance is comparable to achieving a kind of "cognitive homeostasis." John, for instance, perceives himself as an able student and yet does poorly on an examination. He may try to reduce the resulting cognitive dissonance by intellectualizing that grades do not measure the most important outcomes of a college education, that the most successful people are not always those who received the highest grades, that the instructor has a reputation for being unfair, or that he is a good student in every subject except this one. John's intellectualization has enabled him to reduce cognitive dissonance by devaluing the importance of grades and modifying his self-concept.

Concept of Competence

Curiosity, exploratory activity, and manipulative behavior, according to White,[22] all play important roles in the attainment of *competence*. Competence, or *effectance*, is not acquired through behavior instigated by drives based on physiological deficits. Rather, it is a process through which animals and human beings actively seek environmental stimulation. Monkeys manipulate objects placed in the cage, infants shake rattles, and men and boys explore caves. Exploration and manipulation increase one's level of competence and are motives in their own right.

Earlier, Harlow[23] took a similar position. He found no evidence that intensity of drive state and the correlated amount of drive reduction are positively related to learning efficiency in primates. In fact, rather than being influenced by food deprivation, monkeys seemed to learn more efficiently if they were given food before testing. Harlow concludes that a drive-reduction theory of learning is untenable and that curiosity is a first-order motive, not a derived drive.

---

[21] Leon Festinger, *A Theory of Cognitive Dissonance* (Stanford, California: Stanford University Press, 1957).

[22] Robert W. White, "Motivation Reconsidered: The Concept of Competence," *Psychological Review*, 66 (September 1959), 297–333.

[23] Harry F. Harlow, "Mice, Monkeys, Men and Motives," *Psychological Review*, 6 (1953), 23–32.

Motivation and School Learning

The previous section makes clear that a number of intrinsic motives (such as curiosity, exploration, and manipulation) significantly influence learning. Certain other intrinsic motives, however, play a particularly important role in school learning.

Social and Affiliative Motives

Pupils desire acceptance, approval, and recognition by parents, teachers, and peers. The social and affiliation motives are very effective in stimulating participation in learning activities. The first grader who has mastered his first reader often appears to experience as much satisfaction from demonstrating to his parents that he can read as he does from an inner sense of accomplishment.

The influence of social and affiliative motives on learning is revealed in several studies. Bandura and Huston[24] studied the effect of various adult-child relationships on the child's subsequent learning. Nursery school children who experienced consistently warm and rewarding interactions with the adult model imitated this model to a greater extent than did children who had not experienced this nurturing relationship. Sears,[25] in a study of learning conditions and children's behavior in fifth- and sixth-grade classrooms, found that the children who score high on creativity have usually received a great deal of personal attention and praise from their teachers. The satisfying of social and affiliative motives appears to facilitate learning among older students as well. High school students produce a greater number of original poems and art work for teachers whom they view as warm and considerate than they do for teachers whom they perceive as less warm.[26] Teachers who communicate personal warmth in their relationships with others also tend to make increased use of intrinsic motives and to promote pupils' interest in science.[27]

There is some evidence, however, that continuous nurturance on the part of teachers may be less effective than intermittent nurturance and nurturance withdrawal. Hartup[28] compared two groups of four-year-old chil-

[24] Albert Bandura and Aletha C. Huston, "Identification as a Process of Incidental Learning," *Journal of Abnormal and Social Psychology,* 63 (1961), 311–318.

[25] Pauline S. Sears, *The Effect of Classroom Conditions on the Strength of Achievement Motive and Work Output on Elementary Children,* Cooperative Research Project No. 873 (Washington, D.C.: Office of Education, U.S. Department of Health, Education, and Welfare, 1963).

[26] Morris L. Cogan, "The Behavior of Teachers and the Productive Behavior of their Pupils," *Journal of Experimental Education,* 27 (December 1958), 89–124.

[27] Horace B. Reed, "Implications for Science Education of Teacher Competence Research," *Science Education,* 46 (December 1962), 473–486.

[28] Willard W. Hartup, "Nurturance and Nurturance Withdrawal in Relation to the Dependency Behavior in Preschool Children," *Child Development,* 29 (June 1958), 191–201.

dren who were asked to learn a simple concept and a memory task. One group received consistent support and affection from a female experimenter during a ten-minute period of interaction. The other group received five minutes of such nurturant interaction followed by five minutes of nurturance withdrawal, wherein the experimenter ceased to interact with the child and responded to his supplications by saying she was "busy." Hartup found that children in the nurturance-withdrawal group needed fewer trials and made fewer errors in learning. These results suggest that nurturance withdrawal produces greater motivation than consistent nurturance. After a child has experienced warm interaction with an adult, withdrawal of nurturance arouses him to take action toward restoring the warm relationship.

Achievement Motives

The importance of achievement motives in school learning is self-evident. The need-for-achievement motive, often shortened to *nAch*, has been studied extensively by McClelland and his co-workers.[29] Their *nAch* measure consists of four TAT ambiguous-picture cards; the cards are projected on a screen, and the subjects are asked to write stories about the pictures. Children whose stories contain many achievement-related themes score high in *nAch*, the high score being interpreted as evidence of a strong need to achieve. McClelland found that persons high in achievement imagery (high *nAch* scores) complete more tasks when told that such tasks are measures of intellectual ability, solve more simple arithmetic problems in a timed test, get better grades, recall more uncompleted tasks, and have a higher level of aspiration.

Since the need-for-achievement motive is learned by the child as part of his socialization, the strength of this motive must depend on the parents' expectations and values and on the strength of the child's identification with parents and teachers. Winterbottom[30] found that the children of relatively demanding mothers scored higher in need for achievement than did children whose mothers made few demands on them. For example, mothers of offspring scoring high in *nAch* were more likely to expect their children, even before age eight, to know their way around the city, to try new things for themselves, to do well in competition, and to make their own friends. In a later study of middle-class mothers and sons, Winterbottom[31] found the strongest achievement motivation among boys whose mothers expected them to be self-reliant at a fairly early age.

[29] David C. McClelland, John W. Atkinson, Russell A. Clark, and Edgar L. Lowell, *The Achievement Motive* (New York: Appleton-Century-Crofts, 1953).

[30] Miriam R. Winterbottom, "The Relation of Childhood Training in Independence to Achievement Motivation" (unpublished doctor's dissertation, University of Michigan, 1953).

[31] Miriam R. Winterbottom, "The Relation of Need for Achievement to Learning Experiences in Independence and Mastery," in John W. Atkinson, *Motives in Fantasy Action and Society* (Princeton, New Jersey: D. Van Nostrand Co., 1958), pp. 453–478. See also Bernard C. Rosen and Roy D'Andrade, "The Psychosocial Origins of Achievement Motivation," *Sociometry*, 22 (1959), 185–195, 215–218.

Since parents who have attained high-ranking occupational levels usually attended college and had a certain amount of academic success, they might be more likely to expect their children to attend college than would parents at lower occupational levels. A study by Kahl[32] supports this assumption to a certain extent. In Kahl's study, the percentage of high school boys who expected to go to college was progressively higher for those whose fathers were at successively higher occupational levels.

Self-Enhancement Motives

Self-enhancement motives are manifested in strivings for self-improvement, for becoming a more adequate person, and for learning and understanding which permit one to cope more effectively with his world. Where goals of learning activities are perceived as self-enhancing, this motive becomes a powerful ally of the teacher in promoting learning. The strength of one's self-enhancement motives, together with one's evaluations and perceptions of self, largely determine the levels of aspiration one sets for himself. Studies of levels of aspiration and achievement thus provide further understanding of the influence of self-enhancement motives in learning.

Sears[33] investigated the influence of past experience on levels of aspiration in specific reading and arithmetic tasks. Three groups of children in the fourth, fifth, and sixth grades were studied. The first group, the "success" group, consisted of those who had consistently received high grades and saw themselves as doing well in reading and arithmetic. Children in the second group, the "failure" group, had received low grades and considered themselves poor in reading and arithmetic. A third group, called a "differential" group, consisted of children who had experienced success in reading but lack of success in arithmetic.

All three groups were tested under so-called "neutral" conditions; that is, each child was given a series of twenty individually timed reading tasks and twenty individually timed arithmetic tasks to perform in a situation that corresponded to the usual testing experience in an elementary school classroom. After each task the child was asked to estimate the amount of time it would take him to perform the next task. The relationship between level of aspiration and the level of performance was expressed as a *discrepancy score*. Figure 3.1 shows the mean discrepancy score under neutral conditions for all tasks in the reading and arithmetic series for each child in the three groups (N = 36). In Figure 3.1, score symbols of children who estimated they would take longer to complete the task are on the negative side (since a low goal signifies low aspiration). The score symbols for children

32 Joseph A. Kahl, *The American Class Structure* (New York: Holt, Rinehart and Winston, 1957).

33 Pauline S. Sears, "Levels of Aspiration in Academically Successful and Unsuccessful Children," *Journal of Abnormal and Social Psychology,* 35 (October 1940), 498–536. Figures 3.1 and 3.2 are from this article, pp. 511, 515. Copyright 1940 by the American Psychological Association, and reproduced by permission.

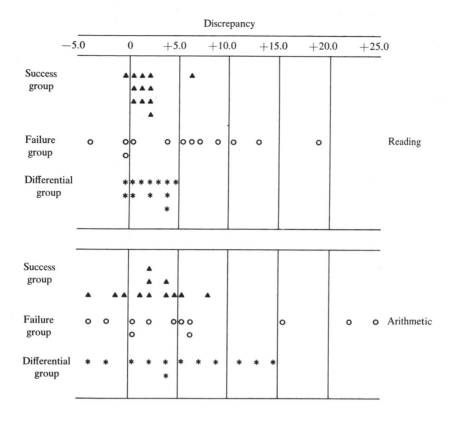

Figure 3.1. Mean discrepancy scores under neutral conditions (from Sears).

who took longer than their predicted times for performing the tasks are on the positive side (a high goal signifies high aspiration). For both the failure and the differential groups, children who had experienced previous failure were more varied in estimating their performance (levels of aspiration) for that series of tasks. The consistently lower discrepancy scores of children who had experienced success in that subject (reading or arithmetic) indicate that they were more realistic in the levels of aspiration they set for themselves in these tasks.

In subsequent testing, half of the children in each group were told they had done well ("success" conditions) on the reading tasks and had done poorly ("failure" conditions) on the arithmetic tasks. The others were told they had done poorly on reading tasks but had done well on the arithmetic tasks. Under "success" conditions, for 75 percent of the tasks the experimenter reported to the child that (irrespective of the actual performance time) his performance on the preceding task was as good or better than his time on the previous one. On each of the other tasks of the "success" series, his performance was reported as being somewhat poorer than his time on the previous task. Under "failure" conditions the child's performance was reported to him as poorer than 75 percent of the tasks and as better for the rest of the tasks.

Figure 3.2 presents data comparing discrepancy scores (levels of aspiration) under neutral, success, and failure conditions for three groups and two tasks combined. The data show that under success conditions, the level of aspiration set by the child is realistic (corresponds with actual performance)

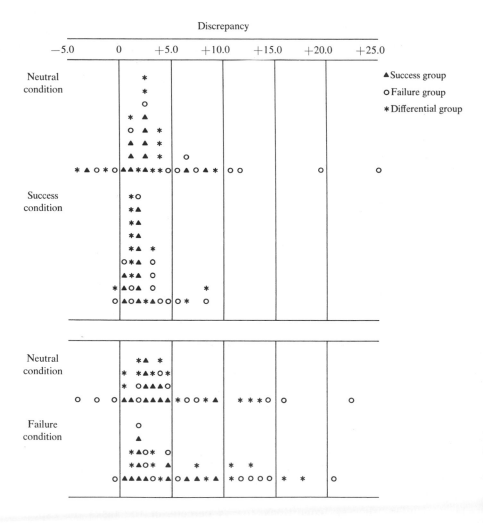

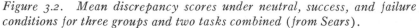

Figure 3.2. Mean discrepancy scores under neutral, success, and failure conditions for three groups and two tasks combined (from Sears).

while under failure conditions, levels of aspiration set by children are less realistic (wide discrepancies between estimates and performance). Sears identified three patterns which different groups of children used in setting levels of aspiration. The first group, a *low-positive-discrepancy* group, consistently set levels of aspiration above the performance level on the last task. For this group, composed mostly of "success" students, the setting of levels of aspiration was realistic and reflected immediately the results of the preceding performance. A second group, the *high-positive-discrepancy* group, consistently showed a large discrepancy between level of aspiration and performance scores. In this group, nearly all were "failure" children who initially set a level of aspiration markedly above their performance scores and maintained this level rigidly, even if their performance never approached it in excellence. If performance did approach this level of aspiration, this level was immediately raised so that a large discrepancy was maintained. Finally, the *negative-discrepancy* group of children—composed of about equal numbers from success, failure, and differential groups—persisted in setting their levels of aspiration below their performance scores.

Sears' study shows the effects of success and failure in strengthening and weakening children's self-enhancement motives (as reflected in their stated expectations for achievement). All children do not respond to success and failure in the same way, however. Some "play it safe" by setting their expectations below the level they can probably achieve, while others set unrealistically high goals.

Self-enhancement motivation is also revealed in a person's strivings to act in ways consistent with his view of himself (self-concept). Empirical observation and research both show that many students who test high in scholastic aptitude but receive average or low marks see themselves as inadequate and not very bright. High achievers, in contrast, generally have positive self-images. Martire[34] investigated the relationships between achievement motivation, discrepancies between self-concept and ideal self-concept, and estimates of level of aspiration. Fifty-three college students were administered a scrambled-words test under neutral conditions (informality and absence of achievement demands) and also under achievement-oriented conditions (subjects were told that the test measured verbal ability). After the testing under neutral conditions, need-for-achievement scores were obtained (by means of McClelland's procedure, described earlier). Ideal self-ratings (desire for achievement) and actual self-ratings (realized achievement) were obtained by having subjects rank a list of personality traits (including five achievement-related traits: intelligence, initiative, motivation, creativeness, and general success). Before taking the test under achievement-oriented conditions, subjects were given average performance scores of previous groups taking the test and were then asked to estimate the number of items they thought they would complete (level-of-aspiration measure). After completing a longer version of the scrambled-words test

[34] John G. Martire, "Relationships between the Self-Concept and Differences in the Strength and Generality of Achievement Motivation," *Journal of Personality,* 24 (June 1956), 364–375.

under achievement-oriented conditions, subjects were administered an alternative form of McClelland's *nAch* measure.

After these measures were administered, subjects were divided into four categories, corresponding to the level of their need-for-achievement scores under neutral conditions and under achievement-oriented conditions (low-high, high-high, high-low, and low-low). A general finding of this study was that the high-high category (those who had high *nAch* scores under both neutral and achievement-oriented conditions) showed a significantly greater discrepancy between ideal and actual self-ratings on the five achievement-related traits than did subjects in the other three categories. This discrepancy suggests that those in this group had developed an unrealistically high achievement motivation. Dissatisfaction in such highly motivated people, caused possibly by low intelligence or lack of opportunity, appears to be reflected in a discrepant self-concept. Martire also found that persons in the high-low category (subjects having a strong, generalized achievement motivation but presumed to be also anxious about failure when in a stressful situation) gave significantly lower estimates—both of the scores they *wished* they would receive and of the scores they *expected* to receive—than did other subjects. This finding suggests that fear of failure is stronger than the striving to achieve.

The Teacher's Influence on Students' Motives

Results of studies already cited, as well as common observation, attest to the central importance of motivation in learning. Thus, in seeking to guide and to promote the learning of students, the teacher is concerned with discovering ways through which they may be aroused to respond actively in learning situations. In general, the way in which one person influences the arousal state of another person is through the use of incentives. An *incentive* is a reward or source of satisfaction which a person *may* obtain. A merchandiser may offer price reductions, service, convenience, or trading stamps as incentives to consumers to induce them to purchase a certain product. A teacher frequently gives praise and high grades to students who perform well in school, the aim of these rewards being to encourage continuous strivings in the recipients and in the other pupils. Anxiety growing out of a fear of failure may also serve as an incentive in arousing the person to expend effort in seeking to avoid failure. Intrinsic motives such as curiosity, need for achievement, or need for self-enhancement may also serve as incentives.

Teachers, then, have a wide choice of incentives: externally controlled incentives such as rewards and punishments, intrinsic incentives such as the student's own need for achievement and self-enhancement, or some combination of extrinsic and intrinsic incentives. Although externally controlled incentives (rewards and punishments) are relatively easy to establish and administer and thus are widely used—by parents in rearing children, by courts and law-enforcement officers, by captains of business and industry, as well as by teachers—such incentives are most effective when they are linked with intrinsic incentives. Thistlethwaite[35] analyzed the effects of praise (in the form of favorable publicity) given to two groups of talented students who took the National Merit Scholarship Test. As a result of this praise (which bolstered their intrinsic need for achievement), a greater number of these students decided to work toward advanced degrees in college.

With few exceptions, studies show that reward in the form of praise, support, and encouragement significantly promotes learning. Page[36] investigated the motivational effects of teachers' comments on test papers. Seventy-four randomly selected high school teachers administered to their 2,139 students an objective test appropriate to the usual course of instruction. After the tests were scored, the papers were randomly assigned to one of three treatment groups: (1) the *no-comment* group, which received no marks beyond those for grading; (2) the *free-comment* group, which received whatever comments the teachers felt were appropriate; and (3) the *specified-comment* group, which received uniform, generally encouraging comments designated by the experimenter for each letter grade; for example, *A:* "Excellent! Keep it up!" *C:* "Perhaps try to do still better?" *F:* "Let's raise this grade!". On the next objective test, students in the free-comment group made slightly higher grades than those in the specific-comment group. However, those who had previously received a specified comment performed significantly better than students who had received no comment.

Kersh[37] studied the influence of teaching strategies on students' subsequent behavior and performance. In his study, each subject in each of three groups of college students was asked to learn the *odd-numbers* and the *constant-difference* rules of addition:

The odd-numbers rule. The sum of any series of consecutive odd numbers, beginning with 1, is equal to the square of the number of figures in the series. (For example, 1, 3, 5, 7 is such a series; there are four numbers, so 4 times 4 is 16, the sum.)

The constant-difference rule. The sum of any series of numbers in which the difference between the numbers is constant is equal to one half the product of the number of figures and the sum of the first and last numbers. (For example, 2, 3, 4, 5, is such a series; 2 and 5 are 7; there are four figures, so 4 times 7 is 28; half of 28 is 14, which is the sum.)

The first group, called the *no-help* group, was required to discover the rules for working the problem without any help from the experimenter. The second group, called the *directed-reference* group, was given some direction

[35] Donald L. Thistlethwaite, "Effects of Social Recognition upon the Educational Motivation of Talented Youth," *Journal of Educational Psychology,* 50 (June 1959), 111–116.

[36] Ellis B. Page, "Teacher Comments and Student Performance: A Seventy-Four Classroom Experiment in School Motivation," *Journal of Educational Psychology* 49 (August 1958), 173–181.

[37] Bert Y. Kersh, "The Adequacy of 'Meaning' as an Explanation for the Superiority of Learning by Independent Discovery," *Journal of Educational Psychology,* 49 (1958), 282–292.

in the form of perceptual aids. The third group, called the *rule-given* group, was told the rules directly and was given practice in applying them without any reference to the arithmetical or geometrical relationships. Thus, the teaching strategies used with the first two groups involved two approaches to discovery learning, while for the third group the teaching strategy involved the use of rote or mechanical learning.

The results of this study showed that students under the directed-reference (some-help) treatment scored highest on measures of retention and on transfer tasks involving use of the two rules. The no-help group scored higher than the rule-given group. Of particular interest in this study were the varied effects of teaching strategies on students' motivations in carrying out and extending the learning task. Subjects in the no-help group who failed to discover the rule during the practice sessions told of their efforts to learn the rule, even going so far as to look up the algebraic formula in the library. On the other hand, one subject in the rule-given group complained that the experimenter had not instructed him to remember the rules, so he promptly forgot them.

An important part of the teacher's task, then, is selecting and implementing strategies that will promote effective learning. Some of the ways which a teacher and the learning experiences she plans may relate to a student's motives are revealed in these excerpts from the case of Heidi, an eight-year-old girl in the third grade. Recorded in Heidi's school records is a listing of straight *A* marks for the first and second grades.

OCTOBER 6

The first part of our afternoon story hour is used for contributions (literary) from both the class and teacher. On certain days a child is allowed to read or tell a favorite story or poem. Yesterday I devoted the period to poetry reading, so today Heidi arrived with a shabby copy of *A Child's Garden of Verses* and asked if she could read two poems to the class. After telling the class that the book had belonged to her great-grandmother, she read "The Land of Counterpane" and "Windy Nights." Before I could compliment her choice of poetry and choose another reader, she continued, "And here's another favorite, 'My Shadow,' " and "I just love this one." She monopolized the fifteen-minute period reading her favorites. After each reading she would give an introduction to the next poem: "My mommy read this to me when I was two," or "I've known this ever since I could talk." Heidi's expression was so good and her animation so infectious that the entire class seemed to enjoy the entertainment.

OCTOBER 8

Today I was reading *Bambi* to the class when Heidi arrived late. She was again clasping her volume to her as she clumped noisily to her seat. As soon as she sat down, she opened her book and, with one hand keeping the place in the book, raised her hand as high as she could reach and kept it up during the entire story period.

NOVEMBER 4

Heidi and Jerry are team captains for our subtraction and addition contests for the month of November, and until today Heidi's team has been scoring ahead. Today, however, Jerry's team won by three points and Heidi made her first mistake at the board. Immediately following the mistake, Heidi complained of a headache, so I had her put her head on her desk. She kept her head down until noon recess, then left the room without glancing left or right.

NOVEMBER 8

Heidi's and Jerry's teams had another contest involving subtraction facts. Each child did five problems at the blackboard when his name was called. I noticed one little fellow glancing at his hand which rested on the chalk tray, and investigation revealed he had the answers to the combinations on a slip of paper in his left hand.

When I questioned the class, three admitted they had cheated in the same way, and another boy said that Heidi had cheated. He said she had looked at the answers which were written on a slip of paper on her desk. (Because she was the leader of her team, her desk was near the board.) Heidi admitted her guilt but said, "I only looked at two answers. I knew the rest." (She turned red, hung her head, and fingered the folds of her skirt.) I stopped the contest and had everyone return to his regular place in the classroom to do the arithmetic test on paper.

Particularly evident in these excerpts are the ways in which some motives (such as need for achievement and self-enhancement) are strengthened and become dominant, with the result that they may endanger the gratification of students' other motives—in Heidi's case, the need for acceptance and belonging.

Summary

Motivation is a process within the organism that mobilizes and directs energy toward some object or part of the environment. Although behavior may be observed directly, motives may only be inferred. Behavior is not the result of a single motive but is influenced by many different and complex motives, some of them unconscious.

Motivation has been defined as an internal energy change that results in affective arousal and anticipatory goal reactions.

Many theories have been advanced to explain motivation. One of these theories, free will, is compatible with many philosophical and theological doctrines but is not useful to psychologists in their attempts to explain the motives underlying behavior because it appears to beg the question. Another theory, hedonism, has had many adherents but fails to explain many things—for instance, why some persons seem to court danger and eschew the easy life.

Instinct theories conceive of motivation as innate and identify specific behavioral tendencies at various levels of animal life; by 1920, however, the instinct theory began to lose adherents because it proved inadequate for explaining the wide range of behavior that could not be classified as instinctual in the usual meaning of the term. *Drive theories* of motivation then attained prominence. A useful model for a drive theory of motivation is Cannon's concept of *homeostasis*—complex physiological processes that maintain most of the steady states in the organism. Various *need theories,* emphasizing specific lacks or deficiencies within the organism, are popular with educators because they point to goals toward which students are striving and provide data useful in curriculum planning. A distinction has been made between *normative needs,* needs that adults believe students *should* have, and *psychological needs,* needs that students actually do have.

Acquired motives (such as fear, anxiety, need for sensory stimulation) play important roles in human motivation. Various theories have been advanced to explain how acquired motives are learned. They may be derived from basic physiological motives (as suggested by Freud's concept of sublimation); they may be functionally autonomous; or they may be evidence of intrinsically motivated behavior.

Intrinsic motives are energy arousals with no known antecedents. Various intrinsic motives are exploratory and curiosity drives, activity and manipulatory motives, and cognitive motives.

Intrinsic motives important in promoting school learning are social and affiliative motives, achievement motives, and self-enhancement motives. The influence of self-enhancement motives in learning is revealed in studies of levels of aspiration and achievement. In general, students who have experienced failure show a greater discrepancy between their levels of aspiration and their performance, while those who have experienced success have lower discrepancy scores and are more realistic and consistent in estimating their subsequent performance.

Teachers who seek to arouse in students positive, active responses toward learning have a wide choice of *incentives* available. Reward incentives appear to be most effective in promoting learning when they are linked with such intrinsic motives as the need for affiliation, achievement, or self-enhancement. Research findings support the teacher's use of praise and encouragement in improving pupil performance. Also effective are teaching strategies that encourage students to find things out for themselves.

Study Questions

1. At the moment of its onset, an individual's behavior is already predetermined. State your agreement or disagreement with this proposition and discuss.

2. Children who begin kindergarten and first grade as eager, enthusiastic, and curious are observed in later grades to be apathetic or uninterested. What facts or principles concerning motivation might explain these changes in their behavior?

3. A teen-age boy has a consuming passion for working on hotrods. What needs are being satisfied by this activity? How might these motives be related to academic learning?

4. "You can lead a horse to water, but you can't make him drink" is a proverb that might characterize the belief that teachers cannot motivate students directly. What can a teacher do to influence a student's motivation so as to effect a change in his behavior?

5. If a student is an underachiever, what should you know about his needs in order to decide whether to place him in a class of like achievers or in a class of lower achievers?

Suggested Readings

C. N. Cofer and M. H. Appley. *Motivation: Theory and Research.* New York: John Wiley, 1964. Presents a comprehensive discussion of the several trends in motivation and research and analyzes the contribution each makes toward a unified theory of motivation.

Abraham Maslow. *Motivation and Personality.* New York: Harper & Row, 1954. Brings together the author's varied writings on the role of motivation in personality development. Of particular interest is Maslow's statement of a theory of motivation in Chapter 5 and his discussion of the qualities and characteristics of self-actualizing people in Chapters 12 and 13.

David C. McClelland, John W. Atkinson, Russell A. Clark, and Edgar L. Lowell. *The Achievement Motive.* New York: Appleton-Century-Crofts, 1955. Summarizes a five-year study of the achievement motive. Of special interest is the description of the development, scoring, and interpretation of a projective test for measuring the achievement motive. Chapter 2 presents a statement of the authors' theory of motivation.

Frederick J. McDonald. *Educational Psychology.* Second Edition. Belmont, California: Wadsworth Publishing Co., 1965. Chapter 4 draws distinctions between motives, needs, and incentives. How motives and needs are learned, the effects of school experiences on goal setting, and the relationship of motivation and teaching strategies are discussed.

Edward J. Murray. *Motivation and Emotion.* Englewood Cliffs, New Jersey: Prentice-Hall, 1964. Integrates various theoretical viewpoints and research studies on motivation. Discusses the origin, nature, and characteristics of homeostatic, sexual, and emotional motives, intrinsically motivated behavior, and derived social motives for achievement and affiliation.

Robert W. White. "Motivation Reconsidered: The Concept of Competence." *Psychological Review*, 66 (September 1959), 297–333. Discusses the widespread discontent with theories of motivation built upon primary drives. Advances the concept of competence as an explanation for the apparent tendency of people to explore their environment and interact effectively with it.

Films

Focus on Behavior: The Need to Achieve, 16 mm, sound, black and white, 30 min. Bloomington, Indiana: Audio-Visual Center, Indiana University (rental fee, $5.40). In this film, Dr. David McClelland demonstrates the tests with which he seeks to verify his psychological theory—that the economic growth or decline of nations is dependent to a large extent upon their entrepreneurs. The *need to achieve* is one of a variety of phenomena studied in motivation research.

Focus on Behavior: The Social Animal, 16 mm, sound, black and white, 29 min. Bloomington, Indiana: Audio-Visual Center, Indiana University (rental fee, $5.40). This film portrays some of the ways in which man is influenced and changed by his society. The effect of group pressure to conform is demonstrated through the experimental work of Dr. Stanley Schachter. The consequences of publicly stating ideas contrary to one's private belief illustrates Dr. Leon Festinger's theory of cognitive dissonance. The influence of motives of competition and cooperation in the bargaining process is explored by Dr. Morton Deutsch.

forces that shape development and learning

4

the physical organism and its growth

In complexity of organization, in structural intricacy, in harmony and balance of pattern, living things are in a separate category from the non-living.

≡   RALPH W. GERARD

In beginning a study of the human organism, we might do well to relate what we know about organic life in general to what we know about the universe. Our universe appears to be governed by natural laws of order, organization, unity, evolution, and change. Some of these natural laws are expressed in the physical sciences by the first and second laws of thermodynamics. The first of these laws relates to the conservation of energy: Energy can neither be created nor destroyed; it can only be changed. Since life, including human life, is a part of the universe, life is a manifestation of unique organizations of energy.

The second law of thermodynamics states that energy is becoming less organized, less available, and more random. The tendency toward the degradation of energy implied by this second law is called *entropy*. An example of the degradation of energy is the operation of machines wherein 30 to 50 percent of the fuel energy is converted into work and the remainder is degraded as friction and heat. The life impulse manifested in growth and development at the beginning of life and in adulthood constitutes a major countertendency to this second law of thermodynamics. However, with the increasing rate of catabolism (the breakdown of tissues and decrease in body efficiency) beginning in middle age and the consequent diminishing of vigor, life increasingly fulfills this second law.

Our knowledge of life in general and of human life in particular is increasing rapidly, but much remains to be known. Biologists became convinced a long time ago that it is not particularly useful to try to define life. Quite marvelous mechanical kidneys, hearts, and brains have been constructed, which—although they fit some of the definitions of life—are clearly not alive. Someone has said that the problem of defining life is a lot like trying to define your wife. You recognize her and you can describe her many features, characteristics, and habits—but just try defining her.

Characteristics of Life

We frequently find it useful to study life in relation to the qualities and characteristics shared by all living organisms. Both the amoeba and man metabolize, grow, reproduce, and adapt to their respective environments; and both possess a dynamic organization. Man differs from other living things only in that he is infinitely more complex. We now turn to an examination of five major characteristics of life, with special focus upon the ways each of these is manifested in man.

Metabolism

Some may wonder why, in enumerating the characteristics of living things, we begin with metabolism. We do so because of a basic law of life: Function precedes structure. The processes of metabolism and growth determine the emergent physical structure—not vice versa. The structure of the body, then, is a response to fundamental processes of metabolism and growth.

Living things take in materials from their environments, change them chemically, and convert them into new products. All of the changes which take place within cells and within the total organism in the synthesis of new materials are subsumed under the general term *metabolism.*

The process of human metabolism may become clearer if we relate it to the carbon cycle of plants and animals. Figure 4.1[1] shows that through the process of *photosynthesis* green plants take carbon dioxide from the air, take water from the soil, and in the presence of sunlight manufacture carbohydrates and give off oxygen. In animals this process is reversed: Carbohydrates and oxygen are taken in and carbon dioxide and water are given off.

[1] Adapted from Paul B. Weisz, *The Science of Biology* (New York: McGraw-Hill Book Co., 1963), p. 396. Used by permission.

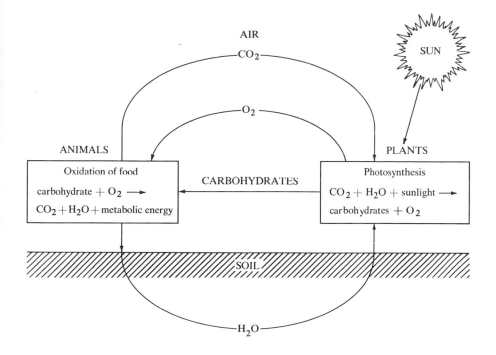

Figure 4.1. The carbon energy cycle (from Weisz). The ultimate source of energy is the sun, some of whose energy is trapped by photosynthesis and formed into carbohydrates and other organic molecules. In animals, organic molecules are broken down by respiration, resulting in metabolic energy.

In this process, metabolic energy is released. Figure 4.1 thus shows the interdependence of plants and animals. The carbohydrates produced and the oxygen given off by plants are sources of food and oxygen necessary to the life of animals. In turn, the carbon dioxide and water given off by animals are essential to the existence and growth of plants.

The chief product of animal metabolism is freed energy, which is used to satisfy the body's energy requirements for maintenance, growth, tissue repair, and movement. Man has a particularly elaborate, highly differentiated, complex mechanism for obtaining energy from the oxidation of sugar. Digestive enzymes break down complex food molecules into glucose, which is then assimilated into the blood stream and carried to each of the billions of cells of the body. The energy freed by the oxidation of glucose in the cell is transformed into phosphate bonds of the adenosine triphosphate (ATP) molecule. This ATP molecule is involved in all of the energy-expending processes of the cell. ATP molecules are formed by two processes. In the first process, called *glycolysis,* a single glucose molecule is broken down into two molecules of lactic acid through a series of at least eleven chemical changes. In the second process, the two lactic acid molecules are changed chemically, in a series of steps known as the *Krebs citric-acid cycle,* to produce thirty-six energy-charged ATP molecules and the by-products carbon dioxide and water. These ATP molecules are sources of energy available to the cell for carrying on life processes.

We should not conclude this discussion of metabolism without giving special emphasis to the key role which enzymes play in all life processes. The key to many of the secrets and complexities of life lies in the number and specificity of enzymes, protein-like agents which act as catalysts in an enormous number of chemical changes at every level and in every system of the body. Enzymes play such a dominant role in the chemistry of life that it is exceedingly difficult to imagine the synthesis of living material without their help.

Growth

One of the important functions of metabolism is the synthesis of new cells and tissues. By this process, the organism increases in size and complexity in accordance with an overall pattern of growth and development. The growth impulse is closely identified with the life impulse itself: Life is assured only when the anabolic building-up processes greatly exceed the catabolic tearing-down processes in the organism. Although this inherent metabolic urge to grow and to develop is very strong in young children, it may be blunted by many factors (malnutrition, various acute and chronic infections, endocrine disturbances, and congenital anomalies and malformations).

The different aspects of growth and development are contained in Krogman's statement, "We grow, we grow up; we grow older."[2] The child increases in size, he changes in proportions, and he progresses toward maturity. The changes in size of the body or of any of its parts is known as *physical growth*. It is measured in inches or centimeters (height) and pounds or kilograms (weight). But increase in size, however important, is only one kind of growth. One also grows up. At the same time that he is increasing in size, he is experiencing changes in proportion, differentiation, and complexity in his body as a whole and in one or more of its parts. A child's growing up is a developmental aspect of the growth process. *Development* refers to the increasing skills and complexity of function which result from increased tissue specialization. Progressive changes in nervous system, muscles, bones, and tissues, for instance, are manifested in motor development, while progressive changes in body physique, sex glands, and associated tissues are manifested in sexual development.

[2] Wilton M. Krogman, "Physical Growth as a Factor in the Behavioral Development of the Child," in Walter B. Waetjen, ed., *New Dimensions in Learning: A Multidisciplinary Approach* (Washington: Association for Supervision and Curriculum Development, N.E.A., 1962), p. 9.

The peak of the anabolic phase of growth is reached soon after attainment of physical maturity, but changes within cells, tissues, and the body as a whole continue to occur. Thus begins the catabolic phase, the slow but inexorable decline of body efficiency brought about by aging of organs and tissues. A wound or bruise in a young child heals quickly; in an adult, the wound heals more slowly; in a very elderly person, it takes a long time to heal and sometimes does not heal at all. The loss of physiological efficiency brought on by processes of aging is particularly evident in the world of sports. Most professional baseball and football players are beyond their peak by the age of thirty; the boxer's legs have begun to slow him up long before he is thirty. We grow, we grow up, we grow old.

Dynamic Organization

The processes of metabolism and growth do not occur in haphazard fashion; they are coordinated processes within a dynamic living system. Dynamic organization—whereby living things maintain internal order while changing, growing, developing, and learning—is one of the foremost characteristics of the life process. Movements and changes within cells, tissues, and the body as a whole are governed by principles of dynamic organization which allow the organism to maintain equilibrium while performing its functions of respiration, digestion, circulation, and elimination and while adapting to lowered caloric intake, growth, infection or disease, or psychological stress.

The maintenance of dynamic organization in organic life is best exemplified by Cannon's concept of *homeostasis*,[3] a term for the coordinated physiological processes that maintain most of the steady states in the organism. One homeostatic process maintains even body temperature by causing heat-producing muscle contractions (shivering) and constriction of blood vessels in cold weather. In hot weather, this process causes dilation of blood vessels, permitting body heat to be brought to skin surfaces where it can be released through evaporation of perspiration. In comparable ways, homeostasis of the sugar, water, salts, calcium, and acid-base levels is maintained within established limits through the action of blood, heart, vascular system, lungs, liver, kidneys, spleen, brain, and nervous system. The advantage which homeostasis offers man is that of relegating to lower brain centers the mundane but vital tasks of maintaining the dynamic organization of life processes. This frees higher brain centers to coordinate the more complex activities involved in development, cognition, and learning.

Reproduction

At the moment of conception, the pattern of organic propensities for functioning, growth, and structure is established by the hereditary contributions of each parent. The extent to which the potentialities represented by

[3] Walter B. Cannon, *Wisdom of the Body* (New York: W. W. Norton & Co., 1939).

this pattern will be realized depends upon the environment. We are able to understand more clearly the difficulties of assigning causes of behavior exclusively to heredity or exclusively to environment when we realize that the internal environment of the mother's body begins to influence the fertilized egg immediately following conception.

Within the nucleus of the fertilized egg are 46 *chromosomes,* which comprise the heredity of the individual—including his potentialities for development. These 46 chromosomes consist of 23 pairs, which differ in size and shape. One set of 23 chromosomes is contributed by the father, and the other set is furnished by the mother. One pair, the sex chromosomes, is homologous in the female (XX) and nonhomologous in the male (XY). Since the sex chromosome of the mother is always X, the sex chromosome of the father determines the sex of the child (X from the father making XX = girl, Y from the father making XY = boy.)

In each of the 23 pairs of chromosomes are smaller substances (called *genes*) arranged in linear sequence along the length of the chromosome. The genes, the carriers of heredity, consist of molecules of desoxyribonucleic acid (DNA). DNA is present in the nuclei of all cells in the human body and in all other forms of life.

Genes do not act independently; rather, they interact with one another and with the environment in the formation of specific hereditary traits. Each body characteristic, such as eye color or body physique, is the result of the action of many different enzymes—each formed according to the genetic instructions contained in a pair of genes. A gene that has a greater capability for producing its own effect over that of its paired gene is called *dominant,* while the one with lesser capability is called *recessive.* The appearance of a specific physical trait in offspring will favor the dominant gene by the familiar 3-to-1 ratio first observed and reported by Mendel. Gene-linked abnormalities may be reproduced by a dominant gene, as in sickle-cell anemia; a recessive gene, as in diabetes mellitus; or a sex-linked gene, in which the gene causing an affliction such as hemophilia or color blindness is carried by the mother but appears only in male offsprings. The genetic makeup of the individual is called *genotype* while the term for the characteristics of appearance or body form produced by genes is *phenotype.*

Sexual reproduction in higher animals makes possible a mixing of genes which ensures the uniqueness of each member of the species. The number of gene combinations possible makes it highly unlikely that any two persons (other than identical twins) will ever have the same constellation of genes.

Adaptation to the Environment

The survival of an individual and a species is dependent upon their ability to adapt to the environment. The adaptation of each species to its environment involves evolutionary changes extending over countless generations.

The flexibility provided by man's highly developed brain and nervous system gives him an incomparable advantage in his efforts to cope with his environment. Contrast the Eskimo's igloo, kayak, sealskin clothing, and ingenious ways of obtaining food in Arctic climates to the herdsman's tent, loose-fitting clothing, and continuous movement in search of food and water in desert climates. As individuals change in adapting to changes in weather, climate, geology, and ecology, their adaptive behaviors are marks of increased maturity, development, and learning.

Energy and Behavior

Every part of the body plays an essential role in maintaining the flow of energy into and through the body. The human energy system ingests, transforms, and transports energy to every cell in the body. Within the cells, energy is utilized in carrying out three major activities of life: (1) maintenance of organization, (2) growth, and (3) physical activity.

Most of the energy available to the organism is utilized for maintenance of organization. Approximately half of the average person's caloric intake each day is expended in basal metabolism. *Basal metabolism* is the irreducible amount of energy required by the body for circulation, respiration, secretion, and the maintenance of the metabolism of all cells during sound sleep or during rest several hours after the intake of food. The concepts of body maintenance and basal metabolism remind us that it takes energy just to stay alive.

Approximately 6 percent of the body's energy intake is accounted for by the increase in metabolic rate following a meal (*specific dynamic action*), and 10 percent of the energy value of foods is lost through excreta. For the remaining 84 percent of the body's energy intake, the proportions utilized for basal requirements (maintenance), growth, and physical activity vary with age and sex. Prior to pubescence, the 84 percent is divided approximately as follows for both sexes: maintenance, 45 percent; growth, 10 percent; and physical activity, 29 percent. For the average fourteen-year-old boy, these proportions change to 40 percent for maintenance, 15 percent for growth, and 29 percent for physical activity. This is in marked contrast with the percentages for the average sixteen-year-old girl, who uses 55 percent of her caloric intake for maintenance, 5 percent for growth, and 24 percent for physical activity.[4]

The amount of energy expended in muscular activity depends upon the type of work in which the individual is engaged, his size, and the energy needs required for growth at his stage of development. If an individual's muscular activity is at a low level compared to his intake of food energy, his body will store the unused calories as fat. If, on the other hand, his muscular activity requires more than 33 percent of his total energy intake, he will register a loss in body weight.

[4] Ernest H. Watson and George H. Lowrey, *Growth and Development of Children* (Chicago: Year Book Publishers, 1951), pp. 219–224.

In mental activity, the amount of energy expended by the brain is believed to be quite small. The fatigue that accompanies extended mental activity appears to be caused by expense of energy in tension in muscles and nervous system.

Nutrition

The amount, quality, and kinds of food taken into the body vitally affect the growth and behavior of the individual. Hunger in young children often produces irritability and restlessness. Poor nutrition at any age can affect behavior and social adjustment.

Of particular concern are the diets of teenagers, who, at this critical stage of development, are often malnourished because of poor choice of foods and irregular eating habits. One study of adolescent girls found that those who scored relatively low on the Minnesota Counseling Inventory Scales for family relationships, emotional stability, conformity, and adjustment to reality had poorer diets and missed more meals than girls with higher scores.[5] Other studies show that adolescents with poorer psychological adjustment have aversions to a greater number of foods.

Studies also reveal that children with nutritive deficiencies lasting three years or longer show a substantial lag in height and weight. There is evidence, too, that these lags in height and weight increase progressively for boys throughout early adolescence. Girls show a progressive lag in weight but not in height.[6] During the first stages of undernutrition, some children are apathetic. Others reveal an increased restlessness; they find it more and more difficult to sit still or to refrain from talking, whispering, and giggling. But an inadequate diet over long periods of time leads eventually to a decrease in motor activity, lack of endurance, and physical exhaustion. Lack of adequate nutrition prevents or severely limits ability to concentrate in the classroom. It is no wonder, then, that lack of energy is cited as a principal cause for retarded learning.

The effects of human starvation on behavior are clearly shown in the results of the Minnesota Study of Human Starvation.[7] During twenty-four weeks of semi-starvation a group of mentally and physically healthy young men experienced lowered circulation, moderate anemia, reduced sex drive, loss of strength and endurance, and some loss of coordination involving the total body. More marked, however, were the psychological changes. Men who initially were even-tempered, humorous, tolerant, and enthusiastic became irritable, apathetic, tired, uninterested in their personal appearance, more concerned with themselves than with others, and unsociable to the point that they stopped having "dates." Their hunger was so great that all they could

[5] Maxine A. Hinton et al., "Influences of Girls' Eating Behavior," *Journal of Home Economics,* 54 (December, 1962), 842–846.

[6] T. D. Spies et al., "Skeletal Maturational Progress of Children with Chronic Nutritive Failure," *American Journal of Diseases of Children,* 85 (1953), 1–12.

[7] A. Keys et al., *The Biology of Human Starvation,* Vols. 1 and 2 (Minneapolis: University of Minnesota Press, 1950).

think about and dream about was food. Only after thirty-three weeks of adequate nutrition were the men back to normal in all respects.

Health

The effects of extended illness and such chronic diseases as rheumatic fever, polio, tuberculosis, and diabetes in limiting learning are visible and very real. (In more fortunate situations many such afflicted students are able to continue their education with the help of visiting teachers and home study.) Of still greater concern to educators, however, are disorders that often go undetected—such as anemia, endocrine disorders, poor teeth, and chronic infections. Undetected physical ailments can rob a student of enough energy to be a chief cause of mediocre or poor academic performance.

The effects of chronic and severe illness in retarding growth and development are dramatically shown in successive X-ray measurements of skeletal growth. Some children, after a severe illness, will show bone scars indicating an interruption of normal growth; and transverse lines which appear on X-rays of certain long bones—for example, along the shaft of the diaphysis—are frequently related to past illness.

The importance of good physical and mental health for the development of children and youth is reflected in the increased emphasis which schools have placed on expanding health services and health education.

Physical Defects

Many kinds of physical defects may affect a child's development and learning. Often, children who seem unable to respond appropriately in the learning situation are labeled "dumb" when poor eyesight or hearing is actually the major cause of their poor performance.

In other cases, poor performance may be attributable to neurological impairments. Injury, either through accident or disease, may result in a permanent disability (such as cerebral palsy or organic epilepsy) to a brain that was previously normal.

Still other children may suffer from neurological nonalignment. In their neurological organization, normal persons tend to have *unilateral dominance*. If they are right-eyed, right-handed, and right-footed, the dominant right side of the body is controlled by the left hemisphere of the brain. Conversely, if the left side of the body is dominant it is controlled by the right hemisphere of the brain. A person whose dominant eye, say, is controlled by the right cerebral hemisphere but whose dominant hand is controlled by the left hemisphere is referred to as *crossed dominant*. Children with crossed dominance often appear to be normal except for their behavior, which may be impulsive, hyperactive, irritable, and unpredictable; and they frequently experience difficulties in learning, many of which seem to be perceptual in origin. Some of these children, for instance, confuse *p* and *q* and *was* and *saw;* others persist in writing *3* backward. Teachers should be alert to the hyperactive, impulsive child whose behavior and learning difficulties do not seem to be explained by commonly known causes. Such a child can be recommended for a neurological examination. He may also benefit from efforts in the relatively new field of special education, a rapidly expanding discipline which is continuously seeking to understand and to educate the many kinds of atypical children and youth in our communities.

Emotional Factors

There can be little doubt that emotions and trauma produced by threat, conflict, and frustration do affect in unique ways the body's patterns of energy expenditure and the development and learning of people. A further discussion of the physical-psychological factors involved in the individual's response to emotional situations is to be found in Chapter 9.

Rest and Activity

Fatigue is a common bodily condition of persons of all ages; as the normal result of vigorous physical exercise or mental activity, it is harmless. Chronic fatigue, however, is a more dangerous condition; it reduces the body's capacity for work, causes damage to tissues, and reduces the body's resistance to infection. The health and efficiency of every human being's dynamic energy system depend on the avoidance of chronic fatigue through a balance between rest and activity. The energies of most school children seem irrepressible. The task of the teacher is to plan a program of activity—adapted to the individual energy needs of each student—which provides for changes of pace, changes of activity, and opportunities for pursuing restful and relaxing activities following periods of intense physical or mental activity. Such an individually tailored, balanced program will help to improve the student's respiration and circulation, stimulate his appetite, and improve his muscle tone. These in turn lead to better posture, normal elimination, reduced tension, and increased body strength, endurance, and coordination. The maintenance of all of these physical conditions is vital to the efficiency of learning and development.

Levels of Energy Output

Knowing something about the level at which a particular child expends energy is extremely useful to teachers and parents as they seek to help children and youth develop and learn. The following excerpts make abundantly clear the need of teachers to understand the energy needs of their students.

Jimmy burst into the room at 8:45 this morning and seemed to be in perpetual motion until I called the class to order to begin the day's work. During the arithmetic lesson Jimmy kept popping in and out of his seat like a jumping jack. First, he popped out to sharpen his pencil, then he asked me which page we were working on, and frequently he made trips over to Ted's desk to borrow his eraser. Twice I escorted Jimmy to his desk, but as soon as my back was turned, he was up and away again. Each time his row was excused to line up for recess, lunch, and at the end of the day Jimmy shot out of his desk in an attempt to be the first of his row in line.

Phil clumped into class today at 9:10, late for the second time this week. He moved slowly to his desk and took another five minutes to find his book, paper, and pencil. Most of the class finished the ten fraction problems in about twenty minutes while Phil had only finished four problems after thirty minutes, but all of his were correct. Phil is usually the last one out of the room for recess and lunch. In games on the playground his running is labored and awkward. Phil is big for his age, he is above average in intelligence, and he eats a good lunch at school each day. In response to nicknames of "Pokey" and "Speed," Phil smiles and responds good-naturedly, "I'm trying to hurry."

Teachers frequently wonder what to do about their Jimmys and Phils. In flights of fancy, some teachers may wish that the school health services would provide long-lasting shots of adrenalin for such as Phil and tranquilizers for such as Jimmy. However, both Jimmy and Phil may be well within the normal range of energy output for their ten-year-old age group.

The fact is that normal children of the same age may vary greatly in their rates of energy output. Some of these wide variations may be due to differences in nutrition, health, patterns of rest, physical defects, and emotional factors that were described earlier in the chapter. For instance, some children from families where emotional tension is high and great demands are made upon them become accustomed to responding quickly and vigorously in a wide variety of situations. The sluggish responses of a Phil and the hyperactivity of a Jimmy may be due, respectively, to an underactive and an overactive thyroid gland. Frequently, both medical tests and observational data are needed to ascertain the reasons for a child's marked overactivity or underactivity.

After all environmental factors and all the physical factors so far mentioned have been considered, however, teachers will still have children in their classes who differ markedly in rates and levels of energy output. These differences are likely to be related to three factors: (1) age, (2) expectancies of normal distribution, and (3) sex.

Age. Figure 4.2[8] reveals that the basal energy production of infants and young children, per unit of weight, is one and a half to two times greater than that of older children, adolescents, and young adults. These data merely confirm observations, common to mothers and teachers, that the energy

[8] From Norman C. Wetzel, "On the Motion of Growth, xvii. Clinical Aspects of Human Growth and Metabolism with Special Reference to Infancy and Pre-School," *Journal of Pediatrics,* 4 (1934), 465–493. Reproduced by permission of The C. V. Mosby Company, St. Louis, Missouri.

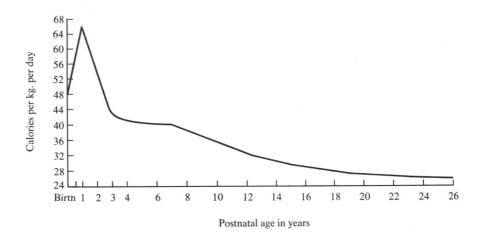

Figure 4.2. Curve for rate of basal heat production per unit of weight (metabolism) from birth to age twenty-six years (from Wetzel).

levels and energy expenditures of most young children are high and that these levels and rates decrease as individuals mature.

Differences in energy output in middle and late childhood were dramatically revealed in a visit by this writer to an elementary school. First, he visited a sixth-grade class which was busily engaged in working on a large mural. Activity was evident in the painting, drawing, measuring, and group work in which all class members participated. Later he moved on to a fifth-grade classroom. Although these fifth graders were engaged in work at their desks, an increased tempo of activity—twisting, turning around, and talking—was evident. Finally the writer looked in on a fourth-grade classroom. Here the surge of energy was irresistible. Arms, legs, and bodies seemed to be in continuous movement as the teacher tried valiantly to lead a discussion, for the benefit of the visitor, on the class project for beautifying the school grounds.

The energy levels of adolescents as a group are variable, and thus are difficult to characterize. Some adolescents' energy levels are fluctuating and erratic. At times they show great bursts of energy, some of which may be sustained. At other times they appear to be practically immobilized. Physical changes associated with the adolescent growth spurt make great demands on the adolescent's energy. Added to these requirements is the energy needed for active participation in games and activities and the energy required for doing homework and household chores. Trying to keep up with so many demands, many adolescents are literally exhausted.

Expectancies of normal distribution. People who are the same age or at the same maturity level also differ markedly in their rates of expending energy. This was clearly evident in the behavioral descriptions of Jimmy and Phil. One of the fundamental facts concerning individual differences in rate of energy output is that the scores of individuals in a randomly selected population will, with respect to a given trait, approximate a *normal curve of distribution*. The concept of the normal curve is best illustrated in relation to intelligence, where the IQs of 68 percent of the general population fall between 85 and 115. Each slope of the curve tapers, so that about 2 percent of the population is expected to measure above 130 and a like percentage below 70.

In similar fashion, an unselected group of students of approximately the same age and maturity will vary in the rates with which they expend energy. Jimmy's high rate of energy output places him near one end of the distribution, while Phil's low rate of energy output places him near the other extreme. Since both are within the normal range, albeit at the extremes, we should not be surprised to find Jimmys and Phils in most classrooms. Most of their classmates may be expected to expend energy at rates somewhere between Jimmy and Phil. (See Figure 4.3.)

Sex. From observations of both sexes we might conclude that boys expend energy at generally higher rates than do girls. Research appears to support this conclusion. Lewis and his associates[9] found that boys have a higher rate of oxygen consumption under basal conditions than do girls. These differences in rate of oxygen consumption were found to be so marked as to require separate norms for boys and girls beginning at age seven. The question of whether sex differences in metabolic rate may be due to boys'

[9] R. C. Lewis et al., "Standards for Basal Metabolism of Children from 2 to 15 Years of Age Inclusive," *Journal of Pediatrics,* 23 (1943), 1–18.

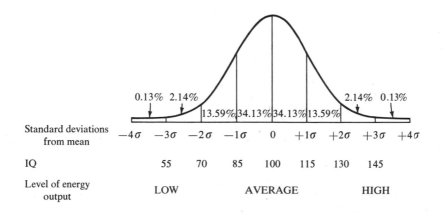

Standard deviations from mean	-4σ	-3σ	-2σ	-1σ	0	$+1\sigma$	$+2\sigma$	$+3\sigma$	$+4\sigma$
IQ			55	70	85	100	115	130	145
Level of energy output			LOW			AVERAGE		HIGH	

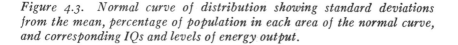

Figure 4.3. Normal curve of distribution showing standard deviations from the mean, percentage of population in each area of the normal curve, and corresponding IQs and levels of energy output.

larger body mass interested Garn and Clark.[10] They found that at all age levels boys consume more oxygen than girls. Girls between ages six and seventeen increased their oxygen consumption 30 percent, while boys increased their oxygen consumption 60 percent during the same period. Garn and Clark concluded that sex differences in metabolic activity are not due to differences in size or internal composition, but that the male's increase in oxygen consumption begins early and persists through adult life. In a later study,[11] they found a close relationship between ketosteroid hormone and higher oxygen consumption in boys, a relationship not found in girls. It appears, then, that males possess an energy-stimulating hormone associated with sex, which may account in part for their seemingly greater physical activity.

The evidence appears to provide ample support for the generalization that individuals vary in rates of energy output on the bases of maturity level, normal variation within the same general age group, and sex. Since differences in energy levels can be expected in every classroom, the resourceful teacher will seek to develop activities and programs that utilize the different energy levels of children in the group. To expect some students to slow down and others to speed up in order to conform to some norm would be a denial of individual differences.

In the preceding discussion, only the physiological bases for differences in energy expenditure have been considered. For a more complete understanding of any individual's behavior, the physiological bases of behavior must be related to cultural and psychological factors. These will be considered in subsequent chapters.

Physical Growth

For our present considerable knowledge of physical growth and development we are indebted to numerous researchers working in the past fifty years. The findings of these researchers substantiate the following generalizations[12] concerning the nature and processes of human growth.

1. *Growth is a continuous process, but it does not proceed at a uniform rate.* The individual is growing all of the time, from conception to maturity and beyond into adult life. Though few would question the continuity of the growth process, many adults seem to forget this fact when they work with children and youth. We are well aware of the process of growth when we observe the enormous changes that occur in babies or early adolescents during the period of a few weeks; but when changes are less obvious, we tend to forget that growth is still going on.

[10] S. Garn and L. Clark, "The Sex Differences in the Basal Metabolic Rates," *Child Development,* 24 (1953), 216–222.

[11] S. Garn and L. Clark, "Relationship between Ketosteroid Secretion and Basal Oxygen Consumption in Children," *Journal of Applied Psychology,* 6 (1954), 546.

[12] Adapted from Marian E. Breckenridge and E. Lee Vincent, *Child Development,* 4th ed. (Philadelphia: W. B. Saunders, 1960), pp. 1–15. Used with permission.

Like the rate of growth of the body as a whole, the rates of growth of particular parts of the body vary at different periods in an individual's life. One evidence of this variation comes from the observation that the infant is not a miniature adult. His head appears oversized, while his body and legs appear undersized. As he grows older, these body parts become better proportioned. These changes in the rates of growth of head, body, and limbs parallel changes in rates of growth of the primary body systems.

The four curves in Figure 4.4[13] show the progress of growth toward maturity of four systems of the body: the lymphatic system, the brain and nervous system, the general system (skeleton, muscles, and internal organs), and the genital system. Following the neural curve in Figure 4.4, we note

[13] After R. E. Scammon, in J. A. Harris et al., *Measurement of Man* (Minneapolis: University of Minnesota Press, 1930). Used with permission.

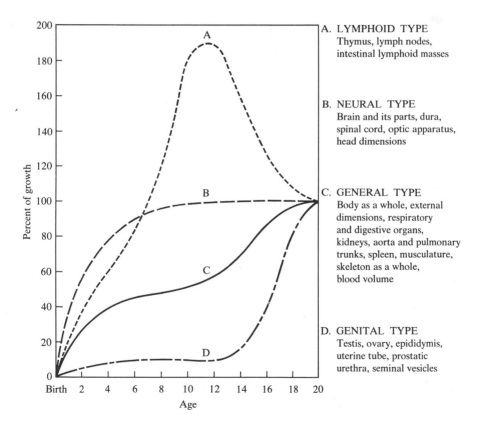

Figure 4.4. A graph showing the major types of postnatal growth of various parts and organs of the body (from Scammon).

that the brain and nervous system grow faster and mature earlier than other parts of the body and appear to be 90 percent complete by the age of six. The growth of the skeleton, muscles, and most internal organs is relatively slow until pubescence, when it begins to accelerate. The lymph masses appear to be proportionately nearly twice as large during ages ten to thirteen than at maturity. (Between the ages of seven and twenty, the thymus gland is larger than its adult size.) The sexual system is almost dormant prior to the pubescent period. After this, genital growth accelerates sharply.

Human growth might be compared to a huge engine that runs continuously. In the process of building up to peak performance, different parts of the engine work at different rates of speed, some idling at five miles per hour while others are racing at eighty miles an hour.

2. *There is a general growth pattern for human beings.* Numerous studies of physical growth show that human beings follow a general pattern: a sequence of decelerated, accelerated, and steady periods in growth. These sequential changes are best represented by a curve showing the velocity of growth (see Figure 4.5[14]). We note that the highest velocity of increase in height per six-month period is about 17 percent and occurs at birth. Though

[14] The curve for boys in Figure 4.5 is adapted from Lois H. Meek et al., *The Personal Social Development of Boys and Girls with Implications for Secondary Education* (New York: Progressive Education Association, 1940), p. 34. Reproduced by permission.

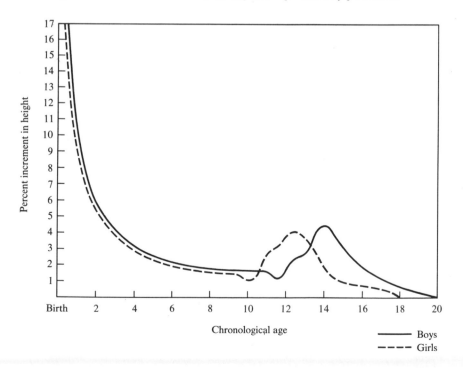

Figure 4.5. *Velocity of average increase in height each six months for boys and girls, birth to age twenty.*

the infant increases 50 percent in length during his first postnatal year, his increases in height during each successive six-month period are progressively smaller, so that the period from birth to age three is one of sharp deceleration. From age three to about age eleven in girls and age thirteen in boys there is a relatively steady 2 to 4 percent increase in height every six months. Girls at about age eleven and boys at about thirteen enter their pubertal growth spurt. Prior to pubescence there is usually a marked period of accelerated growth lasting for one to three years, followed by a long period of gradual deceleration. Menarche in girls and the comparable point of sexual maturation in boys usually occur at or just beyond the peak of the pubertal growth spurt.

3. *Each person has an individual growth cycle which only roughly approximates the general pattern of human growth.* Measures of growth for a large number of persons in a given population will be distributed in accordance with the bell-shaped normal curve (see Figure 4.3). In other words, the "normal" growth pattern is a generalization based on a range of widely varying individual growth patterns. Each individual's pattern is the result of his own body's progressively changing balance of forces. These forces include heredity, characteristics of sex, endocrine factors, and other factors peculiar to each growth dimension.[15] It is characteristic of the delicacy of this balance of forces to produce in the population a broad continuum of growth patterns, including at one end the pattern of the "early maturer" or "fast grower," and at the other end the pattern of the "late maturer" or "slow grower" (see Figure 4.6).

Late-maturing youth do not grow quite as fast as the early maturing, but their growth is continued over a much longer period of time. Rather marked differences may be noted in physique between early-maturing and late-maturing adolescents. Early-maturing boys tend to have relatively broad hips and narrow shoulders, while late-maturing boys tend to be very long legged and to have slender hips and broad shoulders. Early-maturing girls tend to have narrower shoulders than late-maturing girls. From these data it appears that early-maturing boys and late-maturing girls tend to deviate slightly in body proportions from the norms of their own sex group toward those of the opposite sex.[16]

Wide differences in physical growth patterns are particularly evident in the junior-high-school population, where boys and girls of all sizes, shapes, and degrees of physical maturity may be observed. At this age in particular, differences in size and maturity are felt keenly, and those who deviate most from the group norms often suffer acutely. Early maturers tend to feel self-

[15] Frank K. Shuttleworth, "The Physical and Mental Growth of Girls and Boys Age Six to Nineteen in Relation to Age at Maximum Growth," *Monographs of the Society for Research in Child Development*, 4 (1939), 216–221. Figure 4.6 is reproduced from this article by permission of the copyright owner, The Society for Research in Child Development, Inc.

[16] Nancy Bayley and Read D. Tuddenham, "Adolescent Changes in Body Build," in Nelson B. Henry, *Forty-third Yearbook, Adolescence, Part I*. National Society for the Study of Education (Chicago: University of Chicago Press, 1944), pp. 33–55.

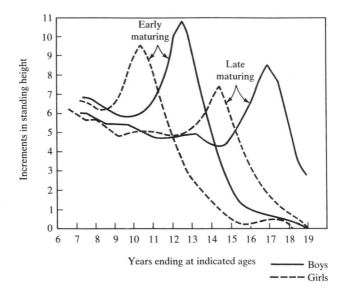

Figure 4.6. Velocity of increase in height of early-maturing and late-maturing boys and girls (from Shuttleworth).

conscious among classmates who are less mature, while late maturers often worry about whether they are normal and whether they will ever grow up. Adults who recognize and accept the fact that most growth deviations are perfectly normal can provide much-needed reassurance and support to students whose growth patterns deviate from the norm. Adult understanding and affection can do much to help adolescents accept their physical selves and their own particular patterns of growth.

4. *Girls on the average are more advanced in physical maturity than are boys at all stages of growth.* The greater physical maturity of girls over boys of the same chronological age is an empirical fact widely recognized and accepted long before its scientific confirmation. Skeletal growth, the rate at which cartilage ossifies in becoming bone, is more advanced in girls at all stages of development. X-rays of the wrist, for example, show that the average six-year-old girl has almost the same skeletal growth as the average seven-year-old boy. By age twelve, the average girl may be as much as two years ahead of the boy in skeletal growth.

Sex differences in the timing of the onset of the pubertal cycle of growth are shown in Figure 4.6. Early-maturing girls achieve their peak velocity of growth about two years before early-maturing boys, and a similar difference is shown between late-maturing girls and boys. Figure 4.6 also shows that not all girls mature ahead of all boys: The early-maturing boys mature about the same time as the average-maturing girls and ahead of the late-maturing girls.

5. *In general, all aspects of growth are interrelated.* The concepts of unity and dynamic organization of the organism, which were presented earlier in the chapter, are particularly relevant to an understanding of the processes of growth. For example, when the arm or leg grows longer, the increase in bone length is accompanied by proportionate growth in nerves, blood vessels, muscles, connective tissue, and skin covering. During pubescence, physical growth is interrelated with sexual maturation; the hormones secreted by the maturing gonads exert a slowing effect on the growth of the long bones. Studies have shown that boys and girls who are further advanced toward sexual maturity than are others of the same age and sex may be as much as 20 pounds heavier and more than 4 inches taller than those who are maturing more slowly.[17]

The question has frequently been raised as to whether changes in a child's mental development parallel changes in physical growth. Olson and his associates[18] have studied large numbers of children from ages eight to thirteen in an effort to ascertain the interrelationships between various kinds of development. In these studies the following physical and mental measures were used: height age, weight age, dental age, calcification (skeletal) age, grip age, reading age, and mental age. A diversity of growth patterns emerged from the data for children at any given age. When the researchers examined the data from the standpoint of the child as a whole, however, they discovered an underlying unity in structures, functions, and achievement. Lorusso,[19] on the other hand, studying an elementary school population (grades one to eight), found that physical and mental maturity, frequency of being chosen by classmates, and interest measures are not adequate predictors of achievement or athletic performance. In individual classrooms, children generally maintained their relative positions in school achievement, classroom status, and verbal-interest measures, but this was not true for the total sample. Lorusso suggests that too strong a reliance on the principle "all aspects of growth are interrelated" may oversimplify processes and events that are in reality quite complex.

Growth, Development, and Learning

Earlier in the chapter we stated that any factor influencing the status or operation of the human energy system will have an effect on development

[17] H. S. Dimock, "A Research in Adolescence. I. Pubescence and Physical Growth," *Child Development*, 6 (1935), 176–195; Herman G. Richey, "The Relation of Accelerated, Normal, and Retarded Puberty to the Height and Weight of School Children," *Monographs of the Society for Research in Child Development*, 2 (1937).

[18] Willard C. Olson, *Child Development* (Boston: D. C. Heath & Co., 1949).

[19] Rocco E. Lorusso, "A Study of the Interrelationships of Selected Variables in Child Development in an Elementary School" (unpublished doctor's dissertation, University of Maryland, 1960).

and learning. In this section, selected studies of the interrelationships of physical maturity and various aspects of learning are reviewed so that the reciprocal influences of each set of forces on the other may be seen.

Of particular interest to elementary school personnel are studies that show positive relationships between selected physical-maturity indexes and academic success. Zeller,[20] a German physician, suggested in a study of first-grade children that school readiness is related to body configuration. Zeller identified two types of body configuration that may be observed in children from ages five to seven. In the first of these types, the early-childhood figure, prominent characteristics are a head and trunk dominating the extremities; a relatively large, rounded, prominent forehead; a short, stocky neck that merges with a sloping shoulder line; a trunk that is sacklike, with no apparent waist; a protruding abdomen; narrow shoulders; and a lateral body outline formed by adipose tissue rather than by muscles and joints. In the second type of figure, a more mature body configuration called the middle-childhood figure, head, trunk, and forehead are better proportioned, neck is longer, trunk is cone-shaped, shoulders are broad, hips are narrow, abdomen is flat, waist is clearly indicated, muscles and joints of arms and legs are clearly visible, adipose tissue has decreased, and linear body is clearly evident. Figures that cannot be classified as either type because they have mixed characteristics were termed *intermediate figures* by Zeller. The contrasting early-childhood and middle-childhood figures are shown in Figure 4.7.[21] So strongly did Zeller associate the early-childhood figure with a lack of school readiness that he urged parents not to enter these children in school.

Simon[22] used Zeller's procedure in a further test of relationships between body configuration and school success. She selected 50 highly successful and 50 failing first-grade American Caucasian students ranging in chronological age from six years, four months to seven years, six months. These students were drawn from five metropolitan public schools and represented all socioeconomic groups. A battery of standard body measures indicated that failing students were less mature than successful students. When failing students were matched by age and IQ with successful students, the failing students still showed up as physically less mature. Simon found that of the measures studied, the ratios of head circumference to leg length and waist circumference to leg length were the most sensitive indicators of school readiness.

A study of the relationship between physical maturity and behavior of adolescent boys was made by Jones and Bayley.[23] They used assessments of skeletal age to identify two groups of adolescent boys—a group of early

[20] W. Zeller, *Der erste Gestaltwandel des Kindes* (Leipzig: Barth, 1936).

[21] Figure 4.7 is reproduced from this article by permission of the copyright owner, The Society for Research in Child Development, Inc.

[22] Maria D. Simon, "Body Configuration and School Readiness," *Child Development,* 30 (December 1959), 493–512.

[23] Mary C. Jones and Nancy Bayley, "Physical Maturing among Boys as Related to Behavior," *Journal of Educational Psychology,* 41 (1950), 129–148.

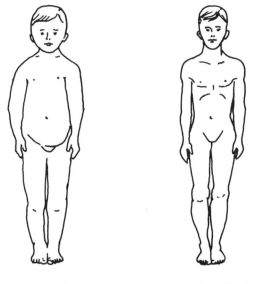

Early childhood　　　　Middle childhood

Figure 4.7. Contrasting body configurations of children five to seven years of age (from Simon).

maturers and a group of late maturers. These two groups were studied and contrasted in relation to social behavior and reputation among classmates. The early-maturing adolescent boys were rated by others as significantly more attractive physically, better groomed, and more unaffected and relaxed. Early-maturing boys were accepted and treated by adults and peers as mature; although several became student leaders in high school, they appeared to have little need to strive for status. The late-maturing adolescent boys, on the other hand, tended to be more·active and attention seeking and thus were treated by adults and others more like the little boys they seemed to be.

In another study, Mussen and Jones[24] investigated the self-conceptions and motivations of adolescent boys who differ in physical maturity. A group of 16 adolescent boys who were accelerated in physical growth and a group of 17 adolescent boys who were retarded in growth made up stories in response to Thematic Apperception Test picture cards. Analyses of these stories revealed that the generally unfavorable sociopsychological environments of the late maturers do appear to have adverse effects on their personality

[24] Paul H. Mussen and Mary C. Jones, "Self-conceptions, Motivations, and Interpersonal Attitudes of Late- and Early-Maturing Boys," *Child Development,* 28 (June 1957), 243–256.

development. Late-maturing boys more frequently revealed negative self-conceptions, feelings of inadequacy, strong feelings of being rejected and dominated, prolonged dependency needs, and rebellious attitudes toward parents. The early maturers, on the other hand, presented a more favorable psychological picture. They appeared to be more self-confident, independent, and capable of playing an adult role in interpersonal relationships. Relatively few seemed to feel inadequate, rejected, dominated, or rebellious toward their families.

These findings were generally corroborated in a later study by Mussen and Jones[25] of the behavior-inferred motivations of late-maturing and early-maturing boys. Strong aggression drives and drives for social acceptance were found to be more characteristic of the physically retarded than the physically accelerated adolescent boy. In interpreting their findings, Mussen and Jones suggest that the late maturer's strong social drives may stem from feelings of insecurity and dependence which are frequently manifested in childish, affected, attention-getting social techniques. Highly aggressive drives among late maturers also tend to be associated with social behavior and personality characteristics indicative of social and emotional maladjustment.

The differences in social and personality variables between early-maturing and late-maturing girls are less marked than those for boys. Though late-maturing girls appear to enjoy greater popularity than early-maturing girls,[26] early-maturing girls reveal in general a more favorable psychological adjustment. Early-maturing girls tend to evince a more positive self-conception, while late-maturing girls tend to reveal a greater need for recognition.[27] A study by Tryon using a self-report inventory also reported higher scores for early-maturing girls on total adjustment, family adjustment, and personal adequacy.[28]

More[29] studied the relationships between puberty and the emotional and social development of both boys and girls. His data show that the American girl at puberty appears to go through a period of abrupt changes in her emotional life and in the patterns of her social behavior. Girls generally are able to handle these new emotions and social patterns but they seem to do it through considerable repression of sexual feelings. More's data reveal that a socially successful girl is one who acts *as if* she were sophisticated and sexually mature but at the same time does not allow herself to feel the emotions she acts out.

25 Paul H. Mussen and Mary C. Jones, "The Behavior-Inferred Motivations of Late and Early Maturing Boys," *Child Development,* 29 (March 1958), 61–67.
26 Robert Ames, "A Longitudinal Study of Social Participation" (unpublished doctor's dissertation, University of California, 1956).
27 Mary C. Jones and Paul H. Mussen, "Self-conceptions, Motivations, and Interpersonal Attitudes of Early- and Late-Maturing Girls," *Child Development,* 29 (December 1958), 491–501.
28 Caroline M. Tryon, *Adjustment Inventory I: Social and Emotional Adjustment* (Berkeley: University of California Press, 1939).
29 Douglas M. More, "Developmental Concordance and Discordance during Puberty and Early Adolescence," *Monographs of the Society for Research in Child Development,* 18 (1953).

Among the boys whom More studied, puberty appears a more gradual affair. That is, the impulses experienced by adolescent boys may be as strong as or stronger than those of girls, but these impulses apparently develop more slowly and gradually. In addition, the sexual impulses of adolescent boys are not as repressed as they generally are in adolescent girls. For these reasons, the adolescent boy is perhaps better able to adjust to sexual changes when they appear.

These several studies seem to show that physical-growth changes do exert a pervasive influence on the behavior, development, and learning of children and youth. The powerfulness of that influence may be seen in the following excerpts from the case records of a late-maturing boy and an early-maturing girl.

A LATE-MATURING BOY

Shorty was a dark-haired, chunky boy with a rather large head, legs rather short in proportion to his trunk, and muscular strength markedly above average for his years. He rated well above average in IQ tests in spite of careless answers, and his motor coordination was rated superior. He was aggressive and mischievous in his relations with other boys and adults, but no more so than some of the other boys of his sixth-grade class.

Shorty was a leader of sorts. When a social situation was unorganized, he talked the most and the loudest and made more than his share of suggestions of things to do. But when the group organized for a game, Shorty's pseudo-leadership vanished, and he resorted to clowning as his chief contribution. His teachers in elementary school described him as restless, talkative, and easily distracted from the task before him.

At first, Shorty found junior high school exhilarating, but his enthusiasm waned as the gap between his goals and his achievement in social significance grew wider and more evident. His attention-seeking and clowning techniques, which had previously given him status, were less acceptable in junior high school. It was during his second year in junior high school that he started talking about his height. Each time he was measured, he stretched himself as far as he could but was always disappointed by the answer to his question "How much have I grown?" The growth situation was hard to accept. Shorty was not only distinctly short but in his overall development he was about a year behind his classmates. He took to hanging on bars and rings every day to "stretch himself," and he asked the examining physician what medicine he could take to make himself grow. His concern over his lack of appropriate male characteristics was reflected in wisecracks and comments he made about these changes in other boys.

In informal social experiences with classmates, Shorty indulged in childish horseplay. The physically more mature girls and boys criticized and rebuffed him. He withdrew to a group of less mature boys, who expressed their frustration by engaging in exaggerated little-boy antics.

In senior high school Shorty was most interested in shop and began working on an old car in an effort to make it run. The days when the "heap" actually ran were few, and the process of repair and replacement went on continuously for months. One day toward the end of this year Shorty was caught stealing auto parts from a junk yard, and during his brief detention by the police Shorty seemed to go berserk. After he was released to his mother's custody, the symptoms of acute mental disturbance subsided, and he returned to school.

With wise understanding and help, Shorty built a new, more realistic pattern of self-expression. He was appointed an assistant football manager, and he was helped in getting a part-time job after school. Following graduation he got a full-time job and was going steady with a very nice girl.

With the wise, sympathetic understanding of interested adults, Shorty Doyle finally came to terms with himself and his world.

AN EARLY-MATURING GIRL

Betty, fourteen years old and in the ninth grade, was referred to the guidance office for doing unsatisfactory work in class. She was described by her teachers as an extremely lively girl who seemed proud of the "tough" things she did.

[Results of tests administered by the guidance department showed that Betty had an IQ of 129; her superb performance on a reading test carried her beyond the point where achievement can be reliably measured. Nothing in these test results gave a clue to Betty's educational maladjustment.]

Prior to the testing, Betty asked Miss M., the guidance counselor, "How tall are you?" Betty measured herself against Miss M. and then said, "I am taller than you are, but I don't believe I look any taller. I quit letting them measure me when I got to be five feet eight, so I don't know exactly how tall I am, and I don't want to know." Betty continued, "Will this work show whether or not I'm nuts? They think I am nuts around here, but honestly sometimes I think I will go crazy with all those little kids all day. There are a couple of girls who have some sense, but do you know what we do in gym now? We dance sometimes with the ninth-grade boys. Can you imagine me dancing with those little squirts of boys? No, I don't dance at all. Quote. Dancing is a trapdoor to hell. Quote. That's father speaking, and he ought to know—he was a sailor!"

Betty was asked if she went to movies with other junior high school boys and girls, and she replied, "Those infants? No! My boyfriends are out of high school, and that's another thing I have trouble over at home. The other day I wanted to go some place, and mother said, "Betty, you aren't old enough to do those things. You are just a little girl. You are only fourteen and you ought to be playing with dolls. Imagine me playing with dolls! I always hated dolls! Me, five feet eight and just a little girl. I feel eighteen or nineteen. I can't stand this kid stuff. I want action!'"

The nurse came into the guidance office very much excited because Betty had offered to bring some marijuana for a project on tobacco and intoxicants. The nurse wanted to have Betty questioned by state narcotic agents. Betty seemed to take special delight in doing things that would cause the nurse to "flip."

The guidance counselor reported that Betty staged a crying jag in the office which lasted for an hour and a half, during which time she went on a regular tirade against her home, her parents, her brother, and everything in general. Her parents are from the mountains and are strictly religious; they believe that almost all recreation is sinful and that anyone who attends movies will go to hell. Betty has evidently made up her mind that if she is going to hell anyway, she might as well go all of the way.

Assessing Growth

Our understanding of an individual's growth and its relation to his behavior and learning is facilitated by our acceptance of the principle that individuals mature at different times and at different rates in accordance with their own patterns of growth. Given these differences in growth and maturity, the educator or parent may ask, "How can one know whether a particular child or adolescent is growing and maturing as he should?" "How can needed information concerning a student's growth be obtained and analyzed in order to forestall or alleviate some of the problems faced by Shorty Doyle and Betty Burroughs?"

A number of available growth grids permit an assessment of a child's growth in relation to his own growth pattern. One of the best instruments for assessing growth is the *Grid for Evaluating Physical Fitness,* developed by Wetzel.[30] The effectiveness of this grid depends upon the use of standard procedures of measurement (with accurate instruments and under similar measurement conditions) of height and weight at six-month intervals. A Wetzel Grid is shown in Figure 4.8.[31] On it have been plotted growth curves from the physical-growth data for Betty Burroughs and Shorty Doyle. The grid at the left enables one to ascertain direction, level, and speed of growth. Height (horizontal scale) is plotted against weight (vertical scale), with each pair of coordinates marked by a dot. Successive coordinates are plotted for successive measurements of height and weight. The coordinates are expected to move up the physique channel that corresponds to the child's body type. Successive parallel lines across the physique channels designate *isodevelopmental levels,* which are used as a standard measure of growth rate. Through much of school life, the normal speed of moving up a physique channel is one developmental level per month or twelve per year. Figure 4.8 shows that Shorty Doyle's rate of growth falls short of this norm during the

[30] Norman C. Wetzel, *The Wetzel Grid for Evaluating Physical Fitness* (Cleveland: NEA Service, 1940).

[31] From Wetzel. Copyright 1940, 1941, 1948 by Dr. Norman C. Wetzel. Reproduced by permission of Dr. Wetzel and Newspaper Enterprise Association.

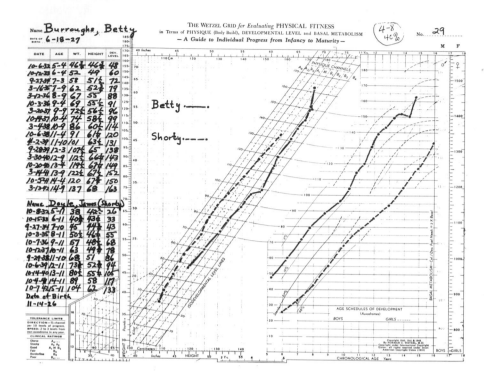

Figure 4.8. Growth curves plotted on Wetzel Grid from physical-growth data for Betty Burroughs and Shorty Doyle.

early and late parts of elementary school, while Betty Burroughs' rate of growth approximates or exceeds the norm during most of her growing years.

The right grid measures the comparative level of development according to age. The measure of isodevelopmental level is carried over from the left grid and is plotted against chronological age. The individual's curve on the right grid may be compared with the nearest *auxodrome,* which indicates the percentage of persons at any given chronological age who are physically more mature than persons whose coordinates are at or below that auxodrome. Figure 4.8 shows that Betty is among the most mature 15 percent of her age group, while Shorty is consistently among the least mature 10 to 20 percent of his age group.

The Wetzel Grid is but one of several instruments available for evaluating the status and quality of the individual's growth. Information obtained from such an instrument is especially useful when it is related to other kinds of data from school—anecdotal records, sociometric choices, parent conferences, and records of home visits.

Summary

Human development and learning are profoundly influenced by the physical processes consonant with life itself—the processes of metabolism, growth, dynamic organization, reproduction, and adaptation to environment.

Physiologically, the human being is an open, complex, dynamic energy system. Energy is used by the body for maintenance of organization, growth and tissue repair, and physical and mental activity. Any process or event which influences the status or operation of the human dynamic energy system affects development and learning. Variables which most frequently influence energy and behavior are nutrition, health, physical defects, the balance of rest and activity, and emotional factors. Individuals vary widely in rates of energy output. Differences in energy levels not directly due to physical causes may be related to differences in maturity, the normal population, and/or sex.

Physical changes of profound significance in the development and learning of children and youth are those associated with physical growth and maturation. Numerous studies of physical growth support the following generalizations regarding physical growth.

1. Growth is continuous but does not proceed at a uniform rate.
2. There is a general growth pattern for human beings.
3. Each person has his own unique growth pattern.
4. Girls on the average are more advanced in physical maturity than are boys.
5. In general, all aspects of growth are interrelated.

Studies of differential physical maturation and early school performance show that physically less mature students usually perform less adequately in academic tasks. Early-maturing adolescent boys are more advanced in social and emotional development and reveal better personal adjustment than their late-maturing peers. While a number of personal and social problems are posed for early-maturing adolescent girls, the effects of differences in maturity on behavior are less evident for girls than they are for boys. In general, the adolescent boy accepts and expresses the impulses which result from physical and sexual maturation, while the adolescent girl represses these impulses.

Excerpts from the case records of a late-maturing boy and an early-maturing girl show the impact of physical growth and maturity on adolescent development, behavior, and learning. The Wetzel Grid, an instrument for assessing the status and quality of physical growth, can be used to evaluate the physical growth and maturation patterns and to record the growth changes of such students as Shorty and Betty.

Study Questions

1. Barbara Anne, age nine, appears listless in class. A large, heavy girl with an IQ of 110, she often does not complete her assigned work and does not participate in games on the playground. What hypotheses would you suggest to explain the possible physical causes of Barbara Anne's listless behavior? What kinds of information would you need to substantiate or refute each of your hypotheses?

2. Mary Tompkins has five boys in her first-grade class who are short and chubby with round faces and prominent foreheads. All of these children have a short attention span, tend to be hyperactive, and have difficulty expressing themselves in front of the class. What do these facts suggest with regard to the timing and the kinds of learning experiences which may be appropriate for these boys?

3. The term *maturity* is frequently used and misused. The concept of physical maturity refers to the appearance of certain physiological and growth changes in body function and structure. What meaning does the term have in reference to an individual's social, emotional, or intellectual development? Does it have a meaning comparable with physical maturity in these other areas of development? Discuss.

4. You are helping a student committee plan a party for members of your eighth-grade homeroom class. With your knowledge of the wide variations in physical growth and maturity which may be observed in a class of eighth-grade students, what suggestions would you offer the committee regarding the types of activities and recreation they might plan for this party?

5. At what point should Shorty have been given help in understanding the realities of his own physical growth? What might a teacher do to help Shorty with his problems?

6. As one of Betty Burroughs' teachers, what would you have done to help Betty adjust to ninth grade in this junior high school?

Suggested Readings

Marian E. Breckenridge and E. Lee Vincent. *Child Development*. Fourth Edition. Philadelphia: W. B. Saunders, 1960. Chapters 1 and 2 present and discuss basic generalizations relating to physical growth and the relationships between physical growth and other aspects of development. Chapters 7 and 8 report research findings relative to growth of the body and motor development.

Dorothy H. Eichorn. "Biological Correlates of Behavior," in Harold W. Stevenson, ed. *Child Psychology*. Sixty-Second Yearbook of the National Society for the Study of Education. Chicago: University of Chicago Press, 1963.

Pages 4–61. Reviews research on human genetics, vision, and rate of maturing relating to human behavior and development.

William E. Martin and Celia Burns Stendler. *Child Behavior and Development.* New York: Harcourt, Brace & World, 1959. Chapter 1 identifies and describes the characteristics and qualities of physiological functioning and behavior that mark the child as distinctly human. Chapter 3 discusses individual differences among children that may be ascribed to biological inheritance rather than to societal influences. Chapter 4 describes the processes of growth and development which apply generally to all children.

Bernice Neugarten. "Body Processes Help to Determine Behavior and Development," in Caroline Tryon (Chairman), *Fostering Mental Health in Our Schools.* Washington: Association for Supervision and Curriculum Development, 1950. Pages 52–63. Discusses the potential effects on behavior and learning of physiological differences in energy output, body build, and patterns of physical growth. Examines the implications of this information for children's learning and adjustment in school.

Ernest H. Watson and George H. Lowrey. *Growth and Development of Children.* Chicago: Year Book Publishers, 1951. Presents factual information on the several phases of physical growth and development. Includes discussions of fetal development, methods of assessing growth evidenced by behavior, organ development, and bone development. Included are discussions of the roles of endocrines, metabolism, and nutrition in growth and development.

Films

Human Growth, 16 mm, sound, color, 19 min. Bloomington, Indiana: Audio-Visual Center, Indiana University (rental fee, $6.65). Pictures changes which take place in the human growth cycle from fertilization of the egg through adulthood. Special emphasis is placed on body changes that occur during adolescence.

Physical Aspects of Puberty, 16 mm, sound, black and white, 18 min. Bloomington, Indiana: Audio-Visual Center, Indiana University (rental fee, $4.15). Describes, with the help of diagrams of the human body, the physical changes in a girl and a boy from the age of ten to puberty. Explains the functions of the endocrine system and its effects on the ·development of primary and secondary sex characteristics. Discusses the effects of rapid physical growth on emotional, social, and mental development.

5

the interpersonal environment

He drew a circle that shut me out—
Heretic, rebel, a thing to flout.
But Love and I had the wit to win:
We drew a circle that took him in!

≡   EDWIN MARKHAM

Man's most significant learning and development take place in a context of social interaction with other human beings. The infant's fumbling efforts to grasp a ball, to feed himself, or to take his first tottering steps are made in response to the friendly encouragement of parents, siblings, and others. The ten-year-old who practices long hours alone in throwing and catching a ball has before him the goal of showing his teammates in the next game how well he can play. The adolescent and the adult learn facts and concepts at least partly in order to deal more effectively with people and their concerns. Most important, the individual's beliefs, attitudes, values, and self-concept are all developed predominantly in social interaction.

Personal observation and clinical studies clearly reveal that man's mental and physical health are profoundly affected by the quality of his relationships with others. Abandonment, rejection, or deprivation of human contact pose the greatest threats to self and to man's will to live; over an extended period of time such threats lead first to insanity and eventually to death.[1]

Why is contact with others so important to man? Erich Fromm[2] gives one answer. According to Fromm, man is constantly searching for meaning and purpose in his existence. In this search he is confronted with the anomaly of his own existence. He is a part of nature, subject to the processes of growth, aging, disease, and death, as are all other living things. Yet, the complexity of his brain, nervous system, and total organism endows him with qualities that enable him to transcend the rest of nature. He possesses capacities to remember, to visualize future events, to symbolize his experience, to conceptualize, to reason, and to use imagination. The realization that no other human can fully share the thoughts, feelings, doubts, and perplexities of his own inner, private world causes him to feel a "separateness," which he may translate as "aloneness." This threat of aloneness, and the uncertainty it creates, is most fully assuaged by the bonds of human relatedness that join each individual with the rest of mankind.

As the human being grows and develops, the dependence of his early life gives way to a relatively high degree of independence in adulthood. Man, however, is never completely independent; he continues to share an interdependence with other persons, other living things, and the resources of his environment. He is dependent upon other human beings to assuage his "core of aloneness" in the same way that he is dependent upon the other resources of his environment for materials that sustain life and promote growth and development. The needs for independence and dependence are not antagonistic but complementary. Each individual achieves independence as he gains a greater understanding of and control over his environment. At the same time, he remains dependent upon other human beings for sustenance and support and for love and security.

Concepts of Love and Security

Love (or, as we shall call it, affection) connotes valuing, fondness, and a feeling of strong personal attachment. Its specific and subtle meanings vary for different cultures and different relationships. Although the search has frustrated philosophers and writers throughout the ages, men still seek to discover and to describe the meaning of love. Fromm speaks of love as the active concern for the life and growth of another. Productive love, according to Fromm,[3] embodies four qualities: care, responsibility, respect, and knowledge. Prescott[4] identifies eight qualities of the love relationship, including

[1] Rollo May, *Man's Search for Himself* (New York: W. W. Norton & Co., 1953), pp. 13–45, 146–148.
[2] Erich Fromm, *Man for Himself* (New York: Holt, Rinehart and Winston, 1947); *The Art of Loving* (New York: Harper & Row, 1956).
[3] Fromm, *The Art of Loving*, p. 26.
[4] Daniel A. Prescott, "Role of Love in Human Development," *Journal of Home Economics,* 44 (1952), 173–176.

empathy with the loved one, concern for his welfare, happiness, and development, and expression of this concern through an offer of personal resources by the lover to the loved one. Love may include sexual components, but it is not dependent upon them. Symonds[5] views sex as one form of sharing and joint activity—the most complete union of which a man and a woman are capable. But sex in which partners do not esteem and value each other as separate personalities is not a component of love.

Love or affection, then, refer to those acts, feelings, and responses in a human relationship which are perceived as connoting personal valuing and acceptance. Though individuals often feel valued and accepted as members of a group, these feelings seem to be experienced more intimately in *one-to-one* relationships between two persons, wherein the feelings and responses of each are focused exclusively on the other. Within this one-to-one relationship, affection reaches its full meaning and value only when expressions of affection are mutual. Relationships in which affection is not reciprocal soon become empty and begin to dissolve.

The feeling that one is valued and accepted by others leads one to value and accept himself. A sense of personal value and self-worth comes to be reflected, often covertly, in an individual's responses to life situations. The term *security* has become associated with this sense of self-worth. A conviction of self-value gives one, in the psychological sense, a feeling of safety and freedom from fear and anxiety which the word *security* connotes.

Sensations of security begin in infancy. Pleasant feelings which accompany the satisfaction of physiological drives tend to become associated with the kinds and quality of human relationships existing between the child or adolescent and the significant persons in his life. Thus, a feeling of security may be experienced initially in the strong affectional bond which develops between a mother and her child as she nurses and cares for him. Qualities of valuing and support expressed in other ways will also characterize the relationships which the child has with his teachers or friends. The need to feel secure is a need which continues throughout life.

The term *security* has become associated with various behavioral symptoms which reflect the individual's responses to feelings of safety and certainty. The secure individual, sure of his own value, is free in his relationships with others. Indeed, studies of persons undergoing counseling reveal that those who have positive feelings about themselves also tend to respond positively to others.[6] Children who feel secure are outgoing, confident, curious, accepting, and self-assured. This positive orientation toward life also facilitates an individual's development and learning.

[5] Percival M. Symonds, *The Dynamics of Human Adjustment* (New York: Appleton-Century-Crofts, 1946), pp. 548–549.

[6] Elizabeth Sheerer, "An Analysis of the Relationship between Acceptance of Self and Acceptance and Respect for Others," *Journal of Consulting Psychology*, 13 (June 1949), 169–175; Dorothy Stock, "An Investigation into the Interrelations between the Self-Concept and Feelings toward Other Persons and Groups," *Journal of Consulting Psychology*, 13 (June 1949), 176–180.

Insecurity may also manifest itself in a variety of ways. Commonly, the insecure child is outwardly aggressive, physically or verbally, toward others or toward himself. His dependence upon others or his preoccupation with the uncertainty of his self-worth is manifested in attention-seeking, bragging, demanding, dominating or exploiting others, or in other selfish and self-centered behavior. When faced with unfamiliar situations, tasks which are too hard, or situations involving competition, the insecure child often becomes panicky, gives up easily, or runs away.[7]

Some children who feel insecure withdraw from contact with other persons. A child whose valuing and acceptance of himself has been damaged by lack of affectional relationships seeks, by withdrawing, to avoid further emotional pain. The insecurity behind this behavior may not be easily detected by adults, because the withdrawn child causes no trouble in the group. Undetected, however, withdrawal, through increasing loss of contact with reality, often leads to mental illness.

The specific behavior patterns and roles that one learns in interaction with others are those which he judges will be most effective in fully satisfying his need to feel secure. Each child learns highly individual ways for dealing with this important need, and probably no learning in the individual's life is so crucial to his overall development and adjustment as is the learning which enables him to achieve a feeling of security.

Affectional Needs in Infancy

Emergence of Relatedness Needs

During the first several weeks of life, the human infant is dependent upon others for the satisfaction of physiological needs. These needs provide his first interpersonal experience. His success or lack of success in satisfying his hunger through nursing, for example, is expressed in reactions of satisfaction and contentment or of dissatisfaction and pain. These pleasant or unpleasant feelings and responses become associated with and directed toward the person (usually the mother) most responsible for them.[8]

The infant's ability to register and associate sensory impressions from personal contacts with his mother extends to other experiences as well. So closely related are a child's physical and psychological needs that anything that makes him more comfortable physically (such as nursing, changing diapers, or picking him up) also improves his psychological well-being. Particularly important to his psychological well-being, in Ribble's[9] view, are

[7] James S. Plant, *Personality and the Cultural Pattern* (New York: Commonwealth Fund, 1937), p. 101.

[8] The critical importance of nursing experiences on the child's later personality development is emphasized in Harry Stack Sullivan, *The Interpersonal Theory of Psychiatry* (New York: W. W. Norton & Co., 1953), pp. 75–91.

[9] Margaret A. Ribble, *The Rights of Infants* (New York: Columbia University Press, 1943), p. 9.

closeness, warmth, support, and acts of mothering, such as fondling, caressing, rocking, and singing or speaking to the baby while caring for his physical needs.

Studies of Maternal Deprivation

Evidence of the crucial importance of relatedness and security needs to the growth and development of young children comes from many sources. One important source is controlled experiments investigating the effects of maternal deprivation in animals.

In a study cited by Bowlby,[10] a pair of goat kids lived with and were fed by the mother except during a daily forty-minute experimental period when one kid was separated from the mother. During the experimental period, the lights were periodically extinguished, a situation which is known to create anxiety in goats. This treatment produced very different behavior in the twins. The one with its mother appeared at ease and moved about freely, while the isolated one cowered in a corner.

A number of experiments investigating the development of affectional responses of neonatal and infant monkeys to an artificial, inanimate mother have been reported by Harlow.[11] Two different mother-surrogate figures were constructed. One was made from a block of wood covered with sponge rubber and sheathed in tan terry cloth, with a light bulb in its back radiating heat. The second mother surrogate was made of wire mesh and was warmed by radiant heat; it differed from the cloth mother surrogate mainly in the quality of contact comfort which it could supply.

In the initial experiment, a cloth mother and a wire mother were placed in different cubicles attached to the infant monkey's cage. For four newborn monkeys the cloth mother lactated and the wire mother did not; for another four the condition was reversed. In either case the infant received all of its milk through the mother surrogate as soon as it was able to. The infants had access to both mothers, and the time spent with each was automatically recorded. The infants fed by the cloth mother spent fifteen to twenty times as much time with her as with the wire mother; and those fed by the wire mother spent five to eight times as much time with their nonlactating cloth mother as with the wire mother. These findings clearly show that contact comfort is of fundamental importance—greater importance even than nursing—in the experiencing of affection. Indeed, Harlow suggests that "the primary function of nursing as an affectional variable is that of insuring frequent and intimate body contact of infant with mother."[12]

In other experiments Harlow studied the role of the mother or mother surrogate in providing infants with a source of security, especially in strange

[10] John Bowlby, *Child Care and the Growth of Love* (Baltimore: Penguin Books, 1965), p. 22.

[11] Harry F. Harlow, "The Nature of Love," *American Psychologist,* 13 (December 1958), 673–685.

[12] Harlow, p. 679.

situations. When placed experimentally in a strange environment, infant monkeys always rushed to the mother surrogate when she was present, clutched her, rubbed their bodies against hers, and frequently manipulated her body and face. A little later, the infants began to use the mother surrogate as a source of security and a base of operations to which they would return from explorations of their new world. When the mother was absent from the room, however, most of the infants would freeze in a crouched position, frantically clutch their bodies, and begin crying, rocking, or sucking. A few monkeys would rush to the center of the room, where the mother was customarily placed, and then run rapidly from object to object, screaming and crying all the while.

The effects of maternal deprivation on human beings have been observed mainly in individuals growing up in institutions. The literature is replete with cases reporting the effects of maternal deprivation on human growth, development, and mental health. Ribble[13] cites the case of an infant left by the mother in an understaffed hospital. Lack of mothering was accompanied by an inability to retain and assimilate food, a continuing loss of weight, a suspension of growth development, and a slipping backward in physiological functioning that threatened the child's life. Although subsequent mothering and attention did restore normal body and growth processes, development was retarded and the child's emotional life was severely damaged. Bowlby[14] cites numerous reports of British children separated from parents for long periods during World War II. These children developed numerous symptoms of emotional maladjustment: inability to love or to form lasting relationships or to care for others; avoidance and rejection of those who sought to help; lack of normal emotional responses; deceit, evasion, stealing, and lack of concentration at school.

Spitz[15] found a dramatic contrast between children reared under conditions of adequate social stimulation and contact and those reared in a socially impoverished environment. One group, consisting primarily of children whose mothers were unable to support them, lived in a foundling home; a second group lived in a nursery attached to a women's prison. In both institutions, the children were admitted shortly after birth, and in both they were given excellent physical and medical care. The two groups differed markedly in the amount of human association they experienced. Babies in the foundling home were kept in cribs where they could see only walls, ceiling, and corridors. These children were raised from the third month by overworked nursing personnel, who fed and washed them but had no time to play with them. Mothers of babies in the prison nursery, however, were available to

[13] Ribble, pp. 4–7.
[14] Bowlby, pp. 18–49.
[15] Rene A. Spitz, "Hospitalism: An Inquiry into the Genesis of Psychiatric Conditions in Early Childhood," *The Psychoanalytic Study of the Child*, 1 (New York: International University Press, 1945), 53–74; Rene A. Spitz and K. M. Wolfe, "Anaclitic Depression: An Inquiry into the Genesis of Psychiatric Conditions in Early Childhood," *The Psychoanalytic Study of the Child*, 2 (New York: International University Press, 1946), 313–342.

spend a few hours each day with their babies, so that these children had more social experiences than those in the foundling home. Spitz's findings revealed that in an infant personality test the foundling-home babies registered a precipitous decline in their monthly developmental quotient from 130 in the third month to 70 at the end of the first year and 45 at the end of the second year. The developmental quotient of children in the prison nursery, on the other hand, averaged 95 to 110 each month during the first year.

A more serious condition associated with maternal deprivation in the foundling home is *anaclitic depression,* which Spitz observed in 19 of 23 foundling-home infants. The principal behavior symptoms included mourning, withdrawal, inability to act, and loss of appetite, sleep, and weight. The children eventually became extremely lethargic and withdrawn and showed a general physical deterioration. This condition Spitz called *hospitalism.* Associated with this general decline was a high mortality rate among the foundling-home children. During a two-year period, 37 percent of these children died, whereas none of the nursery infants were lost by death.

Later writers[16] have been critical of the research methodologies and the interpretations of Spitz and Ribble. When all is said, however, the evidence does suggest that lack of maternal contact and love—although it does not produce invariable effects in all individuals—can cause marked retardation in development and severe damage to physical and mental health.

Affection and Socialization

Since the child learns the ways of his culture primarily in interaction with others, his socialization experiences will influence and be influenced by affectional ties with significant persons in his life. In many cultures, including our own, it is these significant persons—members of the family, the kinship group, the peer group, and neighbors—who fulfill the dual and inseparable functions of teaching the customs and mores of the culture to the child and at the same time of giving him affection and helping him to feel secure. This dual role often creates conflict and confusion for child and elder alike. The affection the child seeks and needs should be unconditional—a valuing of the individual for himself alone, regardless of his particular qualities or characteristics. But sometimes the affection seems to be contingent on good behavior—so that lapses in acceptable toilet habits, aggression toward a sibling, or a violation of any of the middle-class mores brings about disapproval, censure, or punishment by the elder. The child often interprets such acts as personal rejection or the withdrawal of love. On the other hand, the overindulgent elder, who avoids correcting or curbing a child's antisocial behavior for fear that such action will cause the child to feel unloved, can contribute to an increase in a child's self-centeredness and lack of respect for

[16] S. M. Pinneau, "A Critique of the Articles by Margaret Ribble," *Child Development,* 21 (December 1950), 203–228; "The Infantile Disorders of Hospitalism and Anaclitic Depression," *Psychological Bulletin,* 52 (September 1955), 429–452; and H. Orlansky, "Infant Care and Personality," *Psychological Bulletin,* 46 (January 1949), 1–48.

elders. On the whole, however, children who early and continuously experience love and a feeling of being valued are usually able, with increased maturation and experience, to distinguish between the two functions of adults. The secure child or adolescent has the support necessary to accept correction and can work toward meeting and accepting the ways imposed by the culture.

Affection and Patterns of Child Training

Two major approaches to child training, the behaviorist and the psychoanalytic, differ substantially in the emphasis they place on the child's feelings and need for affection. Dominating the scene during the second and third decades of this century was J. B. Watson's behavioristic view that nearly all human behavior and development are the result of *conditioning*. The theory of conditioning describes learning as a series of events wherein a stimulus (such as a loud noise) becomes associated with and evokes a response (such as a startle or fear reaction). Under behaviorism, the environment is controlled in so far as possible by parents and other socializing agents, who introduce stimuli designed to evoke desired behaviors in the young. Behaviorism gives little attention to events that intervene between stimulus and response, and it excludes from consideration consciousness, feelings, cognitions, and introspection.

In applying behaviorism to problems of child rearing, mothers were instructed to feed the infant on a strict schedule, to refrain from picking up a fussy child, and to place him on the toilet at regular times after meals—so that in each case the appropriate stimulus-response associations would be formed. Child training under behaviorism is little concerned with a child's feelings, his relationships with others, or his psychological needs. Focusing on these is equivalent to "spoiling" the child; effective development and learning depend wholly upon the child's forming appropriate stimulus-response patterns.

The principles of psychoanalysis began to be disseminated more widely and to exert increasing influence on psychological thought in the United States beginning about 1930. Freud, and later psychoanalytic theorists, placed great emphasis upon the quality of the early interpersonal relationships of the child because of the influence of these relationships on later personality development. The damaging effects of early emotional deprivation—neuroses, maladjustment, and mental illness—were shown in studies of maternal deprivation, such as those cited earlier. Ribble and Sullivan,[17] therefore, advised mothers to satisfy fully the emotional needs of their children by cuddling, mothering, rocking, and playing with them. These writers also indicated that the parent's own feelings toward the child are extremely important; that is, the parent's acceptance or rejection of the child may be communicated to him through psychomotor tensions. For instance, if the

[17] See notes 8 and 9.

parent holds his child firmly, the child has comfortable, pleasant feelings associated with security; if the child is held loosely or carelessly, he feels fearful and insecure. According to these writers, satisfying the child's physical needs contributes to relieving his tension and to making him feel more comfortable and secure.

Psychoanalytic writings have tended to make parents more aware of and concerned about the affectional needs of children. Thus, psychoanalysis has made a major contribution to an understanding of human development, even though many of its claims have not as yet been fully substantiated by research.

Characteristic Emotional Climates

Children may experience any one of four general types of emotional climates: affection, rejection, inconsistency, or overprotection. Since the description of each climate is rather general, the emotional climate in the home of any particular child is likely to vary somewhat from the description of the type.

Climate of affection. In a home that provides a climate of affection, family members express toward one another the fundamental qualities of acceptance and valuing. A child who grows up in such a climate feels wanted and valued. His relationships with others, especially his parents, are pleasurable and satisfying; he learns that he can depend upon others for support and help. Such a child gains a certainty of his own worth and thus is freed from anxiety. He is able to express affection for others and to work to progress toward growth and maturity. In short, his interactions with others confirm and reinforce his conception of his own value, thereby providing him with a firm feeling of security.

Climate of rejection. Some children live in homes wherein family relationships are cold, indifferent, hostile, or rejecting. In such a climate, the child feels uncertain of his own worth and, consequently, feels threatened, anxious, and in constant conflict. Burdened by these emotions, he cannot make optimum progress in learning and development, and often behaves aggressively. Thus, the child who tries intentionally to hurt others or himself or to behave in other ways which are sure to result in punishment is really grasping for crumbs of attention as a substitute for the affection and acceptance he has been unable to secure. Such a child is emotionally crippled; he has simply not learned that he can gain love and acceptance by socially acceptable behavior.

Climate of inconsistency. In some families, the relationship between child and parents is variable and inconsistent. On some days the parent may be overindulgent, generous, and affectionate toward the child; at other times, for no apparent reason, the parent may be critical, punishing, hostile, or rejecting. This inconsistency deprives the child of adequate perceptual cues to the behavior desired of him. Not knowing for sure how his parent will respond to his behavior in any given situation, he becomes anxious and immobile. Although he is loved and valued at times, the overall inconsistency of the treatment he receives from his parents creates within the child an uncertainty and a fear of taking chances—qualities that are inimical to learning and the development of a well-integrated personality.

Climate of overprotection. Some children are smothered in love. Their parents overindulge them, establish no firm or realistic limits for their behavior, or accede to their every whim. As a result, they become overdependent and self-centered and gain a distorted perception of their own importance.

The indulgent and overprotective adult often has emotional problems of his own. Overprotection may be evidence of irrational fears concerning the safety and health of an only child or a handicapped child, or it may serve as compensation for emotional needs left unfulfilled by the marriage. Robert's mother, in the following case record, manifests both the irrational fears and the unfulfilled needs.

> Robert's mother had had several miscarriages before Robert's difficult birth, and she was past forty when Robert was born. Robert's father spent most of his time with his business, thereby continuing a distant relationship with his wife which had existed since early in the marriage. During Robert's growing years, his mother scarcely let him out of her sight. She nursed him until he was two, boiled his bottles until he was four, and would not let him play with other children for fear he would catch some dread disease. Both shared the same bed until Robert was eight.
>
> Early, Robert sought to feed and dress himself, to build with blocks and to color pictures, but he soon gave up when his mother insisted on their doing things together. As time went on, Robert learned that he could get what he wanted from his mother by screaming his demands or by lying down on the floor and kicking. His social adjustment to kindergarten and first grade was difficult. He demanded the teacher's total attention, grabbed toys and materials from other children, and generally failed to conform to school expectations. During the whole of first grade, Robert's mother brought him to school and came each afternoon to take him home in the car. In response to the teacher's note concerning Robert's messy desk, his mother appeared at school one afternoon and proceeded to clean out his desk while Robert chased other boys around the room.

This case illustrates the characteristics of overprotection noted by Levy:[18] excessive contact between mother and child, infantilization of both mother's and child's behavior, and prevention of independent behavior on the part of the child. For Robert, overprotection blocked healthy emotional relationships with others, frustrated growth toward independence, and severely

---

[18] David M. Levy, *Maternal Overprotection* (New York: Columbia University Press, 1943).

limited development and learning. Overprotection distorts a child's perceptions of himself and the world, thereby creating adjustment problems which must be overcome if learning and development are to proceed.

The Development of Affectional Relationships

The feeling of security that emerges from shared affectional relationships is not gained at once but is developed gradually. The child changes and matures in his way of giving and receiving affection just as he changes and matures in physical size and complexity. The development of the child's affectional life has three aspects: (1) psychosexual development, as shown in a change from self-love and self-centeredness toward increased acceptance and valuing of others; (2) social development, as the child broadens his base of affectional relationships from the family to an ever increasing and widening circle of friends and associates in adolescence and adulthood; and (3) individual development—the change from a state of complete helplessness and dependence upon others to a state of relative independence, which enables the child to help and to share with others.

Psychosexual Development of the Child

The first aspect of the development of the affectional life of the child is described by Freud's theory of psychosexual development. The account that follows is confined to those parts of the theory which assist in explaining the changes in the child's feelings toward self and his relationships with others.

Freud names the initial stages of the infant's psychosexual development for regions or parts of the body whose stimulation bring pleasure. The period of the first few months of life—when the infant gains pleasure from nursing, putting things in his mouth, and biting—is called the *oral phase*. The later months of the first year—when the child's attention comes to be directed to the anus—is called the *anal phase*. Tensions arising in the anal region as a result of the accumulation of fecal material are pleasurably released with the expelling of this material. These physical pleasures produce in the child a fondness for his own body, a fondness manifested in feelings of self-love which Freud calls *narcissism*. Initially, the young child is literally in love with himself. He is wholly self-interested, self-willed, and selfish. Later, as he learns to respond to others, he tends to choose as love objects persons who accede to his wishes and persons who appear to be as fond of him as he is of himself. Thus, his fondness for love objects during this secondary stage of self-love is contingent upon what they can contribute to his comforts and satisfactions. The period of narcissism, wherein the child exercises his self-will in manipulating the people and objects of his environment to his own purposes, has been aptly called *the age of infantile omnipotence.*

For most children the age of infantile omnipotence comes to an end during the preschool years, when parents stop acceding to the demands of the

child and instead place demands upon him. He is not pe[r]
defecate, or strike at others according to his wishes bu[t]
tion of these needs in ways approved by his parents. A[t]
years of age, the centering of the child's attention on
with his stroking and manipulating his sex organs mark[s]
psychosexual development. For a boy, affection for his p[arent]
through close emotional ties with his mother and respe[ct]
of his father. With the onset of the phallic stage, however, the young boy
experiences a rivalry with his father as he seeks the exclusive love and
possession of his mother. In interpreting this behavior, Freud theorized that
the boy's love for his mother becomes incestuous, and, as a result, the boy
becomes jealous of his father. Freud called this psychological phenomenon
the *Oedipus complex*. Strong incest taboos and fear of the father generally
lead to the boy's repressing both his incestuous love for his mother and his
rivalry with his father, with the result that the Oedipus complex gradually
disappears.

During the phallic stage, parallel but quite different changes in relationships between a girl and her parents occur. The girl's perception of male
dominance leads her to express love for her father and to feel jealousy of and
to reject her mother. This shift in feelings and relationships is called the
Electra complex. If the daughter experiences a warm, affectionate relationship with each parent, and if both encourage her to develop her femininity,
the Electra complex is gradually replaced by a strengthened identification
with the mother. This enables the daughter to maintain and to develop warm
affectional ties with both parents.

A major step toward achieving mature affectional ties with others occurs
when relationships reflecting narcissistic self-love and Oedipus or Electra
complexes are no longer satisfying or appropriate to the maturing child.
When the child has reached five or six years of age, the cultural forces of
home, neighborhood, and school openly disapprove of and discourage his
selfish, self-willed ways. Recognizing that he has fallen short of the standards
that parents and teachers have set for him, he tends to feel inadequate and
dissatisfied with himself. He seeks to relieve these feelings of inadequacy and
dissatisfaction by accepting and identifying with the standards of his parents
and teachers and by centering affection on another person. By freeing himself from the persistent demands of self-love, the child becomes able to give
himself fully in relationships with others. He expresses concern for others
and a willingness to help not only parents and siblings but persons outside of
his family as well. This increasing capacity for love, and a sense of fulfillment in loving another person without guilt or anxiety, are the characteristic
marks of mature affectional relationships. One cannot freely love another,
however, unless he first feels loved and valued. Thus, the acceptance and
value that one feels beginning in early life are crucial variables that determine his capacity for achieving mature affectional relationships later.

Between the age of five and the beginning of pubescence (for girls,
between the ages of eight and fourteen; for boys, between the ages of ten and

n) is a period of relative quiescence in sexual development which ud calls the *latency period*. It is a period of vigorous physical activity and development during which the child moves beyond the home to form affectional ties primarily with a group of peers and secondarily with selected adults in the school and community.

Puberty, marking the attainment of sexual maturity, signals the beginning of the *genital stage,* the final phase of psychosexual development. This psychological development, and the physical-growth changes which mark entrance into adulthood, exert a profound influence on the formation of affectional ties during adolescence. The young person is faced with the problem of sublimating his awakening sex drives, the direct expression of which is blocked by the culture. Initially, the adolescent achieves this sublimation by establishing friendships with persons of his own sex and age. Boys may spend long hours together hunting, fishing, bowling, playing tennis, or working on bicycles or an old car. Girl chums frequently spend long hours talking about boys, other girls, favorite movie or singing stars, clothes, grooming, teachers, and parents, doing homework together, and tying up the family telephone.

These close attachments with chums and others of the same sex fail, however, to provide complete satisfaction. The attainment of physical and sexual maturity in adolescence, together with mounting cultural pressures, results in the young person's seeking strong affectional ties with one or more members of the opposite sex. One such attachment with a particular man or woman becomes regarded as permanent and is formalized by marriage. With the centering of the most intense expressions of affection in one's relationship with one's mate and children, the cycle of the development of affectional relationships reaches fulfillment. This maturing of affectional relationships is related only in a very general way to chronological age. Many adults remain dependent and self-centered throughout life, while many children and youth reveal considerable maturity in achieving mutually shared affectional relationships.

Broadening of Affectional Ties

The rather marked changes in one's interpersonal behavior from birth to maturity are paralleled and facilitated by a broadening of one's base of affectional relationships. Strengthening of the child's feeling of security is dependent not only upon the personal acceptance and valuing he experiences with his mother, his father, or a nurse, but also upon the continuing formation of additional one-to-one relationships with significant others, together with other affectional relationships of a less intense nature.

The first and primary relationship with the mother or nurse grows out of the nurturance and care which she provides in satisfying the infant's physiological and dependency needs. As his ability to differentiate objects in his environment and to make social responses increases, the infant establishes relationships with father, siblings, and in many cases with grandparents, aunts, and uncles. These are personal relationships of varying intensities and meanings. Relationships with siblings, as will be noted later, are likely to be mercurial—reflecting contrasting feelings of love and envy, fear, or hate.

In early childhood, after the child has learned to walk and to talk, the base of affectional relationships broadens to persons beyond the family. Characteristically, the young child seeks out a neighbor child of approximately the same age. Playing near one another, each engrossed in his own play activities, the children experience acceptance. The importance of these early childhood relationships is shown in the strong identifications revealed in children's language, dress, interests, and shared activities. One two-year-old girl, for example, would not give her mother a moment's peace until she had a coat with a fur collar like the one her little friend had.

Adults outside the family are often important sources of a child's security throughout childhood and adolescence. Among the most prominent of these are the succession of teachers whom he has in his years at school. School is a significant experience for every child regardless of the particular personal meaning each gains from it. A special bond of affection usually forms between the kindergarten and first-grade teacher and the children. The teacher becomes a kind of second mother to her children, and many will forget and call her "mother." The warmth and support the kindergarten or first-grade teacher gives the child influences to a considerable degree his adjustment and progress in school. In subsequent school experiences, as the teacher-pupil relationship becomes less close and more formalized, the student still looks to the teacher for acceptance and understanding.

As the child grows into late childhood and early adolescence, his base of affectional relationships broadens to include ties with other children and adults in many different groups and situations. The peer group becomes an important influence in the life and development of the student during this period (see Chapter 7). His participation as an accepted member of the peer group not only gives him a feeling of belongingness but also contributes to his feelings of value and self-worth. At this time, as we have noted, the child often shares a special chum relationship with a same-sexed member of the peer group. For many, this chum relationship remains a strong affectional tie even into adult life.

Identifications with older persons of the same sex provide a further broadening of one's affectional ties. Often the older person is a favorite teacher, a scout leader, a baseball or football coach, or an older brother or sister or aunt or uncle whom the child or adolescent greatly admires and emulates. Children and youth also experience a feeling of oneness in make-believe relationships with movie, TV, or athletic stars or fictional heroes.

Affectional ties with members of the opposite sex, leading to the selection of a mate in courtship and marriage, mark a shift toward a new base for one's affectional life. For those who do not marry, a new base of affectional relationships will include the close, lasting friendships they establish with members of both sexes. Each person's affectional base continues to broaden throughout life, as friendships and associations with others are built with members of community, civic, and church groups and with associates on the job. Thus, one develops through the years a widening circle of relationships in which valuing and concern are mutually experienced. This circle of friends and associates changes in membership from time to time, but it continues to serve as an important source of personal valuing and support throughout one's adult life.

Varying kinds of relationships and activities may contribute to one's feeling of security. Some will seek to satisfy their affectional needs through dedicating their energies and lives to an organization, movement, party, or cause, while many others will experience acceptance and a sense of security through a personal relationship with God. Children, and many adults, often experience a special kind of acceptance and affection in their relationships with a pet. These take on added significance when human relationships fail to provide for full satisfaction of this need.

The importance of a broad base of affectional relationships cannot be overemphasized. The individual needs to feel secure not only with his family and close friends but also in the other areas and activities of his life. One's feeling accepted, valued, and supported enables him to respond freely and creatively in all of life's situations. Failure to maintain or to extend a circle of affectional ties results in a narrow affectional base which the changes wrought by time will slowly erode away. For human development and learning to proceed at optimal levels, there must be a broad and expanding base of affectional ties.

Growth toward Independence

We noted earlier that progress in human development is evidenced in change from dependence upon others toward relative independence of action and functioning. One is independent to the degree that he is able to act and to express himself freely without feeling obligated toward or dependent upon others—although one continuously needs support and valuing from other human beings and therefore is always in some degree dependent upon others.

Threats to Security

Parental Rejection

The first and most devastating threat to a child's security is the threat of being unwanted or rejected, particularly by his parents. Parents—one or both of them—may reject a child for a number of reasons: The mother may have feared pregnancy; the birth may have been difficult; the child may add to an already unbearable financial strain; the child may not have been planned; there may be some real or imagined defect in the child himself; the child may interfere with the parents' own pleasures or goals; or the parents may have no real interest in or desire for children.

Parental rejection of a child may be manifested in a variety of ways. Often the parents will constantly criticize the child and set unreasonably high expectations for him. Or they may avoid any show of care and responsibility, leaving him to be cared for by others and having as little contact and association with him as possible. Many times overprotection is a mask for parental rejection; a parent who overindulges his child may be trying to convince others and himself that he or she is a good parent. The child quickly senses, however, the lack of acceptance and valuing which is communicated in the relationships with the parent. The effects of parental rejection may be seen in the case of Louise:

Louise, age nine and in the fourth grade, had many unhappy experiences with other children at school. They called her dumb and made biting remarks about her appearance and dress. Yet the teacher noted that she was attractive, her dresses were similar to those worn by the other girls, and she was above average in her school work.

Louise tried very hard to please the other children by sharing her bicycle and other possessions, by giving in to their wishes, and by inviting a few children to her home to play. Their play was harmonious for a while until one or more started to call Louise names and to exclude her from their games.

In looking into Louise's home background, the teacher learned that Louise was born when her mother was forty-six, and her only sister was seventeeen years older than Louise. The mother was quite upset at becoming pregnant when she had looked forward to freedom from child rearing. During Louise's childhood her mother was very critical of her, and Louise finally gave up trying to please her mother.

An analysis of this case revealed that Louise had felt unwanted from an early age. She tried very hard to gain acceptance, especially from her agemates. Somehow her peers sensed and exploited her lack of a feeling of self-worth, and their cruel treatment added further to her feelings of rejection. Since rejection is something that the child or adolescent is unable to prevent or to understand, he does not know how to cope with it or to acquire the love and acceptance that others have denied him. There is considerable evidence that mental illness, delinquency, and failures in many areas of development and learning are often caused by the feelings of insecurity that follow rejection. A major responsibility falls to the school and other agencies of the community to undergird the home in providing security—giving acceptance and affection to all children, especially those whose homes fail them in this important need.

Sibling Rivalry

Sibling rivalry—the envy, dislike, or even hate of a child for a brother or sister who appears to usurp the parents' love—is a frequent phenomenon in American culture. Its manifestations are varied and well known. They include aggressive feelings and actions, directed toward the sibling and toward the parent, and regressive behavior toward more infantile patterns—wanting to be treated like a baby, resuming bottle feeding, and sometimes failing to control defecation. In a study of the responses of twelve three- and-four-year-old children in standardized doll-play situations, Levy[19] found that hostility expressed as attacks on doll figures followed a consistent pattern. Children with feeding problems, for example, attacked the breasts of the mother doll, and the very repressed child preceded each attack on the baby doll by a self-punishing act. In order to feel comfortable while continuing to express hostile feelings, the child tried to atone for his aggression toward dolls through self-punishment, restitution of the damage, or various defensive measures, such as lies, evasions, and justifications. Completion of these cycles of behavior eventually brought a reduction of feelings of hostility, thereby allowing positive feelings to be expressed toward the rivalry object and the growth of other forms of response to take place.

When the child experiences affection and feels valued for himself alone, rivalry and envy toward a sibling tend gradually to subside. Children can be helped to resolve sibling conflict and rivalry satisfactorily by parents who set aside particular occasions when each child individually can have the parent completely to himself—in reading a story, in helping and working together in the kitchen or the yard, or in going shopping. Some traces of rivalry may persist into adult years, often at the unconscious level, as when a girl tries to surpass her sister in making a better marriage or having a finer home or when a brother feels compelled to achieve a higher position or salary than his sibling rival.

Ordinal Position and Size of Family

Birth order and size of family also influence a child's feeling of security. The only child has the undivided attention of his parents; but, contrary to popular opinion, he may not necessarily be overindulged. In a study of 46 pairs of children whose mothers had been rated on the Fels Parent Behavior Rating Scales, Lasko[20] found that parent behavior toward first children is on the average less warm and more restrictive and coercive than behavior toward second children. She also found that parent behavior toward second children does not tend to change markedly as the child grows older. Shifts do occur, however, in the parents' treatment of first children as they grow older, mainly in the direction of less approval and affection.

In a study of the relationship of ordinal position and school achievement in two-child families, Blustein[21] found that although first-born and

[19] David M. Levy, "Studies in Sibling Rivalry," *Research Monograph of the American Orthopsychiatric Association,* 2 (1937).

[20] Joan K. Lasko, "Parent Behavior toward First and Second Children," *Genetic Psychology Monographs,* 49 (1954), 97–137.

[21] Esther S. Blustein, "The Relationship of Sibling Position in the Family Constellation to School Behavior Variables in Elementary School Children from Two-Child Families" (unpublished doctor's dissertation, University of Maryland, 1967).

second-born children did not differ in scholastic aptitude, first-born children made higher grade-point averages and higher achievement-test scores than their second-born siblings. In addition, first-borns were perceived by their teachers as working harder or more effectively; and first-born boys were rated as more conforming to classroom standards of behavior than second-born boys. In spite of differences in school achievement, first- and second-born boys and girls did not differ in self-ratings of school ability. Oldest children generally reveal higher levels of achievement motivation.[22]

Koch[23] found that second-born boys with an older sister tend to be more dependent and sissyish than first-born boys with a younger sibling of either sex. She also found that boys or girls with an older or younger brother are more competitive, ambitious, and enthusiastic, and less wavering in their decisions than are children who have a sister. However, Koch cautions against making any sweeping generalizations about the effects of a single factor, such as birth order, sex of child, age difference, or sex of sibling. These variables are important in understanding particular children only if they are studied in interaction with one another.

In a study of variables related to adolescent-parent adjustment, Nye[24] found more satisfactory adjustment in smaller families. This finding contrasts sharply with the popular notion that there is more love to be found in larger families.

In many ways, the middle child may be the "forgotten child" in the family. He has neither the privileges nor the prestige of being the oldest, nor is he likely to get the attention the youngest child enjoys. Moreover, in many families, the middle child finds himself the recipient of hand-me-down clothes and toys and thus may feel less valued by parents, since they seldom buy new clothes or toys just for him. The case of Lavonne illustrates the feelings of a middle child in this regard:

Lavonne is ten years old and in the fifth grade. She has one older sister and one younger sister. One morning at school she called the teacher's attention to a dress she was wearing. She said, "Of course, it isn't new. I always have to take Alice's old clothes. I'll certainly be glad if I can ever have a new dress. I bet when I grow up I'll get a job and buy all kinds of pretty clothes." Two weeks later the teacher tested Lavonne's eyes. Afterward Lavonne wanted to know if her eyes were all right. The teacher assured her everything was fine. Lavonne said, "I wouldn't care if I did have to buy glasses. If I had to wear glasses, at least they certainly would have to be new!"

[22] James V. Pierce, "The Educational Motivation Patterns of Superior Students Who Do Not Achieve in High School" (Quincy, Illinois: Youth Development Project, 1960). Mimeographed.
[23] Helen L. Koch, "Some Personality Correlates of Sex, Sibling Position, and Sex of Sibling Among Five- and Six-Year-Old Children," *Genetic Psychology Monographs,* 52 (1955), 3–50.
[24] Ivan Nye, "Adolescent-Parent Adjustment: Age, Sex, Sibling Number, Broken Homes, and Employed Mothers as Variables," *Marriage and Family Living,* 14 (1952), 327–332.

Lavonne's parents probably valued her as much as they did her sisters, and passing on Alice's outgrown clothes enabled the family to make full use of its limited financial resources. To Lavonne, however, this meant that she did not stand as high in her parents' affection.

Failure to Live up to Cultural Expectations

All societies expect their young to learn the behaviors, customs, and values that are of central importance in that culture. By internalizing the ways of his culture, the child gains approval, acceptance, and a feeling of belonging and identification with his social group. Since acceptance and approval are rewards for learning one's culture, the kinds of socialization experiences which children and youth have will clearly be an important factor influencing their feelings of security. Many children experience a threat of loss of parental love and approval because of their failure to conform to expected standards of behavior.

Many children and adolescents feel less secure because of the disapproval and punishment they receive from parents for failure to master a developmental task. This threat of loss of love often weighs most heavily upon the middle-class child, whose culture expects fast and early achievement. Davis and Havighurst[25] note that the middle-class child often suffers parental disapproval when he has setbacks in learning toilet training and fails to take proper care of personal property. Similarly, they point out that the lower-class child also experiences disapproval from family or gang for avoiding a fight or for being too submissive and secretive.

Perhaps the most common threat to the middle-class child's feeling of being loved by his parents is his failure or inability to fulfill the image his parents hold of the kind of person they want him to become. The child who fails to make the honor roll, to be elected homecoming queen, or to follow his father's footsteps in becoming a doctor or lawyer is likely to interpret the disappointment and dissatisfaction expressed by parents as meaning that he is less worthy or less lovable. Acceptance and love must be unconditional and must not be dependent upon how handsome, popular, intelligent or well-behaved a child is. Parents and teachers should recognize that every individual needs to feel valued for himself alone, and that his security should not depend upon the system of approval and rewards used in teaching the culture.

Absentee Fathers

The demands made upon fathers by their corporations, businesses, or the armed services cause them to be frequently separated from their families, thus limiting the opportunities for contacts and the formation of affectional

[25] Allison Davis and Robert J. Havighurst, *Father of the Man* (Boston: Houghton Mifflin Co., 1947).

relationships between them and their sons and daughters. Middle-class suburban fathers often become so preoccupied with their jobs or with civic responsibilities that they come to be seen by their families as "weekend guests." Similarly, many working-class fathers are away from home on construction jobs or driving trucks or buses. Other fathers are in the armed forces and assigned to sea duty or to overseas posts. Thus, increasing numbers of families experience separation from the father.

The love of both parents increases the young person's feeling of security, since the affection of each parent reinforces and complements that of the other. Affectional relationships with a father are crucial in the learning of the appropriate sex role by both son and daughter. In the relationship with his father, the son learns more than how to express his masculinity; he also learns the qualitative difference between expressing affection toward a woman and toward another man. The daughter in her relationship with a father learns appropriate patterns of giving and receiving affection in her relationship with a man; in addition, her relationship with her father contributes to a feeling of security which will find more complete fulfillment later, in her relationship with her husband.

Working Mothers

Since World War II, increasing numbers of women have entered the working force. By 1957, 30 percent of mothers with children under eighteen years of age were working outside of the home.[26] The lack of supervision and care caused by the daily absence of both parents would appear to limit the opportunities for mother-child interaction and hence contribute to children's insecurity. The evidence, however, is inconclusive. The many studies of the effects on children of mothers' working have produced conflicting results. Few broad generalizations emerge, and the effects on the child appear to be influenced by his age at the time when his mother takes a job, by provisions made for child care, and by the unique dynamics and relationships within the particular family.

In an extensive review of the literature, Stolz[27] found no differences between the cases of working and nonworking mothers in (1) incidence of delinquency among children (only mothers who worked sporadically had more delinquent sons), (2) incidence of psychosomatic symptoms and quality of adjustment of adolescent sons and daughters, (3) incidence of dependency behavior shown by elementary school children, (4) sons' achievement-test scores and sons' and daughters' school marks for grades nine through twelve, and (5) expressions of dependent and independent behavior among preschool children.

In an earlier study of adolescent-parent adjustment, Nye[28] found that

[26] Lois M. Stolz, "Effects of Maternal Employment on Children: Evidence from Research," *Child Development,* 31 (December 1960), 749–782.

[27] Stolz, p. 773.

[28] See note 24.

adolescents whose mothers worked part time revealed better adolescent-parent adjustment than did those whose mothers worked full time or were not employed at all. In a later study, Nye found no differences in adolescent-parent affection for mothers who worked and those who did not work.[29]

Broken Homes

The home broken by divorce, separation, or desertion has been pictured generally as a tragic situation, damaging to the affectional relationships and the feelings of security of family members. Similar though less devastating are the effects on families broken by the death of a parent.

Studies of the adjustment of children and youth from broken homes appear to substantiate the proposition that a break in the family will have different effects on different children, different families, and in different situations. Clancy and Smitter[30] reported that children from broken homes had more serious problems of adjustment. Reyburn,[31] in a study of two matched groups of high school students, found no differences between the two groups in school marks or in scores on standardized achievement tests; but the group from broken homes did report 50 percent more problems of adjustment. Nye[32] found, in general, poorer adolescent-parent adjustment in broken homes. He concluded, however, that not all broken homes have the same impact on adolescents, since some of the adolescents who were best adjusted to their parents came from broken homes. In addition, the child whose main affectional ties have been with persons outside the family is likely to be less threatened by a break in the home. Finally, when divorce or separation resolves a long-standing conflict in the home, the break may actually lead to more stable affectional ties with remaining family members and thereby help the child to feel more secure.

Lack of Teacher Sensitivity and Understanding

Students bring to school with them the feelings and anxieties they have acquired in their homes and in their previous school experience. As learning and classroom activities proceed, the perceptive teacher will come to know and to respond to the perceptions and feelings of his students. Frequently, the teacher will have his attention drawn to a child who appears to be having considerable difficulty in adjusting to the school experience. The child may continuously call attention to himself by calling out, demanding help,

[29] Ivan Nye, "Employment Status of Mothers and Adjustment of Adolescent Children," *Marriage and Family Living*, 6 (1959), 260–267.

[30] N. Clancy and Faith Smitter, "A Study of Emotionally Disturbed Children in Santa Barbara County Schools," *California Journal of Educational Research*, 4 (1953), 209–218.

[31] H. Reyburn, "Guidance Needs of Students from Broken Homes," *California Journal of Educational Research*, 2 (1951), 22–25.

[32] Nye, "Adolescent-Parent Adjustment: Age, Sex, Sibling Number, Broken Home, and Employed Mothers as Variables."

refusing to conform to classroom rules, failing to complete his work, show-ing disrespect toward the teacher, or being aggressive toward others. Often a teacher will respond as if he believes such behavior is caused by the child's not having learned acceptable ways of acting. He is puzzled and bewildered when the usual punishments fail to change the undesirable behavior. If the teacher does not recognize the need for accepting and helping the child over an extended period of time, the emotional scars the child already bears will not heal and his feelings of insecurity will continue to increase. The amount of time required to help him and the degree of success of efforts to help him will depend upon the unique dynamics and the severity of his particular case.

Lack of Peer Belongingness

A major threat to a child's sense of security in school is lack of ac-ceptance by his peers. Children and adolescents who have had difficulties in gaining acceptance in their families frequently are handicapped in relating to peers. These children are less able to give themselves unreservedly to group purposes because the question of their own self-value has not been resolved. The insecure child often will insist on having the most desired role in the game, will interpret the rules of the game to his or his team's advantage, and will act more in his own self-interest than in the group's interest. Children whose behavior is contrary to the group's interests experience disapproval and rejection.

Poor Academic Performance

High among the values of most teachers is their perception of them-selves as adequate and competent teachers. Students who perform well academically confirm these teachers' perceptions of themselves. Not only do such students receive high grades, but they frequently earn the personal recognition, interest, and approval of their teachers. This contributes much to the student's feeling of security. On the other hand, children of lesser abilities and lower achievement motivation are likely to receive less recogni-tion and approval from the teacher. Poor academic performance, therefore, may constitute a threat to a student's security, because he is less likely to win the teacher's approval.

When the teacher centers his attention and interest upon the individual student and his learning and development, poor academic performance is less likely to pose a threat to these students' feelings of security. In fact, as Burrell[33] found, students' performance may actually improve. In Burrell's study, when teachers focused on meeting children's individual emotional

[33] Anna P. Burrell, "Facilitating Learning through Emphasis on Meeting Children's Basic Emotional Needs: An In-service Program," *Journal of Educational Sociology*, 24 (1951), 381–393.

needs, the children made significant gains in achievement-test and IQ scores. Moreover, the effectiveness of their work increased, their social relationships improved, deviant behavior decreased, interest in school increased, and truancy declined. The teachers, in giving attention to the emotional needs of a few students, found that they also learned more about how they might meet the needs of their other students.

Teachers' Conceptions of Their Role

A further block to a student's achievement of a feeling of security in school is a teacher's limited conception of his role and of his opportunities for helping students to feel more secure. Too often the teacher's role is viewed only in relation to instruction, to guiding and evaluating learning activities. Many teachers are influenced by traditional stereotypes and believe they should remain aloof from their students. They fear that becoming friendly with and close to a student will result in poor discipline or will give the appearance of partiality. Moreover, in the minds of many teachers, the giving of affection is viewed only in terms of those overt, demonstrative evidences of affection which one uses in greeting members of one's family or close friends.

The conception of teaching presented in this book is one of an open, sympathetic, supportive, helping, facilitative relationship between teacher and pupil, a relationship that focuses on activities that promote individual learning and development. The facilitative effect on learning of a social-emotional climate characterized by warm, accepting, supportive teacher-pupil relationships has been amply demonstrated by research.

Lewin, Lippitt, and White,[34] in their study of three experimentally created social climates, found that under democratic leadership boys more freely praised each other's work, while under an autocratic leader the only way to receive praise was to get it from an adult. As competition for "the leader's" approval increased in autocratic groups, the boys became less inclined to approve the work of fellow members. Under democratic leadership, recognition was more readily gained from both leader and peers; as a result, the greater incidence of cooperative behavior benefited the individual as well as the total group.

Anderson and his associates,[35] in their studies of teachers' classroom personalities, found that dominating teachers usually produced antagonistic and aggressive behavior in children, while flexible teachers more frequently elicited facilitative, cooperative, and self-directive responses from their stu-

[34] Kurt Lewin, Ronald Lippitt, and Ralph K. White, "Patterns of Aggressive Behavior in Experimentally Created 'Social Climates'," *Journal of Social Psychology,* 10 (1939), 271–299.
[35] Harold H. Anderson, Joseph E. Brewer, and Mary F. Reed, "Studies of Teachers' Classroom Personalities, III. Follow-up Studies of the Effects of Dominative and Integrative Contacts on Children's Behavior," *Applied Psychology Monograph No. 11,* Stanford University Press, Stanford University, 1946.

dents. A study by this writer[36] of social-emotional climate and group learning revealed that teachers in groups where the leader used a high proportion of accepting, clarifying, and problem-centered statements indicated a greater understanding of students' behavior than did teachers whose group leaders used higher proportions of information-giving, directive, and critical statements. (This study and the study by Lewin, Lippitt, and White are reported in greater detail in Chapter 17.)

Human beings communicate an acceptance and a valuing of each other not by overt and demonstrative displays of affection but by the concern, interest, support, and valuing expressed in relationships. The manner of communicating this valuing of another person will vary according to the roles of the persons involved, the culture, and each person's own conception of the appropriate response in a particular situation. A teacher's expression of affection for his students need not be limited to a pat on the head, a hug, or holding of hands, which often means so much to preschool and primary-school children. The teacher communicates his interest, concern, and valuing of a student of any age through his ready smile, warm greeting, responsiveness to the student's interests and concerns, and willingness to listen and to help the student. The true measure of a teacher's affection for a student is his full acceptance of the student as a person regardless of his ability, IQ, achievement, or behavior. For many students, approval and praise by the teacher are stronger incentives for learning than are grades, honors, or prizes.

Insecurity: An Example

An indication of the specific ways a child's feeling of insecurity influences his learning is revealed in the case of Jane:

> Jane is ten years old and in the fifth grade. The teacher describes Jane as a rather nice-looking girl with brown hair and eyes, well dressed, and neat. She wears glasses and has crowded teeth. Often in class she sits chewing her fingernails or a strand of her hair. Her score on the California Test of Mental Maturity in the fourth grade yielded an IQ of 117. Jane's father is a college graduate and works as a chemist. Her mother had two years of college. There is a sister, Marcia, age seven, who is in the second grade at the same school.
>
> Several times during the early part of the school year Jane came to the teacher and stated that the other girls did not like her and were mean to her. Later the teacher noticed Jane talking to Lee, Prue, and Audrey. Later in a conference the teacher commented to Jane that she was glad Jane was having a good time with the other girls. Jane's reply was "Oh, I wasn't having a good time. They weren't nice to me. They didn't want to talk to me."

---

[36] Hugh V. Perkins, "The Effects of Climate and Curriculum on Group Learning," *Journal of Educational Research,* 44 (1950), 269–286.

OCTOBER 24

Today the class was illustrating poems and Jane was the first one to hand hers in. The teacher noticed that the title was written and suggested that it would look nicer if it were printed. Jane reddened, grabbed the picture from the teacher's desk, took it to her seat, and tore it into tiny pieces.

After school the teacher talked to Jane about her picture and Jane said, "Oh, I was so mad I tore it up and then I told Gwen. I always do things like that. I get awfully mad. especially at home at my little sister." She frowned, screwed up her face, and said, "She is the meanest, horridest little brat. I just hate her. She won't do a thing I want."

OCTOBER 29

Yesterday the class had planned to make maps of an imaginary land to show such geographical terms as *capes, bays,* and *isthmuses.* Jane and Weldon each came in today with maps they had made at home. The teacher praised both maps and showed them to the class. Jane seemed pleased when the class showed interest but frowned when they offered some criticism. As the class started to work, Jane sat and looked at hers, grumbling, "It isn't fair. They had more help than I had. They got to look at the maps in the room." The teacher went to her and said, "Yours is fine, but some of the formations are not shown. Wouldn't you like to make a perfect one now?" Jane continued to grumble. Finally, she walked across the room to the teacher with her map in her hands. Her face was red. She said defiantly, "I'm going to tear mine up." The teacher looked at her and smiled and said, "Why, Jane, it's your paper." Jane went back to her seat, stood there a minute, tore the paper in shreds, and sat down. The teacher didn't look at her. The children smiled at the teacher, shrugged their shoulders, some shook their heads, and then went on with their work. Jane sat with her head in her hands the rest of the period. Later the teacher said quietly to Jane, "I'm not sure you belong with us today. You have not been helping." In a few minutes Jane came up to the teacher and said she would like to stay after school and help. The teacher smiled and said she was sorry but that she had a meeting at three o'clock.

NOVEMBER 12

Today Jane couldn't get one of her examples in arithmetic. She came to the teacher, but the teacher could not help her because she was with another group. Jane returned to her seat, grumbling. Soon she began tearing her paper in pieces and stuffing it in her desk. No one paid any attention to her. After school Mrs. S., the teacher, detained Jane for a moment and said firmly, "Jane, there is one thing we are through with and that is tearing up papers. Tearing up papers is only something a very small child would do and you are much too big for that. I don't want to see any more of tearing up papers." Then the teacher walked away without giving Jane a chance to talk about it.

In late January the teacher had a conference with Jane's mother at the mother's request. In the conference, Jane's mother expressed concern over Jane's social relationships. She reported that Jane had never had any friends and had never been able to get along with children. The only ones Jane plays with are younger children whom she can dominate. She also plays with a rejected sixth-grade girl. Mrs. J. feels that Jane is learning to handle adults but that she has no idea how to get along with children. The mother is sure that Marcia, the little sister, is back of a great deal of Jane's trouble. "Marcia is friendly and liked by everyone, adults and children. Marcia often brings home friends and is always having a good time. This makes Jane extremely jealous and she treats her sister mean, and openly says she hates her."

The mother believes that Jane's difficulty is also largely caused by the fact that she and her husband tried too hard to be model parents. "We read all of the books on child rearing at the time and tried from her birth to follow every schedule to the letter. The books at that time were poor, I am convinced, and I am afraid that kind of training has harmed Jane. We expected to have a model child, perfect in every way. We stressed perfection so much that I am afraid we made Jane feel inadequate."

The reader may wish to study these excerpts from the case of Jane as they relate to the concepts of affection and security presented in this chapter. The questions listed at the end of the chapter will aid in the analysis and discussion of the case of Jane in relation to these concepts.

Summary

Man's most significant learning and development take place in a context of social interaction with other human beings. He becomes human only as he relates himself to other human beings. Through his relationships with others he assuages his feelings of aloneness and separateness and discovers meaning and purpose for his life.

The meaning of human relatedness is communicated in the personal valuing and self-worth one feels in one-to-one relationships with others. In a human relationship, acts, feelings, and responses that are accepting and valuing define the term *affection*. *Security* has the deeper meaning to the self of feeling personal value, self-acceptance, and self-worth. So pervasive is a feeling of relative security or insecurity that it is reflected in the individual's general behavior and in his responses to life situations.

The human need for affection begins in infancy as pleasant feelings accompanying the satisfactions of the child's physical needs become associated with mother, nurse, and others who care for and nurture the child. A warm mothering relationship in early life exerts a positive and vital influence on all aspects of the child's development and learning. Some differentiation should be made by parents and teachers between socialization roles and security-giving roles, so that disapproval and punishments related to child training are not interpreted by the child as a loss of love. Children grow up in social-emotional climates of affection, rejection, inconsistency, or overprotection. Each emotional climate will communicate different meanings to the child in relation to his personal value and self-worth, and these unique meanings will be reflected in his behavior.

The development of the child's affectional life may be viewed in three dimensions: (1) the psychosexual development of the child from a stage of self-love to an acceptance and valuing of others in mutually shared relationships, (2) the broadening of the base of affectional relationships to include a widening circle of persons with whom he shares affectional ties, and (3) the change from strong dependence on others to a considerable degree of independence, wherein relationships with others are characterized by mutual acceptance and valuing.

A child's security may be threatened by events and dynamic relationships at home and in the school. Major threats to his security related to his home and family are parental rejection, sibling rivalry, difficulties associated with ordinal position and size of family, failure to live up to cultural expectations, absentee fathers, working mothers, and broken homes. Some children may find their security at school threatened by an adjustment problem that hinders their acceptance by others, by a lack of peer belongingness, by poor academic performance, or by the teacher's limited understanding and conception of his role in giving affection and providing emotional support to his students.

Study Questions

1. Ted is rejected by his parents. He is intelligent but frequently is in trouble at school. His teacher says, "There is no way I can help this boy because the problem is in the home." Do you agree or disagree with the teacher's comment? Discuss.

2. Edgar's father is sharply critical of his son's performances in school, in sports, and in his completion of duties at home. He ignores Edgar's good performances. Edgar's mother openly shows a preference for his older brother. Edgar fights continually with other children, and the teacher has isolated him from them "until he has learned how to behave in the group." Discuss this situation and the teacher's handling of Edgar.

3. Some would say that a good teacher possesses among other qualities a sense of being fair, impartial, and objective. Is it possible for a teacher to maintain these qualities and still show a subjective liking for his students? Discuss.

4. A student's developing a crush on his teacher may be a symptom of what stage in his development of affectional relationships?

5. A father gives in to his teenage son's requests and demands and refuses to correct or to discipline him for his disrespect and misbehavior. The father believes that his permissive and generous treatment will contribute to the boy's feeling secure and will cement an affectional tie between parent and son. In time, however, the son comes to ignore his father and to express increasing hostility toward him. What explanations would you offer for the son's behavior?

Suggested Readings

John Bowlby. *Child Care and the Growth of Love.* Baltimore: Penguin Books, 1965. Summarizes evidence involving large numbers of children from different cultural settings showing the damaging emotional effects precipitated by the children's separation from their mothers.

Erich Fromm. *The Art of Loving.* New York: Harper & Row, 1956. Points to the separateness of man's existence and to his need for developing his capacity to love. Discusses and contrasts brotherly love, mother love, erotic love, self-love, and love of God.

Harry F. Harlow. "The Nature of Love," *The American Psychologist,* 13 (December 1958), 673–685. Describes a series of experiments which investigated the responses of infant monkeys toward wire-mesh and terry-cloth mother substitutes. The need of these infant monkeys to seek contacts with something soft and warm was evident throughout the experiments.

James S. Plant. *Personality and the Cultural Pattern.* New York: The Commonwealth Fund, 1937. Chapter 5 points out that one's feeling of security is based upon who one is, whereas a sense of adequacy is formed on the basis of what one is or what one can do. Characteristics of the secure and insecure child are described and related to the development of personality and the maintenance of mental health.

Daniel A. Prescott. "The Role of Love in Human Development," *Journal of Home Economics,* 44 (March 1952), 173–176. Synthesizes contributions by writers from many different fields in the development of a series of statements describing the characteristics and qualities of love. Five hypotheses are offered relating to the role of love in human development.

Margaret A. Ribble. *The Rights of Infants.* New York: Columbia University Press, 1943. Describes the needs and conditions that contribute to an infant's physical and mental development. Special emphasis is given to mothering, permissive training, and warm personal contact.

Films

Mother Love, 16 mm, sound, black and white, 26 min. Bloomington, Indiana: Audio-Visual Center, Indiana University (rental fee, $5.65). Presents the experiments of Dr. Harry Harlow, who studied the responses of newborn rhesus monkeys to two inanimate substitute mothers, one made of wire and the other of cloth. These experiments demonstrate that the single most important factor in an infant's love for its mother is body contact. Deprivation of this contact can cause deep emotional disturbances and even death.

Preface to a Life, 16 mm, sound, black and white, 29 min. Bloomington, Indiana: Audio-Visual Center, Indiana University (rental fee, $3.65). Portrays the influence parents have on a child's developing personality. This is illustrated by a series of episodes in the childhood and adolescence of Michael, whose mother is over-solicitous and whose father is overdemanding, with the result that Michael becomes an ill-adjusted young man. Portrayed also is a healthy childhood, which results when both parents accept their child as an individual.

6

the cultural environment

Tis education forms the common mind:
Just as the twig is bent the tree's inclined.

≡ ALEXANDER POPE

Children the world over are at birth much more alike than
they are different. A Chinese infant exchanged at birth with
an American infant would start on equal footing with
native-born sons and daughters in learning the language,
customs, and ways of his adopted country. Children become
increasingly different as their hereditary potentials interact
with their environment to produce varying patterns of
development. By far the most important differences between
people are those resulting from differences between environments—the ways of feeling, thinking, and behaving each
has internalized from his society as the result of growing up
in that society.

The influence of the immediate environment and its
people on the language and behavior of individuals, irrespective of national origins, is described by Laurence
Wylie:[1]

---

[1] Laurence Wylie, "Bringing up Children—French Way, Our Way," *New York Times
Magazine* (June 30, 1957). Copyright 1957 by the New York Times Company. Reprinted
by permission.

From our house we could hear the children down in the school yard, and it sounded as though our ruse had worked. We lived in a village I will call Peyrane, a few miles east of Avignon, for two months, and our children had not learned French as fast as children are rumored to pick up a foreign language. On that Sunday morning we had suggested that the two boys take their soccer ball down to the school where they might attract some French friends to play with them.

To see what was up I walked down and looked around the corner of the building. The situation was not what I had expected. An exciting soccer game was in progress—but Jonathan and David were not learning French phrases. On the contrary, all the children in the neighborhood were shouting at the top of their lungs: "Keek eet to me!!! Keek eet to me!!!"

In spite of their American aggressiveness the boys did learn French before the village children learned English. Within five months both of them could express themselves effectively, if not grammatically, in the language. Little by little they came to prefer French to English and French customs to American ones. We tried to cling to some parental tenets from home—no eating between meals, getting to bed by 8 o'clock. As our children rejected these sacred institutions, they began to reject us, too. We were immigrants.

Perhaps if we had stayed in France longer, our family unit would have become French enough, that is, a sufficiently tight unit, to withstand this attack, but we were not put to the ultimate test. After almost a year in Peyrane, our leave was up and we left for home. When we stopped in Paris, our two children, so obviously American in appearance but with the most exaggerated of southern French accents, were a delight to French friends and to the *liftiers* of the Hotel Lutetia. The wonder grew to amazement among relatives back in this country at these two little boys who politely shook hands with everyone and who spoke French when playing together.

But this Gallic behavior did not last long. First went the handshake which had caused American adults to laugh and make coy remarks. Then it became apparent that the French language could not resist the corrosive influence of different surroundings. Day by day chunks of it dropped out and were replaced by English.

This excerpt raises an age-old question: Which exerts the greatest influence in shaping human behavior—heredity or environment? Though human heredity and the processes of growth and development give the child a body that is human in appearance and structure, the behavioral qualities that mark him as distinctly human are acquired as he grows up in the company of other human beings. The few accounts of lost or abandoned children who have somehow survived and grown up without human care, presumably having lived with animals, report that their behavior is more like that of animals in their natural environment than of human beings. These children are described as ferocious; they bit their captors, crawled on all fours, ate raw flesh, and seldom if ever were able to use or understand a human language.[2] Thus, man becomes human only as he internalizes his culture's ways of thinking, behaving, and feeling—as taught to him by parents, siblings, teachers, and others.

Concept of Culture

In the preceding chapter it was noted that an individual's affectional relationships with significant people in his life are important because of the much-needed feeling of security they provide. Interactions with others, however, are important also because through them children learn a great deal about behavior in society.

The set of feelings, behaviors, and ways of perceiving, thinking, and valuing which one is taught by his social group is what is meant by the term *culture*. In the anthropological sense, the term refers to much more than architecture, art, music, dance, drama, and literature. It comprises everything that contributes to a total way of life: communication, food and housing, sex, marriage, child rearing, various interpersonal relationships, transportation, economic organization, social organization, government, and dealings with the supernatural. National and racial cultures differ from one another mainly in the ways they have learned to cope with such problems of life as these. They differ to the degree that their responses to these problems are different. Within a culture these responses are handed down from one generation to the next in the process of socialization. In this way, one comes to have built into him the patterns of thinking, feeling, and behaving that characterize his culture. In its broadest sense, then, culture may be defined as *those customs, beliefs, ways of behaving, and values which evolve from cumulative group experience and which are passed from generation to generation as the best or the most acceptable solutions to problems of living.*

Cultural Institutions

Every society has established formal and informal agencies or institutions charged with preserving the status quo and communicating the ways of the culture to each oncoming generation. Although simpler cultures may employ fewer institutions to carry out these tasks, Western, industrialized culture has six major cultural institutions: (1) the family, (2) the church, (3) the school, (4) the peer group, (5) the community, and (6) the mass media. These cultural institutions contribute to the socialization of each individual in the culture.

[2] Wayne Dennis, "A Further Analysis of Reports of Wild Children," *Child Development,* 22 (March 1951), 153–158.

The Family

Some type of family organization is found in every culture. The help-lessness of the child at birth, his dependence on others for sustenance and life, makes it nearly inevitable that much of the child's early socialization will take place in the family setting. It is within the family that most children gain their first perceptions of what the world is like.

The cultural behaviors and values taught by the family relate to every phase of human living, including the infant disciplines of weaning and toilet training, the acceptance and learning of one's sex role, language, courtesies governing interpersonal relationships within and outside the family group, religious observances and rituals, and vocational preferences reflected in children's play. Family influences also are conveyed through the choice of a neighborhood, the formal and informal clubs and associations which the parents join and those they permit their children to join, and the kinds of TV programs which parents allow their children to watch. Many of the behavior patterns and values that the child learns are consistent with and reflect the larger culture; others are characteristic of the particular family; still others, as we shall note in a later chapter, are unique to the individual himself.

The family may also be viewed as a group bound together by reciprocal ties manifested in culturally determined roles and patterns of interaction. Each role carries a status which defines the ways in which the individual will respond and relate to other people. The father's role in child rearing may require him to forbid the adolescent to visit an unsavory bar or pool hall. The father expects his son to comply with his wishes. The culture may also expect the son to comply. Whether the son does comply, however, will depend in part upon the role he believes his culture expects him to play. Many of the roles which the individual is taught by the culture at different stages from infancy to adulthood are contradictory to one another, and the adolescent may be caught between two of them. For example, as Benedict[3] points out, children are expected to be dependent and compliant, whereas adults are considered immature and not quite grown up if they do not exhibit independence and self-reliance. By recognizing and responding to the dis-continuities within our culture, we are better able to understand the atypical and immature behavior of some youth and adults in our society.

The Church

The church may be viewed as a separate institution apart from the community, or it may be seen as one of the forces within the community. Whether and to what extent the church influences the socialization of chil-

[3] Ruth Benedict, "Continuities and Discontinuities in Cultural Conditioning," *Psychiatry*, 1 (1938), 161–167.

dren and youth seems to depend upon the religious beliefs and commitments of family members, especially the mother and father. When parents participate actively in the church, the child, through his identification with his parents, also is likely to become involved. In families that lack an affiliation with a church, the influence of the church in the socialization of the child is likely to be limited or nonexistent.

The problem of ascertaining what children learn from experiences with religious education is extremely complex. Since one's religion is an individual and personal matter, what one learns from religious experience may also be presumed to be unique and personal. In a study of a midwestern community, Havighurst and Taba[4] found that church affiliation seemed to influence one's reputation in the community, but they could not determine whether an individual's character was changed because of his affiliation with a church. The study showed that the stricter the codes of conduct of a denomination, the higher the character reputations of persons affiliated with that denomination. Hartshorne and May,[5] in a study of honesty in children, developed ingenious tests that could be passed only if one cheated, and gave these tests to one group of students who attended Sunday School and to another group who did not go to Sunday School. Both groups attended the same public school. Hartshorne and May found that the percentage of children who cheated on these tests was about the same for both groups (approximately 30 to 40 percent). Neither the length of time children were enrolled in Sunday School nor the regularity of their attendance was found to be associated with their tendency to cheat.

What conceptions of their religion and their church do children acquire? Elkind[6] found, in studies of children, ages six to fourteen, of all three major denominations that these children's concepts of (1) what it means to be a Protestant, Catholic, or Jew, (2) the features of one's sect, (3) how membership in the sect is attained all appear to develop according to Piaget's three age-related stages of intellectual development.[7] In stage one, at about age six, children had only a vague, confused awareness of what being a Protestant, a Catholic, or a Jew really meant. At stage two, usually between ages seven and ten, the child understood the word Protestant, Catholic, or Jew to be the name of a group of people with characteristic ways of behaving ("A Catholic goes to mass and goes to Catholic school"). Finally, at stage three, about age eleven or twelve, children have developed an abstract conception of their denomination. Being a Protestant, Catholic, or Jew meant believing in

---

[4] Robert J. Havighurst and Hilda Taba, *Adolescent Character and Personality* (New York: John Wiley, 1949).

[5] Hugh Hartshorne and Mark A. May, *Studies in the Nature of Character, Studies in Deceit I* (New York: Macmillan Co., 1928).

[6] David Elkind, "The Child's Conception of his Religious Denomination: I. The Jewish Child," *Journal of Genetic Psychology,* 99 (1961), 209–225; "The Child's Conception of his Religious Denomination: II. The Catholic Child," *Journal of Genetic Psychology,* 101 (1962), 185–193; "The Child's Conception of his Religious Denomination: III. The Protestant Child," *Journal of Genetic Psychology,* 103 (1963), 291–304.

[7] Jean Piaget, *The Child's Conception of the World* (London: Kegan Paul, 1951).

the teachings of one's church ("A Protestant is a faithful believer in God and doesn't believe in the Pope").

While church affiliation provides the individual with a sense of group identity, there is little scientific evidence as to what beliefs and values he acquires from religious experience and denominational life. Part of the difficulty is that the specific influence of the church in the socialization of children and youth cannot always be separated from the influence of family and community. In some communities, such as those of the Amish of the Pennsylvania Dutch country, religious beliefs are dominant in guiding the lives of the people. The Amish's ways and values—his plain black clothes, his thrift and hard work, and his eschewing of the use of the automobile—all are based on religious beliefs and church teachings. For most Americans, however, the church's influence, if any, in inculcating beliefs and values is likely not to be consistent across the board of church teaching but to be very personal, highly variable, and difficult to measure.

Complicating attempts to measure the church's influence in communicating beliefs and values is the tendency in America to minimize the differences between religious sects. Evidence of this is revealed in the ecumenical movement toward Christian unity that is being urged and worked for by many denominations. Increasingly, America is pictured as a pluralistic society in which Protestants, Catholics, Jews, and secularists live side by side as citizens. Religious affiliation has been rejected as a test both for citizenship and for holding public office. The United States Supreme Court's decisions against mandatory prayer and Bible reading in the public schools reflect the trend toward strengthening the concept of pluralism in our society.

The School

As technology and rising standards of living induce more women to work outside the home, the school has been called upon to assume increased responsibilities for the socialization of children and youth. Greater numbers of nursery schools and day-care centers are being organized for young children, and more and more teen clubs and extracurricular clubs are being formed for older students. The stated purposes of American education frequently reflect its socialization functions:

1. To provide a basis of communication and a common core of traditions and values.
2. To teach children to work and live together.
3. To help people find ways of realizing their social ideals.
4. To teach skills for carrying on the economic life of society.
5. To select and train children for upward mobility.[8]

[8] W. Lloyd Warner, Robert J. Havighurst, and Martin B. Loeb, *Who Shall Be Educated?* (New York: Harper & Row, 1944), pp. 54–57.

The school tends to mirror the culture of the power group that controls it. In most communities the power controls over schools are centered in persons of middle-class status. As a consequence, in what the school teaches, in the standards it enforces, and in relation to the group it is best adapted to serve, the typical American school has often been labeled a middle-class institution. School administrators and teachers, as members of the middle class, generally support middle-class aspirations, values, and mores. In schools where middle-class behavior, language, dress, and high academic achievement patterns are the norm, children from lower-class groups often become alienated because of their different motivational patterns and vocational aspirations. Only as recent social revolution and war-on-poverty programs have brought these discrepancies in cultural background to the attention of the American people have steps been taken to make the school programs in depressed areas more responsive to the needs of the cultural groups they serve.[9]

The Peer Group

Children learn much from each other. Skills and knowledge required in sports and hobbies as well as attitudes and values of fair play, trust, and loyalty are most frequently acquired through interaction with one's peers. During adolescence the fads of hair style, hit songs, dancing, dress, language, and social behavior are among the most obvious ways in which peer group codes and customs shape the responses of individual group members. The peer group is a force of sufficient importance in human development and learning that we shall devote the next chapter to a discussion of its influence in childhood and adolescence.

The Community

The community consists of many organizations and agencies, both visible and invisible, which exert influence, both direct and indirect, on the socialization of children and youth. The immediate social and physical environment of the community, mediated in part by family, peer group, and school, provides the child with an initial, often lasting view of the world. The child and his family tend to be influenced by the behavior and attitudes of other children and adults who reflect the prevailing mores of the community. A stranger may quickly determine a community's attitudes toward race relations, religion, jobs, economic growth, welfare, politics, zoning, community planning, and a host of other problems simply by a visit to the local barbershop or beauty salon.

The community also plays a role in the socialization of children and youth through its cub scouts, girl scouts, boys' clubs, little league baseball

---

[9] A. Harry Passow, ed., *Education in Depressed Areas* (New York: Teachers College Press, Columbia University, 1963).

teams, teen clubs, and other youth organizations. This is revealed in Barker and Wright's investigation of the everyday behavior and the social participation of the children and youth of a midwestern town.[10] The focus of this ecological study was on the *behavior setting*—the place, event, or occasion (Kane's grocery, 4H club picnic, Thanksgiving Day) where or when social interaction among members of a community occurs. Barker and Wright found that children in the town they studied participated in a large proportion of the behavior settings available to them, including food sales, parades, paper routes, funeral services, club meetings, town elections, restaurants, and school classes. By participating in a large number of activities, many of them essentially adult activities, children learned the ways and mores of the community.

Mass Media

One of the concomitants of a technological culture is an increase in the kinds and uses of media of mass communication. Indeed, the growth of the economy depends upon the wide dissemination of information through newspapers, magazines, comic books, movies, radio, and television, so as to promote popular consumption of products created by the technology. The newspaper editorial, the mass-circulation magazine article, and the TV program are written and produced for a mass heterogeneous audience. Although the individual can, of course, decide whether he will read the editorial or the article or watch the TV program, the family and the peer group exert considerable influence in popularizing and in some cases influencing the content of magazine articles, radio, and TV programs.

Because of their impersonal nature and the diversity of their offerings, the impact of mass media on the socialization of children and youth is difficult to assess. Television, movies, and comics teach many of the ways of society as portrayed by the sheriff, policeman, private investigator, defense attorney, judge, doctor, nurse, sergeant, colonel, nightclub hostess, business tycoon, secretary, and gangster. Idealized portrayals of these roles and of the courts, hospital, industrial corporation, city hall, and armed forces, however, frequently communicate to children and youth inaccurate pictures of the culture. Because of the strong fantasy and comedy content of many TV programs, movies, and comic strips, children may be expected to respond to these for their entertainment rather than their educational value. For some children, knowledge of TV, movie, and comic strip characters and plots assists them in gaining or maintaining acceptance and status in the peer group. Thus, in spite of the wide exposure of children and youth to mass media, what is learned from this exposure is likely to vary from child to child and, consequently, will be difficult to measure.

Exposure of children to mass media may have undesirable effects. Com-

---

[10] Roger G. Barker and Herbert F. Wright, *Midwest and Its Children: The Psychological Ecology of an American Town* (New York: Harper & Row, 1954).

mercial television, for instance, is criticized for its portrayal of sex, crime, and violence. However, the impact of this portrayal on children's personalities and development is not consistent. A study by Himmelweit, Oppenheim, and Vince,[11] conducted in England, concluded that the effect of television on a child varies not only with the programs and the time spent viewing TV but also with the personality of the child and the context in which the viewing takes place. In this connection, Riley and Riley[12] found that children who are more oriented to the family are more likely to prefer programs of violence than are those who are more oriented toward the peer group. Among older boys, peer-group members tend to relate adventure stories to their own lives while non-peer-group members ascribe to these same heroes invincible or even superhuman qualities. This evidence suggests that the child's preferences and reactions to TV programs are strongly influenced by his interpersonal relationships.

Himmelweit and her associates analyzed both the values and the limitations of TV viewing with regard to its effects on the personality development of children and youth. On the positive side, television can implant information, stimulate interests, improve tastes, and widen the range of the child's experience, so that he is able to gain a better understanding of issues and people different from those with whom he customarily associates. Teachers have found that the knowledge and attitudes that students acquire from watching television are valuable adjuncts to the learning of science, history, literature, and current events at school.

On the negative side, television, depending on the content of programs, may frighten or disturb those children who are emotionally insecure or are preoccupied with a particular problem. Television viewing also can lead to lessened acquisition of knowledge by limiting one's participation in other developmental activities, such as reading books, outdoor play, and peer activities. Children ten to fourteen in the Himmelweit study viewed television for an average of eleven to thirteen hours a week, and this was more time than they spent in any other leisure-time activity. Witty's[13] study of American children showed that the elementary-school child averages twenty hours of television viewing per week.

Cultural Diversities

There are more than 200 million people in the United States. These 200 million people, although bound together in a common culture, nevertheless represent many diverse cultural subgroups. The diversities of these groups would soon become apparent if a cross section of Americans were to try to

[11] Hilde T. Himmelweit, A. M. Oppenheim, and Pamela Vince, *Television and the Child* (London: Oxford University Press, 1958).

[12] Matilda W. Riley and John W. Riley, "A Sociological Approach to Communication Research," *Public Opinion Quarterly,* 15 (1951), 445–460.

[13] Paul Witty, "Sixth Report on TV," *School and Society,* 83 (May 12, 1956), 166–168.

reach agreement on a set of values representative of American society. Cultural diversities characteristic of subgroups highlight differences between people which relate to (1) sex, (2) geographical region, (3) urban-suburban-rural background, (4) social class, (5) ethnic background, (6) race, (7) religion, and (8) age.

Sex Roles

Differences between males and females in patterns of feeling, thinking, and behaving go far beyond the physical differences related to sex. The culture into which each boy and girl is born defines for each the norms of sex-appropriate behavior which the boy or girl is expected to internalize. Failure to act in accordance with sex-appropriate modes of response frequently brings social disapproval and leads to social and personal maladjustment.

At an early age, each child is expected to accept his sex role and to behave appropriately as a boy or a girl. This means for boys that being active, aggressive, and engaging in rough play is not only tolerated but subtly encouraged. The American father's covert fear of his son's becoming a "sissy" is reflected in the father's admonition "Stick up for yourself, Mike. Punch him back if he starts anything!" In this context, differences in the middle-class socialization of the two sexes are revealed in our tendency to condone fisticuffs and wrestling between evenly matched young boys, but to disapprove of physical aggression among girls of any age.

Girls in our culture are presumed to experience less difficulty than boys in learning sex-appropriate behavior. Girls are surrounded from an early age with female models with whom they can identify. Mother, older sister, aunt, grandmother and a succession of woman teachers all communicate and reinforce the feminine ways and mores of the culture. Another important factor influencing achievement of femininity, however, is the relationship of a girl with her father. Mussen and Rutherford[14] found that a daughter's acceptance of her feminine role is facilitated not only by the presence of a highly adequate mother as a feminine model but also by the presence of a father who is aware of the behavior expected of young girls and who encourages his daughter to act in feminine ways and to participate in feminine activities. An unexpected finding of this study was that feminization of young girls involves less clear-cut determinants than does the masculinization of boys. Behaviors and activities considered appropriate for boys are distinctly defined, while for girls greater latitude is allowed in the definition of sex-appropriate behavior. It is, for instance, much more acceptable for girls to wear masculine clothes, compete in athletics, and follow many predominantly masculine pursuits than it is for boys to engage in predominantly feminine activities.

While the process of self-identification is important in the learning of

---

[14] Paul H. Mussen and Eldred Rutherford, "Parent-Child Relations and Parental Personality in Relation to Young Children's Sex-Role Preferences," *Child Development,* 34 (September 1963), 589–607.

sex-appropriate behavior, the type of process followed by each sex group is quite different. Lynn[15] hypothesizes that both male and female infants learn to identify initially with the mother but that with boys this early identification with the mother later weakens and is replaced by identification with a culturally defined, somewhat stereotyped masculine role.

The girl, on the other hand, continues to identify with the mother. That is, she identifies not with a feminine role but with the mother in person.

From this general premise—that boys learn their sex role by identifying with a culturally defined, stereotyped masculine role, while girls identify directly with their mothers—Lynn goes on to suggest that the learning method used by girls involves (a) a personal relationship and (b) imitation. The method used by boys, by contrast, involves (a) finding the goal, (b) restructuring the field, and (c) abstracting principles. These differences in learning methods lead Lynn to several further hypotheses:

1. Females will demonstrate a greater need for affiliation with others than will males.
2. Females are more likely than males to rely on the approaches of others to a particular situation instead of working out an approach of their own.
3. Males generally surpass females in problem-solving skills.
4. Males are more concerned with internalized moral standards than are females.
5. Females are more receptive to the standards of others than are males.

These hypotheses await further scientific verification.

Regional Diversities

The culture an American child learns reflects in some degree the language and ways of the part of the United States in which he grows up. Most Americans are aware of the differences in speech, attitudes, and social behavior of persons who live in different regions of the country. A major difficulty one faces in analyzing regional differences is the tendency to be blinded by stereotypes. It must be kept in mind that all Texans, for instance, are not tall, slender men wearing cowboy boots and ten-gallon hats, and that all New Englanders are not reserved, serious, and aloof.

People do, of course, reflect the speech, dress, customs, and behavior patterns generally characteristic of the region where they grew up. However, the amount of regional culture a child internalizes varies and can be ascertained only by careful observation and study of that individual. Many children do not assimilate some of the regional culture patterns of their area because of the influence of parents who grew up in another area. Moreover,

---

[15] David B. Lynn, "Sex Role and Parental Identification," *Child Development,* 33 (September 1962), 555–564.

due to the high geographical mobility of American families, a child may be exposed to a series of different regional cultures as his family moves from place to place and could assimilate elements of each of these cultures. In short, while differences in regional culture are very real, these differences do not appear to have a predictable effect on any particular individual.

Urban-Suburban-Rural Diversities

Not only the region but the type of community a child lives in—urban, suburban, or rural—influences what he will learn in the process of socialization. Farm children early assume responsibilities for the care and feeding of animals, for the cultivation and harvesting of crops, and for the preparation of food, all of which contribute to the farm family's health and economic well-being. Because of their chores, these children find it more difficult to participate actively in programs for youth sponsored by the school, community, or peer group. Much of the socialization of farm youth centers in learning the skills and attitudes related to making a success at farming. Rural youth will spend more of their free time by themselves, with siblings, or perhaps with one or two children from neighboring farms. With improvement of roads, increased use of automobiles, and rural electrification, however, some of the cultural differences between rural and urban youth have tended to disappear.

The urban child is usually less of an economic asset to his family than is the rural child. The urban child tends to spend considerable time in his and other children's homes playing games familiar to his age and peer group. If he lives in an apartment house or slum dwelling, he will be in physical proximity to dozens, perhaps hundreds of other human beings, but he will probably be able to relate himself emotionally only to a very few. The socialization task for the urban child is to achieve personal meaning and integration in a complex milieu of smells, sounds, and visual images and a mélange of nationalities, races, languages, and religions.

Both the social and the geographical mobility of Americans is reflected in the flight of middle-class families to suburbia. Presently, it has been estimated, one fourth of the population of the United States lives in the suburbs surrounding large and medium-sized metropolitan areas.[16] Although there are industrial and working-class suburbs adjoining nearly every city, most suburbs are predominantly middle class. A nice home in the suburbs is a cherished goal of upwardly mobile families who aspire to respectable middle-class status. When asked why they prefer the suburbs, their rationalizations may be that in the suburbs there is more room for the children to play, more privacy, better schools, nicer people, or less traffic and noise.

Suburban culture appears to center around the family, the home, and the activities of the children. Neighborliness among mothers of young children is promoted through morning kaffeeklatsches in each other's homes. Subur-

[16] Frederick Elkin, *The Child and Society* (New York: Random House, 1960), p. 97.

banites tend to participate actively in community organizations, with mother serving as PTA chairman and den mother, while father is coach of the little league team; both are active in church work and the civic association.

Suburban culture tends to be characterized by trends toward conformity and a limited degree of tolerance. William H. Whyte, in *The Organization Man*,[17] describes the ways and the extent to which conformity has become imbedded in the character and ways of life of young suburban business executives and professional men. While there is generally a tolerance in suburban culture of people who differ in religious and ethnic background, the suburbanite's response to Negro-white integration has been mixed. Some suburban residents have welcomed Negro families into their communities and a few have sold their homes to Negroes. Other suburban residents, however, have expressed strong opposition to integration and civil rights for Negroes.

Generally, then, the socialization of the suburban child takes place in a sheltered, homogeneous setting. He grows up with other children who are very much like himself. In his socialization he tends to take over the suburban, middle-class ways of his parents and in time becomes indistinguishable from thousands of other suburbanites.

Social Class

In spite of the fact that equality is a professed national value, American communities exhibit a hierarchical status system of socially ranked classes or groups. Various studies have identified these classes and estimated the proportion of a town's population belonging to each class. Warner and Lunt,[18] in an early study of a New England town, developed an "Index of Evaluative Participation," which yielded a measure of social-class status. The designation of the specific social classes and the percentage of the population found to belong to each class in "Yankee City" (the name given to the New England town studied by Warner and Lunt) is as follows:

Upper upper class	1.4%
Lower upper class	1.6%
Upper middle class	10.0%
Lower middle class	28.0%
Upper lower class	33.0%
Lower lower class	26.0%

Other studies generally group the two upper classes into a single upper class, making a total of five classes altogether. Some studies, too, have found a higher proportion of the community in the middle class than did the investigators in Yankee City.

The ways of life of the middle class and the lower class, each having a prominent identity in American culture, have frequently been analyzed and

[17] William H. Whyte, *The Organization Man* (New York: Simon and Schuster, 1956).

[18] W. Lloyd Warner and Paul S. Lunt, *The Social Life of a Modern Community* (New Haven: Yale University Press, 1940).

compared. The socialization of the middle-class child, in contrast to that of the lower-class child, has been described as "conscious, rational, deliberate, and demanding."[19] Middle-class parents tend to have a very clear idea of what they want their child to become. They are constantly checking the child's developmental progress and academic achievement in relation to age-graded norms, and their anxieties concerning his progress are communicated to the child.

The middle-class child tends to be oriented to the future. He is urged to observe accepted moral values, to work hard and to achieve in school, and to delay marriage until he has completed the education which will assure him of a middle-class job and status. Self-discipline and sacrifice are virtues which the middle-class child is expected to emulate. His parents willingly make financial sacrifices to provide him with toys, books, music lessons, clothes, social advantages, and a college education. They evaluate and exert close supervision over his choice of friends. Middle-class parents teach their children to respect and value property, order, cleanliness, punctuality, and thrift, and to recognize the dignity of work and the value of money. The parent cooperates fully and stands shoulder to shoulder with the school, church, and other agencies that have a part to play in instilling middle-class mores and values.

The middle-class child is strongly motivated to conform to his parents' expectations. Love and approval by parents are his reward for achievement and "right living." Failure or fear of failure is always in the picture, so that the middle-class child is seldom free from the anxieties that lie just below the surface of his consciousness. In short, the middle-class child is given early, rigorous, and long-term training in learning the skills, social graces, and habits that will enable him to perform successfully in a highly competitive society.

The socialization of the lower-class child is more informal, less exacting, and less routinized. The child of the slum is oriented to the present. The memories of the past may be too painful to dwell upon, and the future appears too remote and uncertain. What the lower-class child does and learns is frequently governed by his own inclinations, his parents' convenience and impulses, and the needs of the family. The lower-class child is less closely supervised and thus spends many hours with peers in group-initiated activities. He fails to learn the value of self-discipline and postponement of pleasure, because such behaviors are seldom rewarded or seen as important.

Physical strength and toughness as a fighter have special significance for the lower-class child. Fighting occurs in both middle- and lower-class cultures, but it is more likely to be recognized as an acceptable way of settling disputes in lower-class culture. Where the middle-class child is anxious about whether he is achieving in school as well as he should, the lower-class child's anxieties grow out of the uncertainty of whether others consider him a good

[19] Albert K. Cohen, *Delinquent Boys: The Culture of the Gang* (New York: Free Press, 1955), p. 98.

and fearless fighter. Physical punishment or the threat of punishment is more frequently employed in the socialization of lower-class children and youth, while fear of loss of love or approval by parents acts as a powerful motivating force' in the socialization of the middle-class individual. Thus, the affectional ties of the middle-class child are primarily with his parents, while those of the lower-class child are mainly with his peers.

The reader should be cautioned against accepting these generalized descriptions of middle- and lower-class socialization patterns as characteristic of all members of these groups. In reality, each person and each family is unique, so that each family will express its own unique variations of these patterns. One may observe some middle-class persons, for example, who frequently appear disheveled and unkempt, and others whose indifferent care of house or car expresses a lack of valuing of personal property. Some children from lower-class homes, on the other hand, may be observed to have attractive clothes, good grooming, polite manners, and good work habits. Such children are often erroneously judged by their teachers to be from middle-class homes.

Patterns of child rearing in these two social classes have frequently been compared. Davis and Havighurst's[20] study of child-training patterns reported by middle- and lower-class parents in Chicago revealed that in middle-class families, children are weaned and toilet-trained earlier, must be in the house earlier at night, are permitted less free play, are expected to assume home responsibilities earlier, and engage in two to three times as much thumb sucking as do lower-class children. The general picture presented in the Davis and Havighurst study is one of greater permissiveness and longer periods of training among lower-class families, and earlier, more rigid training patterns followed by middle-class parents.

A similar study of child-rearing practices among upper-middle-class and upper-lower-class families in Boston, conducted by Maccoby and Gibbs,[21] produced somewhat different results. This study revealed that upper-lower-class parents are more severe in toilet training and training in sex modesty, employ more physical punishment and ridicule as a method of controlling children, and disagree with each other over methods of child training more than upper-middle-class parents do. Upper-middle-class parents, on the other hand, are warmer, more permissive, and more demonstrative. In contrast to upper-lower-class parents, they use more praise and reasoning and reveal more mutual respect and affection for each other. Other more recent studies have revealed similar trends in patterns of child training.[22]

[20] Allison Davis and Robert J. Havighurst, "Social Class and Color Differences in Child Rearing," *American Sociological Review*, 11 (1946), 698–710.

[21] Eleanor E. Maccoby and Patricia K. Gibbs, "Methods of Child Rearing in Two Social Classes," in William E. Martin and Celia B. Stendler, *Reading in Child Development* (New York: Harcourt, Brace and World, 1954), pp. 380–396.

[22] See Elinor Waters and Vaughn J. Crandall, "Social Class and Observed Maternal Behavior from 1940 to 1960," *Child Development*, 35 (December 1964), 1021–1032; Bernard C. Rosen, "Social Class and the Child's Perception of the Parent," *Child Development*, 35 (December 1964), 1147–1153.

Ethnic Differences

The American people are the product of fusions of many races, nationalities, cultures, and religious groups. Immigrants to this country usually settle in areas inhabited by others of similar language, national origin, religion, and racial background. As a result, Old World patterns persist in these ethnic communities, and assimilation into the mainstream of American life is delayed. In ethnic groups where assimilation has lagged, the second- or third-generation child frequently finds that he has a dual status and a dual identity. In his family and community Mario is an Italian, but at school and in the world beyond the ethnic community Mario wishes to be identified and accepted as an American like everyone else. However, if he accepts the language, manners of dress, food preferences, patterns of dating and courtship, and religious observances characteristic of his ethnic culture, he is set apart as "different" by the larger non-ethnic peer group; on the other hand, if he abandons these ethnic patterns, he has difficulty maintaining his own self-identity and his emotional ties with his family.

Children whose ethnic cultures are more compatible with American ways and values are assimilated more quickly and more easily into the American way of life. Strodtbeck[23] contrasted the cultural values and achievement motives of Jewish and Italian adolescents and their families. He found that Jews more frequently than Italians expressed achievement-related attitudes, attitudes reflected in expressed beliefs in one's own efforts and a willingness to live some distance from parents if educational or job opportunities required it. Rosen,[24] in a study of selected ethnic groups in four Northeastern states, found that in achievement motivation, value orientation, and aspiration level, white Protestants, Jews, and Greeks ranked higher than did French Canadians and Italians. Parents of white Protestants, Jews, and Greeks more frequently set higher goals, upheld higher values for individual responsibility, future planning, and striving for goals and had higher vocational aspirations for their children. For example, 48 percent of the Italian mothers and 52 percent of the French-Canadian mothers indicated that they would be satisfied to have their sons become department-store salesmen, while only 12, 22, and 29 percent, respectively, of the Jewish, white Protestant, and Greek mothers expressed satisfaction with this level of occupational aspiration for their sons.

It appears that varying degrees of "ethnicity" (a classification designating the length of time one's forebears have lived in the United States) characterizing the mother and father have a direct influence on the child-rearing

[23] Fred L. Strodtbeck, "Family Interaction, Values and Achievement," in David C. McClelland et al., *Talent and Society* (Princeton, New Jersey: D. Van Nostrand Co., 1958), pp. 135–195.
[24] Bernard C. Rosen, "Race, Ethnicity and the Achievement Syndrome," *American Sociological Review,* 24 (1959), 47–60.

practices each parent employs. Eron and his associates[25] found that a high-ethnic mother (one whose family has been in the United States a short time) married to either a high- or low-ethnic husband may bring Old World values into her relationship with him and defer to him as the decision maker. On the other hand, a low-ethnic woman married to a high-ethnic man is likely to experience confusion of roles and value conflicts. Children from such families were viewed as more deviant as far as peer ratings were concerned.

The ethnic child initially must learn the ways of both the ethnic culture of his family and the American culture of his teacher and peers at school. Although the competing cultures frequently pose conflicts for the ethnic child, these conflicts tend to decrease as successive generations become more completely assimilated into the American way of life.

Religious Differences

For many Americans, differences in religious affiliation, practices, and beliefs are yet another cultural difference. While people of different denominations do learn different dogmas, rituals, responses, and symbols, the traditions of religious freedom and tolerance in the United States tend to make religious group identities less distinct and less subject to stereotyping.

Religious affiliation in the United States has increasingly become an aspect of one's social class or ethnic identity. Within Protestantism, Episcopalianism tends to be associated with upper-class status and to be more formal in its religious observances, while fundamentalist sects tend to attract lower-class adherents and to be more emotional in their appeal. The Irish, French, Italians, and Spanish are predominantly Catholic, while Scandinavians and Northern Europeans are predominantly Lutheran. Religious affiliation does appear to give one a sense of identity with yet another institution and subcultural group. However, the problem of ascertaining what individuals gain from their religious experience is formidable, and little is known concerning the outcomes of religious observance and instruction.

Race

Differences in physical appearance, culture, and economic and social status have tended to keep racial groups separated from one another, often in segregated communities. With continued segregation, the cultural differences and the inequalities between racial groups have tended to persist and in some cases to increase. In the United States, the cultural differences between Negroes and whites, for example, are in part the result of the limited participation of Negroes in American life, the lack of real communication between the races, and the long subordination of the Negro group.

In a segregated society, the learned behaviors and attitudes governing social interaction between two racial groups are clearly defined and rigidly

[25] Leonard D. Eron, Thomas J. Banta, Leopold O. Walder, and Jerome H. Laulicht, "Comparison of Data Obtained from Mothers and Fathers on Child-rearing Practices and Their Relation to Child Aggression," *Child Development,* 32 (September 1961), 457–472.

enforced. In geographical areas where white and Negro groups have moved toward integration, many of the cultural differences between whites and Negroes have begun to disappear. Davis and Havighurst[26] found that Negro middle-class families are much more similar to white middle-class families than they are to Negro lower-class families in patterns of child training. Similarities were also found among white and Negro lower-class families. Other findings of this study revealed that Negro parents as a group are more permissive than whites in weaning and feeding their children but are earlier and more strict in toilet training than are white parents as a group.

In other ways, however, such as in conformity and sex role behavior, Negro and white cultures differ. Iscoe, Williams, and Harvey,[27] in a study of white and Negro children in the South, found Negro females between the ages of seven and fifteen less conforming than like-aged white females. Among lower-class Negro families, where the father is often absent from the home, the mother is the chief authority. Negro females who play a dominant role in the family are observed to be more independent in dealing with whites than are Negro males. White females, on the other hand, have been taught from an early age to conform and to get along with people.

Differences in Age and Maturity

A further cultural diversity is based upon differences in age and maturity. One learns to behave in ways that are appropriate to one's age and level of maturity as well as in ways that are appropriate to one's sex, regional, rural-urban-suburban, social class, ethnic, religious, and racial subcultures. Since differences in the learned behaviors of persons of different age and maturity are in part a function of development, these differences will be discussed in later chapters on childhood and adolescence.

Methods of Socialization

Four general methods of socialization will be discussed here: (1) parental control, (2) imitation, (3) identification, and (4) group membership.

Parental Control

Parents' own socialization experiences in early life influence their attitudes toward child rearing.[28] In addition, the personalities of the parents

[26] See note 22.

[27] Ira Iscoe, Martha Williams, and Jerry Harvey, "Age, Intelligence and Sex Variables in the Conformity Behavior of Negro and White Children," *Child Development,* 35 (June 1964), 451–460.

[28] Percival M. Symonds, *The Dynamics of Parent-Child Relationships* (New York: Appleton-Century-Crofts, 1949); Wanda C. Bronson, Edith S. Kalten, and N. Livson, "Patterns of Authority and Affection in Two Generations," *Journal of Abnormal and Social Psychology,* 58 (1958), 143–152; I. D. Harris, *Normal Children and Mothers* (New York: Free Press, 1959).

influence their patterns of child rearing and the adjustment of their children. In a study of 25 Jewish, urban, lower-middle-class mothers and their first child of preschool age, Behrens[29] found that the quality of the child's adjustment (measured by judgments of his responses to feeding, weaning, and toilet training) is more dependent upon his total interaction with his mother than upon whatever specific methods of child training she uses. That is, the kind of a person the mother is seems to be more important in promoting favorable adjustment of the child than are her specific techniques of child training.

Several studies have found relationships between authoritarian parental personalities and the use of restrictive patterns of child training. Block[30] identified two groups of fathers, one restrictive and the other permissive in patterns of child training. The restrictive fathers were found to be indecisive, overly self-controlled, conforming, stereotyped, submissive to authority, and lacking in self-confidence. Restrictive fathers scored significantly higher than permissive fathers on measures of ethnocentrism (exclusive concern for one's own group) and fascism. In a test of independence of judgment, restrictive fathers yielded to group opinion significantly more often than permissive fathers, who tended to stand by their own opinions.

The methods of control which parents employ in their socialization of children and youth vary widely. Direct methods used by parents include a broad range of rewards and punishments, including praise and criticism and approval and disapproval, these verbalized in the form of encouragement, reasoning, or exhortation. What effects have these various methods had in influencing positive change in children's behavior? Whiting and Child[31] studied the effect of severity of training upon personality in seventy-five societies, including our own. Especially significant was their finding that love-oriented techniques ("Mama won't love you if you're bad") frequently result in guilt feelings, because they threaten the child's attainment of the goal of parental love yet keep him oriented toward that goal rather than encouraging avoidance of his parents.

The effect of feelings of guilt at age five and six on resistance to temptation by the same children at age eleven or twelve was studied by Grinder.[32] Sixth-grade students were given the task of operating a "ray gun" shooting gallery with no one in the room, thus tempting them to report better scores than they actually made, since a high score earned them an attractive badge. Results of the study showed that children who had shown signs of a conscience in early childhood were most successful at resisting temptation to cheat at age eleven or twelve. It would appear from the results

[29] Marjorie L. Behrens, "Child Rearing and the Character Structure of the Mother," *Child Development,* 25 (September 1954), 225–238.

[30] J. Block, "Personality Characteristics Associated with Fathers' Attitudes toward Child Rearing," *Child Development,* 26 (March 1955), 41–48.

[31] John W. M. Whiting and Irving L. Child, *Child Training and Personality: A Cross-Cultural Study* (New Haven: Yale University Press, 1953).

[32] Robert E. Grinder, "Parental Child-rearing Practices, Conscience, and Resistance to Temptation of Sixth-Grade Children," *Child Development,* 33 (December 1962), 803–820.

of this study that the conscience formed in early childhood tends to serve as a strong reinforcement for acting in accepted, approved ways in later life.

The relative effects on children's personalities of strict and permissive discipline were studied by Watson.[33] Forty-four children brought up in good, loving, but strictly disciplined homes were compared with 34 children in the same community who were reared in good, loving, but extremely permissive homes. In general, children from permissive homes showed more initiative and independence, except in school tasks; better socialization and cooperation; less inner hostility and more friendly feelings toward others; and a higher level of spontaneity, originality, and creativity. Both Peterson and Hoffman[34] conclude that, although parental firmness is necessary for older children, younger children primarily require kindness. Hoffman also points out that whereas the socialization of the young child is more a matter of unquestioning conformity to specific do's and don'ts, the standards of the older child tend to be generalizations from many previous experiences.

Imitation

Imitation is a less formal and more subtle method of socialization than is parental control. One imitates by modeling his behavior on that of another person. When pretending to feed her dolly, the three-year-old girl holds it and talks to it in the same way her mother does with baby brother. Jim, a ten-year-old boy new in the class, watches the behavior of Joe and Mike, the leaders of the boys in the class. Jim laughs at the things Joe and Mike laugh at and asks his mother to get him the same kind of jeans as Joe and Mike wear. During the following weeks Jim's teacher observes that Jim seems to strut like Joe and Mike. Similarly, the tenth grader and the college freshman look to and imitate the ways of the upperclassmen in learning what a person in that school should be like.

Rosenblith,[35] in a study of learning by imitation, found that kindergarten children made greater improvement in copying a maze when they imitated an adult model than when they were only given additional turns without a model. Hartup[36] studied the imitative behavior of kindergarten children in forced two-choice situations in which the two potential models were always a mother and a father doll. The experimenter manipulated the mother and father dolls so that they appeared to act; the child manipulated a child doll in imitation of one of the parent dolls. Both boys and girls

---

[33] Goodwin Watson, "Some Personality Differences in Children Related to Strict or Permissive Parental Discipline," *Journal of Psychology,* 44 (1957), 227–249.

[34] Donald R. Peterson, Wesley C. Becker, Donald J. Shoemaker, Zella Luria, and Leo A. Hellmer, "Child Behavior Problems and Parental Attitudes," *Child Development,* 32 (March 1961), 151–162; Martin L. Hoffman, "Child-rearing Practices and Moral Development," *Child Development,* 34 (June 1963), 295–318.

[35] Judy F. Rosenblith, "Learning by Imitation in Kindergarten Children," *Child Development,* 30 (March 1959), 69–80.

[36] Willard W. Hartup, "Some Correlates of Parental Imitation in Young Children," *Child Development,* 33 (March 1962), 85–96.

imitated the like-sex parent more frequently than the opposite-sex parent. Girls who imitated their mothers were rated higher in femininity. Masculine behavior of kindergarten boys, however, is less influenced by their imitation of their father than it is by their contacts with older brothers and male peers.

Identification

One of the most important and most effective ways one learns his culture is through identification. Identification is the process through which the individual incorporates into his own feeling, doing, and thinking the behavior, attitudes, and characteristics of another person whom he wishes to be like. It involves more than imitation, although the tendency of the child or adolescent to model himself after another is a frequently observed characteristic of identification. Identification appears to be largely an unconscious process wherein one comes to feel like and to perceive the world like the model with whom he identifies.

In the preceding chapter, it was noted that Freud viewed development as movement through a series of fixed stages. Early in life the child attempts to overcome his weakness and immaturity by trying to be like someone who is able, mature, and successful. The child's initial identification is with both parents. During the period of the Oedipus complex, beginning about age three, the boy establishes a relationship with his mother and the girl reveals a strong attachment for her father. The resolution of the Oedipus complex occurs when at four or five the boy changes his perception of his father— seeing him no longer as a competitor for his mother's love but as someone to be emulated and admired. In identifying with his father, he shares with him the mother's love.

The child identifies with those whom he fears as well as those whom he loves. He will usually identify with the parent who is most dominant in dispensing rewards and punishments. However, as Mussen and Distler[37] suggest, young boys are more likely to identify strongly with their fathers— and thus acquire appropriately sex-typed responses—if their relationships with their fathers are rewarding, warm, and affectionate.

The child not only identifies with the model's way of behaving, but he also accepts the model's definition of what he, the child, should be. In the process of growing up, he learns to change his picture of himself so that it conforms more closely to what others expect of him at successive age levels. The child, by becoming more skillful, more knowledgeable, and more socially responsible in ways expected by the model, is also learning his culture, though he may not be conscious of being socialized.

Early in the child's life at school, he identifies with the teacher and other adults who play important roles in his life. During middle childhood, the

[37] Paul H. Mussen and Luther Distler, "Child-Rearing Antecedents of Masculine Identification in Kindergarten Boys," *Child Development,* 31 (March 1960), 89–100.

child's identification is often with real life and story book heroes. During early adolescence, the young person frequently admires an attractive young adult whom he knows personally. Coaches, teachers, scout leaders, youth leaders, and athletes are some of the people whom adolescents wish to be like. Identification in late adolescence frequently involves forming an integrated picture of what one wishes to be like from the many people he has known and admired.[38]

Identification plays a crucial role in all areas and levels of socialization. People learn the ways of their culture more quickly, effectively, and completely through the process of identification than through the external controls of reward and punishment. The critical lessons in the development of self are more readily learned through identification than through the exhortations of parents and teachers.

Group Membership

The ways of the culture are also learned as one conforms to the expectations of the social group of which he is a member. Identification, imitation, and reward and punishment all play a part in ensuring conformity of members to the group's codes and standards. The culture of the group is a configuration of patterned ways and values abstracted from the culture at large. Socialization, thus, may be facilitated by learning the organized patterns and values of the group in place of the piecemeal learning to which the individual would have to resort if he were not a member of a group. The advantages of group membership in learning one's culture will receive further elaboration in the discussion of the peer group in the next chapter.

Socialization of the Middle-Class Child

Because most middle-class students achieve satisfactorily in schools that reinforce and epitomize middle-class values, many persons may mistakenly conclude that the middle-class child has few if any problems related to socialization and learning. Earlier, in the discussion of social-class culture, it was pointed out that the middle-class child undergoes early, long-term, rigorous training to prepare him for success in a highly competitive society. It may be recalled, too, that middle-class culture is strongly oriented toward success, achievement, cooperation, and participation in the community; this culture places great emphasis on education—especially a "good education," as evidenced by attendance at the "right" school or college.

Middle-class parents, in reflecting upon their own successes, often see themselves as living confirmation of the values that made these successes possible. Such parents are likely to bring to bear on their children pressures

---

[38] Robert F. Peck, "The Child Patterns Himself after His Favorite Models," in Caroline M. Tryon, *Fostering Mental Health in Our Schools* (Washington: Association for Supervision and Curriculum Development, N.E.A., 1950), pp. 146–157.

for achievement based on the parents' own "proven" values. These pressures—particularly those applied to academic performance—can become quite intense, as these excerpts from the case of Skippy reveal:

Skippy is a tall, dark, curly-haired, brown-eyed boy in my fifth-grade class at Broadmoor Hill School. He dresses casually but neatly. He is ten years, two months of age and was born in Midwest City of Jewish parents who were also born in Midwest City. His father is a part owner of a winery in Kentucky. The father is Skippy's favorite because he spends some time with his children every evening helping with home work and in boxing sessions. In Skippy's language his mother is "just like anyone else's mother," but his dad is "better than anyone else's." He has one brother, age fourteen, for whom school success has always been quite easy. The brother is in grade nine at Winchester Hill, a college preparatory high school. Skippy also has a cousin in the A section of grade five in Broadmoor Hill School. Skippy's school achievement records through the first four grades reveal average or below average grades, and he has always had some difficulty with reading. His IQ, according to the Kuhlman-Anderson test given in grade four, is 110.

SEPTEMBER 12

An agitated well-dressed woman interrupted my classes at two o'clock and introduced herself as Skippy's mother. She wished to know how Skippy was doing, if he were prepared for grade five, if he had passed the test I gave, and if he would fail this year. It took me some time to identify Skippy as I was not yet acquainted with the seventy children who came to me. But as Skippy's mother was most insistent I finally managed to identify him by the vivid coloring of a shirt she described him as wearing. I attempted to explain that inasmuch as I didn't know who the child was, I was in no position to judge his work so soon and I didn't know to what test she referred. I had given several small written exercises but no full-scale tests.

I quote Skippy's mother: "But Miss Denham, that test made Skippy ill. He is positive he didn't pass it. He wouldn't eat his dinner last evening and cried practically all night. I considered it important enough to break a dental appointment to come up and see you, and you know how hard they are to get."

I asked her to send Skippy to me and promised to do everything I could to relieve his worry and suggested that she treat the matter lightly.

In the background of this episode is the familiar pattern of parental pressures on a middle-class child for high academic performance. The acuteness of the mother's concern for Skippy's progress in school is revealed in her anxiety and agitation.

A child who fails to live up to his parents' expectations for academic success may react to parental pressures in a variety of ways. Some may rebel, give up, and become labeled as "underachievers," a designation that refers to a variety of types of students whose academic performance is below their expected or measured ability. Fink[39] found that underachieving boys were among the most inadequate and immature groups he studied. They feel alienated from society and family and do not accept the ideals and goals of the culture. Often such students become tense, frustrated, and hostile, and may develop various symptoms of maladjustment. Bright male underachievers have been found to express more hostility than bright male achievers,[40] and conferences with junior high school underachievers revealed that in general they complain more than achievers and express more dissatisfaction and self-pity. They also feel a strong urge to escape from situations which place pressures on them to achieve.[41] Skippy's anxieties and doubts concerning his abilities and adequacy as a student are revealed in the following anecdote.

DECEMBER 23

Skippy remained after school to help arrange the room for the Colonial Christmas Ball. During the day the children had left many gifts on my table for me. As I was preparing to leave I gathered them up and remarked to Skippy that I was afraid Broadmoor Hill children felt a necessity to give teachers Christmas gifts.

Skippy, with an alluring twinkle: We give 'em to the ones who give us important grades.

Teacher, returning the twinkle: So that's it, is it? I've often wondered why you didn't work for them.

Skippy: Now, Miss Denham, I've worked and you know it. My dad says this is the first year I've really worked since I've been in school.

Teacher: Well, it's better than worrying, isn't it? I've often wondered why you got so upset the first week of school and sent your mother up here. What was it all about?

Skippy: Well, kids talk, and the guys that had you last year said a guy had to learn to read in your room and I couldn't read and I didn't believe you when you said that reading test wasn't important. I knew it meant the lowest reading group for me and Dad was getting sore again.

[39] Martin B. Fink, "Objectification of Data Used in Underachievement Self-Concept Study," *California Journal of Educational Research,* 13 (1962), 105–112.
[40] Merville C. Shaw and J. Grubb, "Hostility and Able High School Underachievers," *Journal of Counseling Psychology,* 5 (1958), 263–66.
[41] B. B. Williams et al., "Identifying Factors Related to Success in School" (Rochester, New York: West Irondequoit Central School, April 20, 1962). Mimeographed.

Teacher: But there isn't a lowest reading group.

Skippy: Yeah, but I didn't know that then. There always had been and I always was in it. Being in a low comprehension group was different. You told us things to do about that and I tried to do them. Before I just read and hated it.

Teacher: Do you like to read now?

Skippy: Some books I do. I don't like fairy tales.

Teacher: Well, Skippy, you should be proud of your success this year. Both Mrs. Andrews and I think you are doing as well as the children in 5A.

Skippy (in tears, overcome with joy): Gee, do you mean it?

Teacher: If it means that much to you I can see about having you transferred after the holidays, but there are drawbacks to it.

Skippy: What do you mean?

Teacher: Those children read better than you do so you'd still have the same problem, although I'm sure you can keep up with them. But you would be at the bottom of that group while you are at the top of this one.

Skippy: I like the kids in this group, too.

Teacher: You'd like them, too.

Skippy: I don't care about being there if you just tell my dad I'm good enough.

Teacher: I'll be happy to do that, but I think you are more interested in the grades you are getting than what you are learning. Why?

Skippy: Because a guy has to get ahead in school and that's grades, isn't it? Gee, I even get test colds.

Teacher: What?

Skippy: Yeah, I get a cold just thinking about a test.

This anecdote reveals vividly the effects of pressures for achievement on one middle-class child. Note that while the primary pressures on Skippy for academic performance are being exerted by his parents, Miss Denham and the school are reinforcing these pressures by the emphasis they give to academic skills and by their offer to place Skippy in the A section of the fifth grade. Skippy has clearly internalized the importance and value of high scholastic achievement. This is reflected in his concern about grades. His anxieties, his doubts about his own adequacy, and his uncertainties regarding his own abilities to do satisfactory school work are deeply felt. Skippy reveals a measure of self-insight when he relates his feelings of inadequacy regarding school work to physical ailments such as catching a cold.

The case of Skippy is an illustration of the fact that too often parental and teacher pressures and expectations for school success take little account of a child's abilities, background, and developmental needs. Many of the methods of socialization employed by the adult culture serve to constrict the student's responses rather than to free him to use his capacities and abilities.

Socialization of the Culturally Disadvantaged Child

The problems associated with the socialization of the culturally disadvantaged child can perhaps be best understood in relation to the geographical mobility that has literally changed the face of America. Riessman[42] points out that in 1950 about one child in ten attending public schools in the nation's fourteen largest cities was culturally disadvantaged. By 1960, the proportion had risen to one in three, and by 1970, it is predicted that the ratio will be one in two.

Since 1940, both rural and urban areas have lost population to the mushrooming suburbs. Changing economic conditions and opportunities have brought Negroes from the rural South, whites from Appalachia, Puerto Ricans, Mexicans, and most recently Cuban refugees to the cities, causing middle-class families to flee to the suburbs and beyond to exurbia. Between 1950 and 1960, the population in areas surrounding our large cities has increased by 47 percent, while the population of the central cores of large cities has increased by only 8 percent. Presently about one third of the nation lives in suburban areas.[43]

Passow[44] points out that whereas previous generations of slum inhabitants lived in the city for many years before moving to the suburbs, recent immigrants to slum areas are highly mobile and transient. The influx of less stable families into slum communities and the continuing physical and economic deterioration of these expanding areas have resulted in these communities being designated as "depressed areas." It is in these areas that the incidence of crime, alcoholism, poverty, illiteracy, disease, unemployment, and broken homes is highest.

[42] Frank W. Riessman, *The Culturally Deprived Child* (New York: Harper & Row, 1962).
[43] Frederick Shaw, "A Major Urban Problem: Educating Disadvantaged Youth." (Speech to Human Development Workshop, University of Maryland, August 1962.)
[44] A. Harry Passow, ed., *Education in Depressed Areas* (New York: Teachers College, Columbia University, 1963).

There is pressing need for innovation in the education of children from these depressed areas and for rapid improvement of their schools. A particularly acute problem for these children is their lack of experience with the culture for which most educational methods and materials are designed. Especially crucial for many slum children is their unfamiliarity with the language of the culture into which they have immigrated. For lack of familiarity with the language, many slum children are doomed to scholastic retardation and failure before they even start to school.

The retarding effects of cultural handicaps increase as slum children grow older. Shaw[45] reports that the median IQ scores of children in certain disadvantaged districts of New York City declined from 95 in the first grade to 82 in the eighth grade. Goldberg[46] found that the sharpest drops in mean IQ scores between the third and sixth grades were registered for immigrant Negro children (from 88 to 86) and Puerto Rican children (from 85 to 79). Something of what the lower-class slum child is up against is revealed in these excerpts from the case of José:

José is one of thirty-four children in my third-grade class, which is made up predominantly of Puerto Rican and Negro children. He is olive-skinned, has dark hair which is long, and he usually comes to school in a soiled T-shirt, blue jeans, and sneakers. José is ten years old, is $52\frac{1}{2}$ inches in height and weighs 56 pounds. He is the third of nine children of Mrs. Alvarez. The family arrived in New York from Puerto Rico when José was five. His father is dead and the mother works as a domestic and appears to be the sole support of the family.

OCTOBER 29

In spelling today I asked the class to read four sentences of instruction and to do as each sentence directed. When the noon bell rang, José and a few others had not finished. B told me after lunch that José would not come back because he didn't know how to do his spelling.

NOVEMBER 7

José's pronunciation in reading is very poor. He calls *here* "her" and *do* or *does* "doez." *Th* and *wh* words are very hard for him.

NOVEMBER 12

After school was dismissed I heard some of the children outside of my window speaking Spanish. I walked over and told them that since they

---

[45] See note 43.

[46] Miriam L. Goldberg, "Factors Affecting Educational Attainment in Depressed Urban Areas," in Passow (see note 44), p. 83.

were Americans they should try very hard and practice speaking in English. José said "Like you, Miss?" I said, "Yes, Americans the same as I." He said, "But we are black, not white like you."

NOVEMBER 19

During reading, José was sitting very near the blackboard. When I investigated, he had drawn a picture of the devil, horns and all. I asked, "Who drew the picture?" He immediately said, "Benny." All the children said, "No, Miss, José drew it." He denied it completely and repeated that Benny had drawn it. I gave them a little lecture on the importance of telling the truth. Drawing the picture wasn't nearly so bad as denying it. In Spanish José said to me, "Go fly a kite."

MARCH 22

José missed four words out of twenty-two in our spelling review today. I had all the children write each word they missed ten times and learn how to spell it. When the bell rang, José had not finished. When I called on José to spell words he had missed, he still couldn't spell two of them. I sent him back to his seat to study. The next time I called on him to spell his words, he still couldn't spell them. Once when I reminded him he wasn't studying he ducked his head and frowned.

Finally, I told him when he was sure he knew how to spell his words to put his paper on my desk and he could go. He left right away, twirling his book in the air and catching it. I walked out of the room for a minute. When I got back the other children left in the room told me that José had thrown his book through the window into the room.

These excerpts from the case of José illustrate many important problems. Clearly evident is the wide gulf between the world of the teacher and the world of the lower-class Puerto Rican student. The teacher was strongly motivated to help these children, but she was at a loss to cope effectively with their language and learning disabilities. Finally, deep feelings of inadequacy, futility, and hopelessness seemed to be reflected in many of José's responses to the teacher's demands.

It would be impossible to catalog all of the disabilities and privations of the slum child, but some of the most common ones should be mentioned. Among them are overcrowded living conditions, lack of privacy, substandard housing, and lack of adequate sanitary facilities. But perhaps the greatest deprivation suffered by the slum child is his impoverished sensory environment, which severely handicaps and retards his linguistic prowess and his emotional development. Families living year after year at the subsistence level simply do not have enough money for the toys, books, pictures, crayons, scissors, and paper which enable the young child to express himself. The lower-class child has also seldom traveled beyond his immediate community. He has seldom visited the zoo, the museums, walked in the woods, or seen the ocean. This sensory and experiential deprivation, coupled with a language pattern that differs markedly from that of the middle-class teacher, makes the marked retardation in school achievement of large numbers of slum students all but inevitable.

Summary

The processes of internalizing the ways of the world are learned. The feelings, behaviors, ways of perceiving, thinking, and valuing which an individual learns in conformity to society constitutes his *culture*. In its broadest sense, culture evolves from cumulative group experience; it arises from solutions passed on from generation to generation as the best or most acceptable solutions to problems of living. The term *socialization* refers to the processes and experiences through which one internalizes his culture.

Every society has established formal and informal institutions which are charged with preserving the culture and communicating it to each oncoming generation. The family has a primary role in meeting the child's dependency needs, in inculcating a set of fundamental beliefs and values, and in defining the roles, status, and expected behavior of each person within the family group. Church affiliation tends to influence one's character reputation, but the church's overall influence on children and youth appears to depend upon the religious commitment of parents and family. The school, as a cultural institution which affects the lives of nearly all children, tends to communicate predominantly middle-class values and thus is not always responsive to the needs of children from lower-class and ethnic cultures. The peer group and the community provide experiences through which children and youth develop and modify their understanding of the social world and their relations to it. Although the exposure of children and youth to the mass media is considerable, it is not clear what effect this exposure has on their socialization.

American culture may be divided into subcultures on the basis of differences in (1) sex, (2) region, (3) rural-urban-suburban residence, (4) social class, (5) ethnic background, (6) race, (7) religion, and (8) age. These subcultural variations influence profoundly the behavior, cognition, and feeling a particular child learns and uses.

The parents' own socialization experiences in early life tend to influence the practices and methods of socialization they use with their own children. Permissive methods of discipline appear to be more fruitful and to have more favorable effects on children's personalities than do strict methods of child rearing. Other means of socialization are imitation, identification, and group membership.

The middle-class child experiences anxieties concerning whether he will perform well enough socially and academically to earn his parents' love and approval. Often these anxieties are increased when the school reinforces parental pressures. The lower-class child can be helped to develop his talents and skills if he is provided with opportunities for language development and for experiences with other cultures.

Study Questions

1. Cultural anthropologists tell us that in an absolute sense no culture is superior to any other culture. Why is it then that among the educated as well as the less educated some persons talk and act in a manner which suggests that they believe some groups and cultures are clearly superior to others? Discuss.

2. Describe an example of a beatnik or hippie culture which you know of or have read about. What motives, experiences, and events have led to the development of the beatnik's or hippie's solutions to problems of living? Discuss.

3. Select a subculture—geographical, urban-rural, social class, ethnic, or religious—with which you are well acquainted. Describe the changes that have occurred in this subculture during the past ten years. Analyze the forces and events that have contributed to the culture change you have noted.

4. The children in Miss Tyler's fourth-grade class all are from the same homogeneous middle-class community, yet wide differences may be noted in the expectancies various parents have for their children. Frank is restricted to his own street, while Fred has the run of the neighborhood. How would you account for these differences?

5. What are some of the ways through which contemporary schools may become more responsive to the needs of culturally disadvantaged children?

Suggested Readings

Ruth Benedict. *Patterns of Culture.* New York: Mentor Books, 1946. Describes with illustrations of three primitive cultures how analyses of other cultures can assist one in understanding how customs, institutions, and life experiences shape personality and development. Through such analyses one gains clearer insights into his own culture.

Frederick Elkin. *The Child in Society.* New York: Random House, 1960. Describes the process of socialization in relation to current social theories. Discusses the influence of cultural agencies, family, school, peer group, and mass media and the influence of social-class, ethnic, and suburban subcultural patterns on the socialization of American children and youth.

Michael Harrington. *The Other America.* Baltimore: Penguin Books, 1963. Describes the conditions and patterns of a culture of poverty. Describes how inadequate education, medical services, housing, unorganized workers, lack of political power, and discrimination conspire to keep individuals and families in a state of poverty from one generation to the next.

Ralph Linton. *The Cultural Background of Personality*. New York: Appleton-Century-Crofts, 1945. Develops a concept of culture and describes how hereditary and cultural influences interact in the personal life experiences of the individual in shaping his personality.

William E. Martin and Celia B. Stendler. *Child Behavior and Development*. New York: Harcourt, Brace & World, 1959. Chapters 6–9 discuss the process of socialization, with emphasis upon the impact of society and culture, contrasting theories of socialization, and the effects of early life experiences. Chapters 10–13 describe the role of socialization agents, family, school, peer group, and community, in shaping behavior and development.

A. Harry Passow, Editor. *Education in Depressed Areas*. New York: Bureau of Publications, Teachers College, Columbia University, 1963. A series of papers analyzing the unique characteristics and roles of the school in the urban setting and in urban development, the nature of existing and required instructional procedures, the characteristics of personnel and material resources, and other aspects of the problems faced by schools in depressed urban areas.

Robert R. Sears, Eleanor E. Maccoby, and Harry Levin. *Patterns of Child Rearing*. New York: Harper & Row, 1957. Analyzes interviews with 379 mothers of kindergarten children, with separate chapters devoted to feeding, toilet training, dependency, sex, aggression, restrictions and demands, techniques of training, the development of conscience, and sex and birth order of child. Each chapter reviews current theoretical formulations and research findings.

Films

Four Families, 16 mm, sound, black and white, 59 min. Bloomington, Indiana: Audio-Visual Center, Indiana University (rental fee, $8.90). Explores the generalization that the care a child receives during his early years has an effect upon the continuation of the national character of a people. Shows a day in the life of a rural, middle-class family in India, France, Japan, and Canada. Cultural patterns emphasized include infant dress, differing roles of family members, eating patterns, means of discipline, modes of bathing the baby, and the special place of the child in the family.

The High Wall, 16 mm, sound, black and white, 30 min. Bloomington, Indiana: Audio-Visual Center, Indiana University (rental fee, $4.90). Shows that social forces, especially within the home and school, can create conflict between races and cultural groups. When an outbreak between two teenage gangs sends the two leaders to the hospital, a psychiatrist, with the help of a social case worker, reconstructs the backgrounds of the two boys and their families. He finds that fear, frustration, and deep-seated prejudice have been communicated subtly and directly in the boys' home life, at school, and in the adult club of the parents.

Portrait of the Inner City, 16 mm, sound, black and white, 17 min. Bloomington, Indiana: Audio-Visual Center, Indiana University (rental fee, $4.65). Shows the streets, the schools, and the living quarters in the inner city of a large, urban community in the United States. Shown are the inhabitants who serve as models for young Tommy Knight: the shoeshine man, the porter, the carwash man, and the junkman. In contrast is shown the more positive model of Tommy's older brother, who works as a salesman in a store after school. Some of the techniques of communication between school and inner city community are portrayed.

7

the environment and culture
of the peer group

Just children on their way to school again?
Nay, it is ours to watch a greater thing.
These are the World's Rebuilders!

≡   THEODOSIA GARRISON

Few goals or aspirations so fully engage the attention and
energies of children and youth during their years at school
as gaining acceptance in their peer group. Knocking in the
winning run, being invited to the party of a popular classmate, or being asked by a small clique to join in building a
secret clubhouse may be a more important event in a child's
self-development than anything he learns at school that
week. A young person frequently will work day and night
for weeks and months to achieve a place in the peer group.
Many children will not hesitate to break the rules established by adults if it enables them to gain a place in the
group.

The term *peer group* refers to a number of persons (of
about the same age) who are linked together in some kind
of group structure involving reciprocal relationships among
group members and probably some hierarchical ordering of
roles within the group.[1] A child or adolescent may be a *peer*

[1] Although the term *peer* is also used with reference to adults, as in a "jury of one's
peers" the terms *peer* and *peer group* here refer only to preschool and school-age children,
adolescents, or young adults.

(an equal) without being accepted as a member of a peer group. We also speak of the *peer society*—a set of children or adolescents who share certain common characteristics—and the *peer culture*—the beliefs, feelings, thought, behavior, language, dress, activities, interests, codes, and values of a specific peer group. An entity within the peer group is the *clique,* an exclusive and relatively stable subgroup composed of only a few individuals.

A person may belong to many different peer groups at the same time—his class at school, the neighborhood clique, Little League, a Sunday school class, scouts, and summer camp. His status may be different in each group, but the mere fact of membership in some such groups is vitally important in his socialization and his self-development.

Emergence of the Peer Group

The child's first meaningful interactions with peers begin during the second year of life, after he has made progress in walking and talking, has achieved some independence, and has had experiences interacting with persons outside of his immediate family. During early childhood the young child is usually immersed in his own play; increasingly, however, he indicates a preference for playing in close proximity to a peer, though he may not wish actually to play in collaboration with the other child. The two children play near one another, but each builds his own tower of blocks or digs his own tunnel in the sand. (Such children are engaging in *parallel play,* a characteristic of early childhood.) The young child continues to carry on self-initiated independent activities as he grows and develops increased strength and motor coordination and learns to run, jump, climb, ride a tricycle, and perform many other skills appropriate to his age and level of maturity.

Between the ages of three and five children begin to engage in collaborative play. This marks the onset of an age of *peer relationships.* During this period, children are limited in the number of peer relationships they can handle in a play situation. Two preschoolers of approximately the same age will often play together quite peacefully in the play corner; but should a third child enter the play situation, a conflict frequently arises as two become allied against one over whose turn it is to play with the toy bulldozer. Early childhood is also a period of experimentation with different roles. In a single play session four- and five-year-old boys may play at being, in turn, Superman, G-man, the Lone Ranger, and astronaut; girls at this age may shift during a play session from mother to teacher to nurse to cowgirl. *Fantasy,* exemplified in this experimentation with roles, is another characteristic of early childhood.

When children enter kindergarten and first grade they begin to have greater and more varied opportunities for forming peer relationships and broadening their social horizons. The child at this age is adult oriented. His most important relationship in school is with the teacher, who serves as a mother substitute in providing help, understanding, and support. For most children in first grade, the friendship and support of the teacher is even more important than the relationship with peers. Tryon[2] suggests that the teacher in kindergarten, first grade, or second grade, by her standards and values and by her assigning or withholding of roles, can influence children's responses in ways that affect their relationships with peers in later grades.

The second grade is a period of change in children's groups. During their second year at school, as they increase their physical coordination, strength, and control, children learn new skills and assume new roles. Organized games of jump rope, tag, tetherball, and hopscotch require children to collaborate in coordinated group effort and to learn the rules of the game that are essential for continued team effort in competition with opponents. Children at this age often invent games, making up rules for these games and seeing that others observe the rules.

At this time also, children begin to be more independent of adults. They are more adept at dressing themselves, organizing their own play, and solving their own problems. At the same time many have learned that adults are fallible and do not always carry out their promises.

Friendship choices become more stable during second grade, and cliques begin to form that may persist for several months. Toward the end of second grade there emerges a true peer society, characterized by common goals and purposes and sustained collaborative group activity. The following anecdotes show the increase in group feeling that was observed in one second-grade classroom.

OCTOBER 29

Davy was swinging as high as he could and as fast as he could, singing "You're nothing but a Houn' Dog." Previous to this Davy had asked the teacher, "Do you like Elvis Presley?"

Teacher said, "I do not like that kind of singing. Do you?"

Davy said, "Of course I like him." (He giggled) "My big brother likes him, too. Mom just has a fit sometimes. She says, 'Turn that thing off, or I'll throw out the radio.' She means it, too."

OCTOBER 30

Billy sat across from Davy at lunch. Davy said to Billy, "Say, do you want to hear a good joke? You know my big brother's boy friend likes my jokes. Well, Bill, here it is. Knock, knock." Bill frowned and looked up. Davy said, "Ask who's there." Billy finally said, "Who's there?" Davy said, "Red. Now ask who is Red." Billy said, "Who is Red?" Davy said,

---

[2] Caroline Tryon, "Youngsters Learn Social Roles," *Educational Leadership,* 3 (April 1946), 325–28.

"Red Pepper, that's a hot one." At that he laughed. Others at the table laughed. Billy finally smiled and said, "Oh, you!"

Davy said, "Oh, I have another one. Knock, knock." Bill said, "Who's there?" Davy said, "Boo." Billy said, "Boo who?" Davy said, "Well, don't cry about it." They laughed. Both proceeded to eat lunch.

NOVEMBER 8

At lunch. Davy said, "Oh say, gee whiz, I sure have a lot to tell you about our playhouse or clubhouse we made. Sometimes we call it 'the shack.' We sure have fun there."

Teacher: "I'd love to have you tell me more about your clubhouse."

Davy: "You see there's a creek and a steep bank, and you cross the log to get over to the shack. There's water in the creek, too. One boy's father put a light in it. You know we get demerits if we don't behave. If we get twenty-four, we get kicked out. Then Mike, he's another boy, he goes out on the log. You can guess what happens," he haw-hawed. "Yes, he fell into the water. You see, we got a bucket to bring up water. So he lost our bucket. We haven't figured how to get the bucket yet. I went down all the way to the bank of the creek in my wagon. We sure have fun in that place."

Teacher: "It sounds very interesting. Perhaps I can see it sometime."

Davy giggled, nodded head, eyes danced, and he said, "Well, yes, I guess we can have visitors."

The peer group, with its emerging codes and culture, is a going concern by the time children reach the intermediate grades of elementary school. The boys' interest and increased skills in football and baseball are evident in the long hours spent on the playing field. Girls engage in games of their own—jump rope, four-square—or in just walking and talking in pairs or groups. In most fifth grades, a definite sex cleavage may be observed. Boys avoid talking to girls at this stage for fear of being called a sissy by the other boys. Girls look on disdainfully as boys strut around in the role of rough, tough, rugged he-men who wouldn't be caught dead talking to a girl.[3]

Peer interactions characteristic of the fifth and sixth grades are illustrated in these excerpts from the cases of Skippy and Andy:

NOVEMBER 22

I was invited to the boys' football game after school. The game progressed smoothly until Skippy was downed and an argument arose between him and a player of the opposite team as to where the ball should be put into play.

---

[3] For data on a variation in this pattern of sex cleavage, see Lawrence E. Kanous, Robert A. Daugherty, and Thomas S. Cohn, "Relation between Heterosexual Friendship Choices and Socio-economic Level," *Child Development,* 33 (March 1962), 251–255.

His opponent: I got you here. You're cheating.

Skippy: I'm not. You touched me, but didn't down me until I got here (indicating a line about 12 feet distant).

Opponent: You're a liar! I downed you here.

Skippy: Well, ask the other guys. (General opinion was that Skippy was correct.)

Opponent: You're a liar!

Conversation stopped at this point and Skippy landed a good left which started his opponent's nose bleeding. His opponent started to cry and the game went on with the ball where Skippy had placed it. The two boys went home together (apparently the best of friends).

DECEMBER 10

Ellen H. returned at lunchtime and came into the room laughing. "Guess what I saw at lunchtime," she said, "Andy sitting out in the road smoking a big cigar." About this time Andy came into the room and saw Ellen standing near me and laughing. "Go on, horse-mouth," he said, "tell her." I asked him what he meant. He answered, "A horse has a big mouth, and so does she."

The crescendoing of peer-group activity and influence during adolescence is a phenomenon with which nearly all adults are familiar. Early adolescents, in adjusting to new feelings associated with the change that puberty is making in their bodies, frequently find greater understanding and support among their agemates than among parents and teachers. Most early adolescents at first are still engrossed in activities and relationships within their own sex group. Twelve- and thirteen-year-old boys are active and aggressive and prefer to be with other boys, playing or watching sports, working on their hobbies, going to movies, or wandering uptown to see what is happening. Girls prefer to be with girls as they play records, go shopping, or talk about boys. Many students maintain a strong chum relationship with an agemate of the same sex during these years of early adolescence.

In later adolescence, interactions between the sexes become freer and more frequent as dating and other heterosexual activities come to predominate over activities limited to one's own sex group. Now status depends upon one's acceptance by the other sex as well as by his own sex, and acceptance by the other sex depends on how well one learns a whole new repertoire of social skills—dating, dancing, carrying on a conversation with the opposite sex, and knowing how to act in a heterosexual setting.

Kuhlen and Lee[4] noted a striking increase in heterosexual relationships as age increased in their study of 700 boys and girls in grades six, nine, and twelve. Students were asked to indicate first and second choices of companions in their grade for each of eight activities (such as going for a walk, playing outdoor games, or studying). At the sixth-grade level, 45 percent of the boys and 39 percent of the girls chose members of the opposite sex; by the twelfth grade, 75 percent of the boys and 63 percent of the girls chose persons of the opposite sex. The general picture, then, is one of association with the opposite sex in early childhood, gradual withdrawal of opposite-sex contacts in late childhood, and reestablishment of heterosexual relationships as development proceeds into adolescence. (See Figure 7.1.[5])

As age increases, boys show greater activity and greater daring than girls and begin to take over domination of the adolescent social scene. At the sixth-grade level, girls are more frequently mentioned than boys as being popular; at the twelfth-grade level, boys are mentioned more often than girls. The highly accepted persons in both sexes and at all ages are those who are judged to be popular with others, those who appear to be cheerful, happy, enthusiastic, and friendly, those who enjoy jokes, and those who initiate

[4] Raymond G. Kuhlen and Beatrice J. Lee, "Personality Characteristics and Social Acceptability in Adolescence," *Journal of Educational Psychology,* 34 (1943), 321–340.
[5] From Kanous et al., with extrapolations made from data from Kuhlen and Lee. Reproduced by permission of the copyright owner, The Society for Research in Child Development.

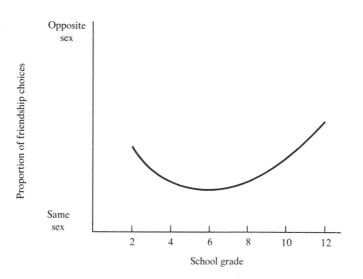

Figure 7.1. Hypothetical curve showing changes in proportion of same-sex and opposite-sex friendship choices at various grade levels (from Kanous et al.).

games and activities. Descriptions such as "talkative," "seeking attention," and "bossing others" do not differentiate between the highly accepted and those not accepted at the sixth-grade level, but these traits do differentiate between the two groups at the twelfth-grade level.

As adolescence continues, the peer culture becomes exceedingly elaborate, developing definite codes of dress, grooming, and behavior, a language which is continually changing, and a set of attitudes and values which defines who and what is "cool," "hoody," or "square." Most children and youths seek to avoid becoming the object of negative references by peers by strongly conforming to the moral codes, standards, and values of the peer culture.

Other changes may be noted as young people move from early adolescence to late adolescence and early adulthood. The early adolescent, for instance, appears to be concerned mainly about his status with the larger peer group of the classroom or school, whereas the late adolescent and young adult seem to be more interested in being identified and gaining status with a smaller group, such as the high school clique or the college fraternity or sorority. All young people moving toward adulthood, however, individually and as a group, may be observed to explore, sift, and test appropriate standards, values, roles, and skills needed for building a philosophy of life, getting started in a vocation, and choosing a desirable mate. The following anecdotes document some of these explorations as well as some of the changes we have described in the peer group.

SEPTEMBER 12

The bell had rung for classes to reconvene after the lunch hour. Three of the high school girls, Alice, Janet, and Nora, were ascending the steps. Dennis, a ninth-grader, was following, and I followed Dennis. I did not hear one sound from any of the group; but, as I watched, Dennis proceeded to flip Alice across the posterior extremity.

Immediately, Alice yelled, "Dennis, don't ever let me see you do that again, or I'll slap your face until it blisters."

Dennis laughingly replied, "Oh! What did I do? Don't tell me you haven't had that happen before?"

After the girls were in their room, I called to Dennis, "Somehow I feel that a public display of this type is not in order."

Dennis did not answer. He merely smiled and went into his room.

NOVEMBER 8

Tonight was the Homecoming Game for us. It was really a hot contest because it was being played between us and the neighboring school. We were behind 13 to 0.

I noticed a long, lanky fellow jump from the wall around the stands to the bench of cheerleaders. It was Dennis. He grabbed the megaphone and yelled, "Give the old fight yell, and yell it."

Dennis kept the megaphone to his mouth and used his right arm in a beating-time motion as he spelled, "F-I-G-H-T, F-I-G-H-T, F-I-G-HT, Fight, Fight, Fight!" At the end of the last "fight!" he gave forth with a big scream. From here Dennis left for the concession stand, where I lost him in the crowd.

NOVEMBER 17

Dennis appeared in class today with a radio. He brought it to my desk and said, "This is what I've been working on for months." I asked, "Did you do all the construction yourself?"

"I certainly did," he said.

"Do you want to tell the class about it?" I asked.

Dennis shook his head and said, "They wouldn't understand!"

I was afraid someone would resent the statement and Becky spoke: "Don't measure my corn in *your* half bushel!" The class laughed.

OCTOBER 9

Although this is only the fifth week of school, I have noticed that Suzy, age seventeen, is one of the more spirited discussants in my senior social problems class. Today we were discussing how students should dress tomorrow for individual visits to industry. Some boys felt that the girls should wear heels and hose. Suzy protested, saying, "We are high school students, not debutantes." She added, "People whom we are visiting may get the idea that the students are trying to act older than their age." The class decision was finally to wear hose and low heels.

OCTOBER 14

Overheard on the field trip.

Helen (to Susan, looking at Susan's left shoulder): No pin?

Susan: No, I gave it back to him.

Helen: Did you have a fight?

Susan: Oh, no. By mutual agreement. We still see each other.

OCTOBER 26

In class today, Suzy challenged the validity of a question I had used on a quiz. Many of the other students also felt it was not a fair question.

There was a good deal of discussion, and finally I showed the class that it was taken almost word for word from the textbook. Suzy then said that she thought the students did not understand one of the words used in the text and in my question. In reply I said that the text was written for high school students and that I had often told the class to look up new words or to ask me. Then I said to the whole class, "I never saw a group so intent on raising one quiz grade by three points." Suzy quickly replied, "Oh, I'm not. I got the question right." At this point we all laughed very heartily and I said, "That's too much!" and we moved on to another subject.

The preceding discussion and case illustrations reveal that peer relationships and peer culture at successive maturity levels mirror the changes that occur as children and youth grow and develop. For example, the motor development of boys during late childhood and early adolescence facilitates and in turn is enhanced by peer-group interest and participation in sports and games. Similarly, physical and sexual maturation is manifested in increased sex-role behavior and heterosexual relationships and activities during adolescence. Thus, the study of the peer group affords us opportunities to increase our understanding of the individual as well as the group.

Functions of the Peer Group

Provision of Emotional Support

One's relationships with peers is a source of emotional support. The extent to which the child gains emotional support from relationships with peers and with the group will depend, as in all human relationships, on the qualities of human acceptance, interest, and concern which are manifested in these peer relationships. A child or adolescent who wins a place in the peer group gains from these experiences increased feelings of value, self-worth, and self-esteem. Acceptance by the peer group enables the student to broaden his base of affectional relationships beyond his family and the world of adults to include a much more discriminating group—his peers.

Another important kind of support is that which the peer group gives any of its members who have been treated unfairly by an adult. The teacher may find that the way he responds to one student markedly influences his relationship and rapport with the whole group. Frequently, the group may show its support of a peer against a teacher by responding with criticism, hostility, or general restlessness and resistance to the teacher and the learning activity.

Identification with Peers

In the last chapter we discussed the process by which the individual learns the ways of his culture through his identifications with a variety of cultural groups—family, church, school, community, social class, ethnic group, and race. One's identification with his peers and peer group during childhood and adolescence is a further important influence in his cultural development. In one's identification with peers, their ways, goals, purposes, and values become internalized into his own patterns of feeling, thinking, and behaving.

Unlike his identifications with many other cultural groups, the young person's identification with peers is an identification with equals, with persons who share a commonality of interests, goals, attitudes, and points of view. As one teenager put it:

> Our crowd is made up of kids who are about my age, who like the same TV programs and games I like, who have about the same feelings toward the teacher, principal, and school that I have, and they are the kids I'd like to spend most of my time with.

The group's ways and values are perceived to have greater meaning and relevance for the young person because they are the ways and values of persons just like himself, rather than of some more distant authority figure. This kinship with equals is, as we shall see, a powerful influence in the development and learning of the individual.

A Setting for Important Learning

As a member of the peer group, the young person learns skills, concepts, attitudes and values which are vital to his own development as a person. It is probably no coincidence that the peer group develops as a significant social force during the intermediate years of elementary school—the time when children are making great strides in motor development and in skill at games. The individual activities of the primary years, running, jumping, swinging, and climbing, give way in elementary school to jump rope, hopscotch, tetherball, four-square, kickball, baseball, and other group and team sports. The rules of these games provide an important learning experience for the individual, and differences in interpreting the rules serve as a test of the group's cohesiveness and skill in resolving conflicts.

The peer group is also the setting for important socialization experiences. Many of the things which the child or adolescent learns from his peer group fulfill the needs and objectives of the larger adult culture. The family, church, school, and community give strong approval to the motor and game skills, the social skills, the skills of dating and courtship, and the skills and attitudes involved in teamwork, cooperation, and loyalty which are learned and reinforced in group interaction. Adults frequently attempt to teach these attitudes and skills through exhortation and advice, but children and youth learn them most quickly and effectively by participating as equals in the activities of the group.

Probably the greatest contribution of the peer group in the socialization of children and youth is its serving as a training ground for learning a democratic way of life. Peer groups in the United States enjoy a considerable degree of autonomy in carrying out activities that promote the group's goals. Neighborhood clubs, cliques, and gangs are probably most autonomous, but even the clubs and extracurricular activities of the high school are organized and carried out mainly by young people under adult supervision. By assuming roles and responsibilities and by participating actively as equals in peer activities, children and youth acquire early and continuous training in the rights, duties, and responsibilities of citizens of a popular, freely elected, representative democracy.

The knowledge, skills, and values which middle-class children and youth learn as members of peer groups differ from those which lower-class children and youth learn in their peer groups. In middle-class culture, the peer group provides children and youth with opportunities for assuming a variety of group roles and responsibilities and for learning cooperative group action in achieving goals. The importance of these group skills is communicated to the middle-class child through his observing that many of the goals and achievements of his parents have been gained through their active participation in business, professional, social, civic, and community associations and groups. The middle-class adolescent gains from the group understanding and support and acquires new attitudes and skills when, singly and in cooperation with others, he resists and rebels against the mounting pressures and expectations of his culture. The group in these instances not only acts as a safety valve for reducing individual and group tensions but provides youth with valuable experiences which they can later use as citizens to influence the changes that are necessary to keep democracy strong and viable.

Since the lower-class culture tends to be more permissive, more informal, and in many ways less exacting, the lower-class child is more often thrown upon his own resources or the resources of an autonomous group of peers. Even more than the middle-class child, the lower-class child becomes emotionally dependent upon his peers, and much of what he does and learns in the group centers in having fun or solving immediate practical problems. For many lower-class youths, the emotional relationships, satisfactions, and rewards of the peer group frequently outweigh those of the family.[6]

Ways of Achieving Peer Acceptance

Identification with Group Goals

Children and youth, as well as adults, come together to achieve individual and group goals. Frequently, a child will fail to gain acceptance in the

---

[6] Albert K. Cohen, *Delinquent Boys: The Culture of the Gang.* (New York: Free Press, 1955), pp. 100–101.

group because his personal goals differ from those of others in the group. Because of this potential conflict between individual and group, much of the interaction and activity in every group focuses upon achieving compatible individual and group goals.

Group goals are more frequently implicit than explicit. Clues to the group's goals are revealed in answers to the question "What does the group do?" From a group's activities one may infer its goals and purposes. The delinquent gang, for example, seeks to enhance its own and its members' self-esteem by defying authority, stealing, destroying property, or by physical violence. A middle-class clique achieves a measure of self-esteem by pledging the same fraternity, becoming active in school politics, or by organizing teams and competing with other groups in bowling, baseball, or basketball. In each case, the activities reflect the group's purposes.

Participation in Group Activities

In order to become a part of the group, the individual must participate to some degree in its *preferred activities* (those activities which a group organizes and pursues that are most significant in relation to the group's purposes and goals). Phillips, Shenker, and Revitz[7] observed that assimilation of a new child into a group of six- and seven-year-old children requires that the new child move from nonparticipation and nonacceptance, through a series of steps of limited participation in strictly defined, limited roles, to full participation, varied group roles, and group acceptance. At first, the new child attempts to get into the group's activities by doing things that another child in the group has done but doing them only after the leader or other member of the group has initiated the activity. If the new child should attempt to initiate, direct, or influence the group's activities himself, he is rebuffed or ignored. In successive interactions with the group, however, the new child achieves partial success—at least one child in the group follows the new child's direction. Later, the new child is included in the group activity by the choice or tacit consent of the group; and finally, the new child initiates and directs group activity with success.

Participation in group activities is particularly important in achieving acceptance among older groups of children. Bud was an awkward, poorly dressed thirteen-year-old who attended school in a mining community. The difficulties Bud faced in achieving a place in the peer group stemmed in part from his lack of participation in the group's activities, as the following anecdote reveals.

APRIL 8

Today we were planning what each group was going to do during recreation period. I remarked to the boys I had not noticed Bud taking

[7] E. Lakin Phillips, Shirley Shenker, and Paula Revitz, "The Assimilation of the New Child into the Group," *Psychiatry*, 14, (August 1951), 319–325.

part in playing ball. Lynn said, "We asked him to play with us, but all he wants to do is to swing or just sit around." Sometimes he plays marbles with Gary. (Gary is about eight years of age.)

Bud seems to lack energy. He takes very little part in active games. The children coax him to play with them, but he refuses. He looks tired and haggard.

Lynn said, "We would like for Bud to play with us because we need him to make two teams. He could learn to play ball if he would practice, even if he is left-handed. He can bat right-handed."

The preferred activities of delinquent gangs often appear to be nonutilitarian, malicious, and negativistic. Stealing, for example, is nonutilitarian when gangs neither need nor use the things they steal. In spite of the effort expended and the danger incurred in stealing, stolen goods are often discarded, destroyed, or casually given away. Malice is expressed in hostility toward non-gang peers as well as adults, in engaging in gang wars, and in taking keen delight in terrorizing "good" children by driving them from playgrounds and gyms for which the gang may have little use.

Two other characteristics of delinquent gangs, as well as of peer groups in general, are *short-run hedonism* and *group autonomy*. Delinquent gangs tend to be impatient, impetuous, and out for fun, paying little attention to the less obvious gains or costs to themselves or others. Gangs display an intolerance for restraints except for those arising from the informal pressures within the group itself. Their autonomy is shown in their active resistance to the home, school, and other agencies which seek to influence or regulate the gang's activities or to compete with the gang for the time or other resources of its members.[8]

Contributing Knowledge and Skills

Individuals who contribute knowledge and skills needed by the group gain added opportunities to participate in group activities and to gain group acceptance. The kinds of knowledge and skills which the group values and needs will again depend on the purposes, goals, and activities of the group and on the maturity level of its members.

An early study by Tryon[9] identified the qualities and values of their peers which were most admired by adolescent boys and girls in the seventh, ninth, and twelfth grades. Seventh-grade boys value expertness in organized games, willingness to take a chance, and skill in leading or directing games. Aggressiveness, boisterousness, and unkemptness are also admired by boys in seventh grade. The seventh-grade girls who are most admired reflect the standards of their mothers and women teachers in being docile, prim, ladylike, and only mildly interested in organized games.

[8] Cohen, pp. 24–32.
[9] Caroline M. Tryon, "Evaluations of Adolescent Personality by Adolescents," *Monographs of the Society for Research in Child Development*, 4 (1939).

In the ninth grade, boys continue to admire physical skills, strength, bravery, and aggressiveness, but social ease and poise, personableness, and likeableness are now also important. The ideal girl is now someone who is a good sport; is popular, friendly, enthusiastic, happy, and daring; and has a good sense of humor.

By the twelfth grade, the girl most admired is the well-groomed, pretty girl who has accepted and fulfilled her feminine role. She is one who belongs to a popular clique, dates a desirable boy, and is liked by the best people, though not necessarily by the most people. Twelfth-grade boys still admire athletic skill, but in addition they value interest and leadership in group activities, good looks and good grooming, intellectual achievement, and social maturity.

Tryon's study, while delineating the range of skills and personal qualities which enhance one's prestige in the group, also emphasizes the dynamic quality of group culture by showing that values important at one maturity level frequently fade and are replaced by other values as the group becomes older.

In a more recent large-scale survey of adolescent values in several large high schools of the Midwest, Coleman[10] found that higher value is attached by boys to being a star athlete and by girls to being an activities leader than by either group to being a brilliant student. In order to get into the top crowd, a girl needs to have a nice personality, good looks, nice clothes, and a good reputation. For boys, athletic ability and having a car are important for being accepted into the top status groups. Good grades count for something with one's own sex group, but cars or clothes count for more in popularity with the opposite sex.

Although different generations of students are represented in these two studies, the valuing of athletic skills in boys and social skills and good grooming in girls is clearly evident in both studies.[11]

However, one should not overstate the importance of any one characteristic, such as athletic skill, in gaining acceptance and status in peer groups. Not all groups place the same value on the same talents. Whyte,[11a] in his analysis of culture, roles, and status among lower-class Italian young-

---

[10] James S. Coleman, *The Adolescent Society* (New York: Free Press, 1961).

[11] For additional data on personal factors contributing to peer-group acceptance see: Lois H. Meek, *The Personal-Social Development of Boys and Girls with Implications for Secondary Education* (New York: Progressive Education Assn., 1940), pp. 43–51; Margaret S. Faust, "Developmental Maturity as a Determinant in Prestige of Adolescent Girls," *Child Development*, 31 (March 1960), 173–184; L. W. McCraw and J. W. Tolbert, "Sociometric Status and Athletic Ability of Junior High School Boys," *The Research Quarterly of the American Association for Health, Physical Education and Recreation*, 24 (March 1953), 72–80; H. Harrison Clarke and David H. Clarke, "Social Status and Mental Health of Boys as Related to Their Maturity, Structural, and Strength Characteristics," *The Research Quarterly*, 32 (October 1961), 320–334; H. Harrison Clarke and Walter H. Greene, "Relationship between Personal-Social Measures Applied to 10-Year-Old Boys," *The Research Quarterly*, 34 (October 1963), 288–298.

[11a] William H. Whyte, *Streetcorner Society* (Chicago: University of Chicago Press, 1943), p. 259.

adult peer groups of Boston, found that the leader need not be the best baseball player, bowler, or fighter, but must have some skill in whatever activities are of particular interest to the group. The leader's ability to influence the group depends in considerable part upon his competent performance in those activities, and he is likely to promote activities in which he excels and to discourage those in which he is not skillful.

A poignant example of a girl who utilized her skill in art to gain some measure of group recognition is that of Ada Adams in the film *Learning to Understand Children* (see p. 43). Ada, a lower-class girl in shabby clothes, won peer recognition by her sketches of the characters of Shakespeare's *Twelfth Night*, which the class had been studying. Her work on the costume committee in the class's presentation of the play led to closer association with and acceptance by some of the popular middle-class girls in the class. In addition to gains in peer acceptance, Ada's changed hair style and improved grooming seemed to be accompaniments to a more adequate self-concept.

Personal Qualities

The personal qualities which elicit positive responses from others are frequently those associated with good mental health. Persons quickly and warmly welcomed into the group are likely to be those who have achieved some measure of personal security and self-esteem, who have developed effective ways for dealing with psychological threats, and who are emotionally independent. Emotional dependence on adults has been found to be related rather consistently to low status among peers.[12]

There is also evidence that high popularity with peers is enjoyed by young people who are able to play a nurturant role in satisfying the dependency needs of others. Among underprivileged adolescent girls in a state training school, for instance, the qualities of self of the most widely accepted girls included being concerned and helping others to develop, to improve their skills, and to achieve goals; expressing impartial fairness and a strong adherence to personal values; and being able to establish rapport quickly and effectively with a wide range of personalities.[13]

Adherence to Group Codes

Some children and adolescents appear to have the knack of melding their personal interests and goals with those of the group; others lack finesse

[12] H. R. Marshall and Boyd R. McCandless, "Relationships between Dependence on Adults and Social Acceptance by Peers," *Child Development,* 28 (September 1957), 413–419; Boyd R. McCandless, Carolyn B. Bilous, and Hannah Lou Bennett, "Peer Popularity and Dependence on Adults in Pre-School Age Socialization," *Child Development,* 32 (September 1961), 511–518; Shirley Moore and Ruth Updegraff, "Sociometric Status of Pre-School Children Related to Age, Sex, Nurturance-giving and Dependency," *Child Development,* 35 (June 1964), 519–524.
[13] Helen H. Jennings, "Leadership and Sociometric Choice," in Theodore M. Newcomb and Eugene L. Hartley, *Readings in Social Psychology* (New York: Holt, Rinehart and Winston, 1947), p. 410.

to such an extent that they quickly antagonize other group members and create dissension in the group. In order to maintain unity and harmony, the group develops a set of group codes, standards, and values and enforces group members' adherence to them.

The group's codes, standards, and values often conflict with the expectations of adults, and this poses a severe dilemma for those children and adolescents who wish to maintain the acceptance and good will of both adults and peers. Frank[14] counsels parents to remain flexible and to work toward compromising their differences with their adolescent offspring. He cautions that the young person does not actually want total freedom; he simply wishes to be released from parental control enough to comply with the often more exacting expectations of his own age and sex group.

The codes, standards, and values of the peer group may be implicit or explicit; at times they may be expressed only covertly and unconsciously. Frequently, group codes or values may be identified in a group's response to an individual's behavior. This is particularly evident in this anecdote from the case of Billy:

MARCH 20

During the morning recess, Billy, age nine, jumped on Bradley's back, threw him down on the concrete, and hurt him pretty badly. The children came rushing in ahead of Billy to tell me about it. Finally, Bradley came in, limping and crying. Billy came in white-faced and shaky and told me, "Mrs. R., I didn't aim to hurt Bradley. I was just playing." Again, I had to remind him that he played too rough. About fifteen minutes passed and Bradley became worse. I was afraid his leg was broken so I had two boys make a hand saddle and carry him downstairs to the cot. Miss B. called his mother to come for him. Billy made several trips to ask how I thought Bradley was. I promised I would call his home at noon and find out. He was really sorry and very upset over it.

At noon he came in to see me. Miss B. called me in from the lounge and there stood Billy with a grin on his face and very matter-of-factly told me that the boys had run him through the belt line for hurting Bradley. Bradley is their favorite. He is a good-natured and even-tempered child. He was in my room last year and due to illness and loss of time at school he didn't pass.

After lunch I had a long talk with the boys about the belt line affair and told them that they would have to be punished for it since it is strictly against school regulations to have such a thing happen. They took their punishment nicely, but were surely off Billy for several days. Bradley was out of school two days. It proved to be a bad bruise, no broken bones or sprains.

[14] Lawrence K. Frank, "The Adolescent and the Family," in Nelson B. Henry, *Forty-third Yearbook, Part I, Adolescence,* National Society for the Study of Education, (Chicago: University of Chicago Press, 1944), pp. 240–245.

Roles and Status in Groups

Roles

Certain expected behaviors, tasks, and jobs must be performed by group members in order for the group to carry on its activities and to achieve its purposes. The pattern of expected behavior which an individual performs in relation to another person or group of persons is known as his *role*. In order for each individual in a group to perform his role effectively and in harmony with others in the group, he must know the roles of every member of the group. Just as the quarterback is unlikely to complete a pass unless he anticipates and responds to the moves of his blocking linemen and his pass receivers, the group member's efforts to achieve individual and group goals are likely to be frustrated unless he can anticipate the response of other members of the group.

When observing children and youth, adults frequently dichotomize peer-group roles simply in terms of leaders and followers. An analysis of students' social behavior, however, reveals many far more subtle differentiations of role. Caldwell,[15] in an analysis of over 4,000 case records written by teachers, identified eighteen social roles of children in kindergarten and grades two, four, and eight. Three are active roles: the *director*, the take-charge person who directs and dominates the activities of others; the *bully*, who secures compliance by threatening and intimidating others; and the *initiator*, who has ideas and frequently suggests what ought to be done. Roles that facilitate group processes, group harmony, and group cohesion are those of the *clarifier, morale builder, mediator, catalyzer*, and *nurturer*. The *sustainer* is a child who sticks up for and identifies with the leader, while the *attendant* is one who follows constructively and cooperatively the dictates of the leader and may also enjoy the confidence and share the secrets of the leader. The *clown*, the well-known wit or jokester, is expected to provide humor. The *imitator* is seen as lacking in initiative but is capable of persistent effort and sacrifice. The *subverter* is one who manipulates people or situations to serve his own self-interest. The remaining five roles identified by Caldwell reflect status in the group: *rejectee, fringer, isolate, scapegoat*, and *dependent*.

A distinction should be made between the roles a person desires to play and the roles the group permits him to play. These may be quite different, as the following anecdote from the case of Horace reveals.

Horace, age eleven and in the fifth grade, has on several occasions displayed a quick temper, which has led to altercations with children on the playground.

[15] Charles G. Caldwell, "The Social Behavior of Children: Studies in a Child Study Program," (unpublished doctoral dissertation, University of Chicago, 1951).

NOVEMBER 21

Our softball had been missing for two days until Horace found it behind some boxes in our supply closet. In finding it Horace announced gleefully, "I'm going to be pitcher for our team at recess." Several boys in the room disagreed. At recess Horace failed in four pitches to get the ball over the plate. Jimmy walked over and told him to stand aside and he would pitch for him. Horace said, "No," and Jimmy pushed him away while the other boys yelled, "Get out of the way, Horace." Horace frowned deeply, put his hands in his pockets, shrugged, and walked to a position in the outfield.

In the contrasting setting of an East Side New York delinquent gang, Bloch and Niederhoffer[16] observed that roles of leadership and influence were shared by four individuals, each of whom operated with autonomy in his own sphere of interest. Paulie masterminded some of the gang's most impressive burglaries and had the final say in all important decisions. Lulu's knack for working with tools and electricity made him a natural for taking care of the technical details connected with a burglary job. Solly was public relations expert and spokesman in encounters with the police. Blackie was preeminent in matters relating to girls. This differentiation of leadership roles was accompanied by a division of power that allowed different personality types to function efficiently in the spheres of interest allotted to them. In this way a clash of rivals was avoided because each had enough autonomy to satisfy him.

Status

Each role carries with it a certain status or prestige, the amount of which depends on the importance of that role for the group. Roles which require greater knowledge and skills or entail greater responsibilities are generally accorded higher status and prestige because they are more valued and needed by the group for the achievement of its purposes. An individual's status in the group can be ascertained by observing the effects of his actions on the rest of the group, the responses of the group toward him, and the roles the group permits him to play.

A number of studies have investigated the characteristics, abilities, and personality traits associated with peer status at various maturity levels. Bonney[17] found that status in the second grade is concentrated among a few individuals and that as children in the second grade become recognized as good readers, their status increases. At the sixth-grade level, play activities

[16] Herbert A. Bloch and Arthur Niederhoffer, *The Gang: A Study in Adolescent Behavior* (New York: Philosophical Library, 1958), pp. 193–219.

[17] Merl E. Bonney, "A Study of Social Status on the Second-Grade Level," *Journal of Genetic Psychology,* 60 (1942), 271–305.

provide a better medium than academic activities for establishing close interpersonal relationships. Children chosen as playmates are accorded greater acceptance than those chosen as partners on a quiz-kid program.[18] Laughlin[19] found that favorable personality traits are a more important determiner of peer status at the sixth-grade level than is mental ability. Children who are well liked tend to be described as friendly, enthusiastic, good-looking, and cheerful, while those who are not well accepted are described as talkative, restless, and attention-seeking.

Other researchers have studied the relationships of academic achievement, IQ, socioeconomic status, and occupational status of father to a child's peer status. In a study of peer status in classrooms of grades five through eight, Morgan[20] found that children whose fathers have higher occupational prestige are preferred in social activities over children whose fathers have lower occupational status. Morgan also found that children who score high in achievement are preferred over children who have lower achievement-test scores. In a study of 37,000 boys and girls in grades three to six, Roff and Sells[21] found that the most frequently chosen children had IQs 15 to 20 points higher than children of the same sex and socioeconomic group who were less frequently chosen.

The accuracy of an adolescent's self-perceptions also appears to influence his peer acceptance. Goslin[22] found that adolescents who perceive themselves differently than they are perceived by the group or who are unable to predict how others will rate them are likely to be accorded a low degree of acceptance by others. Occupying a relatively uncertain place in the larger group, these rejected adolescents frequently encounter considerable inconsistency in the behavior of their peers. This, in turn, causes those who are rejected to have still less accurate perceptions of themselves and others.

Sociometric Testing

Adults frequently make judgments concerning a student's status in the peer group based upon observations of the roles he plays and the behaviors and feelings revealed in his interactions with peers. Judgments based on these observations, however, are subject to error. Children and youth often mask their true feelings toward peers, making it more difficult for adults to

[18] Merl E. Bonney, "A Study of the Sociometric Process among Sixth-Grade Children," *Journal of Educational Psychology,* 37 (September 1946), 359-372.

[19] Frances Laughlin, *Peer Status of Sixth and Seventh Grade Children* (New York: Teachers College Press, Columbia University, 1954).

[20] H. Gerthon Morgan, "Social Relationships of Children in a War-Boom Community," *Journal of Educational Research,* 40 (December 1946), 271–286.

[21] Merrill Roff and S. B. Sells, "Relations between Intelligence and Sociometric Status in Groups Differing in Sex and Socioeconomic Background," *Psychological Reports,* 16 (1965), 511–516.

[22] David A. Goslin, "Accuracy of Self-Perception and Self-Acceptance," *Sociometry,* 25 (September 1962), 283–296.

learn about the actual relationships within the peer group. Adults are most likely to be inaccurate in judging the peer status of older students. Moreno[23] found that teachers' judgments of children's status in kindergarten and first grade are 65 percent accurate, but that at the seventh-grade level they are only 25 percent accurate.

Sociometric testing offers educators and social scientists an objective means of ascertaining the status and relationships of members in a group. A *sociometric test* is a technique for obtaining from each group member his choices of persons in the group with whom he would like to interact or with whom he would like to develop or to maintain a relationship. A *sociogram* is a graphic representation of actual or desired relationships within a group. The information presented in a sociogram is based upon data obtained from a sociometric test.

The teacher who desires to obtain data on students' choices first selects a criterion for choosing appropriate to the classroom situation. Generally, students choose with less hesitancy when they see that the reason for choosing is to enable the teacher and class to organize for play or instruction. Teachers, then, might ask students whom they would like to sit beside, whom they would choose to work with on a committee, or whom they would choose as a work or play partner. It is important that the teacher use the students' choices for the purpose for which they were requested; that is, in the assignment of trip partners, the arrangement of seating, or the organization of committee work.

Collecting the choices of each member of the class is facilitated by the preparation of a duplicated form which explains briefly the use the teacher will make of student choices. One form that can be used or adopted is shown in Figure 7.2. Some teachers prefer not to solicit choices of rejectees. If these choices are desired in order to gain a clearer picture of relationships within the group, the request for last choices in the second paragraph of the form shown in Figure 7.2 is the kind of approach likely to elicit information.

When sociometric choices have been obtained, they are recorded on a Sociometric Matrix Summary Sheet (a form for recording each student's sociometric choices).[23a] Next, the teacher selects the type of sociogram that will display the relationships within the group most clearly and effectively. Symbols representing children who have chosen each other or have both chosen the same child are placed near each other on a piece of paper as a first step in constructing a sociogram. In successive steps, the symbols for other children are positioned on the graph near symbols for persons whom each chooses or persons who choose him. Another way of portraying the choices and the position of each student in the group is to use a target sociogram, in

[23] J. L. Moreno, *Who Shall Survive?* (Washington: Nervous and Mental Disease Publishing Co., 1934).

[23a] For further details on procedures of sociometric testing, see Mary L. Northway and Lindsey Weld, *Sociometric Testing: A Guide for Teachers* (Toronto: University of Toronto Press, 1957); and Norman E. Gronlund, *Sociometry in the Classroom* (New York: Harper & Row, 1959).

Your name_____

Date_____

Boys and girls:

   Next week we will take our trip to Washington D.C.
In order for us to stay together and avoid getting lost,
it will be necessary for each of us to have a partner for
this trip. Please write the names of three classmates,
any of whom you would like to have as a partner on the
trip.

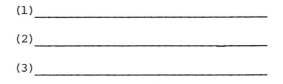

   Many of the persons whom we do not choose will be
chosen by other members of the class. In order that I
may place persons closest to classmates whom they would .
like to be near on the bus, please indicate whom you
would choose last as a partner on this trip.

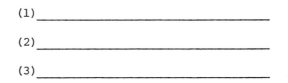

Figure 7.2.   A form for eliciting classmate choices.

which symbols for persons receiving the most choices are placed in or near
the bull's-eye, with those receiving fewer choices being positioned in areas
between the bull's-eye and the periphery of the target in accordance with the
number of choices received. Those with fewest or no choices are placed at the
periphery of the target sociogram.

   Another sociometric instrument is the Classroom Social Distance Scale
developed by Cunningham and her associates.[24] Each student in a class is
asked to place every other student in that class in one of five categories from
(1) "Would like to have him as one of my best friends" to (5) "Wish he
weren't in our room." Using this scale, one is able to obtain information on

---

[24] Ruth Cunningham and Associates, *Understanding Group Behavior of Boys and Girls*
(New York: Teachers College, Columbia University, 1951), pp. 401–406.

the social group as a whole and to ascertain the degree to which individuals and subgroups accept the larger group and the extent to which the larger group accepts them.

Sociometric procedures enable teachers and adult group leaders to acquire useful information concerning interpersonal relationships within a group. These procedures are most useful, however, when they supplement the knowledge of peer relationships which the teacher has acquired from direct observations of group members in daily interaction with one another. The following anecdotes reveal how Miss T. used these sources of information to understand and to help Horace. Horace, it will be recalled, is the fifth grader who wanted to be the pitcher but was sent to the outfield instead.

NOVEMBER 26

Horace came back from lunch early today and was waiting when the boys and girls came out of the building. He had the bat in his hand and declared he was going to be a batter. Two other boys and one girl demanded the position because they had been up at recess and the game was a continuing one. Horace protested by saying, "No, it isn't fair. I was here first." All the other children yelled to him to give up his place and become pitcher. He finally took the bat and walked to the pitcher's mound while Jane stood in the batter's box with her back turned toward him. When he reached the mound, he turned around and threw the bat high in the air toward home-plate. It came down and struck Jane in the back of the head. She cried a while but finally took her turn at bat. After five more minutes of playing, however, she suddenly began to lose her sight. She was taken to the hospital by her mother about an hour later. When Horace went back to the room he had tears in his eyes, his mouth was drawn down at the corners, he kept his head down, looked at the floor, and scuffed along.

DECEMBER 1

Horace was standing on the walk outside the building surrounded by five boys smaller than himself. Every now and then one of the boys would run up and shove him or hit him and he would shove them or hit them back. One of the boys kept saying, "You big stiff, I'll beat you up." Another said, "I'll bash you." One of the boys hit him and Horace chased him around the corner of the building.

DECEMBER 17

In physical education today, Horace was playing center on his basketball team. The girl who was playing opposite him could outjump him when the ball was tossed up for the tip off. He became very disturbed about this. Each time he would grit his teeth, grunt, and jump as high as he could but he was never able to beat the girl.

After the fourth or fifth attempt, instead of trying to hit the ball, he batted the girl on the arm. This caused his team to have a foul called against them. The other members of the team all growled and fussed at him for it. He walked around looking at the floor for a short time and remarked, "I couldn't help it." I noticed that the next time he jumped for the ball it was against a shorter opponent and he slammed the ball clear out of the court.

JANUARY 5

The children in the room were telling about interesting things they had seen and done over the holidays. Horace sat and read a book through the whole series of reports.

On December 10, Miss T. asked the class members to write the names of up to three classmates whom they would like to work with on committees to plan the Christmas party. The choices of the boys in the class were used to construct the sociogram in Figure 7.3. Not only was Horace not chosen by any child in his room, but he was rejected by eight boys (as well as by two girls, who were not recorded on the sociogram). Horace did not choose anybody and handed in a blank piece of paper. When Miss T. asked him about this later, he said, "There isn't anybody I particularly want to work with on a committee."

FEBRUARY 15

During the past three or four weeks, Horace's behavior and attitude have changed markedly. He appears happier, more at ease, and conflicts with his classmates appear to be fewer. During the morning, we planned our newspaper collection for the week. One of the girls needed help to bring a wagonload of papers up Fourth Street hill, which is very steep. Horace quickly offered to help her and made the necessary arrangements.

During our game period today, Horace did not try to catch the ball himself all of the time. Several times he actually gave his teammates the ball so that they might throw it.

The whole day Horace has really worked with the group. I asked the children if they had noticed how much Horace had helped us. One boy replied, "He certainly is full of energy today."

FEBRUARY 20

Today Horace was chosen by the class as one of the fifth-grade representatives on the safety patrol. He grinned broadly when the results of the election were announced. I congratulated Horace on his being elected.

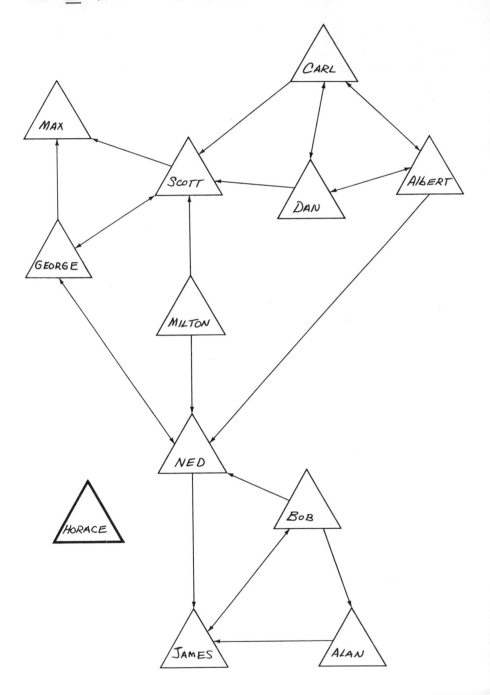

Figure 7.3. Sociogram showing choices made by children in Miss T.'s fifth-grade classroom on December 10 in response to the question "With whom would you like to work on a.committee?"

"Whew," he said. "I didn't think I would ever make the patrol."

"The class must think you'll make a good patrolman or they wouldn't have voted for you," I said.

"This is the first time I have ever been chosen for anything by my class."

MARCH 12

Horace has been performing his patrol duty unsatisfactorily for the past week. He hasn't worn his belt, has been late, and has talked while on his corner. Several times I have talked with him about his patrol work. It seems that he just can't do everything right. If he has his belt and is on time he talks to the girls on the other corners. Today I talked with him again, and he said that he would try not to talk while on duty.

APRIL 8

A group of about fifty boys and girls were gathered around Horace on the playground. He had drawn a line on the ground and started a broad-jumping contest. He had a tape measure and was measuring each jump. He lined the boys and girls up so each would have a chance to jump in turn. After each jump, he would measure it and shout out the distance jumped, then call for the next jumper. He was in complete control. The children who were watching were lined up on each side of the jumpers path and Horace kept waving his arms and yelling to them to stand back and give the jumpers room. This went on until the bell rang, at which time Horace declared Joe the winner with a jump of 13½ feet.

On March 24, Miss T. obtained choices from the children which enabled her to construct a second sociogram. The responses of boys (and one girl) in the room to the question "Who would you like to sit beside?" are shown in Figure 7.4. This time Horace was chosen by two boys and was rejected by only four classmates.

These few brief anecdotes cannot give us the full flavor of the case of Horace, but they do reveal some of the ways Miss T. tried to help him in his efforts to relate to the peer group.

The Teacher's Role

When we consider the ways in which a student can be helped to achieve a place in the peer group, one thing seems clear: The adult cannot win group acceptance for a student who is ignored or rejected; group acceptance is something that must be achieved by the pupil himself. Even when the adult is highly regarded by the group, his efforts to persuade the group to accept a rejected pupil are usually ineffectual. Most peer groups are quick to

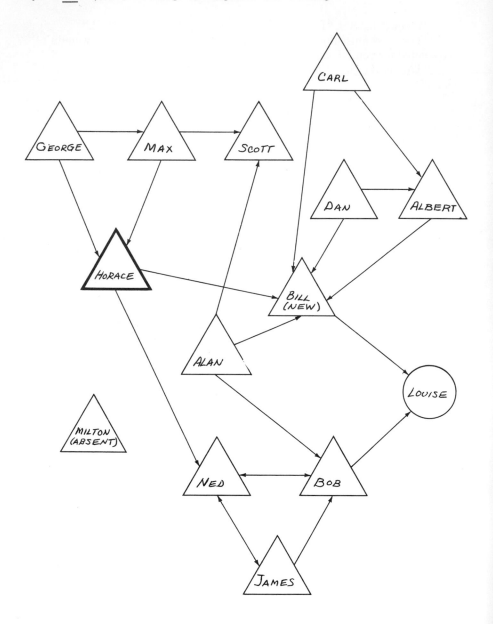

Figure 7.4. Sociogram showing choices made by children in Miss T.'s fifth-grade classroom on March 24 in response to the question "Which children in this class would you like to sit beside?"

see through the adult's subtle efforts to maneuver, manipulate, or control the group. Often, group resentment toward the adult is directed toward the child the adult is sponsoring, thereby making it even more difficult for the child to win group acceptance.

Elliott[25] has suggested three ways in which a teacher may assist a student who is seeking a place in the group: (1) by providing opportunities for development of friendly relations, (2) by helping the student to improve his social skills, and (3) by helping him to build a sense of accomplishment and adequacy. Providing opportunities for pupils to become better acquainted may be accomplished by seating arrangements, by forming committees, and by a variety of other ways. Jane's teacher, in the case introduced in Chapter 5, suggested Jane's name to a mother who was planning a birthday party for her daughter, a popular girl in the class. The teacher's suggestion was readily accepted.

Helping a student improve his social skills is sometimes a bit more difficult, because adult exhortations to a student to be kind, courteous, and considerate seldom change his behavior. For students who strongly desire to improve their status in the group, individual and group counseling frequently may help them to become more sensitive and perceptive of the feelings of others in the group. Quite often, the child's improvement of social skills is dependent upon his having available appropriate models in the persons of peers, older children, or the teacher.

Helping the student to experience an increased sense of adequacy and competency is one of the most effective ways of helping him to improve his position in the group. Ada's teacher, in the film cited earlier, increased Ada's feeling of adequacy and brought her favorable group recognition by showing the class Ada's sketches of the characters of *Twelfth Night,* which the class had been studying. Bud's teacher encouraged him to demonstrate before the class his hobby of taking apart and repairing old clocks. Another teacher, who was reassigned after the beginning of school to a combination grade, kept with her eight students who were less frequently chosen on a friendship chart. These children, older and more mature than the children coming from the lower grade, were given responsibilities in the new class which helped them to feel more adequate and secure.

Probably the most important thing a teacher can do is to accept the child who is ignored or rejected by the group. A teacher who genuinely accepts and values children earns his children's respect and affection. A teacher who has gained the group's esteem is often able to influence the feelings of the group toward persons whom the teacher accepts and values.

It is doubtful that the teacher can change or influence the peer group to any great extent by direct manipulation. Rather, the teacher should be genuinely accepting of the group and should work with it as it seeks to evolve and mature. At times the peer group may appear to be engaged in

[25] Merle H. Elliott, "Patterns of Friendship in the Classroom," *Progressive Education,* 19 (November 1941), 383–390.

activities and to be moving toward goals that are opposed by the adult culture. The best way for adults to influence the group is not to interfere with it but to conduct adult society in a manner and toward goals that the peer group will emulate and move toward.

The teacher's acceptance of each student and of the group as a whole is the basis for the mutual trust and respect essential for cooperative, democratic group living. In the classroom, the teacher is free to focus on the broad aspects of the learning experience and to leave to the group the planning of details, activities, and ideas, which the students are eager to contribute. This increased involvement of students in the learning experience facilitates their development by making them active partners in the educative process.

The Peer Group and Conformity

The peer group can help each individual member gain skills, emotional support, and a sense of self-identity; it can also, however, dull his individuality and compel his adherence to group standards so rigidly that he may become an unquestioning conformist.

As our society has become more highly industrialized and complex, warnings against the dangers of conformity have become more insistent. Riesman[26] describes a trend in the national character away from the inner-directed self-made man of prior generations to an *other-directed* man, whose source of direction and guidance is the group. Riesman sees this dependence upon the group's views and mores as leading to behavioral conformity and an attendant depersonalization and loss of individual autonomy. Whyte[27] documents the erosion of autonomy—in education, business, science, suburbia, personnel practices, and the cultures of the large corporations—as the Protestant ethic is replaced by the social ethic and conformity to the group.

The tendency of persons to conform to group norms is supported by research. Asch[28] conducted an experiment in which each person in a group of eight was asked to give aloud his perceptual judgment as to which of three lines matched the length of a standard line. One member of the group was informed of the true nature of the experiment and was instructed by the experimenter to give as his best judgment an answer which was at variance with his private judgment. Answers of subjects reporting after the "confederate" had reported tended to conform to the "confederate's" judgment, thereby creating and lending support to a "group norm." The judgments of the seven naive subjects conformed to this false "group norm" about 30 percent of the time. Asch's experiment demonstrates the power of social pressure to promote conformity to the group norm, even to encourage rejection of accurate personal perceptions of reality.

---

[26] David Riesman, *The Lonely Crowd* (New Haven: Yale University Press 1950).

[27] William H. Whyte, *The Organization Man* (New York: Simon and Schuster, 1956).

[28] Solomon E. Asch, "Studies of Independence and Conformity: I. A Minority of One against a Unanimous Majority," *Psychological Monographs* 70 (1956).

The peer group, like the other social forces to which it is related, can either ennoble or enslave. Group experiences are essential to the optimum development of every human being, but when the person surrenders his individuality and freedom in blind conformity to the group, human development and learning are likely to become blighted and stunted.

Summary

Interaction and identification with a group of peers are of vital importance in the socialization and self-development of each child and adolescent. One's *peers* are those persons of approximately the same age with whom one interacts or with whom one is associated over a period of time. The *peer group* consists of persons (of about the same age) who are linked together in some kind of group structure. The *peer culture* comprises the patterns of belief, feeling, thinking, behaving, language, dress, activities, interests, codes, and values that characterize a specific peer group.

During the preschool years, peer relationships are formed as the young child interacts and plays with agemates in the neighborhood and at nursery school. The second grade has been identified as a period of change in children's groups. Children during this period show marked gains in physical coordination and independence. During the second grade, *cliques* begin to form that may persist over several months. Toward the end of second grade, there emerges a true *peer society*, in which common goals and purposes are recognized and collaborative activity can persist over a long period of time. Peer-group activity in the intermediate years of elementary school is focused on sports and organized games. A cleavage of the two sexes is characteristic of the peer group during this period.

Early adolescents are engrossed in activities and relationships within their own sex group. As adolescents move toward heterosexual relationships and emotional independence of adults, marked changes occur within the peer group. Interactions between the sexes become freer and more frequent as dating and heterosexual activities come to predominate over activities limited to a single sex.

The peer group has a variety of functions in the development of children and youth. As young people make their way in the world beyond the family, the peer group provides needed emotional support and is a social entity with which young people can strongly identify. The peer group also becomes a setting for important learnings and a significant factor in the process of socialization.

Winning the acceptance and esteem of the peer group is an achievement of great importance for nearly all children and youth. Their success or failure in these endeavors appears to be influenced by the compatibility of the individual with group purposes and goals, by the readiness and the extent of the individual's contributions of needed knowledge and skills to the group, and by certain subtle personal qualities that influence positively or negatively acceptance by the group. The extent to which the individual accepts and adheres to group codes, standards, and values also is an important variable influencing the group's acceptance of him.

The child's or adolescent's acceptance in the peer group is reflected in the roles and status accorded him by the group. Sociometric techniques have enabled teachers and social scientists to study the relationships of members in a group and the structure of that group. Excerpts and sociograms from the case of Horace reveal how his teacher utilized sociometric data in helping Horace to improve his position in the group.

Peer acceptance is an achievement that the child or adolescent must win for himself. Adults, however, can help the student by accepting and working with the peer group instead of trying to control it. Adults can also assist a student in gaining peer acceptance by helping him to develop skills and competencies that bring group recognition. Group acceptance requires that one conform to group customs, standards, and values. However, if the almost overwhelming forces and pressures for conformity in our contemporary culture are not resisted, they may inhibit rather than enhance the development and learning of individuals and groups.

Study Questions

1. Observe a group of teenagers in a snack bar, pizza house, or other teenage hangout. Note their dress, topics of conversation, vocabulary, and the interactions and reactions within the group. What do they talk about? What are the different ways you see individual teenagers relating to this group? What estimates would you make concerning the status of each member of the group?

2. Try to recall one or more of the codes, customs, or fads that were introduced into your child or adolescent peer group. Describe the process through which this fad "caught on." Why was this fad accepted while other similar innovations were not adopted by the group?

3. The peer group, with its insistence upon conformity, serves to deter group members from developing their uniqueness and individuality. Express your agreement or disagreement with this statement and discuss.

4. You are developing a new seating arrangement for your social studies class. During the first six weeks you have noted several peer friendships and cliques among the students in your classroom. Should you arrange the seats on the basis of friendship choices or should you keep friends and clique members separated? Defend your position.

5. If adults register their disapproval of adolescent peer-group behaviors and codes which are in conflict with adult standards and values, adults are likely to lose rapport with and to be ignored or rejected by the peer group. If, on the other hand, adults refrain from taking a stand in opposing those adolescent peer behaviors and codes, adolescents will not receive adult guidance,

through which they might be helped to make better choices. What should the adult do in this case? Discuss.

Suggested Readings

Merl E. Bonney, *Mental Health in Education.* Boston: Allyn and Bacon, 1960. Shows teachers how they can promote mental-health objectives in and through groups. Chapter 8 discusses group conformity and adaptation and suggests ways the school may assist students in achieving group belongingness.

James S. Coleman, *The Adolescent Society.* New York: Macmillan Co., 1963. Reports findings of extensive research which investigated the nature and consequences of adolescent social climates. Characteristics of leaders and the elite in each of ten high schools are identified. Chapter 7 analyzes various peer-group structures and their relation to value systems.

Ruth Cunningham and Associates, *Understanding Group Behavior of Boys and Girls.* New York: Bureau of Publications, Teachers College, Columbia University, 1951. Report of an extensive study of group behavior and interaction of children in an elementary school setting. Various sociometric instruments, including the Social Distance Scale, are described. Authors point to the responsibility of schools for educating groups for group action and for the development of group members.

Norman E. Gronlund, *Sociometry in the Classroom.* New York: Harper & Row, 1959. Presents a comprehensive review of the research literature related to sociometry and its meaning for education. Describes in detail procedures for obtaining and analyzing sociometric data.

David Riesman, *The Lonely Crowd.* New Haven: Yale University Press, 1950. Presents the thesis that social character is related to patterns of population growth. Chapter 3 discusses the change from an inner-directed society, which focuses on production, to an other-directed society, in which consumption, peer group approval, and popularity are major goals.

William F. Whyte, *Streetcorner Society.* Chicago: University of Chicago Press, 1943. An account of peer interaction and culture of a young-adult Italian-American group in Boston. Describes the reciprocal obligations, codes, and leader-follower relationships within the group.

Films

Social Development, 16 mm, sound, black and white, 16 min. Bloomington, Indiana: Audio-Visual Center, Indiana University (rental fee, $3.90). Analyzes social behavior at various age levels, showing how behavior patterns change as the child grows, and depicting the reasons for these changes.

Social Acceptability, 16 mm, sound, black and white, 20 min. Bloomington, Indiana: Audio-Visual Center, Indiana University (rental fee, $4.65). Portrays a high school girl who fails to be accepted by a popular school clique and indicates the importance of social acceptability for successful adjustment and happiness. Shows also how adults may help the adolescent gain social skills.

8

the self: integration and development

To gain in knowledge of self, one must have the courage to seek it and the humility to accept what one may find.

≡   ARTHUR T. JERSILD

The preceding chapters have presented a number of scientific concepts that help to explain how various physiological and environmental forces—the child's level of energy output, his pattern of physical growth, the quality of his affectional relationships, the learnings passed on to him from the adult culture and the peer group—influence human development and learning. Yet this picture is not complete. From even a casual observation of children and youth, we can see that persons with equally high energy levels do not behave in the same ways and that persons who experience a similar lack of affection respond differently. They respond differently because each of them perceives, interprets, and organizes experience in a unique way.

Thus, each individual's unique organization of the personal meanings arising from his experience emerges as a force in its own right—a force we refer to as *self*. Self is a third set of forces emerging from the interaction of the first two, the organism and the environment. Self is a construct, a useful and convenient abstraction not open to direct observation and analysis. The use of this construct enables us to make inferences about the deeper motives of human behavior.

In this chapter and the next, we will be using the terms *self, personality, self-processes, self-structure,* and *self-concept. Self,* in a sense, is that part of the individual that he consciously recognizes as him*self*—his sense of his own continuing identity and of his relationship to his environment. *Personality,* a broader and more inclusive term, refers to the person's total psychological structure—his abilities, capacities, motives, perceptions, traits, habits, and thoughts. *Self-processes* refer to the organized sequence of activities or operations carried out in the development, change, and maintenance of the self. Included in these are motivation, perception, learning, cognition, and adjustment. *Self-structure* refers to the framework or configuration of a particular individual's complex of motives, perceptions, cognitions, feelings, and values. While self-processes are constantly in flux, self-structure is relatively stable through time. Finally, the *self-concept* is made up of the most highly differentiated perceptions, beliefs, feelings, attitudes, and values which the individual holds of or about himself.

Characteristics of the Self

Self as an emergent process. The human infant does not possess a self at birth but does have the capacities for developing a self. Newborn infants differ in temperament and sensitivity to stimuli, but each's development of an organization of personal meanings takes place gradually as receptors, muscles, brain, and nervous system mature. As these structures mature, enabling the child to distinguish between an increasing array of stimuli, self emerges as a dominant process shaping development and learning.

Uniqueness of self. Individuality and uniqueness of self are revealed in the very different ways each person views and responds to the world. Each of us is different, and this makes the understanding of self both an enigma and a challenge. In responding to this challenge, man's study of self centers in a search for understanding of how and why each individual is different.

Maintenance of organization. The word *organization,* connoting order and stability, is probably the most meaningful and descriptive term in any definition of self. In discussing the concept of homeostasis in Chapters 3 and 4, we noted that maintenance of physiological stability is a characteristic of living things. On the physiological level, an individual perceives minimal changes toward imbalance, such as hunger pangs, as cues for action. Similarly, as Stagner[1] points out, changes in the social environment may function as signals for organic disequilibrium, thereby increasing tension, energy mobilization, and action toward restoration of a social-environment constancy. Thus, behavior that reduces tension and restores homeostatic balance exemplifies the maintenance of self-organization.

---

[1] Ross Stagner, "Homeostasis as a Unifying Concept in Personality Theory," *Psychological Review,* 58 (January 1951), 5–17.

Dynamic process. Maintenance of organization does not imply a static quality, nor does it refer to the restoration of some prior equilibrium. Both the term *homeostasis* and our reference to maintenance of organization connote the continuous activity of adjusting and readjusting to changing conditions.

Stability and change, then, are pervasive qualities of both the physical organism and the self. Although these characteristics seem to refer to opposite or conflicting processes, in the context of the living organism and of human behavior they are complementary and interdependent. The child changes in size and structure as he grows taller and as his tissues and body parts become more differentiated; but he is an organized system at all times—before, during, and following these changes in physical growth and development. Change in self is revealed in the changes in the ways one sees himself and sees the world as he acquires knowledge, skills, and roles and experiences shifts in beliefs, goals, attitudes, and values.

Consciousness and self. Consciousness is in some degree a characteristic of the self, since the term self-concept implies a measure of self-awareness. The nature and origins of consciousness are still very much of an enigma to psychologists, but the term generally refers to a level of subjective awareness.

Freudian psychology distinguishes between conscious, preconscious, and unconscious levels and processes. While self is largely formed by the individual's organizing of personal meanings at a conscious level, some meanings of critical importance to self are present in the psychological structure below the level of consciousness.

Self as an inferred process. Since self is an abstraction, it is neither tangible nor visible. Subjectively, I experience self as my ways of thinking, feeling, and behaving, which relate to the way I perceive the objects and events in my life space. An outside observer's perception of another's self is limited to inferences concerning the kind of unique organization of personal meanings the subject is likely to have in order to have responded the way he did to a given stimulus or situation. Since these inferences are at best only hypotheses, they should be checked against all other data available on the subject.

Representative Theories of Self

Freud and Psychoanalysis

Freud conceived of man as a dynamic system of energies. Self, said Freud, is comprised of three major systems: the id, the ego, and the superego. These three psychological systems continuously interact to produce the individual's behavior. The *id,* the original system from which the ego and the superego gradually evolve, is the source of all psychic energy (*libido*). This energy is expressed as *instincts,* inner excitations that drive the organism. Instincts arise out of the inherited biological nature of the organism and are of two kinds: life instincts, which are concerned with survival and are expressed as tensions related to thirst, hunger, sex, or inactivity; and death instincts, which are expressed as destructive impulses and take the form of aggression. When increases of energy produce uncomfortable states of tension, the id serves to discharge the tension so that the organism moves toward equilibrium at a lower energy level. The principle by which the id operates to reduce tension is called the *pleasure principle:* the avoidance of pain and the pursuit of pleasure.

The *ego* emerges as the organism, seeking to satisfy the impulses of the id, comes to grips with the forces and realities of the external world. The ego is a system of forces which redirects id impulses toward gratifications appropriate to the specific environment or situation. The principle by which the ego prevents discharge of tension until appropriate objects for gratification are available is called the *reality principle:* the adjustment of behavior to the demands of the outside world. The principal role of the ego is to mediate between the instinctual impulses of the organism and the limitations imposed by the surrounding environment. It serves as the executive of the self, deciding which instincts will be satisfied and the manner in which they will be satisfied. Its primary objective is to maintain the life of the individual and to ensure the survival of the species.

When the individual attempts to express and to satisfy id impulses by direct action, he tends to be blocked or restrained by the customs, rules, and values of society. As these rules and values are adopted and internalized by the child, they form the *superego.* The superego is a moral arbiter of conduct; it functions to restrain or to inhibit those basic impulses, especially sex and aggression, which society regards as dangerous. In time, the superego becomes the conscience of the child; internalized controls replace those of parents and society in guiding behavior. A well-developed superego enables the individual to maintain adequate control over id impulses.

When the immediate or direct expressions of libidinal energies are blocked, the resulting frustrations, conflicts, and anxieties are reduced through processes such as identification and displacement. In *identification,* as we noted in Chapter 6, the individual incorporates into his own self features of another person. He learns to reduce tension by modeling his behavior after someone else. In *displacement,* id instincts are redirected toward substitute means or objects of satisfaction, as a child directs anger with his parents towards a sibling or a toy. These and other ways of reducing anxieties, often referred to as *defense mechanisms* or *adjustment patterns,* are described in the next chapter.

Social Theories of Self

With the emergence in the early twentieth century of sociology, anthropology, and social psychology as independent disciplines, man began to be viewed as a product of the culture or society in which he lives. Some social theories of self are based on psychoanalytic concepts, but in general they emphasize the role of social forces rather than biological drives in the development of self.

George Herbert Mead[2] describes self as an object of which one gradually becomes aware as he interacts with others. The child is born with no awareness of self, but as other people respond to him he develops an awareness of self by taking over their responses toward him and responding in like manner toward himself. Mead suggests that each individual has multiple selves, varying according to the situation and to the role expectations of different social groups.

For Karen Horney,[3] anxiety, the feeling of being isolated and helpless in a potentially hostile world, is a primary concept. This anxiety is produced by unwholesome early relationships. As the child attempts to cope with his anxiety, he develops irrational patterns of adjustment—"neurotic needs" for such goal objects as affection, power, exploitation, prestige, achievement, or independence.

According to Erich Fromm,[4] the basic conditions of man's existence pose a fundamental contradiction and a dilemma. Man is both a part of nature and separate from it; he is both an animal and a human being. He has specific needs (relatedness, transcendence, rootedness, identity, and orientation) which define his human condition apart from society. Societal demands that are inconsistent with his nature tend to alienate man both from his human condition and from society and to thwart the satisfaction of his needs. Man can rid himself of feelings of alienation either by uniting himself in productive love and shared work with others or by submitting to authority and conforming to society. By selecting the first alternative, however, man helps to create a society that is better adapted for assisting all persons to become fully human.

According to the theory of Harry Stack Sullivan,[5] the individual does not exist apart from his relations with other people; though heredity and maturation do play a part in shaping the individual, all that is distinctly human about him is the product of social interactions. The study of self, then, is a study not of the individual but of the interpersonal situation.

In an interpersonal self theory such as Sullivan's, the conceptions one develops of himself and of other people in symbolizing interpersonal experience are of vital importance. Personifications of mother and of self—especially "good mother" or "bad mother," "good me" or "bad me"—are crucial. Sullivan also places great stress on the role of the cognitive pro-

---

[2] George Herbert Mead, *Mind, Self and Society* (Chicago: University of Chicago Press, 1934).

[3] Karen Horney, *Neurosis and Human Growth* (New York: W.W. Norton & Co., 1950).

[4] Erich Fromm, *Man for Himself* (New York: Holt, Rinehart and Winston, 1947); *The Sane Society* (New York: Holt, Rinehart, and Winston, 1955).

[5] Harry Stack Sullivan, *The Interpersonal Theory of Psychiatry* (New York: W.W. Norton & Co., 1953).

cesses in self-development, and sees experience as occurring in three modes: prototaxic, parataxic, and syntaxic. At the lowest level, the *prototaxic,* are the raw sensations, images, and feelings which are experienced during the first few months of life and have little connection or meaning. Too much of our thinking, Sullivan believes, is *parataxic* thinking, wherein the individual sees causal relationships between experiences that have nothing to do with one another. Finally, the highest mode of thinking, the *syntaxic,* consists of symbols, such as words or numbers, which have a common meaning to a group of people, thereby enabling them to communicate with one another.

Organismic-Existential Self Theories

The organismic theory of Goldstein[6] emphasizes the unity, integration, consistency, and organization of the normal personality. Lecky[7] conceives of personality as an organization of values that are consistent with one another. Behavior is the individual's attempt to maintain consistency and unity in a changing environment.

Angyal,[8] Maslow,[9] Rogers,[10] and Combs and Snygg[11] postulate that human beings move toward a unity of selfhood (variously referred to as *self-actualization, the fully functioning person,* or *the adequate self*). Maslow believes that personality develops as the individual achieves adequate modes of satisfying successive levels of needs that form a hierarchy from basic physiological needs to self-actualization, the highest level of needs. (See Chapter 3 for a discussion of Maslow's hierarchy of needs.)

Every individual, according to organismic-existentialist self theory, is in continuous interaction with a changing world of experience and responds as a whole to this perceptual field. A portion of the perceptual field becomes differentiated as the self. A knowledge of the individual's perceptual field, especially his self-concept, affords the best vantage point for understanding his behavior. The individual behaves in a manner consistent with his self-concept. Perceptions inconsistent with one's self-organization and self-structure may be perceived as threatening to the self and hence be denied awareness or symbolization or be given distorted symbolization. Psychological adjustment occurs when the individual can assimilate at a symbolic level all experience into a consistent relationship with his concept of self. The well-adjusted individual becomes more understanding and more accepting of others, and he tends to replace his existing value system with a continuing value process.[12]

[6] Kurt Goldstein, *The Organism* (New York: American Book Co., 1939).

[7] Prescott Lecky, *Self-consistency* (New York: Island Press, 1945).

[8] Andras Angyal, *Foundations for a Science of Personality* (New York: Commonwealth Fund, 1941).

[9] Abraham H. Maslow, *Motivation and Personality* (New York: Harper & Row, 1954).

[10] Carl R. Rogers, *Client-Centered Therapy: Its Current Practice, Implications and Theory* (Boston: Houghton Mifflin Co., 1951).

[11] Arthur W. Combs and Donald Snygg, *Individual Behavior* (New York: Harper & Row, 1959).

[12] Rogers.

Processes of Self-Development and Change

Stages of Development

Important to an understanding of self and behavior is a conception of the processes through which the self emerges and changes. The psychoanalytic theorists, beginning with Freud, have given considerable attention to this problem. According to Freud, the self develops in specific stages.[13] The first is the *oral stage*. This stage predominates during the first year of life, when the infant gains erogenous satisfactions from sucking. In the *anal stage* of the second and third years, the child seeks gratification through anal activity and experiences anxieties growing out of taboos associated with toilet training and anal eroticism. In the *phallic stage,* the child's interest is in the sex organs and the pleasures associated with their manipulation. At this stage also, the *Oedipus* and *Electra* complexes appear as the child develops erotic feelings toward the parent of the opposite sex. The phallic stage is followed by a *latency period* in late childhood, wherein impulses tend to be repressed. Puberty ushers in the *genital stage,* during which the individual's interests are centered in other people and objects. This stage marks the emergence of heterosexual relationships and the trend toward the more mature interests and activities of approaching adulthood.

Sullivan[14] identifies six stages of personality in the period from birth to maturity. During the first stage the infant moves from a prototaxic to a parataxic mode of cognition, develops personifications in relation to a good or bad mother, begins to develop a rudimentary self system (the psychological mechanism, organized out of interpersonal experience, for coping with anxiety), differentiates between parts of his own body, and learns to coordinate eye-hand movements. Childhood witnesses the emergence of language, the need for playmates, and further integration of the self system (including the identification of one's sex role, dramatic play, anxiety-producing experiences with people, and the use of sublimation for reducing tension). During the juvenile stage, the child becomes social, learns to accept subordination to authority figures outside the family, and gains an orientation to living through interpersonal relationships that enable him to satisfy his physical, social, and psychological needs. The preadolescent stage marks the beginning of genuine relationships with other people. In the early adolescent stage, heterosexual patterns of activity develop. The late adolescent stage is a period of initiation into the satisfactions and responsibilities associated with mature social living. During successive periods of development, interpersonal relationships are formed with many different persons, language becomes increasingly important as a mode of communication, and the self-

[13] Sigmund Freud, *Collected Papers,* Vol. II (London: The Hogarth Press and the Institute of Psycho-Analysis, 1924), pp. 36–75, 244–49, 269–76.

[14] See note 5.

system becomes stabilized as one develops more effective ways of coping with anxiety and maintaining security.

Erikson's[15] theory of psychosocial development distinguishes eight stages in the life cycle of man. At each stage, according to Erikson, a particular issue or problem is most important.

I. *Infancy*—trust versus mistrust (of self and environment)

II. *Early Childhood*—autonomy versus shame and doubt (seeking autonomy in controlling the environment or having to subordinate one's autonomy to the will of others)

III. *Play Age*—initiative versus guilt (activity, curiosity, and imagination in play may be inconsistent with adult expectations, thereby creating guilt in child)

IV. *School Age*—industry versus inferiority (success or failure in school learning accompanied, respectively, by feelings of adequacy or inadequacy)

V. *Adolescence*—identity versus role diffusion (achieving or failing to achieve a sense of self-identity)

VI. *Young Adulthood*—intimacy versus isolation (achieving or failing to achieve close, security-giving relationships with spouse, children, or friends)

VII. *Adulthood*—generativity versus stagnation (expansion of ego expressed in service of guiding the young or regression toward more self-centered activities which limit development)

VIII. *Maturity*—integrity versus disgust, despair (achieving in one's life and work a self-integrity or experiencing despair and disgust in failing to achieve it)

Allport[16] identifies seven aspects of an evolving sense of self. The first aspect, beginning in infancy, is a *bodily sense of self*. Throughout life our bodily sense of self is the concrete evidence of our continuing existence as persons. Continuity of selfhood is also achieved by a growing sense of *self-identity*, beginning in the second year of life. A year or two later the child's increased control over his environment is accompanied by an increased feeling of *self-esteem* and a need for autonomy. There follows from his contacts in the community and school *an extension of self,* which includes the objects, people, institutions, ideas, beliefs, and values with which he is identified. These and the reflected appraisals of the significant people in his life form a *self-image.* The striving of the child for the mastery of physical and intellectual skills is the hallmark of *self as a rational coper.* Like Erikson, Allport sees adolescence as a search for self-identity, but in addition, for Allport, the adolescent's pursuit of long-range purposes and goals constitutes another

15 Erik H. Erikson, *Childhood and Society* (New York: W. W. Norton & Co., 1950).

16 Gordon W. Allport, *Pattern and Growth of Personality* (New York: Holt, Rinehart and Winston, 1961), pp. 110–138.

dimension in the growing sense of selfhood, a dimension that Allport calls *propriate striving*.

A further examination of the development of self during childhood and adolescence will be found in the discussion of developmental tasks in Chapters 10 and 11.

Motivation

Motivational processes are of central importance in the development of self. That part of another person's self that we can observe is expressed in his consistent patterned responses to various life situations. Motivation, as we noted in Chapter 3, is an internal energy change which arouses and directs behavior toward goals. The relationships of motivational concepts and self are shown in Figure 8.1.[17]

[17] Adapted from an earlier model developed by Glenn C. Dildine. Used by permission.

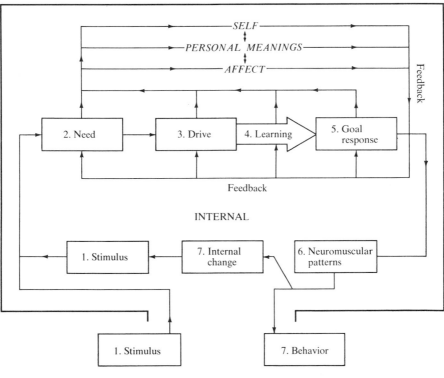

Figure 8.1. A graphical representation of the human behavior cycle (after Dildine).

Motivation begins with (1) a *stimulus,* a pattern of energy discharge from inside or outside the organism which strikes receptor organs, causing a change in energy relationships. This energy change is transmitted from receptors along sensory nerves to higher nerve and brain centers and to the rest of the body. The body condition that triggers this increased activity is experienced as (2) *need,* a disequilibrium or imbalance registered as tension in organs, muscles, neural or cortical tissue, and the organism as a whole. Forces within the organism associated with restoration of balance and maintenance of organization bring about a mobilization of energy that is generally referred to as (3) *drive.*

As the individual searches for, tests, and evaluates possible alternative ways to respond to a drive, he engages in activities which may be subsumed under the general term, (4) *learning.* These activities, like all behavior cycle activities of the brain, the nervous system, and the total organism, are directed toward an appropriate (5) *goal response,* a behavior, decision, or solution which effects a restoration of balance and a reduction of tension. The goal response activates appropriate (6) *neuromuscular patterns,* which translate the goal response into (7) *behavior* to meet the situation.

Self, as the individual's unique dynamic organization of personal meanings, develops and is changed by need, drive, learning, and goal response data. Evaluations of these data as being consistent or inconsistent with one's present organization of personal meanings are expressed as *affect* (feelings and emotions). If these data are consistent with and reinforce one's present organization of personal meanings, the affect experienced is pleasant; if these data are inconsistent with these meanings (that is, threaten self), the affect experienced is unpleasant. On the basis of these evaluations of incoming data, information from the highest centers of control (self) are *fed back* to maintain or modify need, drive, learning, and goal response activities. Feedback from self, for example, will determine the receptor thresholds for various stimuli and hence the degree and intensity of need and resulting drive generated toward a goal response which will restore balance. Likewise, feedback will maintain or modify learning activities of seeking, testing out, evaluating possible alternative goal responses, and selecting the goal response most consistent with self. We should caution the reader that any graphical representation of psychological processes whose descriptions are based largely on inference is at best an approximation of the events that take place and is an oversimplification of the dynamics involved.

The possible uses of this model may be shown in its application to a specific case:

Jim Barnes, a sixteen-year-old high school junior, was a star athlete who made average grades and was popular with his classmates. Jim's father, a prominent physician, had dreams of Jim's entering medicine and joining him in a clinic he had founded. Jim had barely scraped through biology and was presently failing in chemistry and algebra—not only because he lacked aptitude in these subjects but also because he spent most of his time with athletics and in tinkering with things mechanical, especially cars and motor scooters.

The critical blow came when Jim failed his chemistry final at the end of the semester. Mr. Jones, the chemistry instructor, was willing for him to go into second semester chemistry conditionally; but if Jim failed at the end of the year, he would be ineligible for football next fall. The coach, other boys, and the whole school were counting on his playing.

With the help of the high school counselor, Jim saw his alternatives as (a) being tutored in chemistry and algebra to try to pass even though his heart wasn't in the work, (b) dropping his college preparatory subjects over his father's objections and taking shop and mechanical drawing, or (c) following his father's suggestion of transferring to Brookville Prep School, where it was hoped he would be able to improve his scholastic record.

Jim's motivation is reflected in a variety of interrelated needs: his need for self-esteem and recognition as a person and a football player; his need for acceptance by others, including father, coaches, teachers, students, and friends; his need for autonomy and independence; and his need for a sense of achievement. Jim's self reflected the unique organization of personal meanings formed over a lifetime in his relationship with a strong-willed, dominating father, in satisfactions with peers in athletics and work with machines, and in school experiences which provided only a limited sense of achievement. Self not only determined the intensity of each need but also influenced the selection of the most appropriate goal response. Of the three alternatives, Jim finally realized that the substitution of shop courses for academic courses would best fit his needs. This Jim did, even though challenging his father's authority was disquieting.

Perception

Perceptual processes play a central role in the development and adjustment of the self, for it is through perception that meanings are acquired and interaction and intercommunication between organism and environment occur. The term *perception* connotes both a process and a product. It refers to the process of giving structure to stimulation; that is, of ascribing meaning to experience. It also refers to the configuration or pattern of elements produced by the stimulation-structuring process. Like his motivation and self, a person's perceptions may be identified only through inferences drawn from his behavior. We can observe our own percepts, but we cannot know those of another person except by putting ourselves in his place and inferring what he must see, hear, or feel in order to behave in the way he does.

The individual's private world. A study of perception begins with a recognition that each individual lives in a private world of experience. Our perceptions come from us, not from the environment. This idea conflicts with the popular notion that perception is merely the organism's passive, uncritical registering of images formed by environmental stimuli. By now, there appears to be ample evidence, both experimental and empirical, to indicate that the organism is not passive but actively contributes to its own perceptions.

Perception in the objective sense consists of *transactions* between concrete individuals and concrete events.[18] No perception exists independent of a perceiver, and people and objects exist for us only insofar as we perceive them. Nonetheless, we look at people and objects around us with the assumption that they are existing in their own right; and this common-sense view is necessary if we are to communicate with others and carry on our daily activities.

The process by which the things we see, hear, or feel are experienced as outside of ourselves is called *externalization*. Much of our experience has an external orientation, therefore, even though the perceptions of these phenomena occur within the individual. The individual, as we will note, always behaves in accordance with his perceptions, not in accordance with some objective reality that may exist in the external world.

The uniqueness of one's perceptual world, though readily accepted intellectually, is frequently forgotten or ignored in day-to-day encounters. Often, we act as if others all had the same perceptions we do about an object or experience. We feel, for example, that every child wants to work hard in school, or we feel that other nations naturally want our kind of freedom and democracy. We are baffled when we learn that many children see school as a waste of time or that other peoples express disdain for a democracy whose stresses and demands for conformity produce a high incidence of mental illness.

Our perceptions vary in part, then, because of each person's own unique position in space and time and because of his own combination of experiences, needs, and values. Differences in physiological functioning and structure, however, also account for some differences in perception; physiological factors determine the thresholds at which various receptors will be stimulated. For example, while the taste of a weak solution of a chemical substance known as phenylthiocarbamide (PTC) is perceived as intensely bitter by about 70 percent of Americans, the other 30 percent perceive almost no taste at all in the solution.[19]

Culture influences to a considerable degree the meanings we attach to certain stimuli. Responses to Rorschach inkblot card 3 reveal that, typically, Europeans perceive two women quarreling while Moroccans perceive a line of Arab riflemen facing a row of Christian soldiers.[20] Samoans, on the other hand, give a large number of "whole" responses to inkblot cards, seeing

[18] W. H. Ittelson and Hadley Cantril, *Perception: A Transactional Approach* (Garden City, N.Y.: Doubleday and Co., 1954).

[19] L. C. Dunn and T. Dobzansky, *Heredity, Race and Society* (New York: Mentor Books, 1946), p. 8.

[20] M. Bleuer and R. Bleuer, "Rorschach's Ink-blot Tests and Racial Psychology," *Character and Personality*, 4 (1953).

entire blots as maps or animals and seeing the white portions as objects rather than space.[21]

Obviously, then, there is no standard, objective world shared by all persons. However, two or more persons can and often do find similar meanings in the same stimuli or events. People will share common perceptions to the degree that their perceptual fields overlap in time, space, interests, and purposes. This overlap forms the basis for communication and harmonious relationships.

Behavior and perception. Each of us behaves in ways consistent with his own perceptions of reality. This is illustrated by the following anecdote.

> A few years ago Maria, a six-year-old refugee from eastern Europe, was enrolled in an elementary school in the United States. As the class filed out to board the school bus at the end of her first day at school, Maria suddenly screamed and frantically clutched the teacher. The teacher had difficulty in quieting Maria, but eventually learned that Maria was deathly afraid of the yellow bus. It seems that the secret police in her native country had taken her parents away in a yellow bus. Changing Maria's behavior depended upon changing Maria's perception of a yellow bus. Eventually, as she saw the same yellow bus bring her friends and class-mates to school each morning, her terrors and fears subsided.

Similarly, as a member of a minority group perceives that he is accepted, trusted, and valued, he begins to act more openly and naturally rather than defensively or apprehensively. The recognition that people do behave in a manner consistent with their perceptions gives us a new insight into the nature of human development and learning—the insight that there are processes through which people can be helped to modify self-damaging perceptions of reality.[22]

Perception and the self-concept. Among the most relevant and significant perceptions that an individual acquires are his perceptions of himself in various life situations. As we noted earlier, the self-concept is comprised of the highly differentiated perceptions, beliefs, feelings, attitudes, and values that the individual views as characteristic of himself. The self-concept is modified as one incorporates into his self-picture the qualities and traits which the responses and feelings of other people seem to attribute to him.

The individual reveals something of his self-concept in his behavior. Approximations of the child's self-concept may be obtained by inferring how the child must see himself in order to behave as he does. Mike, wearing a big smile after hitting a home run, may be presumed in this situation to see himself in terms of "I can really hit that ball" or "I can come through in the

---

[21] T. H. Cook, "The Application of the Rorschach Test to a Samoan Group," *Rorschach Research Exchange,* 6 (1942), 51–60.

[22] Arthur W. Combs, "Personality Theory and Its Implications for Curriculum Development," in Alexander Frazier, *Learning More about Learning* (Washington, D. C.: Association for Supervision and Curriculum Development, N. E. A., 1959), pp. 5–20.

clutch" or some other appropriate self-picture. Sally, on the other hand, who consistently deprecates her ability by saying, "Li'l ole me, I jus' don't count for much 'cause I can't do anything," may really be saying, in terms of self-concept, "I want people to notice how good I really am."

Not all of the beliefs, qualities, or attributes making up an individual's self-image are of equal value or importance. Mike, for instance, sees himself as, among other things, "a good baseball player" and "a pretty good student." For Mike the first self-percept is of far higher importance than the second, as an observer could tell by noticing that Mike fails to hand in his homework whenever there has been a game the night before. Jerry holds the same two percepts, but, since he is looking forward to a career in engineering, values these percepts in the opposite order.

Self-concept shifts and changes throughout an individual's life; he sees himself, progressively, as a child, an adolescent, a mother or father, a junior member of the firm, the boss, and a grandparent. During childhood and adolescence, the self-concept is particularly susceptible to changes; the individual comes to see himself differently as, for instance, he learns to play a musical instrument and plays in the band, gets the lead in a play, learns to speak French, and becomes popular with the opposite sex. The importance of the teacher's role in the development of his pupils' self-concepts will be discussed later in this chapter.

Selectivity of perception. At any one moment our receptors are being bombarded with many kinds of stimuli. After first responding to the total configuration of these stimuli, we begin to separate out and respond to individual elements of the configuration, a process called *differentiation.* Different people, however, differentiate in different ways. If the same pattern is presented to a number of people, some will focus on one part of it (perceive that part as *figure,* the remaining part as *ground*), and some will focus on a different part. Perception, thus, is *selective.* We perceive whatever is most meaningful and important to us and ignore or give little attention to the less meaningful. Sometimes, however, we may ignore (repress) some elements that are *too* meaningful—so meaningful that they seem painful and threatening.

The defensive aspect of selective perception is shown in a study by Postman, Bruner, and McGinnies.[23] Twenty-five college students were given the Allport-Vernon Scale of Values and then were shown thirty-six value words, presented singly by a tachistoscope at exposures beginning with .01 second. Exposures for each word were increased in steps of .01 second until that value word was correctly recognized. Results of this study showed that high-value words were recognized at shorter time exposures than were low-value words. A subject who scored high in the theoretical-values section of the scale recognized such words as "logical" or "analysis" in .03 second, whereas it might take him .11 second or longer to recognize a word like "reverent," which is associated with religious values. These findings indicate

23 Leo Postman, Jerome S. Bruner, and Elliott McGinnies, "Personal Values as Selective Factors in Perception," *Journal of Abnormal and Social Psychology,* 43 (1948), 142–154.

that people erect barriers against percepts that do not fit or in some way threaten their values and self-concepts.

Perception and the adequate personality. Recently, there has been considerable interest in identifying the qualities of self-development, personal adjustment, and mental health which characterize the adequate personality. A distinguishing characteristic of the adequate personality is the greater clarity, accuracy, and objectivity of his perceptions, in contrast to those of the less adequate person. The adequate personality views himself and others positively. He is able to assess accurately and realistically his strengths and weaknesses and to incorporate these evaluations into his self-picture. The adequate person is also objective and accurate in his perceptions of others. Maslow[24] found that adequate persons, whom he describes as self-actualizing (becoming fully what they are capable of being), were far more likely to perceive people and issues objectively instead of reading into events their own wishes, hopes, fears, anxieties, theories, and beliefs, or those of their cultural group.

The adequate personality is further described as more open to experience than the less adequate person. That is, he is able to accept into awareness a broad range of facts and sense impressions without distorting or rejecting those that are threatening.[25] The adequate person who must drop out of school temporarily, for example, perceives this not as a personal catastrophe, but as an opportunity for clarifying through work experience his vocational and personal goals.

The adequate personality is also less defensive. He accepts failure and disappointment without rationalizing and blaming others. Taylor and Combs,[26] for instance, found that better-adjusted sixth-grade children accepted many more derogatory and unflattering statements as true of themselves than did less well-adjusted children.

Language

The development of self is facilitated by the cognitive processes of remembering, thinking, generalizing, reasoning, imagining, and evaluating. Language is an essential tool in the development of each of these processes. Language enables one to simplify, to abstract, and to generalize from a series of events. This, in turn, enables him to form concepts. By distinguishing between different levels or qualities of performance in solving arithmetic problems, for example, one may develop a concept designating a particular quality of performance and represent that concept by the word "success." This concept may be further generalized to connote a quality of performance (individually defined) in such dissimilar activities as playing golf, rearing children, cooking, and speaking French.

[24] See note 9.
[25] Carl R. Rogers, *On Becoming a Person* (Boston: Houghton Mifflin Co., 1961), pp. 187–188.
[26] Charles Taylor and Arthur W. Combs, "Self-Acceptance and Adjustment," *Journal of Consulting Psychology,* 16 (1952), 89–91.

In the process of abstracting common features from a series of concrete events, the unique character of a specific event is lost. The term "success," for example, does not convey information relative to the difficulty of the task or to how much effort the individual put forth in his successful performance. Abstracting these features would require the forming of additional concepts. The limitations of language for conveying precise, all-inclusive, and universal concepts result in the formation of incomplete or distorted meanings which hamper the development of self. For the slum dweller, the word "policeman" stands for a man to be feared, a man who may arrest you; for the middle-class person, on the other hand, a "policeman" is someone you can call on for help, someone who protects your property. Differences in meanings of words will result in the learning of very different behavior patterns and very different ways of viewing self and the world.

Self emerges and changes as the individual selects and responds to certain stimuli from among the many stimuli that impinge upon his receptor organs. There is considerable evidence suggesting that the selection of stimuli and the organization of behavior patterns bear a close relationship to the structure of the language and the linguistic habits that an individual employs. Bernstein[27] hypothesizes that it is through language structure, even more than content, that values, attitudes, and prejudices are learned. He found that communication in lower-class families leans heavily on the language of bodily contact, gesture, facial expression, and intonation rather than on a complex verbal structure. One characteristic pattern is for the lower-class parent to issue arbitrary commands to the child without giving any reason or explanation. Hess and Shipman[28] cite a hypothetical example of a small child playing noisily among pots and pans on the kitchen floor when the phone rings. The lower-class mother is likely to say simply and imperatively, "Shut up!" while the middle-class mother is more likely to say, "Would you please keep quiet while I answer the phone?" The lower-class child is asked to respond to a simple command, to make a conditioned response. The middle-class child is given the reason why he should make a response (refrain from making noise) and the length of the response. In ways like this, different cultural experiences and patterns of socialization each are linked with a language structure that emphasizes the learning of quite different behavior patterns.

Aspects of the Emergent Self-Structure

Self-structure—the framework or configuration of a particular individual's complex of motives, perceptions, cognitions, feelings, and values—is the product or outcome of self-developmental processes. Self-structure is re-

[27] Basil Bernstein, "Social Class and Linguistic Development: A Theory of Social Learning," in A. H. Halsey, Jean Floud, and C. Arnold Anderson, *Education, Economy, and Society* (New York: Free Press, 1961), pp. 288–314.

[28] Robert D. Hess and Virginia Shipman, "Early Blocks to Children's Learning," *Children,* 12 (September-October 1965), 189–194.

vealed in behavior. One reveals in his behavior the knowledge, skills, and interests he has acquired, the goals he is seeking, the beliefs, values, and attitudes he has adopted, the roles he has learned, and the self-concept he has formed. By interpreting and evaluating the individual's behavior in various life situations, one may describe and assess the status of this person's self-development in relation to each of the aspects of self-structure listed above. Since many of these components of the emergent self-structure, such as concepts, knowledge, skills, attitudes, and values are described in later chapters on learning, we shall not discuss them here. An aspect of self-structure, however, which is particularly relevant to this chapter is the self-concept. We turn now to a discussion of this important dynamic.

The Self-Concept

The *self-concept* is formed as the individual identifies those aspects, qualities, ideas, and things that he regards as "me" or "mine." Basically, the self-concept is made up of a very large number of *percepts*, each of which contains one or more qualities that one ascribes to himself. For example, one may ascribe to himself such qualities as "I am tall," but "I am awkward in games"; "I am pretty," but "I have straight hair." Similarly, one may include in his self-concept percepts of his loving and being loved by family and friends or of his membership in or identification with a culture, subculture, peer group, or other social group.

Each of the percepts one ascribes to himself may have a positive, negative, or neutral value. Thus, the aggregate of attributes, qualities, and abilities one ascribes to himself constitute a hierarchy of personal values. Since the individual behaves in a manner consistent with his self-concept, we would expect his behavior to be determined by his most prized or cherished percept (his highest value). For example, "I am an honest person" is a valued percept in Frank Jones' self-concept. If Frank lies to the teacher to protect a friend, we must conclude that he values more highly self-percepts of "I help my buddies" or "I am not a square" than he does the self-percept "I am an honest person." Behaviors and self-percepts that are inconsistent with the image one holds of himself are threatening and are thus accompanied by emotion and adjustive behavior, topics discussed in the next chapter.

Also included in the self-concept are self-percepts that describe the person as he would like to be. Those qualities, attributes, and roles that the individual does not presently possess but hopes to achieve constitute his *ideal self-concept*. A knowledge of the student's ideal self-concept provides one with clues concerning the direction his behavior is likely to take.

Parents, teachers, and peers strongly influence a young person's self-concept. Many of their views and responses toward him, including the nicknames they give him, become a part of the child's view of himself—a view that often persists over a lifetime. Thus, a teenager who is looked upon and treated by parents, teachers, and peers as a bully or a good sport, as intelligent or dumb, as attractive or homely, as a nice guy or a bad egg, as a cool cat or a square begins to see himself in the roles ascribed to him by others and to behave accordingly. Acceptance and affection at this stage help the individual to form a concept of himself as adequate, secure, well-adjusted, and effective in his relations with others and with the world. The teacher's considerable influence on the student's self-concept is revealed in an excerpt from the case of Jackie.

Jackie is an active, mischievous, twelve-year-old boy who would frequently try things out and test the limits. One day, just before the bell rang, Bob said, "Hey, Mrs. A., somebody's took my money." Mrs. A. said, "Bobby, look in all your pockets and in your desk. You know we don't take things in this class."

Bob looked all around and several boys helped him. The money was gone. He said, "Mrs. A., you saw me put it in my glasses case." Mrs. A. replied, "Bob, somebody's playing a joke on you. Nobody in the fifth grade steals. Now, whoever is teasing Bob, give him his money. It's time for the bell." Jackie reached into his pocket and drew out 65 cents (Bob had lost 75 cents). "Here it is, Bob. I was just teasin' you."

Bob said, "That's only 65 cents, Jackie. Where's the rest of it?" Jackie said, "That's all there was. If you don't believe me you can search me." Mrs. A. told Jackie to stay in a minute after school, but she let him go after discussing catfish for a moment because she was puzzled about what to do.

The issue in this anecdote is not the particular technique used by the teacher in handling the perplexing problem of items reported missing in the classroom. Our interest is rather in the kind and quality of the teacher's response, which showed a deep respect for these children as persons. A different response from Mrs. A. might well have caused these children to see themselves as bad, dishonest, untrustworthy, and thieving. The response Mrs. A. did make in this situation permitted each child to ascribe more positive characteristics to himself and his classmates.

Physical Processes and the Self-Concept

Since self-awareness is first manifested in a bodily sense of self, we might hypothesize that physical processes are an important influence in shaping the self-concept. Several studies have found significant relationships between timing of physical maturation, physical disabilities, body physique, and the self-concept. Mussen and Jones[29] found that early-maturing boys, in contrast to their late-maturing peers, saw themselves as mature, independent, and capable of playing an adult role. Early-maturing girls also reported more

[29] Paul H. Mussen and Mary C. Jones, "Self-conceptions, Motivations, and Inter-personal Attitudes of Late- and Early-maturing Boys," *Child Development* 28 (June 1957), 243–256.

favorable self-concepts, but the differences in personality for early- and late-maturing girls were generally not as marked as those for boys.[30] Physically handicapped children not only see themselves as less adequate physically but also have fewer close friends and are less well-adjusted in comparison with a matched group of non-handicapped children.[31]

In a study of sex differences and body perception, Fisher[32] found that the female has a more definite and stable concept of her body than does the male. The woman perceives her body as related to the fulfillment of her principal life goals, whereas the man is less likely to associate his body attributes with requirements for success and attainment. Consistent with this is the further finding that women reveal stronger feelings of both satisfaction and dissatisfaction with their bodies.[33]

Socialization Processes and the Self-Concept

The self-concept is strongly influenced by one's experiences and socialization as well as by the strength of one's identification with and feelings about his culture. The likelihood that cultural deprivation will communicate a sense of inferiority is clearly shown in studies of the American Negro. The high incidence of unemployment among Negro males and the resultant inability of the Negro father to support his family cause him to see himself as rejected and inferior. The Negro boy's self-picture is unlikely to include high aspirations for achievement when around him he sees men unable to sustain a positive social and economic role. Damage to self-esteem appears to be less severe for Negro girls. Negro girls surpass Negro boys in school achievement, and they reveal greater responsibility for child rearing and greater capacity for keeping a job.[34]

Developmental Changes in the Self-Concept

Numerous studies have described changes in the self-concept at successive maturity levels. Ames[35] notes that during the first two years, the child is primarily egocentric; his sense of self is expressed through obtaining and hoarding objects. By age two and a half, the child's sense of self is strength-

---

[30] Mary C. Jones and Paul H. Mussen, "Self-conceptions, Motivations, and Interpersonal Attitudes of Early- and Late-maturing Girls," *Child Development,* 29 (December 1958), 491–501.

[31] Winifred T. Kinn, *Self-Reports of Physically Handicapped and Non-handicapped Children* (unpublished doctor's dissertation, University of Maryland, 1962).

[32] Seymour Fisher, "Sex Differences in Body Perception," *Psychological Monographs,* 78 (1944), 14.

[33] Paul Secord and Sidney Jourard, "The Appraisal of Body-Cathexis: Body-Cathexis and the Self," *Journal of Consulting Psychology,* 17 (1953), 343–347.

[34] Jean D. Grambs, "The Self-Concept: Basis for Reeducation of Negro Youth," in William C. Kvaraceus, *Negro Self-Concept: Implications for School and Citizenship* (New York: McGraw-Hill Book Co., 1965), pp. 11–51.

[35] Louise Bates Ames, "The Sense of Self of Nursery School Children as Manifested by their Verbal Behavior," *Journal of Genetic Psychology,* 81 (1952), 193–232.

ened in interpersonal relationships, first with the teacher and later with peers, but the focus is still on the acquisition and protection of objects. By age four, the child's excessive boasting and bragging about himself, relatives, and possessions suggest that he is not completely sure of himself and that his sense of self may need strengthening.

In elementary school, the child is striving for a position in his peer group, but he still sees himself as highly dependent upon his parents, particularly for affectional relationships. There is now some growing sense of responsibility and a need to conform to social expectations. At age ten, some interest in the opposite sex is expressed, but few heterosexual relationships are formed.[36] In a study by this writer, fourth- and sixth-grade girls were found to report greater congruence between their self-concepts and their ideal self-concepts than fourth- and sixth-grade boys. During a six-month period in school, however, the self-concepts and ideal self-concepts of both sexes became increasingly more congruent.[37]

Adolescence is marked by an increased stability of the self-concept. In a study by Engel,[38] students reporting positive self-concepts in the tenth grade viewed themselves even more positively when they were retested in the twelfth grade.

Self-Concept and Learning

Learning that effects a positive change in one's self-concept is, perhaps, the most significant learning any of us acquires. For instance, it is not the ability to recognize word symbols as such but the self-percept "I can read" that is most crucial in influencing a pupil's behavior in subsequent reading situations.

The teacher bears a major responsibility for helping students develop positive self-concepts. Staines[39] found that children in a classroom where the teacher helps pupils to clarify their self-concepts and to accept themselves as they are report significantly more positive self-pictures than children taught by a teacher who emphasizes correct answers and the passing of examinations. Children with more favorable self-images see their teachers as expressing positive feelings toward them. The more positive are the children's perceptions of their teacher's feelings toward them, the better is their academic achievement and the more desirable is their classroom behavior as rated by the teachers.[40]

[36] Marjorie B. Creelman, *The C S C Test: Self-Conceptions of Elementary School Children* (unpublished doctor's dissertation, Western Reserve University, 1954).

[37] Hugh V. Perkins, "Factors Influencing Change in Children's Self-Concepts," *Child Development*, 29 (June 1958), 221–230.

[38] Mary Engel, "The Stability of the Self-Concept in Adolescence," *Journal of Abnormal and Social Psychology*, 58 (1959), 211–215.

[39] J. W. Staines, "The Self-Picture as a Factor in the Classroom," *British Journal of Educational Psychology*, 28 (1958), 97–111.

[40] Helen H. Davidson and Gerhard Lang, "Children's Perceptions of their Teachers' Feelings toward Them, Related to Self-Perception, School Achievement, and Behavior," *Journal of Experimental Education*, 29 (1960), 107–118.

Several studies have found positive relationships between self-concept and measures of school achievement. In a study of ninth-grade students, Fink[41] found that underachieving girls feel alienated socially, see themselves as victims of circumstances, and are unable either to accept or to perceive the goals and values of others. Underachieving boys appear to be even more inadequate and immature; they seldom achieve their goals and they complain of powerlessness to improve or to change a situation.

Does one's concept of his general ability or his concepts of his specific abilities exert the greater influence on his academic achievement? Brandt[42] asked sixth- and eleventh-grade students to estimate how well they expected to do, compared to each of their classmates, on each of several academic and physical tasks. The students were then asked to perform these tasks and their estimates were compared with their actual performances. In general, each student's accuracy of self-estimate showed little variation for the different tasks. Brandt therefore concluded that performance is influenced more by one's generalized view of his abilities than by his percepts of his specific abilities. Brookover, Thomas, and Paterson[43] found among seventh-grade students, however, that the specific self-concept relative to a given ability is significantly more accurate than the generalized self-concept of ability in predicting the grade point average of boys in mathematics, social studies, and science. This finding did not hold for girls, except in social studies.

Looking beyond the research evidence, it seems that the self-concept influences a child's learning in at least two ways. First, in order for a child to learn successfully, he must see himself as a learner, as being able to learn. Secondly, one's self-structure—his organization of personal meanings—determines what ideas and facts are relevant for him, and, hence, influences what he will learn. In elaborating the first point, it can be said that one's perception of himself as a learner is probably far more important in influencing his learning performance than is his intelligence, aptitude, or the level of difficulty of the learning material. For many children, early criticisms of their school performance and low grades do much in shaping self-concepts that reflect inadequacy and defeat. They say of themselves, "I never was any good in arithmetic" or "I hate reading." If any of these students is told that he performed well on an intelligence or aptitude test, he may well respond, "There must be some mistake. I never do well on those kinds of tests."

This influence of the self-concept on learning is revealed in an experience reported by Prescott Lecky[44] in which he found that a group of children always made about the same number of spelling mistakes per page of writing, regardless of the difficulty of the material. Since all would be ex-

[41] Martin B. Fink, "Objectification of Data Used in the Underachievement Self-Concept Study," *California Journal of Educational Research,* 13 (May 1962), 105–112.

[42] Richard M. Brandt, "The Accuracy of Self Estimate: A Measure of Self-Concept Reality," *Genetic Psychology Monographs,* 58 (1958), 55–99.

[43] Wilbur B. Brookover, Shailer Thomas, and Ann Paterson, "Self-Concept of Ability and School Achievement," *Sociology of Education,* 37 (Spring 1964), 271–278.

[44] See note 7.

pected to make more errors when given the harder material, the finding that on successive tests each made approximately the same number of errors irrespective of difficulty suggested that each child performed as if he were expected to make a certain number of errors (corresponding to his usual performance) no matter how easy or hard the task was. Lecky wondered whether their test behavior in spelling reflected their perceptions of themselves as spellers and not their actual skill level in spelling. This proved to be the case, for after discussions with a counselor in which feelings about themselves were explored, these children registered a marked increase in their spelling performance even though they had no further work in spelling.

If one is more likely to learn those concepts and skills that are most relevant to his organization of personal meanings, as our second point suggests, this means that how one views himself determines to a considerable extent whether he will learn, what he will learn, and how well he will learn it. Reminding students that Chaucer, quadratic equations, or the history of Greece and Rome are part of our cultural heritage and therefore are important things to be learned may not be enough. These experiences, and others in the school curriculum, should be planned and organized so that each student may gain some personal meaning in the study of each. Thus, a further knowledge of Greek drama may be enhancing to one student, a study of Greek or Roman architecture to another, Greek mythology to another, and perhaps a study of the origin and history of the Olympic Games will be enhancing to a star athlete.

The influence of the pupil's self-concept on his learning performance is revealed in these excerpts from the case of Becky.

Becky is older than any of the other girls in a combination fourth- and fifth-grade class and is one of the larger girls physically. Becky lives in an apartment with mother, sister, and stepfather. The family is Jewish. Following kindergarten, Becky spent one semester in a nonreading group. She was retained in the second grade and during these two years Becky changed schools twice because of moves by the family. After she had finished the third grade she was sent to summer school for strengthening, but she was under the impression she was making up a grade. It was nearly the end of the next semester before she and her family understood her placement. The following June she wanted to go to summer school again. When the teacher explained that she could not send her to a new grade in summer school, Becky lost interest and did not ask any more.

SEPTEMBER 17

The class was organized into three reading groups today. Becky was put into the middle group. When the books were given out the children spent time looking at them and getting acquainted with them. Becky came up to me and said, "This is a fifth-grade book, isn't it?" I replied, "Yes it is, Becky. Doesn't it look interesting? All the stories have been selected to appeal to fifth-grade boys and girls." She relaxed as I talked and said, "I didn't want any fourth-grade book." She returned to her seat smiling and hugging the book.

SEPTEMBER 20

On the basis of the previous week's work, the class was divided into two spelling groups, one an independent spelling group and the other a supervised study group. Becky was put into the latter. As I worked with the group, Becky was sulking. She kept her head down and doodled on her notebook. When I explained that in this group we would learn how to study and to use new words so that we could attack them independently, she sat up quickly and said, "If anyone in this group gets perfect on Friday, can they be put in the other group?" I suggested that it might be wise to work in the group for a steady period to get the full benefit. Getting perfect would mean real progress, but other things would have to be considered. She dropped her head and returned to her doodling.

APRIL 28

We had a very comprehensive test on possessives last Friday. This is a new experience for these children and they reviewed like mad to get ready for it. At the children's request I marked the papers in percentages as in junior high school. Becky made 88 percent, fifth highest in the class. I read the top five names and marks before returning the papers. Becky fairly beamed. She is so proud of her success. The highest mark was 92 percent.

Some of Becky's strongly motivated goals and characteristic adjustment patterns are clearly revealed in these few descriptions of her classroom behavior. She seems to be saying "I am a fifth grader," "I want to make up the grade I had to repeat," "I want to be a good student." Being reassured that she has a fifth-grade book and receiving one of the highest test grades in the room resulted in personal meanings consistent with and enhancing of her self-concept. Her behavior reveals a desire for further learning and achievement, but incidents inconsistent with her self-concept result in apathy, loss of motivation, and little progress with respect to the skills and subjects involved in the incident.

Summary

An understanding of human behavior depends not only upon a knowledge of physical and environmental forces but also upon an understanding of the self, the unique way each person perceives, interprets, and organizes experience. *Self* is defined as a person's unique dynamic organization of the personal meanings arising from his experience.

Self is characterized as an emergent process and as being unique and personal. It is a process in which change takes place while, at the same time, organization is maintained. Much, though not all, of one's knowledge of the activities of the self consists of the inferences one makes about another person's organization of personal meanings. The development of self is facilitated by warm, supportive human relationships with the significant others in one's life.

A brief examination of representative self theories further reveals the abstract and complex nature of the self and makes it evident that self may be viewed from many different vantage points. Freudian theory, which emphasizes the ego's control and redirection of id impulses toward gratifications appropriate to the environment or situation, contrasts with the ideas of social-self theorists such as Sullivan and organismic-existentialist theorists such as Maslow, Rogers, and Combs and Snygg.

The various theories of self-development emphasize the importance of warm interpersonal relationships, the extension of self as the child moves into the broader world, the search for a new sense of self-identity in adolescence, and the seeking of fulfillment in adulthood. The role of motivation in the development of self is shown in the steps of the human behavior cycle. An energy change producing a *stimulus* creates a *need* which activates *drive*. Drive leads to *goal responses* directed toward reducing the drive and satisfying the need.

Perception plays a central role in the development and adjustment of self, for it is through perception that meanings are acquired and interaction between organism and environment occurs. Since each individual lives in a private world of experience, perceptions arise from within the individual and are selective. The *self-concept* emerges as the individual identifies those aspects of his perceptual field that he perceives to be part or characteristic of himself. Selectivity of perception may operate in the defense of self. Adequate personalities, however, are those whose perceptions are more accurate, objective, and realistic and who are more accepting of self and others. Language is the symbolization of meanings, and is thus a fundamental process through which self develops. Language makes possible the development of the processes of reasoning, thinking, and imagining.

From the interaction of self-processes there emerges a *self-structure*— the configuration of a specific individual's complex of motives, perceptions, cognitions, feelings, and values at any given time. The self-structure is revealed in behavior and includes a person's knowledge, skills, interests, goals, beliefs, values, attitudes, and roles.

The *self-concept* is the highest integrative level of the self-structure and is defined as those most highly differentiated perceptions, beliefs, feelings, attitudes, and values which the individual views as part or characteristic of himself. Behavior tends to be consistent with the self-concept and reflects the individual's effort to maintain and enhance the self-concept. The student's self-concept appears to be the most important single factor influencing learning performance—more important than intelligence, aptitude, or difficulty of the material to be learned. Since the self-concept is such a major factor influencing development and learning, the school must assume a prominent role in helping children and youth to develop more adequate self-concepts.

Study Questions

1. Put yourself inside the skin of the student you are studying or of someone else you know well. In the first person singular, write a paragraph describing the self-concept of this person. How would you check the validity of the statements you have made?

2. Try to recall your self-picture at ages five, ten, and fifteen and contrast these with your present self-image. In what ways has your self-concept changed? Is your present self-concept similar or dissimilar to your ideal self-concept of a few years ago? If so, in what ways?

3. Bill Rodgers has been a top student for as long as his teachers and classmates can remember. Yet, prior to every important test, Bill becomes anxious and says he is afraid he will not do well on the exam. He is tense until his test is returned. Upon seeing the high grade on his paper, he exclaims, "Whew, I sure was lucky." How would you account for the seeming inconsistency between Bill's self-concept and his experiences of success on examinations? How might Bill's teachers, parents, and friends help him to modify his concept of his abilities?

4. A dynamic theory of personality, such as Freud's, tends to explain a person's behavior in terms of past experiences and the interactions of inner and outer forces, whereas phenomenological theorists, such as Combs and Snygg and Rogers, state that behavior is determined by the subject's structuring of his perceptual field at that moment. Evaluate the strengths and weaknesses of each position. Which theory is likely to be more useful to educators in helping them to understand the behavior and development of children and youth?

5. How would the phenomenological or perceptual self theorists explain the role of unconscious processes in self-development? How may one's behavior be influenced by motives or meanings of which he has no conscious awareness? Explain.

Suggested Readings

Arthur W. Combs and Donald Snygg. *Individual Behavior.* Revised Edition. New York: Harper & Row, 1959. The authors restate and elaborate the basic postulates of a phenomenological system presented in the first edition of this book. The implications of these principles for education and therapy are examined. Considerable discussion is devoted to the concept of the adequate personality.

Arthur W. Combs. Chairman. *Perceiving, Behaving, Becoming.* Washington: Association for Supervision and Curriculum Development, 1962. The contributions of four phenomenological-existentialist self theorists, Earl Kelley, Carl Rogers, A. H. Maslow, and Arthur Combs, are presented and the implications of their ideas for teaching and learning are explored. The characteristics of the adequate person and the process of becoming are given special emphasis.

Calvin S. Hall and Gardner Lindzey. *Theories of Personality.* New York: John Wiley, 1957. Presents a brief survey and discussion of major psychological personality theories and developments from Freud to existentialism. The last chapter contrasts and synthesizes major ideas from the several theories.

Don E. Hamachek. Editor. *The Self in Growth, Teaching, and Learning.* Englewood Cliffs, New Jersey: Prentice-Hall, 1965. A collection of readings contributed by contemporary self theorists and researchers. The papers grouped in relation to self theory, perceptual processes, formation and development of self, growth processes, teaching, learning, and self-understanding. Particular emphasis is placed upon phenomenological self theory, and a broad range of studies investigating various correlates of the self-concept are reported.

Prescott Lecky. *Self-Consistency: A Theory of Personality.* New York: Island Press, 1945. A brief work which focuses on self as the unifying concept in psychology. Personality is conceived of as an organization of values consistent with one another. The central goal of personality, according to Lecky, is the achievement of a unified, self-consistent organization.

Clark E. Moustakas. *The Self: Explorations in Personal Growth.* New York: Harper & Row, 1956. A collection of papers by writers from many disciplines and many schools of psychiatric, psychological, and philosophic thought. The papers portray the fundamental unity of personality and present a framework for understanding healthy behavior. The emphasis of these writings is on knowing, exploring, and actualizing the self.

Films

Eye of the Beholder, 16 mm, sound, black and white, 25 min. Bloomington, Indiana: Audio-Visual Center, Indiana University (rental fee, $5.90). Shows that no two people see the same thing or situation in the same way. Demonstrates this concept by showing how, through a progression of events, a number of people come to view an artist, Michael Gerard, in quite different ways. The episode culminates with a beautiful girl lying on the studio couch with a red-stained knife at her side. Film shows how people react differently to the artist in terms of how they have been conditioned to view his actions.

Focus on Behavior, 1. *The Conscience of a Child,* 16 mm, sound, black and white, 29 min. Bloomington, Indiana: Audio-Visual Center, Indiana University (rental fee, $5.40). In the laboratory, Dr. Robert Sears shows some of the ways in which psychologists study the growth and development of personality and emotional behavior in children. Focuses on the interaction between parental behavior and attitudes and the emotional development of children.

This is Robert: A Study of Personality Growth in a Preschool Child, 16 mm, sound, black and white, 81 mim. Bloomington, Indiana: Audio-Visual Center, Indiana University (rental fee, $10.40). Traces the development of an aggressive, "difficult," yet appealing child from nursery school to his first year in public school. Robert is confused by adult pressures and his violent and haphazard aggression is seen as a strong, defensive counterattack on the whole world. His mother's steadying support and his teacher's firm, consistent, affectionate treatment enable him to make an outwardly smooth adjustment to school.

9

the self: emotion and adjustment

Emotions, then, are among the most basic, deeply rooted, and biologically useful forms of behavior. They are the modes of physiological integration through which we meet relatively critical situations.

≡   DANIEL A. PRESCOTT

As the individual develops and changes, he also seeks to achieve and to maintain a stable self. Stability of self is manifested in a consistency in one's behavior in response to similar stimuli or situations, in a stability through time of one's self-concept, interests, goals, attitudes, and values, and in a tendency to perceive and to distort events in ways consistent with one's self-concept and views of the world.

Although the process of achieving and maintaining a stable self (self-adjustment) is discussed in a separate chapter, self-adjustment and self-development are in reality complementary processes. Since self-development involves the organizing and reorganizing of personal meanings, a stable self is both a prerequisite to and an outcome of increased self-development. As we noted in the preceding chapter, a student must see himself as able to read if he is to progress in reading. Increased reading achievement, in turn, reinforces and increases the stability of the self-percept, "I can read."

One's evaluation of the personal meaning of an event

or experience is manifested in feelings and emotions. The psychological term *affect* will be used to refer to feeling states aroused by internal and external events. In perceiving and responding to events and situations, the individual evaluates each in terms of its relevance to or its consistency or inconsistency with his view of himself and the world. Events that have little relevance for self arouse little feeling. Events that are consistent with one's self-concept and view of the world evoke pleasant affect (relaxed musculature, minimum tension, etc.). Events that are inconsistent with one's perceptions of self and the world evoke unpleasant affect (discomfort, tension, fear, or anxiety). In this chapter the term *affect* will be used interchangeably with the term *emotion*. Although emotion is a more familiar term, its several meanings makes it less precise for describing the kinds of feeling responses people reveal in evaluating the meaning of events for the maintenance and enhancement of their self-concept and views of the world.

Events that are inconsistent with one's view of self and the world threaten the maintenance of a stable self. Threat to self, however, not only produces tension and anxiety but also prompts the individual to seek to resolve the conflict between self and the world, and so to reduce the threat. *Adjustive behavior* is behavior whose purpose is to reduce threat. Reducing threat, in turn, facilitates the maintenance of a stable self. Emotion and adjustive behavior together constitute the *self-adjustive processes,* which operate to restore and to maintain self-stability and self-consistency. In this chapter, we shall examine these interrelated processes, emotion and adjustment, in greater detail.

Physiology and Affective Experience

Physiological Basis of Emotion

Emotion or *affect* may be defined as the physiological changes which occur in response to the psychological meaning of an event or situation. These physiological changes are initiated by the autonomic nervous system. Under conditions of threat, the thoracolumbar (sympathetic) segment of the autonomic nervous system stimulates marked physiological changes in receptors, blood, muscles, and viscera. These changes include an increase in respiration rate, an increase in pulse rate, a rise in blood pressure, the secretion of adrenalin and release of additional sugar into the blood stream, the release of additional red blood cells into circulation by contraction of the spleen, and an increase in the tension of striped muscles. Other physiological changes occurring at the same time include the dilation of pupils, an increase in perspiration, and a decrease in gastrointestinal activity. These internal changes are reflected in such external reactions as a flushed face, a tense body, and a trembling hand.

The physiological changes associated with heightened affect follow the principle of homeostasis introduced in Chapter 4. The temporary imbalances produced by these physiological changes serve to prepare the organism for actions directed toward restoring and maintaining stability of organism and self. They prepare the organism for "fight or flight,"[1] for the mobilization of body energy resources required to meet the perceived threat. Although this energy mobilization facilitates the organism's making a maximum response in situations which endanger physical life, there is often less opportunity for expending this mobilized energy in vigorous physical movements when psychological threats such as loss of self-esteem or loss of security are involved. The constraints the situation may place upon active responses of skeletal muscles are experienced as tension. As noted earlier, the individual seeks to reduce tension by various modes of adjustment.

Affect may be experienced at any one of four levels of intensity: (1) feeling, (2) mild emotion, (3) strong emotion, and (4) disintegrative emotion.[2] The intensity of affect depends upon the degree of threat involved. Feeling and mild emotion, in general, create a state of motivation which facilitates learning and the optimum functioning of the organism. Strong emotion is manifested in the marked physiological changes described above and the mobilization of energy to meet the threat. Disintegrative emotion is manifested in hysteria, shock, and loss of control of body functions—responses evoked in crises involving great danger or destruction, such as fire, flood, vehicle collision, or war.

Affect may be either pleasant or unpleasant, but in both cases the physiological changes produced are similar. The changes associated with pleasant emotion, however, are usually of shorter duration, since pleasant events (which are perceived as need-fulfilling and consistent with self-concept) are followed by tension reduction and the restoration of physiological and psychological stability. Since the present chapter focuses upon emotions and adjustive behavior evoked in response to threat, the discussion which follows will examine various manifestations of unpleasant affect and the events and situations that arouse them.

Disabling Effects of Stress

The debilitating and disabling effects on the organism of strong, unpleasant emotion continued over long periods of time are well known to clinicians and to those who have studied the effects on animal behavior of experimentally created neuroses. While the gap between animal and human behavior is very wide, the bodily changes occurring in animals and humans under stress are similar. Experiments with animals in stressful situations have, therefore, increased our understanding of the effects of stress on human behavior and adjustment.

[1] Walter B. Cannon, *Bodily Changes in Pain, Hunger, Fear and Rage* (New York: Appleton-Century-Crofts, 1929).
[2] Daniel A. Prescott, *Emotion and the Educative Process* (Washington: American Council on Education, 1938), pp. 10–48.

Masserman[3] describes the behavior of cats who were subjected repeatedly to a physically harmless but "psychically traumatic" stimulus consisting of a mild air blast across the snout or a pulsating shock through the paw. Eventually, the cats developed aberrant responses very much like those manifested in human neuroses. They became "irrationally" fearful of harmless lights, sounds, closed spaces, air currents, and vibrations. In addition to manifesting the physiological changes characteristic of strong emotion, these animals developed gastrointestinal disorders, recurrent asthma, persistent salivation, and sexual impotence. The epileptic-type seizures and muscular rigidities of some of the animals resembled the hysteria and catatonia of humans. These physiological and behavioral responses tended to decrease only after the animals were given a three to twelve months' rest in a favorable environment and were exposed to other types of "therapeutic" treatment.

Other experiments with animals have produced evidence relating emotional stress to increased secretion of stomach acid and the appearance of ulcers. Many people believe that the hard-driving "executive type" person is particularly susceptible to ulcers because of the stress of decision making and the other pressures of his job. Brady,[4] in a series of experiments with monkeys, sought to ascertain whether emotional stress of the type that executives experience does, indeed, produce ulcers. In these experiments, two monkeys, yoked together in restraining chairs, received periodic electric shocks. One monkey, the "executive" monkey, could prevent shocks to himself and his partner by pressing a lever fifteen to twenty times a minute. It was found that long strenuous periods when the animal was in danger of being shocked did not produce ulcers. Rather, it was a schedule of six hours of shock (which could be prevented by continuously pressing the lever) followed by six hours of no shock (shock apparatus turned off) that produced ulcers in the executive monkey. The significant increase in stomach acidity began when the shocking apparatus was turned off, and it increased to a peak several hours later, when the animal presumably was resting. Thus, sustained periods of great stress are not as likely to produce ulcers as an alternation of periods of imminent threat and periods of potential threat, wherein the individual remains tense in anticipation of possible danger.

In another study of the physiological effects of stress, Selye[5] identified distinct physiological changes (which he calls "alarm reactions") that occur when the body is exposed to tissue injury or psychological threat. In studies of animals subjected to stress, he found three characteristic alarm reactions: (1) enlargement of the adrenal cortex, (2) shrinking of the thymus, spleen, and all lymphatic structures, and (3) formation of deep ulcers in the lining of the stomach and duodenum. But these alarm reactions are only the first

---

[3] Jules H. Masserman, "Experimental Neuroses," *Scientific American,* 182 (March 1950), 38–43.

[4] Joseph V. Brady, "Ulcers in Executive Monkeys," *Scientific American,* 199 (October 1958), 3–6.

[5] Hans Selye, *The Stress of Life* (New York: McGraw-Hill Book Co., 1956).

stage of the body's struggle against stress. If stress continues, a second stage, called the "stage of resistance," follows. In this stage, body organs and functions should return to normal as the body adapts to the stressful situation. If the body's responses fail to effect an adaptation to stress in the second stage, a third stage, called the "stage of exhaustion," begins. Here, a repetition of the initial alarm reactions signal a critical weakening of body defenses which, if not arrested, foreshadows collapse and eventual death. Selye calls this three-phase struggle of the body against stress the *general adaptation syndrome* (GAS).

The studies of Masserman, Brady, and Selye show that emotion serves as an efficient alarm system warning the organism of actual or impending danger or threat. If, however, the alarm continues to ring for too long, it produces organic damage to the system it is supposed to protect.

Stress may produce many kinds of organic damage. Psychosomatic medicine has found links between stress and cases of allergies, asthma, gastrointestinal disturbances, hypertension, heart disease, eczema, sexual impotency, infertility, diabetes, and tuberculosis. Certain types of emotional responses and patterns of adjustment appear to be linked to particular types of diseases or disabilities. A competitive, aggressive person suffers from hypertension, migraine headaches, heart trouble, or arthritis more frequently than a person who is not competitive or aggressive. Persons who bottle up their feelings and do not relate easily to others have higher incidences of ulcers, diarrhea, colitis, chronic fatigue, and asthma.[6] Knowledge of such general relationships may be useful in helping some patients, but the uniqueness of each person's organism and psyche usually requires that a detailed study and analysis be made of the patient's life. Only in this way can the sources of stress be identified and the manifestations of stress be treated.

Some Kinds and Qualities of Affective Experience

Fear and Anxiety

Fear and anxiety are feelings of apprehension, pain, or tension that one experiences in facing a real or imagined threat. Although the physiological and behavioral manifestations of fear and anxiety are often quite similar, the feelings themselves differ in ways related to the meaning, source, and duration of the particular threatening experience.

Fear is an affective state produced by threats that are specific, observable, objective, rational, and localized. Examples of fear reactions are the nonswimmer's apprehension of deep water, the marginal worker's worry when he learns of a cutback in production, and the sense of panic aroused in anyone when a fire, flood, tornado, menacing gunman, or careening car poses

---

[6] Franz Alexander, *Psychosomatic Medicine* (New York: W. W. Norton & Co., 1950), pp. 54–80.

a threat to life and limb. Fear is a strong emotion produced by threats that are viewed as real and legitimate by the objective observer as well as by the person experiencing the threat.

Anxiety is a more diffuse feeling of apprehension concerning objects or events that are less specific and less easily identified. Anxiety is often subjective and irrational and is more likely to involve unconscious factors. Because of their nonspecific, diffuse nature, anxieties are generally more chronic, pervasive, and persistent than fears.

A basic form of anxiety is that which is aroused in persons who are uncertain of their own self-worth. As noted in Chapter 5, such persons may remain aloof from others, or they may be cold and hostile. However, anxiety reflecting a sense of unworthiness or rejection may also manifest itself in oversolicitousness and possessiveness, as the rejected one seeks to establish an exclusive friendship tie with another.

The anxious person is more likely than the less-anxious person to see unlikely and remote dangers or catastrophes as real and imminent. A mother becomes anxious when her child does not return home at the expected hour and imagines that the worst has befallen him. Some good students become unrealistically anxious prior to every examination. A high mark relieves their anxieties only until the next examination is announced.

One should not conclude, however, that anxiety is synonymous with abnormality or mental illness. On the contrary, anxiety is experienced by everyone in some degree and thus is a part of normal behavior. That is, it is normal to feel anxious when a threat is real, and anxious behavior is normal when it is appropriate to the degree of threat present. Thus, a mother's concern for the welfare of a critically sick child is a normal anxiety, but a hypochondriac's long list of pains and complaints reflects a neurotic anxiety.

A further distinction between normal and neurotic anxiety is that normal anxiety is generally relieved when the threat is removed. Neurotic anxiety, on the other hand, tends to persist in spite of the removal of the threat. The mother's anxiety is relieved when her child recovers, but the person with imagined ills continues to complain about his pains no matter how many doctors treat him or how many operations he has.

Frustration

Frustration is an unpleasant affect or an internal tension state aroused by prolonged blocking or thwarting of satisfaction of a need or of achievement of a goal. The tension associated with frustration is more disturbing and painful than the initial tension of an unsatisfied need, because continued failure to overcome the barrier tends to intensify the initial tension. These differences in tension states are important, since behavior that follows continued blocking is different from behavior that follows the initial blocking of a need. The anger and resentment of a member of a minority group who, though qualified, has time and again been refused employment is quite different from the disappointment of another man, not a member of a minority group, who has failed to be appointed to a position of higher pay and responsibility.

Dollard and his associates[7] hypothesized that frustration is characteristically followed by aggressive behavior. Support for this frustration-aggression hypothesis comes from studies of children's responses to frustration in the classroom and at home. Preschool children who experienced eight consecutive repetitions of a mildly frustrating situation responded with increased aggressiveness between the first four and last four experiences of the situation.[8] Children and adolescents become frustrated and respond aggressively when they experience rejection or restrictive and autocratic patterns of child training by one or both parents.[9]

People differ considerably in their capacities for tolerating frustration, and these differences reflect differences in self. Differences in student responses to varying degrees of frustration were revealed in a study by Maier.[10] A group of college students were asked to choose between two cards and to indicate their choice by turning a knob to open the door on which the card was mounted. If the subject chose incorrectly, the door would not open and he received a slight electric shock. Subjects were instructed to try to find a basis for choosing between the cards. By prearranging the punishment, varying degrees of frustration were introduced into the experiment, so that different students failed in the task 75, 50, or 25 per cent of the time. Results of this study revealed that people do differ in the degree to which they become frustrated by the same event, that they respond differently to frustration, and that these responses are related to other personality characteristics. The more frustrating was the situation, the greater was the proportion of students who used stereotyped behavior and the greater was their difficulty in learning later discrimination tasks.

A common source of frustration is the blocking that frequently occurs during the course of almost any learning experience. Where the problem or skill to be mastered is appropriate to the individual's capacities, the frustration experienced is often short-lived. Frustration diminishes as the student gains fresh insight with the help of a teacher or peer or from his own further study or analysis of the problem. Mild, temporary frustration, then, often motivates a student to expend further efforts toward achieving a successful performance.

With continued failure, however, the picture becomes quite different.

[7] John Dollard, L. W. Doob, Neal E. Miller, O. Hobart Mowrer, Robert R. Sears, C. S. Ford, Carl I. Hovland, and R. T. Sollenberger, *Frustration and Aggression* (New Haven: Yale University Press, 1939).

[8] Nancy B. Otis and Boyd R. McCandless, "Responses to Repeated Frustrations of Young Children Differentiated according to Need Area," *Journal of Abnormal and Social Psychology* 50 (1955), 349–353.

[9] W. McCord, Joan McCord, and A. Howard, "Familial Correlates of Aggression in Non-delinquent Male Children," *Journal of Abnormal and Social Psychology* 62 (1961), 79–93; A. Bandura and R. H. Walters, *Adolescent Aggression* (New York: Ronald Press, 1959).

[10] N. R. F. Maier, *Frustration: The Study of Behavior without a Goal* (New York: McGraw-Hill Book Co., 1949), pp. 77–122.

When failure follows failure, frustration persists and deepens. Such experiences of continued failure inevitably lead to a modification of the learner's self-concept; he begins to express through his behavior a self-image of "I am dumb" or "I am no good." After a change in self-concept from "adequate" to "inadequate," new experiences of failure prove less threatening and are less frustrating because they are more nearly consistent with the student's revised opinion of himself. In terms of the learning process, however, a downward revision of self-concept is not completely satisfactory, since seeing himself as inadequate constitutes a further block to a student's learning.

Depression

The term *depression* describes a state of inactivity, a feeling of being drained of emotion, and a sense of powerlessness to influence the situation. The characteristic physiological responses associated with depression include lowered pulse rate and blood pressure, slow and irregular breathing, and a loss of appetite. These responses reflect the temporary dominance of the parasympathetic nervous system and have the effect of depressing body activity and change. Depression is most frequently associated with the despair and grief felt when one has lost a family member or a dear friend or when he has witnessed a great tragedy or catastrophe. Normally, persons experiencing depression regain their spontaneity and reestablish their former routines and their responsiveness to others after a few days or weeks of rest and emotional support by family and friends. Depression which recurs or extends over long periods of time, however, is a symptom of personality disturbance and requires professional treatment.

Fear, anxiety, frustration, and depression are characteristic types of unpleasant affective experience. If we are to understand the individual, however, we must become sensitive to the characteristic ways he expresses his feelings and emotions. It is this topic to which we now turn.

Patterns of Emotional Response

Observing the specific ways one expresses unpleasant feelings and emotions provides us with important clues for understanding his behavior and adjustment. Since the term *emotion* refers to the physiological changes that occur in response to threat or frustration, each person's mode of expressing his emotions will be influenced by differences in sensory and neural thresholds and by differences in experience, maturation, and learning. While each person's modes of emotional response are unique, we may identify general patterns of affective behavior which people reveal in coping with threat and frustration.

Physiological changes marking the arousal of emotion frequently affect the face, mouth, eyes, and neck. The flushing of face and neck, the prominence of large veins, and the curling and quivering of lips are all evidences of strong unpleasant emotion. Other evidences of emotional stress are the set jaw, the clenched fist, and the stiffening of muscles of the face and body. As noted earlier, frequent or prolonged "emergency" responses—heightened pulse rate, blood pressure, or stomach secretion of acid—may result in psychosomatic ailments, such as hypertension or ulcers. When the threat or frustration is diminished, the reduction of tension is reflected in a relaxation of muscles that may be expressed in smiling, laughing, greater expressiveness, and freer body movement.

It is especially important for the observer to describe in specific objective terms the emotional responses of the person he is studying. The following description of Craig's behavior provides us with a picture of some of the characteristic ways this sixteen-year-old boy responds to threat.

Craig sat slumped in his seat with feet sprawled out in front of him. As Miss Thomas conducted the review for the grammar test, Craig idly tapped his pencil and gazed out of the window with no change in facial expression. A messenger from the office brought a note which Miss Thomas handed to Craig. As he read the note, Craig flushed deeply, turned quickly, and looked directly at Larry with flashing eyes, lips firmly pressed together, and his fist clenched. When Miss Thomas suggested that Craig better go see what the office wanted, Craig struggled to his feet and walked unsteadily and trembling toward the door. His brows were knit, his face was very red, and as he left the room he glowered at Larry and muttered, "You! You! I'll get even with you if it is the last thing I do."

This description tells us Craig's way of expressing strong unpleasant emotion, but gives no clear picture of the events that precipitated his change in affective behavior. If we are to understand Craig, we must relate his mode of expressing his emotions with the situations or events that aroused those emotions. In the next section, we shall describe characteristic types of situations that evoke unpleasant affect and threaten self.

Situations That Threaten Self

Since one's perceptions are always somewhat different from those of other people who witness the same event, the particular situations that threaten self (and hence are emotion-producing) and the degree of threat inherent in such situations are unique for each individual. We might expect that events involving physical danger, such as fire, flood, or war, would be equally threatening to all persons exposed to the danger. However, even in the face of such clear-cut dangers, the intensity of the threat and the affect it arouses are likely to be different for each individual involved. Some will become hysterical; others will remain calm. Since the sources of threat are different for each person, it is not possible to catalog all of the situations that may threaten self. Instead, we shall identify general situations that pose a threat to most people.

The situations most likely to pose a threat to most people are those where physical flight is impossible, where there is a strong anticipation of punishment, where there is no opportunity to make a rewarding response, or where there is actual or imminent loss of emotional support.[11]

Threats to personal safety where physical flight is impossible are experienced by combat units in warfare and by persons in a burning building or a sinking ship. The anxiety of the student caught stealing or cheating may also reflect the futility of "escape." Persons who commit indiscretions or violate laws or mores often experience continuing anxiety caused by the threat of punishment, whether in the form of imprisonment or in the form of loss of acceptance, power, prestige, influence, or esteem. Indeed, this anxiety may become so great that the embezzler, adulterer, thief, or murderer may surrender or confess in order to gain relief. Anxiety arising from a lack of opportunity to make a rewarding response occurs when a student is torn between withholding or fabricating information to protect a peer and losing by this action the acceptance and goodwill of an adult whose respect he values. This example is also illustrative of the fourth type of emotion-producing situation, the actual or imminent loss of emotional support.

Our understanding of emotional behavior may be increased by identifying the sources of threat faced by children and youth at successive maturity levels.

Sources of Threat in Infancy and Early Childhood

The needs and developmental tasks of the infant are related to growth, physiological functioning, and a sense of security. Situations that produce distress for the infant include hunger, digestive discomfort, fatigue, illness, restriction of physical activities, and deprivation of human contacts and affectional relationships. Beginning at eighteen months, the child experiences increased socialization pressures, and these confront him with many new situations having the potential to produce unpleasant affect. Chief among these situations are learning to use language, to control eliminative functions, to walk and to master other motor skills, and to accept and satisfy a broad range of cultural expectations. Failure, difficulty, or other unpleasant experiences arising from the attempt to master these developmental tasks can transform them into situations of threat.

Since young children are very self-centered, conflicts arising between self and cultural expectations are likely to be particularly threatening for them. The kindergarten and primary-grade child is expected to relate and adjust to persons, groups, and institutions outside of the family. Having to conform to the school's rules and expectations thwarts his desires for activity and inde-

[11] N. Cameron and A. Margaret, *Behavior Pathology* (Boston: Houghton Mifflin Co., 1951).

pendence. The six-year-old playing on the jungle gym expresses annoyance when the bell sounds as a signal to return to the classroom. The eight-year-old becomes upset when his peers exclude him from their game because of his refusal to give others a turn.

As children continue through school, they face the growing expectations of parents and teachers regarding the mastery of a succession of school learning tasks. Failure of the student in any area of school learning is a potential threat and may arouse unpleasant emotion. But emotion evoked in learning situations is not necessarily undesirable. Emotion may have a facilitating effect on development and learning. Mild emotion, or strong emotion of limited duration, often impels the individual to make an optimal effort to perform the task at hand. Emotion of this type is manifested in the physiological imbalance, drive, and arousal that constitute motivation. Such an imbalance or mild tension state is experienced by a student who, for instance, perceives that he cannot do arithmetic or play ball as well as his peers, but believes that it is important for him to strive to equal his peers in these areas and is confident that he can equal his peers.

Stronger emotion of longer duration, however, can jeopardize learning. If, for example, a lack of success in reading is prolonged, the negative feelings aroused in the child can cause emotional disturbances which, in turn, can further interfere with reading performance.[12] Ephron,[13] in treating children and young adults who had reading problems, found that emotional problems, rather than poor reading skills and habits, were invariably responsible for the poor reading performance. Frequently, through counseling and psychotherapy, poor readers were able to resolve personal conflicts and to improve reading performance even though they received no special instruction in the skills and mechanics of reading.

Studies of anxiety and school achievement show that children with higher anxiety have lower mental ages and score lower in school achievement.[14] Underachieving boys reveal feelings of inferiority, are less able to express negative feelings, and are more anxious about expressing physical aggression than are achieving boys.[15] Shaw and Grubb,[16] however, found that bright male underachievers expressed considerably more hostility toward others than did male achievers.

Anxiety among elementary school children has been studied intensively by Sarason and his associates.[17] Their investigations show that the testing

[12] A. F. Grau, "The Emotional World of the Non-Achiever," *Journal of the American Optometric Association,* 28 (1957), 523–531.

[13] B. K. Ephron, *Emotional Difficulties in Reading* (New York: Julian Press, 1953).

[14] Boyd R. McCandless and A. Casteneda, "Anxiety in Children, School Achievement, and Intelligence," *Child Development,* 27 (1956), 379–382; Seymour B. Sarason, Kenneth S. Davidson, Frederick F. Lighthall, Richard R. Waite, and Britton K. Ruebush, *Anxiety in Elementary School Children* (New York: John Wiley, 1960).

[15] Barbara Kimball, "Case Studies in Educational Failure during Adolescence," *American Journal of Orthopsychiatry,* 23 (1953), 406–415.

[16] M. C. Shaw and J. Grubb, "Hostility and Able High School Underachievers," *Counseling Psychology,* 5 (1958), 263–266.

[17] See note 14, Sarason et al.

situation—an almost universal experience in our culture—begins to induce anxiety in students long before they reach high school or college. Sarason and his coworkers developed a Test Anxiety Questionnaire and a General Anxiety Questionnaire and used them to obtain indirect measures of children's anxieties. The Test Anxiety Questionnaire asked children to answer "Yes" or "No" to such questions as "Do you worry when the teacher says that she is going to ask you questions to find out how much you know?" and "Do you worry more about school than other children?"

The General Anxiety Questionnaire asked such questions as "When you are away from home, do you worry about what might be happening at home?" and "Do you sometimes get the feeling that something bad is going to happen to you?"

Sarason found that most elementary school children of high intelligence and high achievement have low test anxiety. He also found that from grade two to grade five, teachers' ratings of a child's anxiety become increasingly *less* accurate in predicting the child's performance on IQ and achievement tests, while the child's own self-estimate of his anxiety becomes increasingly *more* accurate in predicting his performance. Highly anxious boys appear academically less adequate, respond less well to the task at hand, and show greater insecurity in relationships with the teacher than do less-anxious boys. The similarities in the behavior of low-anxious and high-anxious girls in Sarason's studies suggest that in our culture it may be more difficult for boys than for girls to admit that they are sometimes anxious. Sarason's findings consistently favor the low-anxious child. The child with low anxiety is more effective in his school performance, has fewer and less intense conflicts, and is better prepared and better able to cope with problems of emotional development.

Sources of Threat in Adolescence and Adulthood

Any situation that the adolescent perceives as a threat to his feelings of security and adequacy, his acceptance by his own sex, his attractiveness to the opposite sex, or his chances for future vocational success is likely to arouse unpleasant emotion. Situations that are particularly disturbing are those wherein the young person sees himself as possessing an inappropriate physique, appearance, or pattern of growth; a lack of game or social skills; inadequate finances; or a lack of close friends and supportive adults. Restrictions on the adolescent's independence also produce feelings of threat. Lack of success in dating, choosing a life mate, or preparing for and becoming established in a vocation are still further sources of threat for adolescents and young adults.

Situations that arouse unpleasant emotion in adults are those that frustrate the satisfaction of one or more of the human needs described earlier. Situations that most frequently evoke strong, unpleasant affect are those that threaten one's view of the world or his view of himself, including his hopes and aspirations for the future. Experiencing disappointment in love, failing in one's vocational goal, becoming estranged from family or friends, identifying oneself with the failures or problems of family or friends, failing in one's responsibilities as a parent, being unable to provide adequately for one's family, or failing to hold a steady job or to progress in one's vocation are all sources of potential threat for most adults. Similarly, the person who values peace, human brotherhood, and compassion for and tolerance of others will feel anxious and threatened in a world that appears hostile, cruel, cynical, or rejecting. In short, perceptions that are inconsistent with one's views of himself or his views of the world are sources of threat and arouse unpleasant emotion.

The affective state brought on by threat or frustration is manifested in heightened tension or drive which impels the individual to take action toward reducing the tension and restoring equilibrium. As noted earlier, responses made in an effort to reduce tension are called *adjustive behaviors*. It is this important topic to which we now turn our attention.

Adjusting to Threat

One generally uses adjustive behaviors that have in the past proven effective in reducing tension and restoring equilibrium. Thus, the learning of adjustive behaviors conforms to reinforcement theory, which states that behaviors that persist and become habits are those associated with a reduction of drive or tension.

In order to understand other people's adjustive behavior, we must be able to make accurate inferences concerning the ways they see themselves and the world. Adjustive behaviors, for example, which appear to us to be self-defeating, irrational, or incomprehensible, are often seen by the person himself as the only appropriate way he can behave in the situation. Thus, while we may identify general patterns of adjustive behavior, we must remember that each person's adjustive behavior is likely to be a unique variation of a general adjustment pattern. In the following pages we shall describe briefly characteristic types of adjustive behavior.

Adjustment Patterns

Aggression. The purpose of an aggressive act is to remove, control, injure, or destroy a source of frustration or threat. The child's earliest efforts to deal with frustration and threat usually involve direct physical action. The infant who is frustrated by an empty bottle or by being put to bed will often cry and flail his arms in anger. The slightly older child, left at home while his mother goes shopping, may run after his mother or lie down, kick, and cry. Young children learn that grabbing, pushing, hitting, or biting are ways of gaining or retaining a treasured toy. Later, as they develop language skills and a growing vocabulary, children turn to verbal types of aggression, such as name-calling, tattling and teasing. In school, a child may respond aggressively to the teacher's demands by refusing to obey, making faces, or using disrespectful language.

The term *aggression,* however, refers not only to acts of hostility or destruction, but also to efforts to dominate, manipulate, or gain possession of a person, group, or object. The leader who manipulates or controls his followers, party, or organization and the parent who dominates or coerces his child are both using forms of aggression to satisfy their needs and attain their ends. Organized groups such as labor unions, political parties, corporations, or governments may also attempt to manipulate or control the actions of individuals or other groups.

Aggression may be directed toward its source or toward a substitute for that source. Aggression directed toward a substitute, a person or thing totally unrelated to the frustrating event itself, is called *displacement*. This adjustive pattern is frequently used by a child or adult who perceives that an attack on the authority responsible for his frustration is too dangerous. In displacement, aggression is directed toward an innocent victim, as the following anecdote reveals.

Phil returned from the office after lunch today with knitted brows and a downcast face. Bobby, a small boy who is popular with all the children, was standing at the window watching the construction men working on the new wing of the school. As he went to his seat Phil gave Bobby a shove and sent him sprawling to the floor. Phil said angrily, "Why don't you get out of the way?"

When I tried to interest Phil in our social studies assignment, he turned his back on me and said, "No, I won't do it." Later I learned that Mr. Jenkins, the principal, had removed Phil from the safety patrol because of his involvement in a fight that had taken place after school.

Repression. A familiar way of dealing with unpleasant thoughts or feelings is to remove them from consciousness by making oneself believe they do not exist. This adjustive behavior is called *repression*. Repression, a key concept in Freudian psychology, is the act of submerging into one's unconscious certain painful, disquieting, or dangerous thoughts, desires, or conflicts. The adolescent, in response to the warnings of adults, tries to put out of mind disturbing feelings and thoughts about sex. When the conversation turns to recent attacks on women in the neighborhood, Mary says angrily, "Let's talk about something more pleasant." As a war crisis deepens, people go on about their daily activities, not daring to talk or think about events that could disrupt their lives.

All of us repress certain thoughts because not thinking about them reduces our anxieties. But when repression is used by an individual to deal with a deep-seated unresolved conflict, he creates for himself a serious emotional problem, a problem reflected in slips of the tongue which reveal that repression is not complete, in disproportionate effort required to maintain the repression, and in behavior distortions which hamper social relationships and the satisfaction of other needs.[18]

Use of repression is revealed in the following report of a series of counseling interviews with Karen.

In the initial interview, Karen reiterated how fond she was of her mother. She recounted experiences of their going shopping, attending concerts and plays, and taking a trip to Europe together. By the fifth interview, the picture of mother domination of Karen became quite clear. Her mother disapproved of her friends and discouraged her from having dates. In subsequent interviews, Karen's feelings of hostility toward her mother, previously repressed, became increasingly apparent.

Aspects of repression may also be observed in some of the other adjustive behaviors described below, including sublimation, rationalization, and fantasy.

Substitution. When goals are blocked and needs remain unsatisfied, the individual frequently varies his behavior or alters his goals. Adjustment by *substitution* occurs when the individual finds a new behavior or goal to be equally or more satisfying than the original behavior or goal. Thus, the boy whose ambition to become a star athlete is blocked by poor coordination or small size works hard and becomes sports editor of the school newspaper. Through this substitute activity, he satisfies his needs for self-esteem and for identification with sports by writing stories of games, interviewing players, and reporting sports activities. Another student, whose goal of social success has eluded him, may substitute the goal of academic success.

A special type of substitution is *sublimation,* an adjustment pattern in which behavior approved of by society is substituted for behavior which society would disapprove of. Frequently, sublimation tactics are employed to control expressions of sexual or aggressive drives. Many women sublimate their sex drives through church or community activities or in vocations which emphasize service to others, such as nursing, teaching, and social work. Many men sublimate their aggressive drives through participation in contact sports, such as football, boxing, hockey, and wrestling.

Whether a new goal is an adequate substitute for the initial goal depends on the individual's self-organization (his patterns of needs, motives, and values). One coed vying for selection as homecoming queen may easily accept as a substitute being no more than a member of the queen's court, while another coed may accept nothing less than being selected as the queen herself. In general, substitute goals are seldom as satisfying to achieve as the original goal. This lack of complete satisfaction is revealed in the tension one feels and expresses even after substitution has been accomplished.

[18] N. Cameron, *The Psychology of Behavior Disorders* (Boston: Houghton Mifflin Co., 1947), pp. 178–181.

Projection. A common adjustment pattern used by many individuals, especially young children, is projection. In *projection,* one attributes to other persons or groups one's own feelings, attitudes, or motives as a way of disowning them in himself. Usually, therefore, it is one's socially disapproved or forbidden behaviors or motives that are attributed to others. Freddie, who says Jimmie doesn't play fair and cheats, may be ascribing to others characteristics he wishes to disown in himself. Tommy, who was severely chastised for playing in the creek, later told his parents about a bad little boy he saw playing in the creek.

Projection is a common adjustive pattern used by all of us and is not likely to cause difficulty unless it involves a critical aspect of the self-concept.[19] Seeing others as worthy but oneself as unworthy would be one example of self-damaging projection. One minimizes the damaging effects of projection when his responses reflect not only his own perceptions but also the perceptions of others.

Rationalization. An adjustment pattern common in our culture is rationalization. *Rationalization* is giving to oneself and others socially acceptable explanations in place of the real reasons for one's behavior. This pattern is one a child begins to learn at an early age. Giving adequate explanations for one's behavior is expected in our culture, and the child soon learns that he may escape punishment if the motives he reveals in explaining his behavior are acceptable ones.

It takes time, however, for children to learn what constitutes a socially acceptable explanation for their behavior. Thus, three-year-old Susan's explanation that the prized figurine lying in pieces at her feet "slid off the mantel" may bring an inward smile to the disinterested observer, but as a rationalization it is unlikely to be convincing either to the observer or to Susan's mother. As they mature, children become more discriminating in selecting explanations for their behavior.

In rationalization, the individual, consciously or unconsciously, selects from among two or more plausible alternatives the explanation which is most consistent with his self-concept. There must be a valid basis for the explanation in order for the rationalization to be believed and accepted. Of a different nature is *prevarication,* the use of deception and falsehood when no objectively valid basis for the individual's explanation exists. Strong cultural disapproval of prevarication is communicated to children at an early age. Because of this strong disapproval and the penalties associated with prevarication, most persons use it sparingly, and, when they use it, they justify its use as the lesser evil in the situation.

The use of rationalization is usually not harmful, since accurate, valid accounts of one's behavior are usually unnecessary and since rationalization often does help a person to maintain his self-esteem. However, when one uses rationalization almost exclusively as an adjustment pattern, or when his

[19] Roger W. Heyns, *The Psychology of Personal Adjustment* (New York: Holt, Rinehart and Winston, 1958), pp. 62–63.

rationalizations are inconsistent or lack validity, then the delusions created interfere with adjustment.

Withdrawal. Withdrawal is an adjustment pattern that may manifest itself in a variety of ways. There is physical withdrawal, the running away from a problem or threatening situation, which may be observed in adults as well as in children. The child refuses to continue playing the game when he can't get his own way; the adolescent drops out of school or leaves home if conflicts with teachers or parents continue unresolved; the adult resigns his job or withdraws from a club, association, or church as a protest against policies or conditions he cannot accept.

Another type of withdrawal is *insulation,* wherein the individual makes himself inaccessible to others. This type of adjustment may be observed in the student who says nothing and does not participate in class activities. Some adults may insulate themselves by having telephones with unlisted numbers. All of us feel the need at times to insulate ourselves from too much stimulation so that we may have some privacy and time alone to think. However, too much insulation cuts the individual off from interaction with others, and interaction is important for personal development and adjustment.

Still another manifestation of withdrawal is *noncommunication.* This type of adjustment is being used by a student whose response to the teacher's question is to answer "I don't know" or to look at the floor and say nothing. It is also being used by political leaders who respond to reporters' questions with "No comment" and by witnesses before Congressional committees who invoke the Fifth Amendment. The following anecdote illustrates the use of aggression and noncommunication by Harold, age seven.

DECEMBER 9

As the teacher came into the room after 2 o'clock recess she was greeted by an uproar in the cloakroom. Midafternoon recess was just over and the children were hanging up their hats and coats in the cloakroom and coming into the room. Most of the children were already inside, but Harold stood in the middle of the cloakroom surrounded by three children, who were shouting, "You did so!" "Where is my hat?" "Get it down, Harold!" Harold had taken the hats of these children and had thrown them on a very high locker. The teacher was greeted with "Harold threw our hats up!" "We can't get them." The three children were asked to go inside.

When the teacher and Harold were alone the teacher said, "Well, Harold, what are you going to do about it? You have started something now. How are you going to finish it?" There was no answer from Harold. He stood still and looked down. After a little wait the teacher said, "Hadn't you better think of a way to get them down?" Harold tried first with a small chair. Then he got the teacher's chair. Still he couldn't reach the hats. After a few minutes the teacher said, "What can you do now?" No answer from Harold. "Perhaps the other boys and girls can help you to decide." Without a word, Harold got the window stick. He climbed up on the chair and with the stick got the hats down and gave them to the children. The teacher said, "Do you think it was worth all of that trouble?"

Harold said softly, "I don't know" and looked at the floor.

Fantasy. Another type of withdrawal is *fantasy,* wherein the individual seeks to reduce tensions by daydreaming, by creating in his imagination a situation which is less threatening and more comforting than real life. The young child pretends he is a horse or a dog; the homely girl dreams of parties where she is the most beautiful of all the beautiful women present; the boy with few athletic skills dreams of becoming a hero by scoring the winning touchdown against his school's bitterest rival. Fantasy expressed in telling tall tales or in make-believe dramatic play is engaged in by most young children and is quite normal. But fantasy may become a harmful adjustment pattern when a person at any age uses it to avoid or to insulate himself from a threatening situation rather than to face the situation and deal with it openly and objectively.

Regression. When a habitual method of solving a problem proves ineffective, one frequently turns to another method proven effective in the past in solving a similar problem. *Regression* is a pattern of adjustment wherein the individual responds to frustration or threat in ways that were appropriate or effective at an earlier stage of his development. Regression in young children responding to threat may take the form of thumb-sucking, temper tantrums, clinging to mother, rebelliousness, or aggressiveness. The use of regression by adolescents may manifest itself in sulking or having temper tantrums in response to disagreements with adults, in prolonged dependence upon parents for difficult personal decisions, or in the use of various forms of physical or verbal aggression in conflicts with peers. Examples of regressive behavior in adults are the young wife's return to mother after a marital quarrel and the blaming of others for one's own shortcomings and faults.

When the usual adjustive patterns prove ineffective, regression to earlier behaviors is normal and inevitable. Less mature forms of adjustment, however, are seldom as effective or as satisfying as adjustive patterns that have been acquired at a later stage of development. One who makes extensive use of regression is often perceived and treated by others as immature.

Identification. In earlier chapters, we discussed the importance of identification in the establishment of affectional ties and the internalization of cultural patterns and values. Identification, however, is also a process of adjustment. In adjustment through *identification,* the individual reduces tension by attributing to himself "the achievements, characteristics, status, and possessions of other persons or groups."[20] Identifying with a person or group more powerful or successful than oneself is an effective way of coping

[20] Cameron, p. 156.

with threat. The five-year-old is using identification when he says to his tormentor, "My daddy can beat up your daddy." A teenager in conflict with his parents is using identification when he turns to his peers for comfort and support.

One may also adjust to threat or conflict through negative identification with the oppressors or the majority group. A few inmates in concentration camps under Hitler adjusted to torture and incarceration by treating fellow inmates as brutally as did their guards. Members of a minority group adopt the same standards or bases (such as color, mores, or habits) by which they are discriminated against when they, in turn, discriminate against other minority groups. Identification is a pattern of adjustment extensively used by persons in weak or subordinate positions, and sometimes its use is to the detriment of others.

Modifying self-concept. Another way of adjusting to threat is to change one's perceptions of self and the world so that they are more consistent with the reality one has experienced. The high-achieving high school student who does less well in college, the popular student who loses a school election, or the healthy person who suddenly develops a chronic physical impairment may all reduce the tension evoked by the disturbing event by modifying their self-concepts. However, since self is a stable, consistent organization of personal meanings, it is not always feasible or satisfactory to modify one's perceptions of self and the world. Maintenance of self requires a measure of self-consistency. We must be ourselves; we cannot be all things to all people or all things in every situation. Thus, while modifying one's self-concept in response to some threats is an effective adjustive behavior, it is a behavior that cannot be used as a response to every threat.

We noted earlier that the perceptions of psychologically healthy, adequate people are more objective, realistic, and accurate, and that compared to those of less healthy people, psychologically healthy people are more "open" to experience (that is, they are less likely to distort what they perceive). Such individuals are best equipped to adjust to threat by modifying their perceptions of self and the world. They are able to reduce their anxieties by admitting their guilt and atoning for their deeds. This is shown in the following ancedote from the case of Cheryl, age nine.

OCTOBER 3

As the hostess for the week prepared to dismiss the room at 3:15, I took my post at the door of our room. I noticed Sue was crying as she came toward the door. I asked her what was the matter. Sue said, "All the kids are making fun of me. I missed jumping the rope last period and had to take an end. They said I cheated in holding the rope for others to jump as I was mad because I had missed in jumping the rope." I asked, "Who said you cheated, Sue?" She replied through her tears, "Cheryl."

Since Cheryl hadn't been dismissed, I asked her to stay a few minutes after school along with Sue. Cheryl burst into tears and said, "I'm just plain guilty, Mrs. M. I said things I didn't mean. I don't know why I did." I thanked Cheryl for admitting her guilt and assured her that sometimes everyone says things that they are sorry for later. I said, "Let's just forget all about it. Always try to remember that everyone has feelings, and let's not forget it." After I dismissed the girls, I glanced out of the window and saw the two girls going down the sidewalk with their arms around each other talking and laughing.

Criteria for Evaluating Adjustment Patterns

Most individuals have a variety of adjustment patterns available for reducing tension and maintaining self-organization. Our daily experience reveals, however, that some adjustive behaviors are more appropriate or more effective than others for coping with threat in a given situation. The effectiveness of a specific adjustment pattern in a given situation may be evaluated in relation to the following criteria.

1. Does the individual's use of this adjustment pattern result in a reduction of tension?
2. Is the pattern employed appropriate to the situation and to the individual's age, sex, and culture?
3. Does this individual have a variety of adjustment patterns that he can use?
4. Do the adjustment patterns he uses enable him to maintain contact with reality?

Obviously, if the function of an adjustment pattern is to defend the self against threat and anxiety, its effectiveness will be judged initially in terms of how well it performs that function. We have noted, for example, that such adjustive behaviors as withdrawal, fantasy, and insulation are likely to be relatively ineffective, because these patterns tend not to cope with threat or anxiety but to postpone coping with them until a later time. Any adjustment pattern is ineffective to the degree that it leaves conflicts unresolved and thus capable of creating further tension in a later situation.

Adjustive behaviors that are not appropriate to the situation or to one's age, sex, or culture are ineffective because their use is accompanied by social disapproval which produces further anxiety and tension. Thus, overt agression is generally a less effective adjustment pattern for persons of middle-class culture than for members of other culture groups; it is also less effective for adults than for young children and less effective for women than for men. Use of humor to reduce tension may be clearly inappropriate, and therefore ineffective, in situations requiring dignity and reverence. Prevarication is an inappropriate adjustment pattern in most situations.

If, in order to be effective, adjustive behavior must be appropriate to the situation, it is apparent that one must develop a large repertoire of adjustment patterns. This repertoire may be thought of as a "defense in depth." If the first line of defense is breached, there are other lines of defense to fall back on.

Finally, since behavior and development have meaning only in the context of a reality that is shared by other people, one's mode of adjustment should also assist one in maintaining contact with that reality. Living in a fantasy world, regressing toward a less mature adjustment pattern, and repressing or distorting sensory data all tend to disassociate an individual from reality. Exclusive use of these patterns is symptomatic of deepening maladjustment and poor mental health.

The School's Role in Minimizing Threat

Accepting Emotion

The emotion one experiences and the modes of adjustment he has available to respond to threat are vital resources which assist him in maintaining his self-organization. Emotion and adjustment, therefore, should be viewed as assets rather than liabilities. This positive view contrasts with the contemporary attitude that expressing emotions is dangerous or is a sign of weakness. The general public tends to admire the individual who appears cool and unperturbed under fire, who reveals no evidence of strong emotions in physically or psychologically threatening situations. It is possible, however, that such an individual is doing himself damage. There is considerable evidence that people who repress, deny, or distort their feelings hamper their own self-adjustment.

If the school accepts the idea that it is both normal and necessary for children and youth to express emotion and to adjust to threat, then principals and teachers will be better able to help students to understand and to cope with their own emotions and adjustive behavior and those of other people. Recognizing that forbidding a child to express anger or hostility may cause him to repress those feelings or to resort to more damaging or less satisfactory modes of adjustment, the understanding teacher will accept the student's feelings and encourage him to express them in ways appropriate to the situation and to the student's age, culture, and self-concept. The child's progress in development and learning depends as much or more upon the teacher's skill in helping him to learn satisfying and appropriate ways of coping with threat as it does upon the teacher's skill in teaching him reading or arithmetic.

Establishing a Climate of Psychological Safety

The teacher who accepts students and their feelings has taken an important step toward creating a psychologically safe climate conducive to learning. As Rogers[21] points out, conditions of psychological safety and freedom encourage creative behavior. Rogers describes a climate of psychological safety as one in which the individual is accepted as a person of unconditional worth, external evaluation is avoided, and empathic understanding is promoted.

In a climate in which one is accepted as a person of unconditional worth, he knows that whether he feels angry, sad, happy, or indignant, his feelings will be accepted. In such a climate, both teacher and students are free to be themselves.

In a climate in which external evaluation is absent, teachers and students are free to make mistakes without feeling threatened or defensive and without fearing punishment or loss of prestige. Students come to accept their mistakes as a normal and inevitable part of learning; the teacher comes to feel safe in answering "I don't know" to questions for which he lacks information or competence to answer. When the learning climate does not provide psychological safety, students do not take chances; they hold back and do not explore ideas for fear their statements will cause them to appear less intelligent or less able than their classmates. The importance of a psychologically safe climate for facilitating learning is emphasized by Haggard: "The best way to produce 'clear thinkers' is to help children develop into anxiety-free, emotionally healthy individuals who also are trained to master a variety of intellectual tasks."[22]

In a climate of psychological safety, the relationships between teacher and children and among the children themselves are characterized by empathy and understanding. Teacher and pupils learn to accept each other's foibles, shortcomings, irritating habits, and ill-tempered outbursts and grow in their sensitivity to each other's acts of thoughtfulness, interest, and concern. Each will accept and respond appropriately to the other's retort, "I've got problems today. Don't bug me!"

Discipline

The term discipline is derived from the word "disciple," one who follows a leader. The idea of the leader who exerts control "by enforcing obedience and order" is one of the traditional meanings of the word discipline. Other meanings of the term include "training which corrects, molds, strengthens, and perfects"; "punishment"; and "a system of rules affecting conduct and action." These traditional views of discipline are based upon the concept that the human being and his development and learning must be carefully guided, supervised and controlled. This conception further implies that without this guidance, supervision, and control the young person is unlikely to learn the

[21] Carl R. Rogers, "Toward a Theory of Creativity," in Harold H. Anderson, ed., *Creativity and Its Cultivation* (New York: Harper & Row, 1959), pp. 69–82.

[22] Ernest A. Haggard, "Socialization, Personality and Achievement in Gifted Children," *School Review*, Winter Issue (1957), 409.

rules of conduct and action essential to his becoming a mature, effective adult.

Traditional views of discipline applied to the classroom imply that teacher control of student behavior is necessary and desirable for promoting learning. Unless firm control by the teacher is established and is continuously enforced, it is assumed that students are likely to be unruly, disrespectful, mischievous, or obstinate. Failure of the teacher and pupils to maintain discipline results in control of the classroom becoming a contest (and sometimes a battle) between teacher and students. Such a contest is inimical to effective learning, for this type of control creates a restricting, threatening, and uncertain psychological climate which discourages and inhibits free, open, and thoughtful exploration and expression of ideas.

Our discussion of the teacher's role in creating a psychologically safe classroom climate emphasizes a very different view of the human being and a correspondingly different view of discipline. This view of the human being postulates that all of us have inner potentialities, capabilities, and motives for developing, learning, and becoming productive, thoughtful, sensitive, and compassionate human beings. We do not have to be coerced, controlled, or forced into a mold that reflects someone else's conception of what each of us should be like. Rather, each of us is capable of moving in positive directions toward growing and becoming. Positive growing and becoming is most likely to be achieved in a psychologically safe climate characterized by mutual, genuine, empathic acceptance, which affords opportunities for free, open, and thoughtful expression. Thus, discipline, as redefined, is the task of helping students to utilize their abilities, energies, and talents in ways that promote their development and learning.

Continued evidences of tension and unresolved conflicts in the classroom are inimical to the development of a psychologically safe climate and a growth-oriented discipline. Students need help in clarifying and accepting the feelings aroused by disappointments, threats, and frustrations. The sensitive, empathic teacher is accepting of the student and his feelings. This teacher will not dismiss the feelings of concern of the bright but anxious student with the comment "You have nothing to worry about." Rather, he will help the student examine his feelings and the factors that may contribute to his anxiety, thereby assisting him to gain new insights and increased self-understanding.

If the teacher is successful in communicating a genuine, empathic acceptance of the student and his feelings, the student senses, "Here is someone who is concerned and understands how anxious I feel about tests and not being able to satisfy my parents." When the student senses that someone really does care and understand how he feels, his anxieties subside and his negative feelings tend to be replaced by more positive ones. As the student is encouraged to express his feelings, they become clarified. He understands why he feels this way, and his self-acceptance increases as the teacher communicates to him that it is all right to feel this way. Once the student has accepted and clarified his feelings, his anxieties diminish, and he is ready to plan and to take effective action in dealing with the sources of the anxieties.

The qualities of a psychologically safe climate reflect this newer conception of discipline. As students accept and clarify their feelings, they become free to pursue goals that promote the development, learning, and self-enhancement of themselves and others. Through these cooperative endeavors, students grow in self-discipline, a quality that characterizes the maturing human being. Persons guided by an increasing sense of *self-discipline* assume increased personal responsibility and self-direction for engaging in activities and acting in ways that enhance the development and learning of themselves and others.

This newer view of discipline is exemplified in one teacher's response to Tom, a seventh grader:

SEPTEMBER 11

I was giving a diagnostic test in arithmetic. While helping a boy at the next table I heard a commotion and looked over to see Tom bang his desk with both hands until his knuckles were red, tear up his paper, and dash over to the window saying, "I just won't do it."

His face was very red. I waited a few moments for him to cool down, went over to him and asked him quietly if I could help him. "Nobody can" was his reply. I went over to his table with him, sat down, and got him to work several problems. Most of them were not correct. We went over them to find the cause of the mistakes. When I asked if he knew his tables he started to cry. "It's just no use," he said. "I want to do it, but I can't." I told him if he wanted to we could lick the "can't" together.

SEPTEMBER 12

I made a multiplication chart for Tom before school, using very large numbers with red numbers for a guide. He seemed quite pleased and thanked me. Later in the day, after we had been working on arithmetic problems for about fifteen minutes I noticed Tom was getting upset so I asked him if he would help me out by making charts like his for several others having difficulty. He worked on them for the rest of the period and handed me twelve neat copies as he was leaving for P.E. He came back and said, "You know, that was fun."

A teacher holding a traditional view of classroom discipline would probably have silenced or punished Tom for disturbing the class with his outbursts. Such a response would have aggravated a situation that had already produced strong unpleasant emotion for Tom. Tom's teacher, identifying with Tom's goal of increasing his skill in arithmetic ("If you want to, we can lick the 'can't' together.") utilized a more positive approach. Each time Tom's anxiety was aroused by difficulties in solving an arithmetic problem, the teacher wisely suggested a meaningful alternative activity. This reduced Tom's anxiety, yet was a step toward the goal of improving his arithmetic skills.

Summary

As the individual develops and changes, he seeks to achieve and to maintain a stable self. Stability of self is manifested in a consistency of behavior, a stability of self-concept, and a tendency to perceive and to distort events in ways consistent with self-concept and view of the world.

Emotion or *affect* is defined as the complex of physiological changes that occur in response to the meaning of an event or situation for the maintenance and enhancement of self. The effect of these physiological changes is to mobilize the body's energy resources to meet the perceived threat. Physiological manifestations of tension and stress serve as an alarm, warning the organism of actual or impending danger or threat. In humans, certain emotional responses and patterns of adjustment have been linked to particular diseases and disabilities. Although knowledge of these relationships may be useful in helping a patient, the uniqueness of each person's organism and psyche requires that a detailed study be made of the individual's life.

Fear is a strong emotion related to sources of threat that are viewed as real or legitimate, while *anxiety* tends to be a more diffuse feeling of apprehension, a less specific and less easily identified feeling. *Frustration* is an unpleasant affect or an internal tension state aroused by prolonged blocking or thwarting of a need or of achievement of a goal. There is considerable evidence to support the hypothesis that frustration is characteristically followed by aggressive behavior. A common source of frustration is the blocking that occurs during most learning experiences, especially those involving the learning of a complex skill or the solving of a complex problem. *Depression* is a less frequently encountered emotional experience wherein one feels drained of emotion and powerless to influence the situation. Observing the specific ways one expresses unpleasant feelings and emotions provides us with important clues for understanding his behavior and adjustment.

Since one's perceptions are always somewhat different from those of other people who witness the same event, the situations that threaten self will also be different for each individual. An understanding of emotional behavior may be increased by identifying the sources of threat faced by children and youth at successive maturity levels. Although emotion evoked in learning situations is not necessarily undesirable, learning difficulties can cause emotional disturbances, and these disturbances can interfere with learning performance.

Responses made in an effort to reduce tension are called *adjustive behaviors*. One generally uses adjustive behaviors that have in the past proven effective in reducing tension and restoring equilibrium. Although general patterns of adjustive behavior may be identified, the particular adjustive behavior one uses is likely to be a unique variation of a general adjustment pattern. Principal types of adjustive behavior include *aggression, repression, substitution, sublimation, projection, rationalization, withdrawal, fantasy, regression, identification,* and *modification of one's self-concept.* The effectiveness of an adjustment pattern may be evaluated in terms of its success in defending the self by reducing threat and anxiety, in terms of its appropriateness to one's level of maturity, sex, culture, and situation, and in terms of its compatibility with reality.

Since emotion and adjustment are vital resources that assist one in maintaining and preserving self-organization, they should be viewed as assets rather than as liabilities. The understanding teacher accepts the student and his need to express his feelings, though he may not condone adjustive behavior that is clearly inappropriate to a particular situation. The teacher who accepts students and their feelings has taken an important step toward creating a psychologically safe climate, the climate most conducive to and facilitative of students' learning. Rogers describes a psychologically safe climate as one in which the individual is accepted as a person of unconditional worth, external evaluation is avoided, and empathic understanding is promoted.

The qualities of a psychologically safe classroom climate reflect a new view of the human being and a new view of discipline. In this new view of discipline, all persons are seen as having inner potentialities, capabilities, and motives for developing, learning, and becoming productive, thoughtful, sensitive, and compassionate human beings. *Discipline,* therefore, as redefined, is the task of helping students to utilize their abilities, energies, and talents in ways that promote their development and learning. As children and youth assume increased personal responsibility and self-direction, they manifest an increasing sense of *self-discipline,* a quality that characterizes the maturing human being.

Study Questions

1. If maintenance and preservation of self is a high-priority need, how would you explain some persons' voluntarily risking death by mountain climbing, deep sea diving, or parachuting?

2. In the excerpts on pages 127–129, what situations produce unpleasant emotion for Jane? How does she register emotion in the situations and what adjustive behaviors does she use? Put yourself in Jane's place and write down some of the self-referent statements of the self-concept she is trying to defend.

3. Barbara Anne, age seven, is particularly sensitive to any minor slights or correction, and, as a consequence, she bursts into tears two or three times a day. Teacher and classmates apologize and try to console her, but this has little effect on her pattern of emotional response. Following some of these episodes, Barbara Anne's mother comes to school quite upset. As the teacher, what would you do to help Barbara Anne?

4. What explanations would you offer for the wide disparity in the responses of a person who goes into an emotional tailspin over the slightest mishap as contrasted to the person who remains rational and calm during times of great peril or adversity?

5. Ed Barrett, who is a good student, becomes greatly agitated and upset when, for the first time, he has been caught cheating on an examination. Later, in a conference with the counselor, Ed admits he has cheated on other occasions but has not been caught. Does Ed and do each of us have at least two self-images, one of the person we want others to see us as being, and another of the person that deep down we really are? If so, which self-image determines our behavior? Why?

Suggested Readings

Katherine D'Evelyn, *Meeting Children's Emotional Needs*. Englewood Cliffs, N.J.: Prentice-Hall, 1957. Describes the emotional needs of children at successive maturity levels. Analyzes specific symptoms and manifestations of emotional problems, with suggestions of ways teachers may, through working with parents and the school psychologist, help children fulfill their emotional needs.

Roger W. Heyns, *The Psychology of Personal Adjustment*. New York: Holt, Rinehart and Winston, 1958. The first part of the book presents the major concepts of adjustment. Chapter 3 offers a very clear discussion of common adjustment mechanisms. The final section of the book analyzes the adjustment processes that occur at various points of development.

Arthur T. Jersild, *When Teachers Face Themselves*. New York: Bureau of Publications, Teachers College, Columbia University, 1955. The major theme of the book is that education should help children and adults to know themselves and to develop self-acceptance. The achievement of this goal involves a search for personal meaning and an understanding of anxiety, which may distort experience and meaning.

Daniel A. Prescott, *Emotion and the Educative Process*. Washington: American Council on Education, 1938. An early comprehensive analysis of the nature of emotion and its role in education. Chapter VI identifies and discusses basic personality needs whose frustration creates situations that produce unpleasant emotion and a need for adjustment.

Carl R. Rogers, *On Becoming a Person*. Boston: Houghton Mifflin Co., 1961. A collection of papers presenting and interpreting the conditions and goals of client-centered therapy. The task of helping each person to become less defensive and more open to all sensory experience is a central theme of the book.

Seymour S. Sarason, Kenneth S. Davidson, Frederick F. Lighthall, Richard R. Waite, and Britton K. Ruebush, *Anxiety in Elementary School Children*.

New York: John Wiley, 1960. Describes the development of test and general anxiety scales for children, and reports the findings of long-term research investigating the relationships to anxiety of achievement, behavior, and other correlates.

Films

Angry Boy, 16 mm , sound, black and white, 32 min. Bloomington, Indiana: Audio-Visual Center, Indiana University (rental fee, $5.15). Presents the story of Tommy Randall, who has been caught stealing at school and is sent to a child guidance clinic for treatment. The clinic staff identifies Tommy's emotional problem, and, through interviews with his mother, traces the problem to family relationships of mother, grandmother, and father. Tommy's mother learns to understand him, and Tommy does become better adjusted through the help of the clinic.

Fears of Children, 16 mm , sound, black and white, 29 min. Bloomington, Indiana: Audio-Visual Center, Indiana University (rental fee, $5.40). Portrays a parent-child situation in which the mother of five-year-old Paul tends to overprotect him, while the father advocates sterner discipline and encourages him to do things for himself. The resulting conflict confuses Paul and arouses his fears. A friend of Paul's mother points out that it is normal for children to become angry with their parents. Paul's parents make a greater effort to understand the situation and the problem is resolved.

Feeling of Hostility, 16 mm , sound, black and white, 31 min. Bloomington, Indiana: Audio-Visual Center, Indiana University (rental fee, $4.65). Presents the case history of Clare, who develops a feeling of hostility because of a lack of affection and understanding from her family. She compensates by achieving academic success, often at the expense of others. She improves with the help of an understanding teacher, but her capacity for love and friendship is permanently impaired.

the emerging individual

10

developmental tasks

*In order to achieve integration, and at the same time to function accept-
ably in the society of which he is a part, the individual must adjust successfully to key experiences which arise as part of development in our society.*

≡ CAROLINE M. TRYON

Each individual, as he progresses toward maturity, encounters along the way specific *developmental tasks*—"those
major common tasks that face all individuals within a given
society or subculture of society."[1] The successful accomplishment of these tasks—at the time they are encountered
—is crucial for the individual's subsequent development:
"A developmental task is a task which arises at or about a
certain period in the life of the individual, successful
achievement of which leads to happiness and to success
with later tasks, while failure leads to unhappiness in the
individual, disapproval by society, and difficulty with later
tasks."[2] Thus, a developmental task involves two interacting forces: (1) the *maturing organism* and (2) the *expectations of the culture.*

[1] Caroline M. Tryon and Jesse W. Lilienthal, "Developmental Tasks: I. The Concept
and Its Importance," in Caroline M. Tryon, *Fostering Mental Health in Our Schools* (Washington: Association for Supervision and Curriculum Development, N.E.A., 1950), p. 77.
[2] Robert J. Havighurst, *Human Development and Education* (New York: David Mc-
Kay Co., 1953), p. 2.

The physiological maturity of an individual sets general limits for the responses which may be expected of that individual. Lack of adequate strength and motor development makes it impossible for a child to walk much before ten or twelve months of age. Thus, a specific developmental task becomes a necessary learning only at that point in time when the individual has the physiological ability to learn it.

Since individuals vary widely in their rates and patterns of physical growth, developmental tasks cannot be grouped neatly and precisely by chronological age. Instead, these tasks are commonly grouped according to the individual's *maturity level* (for instance, early childhood)—each level encompassing three or more years rather than a single year. This division of the developmental span from birth to maturity includes the following maturity levels (shown graphically in Figure 10.1).[3]

Infancy. Birth to age two or three. Period marks the change from complete helplessness to some degree of independence accompanied by rapid growth and increased stability of physiological processes.

Preschool Childhood. Age two to three to age five, six, or seven. Period of stable growth; large-muscle activity; role exploration through fantasy and parallel play with agemates; and identification with adults. Period of intense socialization in meeting demands and expectations of a different cultural institution: the school.

Early Elementary School Childhood. Age five, six, or seven to eight or nine. Period of slow steady growth; motor development uneven, with large muscles better developed than finer muscles; child becoming more oriented toward and responsive to peers.

Late Childhood. Age eight or nine to beginning of physical changes associated with pubescence (nine to fourteen years for girls, eleven to sixteen years for boys). Continuation of slow steady growth. Child achieves increased coordination of fine muscles and skill in manipulation; increase in social awareness and identification with peers; wider range of interests relating to understanding of the world in which he lives.

Preadolescence. Ages ten to thirteen (covering school grades five to eight). Transition period of one or two years encompassing the latter part of late childhood or the early part of early adolescence. Characterized by hyperactivity, rebelliousness, moodiness, and irritability.

Early Adolescence. Beginning at pubescence and extending to puberty. Period of rapid growth, especially of long bones of legs and arms. Some feeling of restiveness or rebellion against adult controls. Strong identification with peers—at first, with peers of same sex; later, with members of the opposite sex.

Late Adolescence. Puberty to early maturity. Deceleration in rate of growth. Individual more and more looks and acts like an adult, expects to be treated as an adult, but lacks adult's experiences.

[3] From Lois H. Meek, *The Personal-Social Development of Boys and Girls with Implications for Secondary Education* (New York: Progressive Education Association, 1940), p. 34. Used by permission.

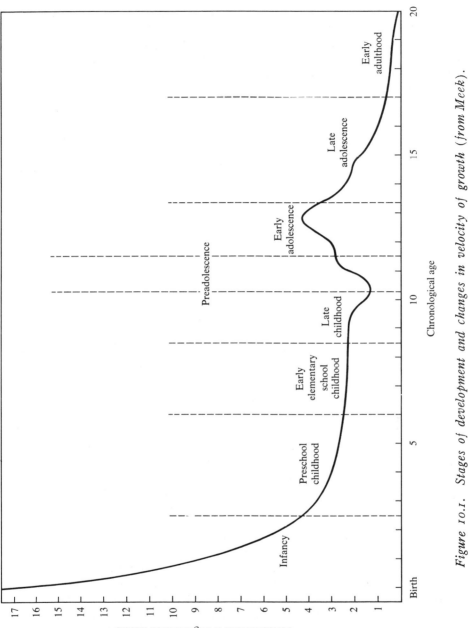

Figure 10.1. Stages of development and changes in velocity of growth (from Meek).

Early Adulthood. Onset of physical maturity to time of marriage and beginning of child rearing or establishment of oneself in a vocation. Period of additional schooling and preparation for a vocation. Induction into world of work. Courtship, marriage, beginning a family.

The second major force in the setting of developmental tasks for children and youth is the culture, which specifies the kinds of learning and development that are expected of its members at successive maturity levels. This means that Jimmy Brown's development in early childhood or early adolescence can appropriately be analyzed only in relation to the developmental tasks of the culture or subculture of which Jimmy is a part. Certain expected developmental learnings (weaning, toilet training, learning to talk, relating to others) are a part of nearly every culture; but differences in the timing and in the manner whereby each is to be learned makes each of these developmental tasks a unique learning in every culture.

In addition to maturation and societal expectations, certain self processes influence the individual's accomplishment of his developmental tasks. For instance, unless Frank sees the task of relating to his peer group as an important step in his own development, he probably will not work at this task even though he has the physiological maturity for it and even though the culture expects it to be learned. If, on the other hand, he perceives this task as important, he will work at it and probably master it to some extent— thereby progressing a step further in his development and enhancement of self.

Each developmental task functions as part of a series of graded, progressive, and interrelated tasks. Consequently, a failure to learn one task often hampers the achievement of related developmental tasks. The child who has not achieved a feeling of security with his family or friends, for example, frequently is unsuccessful in winning the acceptance of others. Similarly, if an individual fails to accomplish a developmental task during the expected period of time, this failure may cause adjustment problems at a later period of his development. If, for instance, he does not achieve emotional independence from his family during his adolescence, he may be unable to develop a stable marital relationship when he becomes an adult.

Conversely, the successful achievement of a developmental task leads to the achievement of related or more complex tasks. As the physical organism matures and new capacities and potentialities emerge, the individual develops a readiness for working on and accomplishing tasks at the next higher stage of development. A child's learning to walk is followed by his learning to run, skip, hop, and jump. In addition, the same task may require increasingly complex behavior as the individual reaches successively higher levels of maturity. The preschooler, for example, works at the task of "achieving independence" by playing with other children in the neighborhood unsupervised by his mother; the early adolescent works at this same task by disregarding the advice of adults on a great many matters; the late adolescent gets a job, thus making himself financially less dependent on his parents. The preadolescent works at the task of "establishing heterosexual relationships" by teasing or by professing dislike of the opposite sex. In adolescence, the same task (or, more accurately, a task with the same label—"establishing heterosexual relationships") calls forth quite different behavior—dating, going steady, courting. Because the specific behaviors that must be learned at each maturity level in achieving such tasks are markedly different, the task itself is virtually a different task at each different level.

Tryon and Lilienthal[4] have identified ten broad categories of developmental tasks:

1. Achieving an appropriate dependence-independence pattern.
2. Achieving an appropriate giving-receiving pattern of affection.
3. Relating to changing social groups.
4. Developing a conscience.
5. Learning one's psycho-socio-biological sex role.
6. Accepting and adjusting to a changing body.
7. Managing a changing body and learning new motor patterns.
8. Learning to understand and control the physical world.
9. Developing an appropriate symbol system and conceptual abilities.
10. Relating one's self to the cosmos.

Each of these tasks calls for the learning of different behaviors at successive maturity levels. Through an analysis of the specific behaviors required for each category of developmental tasks at successive maturity levels, we can gain a clearer perspective of the continuity of human development and learning during childhood and adolescence.

We should note also that each child or youth works on a given developmental task in a unique way. A great many boys in late childhood and adolescence seek peer acceptance by developing athletic skills, but boys who lack athletic skills will strive to gain acceptance of peers in other ways. Tim, a small, underdeveloped twelve-year-old boy, is accepted by his peers in part because he brings his football to school for them to play with. Alex, a studious fourteen-year-old, is accepted because of his skill at leading sing-ins. Thus, although all individuals in a given culture face similar developmental tasks, Tim's or Alex's mode of working on a specific task is *a unique expression of a general pattern of development*.

In the next two chapters we shall present case records describing children and adolescents at successive maturity levels. These behavioral descriptions will be analyzed in relation to the developmental tasks which individuals at each maturity level are striving to achieve.

Summary

The concept of *developmental tasks* (tasks that all individuals within a given society encounter as they progress from infancy to adulthood) permits us to analyze each person's uniqueness in relation to the common patterns of development associated with each maturity level. The maturity levels include

[4] Tryon and Lilienthal, pp. 84–87.

infancy, the *preschool* level, early and late *childhood, preadolescence,* early and late *adolescence,* and early *adulthood.*

The accomplishment of developmental tasks is influenced by the maturing organism, the expectations of the culture, and various self processes (specifically, the processes of perception and motivation).

Developmental tasks are viewed as a series of interrelated, interdependent learnings. Developmental tasks identified by the same verbal labels are encountered at successive maturity levels. Although they might appear to be repetitions of a task first encountered at an earlier maturity level, each is a distinctly different task requiring different behaviors for its achievement at a given maturity level.

Study Questions

1. If you were to visit a primitive culture in another part of the world, what would you look for in seeking to identify the developmental tasks of persons at a given maturity level in that culture?

2. What specific developmental tasks are being worked on by youths who express dissent and opposition through participating in marches and demonstrations? Are these developmental tasks different from those their nonactivist, nonparticipating peers are working on? Discuss.

3. We have presented in this and recent chapters two integrative concepts in human development, the self-concept and developmental tasks. Which concept permits the gathering of more reliable and useful data? Which concept do you feel is more useful in analyzing the behavior and development of children and youth? Defend the positions you have taken.

Suggested Readings

Robert J. Havighurst. *Human Development and Education.* New York: David McKay Co., 1953. Discusses the concept of developmental tasks and identifies the major developmental tasks commonly observed in American culture from infancy to old age. Notes the biological, psychological, and social forces that influence each task and indicates the educational implications of each task.

Caroline M. Tryon and Jesse W. Lilienthal. "Developmental Tasks: I. The Concept and Its Importance" (Chapter 6) and "Developmental Tasks: II. Discussion of Specific Tasks and Implications" (Chapter 7), in Caroline M. Tryon, chairman, *Fostering Mental Health in Our Schools.* Washington: Association for Supervision and Curriculum Development, N.E.A., 1950. Identifies and discusses ten major developmental tasks and learnings which appear in modified form at successive maturity levels. Chapter 7 takes up each major task or area of learning and defines the specific learning behavior at successive maturity levels from infancy to late adolescence.

11

childhood

The childhood shows the man,
As morning shows the day.

≡ JOHN MILTON

Human life begins when a spermatozoon, the male germ cell, penetrates and fertilizes an ovum while it is in the Fallopian tube on its way from the ovary to the uterus. The sperm swim upstream by lashing their tails back and forth, and they move at a rate of 3 inches per hour across the cervix, through the uterus, and up the Fallopian tube to meet the egg. There are more than 200,000,000 sperm in this race, but only one will fertilize the egg. The egg, which carries all of the food and energy, is about 90,000 times larger than a sperm, but egg and sperm each contribute exactly half of the new individual's hereditary material.[1]

The chromosomes of the parent sperm and the egg combine, during the first half hour after fertilization, in the nucleus of the new cell. These threadlike chromosomes carry the genes, which determine the hereditary characteristics of the child: eye and hair color, physique, physical and mental aptitudes, susceptibility, or resistance to various common diseases and disorders (including diabetes, heart trouble, and high blood pressure).

[1] "Drama of Life before Birth," *Life* magazine (April 30, 1965), 54–64.

It takes about three days for the fertilized egg to pass through the Fallopian tube to the uterus and another four or five days for it to become implanted in the uterine wall. Cell division and multiplication begin shortly after fertilization; by the time the fertilized egg reaches the uterus, it is a hollow cluster of more than one hundred cells. The cluster of cells resulting from cell division is known as a *blastocyst*. As the number of cells of the blastocyst increases, three layers of cells are formed, from which further cell differentiations into specialized tissues, organs, and body parts take place. The outer layer, called the *ectoderm*, is the point of origin for the skin, sense organs, and nervous system. From the inner layer of cells, called the *endoderm*, are formed the glands of internal secretion and the alimentary canal. A middle layer of cells, the *mesoderm*, is the point of origin for the muscular, circulatory, and skeletal systems.

During the embryonic period, which extends from the second week to the beginning of the third lunar month, the initial phases of development of the main systems and body organs take place. By the end of the first month the embryo is about ¼ to ½ inches long, and already impressive internal development has begun. At this time the embryo has the beginning of eyes, spinal cord, nervous system, thyroid gland, lungs, stomach, liver, kidneys, and intestines. Its primitive heart has already begun to beat, and bulges on the embryo show that buds of arms and legs are beginning to form. The development of the body from eighteen days to four months of prenatal life is shown in Figure 11.1,[2] with the differentiations and formation of internal organs and structures at four weeks shown in the insert.

At the beginning of the second month it is almost impossible to distinguish a human embryo from any other mammalian embryo. It is a critical time, for the rapidly multiplying cells are especially sensitive to certain chemical substances. During the fifth and sixth weeks of prenatal life the arms and legs may be deformed by thalidomide. The brain, too, is susceptible to damage. During the second and third months the embryo is most susceptible to the ravages of German measles, or rubella virus; should the mother contract the disease at this time, the child may develop heart malformation, cataracts, deafness, or brain damage.

Ordinarily, the embryo is protected against the hazards of viruses and drugs by the placenta, a spongy organ that is attached to the developing embryo by the umbilical cord. The placenta acts as a liver and kidney in removing poisonous wastes; and it serves as a lung for the fetus in the interchange of oxygen and carbon dioxide, which are transported to and from the placenta by the mother's blood stream. The mother's blood and the child's blood do not mix. The placenta acts as a barrier between the two blood streams, allowing nutrients to reach the child in the proper amounts and keeping out most noxious substances. The placenta sometimes fails to prevent the passage of some noxious substances, as in the cases of thalidomide and rubella.

[2] From P. C. Martin and E. L. Vincent, *Human Biological Development* (New York: Ronald Press, © 1960), p. 247. Used by permission.

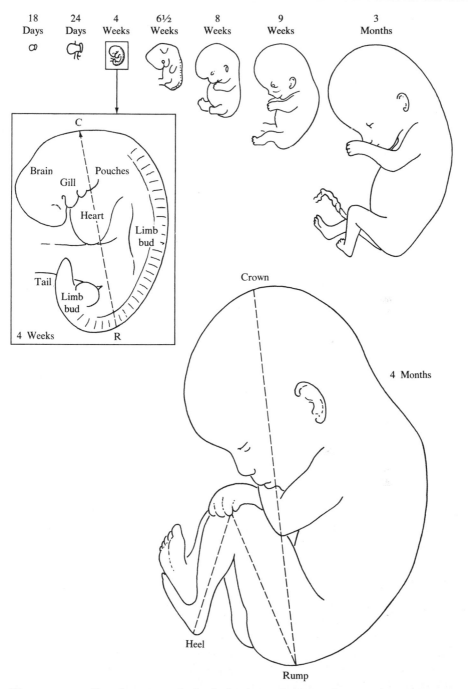

Figure 11.1. *Development of the body from eighteen days to four months of prenatal life (from Martin and Vincent).*

The fetal period extends from the beginning of the third lunar month until the end of gestation. At eleven weeks the fetus, now more than 2½ inches long, floats buoyantly in the amniotic fluid along with the umbilical cord. Although it is totally immersed, the fetus inhales and exhales just enough to send the salty fluid into and out of its lungs. It does not drown because it gets oxygen—not from the air but from the blood brought in by the umbilical cord. By this time all of the body systems are working. Nerves and muscles have become synchronized with the young bones, so that arms and legs can make their first movements.

Beginning at eighteen weeks some fetuses have been known to suck their thumbs, a practice which prepares the child for learning to suck and nurse after birth. At twenty-eight weeks the fetus is more than 10 inches long and weighs 2¼ pounds. In place of earlier generalized patterns of responses, many separate reflexes are beginning to appear. During the last two months of fetal life, deposits of subcutaneous fat cause the fetus to become rounded. Fingernails reach the fingertips, toenails lengthen, and the lower extremities grow rapidly.

Infancy

Birth at full term occurs after 266 to 280 days, when the baby is shoved out of the mother's womb by a hundred-pound propulsive force. Birth is a traumatic experience, since the vital systems must begin to function if the child is to maintain life in the outside world. The newborn infant must now obtain oxygen from the air. If breathing does not occur spontaneously, it may be instigated by a sharp spank by nurse or doctor. The infant's loud cry enables his first breaths to be strong enough to inflate the tiny air sacs in the lungs and get rid of the mucus that has accumulated there. The most dramatic adjustment of all at birth must be made by the heart and circulatory system. At birth the pulmonary circulation system is activated, and the blood entering the right auricle is pumped by the right ventricle to the lungs, where it is aerated. In addition, beginning at birth all waste matter must be filtered and excreted by the infant's own organs. During the first six months of postnatal life the infant is afforded protection from many infections by the immunities obtained from the mother through the placenta.

The neonate's first developmental task, then, is to *achieve stability in physiological functioning*. To assist him in achieving physiological stability the infant has, at birth, *reflexes,* unlearned and involuntary responses to specific stimulation. The respiratory reflex includes a carbon dioxide reflex, which automatically controls the amount of air the infant breathes. No less important for survival are the nursing reflexes, including the hunger cry, active movements in search of food, and suckling and swallowing activities. A characteristic postural reflex, often observed during the sleep of newborn babies, is the tonic neck reflex. When the baby's face is turned to the right, the arm automatically straightens out, while the left arm is bent up so that his clenched fist is against the back of his head. The Moro, or startle, reflex is a defense reaction in response to a sudden loss of equilibrium or a loud noise; the infant's body becomes rigid and his arms extend upward and outward in an arc while his face takes on an agonized expression accompanied by wild shrieks.[3] A related startle pattern may also occur; this response begins with an eye blink and is followed by a thrusting forward of the head and neck and a flexion of other parts of the body.

Being weaned and *learning to eat solid foods* are developmental tasks faced by children in all cultures, although the timing and completion of these tasks vary for different cultures. There is probably no optimum time for the child to be weaned, and children within a culture will vary widely in their accomplishment of this task. In American middle-class culture, weaning may begin as early as the seventh or eighth month, but frequently the baby may cling to his bedtime bottle until eighteen months of age. It may be advisable not to force the child to give up his bottle before he is emotionally ready to do so, since some children seem to need more sucking than others and more of the comfort and security that the bottle appears to provide. During the latter part of the first year, most babies are able to bite and chew well enough to eat solid foods.

Motor Development

Each of a series of steps in motor development and control marks the infant's progress in developing *eye-hand coordination*. By the time the infant is three or four months of age, the nerve cells of the brain are more efficiently connected with the different muscle groups, so that voluntary action is now possible. At four months of age his muscle control enables him to direct his eyes, turn his head, and hold it erect. Gesell and Ilg[4] remind us that a baby can "pick up" a small object with his eyes long before he can pick it up with his fingers. At four months, however, his fingers have become more agile and active, and he spends much time playing with his fingers. During the next three months the child reaches out to approach, to contact, to grasp, to feel, and to manipulate the objects within reach in his environment. The progressive changes in motor development follow the *law of developmental direction;* that is, development proceeds from head to tail (cephalo-caudal) and from trunk to extremity (proximo-distal).

By seven months, the infant begins to manipulate objects. At first he picks up objects like a block or a rattle by closing his fist around them. A little later he learns to bring his thumb and index finger together to pick up a small object. At ten months the baby is likely to reach for a spoon and try to feed himself, but his imperfect eye-hand coordination leads him to get more food on his face and bib and in his hair than in his mouth. Not until he is

[3] C. Anderson Aldrich and Mary M. Aldrich, *Babies Are Human Beings* (New York: Macmillan Co., 1947), pp. 8–10.

[4] Arnold Gesell and Frances L. Ilg, *The First Five Years of Life* (New York: Harper & Row, 1940), p. 101.

two years of age can he use a spoon and feed himself without excessive spilling of food. During his second and third years, the child achieves refinement and versatility in his eye-hand coordination; at the same time, gross motor activity increases.

Learning to walk is an important landmark in the development of every human being. Before it can be accomplished, however, many other steps in motor development must be mastered. Not until the infant is three or four months old have nerves and muscles developed sufficiently to enable him to hold up his head without support. By the fifth month, many infants lying on their backs are able to turn over on their stomachs. The first real crawling occurs when the child is able to lift both his chest and pelvis off the floor at the same time. Following the cephalo-caudal law, the child passes through a series of stages in gaining posture that is required for sitting and later for standing and walking in an erect position. During the period of ten to fifteen months of age, the child, through several stages, learns to walk: He pulls himself from sitting position to standing with support. With back upright and arms outstretched for balance, he places his feet far apart to widen his base as he stands alone. He steps out with wide spacing of legs and a very uncertain gait. Finally, when he is sure of his balance, he puts one foot before the other and acquires accurate control over his equilibrium.[5]

Sensory Development

The young child's varied responses to the world, as he works on his several developmental tasks, depend a great deal upon the messages received through his senses from the outside world. At birth, his sensory equipment is not fully developed. The newborn infant can see black and white but not color, since the cones (which make possible color vision) are not fully mature. The infant's ocular pursuit of a slowly moving object occurs after the second week of life. By the end of the second month, the infant clearly recognizes objects with which he comes into contact. Nerves connecting eyes and brain are entirely formed at about ten weeks, and by about age three months nerves and muscles needed for focusing are fully mature. By age four months, the eyes have become as perfect organs of reception as they will ever be.[6]

The organs for hearing are anatomically complete at birth, and the nerves connecting ears and brain appear to be fully developed. The infant is particularly sensitive to the quality and intensity of auditory stimuli. A loud noise or a sudden loss of equilibrium elicits a startle reflex and is extremely unpleasant. Music or mother's voice can be reassuring, pleasant, and comforting. Recognition of voices and footsteps helps the infant to relate to other people. Little is known about the infant's development in capacity for smell and taste.

Tactual and kinesthetic senses (sensations of pressure, pain, muscles,

[5] Aldrich and Aldrich, pp. 46–48.
[6] Aldrich and Aldrich, pp. 25–26.

joints) are fairly well developed at birth. The infant's habits of toilet and eating are responses to his perceptions of inner-organ sensations. The bladder and rectum, when distended, are accompanied by unpleasant feelings. Moving the bowels is followed by a pleasant feeling. The infant's elimination processes prior to eighteen months are involuntary, since his sphincter-muscle control of bladder and bowels is usually not achieved until after this age.

Learning to control body elimination is a developmental task whose early attainment is eagerly sought by mothers in middle-class culture. The learning of this task is often accompanied by emotional conflict involving both parent and child. Placing the child on the toilet after meals or at regular intervals may bring some successes through the establishment of conditioned responses, but this approach usually fails to teach the child the meaning of toilet training as a social habit. Havighurst[7] points out that the child can be regarded as trained for toilet habits when he recognizes the need to urinate or defecate and has voluntary control over these acts and when he accepts the responsibility for keeping himself clean and dry. These conditions are seldom met before the age of two, and bladder control at night is not achieved by the average child until his fourth birthday.

Social Development

For several weeks after birth, the infant responds to the world in a generalized, undifferentiated manner. Although he is unable to relate to individuals at this early age, the actions of his mother, his nurse, and others, as they care for him and respond to him, become associated with generalized feelings of comfort and security. (In Chapter 5 the qualities of these early interpersonal experiences were shown to exert a pervasive influence on the child's development and learning.) By six months of age, the child is able to notice the differences between familiar people and strangers. His perception of mother is well differentiated, so that he often cries when his mother goes out of the room and leaves him. At other times he will cling to mother's skirts when a stranger comes near him. By ten or eleven months of age, the child has become very responsive to familiar persons, especially mother. He likes to be played with, to throw spoon or toys over the side of the feeding table and to laugh as they are returned. He loves to play games such as patty-cake and peekaboo. In these and later interactions, the child is working on the developmental task of *learning to relate himself emotionally to parents, siblings, and others.*

His relating to people close to him is enhanced at twelve to fifteen months of age with the development of speech. We need to remember, however, that for many months the child has been communicating his wants and feelings by crying, grunting, cooing, fidgeting, and grimacing. A first step in

[7] Robert J. Havighurst, *Developmental Tasks and Education* (New York: David McKay Co., 1953), p. 14.

language development is the random vocalizations that may be observed as early as the third month of life. Initially, these vocalizations are part of the total reactive and expressive system wherein the child is responding to internal and external stimuli. This is followed by a babbling stage, in which the child repeats various vowel and consonant combinations. Learning to push the air over the vocal cords and to coordinate the tongue, lips, palate, and mouth is a very complex operation for the young child.

Hearing his own voice becomes a stimulus to repeat and to continue these vocal patterns. When he is about a year old, the child tries to imitate the speech of others. We observe him imitating "ma-ma," "da-da," and "bye bye." Not only do the child's own sounds become linked to those of others, but the child gains additional practice in speech by interpreting and imitating those sound combinations that persons around him use in conversations. True speech arises during the second year, as the child learns to associate objects with their names, to speak words, to obey simple commands, and finally to communicate with others—first using single words and then simple sentences. Most children at age two have a speaking vocabulary of approximately 300 words. Though learning to talk is one of the most complex and satisfying of human learnings, one's continued social and psychological development requires the broadening of one's language skills at successive stages of maturity.

Preschool Early Childhood

The period between two and three years is a transitional period. Baby softness and roundness gives way to a physique that is larger, sturdier, and more linear. The marked but decelerating increases in height and weight during the first eighteen months of postnatal life are followed by slow steady increases in these dimensions between age two and six. At three years of age, the child has a full set of temporary teeth, and by age six his first permanent teeth begin to arrive.

At two and a half years, the preschooler displays an active curiosity about his physical environment. He gets into, pulls out, and pulls apart everything within reach. By age three, the child is somewhat easier to control. He is beginning to play cooperatively with other children. He shows progress, too, in asking for what he wants instead of snatching it.

Age four is marked by rather stormy activity as well as a growing interest in the world. The child asks numerous questions; at the same time, he rebels against parents and quarrels with playmates. Age five is characterized by strenuous activity, but the activity tends to have more definite direction and purpose. The child reveals greater physical skill and has good control of his body. He is interested in group activities and group play. He is ready to fit into a group, is able to concentrate on an activity for a longer period of time, and is capable of responding to increased opportunities for development and learning in kindergarten.

Something of what a preschooler is like and the developmental tasks he faces is reflected in these excerpts from the case of Tommy:

Tommy is one of 45 morning kindergarten children. He is a very small child weighing 30 pounds and is 42 inches tall. He is five years old.

OCTOBER 20

10:30 A.M. When another child passed Tommy a napkin for his cookie, Tommy put the napkin on his head. The teacher said, "Where does your napkin belong?" He answered, "On my head. I want to look like a clown." "Very well," the teacher said, "everyone likes to laugh at clowns. You may stand up and clown for everyone." After everyone laughed, he ran to his seat. He hasn't done that again. However, others have tried it, and when reminded of Tommy's standing before the class, each one soon puts the napkin on the table.

11:30 This was a rainy day. There were lots of boots to be put on. Tommy couldn't find his boots. The teacher found them and started him out alone working on them. After five minutes he had managed to get one on but it was on the wrong foot. Teacher showed him his mistake, but he insisted on leaving it on the wrong foot. The other was put on the wrong foot. Tommy told the teacher this was the first time he'd ever done it by himself.

FEBRUARY 3

During free-play period the teacher noticed that Tommy was very busy in the corner with a bulldozer. He was alone and making a motor sound with his lips. The teacher inquired, "What are you doing?" He answered, "I'm making tend I'm knocking down trees to build a new road." The teacher asked, "Is that a tractor?" Very disgusted, Tommy answered, "No, that's a bulldozer."

"Tommy, why do you always go to the front of the line instead of taking your place behind the other boys?" He answered, "I like to be first." The teacher answered, "You'll have to take your place behind the others if you don't get here first. That's breaking in line when you get at the beginning of the line."

FEBRUARY 9

The teacher planned for the children to make Valentines this week. Everyone was shown how to cut a heart by folding paper and cutting a half heart. Tommy was completely lost. He could not make the scissors go around and turn the paper at the same time. However, Tommy was not the only one who could not do it. The teacher marked on the paper where to cut, but he still couldn't do it.

FEBRUARY 24

When Tommy entered the room he ran to me to show me his thumb which looked bruised. He said, "See my sore thumb." The teacher asked, "What happened?" He answered, "I caught it in the *door truck.*" The teacher answered, "Gee, I'm sorry you mashed it in the truck door. I know that hurt, but it looks like it's getting well already." Then Tommy started taking off his coat.

There are several word combinations that he reverses such as "awake wide" for "wide awake."

FEBRUARY 25

Tommy helped the teacher carry books and pictures to her car this afternoon. Tommy said, "My, you have a big car." (Teacher has a three-seater station wagon.) Teacher asked, "Do you like my car?" He answered, "Yes, I wish you'd come see me again." Teacher asked, "Why do you want me to visit you?" Tommy grinned sheepishly and said, "Cause I like you." Teacher answered, "Maybe I'll surprise you sometime and go see you again." Tommy and teacher walked hand in hand back into the school.

MARCH 9

The children take turns being helpers for a week to give out napkins, milk, scissors, crayons, etc. Today one of the napkin helpers was absent. Teacher allowed the one present to pick anyone else to substitute for this one day. Tommy was chosen to take the place of the absent child. He threw back his shoulders and strutted to the cabinet to get napkins.

It is seldom that Tommy is picked by his classmates. He seldom is chosen when we play "Farmer in the Dell." I was pleased to see him receive some recognition from his classmates.

MARCH 16

When time came for rhythm band, Tommy said he wanted the cymbals. He said he had not had a turn with them. The teacher asked him why he wanted the cymbals. He answered, "They make the most noise." While the group was marching and playing, Tommy had his teeth "gritted" close together every time he'd crash the cymbals. He has not been able to keep time with any instrument. He can't clap or tap to the time of the music. When the children were putting instruments away, the teacher asked Tommy how he liked playing the cymbals. He answered, "It hurts my ears."

APRIL 7

Tommy was sitting on the floor playing with the oddly shaped blocks. Teacher suggested that he build a high tower. It took him several tries before he could get one to stand. He would try to put a big block on top causing all to tumble. Finally, he chose the biggest one to put down first and build from there.

APRIL 16

After two weeks on the playground equipment, Tommy uses everything with ease and enjoyment. He was slow to try the new equipment, but after watching the others, he has become used to it and climbs to the top of the jungle gym.

Physical Development

Preschool early childhood is a period of vigorous physical activity. Children at this stage are working on *developing their large muscles and gaining control over their bodies*. They like to run, jump, climb, and try to balance themselves. They eagerly respond to music and engage in rhythmic play. Motor skills, however, may be unevenly developed at these ages. Gesell and Ilg[8] remind us that children may do well at one motor skill and poorly at another. By age five, however, the average child has a fairly mature sense of balance, which is reflected in more self-reliant abandon in his motor behavior.

Several entries in the case of Tommy point to his working on gaining control of large muscles. Tommy is the smallest child in the kindergarten, and his motor development seems more like that of a younger child. Tommy has great difficulty in keeping time to the music, but he participates in rhythms and asked to play the cymbals. At first he would not try the slide or jungle gym, but after two weeks he was climbing to the top of the jungle gym.

Preschoolers generally love to color, cut, and paste—activities that require the *learning of fine-muscle control*. Children vary in their timing and progress in mastering this developmental task. Tommy had made only limited progress in learning to put on boots and button his coat; and he, along with several others, was unable to cut out hearts for valentines.

The preschooler also *learns to balance periods of strenuous activity with periods of quiet and rest*. Often children in nursery school and kindergarten

[8] Gesell and Ilg, pp. 65–107.

will withdraw from play or seek a quiet activity. A child's fatigue may be revealed in his irritability and need for a nap. At 10:30 one morning, after a period of vigorous free play, Tommy called out, "Is it time to go home? I'm tired."

Social Development

Preschool early childhood is a period of broadening social horizons. The child is deeply attached to mother throughout this period, but father is becoming increasingly important. His relationships with his family greatly influence his ability to relate to other individuals and groups. A child who feels secure in the knowledge that he is loved usually relates to other adults and to peers quickly and easily. A child who is overly dependent or insecure often has more serious difficulties in relating to others.

We noted earlier that preschoolers learn to relate to peers through fantasy and parallel play. Each likes to be near other children as he acts out his own make-believe story. On February 3, Tommy explained to the teacher that his machine was a bulldozer. In earlier anecdotes he simulated driving a tractor on a farm and pretended that he was a clown.

An important part of the preschooler's social development is *learning and adhering to the rules and expectations of his culture.* In nursery school and kindergarten, the teacher's expectation that he learn to be friendly and considerate of others is an important part of his socialization. Tommy had many things to learn in relations with others in kindergarten. Early in the year he stomped his feet during "grace" before midmorning milk, knocked over a house that other children had built, and put the napkin on his head. He also was unable to put his boots on and button his coat, and the teacher had to speak to him about butting in at the front of the line. These incidents also show that children are *learning concepts of right and wrong.* As the child internalizes standards and mores of the culture, he *develops a conscience.* When reminded by the teacher that people laugh at clowns, Tommy and others refrained from putting their napkins on their heads.

Another important developmental task for youngsters at this maturity level is *learning to relate emotionally with persons outside the family.* Tommy's relating to the teacher is revealed in his responses to her suggestions and corrections and in his helping her carry things to her car, telling her he liked her, and walking back to the class with her. In learning to play and to share with others, Tommy is making progress in relating to a group of peers. He received recognition of his peers the day he was chosen as a helper to pass the napkins.

By means of play, exploration, interactions with others, visits to the zoo or farm, by looking at pictures and listening to stories, and in countless experiences of daily life the child *develops* and *modifies his concepts of social and physical reality.* Tommy learned the principle of beginning with larger blocks in building a tower, but his reversal of the order of words and their modifiers is an example of a concept which has not been mastered.

Children at an early age develop an *awareness of sex differences* from watching younger brothers and sisters being bathed and changed and by noting the different attitudes, behavior patterns, and roles of mothers and fathers and men and women. In learning to cover their genital organs, children acquire attitudes and behaviors which are appropriate to the *development of sexual modesty*. The attitudes and responses of parents toward a child's masturbation and his normal interests in the anatomical differences between the sexes are of critical importance in the child's learning this developmental task. Children need to be helped to develop healthy, positive attitudes toward sex rather than being fearful, anxious, ashamed, or guilty about normal sexual processes and functions. The kinds of sexual behavior one learns and the attitudes and feelings he develops about sex in early years often have a lasting effect on his sexuality throughout life.

By the close of preschool early childhood, the youngster has acquired a certain degree of independence, although mother is still a very important person in his life. He is adult oriented and conforms to adult standards. He is beginning to accept responsibility for his own behavior, to clarify concepts of right and wrong, and to develop a conscience. He is on the threshold of an expanding world of school, neighborhood, society, and the world of varied experiences and ideas.

Early Elementary Childhood

The sixth year in a child's life is an important milestone. His statement "Now I am six and can go to school" signals the taking of a new and important step toward growth in independence. Children in this phase of early childhood make great strides in learning to control their bodies and to direct their energies purposefully; to relate to many different kinds of people, both adults and children; and to use symbols to communicate and to form concepts.

Perhaps we can best obtain a picture of what children in the primary years of elementary school are like by observing two students through the eyes of their teachers. Clare, aged six, is working on many developmental learnings which youngsters face at the beginning of this stage.

OCTOBER 10

At the end of the morning recess period the yard teacher came into the room. "You have a little girl, Clare, who will not listen or obey. She continued to swing after the bell rang. I blew my whistle ten times, and she never paid any attention to me until I walked over to her. I think she ought to sit down for a few recesses until she remembers." When I discussed the matter with the class several children spoke up and said that they felt Clare should get another chance. When it was put to a vote the class voted unanimously in favor of Clare having another chance. "Clare, you see how the class feels, in spite of what the yard teacher said. You have another chance. I hope you will use it wisely."

At recess, many girls from other first grades were jumping rope. Clare was first. She missed. "I get another turn." No comment from the girls. She missed. "I get another turn." No comment. She missed. "I get another turn." Chorus: "You've had enough." Clare went to the side and sat down rather than go to the end of the line. Girls missed and went to the end of the line. Clare stayed seated. Finally she went to the end of the line to get her turn.

NOVEMBER 27

Clare's class was called to the reading circle. Clare was the last to come. She continued to sit at her seat working. When she finally came, although the circle had been formed, she skirted it and drew her chair in next to the teacher. Her book remained closed with the marker remaining in front of it. The other children were studying. Teacher: "Clare, would you like to study the page?" "Oh, I can read it." Teacher let her. She read stumblingly, finally asking on one line, "What does that say?" The teacher suggested she study now. Clare vocalized, "OO-di-do-di-owdy." She turned her back to the circle, discovered some sunflower seeds in the chalk tray. "I like to eat sunflower seeds." She was asked to get her place. Mayer helped her; Clare stood, hands on hips and let Mayer find it for her. Mayer said, "You better stop that fooling around."

She got up, walked over to help Dick with a word. Class at seats were getting noisy. Teacher rang triangle. Before she could say anything Clare chimed in: "Mike, put your head down." When the teacher suggested she would take care of it, Clare vocalized, "Do-di-do-di-do." While the next four readers read, she sat comparatively quiet, helping with words, many times before the child needed it. Then wiggles—she turned and looked away. She wiggled her marker. She stretched in her chair. She wiggled. "Is it lunch time yet? When is it?" When reading circle was dismissed she found work.

JANUARY 31

Clare reported to the class. "We took our rabbits to our friend. He says the reason they didn't make any babies was because they were both does."

"What are does?" asked Glen. "Father rabbits," she replied. The teacher interrupted. "Does are mother rabbits. The father rabbits are called bucks."

"If they were mother rabbits why didn't they have babies?" asked Clare.

"They were both mother rabbits. You need a mother rabbit and a father rabbit," explained the teacher.

Clare was not willing to accept the statement or else she had to think it over. "Well, we didn't have any babies because they were both does," she said and sat down.

MARCH 6

Clare's reading class is the fastest one in a group of four. This year I am giving the children many easy books before they are introduced into a hardback book. The vocabularies are similar in most of the preprimers. Since we have been introducing the second and third of a series of pre-primers Clare has been more interested in reading.

Today as usual she brought her chair up to the circle and placed it next to the teacher. Their new preprimer, *My Little Red Story Book,* had been given to this class the day before to study.

Clare just couldn't get the children into the circle fast enough. "Hurry up, Bunny. Sit here, Sally. Bring your chair over here. Don't sit too close. It's hot. Now, Miss J., everybody is ready. May I read?" She read four pages without a mistake.

Davy is aged seven and a half and in the second grade.

OCTOBER 22

Davy came in this morning smiling. He said, "Ya know, I'm sure glad you're back." The teacher had been absent Friday. Continuing, Davy said, "Do you know what happened when you were out?"

Teacher smiled and said, "Davy, what happened?"

Davy said, "Well, you know Miss Smith was here to teach us, and you know, Robbie wouldn't go up to read." Robbie is a small, immature child. Robbie overheard Davy and rushed up to defend himself. "Miss Jones," he said, "I didn't belong in that group. That's why."

Davy said, "Oh, yes you did, Robbie. All the other kids in your group went up. You cried. Why did you cry?"

Robbie said, "I don't know."

The teacher patted Robbie on the head, looked at Davy and said, "Well, Davy, Robbie is new to our school and it takes time to get acquainted with everyone and learn how we do things here. He did not know Miss Smith as well as you do. Perhaps the next time Miss Jones has to be absent, Robbie will go up to his reading group."

Davy said, "Well, I sure hope so, and Robbie, please, for heaven's sake, don't cry anymore, huh?" He looked Robbie in the eye.

NOVEMBER 6

Davy and June came to the door lunchroom and said, "We've got a place for you again."

Before the teacher could reply Tina went and sat on the "saved" chair. The teacher went back to the third table and sat down. Davy and June looked at Tina with "daggers" and murder in their eyes. After being seated, teacher looked up to observe Tina sitting next to Davy crying. By this time June came back to the teacher and said, "Miss J., Davy hit Tina because she sat down there." Teacher got up off the chair, went up to Tina and said, "Tina, what is the matter?" Tina said, "Davy hit me because I sat here. He wanted you to." Teacher looked at Davy, put her hand on his head, turned him around and said, "Davy, why did you hit Tina? Did she do anything to you?"

Davy sat silent for a minute and then looked up and said, "Oh, she cries if you touch her anyway, but she didn't need to sit there."

Teacher said, "Do you think you should have hit her? Do you hit girls?"

Davy said, "No, I'm sorry, Tina." Tina wiped big tears and said, "Okay." They started eating. After lunch Davy walked back to the room with the teacher.

DECEMBER 6

Davy, leaning over toward teacher, said in loud voice to be heard above noise in lunch room, "Miss J., I just gotta tell you. This is good (giggled, eyes sparkled). You know our club house. We have a couch. Skippy's dad is putting it in. O yes, Jimmy Baker. He is not a member any more. He sure cusses. So-o-o he was kicked out. We have our rules up in a box. We keep it locked."

Miss J. said, "Davy, are there any members left?"

Davy said, "Well, (pause) three now." He started to eat his mashed potatoes and gravy.

JANUARY 6

There are four in this group which includes Davy. All are good readers, enjoy reading, read to the class, and do independent reading. They were finishing "Skippy, the Monkey," a story of a mischievous monkey. Davy began chuckling softly, then a big grin, and eyes sparkled as he read. Then he laughed aloud. Children said, "Where are you reading that makes you laugh?"

Davy replied, "Hurry up to page 26 and you'll see. Wait until you see what Skippy is doing." The rest of the children read as fast as they could. Davy waited for them to catch up. When they reached it, David said, "Ha! Ha-ha! Did you ever see such a monkey. I'd like to have that little devil."

Beth made big eyes and said, "Oh, oh, Davy! What did you say?" Davy said, "Why, that's nothing to blow your top about. It isn't bad, is it, Miss J?"

Teacher replied, "I'm sure you could have used a better word than devil."

Davy said, "Well, the truth is he was a devil or at least acted like one."

Beth laughed. Others joined in. Reading proceeded.

FEBRUARY I

The children had two large basketballs. The girls had one and the boys had one. This was the day they could play anything they chose. Davy ran, jumped, wrestled, bounced basketball, and began shooting at the goal. He made two goals, clapped his hands, and danced when he made them. He told the other boys, "Boy, I made two goals!" They smiled and applauded. Then Davy lay down on his stomach and had James, Bobby, and Dick pull him across the floor as though he were a sled. He was laughing loudly and enjoying it immensely. He had them pull him three times across the end of the gym. Then he saw a group of boys lining up for a race. He dashed to get in line for the race. He ran the race, won, and dashed halfway to the teacher, slipped part of the way, and said, "Boy, I sure put on steam, but I won!" His face was very red and he was perspiring.

FEBRUARY 19

After lunch children hurried with their trays so they could be the first in line next to the teacher. Davy was late today which is unusual. He hurried to the line, not smiling, and looking somewhat angry. Barry, a large boy for his age and largest in the room, said, "O.K., let Davy in line. He is the leader today." Davy smiled at Barry who said, "See, I stuck up for you, Davy." Davy said, "Thanks, Barry. I'll remember this." Then with a smile he took his place as leader of the line and led it back to the room.

Physical Development

Physical growth during early elementary years is slow and steady. Children during this period generally increase 2 or 3 inches in length and 3 to 6 pounds in weight each year; but, as was noted in Chapter 4, there is considerable variation among children at any level in their rates of growth and maturing. The child's face and body are gradually changing shape. The jaw lengthens as baby teeth work themselves loose, come out, and are replaced by permanent teeth. The heart is in a period of rapid growth, but the brain has achieved about 90 percent of its weight. The eyes of the six year old have not reached adult size or shape, and because of their relatively shallow depth, the child at this age is often farsighted. As a consequence, many six year olds are delayed in beginning to learn to read. By the end of early elementary childhood, the dominance of left or right eye and handedness has been established.

The high activity of the preschool years carries over in the early elementary period. There is a great deal of running, jumping, climbing. As children play on the swings, do stunts on the bars, participate in rhythms, learn to swim and to balance themselves in walking a plank, play circle games, tag, run relay races, or play simple games with a large rubber ball, they are *gaining increased skill in using and controlling large muscles*. Clare is working on large-muscle control, as shown by her doing stunts on the bars, skipping rope, running, and initiating active games. This is the period when tag, jacks, marbles, hide-and-go-seek, ring toss, spinning tops, and flying kites are popular. Some girls begin to take dancing at this age, and a few have fleeting dreams of becoming a famous ballerina.

In time, this active play becomes more organized, as children form teams and compete against each other. Then active play is focused on *learning skills required in organized games and sports*, a developmental learning of considerable importance in middle childhood. Davy is already beginning to work on this task, as revealed by his initial successes with the basketball.

In conformity to the law of developmental direction which was encountered earlier, children are beginning to *gain increased control over their fine muscles*. At first, they are awkward in using their hands, but in time they do quite well in coloring, cutting, pasting, painting, drawing, and using simple tools such as hammer and saw.

Social Development

The early elementary period is marked by important changes in children's social development. The child's identification with adults, especially the teacher, which was noted in nursery school and kindergarten, continues into first grade. The child's relationships with his teachers at this stage influence his feelings of security and also shape his whole outlook on life, his feelings of adequacy, and his experiences in relating to peers and other adults.

As young children interact with and respond to their teachers, they are *learning to relate emotionally to adults outside the home*. Davy enjoyed sitting with the teacher and telling her about his gang's clubhouse and activities. At the same time, as children begin to assume responsibilities (dress themselves, go on errands, go to school alone and arrive there on time, and learn to take care of themselves in a new environment), they are taking important steps in *achieving independence of family*. Six-year-old Clare expressed her independence by saying "No" to her mother, by continuing to swing after the yard teacher blew her whistle, and by not working with the teacher and other children in the reading group.

Children's relationships with their peers increase in importance and intensity during the early elementary years. At ages seven, eight, and nine, children spend increasing amounts of time and effort in activities that will enable them to *win acceptance, roles, and prestige in the peer group*. As we noted in Chapter 7, this is the period when gangs and short-lived clubs are formed, complete with secret language and codes. The mania for collecting baseball cards and other objects and paraphernalia begins about this time. As children improve in motor coordination and develop game skills, they begin to play baseball, soccer, basketball, football, and other games involving a group of peers. As children learn the rules of the game and find ways of settling their disagreements over rules, an increase in group cohesiveness may be noted, and peer activities continue over longer periods of time. Further interactions with peers are provided by Brownie and Cub Scout groups.

The child's relationships with his peers during the primary grades are evident in the excerpts from the cases of Clare and Davy. Clare's classmates supported her so that she was not kept in at recess in spite of the yard teacher's recommendation, but they strongly protested her continuing to jump rope after she missed. Another peer warned her against fooling around during the reading period. Clare became more responsive to the reactions of peers as the year progressed. In the excerpts from the case of Davy, the peer group is seen to exert a strong influence in the daily lives of second-grade children. The intolerance of primary children for their less able and mature peers is revealed in Davy's asking Robbie not to cry when the substitute teacher was there. Davy on numerous occasions spoke of his gang's clubhouse, but when the teacher asked to visit the clubhouse, Davy was not sure whether she would be permitted to come. Sticking up for a friend and peer was shown in Barry's holding Davy's place in line.

As children relate to one another, many of their behaviors such as teasing, name calling, and quarreling are strongly disapproved by adults. Children at this stage, as well as at earlier and later stages, continue to work on *learning and adhering to the expectations of the culture.* Clare gradually learned to give her attention to the reading activity, and Davy was made aware of his wrongdoing in hitting Tina when she took the seat he was saving for the teacher. Conforming to the demands of the culture is facilitated by the *development of a conscience,* which began with the child's identification with his parents during the preschool years. Moreover, as peer activities of boys and girls become more divergent, further progress may be noted in each child's *acceptance of his sex role.* Evidence of Davy's developing a conscience and acceptance of his sex role is shown in the anecdote of Davy hitting Tina. The teacher asked Davy, "Do you hit girls?" and Davy said, "I'm sorry, Tina."

Mental Development

When children begin the primary years, they are ready and eager to learn as much as they can of the world about them and to communicate by using the symbols they have observed their older siblings and grownups use. *Learning and gaining increased skill in reading* is a key developmental task of children during their early years in school. At the age of six and a half, most children have acquired adequate breadth of interest and sufficient mental maturity and eye development to be ready to read. Reading vocabulary increases rapidly during the primary years, children learn to read silently, and many children are reading independently by the end of this period. They are acquiring skills that are part of the broad developmental task of *learning appropriate symbol systems and the development of conceptual abilities*. Children during this period not only learn to tell time but, through adapting to the routines of home and school, develop a concept of time. They are beginning to have some awareness of the past and reveal an interest in people who lived long ago. They are acquiring concepts of space and distance beyond their own experience. Differences in sizes and shapes fascinate them. They are gaining a better understanding of spatial relationships, and they show this in the greater realism, proportion, and detail in their drawings and paintings. In these and many other ways children in the primary years are *learning a vast number of physical and social concepts related to their ever widening world*.

The cases of Clare and Davy show that each in his own way was hard at work on the developmental tasks of *mastering a symbol system* (implied in learning to read) and of *developing concepts related to the physical and social world*. Clare's teacher reported that she was in the first reading group and was reading well. Her growth in developing concepts was revealed in her comment that a certain story was silly because it told of rabbits and boys being hatched from eggs. Davy's skill and interest in reading may be inferred from his comments about the monkey in the story. His concepts of what it means to belong to a gang and what constitutes cussing are revealed in several of his comments.

The early elementary childhood years witness important changes as the child begins to interact with adults and peers in a wider world. During these years he becomes more responsible and independent, and develops the skills and understandings that will enable him, through reading, cognitive development, and problem solving, to deal with concepts and phenomena far beyond the space and time of his immediate world.

Late Childhood

Late childhood, as it is to be described here, encompasses the period of development of boys (age nine to eleven) and girls (age nine and ten) in the upper elementary years of grades four, five, and six. (Some writers refer to this stage as "middle childhood"; others use the term "preadolescence.") This period is often referred to as the "latency" period of development. It is a period of slow, steady growth in height and weight; but there is a sharp decrease in rate of growth during the last few months of late childhood, just prior to the onset of the pubescent growth spurt. Wide differences in physical maturity are noticeable among children at this level. Some children in fourth, fifth, and sixth grades appear small and underdeveloped, while many of their classmates—tall, large, and well developed—are in the preadolescent and early adolescent stages of maturity. A few girls begin menstruating at nine and ten years of age.

Late childhood may offer parents and teachers a "breather" from the stresses and problems of earlier periods of development. The youngster in late childhood is more responsible and dependable. He has developed a great many skills, he is more amenable to reason and logic, he is developing a strongly internalized sense of right and wrong, and he reveals a tremendous interest in and curiosity about the physical and social world in which he lives.

During late childhood, the peer group becomes increasingly important in the lives of children, but the interests and activities of boys and girls diverge more and more, as each sex group disdains the other and keeps pretty much to itself. Late childhood is a period of comparative calm wherein children in general adjust smoothly to the problems that confront them.

Before we discuss the changes and developmental tasks of late childhood, it may be useful to observe how two children, Cheryl and Stan, are responding to the demands and changes of this period.

Cheryl is nine years, nine months of age and is in the fourth grade of a third and fourth grade combination class. She has an older brother Tim, who is eleven, and two sisters, Nancy and Paula, who are five and three respectively. Her father was killed the year before in an automobile accident.

OCTOBER 6

For "Show and Tell" this morning Cheryl told about a teenager who goes to the same church as she does. Cheryl said the girl was simply "charming." "Yesterday at church she looked beautiful. She had on a navy blue chemise dress with huge white buttons for trimming. She had on a little blue hat, some blue pumps and even blue hose. She has a real small waistline." Cheryl also stated that she didn't know this girl, "although she has noticed me as she smiles at me." Cheryl hopes to make her acquaintance so she'll get some ideas on how to dress when she gets a little older.

OCTOBER 27

Cheryl was radiant as she rushed into the room this morning. Her eyes were simply dancing as she walked to her desk to put her library book away. She exclaimed, "Do you see anything different about me this morning?" I instantly knew that I'd better look Cheryl over fairly well before I answered. I had no need to worry as Cheryl was bubbling with enthusiasm. She exclaimed, "Oh, Mrs. M., see my new tights! They're robin's egg blue. I simply am crazy about them." Cheryl opened the door and ran outside to show her new tights to all her friends.

NOVEMBER 14

When Miss B. brought her fifth grade to visit our room, one boy wondered why we all had new seats. Cheryl immediately spoke up and said, "We are the most privileged, so—we get new seats." The boy gave Cheryl a "sneering" look and Cheryl answered by a "cool stare."

FEBRUARY 27

Story written for language.

The Measure of Greatness

I think that a person rich or poor could be called great. A person does not have to be smart to be great. I think Abraham Lincoln was great even though he was poor and didn't have any schooling. And also there was George Washington who was rich and had schooling.

The greatest living person I know is my mother. The reason I think she is nice is because she is never cross or mean.

Cheryl Howe

MARCH 31

As I was writing some fourth-grade assignments on the board Cheryl came up and said, "Oh, Mrs. M., I forgot to tell you. During Easter vacation I got a phone call. Guess who it was from?"

I hesitated a few seconds and asked, "Was it a boy or a girl?"

Cheryl: "A boy, and I really wasn't too thrilled. But I guess it's OK."

Teacher: "I give up. You'll have to just tell me."

Cheryl: "W—e—ll, it was Gary Grimes. He called one evening and told me he was moving. He would be going to a new school and wouldn't see me anymore. He said that he liked me very much and he thought I liked him."

Cheryl went on to explain that she was so embarrassed, but she was courteous and kind to Gary.

Stan is ten years, nine months of age and in the fifth grade. He laughs vigorously when something funny happens in the classroom and is always alert to do any favor I might ask of him. Although not a skilled leader in sports he seems to show much enthusiasm and eagerness in participating in all games.

OCTOBER 14

While playing kickball today during recreation period, Stan and Russ were continually getting together and trying to wrestle until the captain of the team said, "What's the matter with you two? You are not keeping your positions."

Stan remarked, "I just guess we aren't too interested today and we'd rather wrestle." Several other boys yelled at them and said, "Come on, Stan and Russ, we need your help." Both boys got to their positions and followed the game a little more closely.

NOVEMBER 17

In a conference with Stan's mother this afternoon I learned that astronomy seems to be his greatest interest. When on a trip to New York with the family, they had taken him to the observatory which he thoroughly enjoyed. Several times his father has taken him and his older brother to the Naval Observatory in Washington.

NOVEMBER 24

Stan was sitting by my desk. Carl asked if he might buy a small picture of one of the girls. (She had returned her pictures without purchasing any.) Stan remarked, "Mrs. T., it's really fun sitting by your desk seeing how goofy some of these guys are. Imagine wanting to buy a girl's picture! I think too much of my money to spend it on a girl's picture. Carl surely must be in love." Carl looked at Stan with a very delighted look on his face and remarked, "Sure, Stan, I want to buy Bee's picture, so what?" Stan shook his head in a negative way and remarked again, "Buying a girl's picture!" I smiled at his remark and said, "Stan, maybe you'll think enough of a girl to buy her picture." Stan replied, "No, not me, that silver smells too good to me."

DECEMBER 21

Stan came up to me and said he had hurt his hand and wrist yesterday. I asked how he hurt himself. He said, "You see, one of my friends and I were playing, and I guess he wanted to see which could be the best in boxing, and this is what I got, a bad hand. I don't think either could be judged the winner for he went home with a bruised shoulder and I with a partly sprained thumb, so that's why I feel gloomy. But one thing, I did come to school today and he didn't, so maybe he couldn't take it as well as I could. The other boy is Frank in the sixth grade, a year older than I am, but I believe I am a little taller and heavier than he is. I'll find out about his pains tonight when I get home. I am glad I could come to school."

MARCH 23

Today we had a spelling contest. Before beginning, several asked Stan not to spell his words so loudly. He observed this suggestion by his peers. He and another boy tied as the best spellers. Stan's face showed an expression of joy. He wasn't boastful, but one could tell that he was pleased when several boys and girls said, "Stan, you are really a good speller." "Thank you" was his only reply.

APRIL 3

Stan seems to be noticing Bee a great deal today. She is one of the most popular girls in the room. He looked over at her and smiled several times. When he passed her desk, he'd pause to say something. While playing circle soccer each time he'd kick the ball in Bee's direction. This seemed to please her for I noticed she smiled each time the ball was kicked to her. When the group was ready to leave at three o'clock, I said, "Stan, I think something has happened to you."

He said, "I am curious to know. May I stay in to find out?" Before I had time to answer, Stan returned to his seat and waited to talk with me. He asked what I had noticed.

I said, "I believe there is a girl in here you are showing a little attention." With a pleased look he replied, "You mean Bee?"

I said, "Yes, Stan, I noticed how you were showing her a little attention."

"You know, Mrs. T, she is right pretty, attractive, a good sport, and good in school work, and I do like her very much, but I am not so sure whether she likes me."

I said, "I am pleased you see these good qualities, and Bee is a fine girl."

MAY 3

Stan's mother came to bring Stan his baseball mitt he had forgotten. I spoke to his mother and she said, "Mrs. T., Stan was so enthusiastic about his new mitt, and now he doesn't want to play with the boys at noontime."

I said, "Stan, what is the trouble? You showed me your mitt and were so happy about it."

He said, "Mrs. T., the boys just don't want me to play because I can't always hit the ball."

I said, "Stan, maybe the boys feel you need more practice. Why not practice with some of the boys after school and at noon until you become more skillful?"

He said, "Mother, don't leave my mitt. I am not going to play." The mother insisted, but knowing the boys on the team, I could see Stan's point of view and I felt if I could talk with some of the boys they could help Stan. Stan said he didn't want me to do that. They'd think he was a sissy if I should arrange to have him play. I asked Al if he'd help him with the skill in batting.

Al said, "I like Stan and even though he isn't such a grand player, I think he should be on the team. He can do some things better than some of the boys." Al urged Stan to play the next day. Stan had his mitt and brought it with him to the ball diamond. Later I noticed that Stan is on the team and seems to be very happy.

Physical Development

Late childhood is the period wherein *physical prowess* and *athletic skills,* especially for boys, are more important than at any other time. Failure to learn the skills which enable one to participate adequately in the games and activities of the peer group is a grave handicap to being accepted by the group. The importance of being able to play well enough to make the team was keenly felt by Stan in the anecdote cited above. Stan recognized that he could not play ball as well as some of the boys; and, after some initial hesitation, he worked hard to improve himself in hitting and fielding.

The rapid *development of fine-muscle control* during this period is revealed in improved athletic skills, skills in playing a musical instrument and use of tools, and in more legible handwriting and quality of art work. Arts and crafts hold considerable interest for children in late childhood. Boys may spend a morning or an afternoon working on a model airplane or car or building things with simple tools. Girls sew and weave, and both sexes reveal interests and skills in leather work, plastics, ceramics, and other art media.

The growth of body organs during late childhood has an important influence on behavior and development. Lungs and the digestive and circulatory systems are still growing. Since the heart lags behind the growth and development of other organs, overstimulation and excessive fatigue should be avoided. The eyes are much better developed and are able to accommodate to close work with less strain.[9]

For boys, this is a period of rough-and-tumble play. It is a time when boys test themselves against other boys by wrestling and occasional fights. Stan and his friend Russ started wrestling during kickball; later he spoke to the teacher of his injured hand, which came from his trying to outbox another boy. In late childhood, girls become physically less active. Cheryl played jumprope with the girls, but already in fourth grade she was more frequently a spectator rather than a participant in active games with boys.

Social Development

The peer group, which emerges in the latter part of the primary years, has by late childhood become an important social force in the lives of most of these children. *Being accepted by one's peers* and *playing roles in the peer group* are among the important developmental tasks which confront the child at this stage of his development. We noted earlier the important relationships between physical skills, physical maturity, and peer acceptance. Cultural differences, however, appear to exert limited influence on peer status during late childhood. If a child's behavior is acceptable to his peers, differences in socioeconomic background, race, and religion influence peer acceptance relatively little unless pressures are exerted on children by their homes.

As noted earlier, the beginnings of a strong conformity may be observed in late childhood. The peer group exerts an increasing influence on the dress, activities, and values of its members. Few children wish to risk rejection because of failure to conform. The peer group at this stage is made up of smaller clubs and cliques. Often these small groups form spontaneously and

---

[9] Gladys G. Jenkins, Helen Schacter, and William W. Bauer, *These Are Your Children* (Glenview, Illinois: Scott, Foresman and Co., 1949), pp. 106–181.

are informal and continuously changing. Frequently, clubs and cliques strive to maintain their identity and structure through use of secret language, secret rules, and secret passwords.

The most striking characteristic of most peer groups in late childhood is that there are really two peer groups, formed by the cleavage between the sexes. In maintaining their preference for rough-and-tumble play, boys disdain weakness and feminine activities as "soft" and "sissyish." Girls perceive boys this age as rough, uncouth, ill mannered, and not quite civilized. Girls and boys in late childhood do work and play together under the leadership of an adult, but in free-play situations each child tends to participate in his own sex activities. At various times, each sex group may respond to the other sex group by ignoring the other group, by criticism, and at times by antagonism and hostility. Stan left little doubt about his feelings toward girls: "Imagine wanting to buy a girl's picture! I think too much of my money to want to spend it on a girl's picture." The mutual disdain which Cheryl and a boy in another class felt for each other is reflected in his "sneering look" and her "cool stare."

The boy's life in late childhood tends to be bound up in the life and activities of his gang. Many gangs center their attention on athletics and sports, some concentrate on maintaining their position and territory vis-à-vis neighboring gangs, while others seem to "have little organized purpose other than to serve as hideouts from adults where fellows may . . . exchange yarns of escapades and plan ever more daring, more dangerous activities."[10] It is from the gang that members gain further information about sex. Often it is communicated through ribald stories accompanied by raucous laughter. Though the stories, antics, practical joking, roughhousing, and secret communications seem silly and pointless to many adults, they are the means through which children in late childhood measure themselves against their peers in the group.

Clubs and formation of cliques are also focal points of girls' social interaction in late childhood. It has been suggested that girls are more concerned with form and verbal imagery than boys at this age and that their clubs exist more for the practice they provide girls to exercise their verbal powers through the forms required by club life than for the sociability it affords. There is some indication, too, that girls' clubs tend to be more exclusive, more autocratic, and more tightly knit than do boys' gangs.[11]

Whereas boys gain prestige at this stage through athletic prowess, girls gain status in the group by their manner of dressing and grooming. They are much more conscious of their appearance than are boys. This strong interest in clothes was revealed in the excerpts from the case of Cheryl. By her detailed descriptions of the teen-ager she had seen in church, Cheryl revealed her strong admiration of this girl. Cheryl bubbled with enthusiasm in showing the teacher her robin's egg blue tights; and, in talking to a girl friend

---

[10] Howard A. Lane and Mary Beauchamp, *Understanding Human Development* (Englewood Cliffs, New Jersey: Prentice-Hall, 1959), p. 277.

[11] Lane and Beauchamp, pp. 281–282.

about her mother's new sweater that she tried on, she sighed, "It looked real dreamy on me."

In spite of the strong influence of the peer group in the lives of children in late childhood, the affection, confidence, and support of adults are still very important. Thus, for these children, *relating to adults*—gaining their friendship, confidence, and approval—is an important continuing developmental task. The need for peer-group belongingness and, at the same time, for the affection and approval of adults may be a source of conflict for the child if the differing expectations of each cannot be compromised or reconciled. Standards of the peer group come increasingly to prevail over those advocated by adults. At the same time, the efforts of adults to dominate, to manipulate, or to overprotect individuals or the group are deeply resented.

Because of the group's increased sensitivity to and fear of adult domination or manipulation, the parent or teacher who wishes to assist a child in gaining peer acceptance needs to exercise unusual tact. Stan was particularly sensitive to the unwanted interference of his mother in bringing his mitt to school and of his teacher's offer to ask the other boys to help Stan on May 3. Stan's ready smile, his willingness to help, and his frequent reporting to the teacher on peer activities and out-of-school experiences revealed a strong liking for his teacher. It was natural for Cheryl to identify strongly with her teacher, since she shared with her teacher her hopes and aspirations. It is also revealed in her statement, "Mrs. M., I think you're a real common person. You usually wear such plain, attractive clothes." The teacher replied, "Thank you, Cheryl. That's the nicest compliment I've received in a long time."

Personal and Intellectual Development

Children register considerable progress during the years of late childhood in their development as persons. They are becoming more skilled in handling their emotions, in relating to others, and in coping with frustration. To the extent that children succeed in mastering developmental tasks of learning physical and game skills and gaining peer group acceptance, they grow in self-confidence. Stan revealed a new sense of self-esteem in his report of his boxing match with Frank.

Children at this stage are *learning more mature and more effective ways of adjusting to threat and frustration*. They can be more objective in seeing and accepting their own faults and shortcomings rather than projecting the blame onto others. Cheryl's progress in learning more appropriate adjustment patterns was shown in a variety of ways. In an anecdote presented in a previous chapter, Cheryl readily admitted her guilt in accusing Sue of cheating, and she apologized. She reported being courteous and kind to Gary, who unexpectedly telephoned and told Cheryl he liked her.

A child's growth in personal development at this stage is also shown in his *increased awareness of the opposite sex* and by his *increased acceptance of his own sex role*. We have noted the attachment for one's own sex and the antagonism directed toward the opposite sex, manifested during much of late childhood. This attachment to one's own sex extends over a longer period of time for boys than it does for girls.

In spite of their efforts to maintain their pose of disdain for the opposite sex, boys and girls are seldom able to mask their growing awareness of and interest in the opposite sex. The physical changes associated with approaching puberty make this growing awareness inevitable. In manifesting an awareness in the opposite sex at this stage, children are taking an important step toward *establishing heterosexual relationships,* an important developmental task faced in early adolescence. Cheryl reported that she wasn't too thrilled by Gary's saying that he liked her. Stan's sudden change in attitude toward girls is not untypical and is rather amusing. One may guess that some boys may be revealing their growing awareness in girls "safely" by teasing male peers who express this interest more overtly.

Boys and girls indicate an acceptance of their sex roles through characteristic behavior and modes of response that have already been described. Thus, boys show their masculinity by being tough and brave, playing hard and rough, and showing interest in sports. Girls express their femininity in their grooming, in their interests in clothes, and in their development of social and verbal skills.

Late childhood is a period of marked *development of intellectual skills* and interests. Most children at this stage have developed sufficient skill in reading to be able to use it to acquire a broad range of knowledge in many different fields. The average nine-year-old has a vocabulary of more than 10,000 words, which increases to nearly 14,000 words by age eleven.[12] However, a range of difference of four or five years in reading ability may be expected in the same classroom and grade at this stage. A few eleven-year-olds will be reading at adult levels.

Most children in late childhood are intensely curious about the physical and social world in which they live. They can distinguish between fantasy and reality, and they are oriented toward the world of reality. They exhibit a keen interest in science, in space travel, in other parts of the world, and in past events. This is a period when interest in collecting reaches a peak. A boy may collect rocks, stamps, or butterflies, while a girl may be adding to her collection of foreign dolls. Children's reading interests center in books about travel, science, nature, and biography.

Their wide interests and the broad scope of their reading enable children to make great strides in cognitive development. They are forming a great many concepts and are capable of abstract thought. Concepts such as gravity, space, power, and freedom are undergoing refinement of meaning. Stan's mother reported to the teacher Stan's strong interest in astronomy and his visits to observatories. Cheryl revealed in her language composition her understanding of the concept of "greatness."

---

[12] Ruth Strang, *An Introduction to Child Study,* 4th ed. (New York: Macmillan Co., 1959), p. 455.

Summary

What the individual is like as he grows and develops during the weeks and months after birth is a response in part to the prenatal development which preceded it. Birth is a traumatic experience; the vital systems must begin to function to maintain life in the outside world. During infancy, the important developmental tasks are the following:

1. Achieving stability in physiological functioning.
2. Developing eye-hand coordination.
3. Being weaned.
4. Learning to eat solid foods.
5. Learning to relate emotionally to parents, siblings, and others.
6. Learning to walk.
7. Learning to talk.
8. Learning to control elimination.

Preschool early childhood, beginning at age two or three, is a period of transition wherein the child begins to interact with and to learn about the world beyond the family. During these preschool years children may be observed working on these developmental tasks:

1. Developing large muscles and gaining control of their bodies.
2. Learning to balance periods of activity with periods of quiet and rest.
3. Learning to relate to peers through fantasy and parallel play.
4. Learning and adhering to the rules and expectations of the culture.
5. Learning to relate emotionally to persons outside the family.
6. Developing and modifying concepts of social and physical reality.
7. Becoming aware of sex differences.
8. Developing sexual modesty.

Age six, the beginning of early elementary childhood, is a time when the child moves from his family into the larger world of the school and community. Some of the key developmental tasks of most American children at this stage are the following:

1. Gaining increased skill in using and controlling large muscles.
2. Learning skills required in organized games and sports.
3. Gaining increased control over fine muscles.
4. Learning to relate to adults outside of the family.

5. Achieving some degree of independence of family.
6. Gaining acceptance, roles, and prestige as a member of the peer group.
7. Further learning of and adherence to the expectations of the culture.
8. Developing a conscience.
9. Accepting one's sex role.
10. Learning appropriate symbol systems and developing conceptual abilities.
11. Developing physical and social concepts which relate to an ever changing world.

Late childhood, often referred to as the "latency" period, is the period of slow, steady growth experienced by children in the upper grades prior to the onset of the pubescent growth spurt. The following developmental tasks engage the energies of most American children during the period of late childhood:

1. Development of physical prowess and athletic skills (especially for boys).
2. Increased development of fine-muscle control.
3. Gaining acceptance and playing roles in the peer group.
4. Developing and maintaining friendly relationships with adults.
5. Developing effective ways of adjusting to threat and frustration.
6. Increasing one's awareness of the opposite sex.
7. Further acceptance and learning of one's sex role.
8. Further development of intellectual skills.
9. Growth in cognitive development and use of abstractions.

Study Questions

1. Children today are learning complex concepts and skills at an earlier age than children of preceding decades and generations. Cite examples to illustrate the changes in timing of onset of certain developmental tasks. What are some new tasks expected of children growing up today?

2. Mrs. Akin is very ambitious for her six-year-old daughter, Marjorie. Marjorie is small and shy, has a short attention span, and appears to be less developed than many others in her class. Miss Hoyt, Marjorie's first-grade teacher, is providing Marjorie and other less mature children in her class with additional readiness experiences while the more mature children are beginning to read from books. Mrs. Akin is quite upset when she learns that Marjorie is not reading from books as is the daughter of her next-door neighbor. If you were Miss Hoyt, how would you respond to Mrs. Akin?

3. Observe a student for twenty minutes in the classroom or on the playground and describe his behavior and interactions with others. What clues do you

have concerning the common expected learnings appropriate to his maturity level that he seems to be working on? How are his behaviors and approaches to working on these developmental tasks different from those of other students?

4. To what extent are the learning objectives and activities of a specific grade level or subject with which you are acquainted consonant with the developmental tasks students at that maturity level are working on? Do school experiences provide opportunities to children for working on their developmental tasks, or are school experiences largely irrelevant to the developmental tasks of children? Discuss.

Suggested Readings

Gladys G. Jenkins, Helen Schacter, and William W. Bauer. *These Are Your Children.* Glenview, Ill.: Scott, Foresman and Co., 1949. Presents a generalized description of the physical, social, and mental development of children for each age from year five to year eight. Later chapters deal with the mature child, the preadolescent, and parent-child relationships.

Howard Lane and Mary Beauchamp. *Understanding Human Development.* Englewood Cliffs, N.J.: Prentice-Hall, 1959. Chapters 8–13 trace the course of human development from pre-memory age through preschool, early childhood, middle childhood, early adolescent, and late adolescent—early adult maturity levels. Using illustrations from their own rich experiences with children and youth, the authors enumerate the characteristics of each stage.

Harper Lee. *To Kill a Mockingbird.* New York: J. B. Lippincott, 1960. Pulitzer Prize novel which portrays the childhood of a captivating young girl, Scout, and her experiences growing up in a small Southern town a generation ago. Vividly portrayed are the human emotions and relationships within a warm loving family and those of fear and hostility aroused in the community by an unfortunate racial incident. A rich, delightful picture of children and childhood.

L. Joseph Stone and Joseph Church. *Childhood and Adolescence.* New York: Random House, 1957. A comprehensive discussion of physical, social, and intellectual development from birth through adolescence. Included is a consideration of the child's capacities, needs, passions, and concerns, and the environmental conditions that help to shape his individuality.

Films

The Terrible Twos and Trusting Threes, 16 mm, sound, black and white, 22 min. Bloomington, Indiana: Audio-Visual Center, Indiana University (rental fee, $3.90). Portrays child behavior at two and three years, showing what to expect from youngsters at these ages and suggesting how parents can deal constructively with these problems.

Frustrating Fours and Fascinating Fives, 16 mm, sound, black and white, 22 min. Bloomington, Indiana: Audio-Visual Center, Indiana University (rental fee, $4.15). A four-year-old boy's behavior in the home is shown as oscillating from childishness to vigorous self-assertion while at kindergarten at age five contrasting behaviors of imaginary craftsmanship and inconsistent destructiveness are revealed. Although the change is gradual, the child appears to be more independent of adult support and has an insatiable curiosity about the world around him.

From Sociable Six to Noisy Nine, 16 mm, sound, black and white, 22 min. Bloomington, Indiana: Audio-Visual Center, Indiana University (rental fee, $4.40). Describes the characteristic behavior of children six to nine years of age. A couple with three children in this age group are shown handling such problems as jealousy, occasional dishonesty, destructiveness, and varying interests and abilities.

From Ten to Twelve, 16 mm, sound, black and white, 26 min. Bloomington, Indiana: Audio-Visual Center, Indiana University (rental fee, $5.90). Shows the characteristic behavior of children this age. Boys are seen as noisy and messy in appearance, belonging to a gang, and having different developmental and personality characteristics. Some girls at this age level are seen as unsophisticated while others are mature, sensitive to relationships with adults, and very talkative. Problems of discipline, guidance, and understanding that confront most parents are shown. Much of the conflicting behavior of pre-teens is seen as a normal part of growing up.

12

adolescence

If youth be a defect, it is one we outgrow only too soon.

≡   JAMES RUSSELL LOWELL

Adolescence is a period of biosocial transition between childhood and adulthood. The adolescent, far more variable than
the infant in his growth and behavior, is at an in-between
stage of development—at one instant displaying the behavior and feelings of a child and at other times acting quite
grown up. So prone are we to dichotomize people as adults
or children that we are perplexed about how to respond to
persons who are in between and something of both.

Adolescence appears to generate mixed feelings and
reactions in adults and in adolescents themselves. Understanding parents and teachers have come to accept elongated, rapidly maturing bodies, awkwardness, self-consciousness, rebelliousness, idealism, and wide swings in mood
and activity as normal characteristics of adolescence. Early
adolescence is a period when young people, because of rapid
growth and maturing, are at times less attractive and less
skillful than they were as children or will be as adults and
they have little experience and few resources for coping
with new problems associated with these changes. For many
adults and youth, adolescence is something to be endured.
Something of the ambivalence of adults in their attitudes
toward adolescence is revealed in this statement by Stone
and Church:

[Adolescence] is a phase that no one looks forward to, that adolescents themselves deny, and that only a few fading athletes and aging women look back on with regret and then usually with the reservation that it is their adolescent bodies they want, leaving their adult mentalities as they are.[1]

Although the awkwardness and anxieties of early adolescence are frequently accompanied by a pervasive feeling of being out of step, the beauty, strength, and vitality of late adolescence and young adulthood are emulated by persons of all ages. Our culture's adulation of and identification with youth is strikingly revealed in the advertising of countless products claiming the ability to help us look or feel younger. Thus, there is a kind of dichotomy in attitudes toward adolescence. Early adolescence is accompanied by an anxious and uncomfortable feeling of being out of step, while late adolescence and young adulthood are focal points for adulation and envy.

Puberty versus Adolescence

Before we discuss further the changes that occur during adolescence, it is necessary to distinguish in our terminology between the physical and sexual maturation of boys and girls (puberty) and certain behavioral characteristics of this maturity level (adolescence), characteristics that appear to be as much influenced by culture as by the physical changes of puberty. In speaking of the physical maturation of boys and girls, we will use the terms *prepuberty* (or *pubescence*), *puberty,* and *postpuberty.*

Pubescence is a period of about two years prior to puberty. During pubescence, physiological development occurs and reproductive organs mature. The onset of pubescence is marked by a spurt in physical growth, followed by changes in body proportion, the appearance of secondary sex characteristics, and the maturation of primary sex organs.

Puberty has been defined as the point of development at which biological changes reach a climax and sexual maturity is evidenced.[2] Puberty occurs in the girl with menarche, her first menstruation, and has been preceded by various body changes, including enlarging breasts, widening hips, and the appearance of pubic and underarm hair. Boys experience no such definite or dramatic sign as menstruation to mark their puberty. Puberty in boys is revealed by a variety of body changes, including growth of long bones of arms and legs, appearance of pubic and underarm hair, and hair on the upper lip and chin. At puberty, boys begin to experience nocturnal emissions. These are irregular, spontaneous expulsions of seminal fluid during sleep. Probably the most valid evidence of sexual maturity in boys is the presence from time to time of live spermatozoa in the urine.

[1] F. Joseph Stone and Joseph Church, *Childhood and Adolescence* (New York: Random House, 1957), p. 268.
[2] Stone and Church, p. 269.

Although puberty marks the beginning of sexual functioning, several more years of growth and development are required before the female menstrual cycle becomes stabilized and the male becomes capable of ejaculating sperm in sufficient quantity to assure procreation. The age at which reproductive maturity occurs varies considerably and appears to be related to socioeconomic as well as geographical differences. Greulich[3] reports that reproductive maturity is earlier among those of higher socioeconomic status, those residing in temperate climates, and those favored by good nutrition. It appears later in those having inadequate diets, those with severe illnesses, and those who reside in tropical climates. Many primitive cultures take official note of the individual's sexual maturity in ceremonial observances called *puberty rites*.

Postpuberty is the name given to the several years following puberty. This period witnesses a progressive decrease in the velocity of growth toward adult body size, proportion, form, and capacities. This is the period during which the menstrual cycle becomes more regular, and during which both boys and girls fill out and develop adult-like contours and physiques.

Adolescence is the period of development extending from the beginning of pubescence to the point at which the individual assumes the roles and responsibilities of adulthood. Culturally, adolescence is the period of transition between the dependency of childhood and the relative autonomy of adulthood. Psychologically, it is a period of adjustment to physical and social changes that distinguish child behavior from adult behavior. Chronologically, adolescence consists of the time span from approximately (depending on the individual and the culture) twelve or thirteen until the late teens or early twenties. The term *adolescence* is probably most imprecise when it is used to refer to stereotyped behavior characteristics of some individuals at this age. The Franks[4] point out that rebelliousness, moodiness, irritability, crying spells, or outbursts of anger may occur before puberty in some children and may not appear at all in other children. A number of different explanations have been offered to explain the behavior changes which occur during the five- to eight-year period separating childhood and adulthood. We shall examine some of these explanations in the discussion of theories of adolescence which follows.

Theories of Adolescence

The marked interest in adolescent behavior and development manifested during this century has stimulated the development of numerous theories of

---

[3] W. W. Greulich, "Physical Changes in Adolescence," in Nelson B. Henry, *Forty-third Yearbook: Part I, Adolescence,* National Society for the Study of Education (Chicago: University of Chicago Press, 1944), p. 29.

[4] Mary Frank and Lawrence K. Frank, *Your Adolescent at Home and in School* (New York: Viking Press, 1956), p. 36.

adolescence.[5] G. Stanley Hall,[6] one of the earliest investigators and writers on the psychology of adolescence, described adolescence as a time of inner turmoil, a period of storm and stress. He perceived the emotional life of the adolescent as oscillating between contradictory tendencies of energy, excitation, laughter, and euphoria and indifference, lethargy, gloom, and melancholy. This emotional turmoil was believed to result from the physiological upheaval associated with puberty. Studies by anthropologists, however, reveal that in other cultures adolescence is not always a period of turmoil. Margaret Mead[7] found that in Samoa adolescence represents no period of crisis or stress but is an orderly development of a set of slowly maturing interests and activities. Little support was found, too, for Hall's law of recapitulation, which postulated that the individual relives the development of the human race from early animal-like primitiveness to more civilized ways of life.

The relationships in pubescence between physiological changes and behavioral changes are recognized in Sigmund Freud's theory of psychosexual development, described in earlier chapters. Pubescent development during the genital period is marked by an awakening sexuality and increases in nervous excitement, anxiety, and personality disturbances. These disturbances and anxieties arise from the continuing struggle during pubescence between the biological-instinctual id forces and the socially responsive superego. Anna Freud[8] identifies two principal defense mechanisms which are typically used during pubescence to reduce anxiety: (1) *asceticism,* a self-discipline and withdrawal reflecting a distrust of all instinctual wishes, and (2) increased *intellectualization,* a repressing of libidinal thoughts through engagement in intellectual interests.

Erik Erikson,[9] in his eight stages of man (presented in Chapter 8), posits the establishment of ego identity during pubescence. He suggests that the rapid body growth, genital maturity, and sexual awareness of pubescence foment a psychological revolution within the adolescent, threatening his body image and ego identity. The adolescent then must reestablish his ego identity, in the light of earlier experiences, and accept his body changes and libidinal feelings as a part of himself. In order to establish ego identity, the individual must integrate his vocational ambitions and aspirations and the qualities acquired through earlier identifications in imitation of parents, falling in love, and admiration of heroes.

Our observations of children and youth strongly suggest that the early and late periods of the five- to eight-year span between childhood and adulthood are rather distinct and qualitatively quite different from one another.

[5] Only a few representative theories are considered here. For a more comprehensive treatment of the topic, see Rolf E. Muuss, *Theories of Adolescence* (New York: Random House, 1962).

[6] *Adolescence* (New York: Appleton-Century-Crofts, 1916). 2 vols.

[7] *Coming of Age in Samoa* (New York: William Morrow, 1939), p. 157.

[8] *The Ego and the Mechanism of Defence,* trans. by C. Barnes (New York: International University Press, 1948).

[9] *Childhood and Society* (New York: W. W. Norton & Co., 1950), pp. 227–229.

In the following sections, we shall highlight some of these differences and at the same time note common trends in preadolescence, early adolescence, and late adolescence.

Preadolescence

Preadolescence, as the term implies, is a period in the developmental span between childhood and adolescence. In our use of the term, *preadolescence* is a period of one to two years encompassing the latter part of late childhood and the early part of early adolescence. Preadolescence has also been identified as the period when the childhood personality is broken up so that it can be modified into the personality of the adult.[10] It is a period of hyperactivity, rebelliousness, moodiness, and irritability. These behaviors, representing temporary developmental discordance and maladjustment, are the young person's responses as he copes with the disorganization of his childhood personality. His disturbing behavior is particularly trying and baffling to adults who live or work with him. Redl expresses this well when he refers to preadolescence as "the phase when the nicest children begin to behave in a most awful way."[11]

Preadolescence, overlapping as it does both late childhood and early adolescence, contains some of the characteristics of each. One of the most striking characteristics of preadolescents is their restlessness and hyperactivity. They appear to be continually in motion—tapping pencils, manipulating any one of the many objects they carry in their pockets, playing with their hair. Preadolescence is the period when the boy and girl, as they begin to mature physically, gain the first glimpses of the man or woman each will become. Both sexes are becoming aware of the grown-up body and the desirability of grown-up attractiveness.

Before proceeding further with a discussion of the characteristics and developmental tasks of preadolescence, we shall present descriptions of two preadolescents found in excerpts from the case of Deke and the case of Babs:

> Deke is a boy twelve years, five months of age who is in the sixth grade. The first day of school he remained rather close to a group of five or six other boys. This was evidenced by their motions of "Here, sit here," and "I saved this for you." In September, Deke was 63 inches tall and weighed 106 pounds.

OCTOBER 29

> Today from 2:00 to 3:15 we had our Halloween party. The group played three team games. While refreshments were served by the students

---

[10] Fritz Redl, "Pre-adolescents—What Makes Them Tick?" *Child Study,* 21 (1944), 58–59.
[11] *Ibid.*

on the committee, Deke, Dan, Fred, Carl, and Earl pulled their chairs in together so they were partially facing each other. They were giggling, talking, seeming to pay no attention to the others. Presently Deke got up and came to the table where the remaining refreshments were placed. He served himself with the balance of about four chocolate-covered peanut butter cookies. He passed them to the boys near him. They continued to giggle.

Later Earl said, "Do you know what we were laughing about at the party?" "No," I replied. "Well, Carl put some ice cream in his cider. Then we all did. We dipped our cookies in that. It was good!" he said.

NOVEMBER 3

Deke is very good in the soccer game. He is after the ball, often getting a kick at it or stopping it. In the punt-ball game, Deke usually gives it a good kick, getting it high in the air; but often it is caught on the fly. He catches the ball frequently. He is taller than any of the other boys but usually jumps up, getting both feet off the ground to catch the ball. He sort of cradles his arms to get it.

NOVEMBER 12

During our short rest period in the classroom we were playing human tic-tac-toe. Alice was leader. After her turn was up, she chose Deke to take her place. The girls chose boys to take their places, and the boys in turn chose girls. Deke was leader in the last part of the game.

DECEMBER 13

Before 9 o'clock, Deke, with about eight boys standing around him, was showing a card trick. They walked closer to show it to me. During this time they were laughing and saying, "How did you do it?" Finally, he began to show another trick about finding it in another's hands. First he tried the left and then the right. Then he pretended to try the arms. The "trick" was finished when the hands were around the other person's neck. They all laughed. Fred said, "He showed that to us yesterday. John tried it on Cora. She got away and ran." They thought this was funny, too, as they laughed again.

JANUARY 4

As I walked by the table where Deke, Earl, Fred, Dan, Carl, and Ben were sitting with their heads close together, Ben said, "Mrs. G., we don't know whether to let John in with us or not." It was then that I realized that John was sitting at the end of the table. There are only six places to sit, but he pulled up a chair. I said, "Why, what do you mean?" "I'm with the six musketeers, and he makes seven," he explained. "He knows some big words and we know some little words. He might get something on us." All the while John was just sitting there, grinning. "Let me know what you decide," I said. "OK," he replied.

I have been under the impression that it was a question as to who was the sixth musketeer, Ben or John. Ben was doing the talking. Apparently, he feels himself pretty well "in" the group. All this time Deke did not say a word.

JANUARY 8 (AT THE TEACHER'S HOME)

I heard children's voices and pretty soon my doorbell rang. Deke, with Helen, the girl who had invited him to the square dance, and Fay, came in. They were all talking in happy voices telling who was at the dance, who went with whom and how much they ate (the latter in some detail). Deke said Carl hadn't come because his mother was "kinda strict on him." Earl had come, but his mother came afterwards to take him home. Deke was to be taken home that night by Helen's father.

MARCH 22

For several weeks, Deke has seemed far more restless. He is growing quite tall and is thin. I have often noticed him stretching his long legs out to rest on another desk or chair. He pushes his desk up and leans back with his hands clasped over his head.

He has found it hard to be still while making a small houseboat model, and he always seems to be talking. His interest in the hunters and trappers in our study of the West has been great. He found a picture of a trapper, and after planning individually with me, he enlarged the picture using the projector. While coloring with chalk and completing the picture, I noticed no need for "help" from his friends. He worked rapidly using big swinging movements with his arms.

He has much to tell, not to me, anymore, but to the boys in the room. Lately he pays more attention to Fred than to any of the others of the musketeer group. In fact, that little group is no longer so much in evidence. Several times recently they have divided up, usually three at one table with other boys and the other three at another table with still others. Over this period of time, the others sitting at the tables with the divided group have not been the same every day.

Babs is ten years, four months old and is in the fifth grade. She is about the same size as the other girls in her class. Babs is in a hurry whenever she does anything. She is always running. Babs wears very attractive clothes. She wears most colors well, but her favorite dresses are pink with ruffles and lace. She said, "I love fancy clothes." She always looks neat and takes very good care of her clothes. She polishes her own shoes and puts her hair up in curlers. She has a shoulder bob.

OCTOBER 27

Babs and several girls pretend they have letters on the playground. They show these letters to certain boys and say, "I have a letter, but you can't see it." Then the boys chase them and try to get the letters. They seem to enjoy this because it goes on almost every recess. Babs told me, "I think the boys are so nosey. They always want to see what we write!"

NOVEMBER 10

Some boys and girls were working on a Thanksgiving play. John said, "I will not have anything to do with the play if Babs is in it; she always wants to be boss, and I won't have an old girl bossing me around." This was said before the whole room, and all the boys agreed with John. The girls said they didn't want to be in it anyway. Babs said, "You will need us to play the Pilgrims' mothers and the girls." John also added, "We would rather wear dresses and be girls ourselves." To which Babs replied, "All right, have your old play, and don't call on me to help you when you get in a tight place." She made a face at him. John was director of the play and picked the characters. When he wanted a Pilgrim mother, he picked Babs and gave her the following reason: "I know you can get the costume and I know you can learn the part, but remember, you are not boss this time."

DECEMBER 7

Today Babs was wearing a very pretty yellow wool skirt and white blouse. She looked very pretty, but I did not say anything about it. At recess she came to show me some dirt she had gotten on her skirt. I admired her outfit and said she looked very nice. She said, "Mother doesn't like me in skirts. She says they make me look too old."
I said, "I guess Mother wants to keep her baby."
She said, "She still calls me 'Baby,' but I think I'm too big for that now."

DECEMBER 8

Babs certainly has a way with the boys. She talks to them a lot, rolls her eyes and smiles when they seem willing to do anything she wants. I watched her this morning getting a boy to do her arithmetic. She told him how to do it, and he did all the work.

JANUARY 11

Babs' sister came in to talk to me this morning. She told me Babs was talking in her sleep last night. They have separate rooms, but they are close. While she was talking Babs came in and heard her. Babs said, "She is just saying that to tease me. She is always teasing me about something. She talks in her sleep all the time about her boy friends." Babs' sister blushed and said, "She means she talks about *her* boy friends."

FEBRUARY 24

Today on the playground, Jackson, a sixth-grade boy, said to me, "Babs is always hitting me and pulling my sweater off." I sent for Babs and asked her about it. She started to cry and said, "He hit me first, and I am going to take up for myself." This is the first time I have seen Babs cry.

MARCH 22

Babs has been acting like a much older girl since she had her hair cut short. Some of the girls told me that Babs likes a boy in the seventh grade. He lives near her and takes her for rides on his bicycle in the evenings.

Today she was with three sixth-grade girls. They were walking past the high school looking up at the windows. Later in the day I heard Babs tell some girls that she had a boy friend in high school.

Physical Development

Preadolescence witnesses a brief slowing down of growth just prior to the onset of the rapid lengthening of arms and legs during pubescence. The physical and sexual maturing of many preadolescent girls is marked by developing breasts, widening hips, a more feminine figure, and the onset of menstruation. An important developmental task of the preadolescent, therefore, is *developing a readiness for and an acceptance of the body changes* that take place as one grows toward physical and sexual maturity. Evidence of these physical changes was revealed in the last entry in the case of Deke, wherein the teacher describes him as growing quite tall and thin. The physical changes Babs is experiencing may be inferred from the several evidences of her strong interest in boys and in grooming.

The restlessness and hyperactivity of preadolescence alluded to earlier are also evident in the descriptions of Deke and Babs. Deke is active in sports and appears restless, while Babs has been described as in a hurry and always running. In spite of his restlessness, the preadolescent's endurance is usually not high, and he may often become overtired. Rather wide swings between hyperactivity and listlessness may be observed in some adolescents.

Emotional Development

A persistent developmental task of preadolescence is the *developing of appropriate ways of adjusting to new feelings evoked by changes in maturity and changes in one's perceptions of parents, peers, and self.* Boys and girls who have great affection for their parents will at this stage, nevertheless, often respond to their elders with irritation, distrust, and suspicion. They are easily offended and are quick to complain that adults do not understand them or treat them fairly. They are very sensitive, self-conscious, and easily hurt. At other times they appear to be unable to control their emotions and frequently lose themselves in anger, fear, or love. Many of the preadolescent's frustrations result from conflicts between parents and peers, or from an awareness of a lack of social skills or a failure to mature at the same rate as others. It will be recalled from Chapter 4 that the late-maturing boy often feels out of place with peers because of differences in his rate of maturing.

Conflict between the preadolescent and his parents often arises over his manner of dress, his friends, the ways he spends his time, the condition of his room, his general behavior, and his seeming lack of respect and consideration for others. His resistance to these demands and expectations is a first step toward *asserting his independence of adults.* Although he may act at times like a child, he resists efforts of adults to treat him as a child. However, even though he is restive under adult prodding and restrictions, the preadolescent is not ready for, nor does he really want, complete independence from family.

In expressing her independence of adults, the preadolescent girl develops new feelings about herself and her relationships with members of her family. She may express her growing independence through criticisms of her mother's choice of clothes and personal grooming, the house decor, or her mother's overprotectiveness. In spite of this criticism, however, the daughter remains dependent upon her mother for evidences of acceptance and affection. The preadolescent girl is often ambivalent in her feelings toward younger siblings. At one moment she may express disdain for their immature behavior, while at the next moment she may be quite affectionate toward and protective of them.

The preadolescent boy's assertion of independence frequently brings him into conflict with his father. These conflicts arise when the son feels unable to meet his father's demands and expectations. If he feels inadequate and is anxious over whether he can meet his father's high standards, he may adjust by simply not trying. It is less damaging to his self-image to appear uncaring and lazy than to appear incompetent. The understanding father can help his son discover his individuality in the family by allowing him leeway in making decisions and by not criticizing his mistakes. The failure of the father to respect the boy's need for independent action causes many boys to struggle for a lifetime to demonstrate their worth to their fathers. The mother's love and admiration continue to be important to the preadolescent son. A boy must be able to feel that he will have his mother's love even if he is different from his father. His love for his parents and their love for him become part of his understanding of others and his whole attitude toward life.[12]

12 Frank and Frank, pp. 55–58.

Every preadolescent faces the important developmental task of *forming and strengthening affectional relationships with adults within and outside of the family.* The giggling, silly behavior of Deke and some of his friends is characteristic of the kind of preadolescent activity that many adults find annoying. Yet the many contacts which Deke and his friends initiated with the teacher indicate their desire and need for her friendship and affection. Similarly, Babs, on several occasions, related to the teacher and sought her support. Frequently, the preadolescent develops a strong identification with a young adult, who becomes the preadolescent's "ideal." For the preadolescent girl, the "ideal" is a paragon of poise and femininity; for the boy, the "ideal" is a model of strength and masculine self-assurance.

Social Development

In preadolescence, the importance of the peer clique or gang is even more evident than it was in late childhood. A continuing developmental task is that of *achieving acceptance and roles in a changing peer group.* Although the need for adult approval is still very important, the preadolescent frequently spends more time with his friends and is more responsive to their ideas and values than to those of parents and other adults.

We have noted, too, that at this stage there is an increased striving to conform to the peer group in matters of dress, language, behavior, and values. A further developmental task posed for the preadolescent is that of *accepting, learning, and adhering to the codes, standards, and values of the peer group.* An unspoken and unwritten code develops among members of the peer group and defines in peer terms what is good and bad, acceptable and not acceptable. In general, the peer code calls for supporting one's peers in conflicts with adults. It also requires that one maintain his independence from adults, and anything that smacks of being teacher's pet is beyond the pale. The pressure on the individual for adhering to the peer code is revealed in the boys' objections to Babs' being in the play because she seemed to want to boss others.

Frequently, the preadolescent must in some way reconcile the sharp differences between peer and adult codes and values. He wishes to be admired by his pals on a peer-group basis; at the same time, he wishes that his parents would relax their demands so that somehow he can maintain the approval of both parents and peers. The wise adult avoids placing the preadolescent in situations that provoke a serious conflict between adult and peer standards.

The marked tendency in late childhood for boys and girls to prefer members of their own sex group and to show disdain for members of the opposite sex may also be observed in preadolescence. Boys see girls as weak and inferior, and frequently judge girls as "okay" only to the degree that they are like boys. Some girls may too readily accept the interpretation of boys and respond with a frantic imitation of boyish behavior in a negation of their feminine role. They dress like boys, play boys' games, and use tomboy language. For most girls, however, this period of identifying and competing with boys is brief. With the onset of pubescence their behavior and interests are increasingly feminine.

The onset of preadolescence is also characterized by a masked but awakening interest in the opposite sex. This interest is manifested in the preadolescent's ambivalent attitudes toward the opposite sex. The preadolescent deals with this ambivalence by maintaining a strong identity with his own sex group while at the same time experimenting briefly with heterosexual relationships and activities. This phenomenon is clearly evident in the cases of Deke and Babs. Deke was most frequently observed in interaction with his close pals, the "six musketeers." We do see Deke and other boys, however, choosing girls in a game of human tic-tac-toe, showing girls card tricks, and accepting from girls invitations to square dances. It is humorous to note in the anecdote of January 8 that in their report to the teacher Deke and his friends talked more about how much each person ate at the square dance than about any other aspect of the boy-girl event. The ambivalence of Babs toward her own sex group and toward boys is strikingly shown. Babs is frequently in conflict with some boys her age, but she seems to have a way with other boys in getting them to do things for her. The interest of the preadolescent girl in older boys is also evident in the case of Babs, who is reported to have boy friends two or three years older than herself.

Psychological Development

In preadolescence, the brain and nervous system have nearly reached adult proportions, but preadolescent youngsters still lack the experiences that would enable them to solve adult problems and to respond in adult ways. Their interest in physical science remains strong, especially for boys, and they show an increasing interest in human relationships. A reexamination of values may begin about this time. Preadolescents reveal a strong valuing of justice and fair play, and they are likely to challenge adults or peers who violate these codes. Preadolescents are developing a stronger conscience, and with this they often experience intense feelings of guilt. Some may begin to question the religious teachings of church and home. They are likely also to be critical of people who do not live up to their ideals.

Blair and Burton[13] have identified three trends in the intellectual development of preadolescents: a strong focus on reality, the capability to use causal relationships effectively in thinking about physical, mechanical, and natural phenomena, and wide reading and rapid educational achievement. The preadolescent's interest in the larger world is manifested in increased awareness of world events, in social and economic problems, and in the advances of science and technology. Through reading and exposure to other mass media, preadolescents learn about their world and explore specific intellectual interests. At this time they are capable of applying a scientific prob-

[13] Arthur W. Blair and William H. Burton, *Growth and Development of the Preadolescent* (New York: Appleton-Century-Crofts, 1951), pp. 148–177.

lem-solving approach to increasingly complex problems. As they pursue intellectual interests, manual and manipulatory skills, such as those required in conducting home experiments in chemistry and building models, are further developed and refined.

In these activities preadolescents are working on the continuing developmental task of *refining intellectual skills, understandings, attitudes, and interests appropriate to a phase of development marked by the beginnings of physical change and increased maturity.* Their interests are influenced by their rapidly changing bodies, their strong feelings and emotional reactions, and their awareness of the new roles and expectations they must fulfill as they progress toward adulthood.

Preadolescence is a relatively brief period of transition from childhood to adolescence. It is a time when boys and girls more and more are oriented to the people, events, and phenomena of the outside world. Parents and home are taken more or less for granted, and one's life and activities center in the peer group. It is a period of marked swings and fluctuations in activity, behavior, and emotions. Games and physical activities are important. It is a time of self-examination and self-assessment. Finally, it is a period marked by idealism, curiosity, a focus on reality, increased interest in causal relationships, and a real growth in intellectual powers.

Early Adolescence

The central theme in adolescence is the rediscovery of one's self. In the transition from the dependency of childhood to the independence of adulthood the adolescent must adjust to an almost new body. The maturing body is the symbol of a new and changing self. The early adolescent must incorporate into his self-concept new feelings, a new body image, and new conceptions of his role and place in a changing world. The search for self is reflected in an intensified self-awareness, frequently manifested in increased self-consciousness.

Early adolescence, as we noted earlier, is marked by the rapid growth of the long bones, changes in body proportion, and evidences of sexual maturation associated with pubescence. Early adolescence extends from the beginning of the pubescent growth spurt until about a year after puberty, when the individual's new biological organization has become stabilized. For most individuals, early adolescence encompasses roughly the years of junior high school and possibly a year or two beyond.

Some writers make little or no distinction between the terms *preadolescence* and *early adolescence*. It is evident, too, that no sharp line separates late childhood from early adolescence. We have preferred to designate by the term *preadolescence* the relatively brief period of transition characterized by swings in mood and behavior and a breaking up of the childhood personality. Early adolescence we would define as the remainder of pubescence, extending about a year beyond puberty, during which time greater stability in behavior, biological organization, and sexual functioning is being achieved. Many of the developmental tasks of preadolescence are encountered in a different form or at a higher level in early adolescence.

The great variation among early adolescents in growth, maturity, and behavior points to the uniqueness of each individual. Excerpts from the cases of Doris and Dennis reveal how two young people attempted to work through the developmental tasks and adjustments of early adolescence:

Doris is fourteen years old and in the ninth grade. She is an adopted child of Spanish ancestry and an only child. Last year a recommendation was sent home that she follow the standard course of study. The next morning she came to me in tears. She said, "Daddy is angry about my low rating. He called me stupid and dumb. He said I must be playing around in school. Daddy always got good grades in school, and he expects me to do it, too."

OCTOBER 16

I have watched Doris several times after school as she was waiting for her bus. She stands around with a group of boys and girls. She does very little talking but laughs a great deal and rolls her eyes. She handles her hair a great deal, lifting it from her shoulders.

OCTOBER 21

Today, in a conference, Doris' father said, "Jim, her boyfriend, came by a week ago Saturday afternoon. She had just washed her hair and had put it up in pin curlers. She asked her mother to tell him she wasn't at home. She didn't want him to see her that way. Her mother finally agreed and lied for her. The boy went on to another girl's house. This girl told him Doris was home. He saw her at church on Sunday and asked why she had her mother lie for her. Doris told him that she didn't want him to see her hair in pin curls. He said, 'Don't ever lie again. I came to see you, not your hair.' "

OCTOBER 22

Doris doesn't talk much in the group. She rolls her big brown eyes, arches her brows, and flashes her teeth, which are large, white, and square. Once she said to me, "My teeth are too big." Earlier this morning I saw her wearing her glasses. I asked her about them, and she said, "I never wear them in the halls, but I always wear them in class."

OCTOBER 31

This afternoon before the Halloween dance Doris went before the mirrors in the home arts room and arranged her hair on her shoulders.

Then she repaired her lipstick. Her bangs were curled, but still reached to her eyebrows. She stood for a moment, rolling her eyes, lifted her shoulders, and continued to primp before the mirror.

She changed to a red skirt for the dance. She had red flowers in her hair. One of the teachers said to me during the dance, "Did you see Doris? She looks more like a gypsy than anything else."

Doris was popular during the dance. She didn't miss one, and she danced better than the average child. Jim was her partner very often.

NOVEMBER 18

In a conference with Doris I told her that her father was very interested in her grades and how she was getting along. "He seems to think a great deal of you," I said.

"Yes, I guess he does," she replied, "but I wish he would let me go."

"Go where?" I asked.

"Oh, I don't know, just be free or something," she said. "Some of the girls in our neighborhood want to get a house to ourselves and go on our own."

I said, "That will take money."

"We are going to get jobs when we are older and try it. I told Mama what we were planning to do. She said we couldn't do it, but when I insisted that we were, she said that she and Daddy would sell the house and buy a trailer and tour the country. They would be free, too." She raised her shoulders, put her head on one side and laughed. "We would all have fun and maybe I would wish I were with them. I like to go places, but I don't want to do it with my parents."

JANUARY 26

This afternoon during our conference she talked mostly without prompting. She laughed now and then, rolled her eyes, tilted her head from side to side, and lifted her shoulders. She has a new bronze rinse on her hair. I noticed how very neat and clean she was. Her yellow blouse was trimmed with lace and was very becoming. Her fingernails were well manicured and tinted with pink polish. I noticed her hands are very beautiful. I asked her how much she weighed.

"Just exactly 100 pounds," she said, "and I'm just five feet tall."

FEBRUARY 6

Doris was elected by her homeroom to be candidate for Queen of the Sweetheart Dance to be held on February 13th. I passed her in the hall and stopped to congratulate her. Her face was all smiles. She thanked me as she lifted her hair from her shoulders, spreading it out carefully. She moved on, swinging her skirts.

FEBRUARY 13

For the dance today Doris was dressed in a red and white dress. Her hair hung loosely on her shoulders and she had flowers in her hair. When the winners were announced, Doris was not among them. I saw her a few minutes after the coronation. She was dancing with a very popular boy. She and her partner later joined in the grand march. They walked along hand in hand grinning at each other. She danced every dance and several times I saw her laughing up at her partner.

APRIL 8

In a conference today Doris said, "My problem is to find the right boy. I don't have a boy friend now. There are three boys in this school who want to go with me, but I don't want any of them. Those boys who want to go with me I don't want, those I want I can't get. There are three high school boys I like, one in particular, but none of them will look at me. I'll have a problem when it comes to finding a husband. I'll have to find one who is a member of the church. Mama wouldn't mind too much if he weren't a member, but it would break Daddy's heart if I married somebody outside the church."

I asked, "What about your Navy career?"

She answered, "I still have that in mind but only if I don't find someone to marry when I finish high school. I really want to get married because I want to have a baby. I love babies. I want to have a lot of kids. I wish I had a brother or a sister. I sure envy the girls who have brothers especially."

Dennis, who was introduced in Chapter 7, is fourteen years old and is in the ninth grade. He is 6 feet, 1 inch tall, weighs 169 pounds, and has wavy brunette hair and blue eyes. The following is the first paragraph of his "autobiography."

On September the 8th, 19—, a future Vice-President was born. He weighed 8 pounds and 8 ounces, and he wasn't wearing a thing. The reason he wasn't born a future President was that his parents had moved out of their log cabin three months before he was born. In short I was born. At least that's what the birth certificate says.

The following are excerpts from Dennis's case record.

SEPTEMBER 11

After giving Dennis his test paper at the end of English period, I added, "Please stay a minute after class." After the other students had gone, I turned around to Dennis and said, "Dennis, you did a right nice job of 'bull slinging' on your test paper yesterday, and I'd like for you to cease trying to make a monkey out of me. Is that clear?"

Dennis laughed and said, "Now don't get mad, Miss Neal. Miss R. and I can't get along at all, and I'd hate to have two against me."

"All right, Dennis," I remarked, "but let's leave our humor for picnics and such."

He asked, "Is that all?" and I nodded in reply. He crushed the test paper in his hands and left the room.

OCTOBER 3

As we left school this afternoon I followed some children down the flight of steps from the second to the first floor. Dennis happened to be right in front of me, and he had gotten a lock of Laura's hair and was apparently pulling at it. At that moment, Laura whirled around and shouted, "Dennis, I don't believe you have a lick of sense. I've a good mind to slap your face." Laura was talking by the time she turned around. However, when she saw me she said, "I'm sorry I yelled, Miss Neal, but Dennis never shows any manners."

Before I could say a word, Dennis shrugged his shoulders and said, as if in disgust, "These women!" He took two large steps and was out of the building.

Laura added, "Don't you think he's rude?"

I said, "I don't think he meant any harm."

Laura replied, "Well, he sure is silly."

OCTOBER 20

This morning just as I arrived at school I met Dennis. I immediately thought of the Halloween Carnival. I spoke: "Hi, Dennis, did you see about any prizes for my Bingo stand?"

Dennis at first clasped his hand over his mouth. Then he remarked, "Gosh! Miss Neal, I forgot, but don't worry. I'll get you some."

I came on in the building with two of my teaching companions, Miss R. and Miss T. When we were out of hearing distance for Dennis, Miss R. stated, "I wonder if you had better rely on Dennis. I'd be afraid to."

NOVEMBER 12

As classes were dismissed today I heard Miss R. say, "Dennis, if you don't keep your hat off your head until you leave the building, I don't know what I'm going to do." Dennis was wearing a long billed straw cap. He lifted the hat about 12 inches from the top of his head and just held it suspended there. I decided to watch, and he kept the cap in this position until he left the building. Then he just dropped it on his head again. It landed sort of drooped over one eye. Joan and Bertha were watching, too, and they laughed.

DECEMBER 11

The class had asked me to chaperone their party which was planned for Saturday night. Today plans were submitted and seemed rather complete except for the Recreation Committee, which had no report. I asked, "Who's chairman of the Recreation Committee?" Dennis raised his hand. I said, "I'll have to see the type of recreation you've planned before I'll okay chaperoning the party."

Dennis said with a giggle, "Oh, we'll play Post Office and Spin the Lid."

"No, you won't under my supervision," I remarked.

Dennis continued, "Well, I guess we'll have to move the party to my house."

"Well, if that's your choice for recreation, I imagine you'll have to," I added.

Doris said, "Miss Neal, we'll just dance if you'll come." I asked if it were agreeable with the rest of the class. It was, so I consented to chaperone.

Physical Development

Earlier in this chapter we noted that the pubescent growth spurt, which begins to taper off after puberty, leaves one nearly an adult in physique and appearance. Sex organs mature, and the secondary sex characteristics of deepening voice, shoulder development of boys, development of breasts and hips of girls, and adult distribution of body hair are clearly evident. The startling physical changes which take place over a summer have a profound effect on the young person himself. In his gawky appearance, his awkwardness, and his sexual maturity, he becomes acutely aware of his changing body. An unavoidable and insistent developmental task faced by every early adolescent is *his acceptance and adjustment to his changing, maturing body.* Contours of the body and face become mature. The face becomes more tapered and elongated. Muscles of boys become firm and hard, and, as sexual maturity is attained, growth of the bones is completed. Toward the end of early adolescence, girls (at about fourteen) and boys (around fifteen) look more like adults than like children.[14]

One will recall that early adolescents are extremely sensitive about their appearance. They tend to evaluate themselves physically against a Hollywood ideal, and it is no wonder that most find themselves lacking and reveal great concern about their physical characteristics. They worry about their stature and size, their muscular strength (boys), their shapeliness (girls), their facial features, their complexions. It will be recalled, too, that early-maturing boys achieved a marked advantage over late-maturing boys in sports competition, social relationships, and personal adjustment.

[14] Edward C. Britton and J. Merritt Winans, *Growing from Infancy to Adulthood* (New York: Appleton-Century-Crofts, 1958), p. 70.

An aspect of accepting and adjusting to a changing body is that of *accepting one's sexual maturing and one's sexuality as a male or female.* In early adolescence, the distinctions between male and female are sharply drawn. It is at this time that one not only accepts maleness or femaleness but also begins to value it. The adolescent boy learns to express his masculinity, and the adolescent girl learns to express her femininity, in ways that are appropriate to the situation. Lack of accurate information about sex may make it more difficult to accept one's sexuality. Because of this lack of information, many adolescent boys and girls become anxious, overcurious, and misinformed about sex. Feelings related to sex become more serious and intense because nothing in the adolescent's experience prepares him for dealing with and accepting his own sexuality. Frequently, parents themselves are embarrassed to discuss the problem.

Adults need to be reminded that sex has a different meaning at each stage of development. Children learn that sex is an act of mating that must occur before a couple can have a baby. In the postpubescent period, interest in sex centers in the physical attraction between men and women. Learning to deal with this attraction and to respond to it appropriately is a continuing interest and concern of adolescents and young people during periods of dating, going steady, and courtship. Following marriage, the procreative aspects of sex take on added significance. In clarifying their ideas and understanding of sex, young people are seeking some assurance that they are sexually adequate and normal.

The adolescent's total personality, his past feelings about his body, his capacities and abilities, and his feelings of self-worth strongly influence his feelings and attitudes toward sex and his approach to the opposite sex.[15] Attitudes that sex is dirty, women are untouchable, and men cannot be trusted not only handicap the young person's heterosexual adjustment, but may make more difficult his later marital adjustment as well.

Acceptance of one's sexuality is also important in one's *acceptance and learning of his sex role,* which was discussed in Chapter 6. Many of the developmental tasks discussed in this section are reflected in the early adolescent's interest in and concern over grooming. This was particularly evident in the case of Doris. She was frequently observed primping, lifting her hair from her shoulders, and swinging her skirts as she walked down the hall. It is reflected, too, in the anecdote of October 21, where it was reported that Doris and her mother lied so that her boyfriend would not see her with her hair done up in pincurlers. It seems, further, that Doris has learned that rolling her eyes and arching her brows are feminine ways of responding in the company of boys.

Social and Emotional Development

Being accepted and playing roles as a member of the peer group is a continuing developmental task, and at no stage of development is this task

---

[15] Frank and Frank, pp. 108–112.

more important than in early adolescence. At this stage, boys and girls will slavishly conform to group codes and standards for no other reasons than that "everyone is doing it."

Strong friendship ties with members of one's sex group continue to be a strong positive force throughout early adolescence. Friendship choices at this stage are based more frequently than heretofore on similarity of physical maturity, abilities, interests, and socioeconomic status. Boys appear to have a wide circle of casual friends, whereas girls are more likely to have a small circle of intimate friends. Girls, throughout their teen years, maintain closer ties with girl friends than with boy friends.[16] For the early adolescent boy, skill in sports earns acceptance and prestige in the peer group, whereas for girls, nice clothes, grooming, and good looks bring peer acceptance and prestige. Social poise and skills in dancing, conversation, dating, and organizing social activities and clubs are also important assets for achieving peer status in early adolescence.

The growing awareness of the opposite sex during late childhood and preadolescence is replaced by the awakening of a strong interest in the opposite sex in early adolescence. As young people learn appropriate ways of responding to peers of the opposite sex, they are working on the crucially important task of *establishing heterosexual relationships*. Early adolescents vary a great deal in the timing of this task and in the ways they work on it. Girls, as compared with boys of the same age, are more advanced in seeking the attention of the opposite sex and taking the initiative in dancing and at parties. A number of boys and the more immature girls tend to hold back in their relationships with the opposite sex. But, by age fourteen, more than half of both the boys and girls are dating.[17]

The cultural patterns of the home and community may make it difficult for the young person to form satisfying heterosexual relationships. Ambitious parents may push early adolescents into heterosexual activities before they are ready. The need to conform and to be popular may force some young people to act in ways that are incompatible with their temperament and interests. Finally, the confusion among both adults and adolescents with regard to feelings and attitudes about sex can impede natural healthy heterosexual development.[18]

We note that Doris is very much aware of boys and is fairly well advanced in heterosexual development. Her heterosexual interests are revealed in her primping, rolling her eyes, swinging her skirts, talking about boy friends, attending school dances, and expressing interest in getting married. Dennis is preoccupied with working on heterosexual development, but because of adjustment problems and failure to live up to peer standards, Dennis appears to be making only limited progress in heterosexual development.

[16] Britton and Winans, pp. 74–75.
[17] Britton and Winans, pp. 76–77.
[18] Howard A. Lane and Mary Beauchamp, *Understanding Human Development* (Englewood Cliffs, New Jersey: Prentice-Hall, 1959), pp. 320–322.

Another developmental task of primary importance in early adolescence is *achieving some measure of emancipation from parents and teachers.* The ease or difficulty the adolescent experiences with this task will depend largely upon his parents' attitudes and expectations. It is common for parents with the best of intentions to expect and require absolute obedience from their children beginning in early childhood. Even when the parent-child relationship is benevolent and loving, the child may seldom be permitted to decide things for himself.

Frequently, the efforts of the adolescent to assert his independence will be reflected in negative and unconventional behavior. The adolescent is likely to rebel against cleaning up his room, to be rude and disrespectful, to appear in sloppy or outrageous dress, to flaunt his parents' wishes concerning his friends, and to give forth with emotional outbursts when met with parental refusal or disapproval. In addition, he may become critical of his parents—their dress, their attitudes, the car they drive, and the appearance of the home. Girls especially want their home to be attractive to friends. Often, they are critical about the house and its furnishings, and they seem to want perfection.[19] All these behaviors, which are frequently so disturbing to adults, are symptoms of the adolescent's striving for independence.

The adolescent's negative behavior and rejection of adults appear in part to be a response to the disorganization that follows the breakdown of the childhood personality (as suggested by Redl[20]) and the need to challenge parental authority "as the price of his own individual maturation and acceptance by his own age group."[21] Frank reminds parents that their adolescent offspring really do not want complete freedom. Rather, they wish to be released from parental control and conformity so that they may comply with the often more exacting requirements of their own age and sex group.[22] Moreover, there is evidence that adolescents really depend upon parents and teachers to set rules and expectations for their conduct, and even though teenagers may protest, they would feel let down by adults if the latter did not establish some limits.

The early adolescent's striving for independence is vividly portrayed in the cases of Doris and Dennis. Doris speaks to the counselor about her conflict with her father and his distrust of her, her desires to be free and to join with other girls in leaving home and living in an apartment, and her desire to get married. We know little of Dennis' relations with his family; but Dennis is working hard on achieving independence of his teachers, as shown in his baiting of teachers, his wearing his hat in school, and his testing the limits of teachers' patience for tolerating his unconventional behavior.

[19] Britton and Winans, p. 78.

[20] See note 10.

[21] Lawrence K. Frank, "The Adolescent and the Family," in Nelson B. Henry, *Forty-third Yearbook: Part I, Adolescence,* National Society for the Study of Education (Chicago: University of Chicago Press, 1944), pp. 240–254.

[22] Frank, p. 247.

Psychological Development

Perhaps the most pressing developmental task facing the adolescent is that of *searching for and achieving a sense of self-identity*. It will be recalled that the integration of self in the form of ego identity in adolescence is the fifth stage of Erikson's eight stages of man.[23] Mention has been made also of the breaking up of the childhood personality evident in preadolescence[24] and of the maturing body as a symbol of new feelings and attitudes toward self, toward others, and toward life.[25]

The adolescent's search for a sense of self-identity is revealed in a variety of ways. Becoming independent of parents and teachers and gaining acceptance of peers are important steps in achieving a sense of personal identity. Possessing the ability to cope effectively with one's environment also contributes to a sense of identity. One's choice of and preparation for a vocation is a particularly crucial step in achieving this task. Whether the boy chooses a career in business, government, or the military service, and whether the girl chooses marriage or a career, will profoundly influence the sense of self-identity of each. Although the quest for self-identity is a significant developmental task of adolescence and early childhood, the elaboration, re-affirmation, or modification of one's self-identity remains an uncompleted task which the individual works on throughout adult life.

There is ample evidence that both Doris and Dennis are working on the task of achieving self-identity. Doris wants very much to see herself as worthy of her father's trust and as feminine, well groomed, and attractive to boys. Her search for self-identity is also reflected in her talk about leaving home, joining the Navy, and getting married. Dennis's search for self-identity appears to be complicated by adjustment problems that bring him into conflict with teachers and peers.

Adolescents are faced with *developing adjustment patterns which are appropriate to their increased maturity*. The complexities and difficulties involved in working on and achieving the developmental tasks of early adolescence make severe demands upon the adolescent's emotional resources. Thus, we may suppose that Dennis's roles of teacher-baiter and peer-group tease are patterns of adjustment to unspecified problems in interpersonal relationships. Whether Dennis continues to play these roles will depend upon the opportunities he has and the satisfactions he gains in playing socially more appropriate roles. Schoeppe, Haggard, and Havighurst conclude from a study of sixteen-year-old boys and girls:

If the adolescent is to accomplish successfully the developmental tasks required in his society, it is imperative that he master his impulsivity and

[23] Erikson, pp. 227–229.
[24] Redl.
[25] Herbert R. Stolz and Lois M. Stolz, "Adolescent Problems Related to Somatic Variations," in Nelson B. Henry, *Forty-third Yearbook: Part I, Adolescence,* National Society for the Study of Education (Chicago: University of Chicago Press, 1944), pp. 80–99.

accept himself, so that he can mobilize his energy to deal effectively with the social and cultural forces which impinge upon him.[26]

Late Adolescence–Early Adulthood

The boy or girl entering late adolescence has many more of the characteristics of adulthood than of childhood. This stage encompasses roughly the chronological ages of fifteen to twenty (senior high school and first years of college or job). Young people in late adolescence–early adulthood represent a broad range of interests, life goals, activities, and achievements. Individual differences in capacities, abilities, and talents have been magnified or blunted by more than fifteen years of environmental differences in family relationships, socioeconomic status, ethnic background, culture, community, and opportunities for higher education.

These young people, who a few years before (in elementary school and junior high school) seemed almost indistinguishable from one another, now differ greatly with respect to present role, situation, and the immediate future. Many in their late teens play adult roles in the adult world—in full-time employment, in the military service, as homemaker and parent. Others of their contemporaries face several years of additional schooling and, for many, continued dependence upon their parents for financial support.

Many of the developmental tasks of late adolescence–early adulthood will be familiar to the reader, since they have been encountered earlier in this chapter. In the context of approaching adulthood, however, each developmental task of late adolescence is a very different learning from its antecedent. In heterosexual development, for example, learning what one does on a date is a world apart from building a relationship of mutual understanding, trust, love, and respect in courtship.

Again, for a clearer understanding of this last developmental stage, we present brief excerpts from case records of a boy and a girl in late adolescence–early adulthood:

> Phil Watson is seventeen years old and a junior in high school. Last spring he was elected president of this year's junior class. He is 6 feet tall and weighs 150 pounds. He has been active in extracurricular activities, but his main interest has been the debate team.

SEPTEMBER 18

The assignment was to write a paragraph related to a picture I passed around the class. The picture was an optical illusion which showed a

---

[26] Aileen Schoeppe, Ernest A. Haggard, and Robert J. Havighurst, "Some Factors Affecting Sixteen-Year-Olds' Success in Five Developmental Tasks," *Journal of Abnormal and Social Psychology,* 48 (January 1953), 42–52.

woman sitting at a dressing table before a mirror. From one view she was a beautiful lady, from the other she was a hideous death's-head. This is Phil's paragraph:

Life is the essence of beauty. Beauty to most means only all; and yet I ask is beauty anything?

I know not for what purpose a person should live if they're not beautiful. For to most beauty is all. To please all is to be happy, is it not? So I have been told. Yet, I ask again, is beauty anything? Why should you try if you are lost and ugly? You cannot win. For to most beauty is all. Still I ask is beauty anything?

Ugly one, try not to change thy face. I am dead and God is ugly like us. I know not for what purpose a person should live if he is not beautiful.

OCTOBER 20

This afternoon Mrs. Thompson, the guidance counselor, indicated that Phil had been in the guidance office to get information about colleges, their costs, and opportunities for scholarship help. He said, "No one in my family has ever attended college, but I would like to." He will need some type of scholarship aid, as his family has very modest means and can give him very little help. He has indicated an interest in being a teacher, but except for English many of his grades have been poor, especially in math and science.

He would like to go away to school but is afraid his limited finances will not permit it. Phil indicated that he earned twenty-five dollars a month with his paper route, but from his earnings he has to buy his own clothes and pay his school expenses.

NOVEMBER 10

In the period between classes, I noticed Phil walking with his friend, Sue Bently, to her next class. She never took her eyes off him as he chatted and smiled at her. He was the last one to enter the classroom just as the bell rang.

Today I played a record of a reading of Walt Whitman's "Song of Myself." After the record I asked, "What connections did Whitman draw between the grass and death?" Phil raised his hand and I called on him.

"He called it the hair of graves at first. Later it is compared to a white-haired old lady, an old man's beard y'know. It is always the hair of the grave. It, well—it's just another part of life."

"Why did he make these comparisons?" I asked.

Phil continued, "It seems like he was looking for a chance to give a new view of death. He was glorifying it. Obviously, he means that death is a lot luckier than people think—that's what the last line says."

Later in the discussion I asked, "What about the image of grass growing from the roof of a dead person's mouth—that's pretty stark isn't it?" Phil's hand shot up, and I nodded.

"Yeah, but like in 'Thanatopsis' where he goes into decomposition—that's not romantic. It seems even more realistic than this. After all, he was trying to be scientific. And he just flat says that death is nothing"—pause and then with greater emphasis—"but mingling of the elements." He continued, "In that poem ya gotta take the essential part—without the two ends he tacked on—they're no good!" Phil and I laughed, but most of the class appeared to have lost the train of thought, as they looked blankly and didn't respond.

FEBRUARY 23

Today I accompanied the debate teams, affirmative and negative, to the State Debate Tournament. Both of our teams were eliminated in the fourth round, but Phil came through with the highest rating in the discussion to win $10.00 in cash and a gold pin.

Out of approximately 500 speech contestants, Phil was also elected president of the State High School Speech Association for the coming year. His acceptance speech was actually a piece of art in my viewpoint. Students from many of the large high schools congratulated him, and he shook hands with many, many students in the meeting. Throughout this period of time, Phil maintained his poise and wore a smile.

One of the members of my group said, "Oh! Miss Foster, aren't you proud of Phil? He's just the smartest and most handsome boy in the entire group."

I nodded and smiled my approval.

MARCH 13

We received word today that Phil's father was taken to the hospital today with a serious heart condition. This afternoon I talked to Phil after school and tried to comfort him. He said, "I don't know whether I can remain in school or not. If Dad is in the hospital for very long, I'll have to quit and get a job to support my mother and brother and sister."

"I believe there are a lot of people who would be willing to help," I countered.

"It looks like this is the end of my hopes to go to college," he said sadly.

"Anybody who has a strong enough desire to get a college education will get there eventually," I reassured him. "I'm sure you will find a way, and we'll help you all we can."

"Thanks for everything," he said as he left to meet his girl friend Sue. Later I spoke to Mrs. Thompson, and she suggested that she was sure Phil could finish high school by participating in the work-study program.

"Phil wants to be a teacher," I said. "I hope he can be helped to reach his goal, for he is the kind of person we need in teaching." She heartily agreed as we said goodbye.

A few brief excerpts from the case of Susan were presented in Chapter 7. She is a high school senior, is seventeen years, nine months of age, and her most recent total IQ on the California Test of Mental Maturity was 104.

OCTOBER 8

In a conference after class, Susan said she disagreed with a statement I had made in class, to wit, that college was not only for vocational training but was also fine for women who had marriage and a family as their only goal in life, if they had college-level ability. Suzy was telling me how she could see no value in college for herself because she would be married in three or four years. She added that most of her boy friends have been college students and that now she is going with a boy who's attending State University. We talked for some time on how she might find more in common with her husband and tastes more consistent with his if she were to go to college. In response she said that she had artistic and cultural tastes already.

I realized more and more that I was in effect persuading her to go to college, so I tried to draw the subject to a conclusion. Finally, she said, "You know, my parents want me to go to college, but I still don't see that it will help me. I will work for a few years, then get married."

NOVEMBER 4

Susan is neither attractive nor homely. She dresses in style and with obvious care. She gives me a pleasant, neat impression. She wears dark horn-rimmed glasses almost all the time, an average amount of makeup, and has a very ready smile. Her teeth are even and well cared for, by appearance. She is 5 feet, 4 inches tall and weighs 130.

For two years, Suzy has had a part-time job as credit interviewer for the Blakely Department Store. She works three evenings a week, taking credit applications and opening accounts for people. She tells me that she enjoys her work very much, mostly because she likes the contact with different types of people. A good part of her job consists of typing forms from information gathered in asking questions of the applicant.

NOVEMBER 24

Just as she was leaving the office today, Suzy came over to me and said, "Look what the turkey brought me." She held her left hand out and on the third finger was a school ring of Bancroft, the private military school Jack had attended.

I said, "It looks like Jack is back." She went on to say that after she had come home from a walk on Thursday her mother said, "Someone's in the living room to see you." She dramatically described her surprise at seeing Jack there. Then she explained that her mother is afraid she will lose the ring because it is too big for her finger. "Jack is going to get a solid gold band to make it smaller."

I said, "That might make it more permanent."

Suzy smiled and said, "I hope so," and was gone out the door.

JANUARY 6

In the course of conversation today, I mentioned that her mother seems to like Jack. She said that both her parents like him very much, but they don't want her to marry until he gets out of the Navy (2½ years). I asked her how she felt about that and she said they both wanted to marry sooner but that they hadn't set any date yet as things were too indefinite with Jack. She added that when they did set a date she thought her parents would agree. I said, "Suppose they don't."

"I'm sure they will," she said, "but if they don't, I guess we'll just go ahead."

FEBRUARY 11

Suzy told me today that Jack sent her a telegram saying he had been selected for Naval ROTC. I congratulated her and remarked how wonderful it would be to have a college education and be paid for it. There were several other students in the office at the time, and I felt she was enjoying impressing them, especially when she said, "I told his mother that I'm going to be an admiral's wife." Then she said she thought there was a requirement that NROTC men could not be married. I gave her a copy of the NROTC handbook so she could look up the requirement. She was still smiling when she read it and said, "Oh, my goodness, four years. He can get married when he graduates." She kept smiling and said, "Well—." She then put the book down and left the office.

Physical Development

During the late adolescent period the individual attains his adult height. It is during this period that boys finally catch up to girls in physical maturity. The late adolescent has come to some kind of terms with the realities of his body type and appearance, and he is likely to have incorporated these realities into his self-image.

Physical size, strength, skill, and daring are desired qualities of manliness. The period of late adolescence is a time when individuals are at their peak of physical efficiency and coordination. Recognition, adulation, and honor tend to be reserved to the few well-developed, well-coordinated boys who participate in varsity athletics.

Every boy needs to see himself as physically adequate. A few boys, as in the case of Shorty Doyle in Chapter 4, attempt to compensate for their felt physical inadequacy by exaggerated attempts at getting attention, boastfulness, and bravado. As young people seek a measure of self-identity in their choice of a vocation, the *development of physical skills required for success in one's chosen vocation* tends to overshadow athletic skills.

Learning vocational skills depends as much upon one's possessing the requisite emotional and intellectual qualities as it does upon physical development and coordination. The late adolescent tends to spend more and more time learning skills in activities closely related to his educational and vocational interests. In short, possessing the necessary physical qualifications will be an important consideration in one's choice of a vocation. Medical students who lack finger dexterity are likely to choose a specialty other than surgery.

As we have noted throughout this chapter, girls assess their physical characteristics and appearance in relation to their contribution in making them attractive to boys. Susan is concerned about her figure, hair, and grooming. She is described as neat, well dressed, and very feminine in her appearance. Her typing skill will enable her to hold a job until she marries, but it is probably secondary to the qualities of feminine appearance and figure described above. Phil is tall and rather good looking. Since most of his energies are devoted to intellectual interests and leadership in extracurricular activities, physical skills appear to be relatively unimportant to him.

Social Development

The peer group, often labeled "the crowd," continues to be important to the late adolescent. At this age, some are becoming independent of the group, but for many, peers remain an important influence in their lives. In a study of ten midwestern high schools, Coleman found that when the elites of the school are faced with the problem of whether to go to a friend's house or to a rally, they turn to the teenage society as a whole, to the pep rally, "a ritual of the adolescent social system surrounding the high school."[27]

From Coleman's findings, cited in an earlier chapter, it may be recalled that in order to get into the top crowd a girl needs to have a nice personality, good looks, and nice clothes, but she also has to have a good reputation. For boys, athletic ability and having a car were important for being accepted into the top status group. Academic success was not valued by either sex group. The leading crowds of boys wanted to be remembered as star athletes; they were far less interested than were the rest of the student body in being recognized as brilliant students. Similarly, leading crowds of girls were oriented away from thinking of themselves as a brilliant student and toward the image of an activities leader or the most popular girl in the school.[28]

The thoughts, efforts, and concerns of the boy and girl in late adolescence–early adulthood center mainly on making themselves acceptable to the opposite sex. The developmental task each is working on is that of *acquiring the skills, attitudes, and understanding which enable one to develop and to grow in a close personal affectional relationship with an esteemed person of*

[27] James S. Coleman, *The Adolescent Society* (New York: Free Press, 1963), p. 142.
[28] Coleman, pp. 143–163, 244.

the opposite sex. This is, of course, a continuation of the task of heterosexual development which began in preadolescence. In early adolescence, heterosexual relationships begin with nondating mixed parties and pairing off, followed by various trials and periods of "going steady" with one or more partners. This culminates for most individuals in *choosing a life mate,* followed by courtship and marriage.

In Coleman's study, a girl's reputation was crucial to her acceptance by both sexes. This posed a dilemma for some girls, since the approaches they used in becoming successful with boys could endanger their good reputations. Middle-class adolescent boys in this study tended to choose active rather than passive girls. Passive girls were those who were seen as conforming to parental expectations and school "assignments" and as getting high grades. Middle-class boys, in expressing their liberation from parental control, tend to seek partners in liberation, not girls responding to the controls of childhood. Coleman points out that traditionally in adolescence, and still more so among working-class boys, the relevant dichotomy is the *good* girl, one whom the boy respects and admires, versus the *bad* girl, one the boy exploits and has fun with. Among modern middle-class adolescents, however, this dichotomy is replaced by the *active* girl versus the *passive* girl—the first to respect and have fun with, the second to ignore.[29]

Success in dating is related to many other developmental tasks. Foremost among these is one's acceptance and learning of his sex role. Being mature, responsible, considerate, and able to relate to others is also important. For girls, good looks, grooming, and nice clothes are important assets that increase their attractiveness to boys. Girls, in turn, expect their beaus to be strong, poised, and self-assured. As the boy grows up, he must ascertain what girls expect of him. He is expected to take the lead, but he must learn the proper balance between leading and being overassertive.

The involvement of the late adolescent in heterosexual relationships which culminate in finding a life mate is clearly shown in the case of Susan. Early in the record, Susan is dating several boys. She wants to get married and seems to feel that going to college will not necessarily further that goal in her case. By Thanksgiving, Susan has a strong involvement with Jack, an involvement she hopes and expects will lead to marriage. Phil and Sue Bently have a strong interest in each other, but for Phil marriage appears to be some years away. His strong desire to attend college and the crisis of his father's illness are far more pressing at the moment. Most late adolescents have numerous experiences of falling in and out of love. Sometimes these experiences are painful, but they also can be helpful and developmental in giving the young person perspective in his choosing a life mate.

Another developmental task in late adolescence, a task encountered earlier, is that of *achieving independence of parents and family.* We noted that in early adolescence the task of gaining emancipation from parents centered in conflicts involving home duties, clothes, and choice of friends. By

[29] Coleman, p. 172.

late adolescence, many of these problems are resolved, or parents come to realize and to accept the limitations on their abilities to control their nearly grown offspring.

However, even though the late adolescent achieves independence from his family, his parents are still important to him. Coleman found that the high school adolescents' allegiance in the ten midwest high schools he studied was shared about equally between parents and peers. When adolescent boys and girls were asked whose disapproval for joining a school club would be hardest to take, 54 percent said parents, 43 percent said friends, and 3 percent said teachers. Thus, adolescents "look forward to their peers and backward to their parents."[30] Where the adolescent and his parents have maintained rapport and mutual respect, the parents' influence tends to remain strong.

The gaining of some measure of financial independence appears to be an important aspect of the task of achieving independence in late adolescence. By age sixteen or eighteen, most young people have the capabilities for holding down a full-time or part-time job. Young people who look forward to several years of additional education beyond high school may have fewer opportunities for gaining economic independence from parents. Most college students, however, earn some portion of their personal and college expenses. Those late adolescents who suffer the greatest frustration from failure to achieve a measure of economic independence are probably members of minority groups and those in disadvantaged areas who are unable to gain employment and have neither the interest, nor the qualifications, nor the financial support for further schooling. It is no wonder that these young people feel bitter at being discarded by society before they have even gotten a start in adult life.

The achieving of independence from parents and families manifests itself in a variety of ways, each of which may be a source of conflict. Besides earning enough money for clothes and personal expenses, there is the selection of clothes, the issue of frequency of going out and the hour of return, the use of the family car, the choice of staying in school or going to work, driving and owning a car, taking a full-time job, living away from home, getting married, joining the armed forces, and voting.

It is important to note that along with the young person's desire for independence goes his desire for developing and maintaining good relationships. As the stresses of growing up diminish, the late adolescent–early adult and his parents may interact with and enjoy each other on more egalitarian terms.

Susan expressed her growing independence in many ways. Case-record excerpts report her decision not to go to college, her voting for girls wearing hose and low heels on the class trip, her working part time as a typist in the Blakely Department Store, and her intention of getting married whether her parents approve or not. Her good relationship with her parents is revealed in

[30] Coleman, p. 5.

her statement that she was sure her parents would approve of her getting married when the time came. The record of Phil states that he earns twenty-five dollars a month from his paper route, from which he buys his own clothes and pays his school expenses. Not reported were his trips taken with another boy the previous summer to New York, Boston, and Atlantic City. It is certain, too, that the increased responsibility he must assume in helping to support his mother and family will give him an increased feeling of being mature and playing an adult role.

Psychological and Personal Development

Although mental development continues throughout late adolescence and beyond, the young person during this period reaches a peak in his capacity to learn. Certainly one of the most important developmental tasks in the individual's life is his *choosing, preparing for, and entering a life vocation*. Late adolescents reveal greater stability and are more realistic in their choice of a vocation.

Considerable shifting in occupational choices occurs during late adolescence and even in the twenties, after one has finished school and gone to work. Of pressing concern to late adolescents is their appraisal of their own abilities in relation to job interests and opportunities. Young people keep asking themselves: "I wonder if I'm good enough for this?" "Will I gain satisfaction in this work and can I continue to grow?" Many youth who go on to college do not have a firm vocational choice, as evidenced by the finding of a large university that prior to graduation 60 percent of the students change their choice of major field and 40 percent change to a different college.

To assist students in making realistic vocational choices, guidance and pupil personnel services in schools and colleges make available to students test results, occupational information, and counseling which provide them with a sounder basis for choosing a vocation. Without adequate occupational information and a realistic assessment of interests and abilities, choices tend to be based less on objective knowledge of self and more on the aspirations of parents or the prestige society attaches to certain vocations.

Vocational choices of girls usually create fewer anxieties. Although most girls look forward to marriage, their immediate focus is upon qualifying for employment in their young adult years prior to and perhaps extending into the early years of marriage. This was the situation that Susan faced as she considered her employer's offer of a full-time job while she waited for Jack to finish his Navy enlistment or complete Naval ROTC. Phil Watson hoped to become a teacher, and he was faced with finding the ways and the means of completing his education while at the same time fulfilling his responsibilities to his family.

Another developmental task which faces most late adolescents is that of *crystallizing a system of values and developing a philosophy of life*. It is natural for youth on the threshold of adult life to feel apprehensive and uncertain as to what is right and what they want their lives to stand for. As they take on the roles and responsibilities of adult life, they face choices and decisions for which there is no sure guide. They long ago were made aware of the fallibility of adults and of the discrepancies between people's verbally expressed beliefs and values and what they do or fail to do in their daily lives.

In late adolescence and early adulthood, a youth searches for and incorporates into his self-image those beliefs, convictions, values, and aspirations which will direct his future activities and give whatever meaning and purpose his life will have. Many would see the frequent bull sessions in the college dormitory, factory cafeteria lunch table, or boot camp as inconsequential or a waste of time. It is in these discussions, however, that a youth seeks to crystallize his values and to formulate and refine his philosophy of life.

The late adolescent tends to be idealistic. He seeks to right inequities and tries to build a more perfect world. In striving to confirm and live his philosophy of life, he may be observed picketing, participating in civil-rights movements, or protesting government policy. A youth seeks to realize his ideals and to live up to his philosophy even though to many adults his behavior appears to be wrong, regrettable, naïve, irrational, or ill advised. Young people work on this task in a variety of ways: fighting for one's country as a member of the armed forces, being a conscientious objector, joining the Peace Corps or performing social service on the home front, or staying home to care for an invalid parent.

Late adolescence is a period when the influence of the church and its teachings diminish for many youth. The late adolescent–young adult looks to fresh sources for answers to age-old questions of what kind of a universe this is and where he stands in it. We may expect him to become disillusioned, perhaps bitter, about the injustices and lack of love which appear to be so prevalent in the world about him. Most young people come to see in clearer perspective the good as well as the bad and to reaffirm most of the values and beliefs taught by their homes, churches, schools, and communities. In the case excerpts, Susan may be observed valuing and trusting her own feelings about college, getting a job, and marriage. Phil, through the encouragement of his teacher, sought to clarify his values and beliefs about the nature of life and the universe through a study of literature.

Our descriptions of the developmental tasks and of the stages of human development are concluded at this point even though the most significant years of one's life have barely begun. Indeed, Havighurst extends the developmental-task concept to include the whole life span from birth to senescence. These two chapters have presented the principal characteristics and developmental tasks from birth to physiological maturity. The reader should again be cautioned that no attempt has been made in these two chapters to arrive at an all-inclusive list of developmental tasks. Different cultures and different levels of society set different demands and expectancies for children and youth, and these demands and expectancies are constantly changing. A knowledge of developmental tasks provides us with a framework for interpreting the information we have about an individual, but permits only a general assessment of his development. The framework of developmental tasks is not a prescription, for each individual works on each common task in his own time and in his own unique way.

Developmental Tasks and Education

Developmental tasks are the milestones on the journey of development and becoming. In achieving these tasks, one moves toward increased independence, self-realization, and self-enhancement. The developmental-task concept, as we have noted, is an integrating concept which the educator may use in assessing an individual student's development. The individual's self-concept, how he sees and feels about himself and about his world, may also be used as an integrating concept in seeking an understanding of development.

Developmental tasks are common learnings which face individuals growing up in a specific society or subculture. The mastery of these tasks is made possible by the individual's achieving the maturation which a specific task requires for its successful completion. The culture in essence says: "This learning (such as walking, reading, gaining acceptance of peers) is an important step in your own development. Learning the task is related to your being approved by society, your personal happiness, and your success with later developmental tasks." Self processes play an important role, for unless the learning of the task is related to an individual's motives, goals, and values, he is unlikely to work on the task or to master it.

Since the culture has an important stake in youth's learning the developmental tasks appropriate to their maturity level, one may ask how the school and its curricula assist students in their learning of developmental tasks. Obviously, there is no simple answer to this question. The curricula of most schools place considerably more emphasis upon students' increasing their knowledge and skills in academic areas than upon acquiring broad general learnings that are related to their growing up.

Most schools do a fairly effective job of helping children to learn to read, to develop concepts related to the physical and social world, and to gain coordination of large and fine muscles. Most schools, however, appear to do little in helping children and youth to accept and to learn their sex roles, win acceptance in the peer group, develop heterosexual relationships, accept a changing body, gain independence, or achieve a sense of self-identity. Because of the limited opportunities for working on developmental tasks through classroom learning experiences, many adolescents may be observed exploiting the three-to-five minute break between periods, the lunch period, and the period after school in working on peer acceptance, heterosexual relationships, and the clarification of their sex roles.

Some would argue that the school provides students with opportunities to work on their developmental tasks in the broad range of clubs and extra-curricular activities the school offers. This may be in part true, but the experiences offered are seldom systematic, nor does the whole student body participate in them. Schools where nonintellectual activities overshadow the academic program may reflect the efforts of students to achieve important developmental tasks outside of an academic program that may not be sufficiently responsive to the developmental needs of students. The following are some of the ways in which developmental tasks and the school program may be interrelated.

First of all, teachers can develop increased sensitivity to and understanding of the sequence of changes and learnings which occur at successive stages of development. Education must be seen as facilitating each student's development and learning rather than only imparting skills and knowledge. Each student brings a unique developmental history and readiness to the common tasks of growing up, and each encounters some problems of adjustment which will influence his ability to master these tasks. A central theme of this book is that guidance of any individual child requires knowledge of the unique and specific features of his life history and of his immediate milieu, as well as recognition of the principles of development, including his developmental tasks. This has been illustrated in the several case illustrations appearing in this and the preceding chapter, as well as in other parts of the book.

Second, in implementing the preceding principle, teachers can incorporate into school experiences many opportunities which permit and encourage students to work on their developmental tasks. The following are suggestions:

1. Provide frequent opportunities for students to form into groups of their own choosing for committees, projects, and panel discussions (peer-group acceptance). Form groups which include both boys and girls (heterosexual development).

2. Plan for student-led discussions of current events, mathematics needed in daily life, analysis of literary works and figures, etc. Encourage all students to express their viewpoints and feelings (achieving independence).

3. Plan and present a high school career conference (planning and preparing for a vocation).

4. Encourage understanding of self and others through autobiographies, themes, written reactions to readings, field trips, and discussion of events of national and international significance. Explore with students the feelings, attitudes, and motives of literary or historical figures, or those which relate to a school problem or situation (achieving self-identity).

5. Assist students, through appropriate questions, comments, and discussions of their statements, to achieve clarification of personal values

and beliefs. Analyze the philosophies and value commitments of historical and literary figures, writers, and artists, and the commitments of
one's own culture in contrast to those of other cultures (achieving self-
identity, clarifying one's values).

Third, teachers can become sensitive to the dangers of overloading children with demands irrelevant to the developmental tasks at hand. They can
also avoid making too rigid the cultural expectations for accomplishing each
task. There has been considerable question regarding the value of homework.
Many students underachieve or drop out of school because school assignments often appear irrelevant to their needs.

Finally, educators can interpret what they know about the student's
developmental needs and progress to parents, other teachers, youth leaders,
physicians, and others who are in positions of being able to help the student.
It is clear that if the optimum development, learning, and mental health of
the individual student is to be realized, all persons and agencies who play
prominent roles in his life must be in communication with one another and
work cooperatively in the best interest of the student.

Summary

Adolescence is a period of biosocial transition between childhood and
adulthood which has been of special interest to parents, educators, psychologists, and the culture at large. Adolescence is a period of feeling out of place
and out of step, but in its later phases it is a period which many children and
adults seek to emulate.

Many theories have been developed to explain the variable behavior and
conflicting tendencies which characterize adolescence in our culture. G.
Stanley Hall described adolescence as a time of inner turmoil, a period of
storm and stress. Freud viewed the developmental process of adolescence as a
dynamic struggle between the biological-instinctual id forces and the socially
responsive superego. In Erikson's formulation, a major task in adolescence is
one's reestablishment of his ego identity in accepting as part of himself his
body changes and libidinal feelings.

Important distinctions have been made between the terms *puberty* and
adolescence. Puberty is the point of development at which biological changes
reach a climax and sexual maturity is achieved. Adolescence is the period of
development and change extending from the beginning of pubescence to the
point at which the individual assumes roles and responsibilities of adulthood.

Preadolescence is a period of one to two years encompassing the latter
part of late childhood and the early part of early adolescence, a period in
which the young person's behavior reflects the temporary developmental
discordance and adjustment to the disorganization of his childhood personality. Developmental tasks identified in preadolescence include the following:

1. Developing a readiness for and an acceptance of body changes which mark one's growth toward physical and sexual maturity.

2. Developing appropriate patterns for adjusting to new feelings about one's changing body, maturation, parents, peers, and self.

3. Asserting one's independence of adults.

4. Forming and strengthening affectional relationships with adults within and outside of the family.

5. Achieving acceptance and roles in a changing peer group.

6. Accepting, learning, and adhering to peer group codes, standards, and values.

7. Developing intellectual skills and concepts appropriate to a period of physical change and increasing maturity.

The central theme in adolescence is the rediscovery of one's self. The early adolescent must incorporate into his self-concept new feelings, a new body image, and new concepts of his roles and place in a changing world. The developmental tasks which early adolescents may be observed to be working on include:

1. Acceptance of and adjustment to a changing, maturing body.

2. Accepting one's sexual maturing and one's sexuality as a male or female.

3. Accepting and learning one's sex role.

4. Being accepted and playing roles as a member of the peer group.

5. Reestablishing heterosexual relationships.

6. Achieving some measure of emancipation from parents and teachers.

7. Searching for and achieving a sense of self-identity.

8. Developing adjustment patterns which are appropriate to one's increased maturity.

Young people in late adolescence–early adulthood represent a broad range of interests, goals, activities, and achievements. Although many of the developmental tasks of this period are similar to those of an earlier period, they often involve very different learnings from their earlier antecedents. These developmental tasks include:

1. Developing physical skills, knowledge, and competencies required for success in one's chosen vocation.

2. Acquiring skills, attitudes, and understandings which enable one to develop and to grow in a close personal affectional relationship with an esteemed person of the opposite sex.

3. Choosing a life mate.

4. Achieving independence of parents and family.
5. Choosing, preparing for, and entering a life vocation.
6. Crystallizing a system of values and developing a philosophy of life.

Achievement of developmental tasks appropriate to one's level of maturity is a strong expectation of one's culture as well as evidence of the individual's developing and becoming. The school as an agency of the culture has an important stake in assisting students to master their developmental tasks. Teachers, in their selection of process and content of learning experiences, are able to help students achieve their developmental tasks.

Study Questions

1. As you look back on your own adolescence, what were the most important events or experiences which were evidence of your achieving independence from adults? How were the behaviors you learned in achieving independence different from those of some of your friends or classmates who were members of a different subculture from yours?
2. In one large public university 60 percent of the undergraduate student body sometime during their four years change their major field, and 40 percent transfer to a different college on campus. What developmental tasks appear to be associated with these decisions to change major or change colleges?
3. Henry Baldwin, age seventeen, is a well-developed, mature looking young man. He is outwardly friendly to all, but appears to have no interest in heterosexual relationships. Should Henry be guided toward taking some first steps in working on this developmental task, or should one wait for Henry to indicate a readiness for working on the task?
4. Chapters 3–9 have portrayed human development and learning as being influenced and shaped by a series of interrelated dynamic processes. Chapters 11 and 12, in contrast, have employed the developmental-task concept to present a normative picture of what boys and girls generally are like during each period of childhood and adolescence. Disregarding differences in amounts of material presented, list the advantages and disadvantages of each approach to studying human development and learning.

Suggested Readings

James S. Coleman. *The Adolescent Society*. New York: Free Press, 1961. A study of adolescent social climates and the relation of these to the behavior, learning, and values of adolescents in ten midwestern high schools. Chapters 8, 9, and 10 are particularly informative in showing the psychological and scholastic effects of the social system on the way adolescents feel about themselves and in indicating the sources of adolescent value systems.

Elizabeth Douvan and Joseph Adelson. *The Adolescent Experience*. New York: John Wiley, 1966. Reports the findings of two national interview studies involving 3,000 adolescents between the ages of fourteen and sixteen. The authors conclude from their findings that the American teenager is less rebellious and disturbed than some would have us believe. Sex differences in adolescent development appear to be far more crucial than has been heretofore realized.

Edgar Z. Friedenberg. *The Vanishing Adolescent*. Boston: Beacon Press, 1960. Proposes and presents supporting evidence for the thesis that the school unwittingly and perhaps unconsciously frustrates the specific emotional processes in adolescents which lead to self-understanding and self-esteem. Analyzes the cases of five adolescent boys, four of whom experienced severe damage to their self-esteem during their school experience.

Arthur T. Jersild. *Psychology of Adolescence*. Second Edition. New York: Macmillan Co., 1963. The central focus of this book is on the adolescent's self. Chapters examine the adolescent's physical development, his thought and fantasy, emotional development, social development, education and vocation, and personality development and fulfillment. Each chapter is a description of the objective aspects of adolescents' growth and behavior with an inquiry into the subjective meanings of what is happening in their lives.

J. D. Salinger. *Catcher in the Rye*. Boston: Little, Brown and Co., 1953. Describes the weekend experiences of Holden Caulfield, beginning with his dismissal from Pency Prep for academic failure and ending with his reaching home in New York City. The raw feelings of this disturbed late adolescent are vividly described as he searches for meaning, understanding, and acceptance in relationships with both friends and strangers.

Ruth Strang. *The Adolescent Views Himself*. New York: McGraw-Hill Book Co., 1957. The focus of this book is upon the ways adolescents perceive themselves and their world. The dimensions of the adolescent's world, his self-concept, and feelings are discussed, followed by individual chapters on adolescents' perceptions and the attainment of each of the major developmental tasks of adolescence. Extensive use is made of the adolescents' own statements of attitudes and values, activities and relationships, and their problems in growing up.

Films

Farewell to Childhood, 16 mm, sound, black and white, 24 min. Bloomington, Indiana: Audio-Visual Center, Indiana University (rental fee, $4.15). The story of an adolescent girl and her relationship with her parents. Her parents are bewildered and confused by her changing moods and apparent inconsistencies, but relationships improve as the parents begin to understand her point of view and she realizes that parents also need to be understood.

Age of Turmoil, 16 mm, sound, black and white, 20 min. Bloomington, Indiana: Audio-Visual Center, Indiana University (rental fee, $4.15). Six teenagers, age thirteen to fifteen, representing different personality types, illustrate the behavior that reflects the emotional turmoil of an early teenager. Adolescent actions which seem odd, inexplicable and annoying to parents are portrayed as normal universal traits. The reactions of different personality types to new situations, adolescents' oft-times unrealistic attitudes toward life, and conflicts and emotional instability are seen as characteristic of this group.

The Teens, 16 mm, sound, black and white, 26 min. Bloomington, Indiana: Audio-Visual Center, Indiana University (rental fee $5.90). Shows the normal behavior of three teenagers in the everyday life of an urban middle-class family. Barry, fourteen, engages in vigorous activity with the gang; his thirteen-year-old brother, Timmy, still likes to be alone or share a hobby with a friend; while fifteen-year-old Joan responds in mature ways, although she still looks to her mother for emotional support.

learning and the
educative process

13

the nature and theories of learning

Learning is but an adjunct to ourself,
And where we are our learning likewise is.

≡ SHAKESPEARE

Learning is a universal, lifelong activity wherein individuals modify their behavior in coping with and adapting to their environment. Learning occurs in a wide variety of situations and at all levels of animal life—from the conditioned reflexes of lower animals to the complex cognitive processes of man.

Early evidence of learning among low forms of life was reported by Day and Bentley,[1] who found that paramecia can, after repeated trials, reduce the time required for them to turn around in a capillary tube. More recently, studies have revealed that the planarium, a simple flatworm, through a series of stimuli involving light coupled with electric shock, can be conditioned to flex its body in response to the light stimulus alone.[2] However, though lower forms of life do learn, their learning is slow, limited, and

---

[1] L. M. Day and M. Bentley, "A Note on Learning in Paramecium," *Journal of Animal Behavior,* 1 (1911), 167.
[2] R. Thompson and J. V. McConnell, "Classical Conditioning in the Planarium, Dugesia dorotcephala," *Journal of Comparative and Physiological Psychology,* 48 (1955), 65–68.

not very important to their existence. Protozoa, for example, are practically mature at birth; instinctive responses which begin functioning at birth provide them with most of the behaviors they will ever use.[3]

Man, on the other hand, the highest form of animal life, is also the most helpless at birth, has the longest period of infancy, and has the greatest capacity for profiting from experience. Learned responses constitute the overwhelming proportion of his behavioral repertoire. The change in proportions between innate and learned components of behavior at various points on the ascending scale of animal life is shown in Figure 13.1.[4]

Learning as Process and Product

The term *learning* refers to both a process and a product. Some of the processes involved in the transactions that take place between the organism and its environment are the familiar ones of sensing, perceiving, feeling, symbolizing, remembering, abstracting, thinking, and behaving. Each of these is anything but simple.

There is evidence, for example, that biochemical changes within the body may influence behavior. When planaria that have been conditioned to

[3] James W. Sawrey and Charles W. Telford, *Educational Psychology,* 2nd ed. (Boston: Allyn and Bacon, 1964), pp. 93–94.

[4] From James M. Sawrey and Charles W. Telford, *Educational Psychology,* 2nd ed. (Boston: Allyn & Bacon, 1964), p. 94. Reproduced by permission.

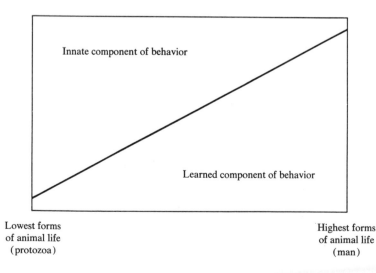

Lowest forms
of animal life
(protozoa)

Highest forms
of animal life
(man)

Figure 13.1. The relationship of components of behavior to level of animal life (from Sawrey and Telford).

respond to light are cut in half, both of the regenerated organisms that are then formed—one from the head segment and one from the tail segment— also respond to light. According to one hypothesis, the memory retention of the planarium is related to the presence in the body of the worm of some biochemical substance. Other investigations appear to substantiate this hypothesis. When conditioned planaria are cut up and fed to unconditioned planaria, the cannibalistic worms learn much faster than those on a less-educated diet. Investigators have hypothesized that RNA (ribonucleic acid, a protein-like substance found in all cells which transmits from the nucleus to the cytoplasm coded genetic information obtained from the DNA, desoxy-ribonucleic acid, molecule) might be the substance responsible for memory retention in the planarium. When the bottom half of the planarium is treated with a substance that destroys RNA, this half becomes a worm with no learning and hence no memory at all.[5] In other experiments, rats trained to walk a tightwire were found to have more RNA in their brain cells than did untrained rats. It is clear that processes of learning involve not only psychological and behavioral components but physiological, biochemical factors as well.

Most of us, however, are more accustomed to thinking of learning as an outcome or product than as a process. Our references to and many of our conceptions of learning are frequently limited to those changes that are acquired in school or other formal teaching-learning situations. Intuitively, however, we know that learning also has occurred when a baby is able to grasp a ball, to walk, or to talk; when a teenager acquires a taste for pizza or learns to ride a motorcycle; and when a young mother learns to distinguish between the different kinds of cries her infant emits. We often overlook these and similar kinds of learning because they are not usually associated with a school setting.

Also included in a broad concept of learning are the formation, modification, and breaking of habits; the acquiring of interests, attitudes, and values; the development of tastes and preferences; and the formation of biases and prejudices. Learning is involved in the synthesis and application of knowledge in reasoning, thinking, theory building, and problem solving, and in our deepest feelings and emotions, our self-concepts, and, indeed, our total personalities. (Further discussion and elaboration of the various kinds and outcomes of learning will be found in Chapters 15 and 16.)

Definition of Learning

The term *learning* does not lend itself to any simple or universally accepted definition, but a common and somewhat useful definition, fre-

[5] J. V. McConnell, A. L. Jacobson, and D. P. Kimble, "The Effects of Regeneration upon Retention of a Conditioned Response in a Planarium," *Journal of Comparative and Physiological Psychology,* 52 (1959), 1–5.

quently cited by psychologists and educators, is that *learning is a modification of behavior as a result of experience or training.*

Some of the advantages and disadvantages of this definition are immediately apparent. By limiting the types of changes under consideration to those resulting from experience or training, the definition excludes behavioral changes due to innate response tendencies, maturation, or temporary states such as fatigue or the use of drugs. The definition also excludes changes that are not manifested in modifications of behavior. All of us, for example, may recall an experience or an idea that has changed the way we feel or think, but in a way that has not affected our overt behavior. The importance of recognizing the existence of both overt and covert behavioral changes is emphasized by Hilgard,[6] who distinguishes between *learning* (covert) and *performance* (overt). He points out that learning can only be inferred from performance.

Since both overt and covert changes constitute learning, some theorists prefer to define learning in terms of "modification in the learner" instead of "modification in behavior." Others limit their definition of learning to the relatively permanent changes associated with training or experience, while still others feel there is no good reason to limit a definition of learning to permanent changes.

Clearly, there are many kinds, expressions, and levels of learning. In substance, however, there is little conflict over the definition of learning between rival theories and points of view. The differences of opinion that do exist have actually arisen from differences in interpretations of the findings of particular experiments.

Theories of Learning

There is a real need for every educator to develop a personal theory of learning. The first step in the development of an adequate, consistent personal learning theory is gaining a basic knowledge and understanding of the major learning theories found in the literature of psychology. An educator may embrace an existing theory in its totality. More frequently, however, he will probably select from various theories those principles, laws, or postulates that correlate most directly and consistently with his own findings, predilections, biases, and speculations. These become organized and synthesized into a personal theory of learning which evolves, changes, and becomes further refined as the educator continues to study and to analyze the processes through which people learn.

Role and Function of Theory

Contemporary American culture too often attaches unfortunate connotations to the term *theory*. Americans in general are a pragmatic people.

---

[6] Ernest R. Hilgard and Gordon H. Bower, *Theories of Learning*, 3rd ed. (New York: Appleton-Century-Crofts, 1966), p. 5.

Although they have made important contributions to basic research, Americans have demonstrated special skill and inventiveness in applying theories and principles from basic research to the development of new technologies and new products. "Being practical" has become an important value in American culture.

Unfortunately, it has been erroneously assumed that theory is detrimental to sound practice. The persistence of this popular stereotype in our culture is both unfortunate and dangerous; both the practitioner and the researcher in any science or discipline recognize that nothing is as valuable as a good theory for improving practice and discovering new knowledge. If a theory is merely a conception of some aspect of reality or of the relationships between entities or events, then whatever the teacher does in the teaching-learning situation reflects the theory he holds, either implicitly or explicitly. In a deeper sense, the teaching act utilizes two kinds of theories: Learning theories, which seek to explain or describe the events that occur in learning, will be dealt with in this chapter; instructional theories, which describe what teachers do to facilitate and to promote the learning of students, will be examined in later chapters.

A theory performs several important purposes and functions. An initial purpose is that of organizing and integrating all that is known into a hypothetical scheme for explaining a given phenomenon or problem. Most important, however, a theory can point to new and as yet unobserved relationships. As a means of synthesizing and extending knowledge, a theory is a frame of reference from which new predictions of events and relationships may be made. Since the development of any science depends upon the discovery of stable empirical relationships between events and variables, a theory is useful and valid to the extent that predictions and propositions generated by it turn out to be true. As theories lead to more valid predictions of events, they permit man to achieve increased understanding of these phenomena and to increase his capacity to cope with his world.

Stimulus-Organism-Response

Three sets of variables must be considered in any study of the learning process: (1) the *stimulus* or situation, which consists of one or more sensations evoked by body or environmental changes; (2) the *organism*—that is, the internal processes that intervene between stimulus and response; and (3) the *response*—the overt and covert activities that modify the initial stimulus (eating candy reduces hunger). Each of the learning theories to be discussed in this chapter varies in its description of and in the relative importance it assigns to stimulus-organism-response (S-O-R) variables in the learning process. Some give primary emphasis to S and R, while others emphasize O and R. As we observe what occurs in learning, S-O-R appear as an interrelated and unified series of events. If we are to understand a given theory, however, we shall need to focus upon individual S-O-R variables and to analyze the influence of each on other variables and on the total S-O-R sequence of events.

The stimulus-organism-response paradigm is similar to the model of the human behavior cycle described in Chapter 8. The impetus for learning, as in the activation of the human behavior cycle, is a *stimulus*. Instead of thinking of a single stimulus, however, we should probably think of a set of stimuli (sensations of touch, sight, hearing, taste, smell, and kinesthesia) impinging on the receptor organs at any given moment. A set of stimuli conveys information. If an organism is to change in ways that characterize learning, it must receive some kind of message, or *input*. Without some kind of patterned stimulation, the individual has difficulty maintaining his psychological organization.

The variables referred to by the term *organism* include all processes and events that occur inside the organism between the onset of the sensation and the emitting of a response. These processes and events are referred to as *intervening variables* in some theories and as *mediating variables* in other theories. The variables labeled "organism" include perception (the process of differentiating, integrating, and ascribing meaning to sensory stimulation); motivation (the arousal and direction of the individual's energy toward specific goals); intelligence and aptitudes; goals and aspirations; concepts, knowledge, and skills previously acquired; and attitudes, values, and self-concept. These variables are psychological, are not open to direct observation and study, and therefore must be inferred from the organism's behavior.

Response is a general term used to refer to whatever the organism does or does not do following the stimulus and organism steps in the S-O-R sequence of activities. Often, we think of response as some observable behavior. We look for some movement or action of the body or its parts—perhaps a verbal response, a nod of the head, a frown or smile, or even a flick of an eyelash. Teachers become alert to actions or words that confirm a student's grasp of the concept of gravity, his mastery of a rule of grammar, or his ability to apply an historical principle to a current political problem. Even when he is making no observable response, however, a learner is probably learning something. A student who registers no movement, comment, or change of expression to the statement "Trade barriers restrict free trade and economic growth" may store the principle in his memory, may try to think of examples of the principle or relate it to other economic concepts, or may view the principle as further evidence that economics is dull. In order to determine whether any learning has occurred, the teacher must await some future situation wherein some statement or application of this principle is relevant. It is possible, of course, that the learner was attending to other internal or external stimuli, so that no stimuli symbolizing trade barriers, free trade, and economic growth were received, no relevant response occurred, and, presumably, the desired learning did not take place.

The nature of the response is far more complex than this brief description suggests. The response consists of much more than a movement or an oral or written statement. It includes activities at various levels—brain, nervous system, muscles, glands, and other internal organs. As we well know, the many activities that comprise a response are different for every learner.

A Taxonomy of Types and Theories of Learning

The history of psychology is studded with conflicts between rival learning theories, but it is increasingly evident that, despite optimistic claims, no one learning theory can at present provide adequate explanations for all of the many types of learning. Some theories have been more successful in explaining psychomotor skills and the learning of attitudes; other theories offer more adequate explanations of cognitive and problem-solving learning. As a result, a number of learning theorists recently have tried to produce a taxonomy of types of learning.

One such taxonomy of types of learning has been developed by Gagné.[7] From observations of everyday occurrences, Gagné has identified eight types of learning, each of which requires a different set of conditions. The conditions of learning are the events that must take place if a particular learning is to occur. The conditions of learning include events within the learner (such as drive level, previous learning, and satisfaction) and events in the learning situation (such as the task itself). Knowledge of these conditions enables the teacher to provide appropriate guidance in promoting learning activities. The eight types of learning identified by Gagné appear in a hierarchy of levels of complexity:

TYPE 1: *Signal learning.* The individual learns to make a general, diffuse response to a signal. This is the classical conditioned response of Pavlov [and the behaviorism of Watson].

TYPE 2: *Stimulus-response learning.* The learner acquires a precise response to a discriminated stimulus. What is learned is a connection (Thorndike) or a discriminated operant (Skinner), sometimes called an instrumental response (Kimble).

TYPE 3: *Chaining.* What is acquired is a chain of two or more stimulus-response connections. The conditions for such learning have been described by [Guthrie,] Skinner and others.

TYPE 4: *Verbal association.* Verbal association is the learning of chains that are verbal. Basically, the conditions resemble those for other (motor) chains. However, the presence of language in the human being makes this a special type because internal links may be selected from the individual's previously learned repertoire of language.

TYPE 5: *Multiple discrimination.* The individual learns to make *n* different identifying responses to *n* different stimuli, which may resemble each other in physical appearance to a greater or lesser degree. Although

[7] Robert M. Gagné, *The Conditions of Learning* (New York: Holt, Rinehart and Winston, 1965).

the learning of each stimulus-response connection is a simple Type-2 occurrence, the connections tend to interfere with each other's retention.

TYPE 6: *Concept learning.* The learner acquires a capability of making a common response to a class of stimuli that may differ from each other widely in physical appearance. He is able to make a response that identifies an entire class of objects or events (Kendler).

TYPE 7: *Principle learning.* In simplest terms a principle is a chain of two or more concepts. It functions to control behavior in the manner suggested by a verbalized rule of the form "If A, then B," where A and B are concepts. However, it must be carefully distinguished from the mere verbal sequence "If A, then B," which, of course, may be learned as Type 4.

TYPE 8: *Problem solving.* Problem solving is a kind of learning that requires the internal events usually called thinking. Two or more previously acquired principles are somehow combined to produce a new capability that can be shown to depend on a "higher-order" principle.[8]

This taxonomy is one way of classifying different kinds of learning and of relating each to the learning theory or theories best suited for explaining it. Gagné suggests that principles and generalizations emerging from learning theory may prove useful only as they are related to the kinds of capability being learned. Other writings by Gagné analyze the individual skills and understandings required at each level or step in a specific learning. Each of these skills and understandings are related by Gagné to one or more of the eight types of learning summarized above. Through an analysis of this kind, what is known about the types or conditions of learning may be used in facilitating specific learning performances.

Prescientific Learning Theories

Man's earliest ideas about the nature of learning were philosophical rather than psychological. A philosophical, prescientific theory which has enjoyed support for more than two thousand years is the *doctrine of mental discipline.*[9] Adherents of this doctrine conceive of education as a process of training the mind, just as one disciplines or trains his body through exercise and practice. Latin, Greek, and mathematics were presumed to have the most value for training the mind; and these subjects continued to be emphasized in education during the nineteenth and well into the twentieth century.

[8] From Chapter Two of *The Conditions of Learning* by Robert M. Gagné. Copyright © 1965 by Holt, Rinehart and Winston, Inc. Reprinted by permission of Holt, Rinehart and Winston, Inc. Bracketed material inserted by this writer.

[9] For a more complete discussion of the doctrine of mental discipline, learning through unfoldment, and apperception, see Morris L. Bigge, *Learning Theories for Teachers* (New York: Harper & Row, 1964), pp. 19–48.

A second prescientific learning theory is *learning through unfoldment*. According to this theory, learning is practically synonymous with development. Emphasis is placed upon freeing the child to develop his aptitudes, capabilities, and skills. This theory assumes that if the child is free to explore and to express himself, he will learn those concepts and skills that are appropriate to his personal needs and to the demands of his environment.

A third type of prescientific learning theory is *apperception*. Two of its adherents, John Locke and Johann Friedrich Herbart, believed that there are no innate ideas, and that everything a person knows is acquired through the senses. Education based upon apperception theory encourages and assists the learner to acquire ideas which build and enlarge his "apperceptive mass "—that is, his storehouse of knowledge.

During the latter part of the nineteenth century, the study of learning began to become a part of a full-fledged science of psychology. In 1879, in Leipzig, Wilhelm Wundt established the first psychological laboratory. There, he and his co-workers used scientific methods of inquiry in conducting studies of consciousness and cognition. William James (1842–1910), America's first eminent psychologist, conceived of learning as perceiving meaning by analyzing, sorting, and cataloging the sights, sounds, tastes, smells, and feelings of one's "stream of consciousness." His work and writings helped to prepare American psychology of the late nineteenth and early twentieth century for the emergence and development of scientific learning theories.

Two Views of Learning

Scientific learning theories and systems of psychology developed in America after 1900 may be roughly classified under two broad headings, (1) association theories and (2) cognitive field theories. These two types of learning theory differ first of all in their philosophical premises and in their conceptions of the nature of man. In general, associationists hold that the learner is essentially passive, that his behavior is controlled by internal and external forces. Cognitive field theorists, on the other hand, believe that the learner's own purposes, motives, perceptions, and cognitions influence and are influenced by interactions with the psychological environment.

Association theories have often been described as molecular, reductionist, and mechanistic, since they study small, irreducible elements of learning and use many of the same terms and experimental procedures emphasized in the natural sciences. Cognitive field theories are frequently described as molar and relativistic. They contend that any idea or object derives its qualities and has meaning only in relation to other components of the total situation. Reality for the cognitive field theorists is the meanings which the individual acquires as he interacts with his environment.

Association theorists and cognitive field theorists both use the methods of scientific inquiry in their study of learning. They differ, however, in the assumptions they make and the ends they seek. The cognitive field theorist relies largely on inferences drawn from data on the learner's perceptions, insights, and cognitions; the association theorist usually restricts his investigations to those events that can be directly observed and measured. In the following pages, we will discuss briefly representative theories from each family of learning theories.

Learning by Association

Association theories focus on behavior, emphasizing conditioning; that is, they seek to discover and to refine the principles or laws whereby a *stimulus,* or *situation,* of an external or internal environment becomes associated with the aspect of behavior called *response.* Association theories of learning may be classified under headings reflecting two traditional points of view: (1) contiguity theories of conditioning and (2) learning by reinforcement.

Contiguity Theories of Conditioning

One explanation of learning by association is that a connection is formed between *sensations* (stimuli or situation) and *behavior* (response) when elements of the two occur in close temporal proximity to each other. According to this view, when stimulus (S) and response (R) are contiguous, learning occurs. The repeated association of a particular stimulus and a particular response—a process which produces habitual responses—is known as *conditioning.* Those behavior patterns or habits learned through their association with given stimuli or situations are called *conditioned responses.* Conditioned responses are often acquired unconsciously; higher brain centers or mental processes often are not involved. Conditioning is a basic type of learning of which we have many examples in our daily experience. The small child's fondness for a special teddy bear or blanket, his fear of strangers and the dark, his anticipation that tying on a bib will be followed by food and that bath will be followed by bed—all are conditioned responses. Similarly, our tastes, preferences, likes, dislikes, fears, and antipathies for certain foods, colors, smells, people, animals, and objects are all acquired largely through conditioning.

Classical conditioning. A basic type of learning occurs when a neutral stimulus is paired with an unconditioned stimulus to activate a reflex response. Classical conditioning consists of the successive pairing of the two stimuli (for instance, a buzzer and a puff of air) to elicit a reflex response (in this instance, blinking of the eye) to the neutral stimulus alone. Learning by conditioning has occurred when the buzzer alone evokes the eye blink (conditioned response). Virtually any neutral stimulus (a color, a bell, even an odor), through successive pairings with the puff of air, can become a conditioned stimulus. The one-time neutral stimulus (now the *conditioned stimulus*), having heretofore served as a signal for the puff of air, is now capable of eliciting the eye blink even when the puff of air is eliminated. The law of conditioning thus states that when a neutral stimulus is paired with an unconditioned stimulus (UCS) over several trials, a conditioned stimulus (CS) results, and this conditioned stimulus has by itself the ability to evoke the conditioned response (CR).

The elements of classical conditioning described above were first identified by Ivan Pavlov (1849–1936),[10] a Russian physiologist whose work profoundly influenced the development of learning theory in the United States. While studying certain digestive reflexes of dogs, Pavlov noted that these laboratory animals would salivate at the mere sight of food. In one of Pavlov's oft-cited experiments, a hungry dog was fastened comfortably, but securely, to a laboratory table in a stimulus-free room and fed powdered meat. Shortly before the meat was given, a bell was rung. The dog's reaction to the food—the extent of his salivation—was measured at each feeding. At first, the dog salivated only upon presentation of the food. After about thirty trials, however, the dog salivated just as much at the sound of the bell. After thirty trials, then, conditioning had occurred, since the ringing of the bell alone was sufficient to elicit salivation (see Figure 13.2).[11] If food was not presented following the ringing of the bell, the conditioned response (salivation) gradually decreased and finally ceased. This process is known as *extinction*.

[10] See Ivan P. Pavlov, *Conditioned Reflexes,* trans. by G. V. Anrep (London: Oxford University Press, 1927).
[11] From Sawrey and Telford, p. 99. Reproduced by permission.

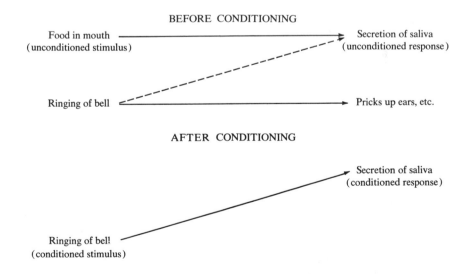

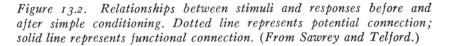

Figure 13.2. Relationships between stimuli and responses before and after simple conditioning. Dotted line represents potential connection; solid line represents functional connection. (From Sawrey and Telford.)

In other experiments, Pavlov discovered a principle of *stimulus generalization*. He found that stimuli similar to but not identical with the conditioned stimulus will also evoke the conditioned response. Thus, the sounding of a tone which is slightly higher or lower in pitch than the original tone has the property of eliciting the same conditioned response. The less similar the new stimulus to the original one, however, the weaker the conditioned response. Pavlov found that stimulus discrimination is achieved when the animal salivates (conditioned response) to a tone of 440 vibrations per minute, but does not salivate to tones of 420 or 460 vibrations per minute. He also demonstrated that *higher order conditioning* occurs when the conditioned response (salivation) is evoked following repeated pairings of a second neutral stimulus (electric shock becoming the new conditioned stimulus) and the first neutral stimulus (the bell becoming the new unconditioned stimulus).

When Pavlov's work was introduced into the United States, it found ready acceptance in a school of psychology known as behaviorism, whose basic ideas were first expounded by John B. Watson (1878–1958).[12] *Behaviorism,* an environmentalist psychology, sought completely objective explanations of behavior, avoiding any consideration of consciousness or other mental factors. Watson extended Pavlov's classical conditioning model, developed from animal experiments, to studies of human behavior, and expanded the reflex-arc concept to include responses that are nonreflective and complex.

Watson believed that if the proper stimuli were presented, specific responses could be elicited in an individual from early infancy; thus, the individual could be molded into any type of person desired. Using the classical conditioning model in one of his most famous experiments, Watson conditioned Albert, an eleven-month-old boy, to fear a white rat toward which he had previously responded in a positive, friendly manner. One day, as the boy reached out to touch the rat, Watson produced a loud noise by striking an iron bar behind Albert's head just as he touched the rat. Albert jumped and fell forward, burying his face in the mattress. With successive repetitions of this procedure, various other fear responses were evoked from Albert. Finally, Albert began to cry and to crawl away whenever he saw the rat. Watson suggested by this experiment that fear is a conditioned (learned) reaction. Later, by showing Albert the rat at a distance, then moving it closer on successive days, and omitting the loud noise, Watson demonstrated that fear as a conditioned response can be unlearned.

The most direct, practical application of classical conditioning to human learning appears to be in helping one to understand that emotional responses such as fears, anxieties, and phobias are learned. As the process of extinction suggests, the fear-evoking stimuli (words, people or objects) that produced these responses, can be detached from the original fear stimulus (a loud sound) and therefore become no longer feared.

[12] John B. Watson, *Psychology from the Standpoint of a Behaviorist* (Philadelphia: J. B. Lippincott Co., 1919).

Guthrie. Perhaps the most representative contiguity learning theory is Edwin R. Guthrie's (1886–1959) theory of *simultaneous contiguous conditioning.*[13] In Pavlov's system, one stimulus becomes a substitute for another stimulus after several trials. In Guthrie's theory, however, learning takes place when stimulus and response occur together. The stimulus of seeing a baseball on the ground becomes linked with the response of grasping the ball (rather than kicking it). Guthrie's theory states that if we once respond to a motionless baseball by grasping it, we are likely to do so again the next time we see a baseball lying on the ground. According to Guthrie, one occurrence is sufficient to establish the S-R connection. Further practice adds nothing to the strength of the connection.

But how can anyone show that we learn to throw a baseball as the result of a single trial? Guthrie deals with this apparent contradiction by stating that behavior is made up of a series of complex movements, a series of stimulus-response units, or what Gagné calls Type-3 chaining. Each minute muscle contraction or movement is a behavior unit. A moment's reflection will remind us that most psychomotor skills such as writing, walking, or driving a car involve a large number of individual movements, which become integrated into a Type-3 chain. Throwing a ball, for example, involves grasping the ball, aiming at the target, releasing the ball, changing position of feet and body while in the act of throwing, and following through after the release of the ball. According to Guthrie, the response that leads successfully to the next unit in the series is the response that is learned; consequently, learning takes place in one trial.

Guthrie contended that what the learner does in a given situation he will continue to do in recurrences of this situation, since there is no reason for his behavior to change unless the situation itself changes. In support of his theory, Guthrie cited his experiments with cats in a puzzle box. After a cat had once escaped from the box, it would repeat the movements that accomplished the initial escape in subsequent escape attempts. We learn what we do.

Although reward may preserve behavior from disintegration, and repetition may facilitate the integration of several movements, neither reward nor repetition, according to Guthrie, is essential for learning. Guthrie's emphasis upon movements suggests that the teacher should break down an assignment into its smallest units. If one-trial learning is to be effective, it is imperative that the teacher make sure that the student's final response in a recitation is a correct one. The attractiveness of Guthrie's theory lies in its simplicity, but since, in our own experience, human learning appears to be far more complex than Guthrie suggests, his theory offers only limited help to teachers.

Learning by Reinforcement

A contrasting view of learning by association is offered by reinforcement theorists, who contend that stimulus-response connections are formed

---

[13] See Edwin R. Guthrie, *The Psychology of Learning* (New York: Harper & Row, 1935).

not because of their proximity to one another (contiguity) but because of the consequences (success or reward) of the connection.

Thorndike. Edward Lee Thorndike (1874–1949)[14] developed the first experimentally based psychological theory of learning in America and did much to influence teaching and learning in American education during the first half of the twentieth century. Thorndike believed that learning takes place at the physiological level: Ideas are associated as a result of the linking of neurons, two or more. An impulse, conducted across the synapses of particular adjoining neurons, forms connections between situations (S) and response (R). Largely through simple trial and error, the learner selects and connects S-R components in such a way as to achieve success or satisfaction. Since Thorndike views learning as the process of selecting and connecting appropriate S-R units in the forming and strengthening of neural bonds, his theory became known as *connectionism* or *bond theory.*

Thorndike's experiments with animals and humans led him to formulate a set of laws of learning which postulate the specific conditions that influence synaptic S-R connections. The most important of Thorndike's laws of learning is the *law of effect* (the basis of reinforcement theory), which states that an S-R connection is strengthened when the connection results in success or satisfaction for the learner. For the child, the synaptic connection between appropriate neurons for the stimulus "9 plus 2" and the response "11" is strengthened because hearing the teacher say "Correct" is accompanied by a pleasant feeling of satisfaction or success. The child may also ascertain the correctness of his answer through self-initiated activities, such as counting on his fingers, and thereby achieve a pleasant feeling of satisfaction or success. In his initial formulation of the law of effect, Thorndike stated that S-R connections which result in dissatisfaction or failure are weakened. However, he rescinded this part of the law when later experiments revealed that non-reward does not decrease the number of wrong responses given. Other laws proposed that connections are strengthened by repetition (later rescinded) and that bonds can be formed only when the organism is in a state of readiness.

According to Thorndike, the greater the number and variety of discrete synaptic bonds or connections one has formed, the more he knows and the more he can do. Learning complex skills and solving difficult problems requires more bonds than are required for simpler skills and problems. Since learning, according to this view, is an accretion of bonds, Thorndike believed that educational methods that proceeded from simple to complex and from part to whole would be most effective in promoting learning. Thus, a student would be more likely to learn to multiply two-digit numbers if he had already learned to multiply one-digit numbers.

A further contribution of Thorndike's is his *theory of identical elements,* which states that one will use in a new situation things he has learned

---

[14] See Edward L. Thorndike, *Educational Psychology,* Vol. 2 (New York: Teachers College, Columbia University, 1913).

in a previous situation to the extent that elements in the two situations are the same or similar. Later studies show, however, that other variables (such as generalizations formed in one situation that are applicable in other situations) may play more important roles in transfer of learning. Many studies show, for example, that transfer is increased when the teacher helps students to see how skills and concepts acquired in one situation may be applied to other situations.

Connectionism's emphasis upon the identification of identical elements and upon moving from the simple to the complex enabled Thorndike and others to organize curriculum into a sequence of graded steps. Thorndike's emphasis upon proceeding from simple to complex and from part to whole, however, has been challenged by cognitive field theories, sparking a controversy which will be discussed later in this chapter.

Hull. Clark Hull (1884–1952)[15] adapted Thorndike's law of effect in developing a theory of reinforcement which has served as a model of theory building. Central to Hull's theory is the concept of *need,* a state of deficiency or disequilibrium within the organism which in some degree threatens its survival. Hunger, for example, is a need that sets up a *drive* to search for food. *Responses,* such as pulling an apple off a tree or getting food from the refrigerator, satisfy the need for food and reduce the drive. Responses which become associated with drive reduction are said to be *reinforced.* As reinforced behaviors are further strengthened, they become habits. For Hull, reinforcement is not merely reward or satisfaction; it is any event that increases the probability that the organism will respond in the same way to similar patterns of stimulus and drive.

To a greater extent than any other learning theorist, Hull identified, defined, and conceptualized some of the variables that intervene between stimulus and response. Principal intervening variables in Hull's system are drive, habit strength, incentive motivation, and excitatory potential. *Drive* is a state of activation which may be expressed quantitatively in terms of, for example, the number of hours or days a hungry person has been without food. *Habit strength* is a measure of the strength of the S-R bond, the strength of the habit being dependent upon the number of times this S-R connection has been reinforced. If the hungry person finds, and continues to find, berries in a patch near the river, his frequent trips to the patch expresses the strength of his habit to make that response. *Incentive motivation* is the amount of reward a given response earns. If the plums in an orchard an equal distance away are sweeter and juicier than the berries, the greater attractiveness of the plums (incentive motivation) may exert a stronger influence on the hungry man's behavior than the strength of his habit to return to the berry patch. *Excitatory potential,* a product of the first three intervening variables, is the learner's overall tendency to make a response to a given stimulus. Thus, the hungry man's response—his trips to the berry patch or the orchard—is determined by the product of his drive (hunger),

---

[15] Clark L. Hull, *Principles of Behavior* (New York: Appleton-Century-Crofts, 1943).

habit strength (the number of times this response has resulted in his finding food), and incentive motivation (the amount of satisfaction provided by the food).

Dollard and Miller[16] have utilized several of the constructs of Hull's theory in developing a reinforcement theory useful in analyzing several different kinds of learning. They describe the application of their theory to a six-year-old girl who is hungry and likes candy. While she is absent from a room, a piece of her favorite candy is hidden under the bottom edge of a particular book in a bookcase. After being brought back into the room and asked if she wants a piece of candy, she is told that she may look for the candy under the books but must replace each book until she finds the candy. After 210 seconds, she discovers the candy under the thirty-seventh book she picked up. With some fluctuation in speed and performance, she improved until on the tenth trial she found the candy in two seconds.

Dollard and Miller analyze this kind of learning in relation to four basic principles. First, a *drive* toward action arises—either from a physiological need or from external pressure. The little girl's drive toward action was hunger. Second, the learner responds to *cues*. At first, the little girl was told where to look; later, she responded to the color, size, and location of the book. Third, the learning situation must provide the learner with opportunities for making the desired *responses*. The little girl was permitted to select and pull out books repeatedly to find the candy. Fourth, the response which is associated with success or satisfaction results in *reinforcement*, because it is accompanied by a reduction of need (eating candy decreases the hunger drive). Finally, the response pattern—in this case, selecting the correct book—if it is strengthened by successive reinforcements, becomes a *habit*.

Dollard and Miller have shown that neurosis and other psychopathologies may be explained by the principles of reinforcement. An adolescent, for example, feels hostile toward adults because he believes they do not accept him. When he expresses these hostile feelings, he is punished by being ridiculed before his peers, being given poor grades, and having privileges withheld. This causes him to become upset and to fear further reprisals from adults. This fear is called a *secondary drive*. Because of it, the adolescent of our example refrains from expressing his hostility even when adults seek to dominate and exploit him. Recurrences of these events place the adolescent in severe conflict, symptomatic of a neurosis. He has a strong drive to express his hostility, but fear of punishment inhibits his expression of this feeling. Dollard and Miller indicate that reinforcement learning theory may be used during psychotherapy to encourage such an adolescent to act in a hostile manner toward the therapist and other adults without fear of punishment. This would extinguish his fear of expressing hostility toward adults, permit him to view his conflict more objectively, and prepare him for the next step—learning to express hostility in situations where a hostile response

[16] John Dollard and Neal E. Miller, *Personality and Psychotherapy* (New York: McGraw-Hill Book Co., 1950).

is appropriate. The adolescent's conditioned fear of his hostile impulses is an example of Gagné's Type-1 learning; his responses to this fear—first complying with adults and later resisting them—are examples of Type-3 learning.

Central to Hull's and Dollard and Miller's reinforcement theories is the presence of drive, a prerequisite for learning. Since humans may be presumed to learn academic skills in response to something other than hunger or thirst, reinforcement theorists have introduced the concepts of *secondary drives* and *secondary reinforcement*. In the example cited above, the fear response becomes a secondary drive because it is aroused at the same time the primary drive, pain, is evoked. Fear, as well as pain, motivates the adolescent to desist from engaging in hostile acts. A neutral stimulus becomes a secondary reinforcer when it is paired with another stimulus or event which is already reinforcing (primary reinforcer). In the above example, the adult's nondominative, nonexploitive behavior is the primary reinforcer in reducing fear, while the adult's smile, if it occurred, would be the secondary reinforcer, because it also reduces fear. Grades, honors, and money are familiar examples of secondary reinforcers.

Skinner. The foremost contemporary exponent of learning by reinforcement is B. F. Skinner (1904–   ),[17] whose psychology has been called a descriptive behaviorism. Skinner focuses upon the external conditions under which learning occurs and upon the behavior of the organism under these conditions. He makes a sharp distinction between respondent behavior and operant behavior. *Respondent behavior* is evoked when a neutral stimulus, after a series of pairings with an unconditioned stimulus, comes to elicit a conditioned response. *Operant behavior* is a response to the environment. No particular stimulus consistently elicits operant behavior; rather, the learner emits responses to the environment, and these responses, if reinforced, tend to be repeated. Thus, an operant is behavior which has been reinforced. The law of operant conditioning states that "if the occurrence of an operant is followed by presentation of a reinforcing stimulus, the strength of the operant is increased."[18]

Although the findings of operant conditioning have been widely applied to human learning, much of the basic research has been carried out with rats and pigeons. Initially, the behavior of an untrained pigeon is shaped toward the desired ends of the experimenter by his rewarding the pigeon with a pellet of food each time it successively turns toward, comes closer to, and finally pecks a circular key (disc). Behavior is shaped through a series of successive approximations, wherein reinforced behavior is gradually brought closer and closer to the desired pattern. Through the technique of *shaping,* animals may be trained to perform complex acts that are outside of their normal range of behavior. The pigeon's behavior may also be shaped by rewarding it only when it recognizes the reappearance of the first stimuli in a

[17] See B. F. Skinner, *The Behavior of Organisms* (New York: Appleton-Century-Crofts, 1938).

[18] Skinner, p. 21.

sequence of three stimuli presented in rapid succession. For example, a cross, a circle, and a cross appear in rapid succession on central, right, and left keys, respectively. If the pigeon pecks the center key and waits until the cross reappears and then pecks the left key, he has learned to discriminate between a cross and a circle, and his behavior is called a *discriminated operant*.

In operant conditioning, the reinforcing stimulus (food) does not occur simultaneously with the response, but follows the response. The initial stimulus (the key) is not the cause of the response, according to Skinner, but is merely one of the conditions under which the behavior occurs. The significant association in operant conditioning is formed between the operant (R) (pecking the key) and the reinforcing stimulus (S) (presentation of the food).

The technique of shaping behavior has been used extensively in human learning. Children's responses are shaped by socialization processes toward desired social behaviors; the responses of retardates and the emotionally disturbed may be shaped in the learning of simple skills; and the classroom teacher shapes students' behaviors toward goals in reciting, preparing a report, learning shorthand, and observing proper deportment. Each of these activities is an example of Gagné's Type-3 and Type-4 learning. Since many of these activities require the learner to make different responses to different but similar stimuli, Type-5, multiple discrimination learning, may also be involved.

Operant conditioning is one of the few systems of learning which has been directly applied to the classroom. Skinner suggests that the inefficiency of some current teaching procedures may be overcome by presenting a series of stimuli to which the child is to respond, by reinforcing the child's response immediately instead of after a time lapse, and by step-by-step reinforcement of a series of progressive approximations toward the final desired behavior. The following account shows how Mr. Phillips, a junior high school English teacher, used operant reinforcement in the teaching of grammar.

In planning for the fall semester following a summer course in learning theory, Mr. Phillips noted that many of his students of above average intelligence were woefully weak in their knowledge of English grammar, as revealed in their oral and written expression. He wondered whether these students would improve if given immediate reinforcement when they used language correctly as suggested by operant conditioning.

He tried giving words of praise and encouragement to students who responded correctly to items in grammar exercises. Mr. Phillips quickly perceived that operant conditioning might work quite well if he were tutoring just one student, but in class recitation only one student at a time could respond and have his response reinforced. It was evident, too, that for a few students some of the principles of grammar presented were not simplified enough or were unrelated to the preceding principle of grammar that had been studied.

Further, he noted that his attention was so focused upon the proper timing and kind of reinforcing comment that he was having difficulty keeping in view the central function of language as a medium of human expression and communication. It was also evident that one third of the class expressed themselves well in English and had little need for the grammar drill.

Mr. Phillips had obtained materials and information on programed learning texts during the learning theory class and at the state teachers' convention. Following a conference with his supervisor, an order was placed for a programed English text which would be used under minimum supervision by students who could profit from a thorough review and strengthening of knowledge and skills in English expression.

Programed Learning

Skinner's system of operant reinforcement has been applied in the selection and programing of material for use with teaching machines or programed texts. Effective learning through the use of programed learning media requires that the student take the initiative in composing his response, rather than selecting his response from among a set of alternatives. In programed learning, again following Skinner's suggestion, the student passes through a carefully designed sequence of small, easy steps toward the desired behavior.

The student using Skinner's machines or programed texts is presented with a graduated series of questions, each of which calls for an answer that has been presented in or suggested by the previous material. Each question is in the form of an incomplete statement, and the student responds by writing a word or phrase which completes the statement. He then moves a device that exposes the correct answer; compares it with his response; and then, if his answer is correct, moves a lever which brings up the next question. Correct answers thus are reinforced by the exposed printed answer. Programed instruction is also presented in the form of a scrambled textbook. Figure 13.3[19] presents items from a page of a book programed for self-instruction in English grammar.

In programed instruction, the choice and the sequential ordering of information and questions are of primary importance. If materials to be learned are properly prepared and presented in sequential order, Skinner finds that they are highly effective. Skinner summarizes the advantages of this type of instruction:

1. Learning is more effective when it involves the active participation of the learner. Since the student is continually reading and answering questions, he is always busy with learning activities. He does not sit passively listening to a lecture or watching a demonstration but must make an overt response in answering each question that is posed.

[19] From M. W. Sullivan, *Programmed English* (New York: The Macmillan Company, 1963). Reprinted by permission.

Only an_____can modify a verb.	adverb
Many adverbs end in_____.	ly
When they modify the verb, these adverbs usually tell us something about the _____ of the verb.	action
Adverbs ending in____seldom modify linking verbs.	ly
Do they often modify verbs of action?	yes

Some of the following sentences contain linking verbs. The others contain verbs of action.	
The linking verbs are followed by adjectives which modify the_____ of the sentence.	subject
The verbs of action are followed by adverbs ending in <u>ly</u> which modify the_____.	verb
In each sentence select the correct form of the adjective or adverb:	
A rose smells - sweet/sweetly.	sweet
This food tastes - bad/badly.	bad
The professor speaks - rapid/rapidly.	rapidly
You sing - good/well.	well
He felt - quick/quickly/ - for the door knob.	quickly
He polished - vigorous/vigorously.	vigorously
The play ended - happy/happily.	happily
The snake struck - vicious/viciously	viciously

Figure 13.3. A page from a programed-learning textbook. The student is instructed to cover up the answers using a leatherette strip which serves as a guide. After answering the question, he moves the guide down so that it reveals the correct answer. (From Sullivan.)

2. The learning of concepts and principles is facilitated when they are presented in small sequential steps, beginning with the simple and leading to more complex concepts and principles. The student is less likely to get "lost" because wherever he is in the program he has been able to answer every question up to that point. The teaching machine operates like a good tutor in making sure that a particular point is understood before the student moves on. Lectures and textbooks, on the other hand, often proceed without ascertaining whether the student understands and thus may leave him behind.

3. Learning is facilitated when the learner is permitted to proceed as slowly or quickly as he is able and as he wishes with no pressure being exerted to complete a question or section within a specified period of time. Thus, the student does not have to cope with concepts until he is ready for them. Programed learning is self-paced, with the only requirement being a correct response before the learner is permitted to proceed with new material.

4. Like a skillful tutor, the machine helps the student come up with the correct answer. The student is helped by the orderly construction of the program and in part by the hints and suggestions which may be derived from the verbal material.

5. Finally, the machine provides reinforcement for every correct response. This immediate feedback enables the student to learn more efficiently with minimum loss of time and effort; it contributes, too, toward maintaining his interest in learning.[20]

Advocates of programed instruction point out that neither teaching machines nor programed texts are intended to replace the teacher. Rather, these media serve to supplement the teacher's activities and to free him to help slower students and those with individual problems. Skinner's method of having all students go through the same sequence of items or frames is called *linear programing*. A contrasting type of program, called a *branching program,* provides several different sequences of items or frames. This type of program seeks to make greater provision for individual differences, since the particular route a learner follows is determined by his response at some preceding "choice point."

Programed learning media appear to be most useful in the learning and recognition of verbal definitions and concepts, and most programed learning materials contain many such items. Thus, Gagné's Type-4 (verbal association) learning appears to be most characteristic of programed learning material. Less frequently, the learner may be asked to identify a concept (Type 6—concept learning), to apply a rule (Type 7—principle learning), or to utilize two or more previously learned principles in solving a problem (Type 8—problem solving).

[20] B. F. Skinner, "Teaching Machines," *Science,* 128 (October 24, 1958), 969–977. Reprinted by permission.

As with so many problems and issues in education, the answers to the question of whether programed learning is superior to traditional patterns of instruction are equivocal, since the findings of different studies are inconsistent. Some studies show that programed instruction may produce greater initial gains in achievement, but that often these gains are not maintained. The chief complaint of good students is that programed material quickly becomes boring; the individual must follow a prescribed series of steps and has little or no opportunity to relate, to evaluate, to reflect, or to make an "intuitive leap" that may short-cut the step-by-step sequence. Advocates of programed instruction contend, however, that improved programs can eliminate many of these disadvantages and deficiencies.

Conditioning and Education

Conditioning is probably a more common and pervasive type of learning in human experience than most persons realize. A child who is bitten or frightened by a ferocious dog can be conditioned to fear all dogs, even small, friendly, tail-wagging puppies. An adult responds with aversion to a particular seafood or vegetable because of its association with a specific traumatic experience. Another loves to listen to an old popular song because it conjures up an old romance.

Conditioning also plays an important part in the learning of language. First through stimulus-response discriminated operants (Type 2), and later through verbal associations (Type 4) spoken words become linked with objects and then with the variety of characteristics, differentiations, and meanings that may be ascribed to particular objects. The pairing of a spoken word with its printed equivalent is a further example of verbal association. Learning to discriminate between several meanings associated with a particular word or idea is an example of multiple discrimination (Type 5).

Conditioned responses may, through reinforcement, become generalized and transferred to an infinite number of stimuli or events. If Ted is sharply criticized for his poor reading, he becomes conditioned to dislike and to avoid reading. He feigns illness and sometimes actually becomes ill when faced with a reading assignment. These responses are reinforced as the result of disapprobation of poor reading shown by parents, teachers, and peers. Over a period of years, Ted's initial conditioned response of anxiety about reading may become generalized to an avoidance and dislike of other school subjects, his teacher, all teachers, all women who look or act like his teacher, this school, this school system, all schools and school systems, education in general, and life in general. This would be an example of the higher-order conditioning of signal learning (Type 1). At the other extreme, each of us has observed how a single positive association may become generalized by reinforcement, so that the individual responds to people and the world in general with cheer, optimism, and confidence no matter how bleak the situation appears. While most learning is probably more than simple conditioning or association, it is nevertheless likely that these processes play some part in almost every learning experience.

Cognitive Field Theories of Learning

Cognitive field theories of learning, with their emphasis upon perception, cognition, goals, personal meaning, and the immediate situation, contrast sharply with association theories—particularly with respect to motivation. Association theorists believe that the learner is motivated primarily by organic drives and by successful (rewarded or otherwise reinforced) learning experiences. Cognitive field psychologists, in contrast, believe that the individual is motivated primarily by his need to grasp the *holistic meaning* of perceived phenomena.

Gestalt Theory

Gestalt psychology began with psychological studies of visual perception. In 1912, Max Wertheimer demonstrated that two fine parallel lines that are close together will be seen as one and that two optical stimuli perceived by the human eye in quick succession convey the illusion of movement. This illusion of motion has been called the *phi phenomenon,* and it is exemplified in the series of individual pictures seen in rapid succession in the modern motion picture. Such experiments in perception became the basis for a radically different view of learning that became known as Gestalt psychology.

Gestalt psychology is based on the premise that there is an essential unity in nature and that each phenomenon of nature is a whole, not merely the sum of its parts. Initially, a perceiver responds to a stimulus pattern as a whole; he perceives a total configuration, or *Gestalt*. Following this response to the whole, the perceiver differentiates the whole into separate components or parts. That part of the perceptual image which the perceiver differentiates most sharply and focuses his attention upon is called the *figure*. The less differentiated portions of the image serve as background and are called *ground*. Figure and ground, therefore, refer to the relationships between more differentiated and less differentiated portions of a perceptual image.

The concepts of Gestalt, figure, and ground are illustrated in Figure 13.4.[21] Some will see the top figure in Figure 13.4 as a comb for holding a woman's hair in place. Others will see it as a traffic officer with a white glove raised in front of his face. Some may see the bottom figure as a black Maltese cross, others, as a white propeller. When one is focusing on one of these images, the other is in the "ground"—and vice versa. Being attentive to anything means perceiving it in its "figural" form rather than as "ground."

Fundamental to a cognitive field theory of learning is the proposition that the individual confers form, configuration, and meaning on what he perceives. A basic law of Gestalt psychology is the law of *Pragnanz,* which states that a person will impose order on a disorganized perceptual field in a

[21] From George W. Hartmann, "The Field Theory of Learning and Its Educational Consequences," in *Forty-First Yearbook,* Part I, of the National Society for the Study of Education, Nelson B. Henry, *The Psychology of Learning* (Chicago: University of Chicago Press, 1942), p. 176. Reproduced by permission.

Figure 13.4.   Conventional "reversible" figures (from Hartmann).

predictable way, a way that produces "good" Gestalts—images that are simple and symmetrical.

Motivational dynamics in Gestalt learning are inferred in the law of *closure,* which states that an individual will seek to complete an open or incomplete figure or design. Thus, he will "see" a 330-degree arc as a circle and a silhouette as a person even when details of face and body are missing. Achieving completeness or closure is satisfying, whereas lack of completion is accompanied by tension and dissatisfaction. Closure represents a goal or end toward which the individual is striving as he seeks to perceive unity, completeness, and stability in the objects and events he encounters.

Another concept emphasized in Gestalt psychology is insight—the "sudden flash" that occurs when an individual successfully grasps the key to a problem which previously baffled him. Evidence that learning occurs only when the learner has achieved insight into the problem was obtained initially by Kohler in a series of experiments with chimpanzees.[22] In these experiments, hungry chimpanzees in a cage had to devise a way to reach a banana placed just beyond their reach. In one experiment, the chimps could solve the problem by using a stick or standing on a box. In other experiments, the solution was made more difficult—the chimpanzee was required to place one box on top of the other or to fit two sticks together in order to reach the banana. In reporting these experiments, Kohler emphasized that the solution always seemed to come to the chimpanzee abruptly, as a flash of insight that occurred when relations were perceived in the entire perceptual field. These successful responses, occurring as flashes of insight, tended to be permanent and to carry over to later experiences.

Learning by insight appears to have important applications to classroom learning. After showing children how to find the area of a rectangle by dividing the rectangle into small squares, Wertheimer asked the children to find the area of a parallelogram.[23] One child, seeing that the projecting ends of the parallelogram made the problem more difficult, asked for scissors, cut off one end, and fitted it against the other end, thus making the parallelogram into a rectangle. Another child achieved the same result by bending the parallelogram into a ring, so that the two ends fit together, and then cutting the ring vertically to make a rectangle. Each child's insight into the correct relationship between two geometric figures permitted him to achieve a solution through a restructuring of the problem. Each child changed the parallelogram into a better Gestalt.

Gestalt theory appears to be most relevant in explaining the cognitive types of learning in Gagné's taxonomy. Recognizing a type of aircraft by its silhouette or grasping the key to a puzzle requires that one distinguish between many different stimuli resembling each other in physical appearance—an example of Type-5 (multiple discrimination) learning. Acquiring the key to a problem usually involves the learning of a new concept (Type 6, concept learning), as, for instance, the chimps learned to "lengthen their arms" in order to obtain food. The solution to most problems involves the development and application of principles exemplified by Type-7 (principle) and Type-8 (problem-solving) learning.

Lewin's Topological Psychology

While the early Gestaltists focused upon the structure and properties of perceptual configurations and on learning by insight, Kurt Lewin (1890–

[22] Wolfgang Kohler, *The Mentality of Apes,* trans. by Ella Winter (New York: Harcourt, Brace & World, 1927).

[23] Max Wertheimer, *Productive Thinking* (New York: Harper & Row, 1945), p. 48.

1947)[24] gave his attention to the individual's subjective structuring of his field and to the psychological variables which influence this structuring. Thus, Lewin's field theory comes close to merging learning theory (how learning takes place) and personality theory (why the individual behaves as he does).

A basic construct of Lewin's theory is that of life space (Lewin's name for cognitive field), the individual's world of reality. *Life space* may be defined as the totality of facts and events which determines one's behavior at any given time. Conceptually and graphically, one's life space is represented as a two-dimensional area containing the person himself, the goals he is striving to achieve, the "negative" goals he is striving to avoid, the forces which push him toward or away from goals, and the paths he may take to achieve his goals. Lewin used the term *topology* (a nonmetrical geometry of spaces which includes such concepts as "inside," "outside," and "boundary") to describe his psychology because he believed that the person-environment relationship could best be presented as topological space.

Life space, a person's psychological space, may or may not include elements of his physical or geographical environment. A person, for example, may be unaware of slow-growing cancer in his body. The cancer is physically present but is not represented in his life space. On the other hand, a person may believe he has cancer though all tests for cancer are negative. In this case, cancer is physically absent but is very much present in the person's life space. His perception of his having cancer will influence his behavior; he may give up his job, go from clinic to clinic for diagnosis and treatment, or bemoan his fate. Thus, a fundamental principle of Lewin's theory is that behavior at the time it occurs is determined by the person's life space. This principle and the main constructs of Lewin's system are illustrated in Figure 13.5, a topological representation of Peter in a classroom situation in which he is required to read.

In Figure 13.5, Peter (P) must improve his reading ($^-$Rdg) in order to pass to the next grade ($^+$G). A is the point at which movement may be initiated. The symbols prefixed $_fA^+$ represent forces acting at point A to push Peter toward the goal while symbols prefixed $_fA^-$ represent negative forces acting at point A to push him away from the goal. Positive forces (on the left) include $^+AP_1$, love and approval of parents, which Peter can maintain by success in school; $^+BL_2$, belonging in the peer group, which he can maintain if he is promoted with his class; and $^+AS_3$, the aspiration to be admitted to a good technical school to pursue his lifelong goal of studying electronics. Negative forces (on the right) include $^-EX_1$, past experiences in reading, in which Peter has done poorly; $^-BK_2$, the uninteresting stories and books he is required to read; and $^-SE_3$, the low self-esteem he feels with respect to reading and to academic situations in general. Peter's locomotion, or movements, in relation to reading and passing to the next grade

[24] See Kurt Lewin, *Principles of Topological Psychology* (New York: McGraw-Hill Book Co., 1935).

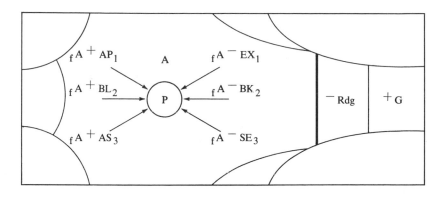

Figure 13.5. Topological representation of the life space of boy P whose goal of passing to the next grade requires that he improve in his reading.

will depend upon the resolution of the vectors of forces, represented by arrows.

It appears that Peter's responses in this situation will depend largely on perceptual and cognitive types of learning. In making some progress in his reading, he has learned that the same printed word symbol often has different meanings (Gagné's Type-5, multiple-discrimination learning). He responds to clearly formed concepts of "reading," "promotion," "teacher," "parents," "approval," "education," and "electronics" (Type 6, concept learning). Finally, the movements Peter makes in dealing with the issue of improving his reading are likely to involve Type-3, Type-7, and Type-8 (chaining, principle, and problem-solving) learning.

Lewin's theory provided the impetus for important breakthroughs in behavioral science research. The influence of his ideas on the development of phenomenological self theory and on investigations of social-emotional climate, group behavior, and learning have been substantial. Discussion of these influences appear elsewhere in this book.

Tolman's Purposive Behaviorism

Edward C. Tolman (1886–1959)[25] developed a theory of learning called *purposive behaviorism* which utilized concepts from both S-R association and cognitive field theories. Insofar as he rejected introspection, treated such variables as consciousness and ideation as inferences from observed behavior, and experimented primarily with laboratory animals in studies of maze behavior, Tolman was a behaviorist. In interpreting his results, however,

[25] See Edward C. Tolman, *Purposive Behavior in Animals and Men* (Berkeley, California: University of California Press, 1949).

Tolman utilized explanatory principles of cognitive field theory: perception, cognition, field, Gestalt, and insight.

For Tolman, behavior is purposive and goal-directed. The specific movements in a behavior are less important than the goal toward which the organism is striving. Tolman contended that in running a maze an animal selects certain stimuli, cues, and features of his environment as signs or guides and utilizes these in learning his way about and forming a "cognitive map." Support for this theory—that learning depends not on S-R chains but upon the learner's cognitive structure—came from studies of latent learning. In these studies, a group of animals, nonrewarded for ten days but rewarded on the eleventh, made markedly fewer errors in running a maze than a group rewarded each day from the first day.[26] The first group had apparently been developing a "cognitive map" of the layout of the maze during the period they had not been rewarded. These and other experiments in latent learning point to an important distinction between *performance* and *learning*. They suggest that individuals are learning even when no change can be detected in their performance.

Tolman's theory has been called "sign-Gestalt" or "sign-significate" learning. The theory identifies three elements in learning: sign–behavior route–significate. The *sign* is a stimulus, a feature of the learner's "cognitive map" (color, appearance, or some other distinguishing feature or junction point in maze). The sign becomes associated with the *behavior route,* the learner's movement or response. The *significate* is the goal of the behavior (food at the end of the maze in the experiment cited above). Tolman's sign-significate (S-S) theory embodied what he called an expectancy principle: When a stimulus (sign) is followed by a second stimulus (significate), the learner will acquire an association between the two stimuli. Thus, for Tolman, learning was a matter of acquiring meanings (signs) from the relationships between behavior (behavior route) and the anticipated goal (significate).

Although Tolman based his theory primarily on studies of animals, his writings imply that human beings also develop cognitive maps and that learning is an outcome of goal-seeking activities. Like Hull's, Tolman's behaviorism focuses upon *intervening variables*—events which occur between stimulus and response. Unlike Hull, however, Tolman used terms referring to mental processes—cognitions, perceptions, beliefs, goals, and purposes—to designate the intervening variables in his system. Central constructs serving as intervening variables in Tolman's theory include a *need system* and a *belief-value matrix.*[27] For a student assigned the task of solving a difficult geometry problem, needs relevant to this task may be presumed to be needs for achievement and affiliation. Also present as intervening variables are the

---

[26] Edward C. Tolman and C. H. Honzik, "Introduction and Removal of Reward and Maze Performance in Rats," *University of California Publication in Psychology,* 4 (1930), 257–275, 282, 283.

[27] Edward C. Tolman, "A Cognition Motivation Model," *Psychological Review,* 59 (September 1952), 389–400.

student's belief that an understanding of geometry is important in becoming an engineer and his valuing of the competence to solve a difficult problem without asking for help. A third set of intervening variables is called *behavior space*. The student's behavior space includes his perceptions of the problem and the possible approaches to solving it. Each of these has its positive and negative valences, corresponding to the probability that a perception or an approach will lead to a solution of the problem. Thus, according to Tolman, what the learner will do (his response) depends not only upon the stimulus situation and the conditions of drive, but also upon the intervening variables: need system, belief-value matrix, and behavior space. Applications of Tolman's theory to human learning would be illustrative of all eight of Gagné's types of learning.

Phenomenological Theory and Learning

Phenomenological self theory (described in Chapter 8) has sought to explain why some persons learn and others do not with a proposition adopted from Lewin's topological field theory: The individual behaves in a manner consistent with his self-concept (or, as Lewin would say, his life space). From this, phenomenological self theorists have derived the proposal that how a person perceives himself in a given learning situation will in large measure determine what he will learn.

Combs[28] rejects the notion that what a person learns is the result of forces exerted on the individual (as the S-R theorists contend). Instead, he proposes that behavior is determined by the meaning one derives from his perceptions and that learning is the exploration and discovery of personal meanings. Teaching then becomes a process of helping students to explore and to discover the personal meaning in the events they experience. Rogers[29] also expresses a phenomenological view of learning:

> I have come to feel that the only learning which significantly influences behavior is self-discovered, self-appropriated learning . . . I realize that I am only interested in being a learner, preferably learning things that matter, that have some significant influence on my own behavior.

In spite of the attractiveness of a phenomenological self theory of learning, there have been few efforts made to develop further and to test such a theory. Snygg[30] made a start on this problem when he proposed a cognitive field model of learning, in which the individual is aware of a need, perceives a

[28] Arthur W. Combs, "Perceiving and Behaving," in Arthur W. Combs, *Perceiving, Behaving, Becoming* (Washington: Assn. for Supervision and Curriculum Development, N. E. A., 1962), pp. 65–82.

[29] Carl R. Rogers, *On Becoming a Person* (Boston: Houghton Mifflin Co., 1961), p. 276.

[30] Donald Snygg, "A Cognitive Field Theory of Learning," in Walter B. Waetjen and Robert R. Leeper, *Learning and Mental Health in the School* (Washington: Assn. for Supervision and Curriculum Development, N. E. A., 1966), pp. 77–96.

goal, and engages in a sequence of activities involving perception of a problem, action or response, and perception of results (evaluation and feedback). The learner, for example, becomes aware of a need to increase his vocabulary so that he may achieve his goal of understanding the contents of a technical manual. He perceives his problem as one of learning the meaning of unfamiliar words. His action or response is to look up these words in a dictionary. If the dictionary meanings of a given word enable him to understand the passage in the technical manual, this particular sequence of search-act-evaluate activities is terminated. If the dictionary meaning does not lead to understanding, then further search-act-evaluate sequences may be required. Snygg suggests that under his theory optimum learning takes place in situations which allow the learner to test his ideas under conditions which provide for immediate feedback.

A number of studies appear to support the proposition that one's perception of himself as a learner will in large measure determine what he will learn. Studies cited in Chapter 8 revealed that boys who have unfavorable self-images also are low in scholastic achievement. Sears[31] and Spaulding[32] found that when children with inadequate self-concepts were matched by intelligence test scores with children with adequate self-concepts, those with adequate self-concepts tended to do better in school. Spaulding further found that, among high-ability children, boys tend to be more realistic in their self-concepts of their own mental abilities than girls. Among low-ability children, however, girls are more realistic in their self-concepts of their mental abilities than boys. In spite of these findings, phenomenological learning theory has not as yet provided any principles indicating how the environment should be arranged in order to facilitate learning.[33]

Phenomenological self theory, as well as the other cognitive field theories discussed here, offer explanations of learning that are especially relevant to Gagné's Type-6, Type-7, and Type-8 (multiple-discrimination, principle, and problem-solving) learning. Other explanations for and examples of these types of learning will be presented in Chapter 15.

Summary

Learning is a universal, life-long process wherein individuals modify their behavior in coping with and adapting to their environment. Capacity for learning and the importance of learning in the life of the species increase with the greater complexity of organization of higher animals. For man, the

[31] Pauline S. Sears, "Accuracy of Self-Perceptions in Elementary School Children." (Paper presented at the California Educational Research Association meeting, 1959.)

[32] Robert L. Spaulding, "Differential Effects of High and Low Concepts Regarding Mental Ability upon Academic Achievement." (Paper presented at the California Educational Research Association meeting, 1960.)

[33] Robert M. W. Travers, *Essentials of Learning* (New York: Macmillan Co., 1963), p. 472.

highest form of animal life, learned responses constitute the overwhelming majority of his behavioral repertoire.

Learning is both a process and a product. Learning has been defined as a modification of behavior as the result of experience or training. A useful distinction may be drawn between the term *performance,* what the learner does, and the term *learning,* which must always be inferred from performance.

A general model of learning useful in any study of the learning process consists of three sets of variables: *stimulus* or *situation* variables; *organism* variables, internal processes or events which intervene between stimulus and response; and *response* variables, overt and covert activities which relate to conditions of stimulation. Each learning theory tends to emphasize and to elaborate certain interrelationships within the situation-organism-response model in preference to other interrelationships within the model.

A growing recognition by psychologists that there are several different types of learning, each of which appears to fit one kind of learning theory more readily than others, has resulted in several attempts to produce a taxonomy of learning types. One such taxonomy, developed by Gagné, identifies and describes eight types of learning, each of which requires a different set of conditions. Types 1 (signal), 2 (stimulus-response), 3 (chaining), and 4 (verbal-association) exemplify stimulus-response association learning; Types 5 (multiple-discrimination), 6 (concept), 7 (principle), and 8 (problem-solving) are explained more readily by cognitive field theories of learning.

Association theories of learning may be classified in relation to two traditional points of view: (1) contiguity theories of conditioning and (2) learning by reinforcement. In the classical conditioning of Pavlov and Watson, when a *neutral stimulus* (bell) is paired with an *unconditioned stimulus* (food), the neutral stimulus becomes a *conditioned stimulus* which has the ability to evoke a *conditioned response* (salivation). In Guthrie's theory of simultaneous contiguous conditioning, the response that leads successfully to the next unit in a series of behaviors is the response that is learned.

What has since come to be known as reinforcement theory was first enunciated by Thorndike in his *law of effect.* Thorndike's law states that the strengthening of an S-R connection depends upon its consequences—success or failure. *Connectionism,* as this theory is called, is a process of selecting and connecting appropriate S-R components in forming neural bonds. His emphasis upon proceeding from simple to complex and from part to whole in forming bonds led Thorndike to organize vocabulary lists and arithmetic concepts into graded steps.

Hull developed a carefully conceived theory of reinforcement that has become a model of theory building. For Hull, learning was reinforcement—the general action of the organism in reducing need which in turn strengthens habits that insure survival. With the prominence they gave to secondary drives and secondary reinforcement, Hull, together with Dollard and Miller, broadened the application of reinforcement theory to include many kinds of learning.

The foremost contemporary exponent of reinforcement theory is B. F. Skinner. Skinner's operant conditioning differs from Pavlovian conditioning in that it withholds the reinforcing stimulus until the learner makes the desired movement or correct discrimination. Thus, a learner's behavior may be shaped toward desired ends by rewarding each response that more closely approximates the desired response. Skinner found that stronger associations are formed if the learner is rewarded intermittently rather than after every response. A direct application to education of operant conditioning has come with the development of programed instructional materials.

Cognitive field theories of learning, with their emphasis on perception, cognition, goals, and personal meaning, offer a view of learning which contrasts sharply with that of the associationists. A fundamental proposition of cognitive field theory is that the individual confers form, configuration, and meaning on what he perceives. Learning, according to Gestalt theory, requires the learner to achieve insight into the solution of the problem. Insight, achieved when the individual successfully grasps the key to a previously baffling problem, may occur quite suddenly.

Kurt Lewin expanded cognitive field theory by drawing into it the psychological variables which influence the structuring of one's cognitive field. A key construct in Lewin's theory is the individual's *life space,* the totality of facts and events which determines the individual's behavior at any given time.

Tolman, a behaviorist who incorporated into his theory constructs from cognitive field theory, postulated that an animal's learning of a maze depends upon its forming a "cognitive map." Tolman emphasized the distinction between learning and performance, and his experiments with latent learning show that subjects are learning even when no changes may be detected in their performance.

Phenomenological self theorists have endeavored to explain why some persons learn while others do not by proposing that how an individual perceives himself in a given learning situation will in large measure determine what he will learn. Although some research supports this proposition, phenomenological approaches to learning have not as yet provided any principles indicating how the environment should be arranged in order to facilitate learning.

Study Questions

1. Describe two or three examples of the best teaching you have ever observed. Identify the common elements in each. What theories of learning were being employed?

2. Mrs. Hendricks, who has taught in the same school for many years, was heard to remark to a younger teacher, "That may be all right in theory, but

it won't work in actual practice." What inferences do you draw from this statement with regard to Mrs. Hendricks' view of teaching and learning?

3. Compare the capacities and responses of a human learner with those of an electronic computer. What are the chief advantages of each with respect to various kinds of learning?

4. During a school day, a fifth-grade class may spend time solving arithmetic problems involving fractions, studying their spelling words by writing them in sentences, writing an original play and preparing to produce it, lining up without being told in coming in from recess or lunch, and practicing shooting goals with a basketball during physical education. What learning theory or theories best explain each of these learning activities?

5. This book has frequently used the terms "development" and "learning." What characteristics are common to both concepts? What distinctions would you make between the two terms?

Suggested Readings

Morris L. Bigge. *Learning Theories for Teachers*. New York: Harper & Row, 1964. Presents in Socratic form a comprehensive view of current psychological learning theories. Contrasts association and cognitive field theories in general and analyzes the contribution of each to learning and teaching.

Thomas E. Clayton. *Teaching and Learning: A Psychological Perspective*. Englewood Cliffs, New Jersey: Prentice-Hall, 1965. Presents basic concepts relative to the teaching process, the nature and conditions of the learning process, and the nature and development of the learner. Chapters 4–8 provide a brief, succinct discussion of the nature of learning and each of the major learning theorists. Provides a useful overview of learning and learning theories for the less sophisticated student.

Alexander Frazier. Editor. *Learning More about Learning*. Washington: Association for Supervision and Curriculum Development, 1959. Contains addresses of four speakers at educational research institutes. The papers by Combs and Bills are forceful statements supporting a phenomenological view of learning.

Robert M. Gagné. *The Conditions of Learning*. New York: Holt, Rinehart and Winston, 1965. Describes eight types of learning, from simple signal, stimulus-response learning to complex problem solving. The eight varieties of learning are fundamental in the development of hierarchical learning sets. These sets identify goals and sequential learning steps required for learning a skill or concept.

James G. Holland and B. F. Skinner. *The Analysis of Behavior*. New York: McGraw-Hill Book Co., 1961. A programed text containing approximately two thousand frames which present and test student's comprehension of concepts related to classical and operant conditioning.

Walter B. Waetjen and Robert R. Leeper. Editors. *Learning and Mental Health in the School*. Washington: Association for Supervision and Curriculum Development, 1966. Discusses mental health in terms of the learning skills and understandings one needs for coping with the environment, communicating, solving problems, and preparing for a vocation. The concepts involved and the ways in which competency, self-actualization, and becoming are fostered are discussed by various writers.

Films

Focus on Behavior: Learning about Learning, 16 mm, sound, black and white, 30 min. Bloomington, Indiana: Audio-Visual Center, Indiana University (rental fee, $5.40). Describes the approaches used by Skinner, Harlow, Spence, and the Kendlers in developing new theoretical concepts about man's ability to learn.

Teaching Machines and Programmed Learning, 16 mm, sound, black and white, 28 min. Bloomington, Indiana: Audio-Visual Center, Indiana University (rental fee, $4.40). Presents Drs. B. F. Skinner, A. A. Lumsdaine, and Robert Glaser as each discusses teaching machines and programed learning. Skinner identifies the main features and rationale behind the use of teaching machines. Lumsdaine discusses various types of machines and current trends in programed material. Glaser describes the impact of programed learning upon the whole educational system.

Skippy and the Three R's, 16 mm, sound, black and white, 30 min. Bloomington, Indiana: Audio-Visual Center, Indiana University (rental fee, $4.65). Shows a teacher-guided excursion of first-grade children into the community. The children later tell stories of their experiences which the teacher writes for them to read. The curriculum is based on things children want and need to learn, for which they are ready, and which have meaning for them.

14

readiness for learning

*Feed the growing human being, feed him with the sort of experience
for which from year to year he shows a natural craving.*

≡   WILLIAM JAMES

Few educators doubt the importance of readiness in human
development and learning. There is ample evidence from
research and from everyday experience that pupils learn
more quickly, efficiently, and effectively when they are ready
for a learning experience. Thorndike, it will be recalled,
clearly perceived the key which readiness plays in learning;
the Law of Readiness became a major part of his connec-
tionist theory of learning. His interest in readiness is also
reflected in his development of sequential organizations of
subject matter for successive grades in school.

Too often, however, teachers think of readiness as something that occurs prior to the learning activity itself. They
assume that if a student is placed in a class or is registered
for a course, he is able and ready to learn the concepts and
skills he will encounter. Further, they assume that if a
student has an average or higher than average IQ, he can
learn. These assumptions are questionable. We know from
our study of human development and learning that individuals differ in every aspect of their development—including their "readiness." Therefore, some students will require

help from the teacher to develop readiness for the learning tasks which the school is expected to teach.

What is readiness? The term in general connotes the presence within the learner of requisite conditions for his effective learning. Attempts to develop more detailed definitions of the term have generated considerable confusion and controversy. Some people hold that readiness is solely an inner dynamic, a product of maturation; to these people, readiness is almost synonymous with maturation. Others believe that readiness is also influenced by environmental, experiential, and psychological variables. A related disagreement has arisen over whether the learner is always in a natural state of readiness or whether readiness is something that must be nourished and developed. Bruner appears to feel that children are always ready to learn; in an oft-quoted statement, he opines that "any subject can be taught effectively in some intellectually honest form to any child at any stage of development."[1] However, the view that readiness is a quality that requires development appears to enjoy wider acceptance.

For our purposes, we will define a learner's readiness in any situation as *the sum of his characteristics which make his behavior amenable to change*. One's readiness for learning depends on the interplay of dynamic processes described in Chapters 3 through 9: one's physical maturity and development; his experiences with adults and peers and his culture in general; and his needs, goals, learned ideas, skills, emotions, and adjustive patterns.

The student's state of readiness, then, is not the same from day to day but changes with increased maturation and added learning and experience. A student's readiness for some activities and skills may decrease, while his readiness for others may increase. For example, the child's readiness for boy-girl relationships is probably greater at ages six and fourteen than at age ten. On the other hand, his readiness for baseball is probably greater at age ten than at either six or fourteen.

Principles of Readiness

Cronbach[2] cites four principles that influence the development of readiness. First, *all aspects of development interact*. We might add that all aspects of development are also interrelated. We noted in Chapter 4, for example, that Betty Burroughs' early physical maturation contributed to her view of herself as out of place in the ninth grade, but gave her a readiness for interacting and learning with older adolescents. In Chapter 8, the case of Becky showed that an inadequate self-concept may influence intellectual

[1] Jerome S. Bruner, *The Process of Education* (Cambridge: Harvard University Press, 1960), p. 33.
[2] Lee J. Cronbach, *Educational Psychology*, 2nd ed. (New York: Harcourt, Brace & World, 1963), p. 89.

development and achievement. Chapters 11 and 12 emphasized the serial appearance and interrelatedness of developmental tasks. Similarly, the development of affectional relationships in early life prepares the individual for satisfying peer relationships at a later age.

Second, *physiological maturing prepares one to profit from experience.* The need to have the physical maturation requisite for a specific learning is self-evident. An individual's readiness, however, is a result of both physical change and learning. One does not automatically begin to walk or read as soon as he is physically mature enough. Many trials, successes, and failures must occur before these activities are mastered.

Third, *experiences have a cumulative effect.* Successes or failures at earlier stages of development usually have a direct influence on related aspects of later development. A child's success in sports, his fascination with history, or his curiosity about stars and planets in elementary school provides him with a predisposition toward and a readiness for experiences and satisfactions in sports or in the study of history or astronomy in high school or college. Conversely, failure or lack of satisfaction in certain activities lessens one's readiness for those activities and leads him to avoid them on subsequent occasions.

Finally, *basic readiness for a particular activity is established during certain formative periods of life.* This principle suggests that there is an optimum time for initiating most learning tasks, a "teachable moment."[3] The formative period for the establishment of readiness for a physical skill, for instance, is age one to four; the formative period for the development of attitudes about one's intellectual ability is the first year or two of school, when success, failure, or conflict influences reactions to all subsequent schooling.[4]

Dimensions of Readiness

Maturation

Initially, the term *maturation* was used by geneticists and embryologists to designate the period of development in which an immature germ cell is converted into a mature one. This significant change, called meiosis, produces a reduction of chromosomes, so that a mature ovum or sperm has only half as many chromosomes as immature germ cells and other body cells. This quite specific definition has given way to more generalized and sometimes ambiguous and confusing usage by behavioral scientists. As a result, the term is now applied indiscriminately to different kinds of maturity—physical, sexual, skeletal, social, emotional, and mental. Furthermore, some of these types of maturation are difficult to assess. For instance, although physical matura-

[3] Robert J. Havighurst, *Human Development and Education* (New York: David McKay Co., 1953), p. 5.
[4] Cronbach, p. 90.

tion can be measured fairly reliably (by level of bone ossification in comparison to norms, chronological age at menarche, or the appearance and measurement of secondary sex characteristics), there is far less agreement about *social* or *emotional maturity*. At best, these terms refer to a score or percentile derived from a test of undetermined validity; more often, they reflect subjective assessments of some individuals by other individuals.

The terms *maturity* and *maturation* also imply the attainment of some end point or final goal, which is accompanied by the cessation of processes of growth and development. This notion too is somewhat misleading; for, as we have tried to show, the human being is an open, dynamic energy system which moves toward optimum development, a development that is limited only by the individual's capacities, his opportunities, and his level of organization (physiological and psychological). Maturation, therefore is an open-ended process, and maturity is a relative rather than an absolute term.

Maturation is not always clearly distinguishable from learning. Maturation, in the strict meaning of the term, refers to that process whereby behavior is modified as a result of the growth and development of physical structure. Learning, on the other hand, is the process by which behavior is originated or changed through practice or training. However, maturation and learning are interrelated processes; if an individual is not yet mature enough to learn a particular skill, practice and training alone will not enable him to learn it.

The negligible effect of practice in the absence of requisite maturation was demonstrated in a study by Gesell and Thompson,[5] who studied learning and maturation in two young girls, identical twins, labeled T and C. At the beginning of the study, the twins, at age 46 weeks, were essentially equal in all fields of behavior, including locomotion. Both were able to pull themselves to a standing position, to creep with equal facility, and to walk when held by two hands, and both were on the threshold of walking alone. Beginning at 46 weeks, twin T was given ten minutes of stimulation and guidance every morning in stair climbing, creeping, pulling herself to a standing position, walking while holding on to a crib, and walking while holding on to the experimenter's hand. After the first three days of this training, the experimenter enticed T to climb as many steps as possible. Twin C was given no specific training until she was 53 weeks old.

At 52 weeks of age (after T had had six weeks of training), the twins were equal in creeping ability and expressed an equal eagerness to stand. T, however, was slightly better than C in standing alone momentarily and in lowering her body. At this time, C made an initial attempt to climb the stairs, while T could already climb them (in 26 seconds). The following week (when the twins were 53 weeks of age) twin C, although untrained, climbed the entire staircase, unassisted, in 45 seconds; the next day she did it in 40 seconds. Twin T had meanwhile reduced her time to 17 seconds.

[5] Arnold Gesell and Helen Thompson, "Learning and Maturation in Identical Infant Twins: An Experimental Analysis by the Method of Co-Twin Control," in R. G. Barker, J. S. Kounin, and H. F. Wright, *Child Behavior and Development* (New York: McGraw-Hill Book Co., 1943), pp. 209–227.

Comparisons in the performances of the twins after T had had six weeks of training (at age 52 weeks) and C had had two weeks of training (at age 55 weeks) revealed that both climbed in a similar manner, but that C climbed more rapidly. C also walked better than T when supported by one hand. Although T's training began seven weeks earlier and lasted three times as long (six weeks as opposed to two weeks), three weeks of added age nevertheless enabled C to surpass T in performance. Gesell and Thompson concluded that the maturity advantage of three weeks of age must have accounted for this superiority of C's performance.

The findings of this and other co-twin control studies suggest that maturation is a function of the passage of time and that practice given too early is likely to be ineffectual and in some cases detrimental. Although such indications of the importance of maturation in motor learning may not necessarily apply to cognitive learning, the idea of postponing practice until the child has attained the requisite level of maturity has nevertheless become well accepted in educational practice.

Several procedures have been developed for studying and assessing the maturity levels of school children. A procedure developed by Olson[6] is based upon the contention that maturity is not a single, discrete variable but a composite measure based upon many different indices of development. His procedure for measuring and describing a child's maturity is to translate longitudinal data on the child into indices which can be plotted on a single graph. Thus, reading tests and mental maturity tests yield reading age (RA) and mental age (MA), height and weight data are translated into height age (HA) and weight age (WA), strength of grip in kilograms yields grip age (GA), the number of erupted permanent teeth provides a measure of dental age (DA), and comparisons of X-rays of hand and wrist with norms provides an assessment of skeletal age which Olson called carpal age (CaA). Figure 14.1[7] records the progress of one child in each of these indices of development. Olson averaged these several measures to obtain an index of the child's overall growth and development, which he calls organismic age (OA).

Olson's work shows that maturity is a more complex phenomenon than the educator's use of the term would suggest. Tyler,[8] however, criticizes the concept of organismic age; in his opinion, morphological, motor, behavioral, and mental maturities are in no way comparable, so that averaging them tends rather to conceal than to reveal intraindividual differences in maturity.

Intelligence

Intelligence is another important aspect of readiness. Students assigned to a particular class are supposed to have sufficient intellectual aptitude to

[6] Willard C. Olson, *Child Development* (New York: D. C. Heath & Co., 1949).

[7] From Willard O. Olson and Byron O. Hughes, "Growth of the Child as a Whole," in R. G. Baker, J. S. Kounin, and H. F. Wright, *Child Behavior and Development* (New York: McGraw-Hill Book Co., 1943), p. 200. Reproduced by permission.

[8] Fred T. Tyler, "Concepts of Organismic Growth: A Critique," *Journal of Educational Psychology,* 44 (October 1953), 321–342.

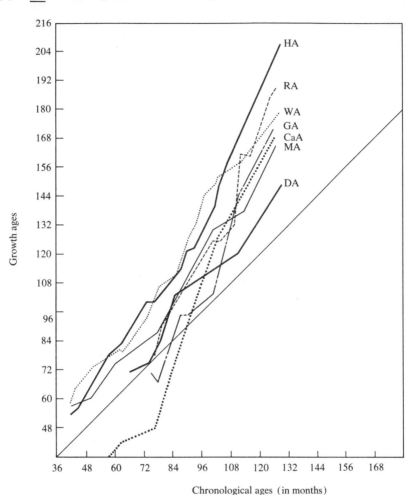

Figure 14.1. Graphs showing one student's progress in different kinds of growth: height age (HA), reading age (RA), weight age (WA), grip age (GA), carpal age (CaA), mental age (MA), and dental age (DA). (From Olson and Hughes.)

profit from that class. But how does a teacher know that all of his students do have sufficient intellectual aptitude? In order to solve this dilemma, psychologists have tried to develop intelligence tests which discriminate between students who are most likely and students who are least likely to profit academically from school instruction. A pioneer in the development of such tests was Alfred Binet. In the early 1900s, Binet and his co-worker, Simon, developed a scale designed to measure complex functions of behavior, while avoiding measures of sensation and simple motor responses. In 1908, the Binet-Simon scale was brought to the United States and translated into English. Here it was modified and from those modifications emerged the well-known Revised Stanford-Binet Scale. This is an individual test consisting of a series of tasks for each year from ages two to fourteen, followed by tasks for the levels of average and superior adult. Included in the scale are tasks which ask the testee to identify objects, to repeat digits from memory, to give the meaning of words, to identify verbal and pictorial absurdities, and to define abstract words. The testee is given a score of so many months for each correct task completed at each year level. When added together, these scores yield a *mental age* (MA), which corresponds to the performance of an average individual of that chronological age (CA). An individual's mental development (his Intelligence Quotient, or IQ) is determined by the following formula:

$$IQ = \frac{MA}{CA} \times 100$$

That is, the individual's mental age is divided by his chronological age, and the result is multiplied by 100. By definition, the IQ is never an absolute measure of intellectual aptitude but an indication of the rate at which the individual is achieving his intelligence. Thus, a five-year-old child with a mental age of eight would have an IQ of 160, whereas a twelve-year-old child with the same mental age would have an IQ of 67.

Another individually administered intelligence test in common use is the Wechsler Intelligence Scale for Children (WISC), a series of performance (nonverbal) and verbal tests used throughout the age range. An individual's performance on the test yields a raw score which may be translated into an IQ score derived from the formula given above.

Individual tests, such as the Stanford-Binet and the Wechsler, permit the testing of only one individual by one examiner at a time. The individual test is frequently administered for the purpose of obtaining an accurate estimate of the intellectual aptitude of a student who has been referred by a teacher or school to psychological services for diagnosis of a learning or behavior problem. When properly administered, such a test yields a more valid measure of the rate of growth in intellectual aptitude than does a group test.

Group tests of intelligence were developed during World War I, when large numbers of recruits had to be classified and screened for various military jobs and assignments. The Army Alpha and Army Beta (nonlanguage) tests proved to be very successful for assessing the mental aptitudes of military personnel.

The period between the two World Wars witnessed a tremendous growth in the development and use of standardized tests of all kinds. These tests yielded quantitative scores which were subjected to a variety of statistical treatments. The tremendous interest in educational measurement gave rise in the 1920s and 1930s to what has been referred to as "the scientific movement in education." Numerous group intelligence, achievement, and other types of standardized tests were developed for use in elementary schools, high schools, and colleges. Some of these intelligence tests yield scores which are readily transformed into IQ scores; but a more common practice, especially in testing older students, has been to translate the raw test score into a percentile score. A person's percentile score indicates what percentage of the comparison group (such as eighth graders or college freshmen) received a lower score than he did. A comparison between IQ and percentile scores is shown in Table 14.1.[9]

Table 14.1.   A Guide for Interpreting the IQ (from Cronbach).

IQ	PERCENTILE SCORE	PROGNOSIS OR INTERPRETATION
140	99	
130	96	
120	87	Likely to succeed in college
110	69	Level of median college entrant
100	50	Average of unselected population
90	23	Unlikely to complete traditional high school program
80	8	
70	3	

The reader may have noted that we have been discussing intelligence and intelligence testing for some pages without having defined the term *intelligence*. There have been many definitions of intelligence, but probably all are for one reason or another incomplete. In general, the term refers to one's capacities or abilities for learning. In discussing intelligence, Binet and Simon wrote, "To judge well, to comprehend well, to reason well, these are the essential activities of intelligence."[10] Nearly three decades later, Stoddard endeavored to include in his definition the then current dimensions of intelligence:

Intelligence is the ability to undertake activities that are characterized by (1) difficulty, (2) complexity, (3) abstractness, (4) economy, (5) adaptiveness to a goal, (6) social value, and (7) emergence of originals,

[9] From Lee J. Cronbach, *Educational Psychology* (New York: Harcourt, Brace & World, 1954), p. 192. Reproduced by permission.
[10] Alfred Binet and T. Simon, *The Development of Intelligence in Children,* trans. by Elizabeth S. Kite (Baltimore: Williams and Wilkins, 1916), p. 42.

and to maintain such activities under conditions that demand a concentration of energy and a resistance to emotional forces.[11]

Stoddard's attempt to develop a comprehensive definition of intelligence falls short in at least two respects. First, its emphasis upon qualities of complexity and abstractness seems to deny intelligence to animals below the level of primates, whereas, as Munn[12] suggests, there appears to be "a more or less gradual transition from relatively simple sensorimotor learning of lower animals to higher types of symbolic processes exhibited by primates." That is, intelligence is not an all-or-none affair; degrees of intelligence may be observed at all levels of animal life.

Second, studies of the structure of the intellect and of creativity (which will be discussed later) strongly suggest that there exist intellectual abilities and qualities which our present intelligence tests do not measure.[13] Consequently, in recent years psychologists have tended to avoid defining intelligence. Instead, they speak of intelligence as "that which the intelligence tests measure." While such a description may be realistic and practical, it, too, restricts the concept of intelligence to human beings, besides being vague and nonspecific.

The notion of fixed intelligence. The view that one's IQ remains relatively constant throughout life permeated much of psychological and educational thinking during the first half of the twentieth century. Hunt[14] points out that this view was based on (1) the belief in fixed intelligence—that is, the belief that intelligence is an innate dimension of personal capacity which increases at a fixed rate to a predetermined level; (2) the belief in predetermined development—that is, the belief that behavioral organizations unfold more or less automatically as a function of physical growth and development.

The belief in fixed intelligence prevailed until fairly recent times. Such a belief appeared to be supported by considerable evidence. It was consistent with the then current belief that development is predetermined by genetic inheritance. Moreover, the average IQ from age to age was found to be quite stable; the IQs of individual children showed considerable constancy from test to test through the school years to adulthood, and the various Binet-type tests gave accurate predictions of school achievement. Finally, this belief in the hereditary determination of intelligence scores seemed to be supported by the comparison of correlations between intelligence-test scores of persons with different degrees of genetic relationship, ranging from .9 for identical twins to .5 for siblings and for parents and their children to zero for unrelated children.[15]

[11] George D. Stoddard, *The Meaning of Intelligence* (New York: Macmillan Co., 1943).

[12] Norman L. Munn, *The Evolution and Growth of Human Behavior* (Boston: Houghton Mifflin Co., 1965), p. 409.

[13] J. P. Guilford, "Three Faces of Intellect," *The American Psychologist,* 14 (August 1959), 469–479.

[14] J. McV. Hunt, *Intelligence and Experience* (New York: Ronald Press, 1961).

[15] Hunt, pp. 10–19.

The belief in fixed intelligence came under strong attack in the *nature versus nurture* controversy of the 1930s. There ensued spirited debate and feverish investigation by both those who contended that intelligence is inherited and fixed (nature) and those who believed that intelligence can be changed if a child is placed in a favorable and stimulating environment (nurture). The nurture point of view was strengthened by studies that investigated IQ changes among identical twins who had been separated and reared apart. Newman, Freeman, and Holzinger[16] found that two of nineteen pairs of twins differed by 24 and 19 IQ points, and that the average difference for all nineteen pairs of identical twins was 8.2 points. Such findings suggested that differences in IQ may be related in part to differences in educational and cultural opportunities.

Further doubt is cast on the idea of fixed intelligence by longitudinal studies of the growth and development of individuals. Jones and Conrad[17] have shown the subsequent variations in the IQs of five boys, each of whom had an IQ of 92 at age seven. At age eleven, their mental ages varied from 105 to 165 months, and their IQs varied from 76 to 129. At age seventeen, the differences in mental age ranged from 160 to 225 months, and IQs varied from 78 to 111. (See Figure 14.2.) Honzik, Macfarlane, and Allen[18] compared performances on intelligence tests for a group of children from age two to eighteen. They found that the IQs of almost 60 percent of the children changed 15 or more points between the ages of six and eighteen, that one third of the group changed 20 or more points, and that 9 percent changed 30 or more points. Changes in mental test scores tended to be in the direction of the family's education and socioeconomic status.

Longitudinal studies carried out in Berkeley, California, by Honzik (cited above) and by Bayley[19] show that correlations between IQ scores on the same individuals in early adulthood are about .9; however, when adult IQ scores are compared with IQ scores made by these same individuals at age seven, the correlations drop to .7. Finally, when adult IQ scores are compared with IQ scores on tests administered during infancy, the correlation is zero. These wide differences between IQ scores obtained for the same individuals in infancy and adulthood are frequently attributed to the unreliability of intelligence tests used in testing infants. Hunt[20] points out, however, that infant tests of intelligence have been found highly reliable when the same infants are retested. Their low correlation with adult IQ scores indi-

[16] H. H. Newman, Frank N. Freeman, and Karl J. Holzinger, *Twins: A Study of Heredity and Environment* (Chicago: University of Chicago Press, 1937).

[17] Harold E. Jones and Herbert S. Conrad, "Mental Development in Adolescence," in Nelson B. Henry, *Forty-third Yearbook: Part I, Adolescence,* National Society for the Study of Education, (Chicago: University of Chicago Press, 1944), pp. 146–163. Figure 14.2 is reproduced from this article by permission.

[18] Marjorie P. Honzik, Jean W. Macfarlane, and L. Allen, "The Stability of Mental Test Performance between Two and Eighteen Years," *Journal of Experimental Education,* 16 (1948), 309–324.

[19] Nancy Bayley, "Consistency and Variability in Growth from Birth to Eighteen Years," *Journal of Genetic Psychology,* 75 (1949), 165–196.

[20] Hunt, p. 314.

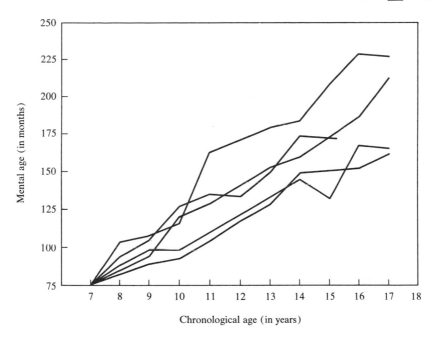

Figure 14.2. Subsequent variation in mental growth for five boys, each of whom had an IQ of 92 at age seven (from Jones and Conrad).

cates not that they are unreliable but that they are not predictive of adult intelligence. Hunt suggests that marked differences in IQ scores for the same individuals between infancy and adulthood point to the development in the child of new intellectual structures at successive maturity levels.

Various studies show that educational and socioeconomic differences are associated with differences in IQ. Children of unskilled workers have an average IQ of about 95. Children from successively higher socioeconomic levels register correspondingly higher IQs, with children of middle-class parents having an average IQ of 125.[21] Studies of children reared in isolated mountain communities or in city slums show that both of these groups score lower in IQ tests than does the population at large, and that the IQs of these children decline as they get older.[22]

Studies of the relationships between foster-home and nursery-school experience and change in intelligence also cast doubt on the notion that IQ

[21] W. S. Neff, "Socioeconomic Status and Intelligence: A Critical Survey," *Psychological Bulletin*, 35 (1938), 727–757.
[22] Mandel Sherman and T. R. Henry, *The Hollow Folk* (New York: Thomas Y. Crowell Co., 1933); Miriam L. Goldberg, "Factors Affecting Educational Attainment in Depressed Urban Areas," in A. H. Passow, *Education in Depressed Areas* (New York: Columbia University Teachers' College Press, 1963), pp. 68–100.

represents a fixed level of mental aptitude. Several studies show that the relationship between the IQs of children and real parents is higher than the relationship between the IQs of children and the IQs of foster parents.[23] Skodak and Skeels,[24] however, found that the IQs of children in foster homes were an average of 20 points higher than those of their true mothers. This finding is difficult to interpret because of a lack of information concerning the IQs of the fathers and the low correlation of the IQ scores obtained at an early age with those obtained several years later. Anastasi and Foley[25] found that children placed in institutions registered lower IQs than those placed in foster homes. The higher IQ scores of children in foster homes suggest that these children benefit from greater intellectual stimulation than do children in institutions. Critics point out, however, that more favorable qualifications were presumably part of the reason the foster children were adopted in the first place, and that this fact may be more important than the quality of the foster home in accounting for their higher IQs.[26]

The question of whether IQ can be increased by nursery-school experience is a controversial one. Wellman[27] found that preschool children who attended nursery school gained an average of 7 IQ points, while matched children who had no nursery school experience lost an average of 3.9 points. Critics have suggested, however, that such a gain may be due in part to the similarity between nursery-school experience and the kinds of aptitudes which IQ tests measure at early age levels.[28]

Several other studies also bring into question the assumption of a pre-determined intelligence independent of environmental stimulation.[29] Such studies suggest that under the stimulation of a favorable environment, children's IQs do increase. Some of the findings and many of the criticisms of these studies seem to indicate, however, that this generalization does not hold true for all children. A few further comments may clarify some of the issues that have been raised.

To begin with, it seems quite pointless to try to ascertain the relative contributions of heredity and environment to the growth of intelligence. There is considerable evidence that the contributions of heredity and environment are interwoven and interrelated from conception onward. The

[23] A. M. Leahy, "Nature-Nurture and Intelligence," *Genetic Psychology Monographs,* 17 (1935), 235–308.

[24] M. Skodak and H. M. Skeels, "A Final Follow-up Study of One Hundred Adopted Children," *Journal of Genetic Psychology,* 75 (1945), 85–125.

[25] Anne Anastasi and J. P. Foley, *Differential Psychology* (New York: Macmillan Co., 1949), pp. 362–367.

[26] Munn, pp. 426–427.

[27] Beth L. Wellman, "Iowa Studies on the Effects of Schooling," *Thirty-ninth Yearbook,* Vol. 2, National Society for the Study of Education, (Chicago: University of Chicago Press, 1940), pp. 377–399.

[28] Munn, p. 427.

[29] Wayne Dennis and Pergrouhi Najarian, "Infant Development under Environmental Handicap," *Psychological Monographs,* 71 (1957), No. 7; Wayne Dennis, "Causes of Retardation among Institutional Children: Iran," *Journal of Genetic Psychology,* 96 (1960), 47–59; Arthur W. Combs, "Intelligence from a Perceptual Point of View," *Journal of Abnormal and Social Psychology,* 47 (July 1952), 662–673.

hereditary factor, while difficult to measure, is, nevertheless, a limiting factor in intellectual development. The finding that children's IQs correspond more closely to those of their true parents than to the IQs of their foster parents indicates that a favorable environment is likely to have a limited influence in raising the IQs of children with low intelligence. The evidence does suggest, however, that good schools or a good home environment will enable a child to raise his IQ above what it would have been in a poorer school or home. Thus, although the IQs of most persons remain relatively stable, the IQs of others vary sufficiently to bring into question the long and strongly held assumptions regarding a fixed, genetically determined intelligence.

"Intelligence" and intelligence test scores. It is important to distinguish between realized or effective intelligence (the intelligence that IQ tests in some degree measure) and the theoretical construct of native intelligence, for which we have no measure. An analogy has often been drawn between those two kinds of intelligence and one's inherited capacity for tallness *versus* his achieved height. Heredity not only sets the limits within which the individual may develop his physical attributes, but also determines the limits of his capacity for intellectual functioning. Realized intelligence is a measure of the extent to which one's inherited capacity for intellectual functioning has been achieved.

Our review of some of the issues and problems related to intelligence leads to the conclusion that educators need a balanced view when interpreting and using intelligence-test scores; either to ignore or to overrely on them is unwarranted. While intelligence is usually thought of in quantitative terms, we need to remember that it is not a substance or an entity within the organism. Rather, it is a *quality* of behavior and should always be interpreted as a descriptive term characterizing an action or an actor. Furthermore, any intelligence- or aptitude-test score is only an *estimate* of an individual's realized intelligence. Since an intelligence test samples performance on a limited number of intellectual abilities, any intelligence-test score is subject to errors of sampling and measurement. Educators, therefore, should not rely on a single test score but should seek several independent measures of the student's intelligence. It is particularly unfortunate when parents or teachers view an IQ score as a fixed capacity rather than as an estimate of a student's rate of intellectual development. The story is told of a teacher who didn't try very hard with a boy whose IQ was 87. She didn't feel guilty about her limited success in helping him to learn until she discovered that she had copied his locker number in the space intended for his IQ score. An IQ score is helpful in planning an educational program, but it should be used as only one of several estimates of a student's mental ability.

The preceding discussion suggests that the intellectual aptitudes of many children can be increased. There is a need to provide students with as stimulating and as enriched a learning environment as possible, for it is doubtful that the optimum intellectual abilities of our students are being realized in present educational programs. (This unrealized intellectual capacity appears to be most common among culturally disadvantaged children, a problem which will be considered in a later section of this chapter.) One should recall, too, that present intelligence tests, in sampling a child's verbal comprehension, word fluency, spatial relationships, and number and inductive abilities, measure only a few aspects of intellectual aptitude. Evidence of this is found in the findings of Getzels and Jackson[30] in their study of a group of private school students whose average IQ was 132. They found that a number of children who scored in the top fifth in IQ did not score in the top fifth in creativity, while some in the top fifth in creativity were below the average IQ for that school.

Intellectual Development

Maturation level and intelligence-test scores, by themselves, are no longer considered adequate indices of readiness for learning. Studies, previously cited, which show that the IQs of many children may be increased by favorable home situations and enriched educational opportunities suggest that a child's *intellectual development*—his acquisition of modes and patterns of thinking in processing sensory data—may provide more useful clues concerning his readiness for learning than his IQ score. The concept of intellectual development focuses not only on the development and functioning of the somatic and cerebral structures involved in processing information, but also on the role of experience in the "development of those central organizations for the processing of information that are required to solve problems."[31]

This view of intelligence has several advantages. It suggests that intelligence is largely the result of nurturance rather than genetic factors. It is also consistent with Piaget's theory of the growth of logical thinking, wherein it is postulated that each stage of development carries with it possibilities for the acquisition of new abilities and new ways of processing information. Piaget further hypothesizes that unless each of these abilities is used, it will not develop fully and will contribute little to the requirements of the next stage.

Although the work of Hebb, Harlow, Guilford, Osgood, Bruner, and others supports this conception of intelligence, Piaget's own empirical observations of the intellectual development of children provide our clearest understanding of the conception. In his studies of intellectual development, Piaget begins not with the learner but with knowledge—what the child learns. He is especially concerned with the structure of knowledge, since he believes that an understanding of the structure of knowledge offers clues to how a child comes to "know" certain facts and how he orders and transforms these facts in performing various mental operations. The action that a child

[30] Jacob W. Getzels and Philip W. Jackson, *Creativity and Intelligence* (New York: John Wiley, 1962).
[31] Hunt, p. 65.

takes in dealing with a fact or concept is called an *operation*. For example, counting, ordering, classifying, or measuring a class of objects are all operations which enable the child to "know" these objects through transforming them. Thus, for Piaget, knowledge may be said to consist of the repertoire of actions the child uses in response to the objects he encounters.

Inhelder and Piaget[32] identify four distinct stages of intellectual development: (1) the sensorimotor period, (2) the preoperational stage, (3) the period of concrete operations, and (4) the period of formal operational thought.

The sensorimotor period. The first period of intellectual development, called the sensorimotor period, begins at birth and lasts until the child is between eighteen months and two years of age. At birth, the child begins to receive information through his sense organs concerning the world about him; initially, however, this information has little meaning for him. Gradually, motor responses develop: the child focuses his eyes on objects, turns his head toward objects or in response to sounds, and coordinates his hand movements with eye and head movements. In time, these visual, auditory, tactual, and kinesthetic sensations become organized into coordinated *patterns of action*. These patterns of action Piaget calls sensorimotor schemata, and in his theory they are said to increase in complexity and relatedness during the first eighteen months or so of life.

As new objects, stimuli, and situations are introduced to the child, he discovers that his existing patterns of action or schemata are not adequate for dealing effectively with new situations. As he varies his response in order to achieve an *accommodation* to the new situation, his old action patterns or schemata are modified and new ones are formed. With increased eye-hand coordination, for instance, the baby picks up a variety of objects, blocks, balls, spoons, and so on. When he picks up a rattle, however, he finds that the rattle makes a noise. His accommodation to this new discovery is to shake the rattle. Through the process which Piaget calls *assimilation,* the child uses in new situations information or responses from previous situations. We say the infant has assimilated the vigorous arm movements he discovered in shaking the rattle when we later observe him using these arm movements to make noise by beating the top of his feeding table with a spoon. Through processes of *self-regulation,* the child seeks to achieve a balance between accommodation (modifying one's behavior in response to changes in the environment) and assimilation (changing inner mental processes so that they reflect and are consistent with the information obtained through accommodation).

Through a series of increasingly complex assimilations and accommodations, the child becomes more and more adept at manipulating and responding to his world. The world becomes increasingly predictable to him. During

[32] Barbel Inhelder and Jean Piaget, *The Growth of Logical Thinking from Childhood to Adolescence,* trans. by Anne Parsons and Stanley Milgram (New York: Basic Books, 1958).

the sensorimotor period, the child comes to recognize a variety of objects, but these recognitions have been preceded by visual explorations of these same objects in a variety of situations. In time, the child is able to "recognize" an object when it is not in sight; that is, he searches for the object when it has momentarily disappeared from view. This "recognition" marks the beginning of the child's ability to "conserve"—that is, to comprehend stability and invariance in his environment.[33]

During the early part of infancy, the child's responses to people or objects take place in the context of a particular moment and situation. Later, as his responses become better adapted to his environment, he no longer needs to respond to objects directly; he is able to remember previous actions and to apply them. He may, for example, search with his eyes for objects that have disappeared from view, lift his arms in anticipation of his mother taking off his shirt, and place his fingers in front of his eyes in response to an adult's invitation to play peekaboo. As he accommodates his vocal productions to those he hears, he begins to assimilate a vocabulary and to acquire labels; as a result, his capacity to store and to retrieve information is greatly increased.

To maximize intellectual development, according to Piaget's theory, a child should be presented with a wide variety of stimuli, the stimuli presented should be matched to the complexity of the reaction patterns the child already has available, and the child should have much time for spontaneous play.

The preoperational stage. The first phase of the preoperational stage extends from about eighteen months to four years of age. During this phase, the child's ways of thinking become increasingly like those of adults. The learning of language provides the child with symbols and labels for processing data from ever more varied experiences. He learns to match new experiences with already available symbols, to distinguish between different aspects of experience, and to deal with relationships through the use of symbols. Thus, the child's statement "go bye bye in car to see Grandma" reveals an awareness, through the use of language, of distinct phases of a fairly complex operation. During this period, the child also invents new categories or schema for storing and classifying information. Through this process, the young child learns not to call all four-legged, furry creatures "kitty" or all men in a naval uniform "Daddy."

The period from about age four to age seven or eight marks the *intuitive phase* of the preoperational stage. In this phase, the child begins to modify his thinking so that his view of things corresponds more nearly with outer reality. The schema used by children in this and succeeding stages of intellectual development involve the principle of conservation. A child demonstrates an ability to conserve when he grasps the idea that number, for

---

[33] For another description of Piaget's theory, see Millie Almy, "New Views on Intellectual Development in Early Childhood Education," in A. H. Passow and R. R. Leeper, *Intellectual Development: Another Look* (Washington: Association for Supervision & Curriculum Development, 1964), p. 16.

example, is not changed when a set of objects is partitioned into subgroups and that mass or substance does not change when the shape or appearance of an object is transformed. In one of Piaget's typical experiments, the child is shown two plasticine balls of equal size and weight and identical in appearance. One of the balls is then rolled into a long, thin sausage and the child is asked, "Which is bigger?" During the intuitive phase children usually perceive change in shape as also being a change in quantity or mass.

Asking children to work on problems of propositional logic also affords opportunities for studying the thought processes children use at successive stages of intellectual development. During the intuitive phase, when four- or five-year-old children are asked to predict whether items such as a plank, a needle, a pebble, or an aluminum cover will float or sink in water, it is quickly apparent that the categories available to the child at this stage are inadequate. Categories such as heavy-light and large-small are inadequate for sorting things into categories of floating and nonfloating objects. The child's explanation that some objects float "because they swim on top of the water" while others sink "because they are big or heavy or stay at the bottom" reveals his lack of a satisfactory organizing principle. Almy[34] reminds us that the big-little schemata must be transformed into a fourfold classification of big-heavy, big-light, little-heavy, and little-light. This step is necessary in order for the young child to develop a concept of relative weight. Thus, during the preoperational stage, the child's thought processes tend to be dominated by his perceptions. His reasoning is based upon a particular instance and he often is not aware that his conclusions are inconsistent and contradict one another.

Stage of concrete operations. The period from seven to eleven years of age is the stage of concrete operations. In this stage, the child's thinking, though increasingly more logical and systematic, is, nevertheless, limited to what he has experienced. When he encounters situations with which he cannot deal on the basis of direct experiences, he reasons by use of analogy to something he has experienced. In the experiment involving conservation of mass, the child is likely to respond that the two amounts of plasticine are equal no matter what shape one of the balls is given. The nine-year-old child is able to conserve weight by applying the principle of reversibility: "Even though the ball is lengthened, what it has gained in length it has lost in thickness." In the problem of propositional logic requiring the child to predict which objects will float and which will sink, the eight- or nine-year-old child strives to overcome the contradiction that certain large objects float while certain small ones sink. In striving for internal consistency, he may answer, "If the wood were the same size as the needle it would be lighter." Thus, during the stage of concrete operations the child, through direct experience, grasps the idea that quantity is not changed by dispersing ten beads over a wider area, nor does mass or substance change when the shape or appearance of an object is altered.

[34] Almy, pp. 18–20.

Stage of formal operational thought. At about eleven or twelve, the child begins to group and to systematize his classifications so that he may consider all possible combinations in each case. In the latter part of the stage of concrete operations, he has made significant progress toward internal consistency in searching for a single explanation, but the discovery of the law or principle (the explanation) must await the stage of formal operational thought. In the problem of the floating bodies and specific gravity, the key to the principle is relating the weight of the object being considered to the weight of an equal volume of water, a relationship the children had no opportunity to observe in the testing situation. At the beginning of the stage of formal operations, the child recognizes that the kind of material (wood, steel, aluminum, stone) and the surface properties or dimensions (thin and flat or long and narrow) influence whether or not a given object will float, but he has not discovered the law of specific gravity. By age thirteen or fourteen, however, the young adolescent not only has discovered the law but can state it and describe a procedure for verifying it. This is revealed in the statement of one subject:

> I take a wooden cube and a plastic cube that I fill with water. I weigh them, and the difference can be seen on the scale according to whether an object is heavier or lighter than water.[35]

Summary of Piaget's theory of intellectual development. Readiness for learning, according to Piaget's theory, is not simply a product of maturation. Rather, readiness depends upon the development of centralized processes that are reflected in patterns of action used by the child in accumulating and organizing information so that he can cope more effectively with his environment. Almy summarizes the main points of Piaget's theory:

> First, *more than maturation is involved.* The increasing complexity and adaptability of the child's thought are contingent on his opportunities to think about something, to have appropriate new experiences.
> Second, *what a child assimilates, what gets incorporated into his repertoire of thought processes, what challenges him to reorganize or reclassify information is in part dependent on the processes and systems he already has available . . .*
> Third, *abstract patterns of thinking, like concrete patterns, do not emerge full blown but are rather the product of a series of encounters with ideas in which the child's thought has accommodated itself to new relationships.*

Experiential Readiness

As our discussion of intellectual development and readiness has indicated, a child's progress from the stage of concrete experiences to the stage of

[35] Inhelder and Piaget, p. 44.

formal operational thought depends upon his having the kinds of experiences which will enable him to develop appropriate thought structures. Experiential readiness has for many years been a major focus of teachers' efforts to help young children to acquire repertoires of experiences upon which academic skills and later learning can be built. If the kinds of experiences students have can increase their readiness for learning, then readiness is something that teachers and parents can do something about.

The crucial role of past experience in facilitating or limiting school learning is most clearly revealed in studies of the performance of children from culturally disadvantaged homes. It is in the area of language development, and especially in the abstract qualities of verbal functioning, that these children are likely to be most retarded. The impoverished home lacks the large variety of objects, utensils, toys, pictures, and other objects that serve as referents for language development in middle-class homes.

Because he is not spoken to or read to very much by adults, and because his home environment is full of noise and distractions, the culturally disadvantaged child's auditory discrimination is often poor.[36] Auditory discrimination and general auditory responsiveness are presumably necessary for good verbal performance and reading ability.[37] The slum child is also inhibited in his development of concepts. His parents' everyday vocabulary is limited; stimulating conversation does not take place in the home; and there are few if any books, newspapers, or magazines in the home. As a result, the lower-class child tends to respond mostly to the concrete, the tangible, and the immediate. Middle-class children, on the other hand, are able to respond to abstract, categorical, and relational properties.[38] For example, if given a number of marbles, the lower-class child will probably simply hold them in his hand and look at them, while the middle-class child may count them and announce how many blue, red, and green ones there are. These cultural differences in the development of language and conceptual thinking become marked with increasing age.

One view of the parents' influence on the child's development of language and modes of thought has been expressed by Basil Bernstein.[39] Bernstein distinguishes between two types of families. One type stresses discipline and control; the other type stresses personal relationships. In the "discipline-and-control" families, a *restrictive* style of language—consisting of short, simple, and often unfinished sentences—predominates. This kind of language is easily understood but lacks the specificity and exactness needed for developing precise and well-differentiated concepts. In "personal-relationship" families, an *elaborate* style of language prevails. In these families,

[36] David P. Ausubel, "The Effects of Cultural Deprivation on Learning Patterns," *Audiovisual Instruction,* 10 (January 1965), 10–12.

[37] Cynthia P. Deutsch, "Auditory Discrimination and Learning: Social Factors," *Merrill-Palmer Quarterly of Behavior and Development,* 10 (1964), 277–296.

[38] See note 36.

[39] Basil Bernstein, "Social Class and Linguistic Development," in A. H. Halsey, Jean Flood, and C. Arnold Anderson, *Education, Economy and Society* (New York: Free Press, 1961).

communication is individualized and specific and provides for a wide range of linguistic and behavioral alternatives in interpersonal interaction.

Hess and Shipman[40] studied the effects of these contrasting family communication styles on children's performance in learning from their mothers a series of simple tasks, such as grouping toys by color or function and sorting blocks according to two characteristics. Their study investigated the relationships between the kind and quality of the mother-child interaction during the time her child worked on these cognitive tasks and the child's performance of the tasks. Mothers and children from four socioeconomic groups were studied: professionals, skilled workers, unskilled workers, and families on public assistance.

Bernstein's hypothesis concerning the relationship of family communication style and cognitive development appears to be substantiated by the findings of this study. Mothers of children who performed tasks correctly were more likely to give explicit information and instructions about the task and to offer support and help. In contrast, mothers of children who performed with less success tended to rely more on physical signs and nonverbal communication and were generally less explicit in their directions and expectations. In general, marked social class differences were found in the abilities of the children to learn from their mothers. Children from middle-class homes ranked above children from lower socioeconomic levels in their performance of the tasks.

The culturally disadvantaged child's retardation in language and cognitive development tends to increase as he progresses through school. At the outset, in elementary school, he lacks readiness for learning because he has not made a complete transition from (in Piaget's terms) the concrete operational to the formal operational modes of thought. As a result, his progress in junior and senior high school subjects which require fluency with language and use of abstractions is limited.

Many programs attempting to overcome in part the experiential handicaps of culturally disadvantaged children and youth have been initiated or are being developed. Smith [41] suggests that slum children may be helped to experience their environment intellectually by being challenged to see, to distinguish, and to know about the objects in it. On a field trip, they should be encouraged to identify cities, buildings, animals, highways, rivers, and historical landmarks along the route.

Brunson[42] describes an approach used by high school social studies teachers to help culturally disadvantaged students to focus their attention on the main ideas of a presentation. Special tape-recorded lectures are produced, together with a guide sheet emphasizing the main ideas of the lecture. The

---

[40] Robert D. Hess and Virginia Shipman, "Early Blocks to Children's Learning," *Children,* 12 (September-October 1965), 189–194.

[41] Mildred B. Smith, "Reading for the Culturally Disadvantaged," *Educational Leadership,* 22 (March 1965), 398–403.

[42] F. Ward Brunson, "Creative Teaching of the Culturally Disadvantaged," *Audiovisual Instruction,* 10 (January 1965), 30–31.

guide sheet follows the sequence of the presentation, and the student fills in blanks as the presentation proceeds. Later, the guide sheet is discussed in class, and the student makes corrections where necessary.

Although such programs are unquestionably helpful, the effects of cultural differences in intellectual development are in part irreversible; a student with this type of background is often less able to profit from enriched and advanced levels of environmental stimulation. To facilitate the culturally disadvantaged child's transition to a more abstract level of cognitive functioning, Ausubel[43] suggests greater opportunities for the physical manipulation of objects, the use of abacuses, schematic models, and diagrams, and the use of illustrations and analogies drawn from everyday experience. In addition, programed instruction is a promising device—if each frame presents a complete rather than a fragmented concept.

Readiness and the Facilitation of Learning

What role does readiness play in the learning of school subjects? We shall next discuss readiness as it relates to reading, mathematics, and science.

Reading

Tinker[44] mentions four factors affecting readiness for reading: (1) intelligence, (2) physical factors, (3) experience and language development, and (4) personal and social adjustment. Correlations of .50 to .65 between mental age and ability to read indicate that children of higher mental ages read better than those of lower mental ages.[45] Physical factors affecting reading ability include fatigue, illness, and physical disabilities, such as hearing loss, poor vision, or lack of acuity of auditory and visual discrimination. The lack of unilateral dominance in children who are, for example, right-eyed and left-handed may influence readiness for reading, but the evidence is not clear. The importance of experience and language development in facilitating skill in reading was noted earlier, in our discussion of cultural factors and readiness. The child's understanding of what he reads depends upon the knowledge he has acquired from his activities, his perceptions, his contacts with people and things, his emotional experiences, and his reactions to all of these. Experiential readiness for reading is measured by the extent to which the child can recall and represent in language the experiences he has had. The limitations on development and learning posed by immaturity in personal and social adjustment have also been discussed at some length in previous chapters.

[43] See note 36.

[44] Miles A. Tinker, *Teaching Elementary Reading* (New York: Appleton-Century-Crofts, 1952), pp. 22–38.

[45] M. V. Morphett and C. Washburne, "When Should Children Begin to Read?" *Elementary School Journal,* 31 (1931), 496–503.

Monroe and Rogers[46] suggest that a child's oral-language skills may be evaluated by an analysis of the child's way of thinking—the quality of his ideas and the nature of his definitions of words; and the child's use of words—his ability to verbalize ideas and his command of sentence structure. Various scales have been developed for evaluating each of the child's oral-language skills.

An issue which frequently arises in any discussion of readiness for reading is the desirability and efficacy of encouraging and helping children to learn to read prior to the first grade. Although most children do not achieve the requisite physical maturity until about six and a half years, some children show an interest in reading and do learn to read before they enter the first grade. In a group of 5,103 beginning first graders in California, Durkin[47] found 49 children from varied socioeconomic levels, with IQs ranging from 91 to 161, who read at grade levels from 1.5 to 4.6. In contrast to the findings of other studies, Durkin found that more than half of the early readers came from the blue-collar class, while only 14 percent were from families of professional status. Family interviews revealed that these early readers had good memories and that they were persistent, curious, perfectionistic, and eager to keep up with older siblings. Even before they started kindergarten, their drawing-scribbling frequently led them to draw letters copied from books or signs. The ability to make letters led to the question "How do you spell _____?" and ultimately to reading.

In a second study,[48] this time of 4,465 first graders enrolled in New York City public schools, Durkin identified 157 children as early readers. At the beginning of the first grade, the median reading level of these early readers was 2.0 and their median IQ on the Revised Stanford-Binet Scale was 133; their median gain in reading during the first grade was 1.4 years. A randomly selected group of 30 of these early readers were compared with a group of 30 matched first graders who could not read when they entered first grade. Comparisons of the two groups revealed that early readers come from smaller families and walk and talk at earlier ages. They are more often content with quiet activities, such as drawing, coloring, and looking at books and pictures. They spend fewer hours watching TV but learn more from TV viewing than children who did not read at the beginning of first grade. The influence of parents of early readers appears to be important in encouraging these children to learn to read. When reading to their children, parents of early readers more often discuss pictures and point out particular words as they read, a procedure which is more likely to help a child learn to read.

Sutton,[49] in a study of the attitudes of kindergarten children who were

[46] Marion Monroe and Bernice Rogers, *Foundations for Reading* (Glenview, Illinois: Scott, Foresman and Co., 1964), pp. 24–48.

[47] Dolores Durkin, "Children Who Read before Grade One," *Reading Teacher,* 14 (January 1961), 163–166.

[48] Dolores Durkin, "Children Who Read before Grade One: A Second Study," *Elementary School Journal,* 44 (December 1963), 143–148.

[49] Marjorie H. Sutton, "Attitudes of Young Children toward Reading," *Education,* 85 (December 1964), 238–241.

given the opportunity to learn to read, found that about half of a group of 134 of these children voluntarily participated in the daily ten to fifteen minutes of reading instruction that was offered. Most of the children who participated looked upon reading as evidence of increased maturity and were highly motivated to learn to read. Results of a standardized reading test given in April revealed that 46 of these kindergarten children (more than one third) had achieved a reading level of at least the third month of the first grade. Their early success in reading increased their enthusiasm, so that by the following year most of them had become independent readers.

These studies suggest that where early reading occurs naturally, without pressure, it does not interfere with subsequent progress in reading at school, and, indeed, may contribute to the child's development of a positive self-image and favorable attitudes toward learning.

Mathematics

With the advent of the "new math," the emphasis on readiness has shifted toward helping students discover the order and structure of mathematics. Less emphasis is placed upon processes and the acquisition of computational skill, and more emphasis is placed upon mathematics as a language or tool for expressing and dealing with ideas and concepts. Mathematical concepts once thought too difficult for young children to grasp are now introduced in the early grades, and these establish a readiness for mathematics experiences at higher grade levels.

Suppes[50] found that readiness among primary grade children for forming mathematical concepts is enhanced when the concepts are presented precisely, with the help of consistent notation. Children early learn the notion of sets by manipulating concrete objects (such as beads, balls, pencils). They learn that numbers are properties of sets and that the operation of addition of numbers is simply a general way of combining families of sets of things without paying any particular attention to the things themselves. The leap in abstraction from groups of objects to numerals is accomplished, in set notation, in three steps. The first step is to portray the objects corresponding to a set (for example, five blocks) within a pair of brackets. The second step is to place the letter N in front of the bracket. This notation names a number and at the same time maintains the pictorial character of the set description. The final step is to introduce the Arabic numeral that corresponds to the set (in our example, 5). Introducing the student first to the easily comprehended operations on performed sets prepares him for the more difficult operations performed on numbers.

Other ways of increasing students' readiness for learning mathematical

---

[50] Patrick Suppes, "The Formation of Mathematical Concepts in Primary Grade Children," in A. H. Passow and R. R. Leeper, *Intellectual Development: Another Look* (Washington: Association for Supervision and Curriculum Development, 1964), pp. 99–119.

concepts and skills have also been suggested. One writer[51] suggests that students' readiness for ninth-grade algebra will be enhanced if mathematics teachers in grades seven and eight emphasize "the factor point of view," "equation type of thinking," and "ordered pairs." Davis[52] ascertained the skills basic to success in algebra and then sought to teach these skills in the elementary grades, so that they would be learned well in advance by prospective algebra students. Brune[53] recommends the introduction of simple geometry in the lower grades, thereby enabling students to develop mathematical motivations that will be helpful in later studies.

Finally, readiness in mathematics as well as other subjects may be facilitated by the analysis of learning sets and hierarchies. It will be recalled (from Chapter 13) that Gagné[54] has developed a taxonomy of eight types of learning, increasing in complexity from signal learning (Type 1) to problem solving learning (Type 8). Mastery of each lower or less complex type of learning confers upon the learner capabilities needed for achieving more complex learnings. For example, a student must have acquired concepts of time, velocity, and gravity before he can solve problems involving the speed of falling bodies. Thus, underlying every major educational objective is a hierarchy of subordinate capabilities that the learner must achieve before the final objective may be attained. Such subordinate capabilities are called *learning sets*. The learning sets that must be mastered before a student is capable of "solving equations" are shown in Figure 14.3. Using the concept of learning sets, the teacher assists students to achieve readiness for particular learning by mapping the sequence of subordinate learning capabilities (such as those shown in Figure 14.3) prerequisite to attaining the desired educational goal, and organizing activities which provide students with opportunities for acquiring each of the subordinate capabilities or learning sets.

Gagné and Paradise[55] tested the validity of the hierarchy of learning sets for solving equations (Figure 14.3) in an experiment which sought to ascertain whether correlations of relevant abilities were higher than those of irrelevant abilities with measures of achievement in equation solving. After administering a learning program on equation solving to a group of 118 seventh graders in four different school classes, Gagné and Paradise found instances of positive transfer to each learning set from subordinate relevant learning sets throughout the hierarchy, with proportions ranging from .91 to

[51] Francis J. Mueller, "Building Algebra Readiness in Grades Seven and Eight," *Arithmetic Teacher,* 6 (November 1959), 269–273.

[52] Robert B. Davis, "The 'Madison Project' of Syracuse University," *Mathematics Teacher,* 53 (November 1960), 571–575.

[53] Irvin H. Brune, "Geometry in the Grades," *Arithmetic Teacher,* 8 (May 1961), 210–219.

[54] Robert M. Gagné, *The Conditions of Learning* (New York: Holt, Rinehart and Winston, 1965).

[55] Robert M. Gagné and Noel E. Paradise, "Abilities and Learning Sets in Knowledge Acquisition," *Psychological Monographs,* 75 (1961), 1–23. (Whole No. 518). Figure 14.3 is from this article. Copyright 1961 by the American Psychological Association, and reproduced by permission.

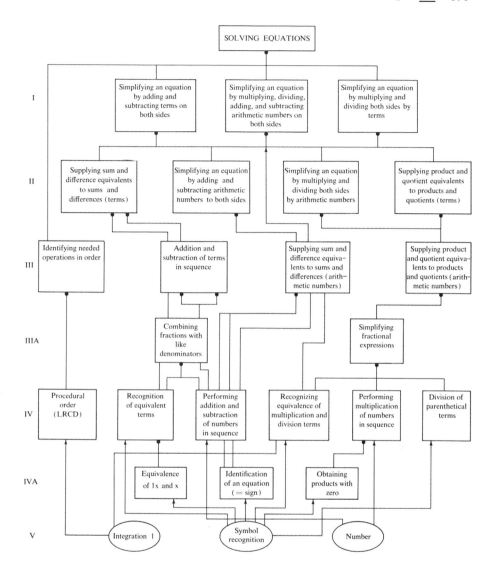

Figure 14.3. Proposed hierarchy of learning sets in a self-instructional program on "solving equations" (from Gagné and Paradise).

1.00. In addition, the rate of mastery of learning sets at progressively higher levels of the hierarchy was found to depend increasingly upon specific transfer from subordinate learning sets.

These and related researches suggest that a pupil is ready to learn the concepts and skills at a given level of difficulty if he has mastered the concepts and skills in the learning sets of the hierarchy below that level.

Science

Considerable study by educators and scientists during the past decade has been directed toward improving science curricula and the teaching of science in the elementary and secondary schools. While readiness for experiences in science is important at all levels, we shall consider here the problem of readiness as it is related to science education in the elementary schools.

Karplus, [56] a physicist, carried out a study of curriculum improvement in elementary science testing by teaching in first-grade classrooms the methods and materials he had developed. For Karplus, the principal objective of the elementary school science program is the development of "scientific literacy," which provides the student with a conceptual structure and a means of communication which will enable him to interpret information obtained by others. Karplus deplores exclusive reliance on textbooks and other secondary sources and failure to use direct experiences to nourish pupils' development of scientific modes of thinking. Too often, he says, "the science course creates a second, separate, and relatively abstract structure that is not much used outside the school situation and which eventually atrophies or even results in resentment against science."[57]

Karplus suggests that one of the first tasks of a science program is to reinforce a child's growing awareness of material objects and their properties. By utilizing children's everyday experiences, the elementary school teacher can assist students to understand such fundamental concepts as interaction, system, equilibrium, reversibility, and irreversibility. Common experiences such as scraping a knee, pulling or pushing a wagon, cutting paper, sticking a stamp or label on paper are all examples of *interaction* (wherein two or more objects affect or influence each other). When children are allowed to examine a display of many *systems* (including, perhaps, a pile of blocks, a burning candle, a spring, an ice cube in water, sugar crystals in water, and a stone in water), they may discover that some systems are in *equilibrium* (the pile of blocks, the spring, and the stone), while others are not in equilibrium (the burning candle, the sugar and the ice cube in water). Noting that undisturbed systems tend to come to equilibrium, the child is better able to cope with the concepts of *reversibility* and *irreversibility*. The teacher can then demonstrate these concepts by showing pupils a film composed of reversible and irreversible scenes and running it in both directions.

The kind of science program which Karplus has described, by introducing concepts that contribute to a scientific mode of thinking, builds a readiness for later science experiences.

[56] Robert Karplus, "One Physicist Looks at Science Education," in A. H. Passow and R. R. Leeper, *Intellectual Development: Another Look* (Washington: Association for Supervision and Curriculum Development, 1964), pp. 78–98.
[57] Karplus, p. 82.

Gagné[58] describes a similar approach used by the Commission on Science Education of the American Association for the Advancement of Science. The Commission emphasizes the teaching of *processes* of science, in place of a science-content approach, beginning in the elementary school. Exercises have been developed to increase children's understanding of such processes as observation, classification, communication, number relations, measurement, space relations, prediction, and inference. Children demonstrate these processes by performing various experiments and exercises. In one such experiment, fifth-grade students formulate a method of measuring the energy of motion of a cylinder when it reaches the bottom of an inclined plane and pushes a block on the surface of a table. The children vary the slope of the plane and the initial position of the cylinder, and note the effects on the distance the block moves. In carrying out this experiment, children utilize processes of observation, measurement, number relations, prediction and inference in discovering a physical law: Work equals force times distance. Using this approach, pupils learn to carry out critical and disciplined thinking in connection with each of the processes of science.

Summary

There is considerable evidence suggesting that pupils learn more quickly, efficiently, and effectively when they are ready for and can profit from a learning experience. Many misconceptions and conflicting views exist regarding the concept of readiness. A major disagreement is whether readiness is an inner dynamic present in the learner or whether it must be developed. By our definition, a learner's *readiness* in any situation is the sum total of all of his characteristics which make his behavior amenable to change.

Maturation, an important dimension of readiness, involves the changes in organic function and structure which precede and are prerequisite to learning. Misconceptions associated with the term maturation are reflected in its indiscriminate application to different kinds of maturity—physical, skeletal, social, mental, and emotional—and in the implication that there exists some end-point of maturation at which the processes of growth and development cease. Studies of maturation and learning indicate in general that practice and training introduced prior to the time a child has gained the required physiological maturity tend to be ineffectual.

Intelligence is a second important dimension of readiness. The Intelligence Quotient, commonly called the IQ, is defined in terms of an equation:

$$IQ = \frac{\text{Mental Age}}{\text{Chronological Age}} \times 100$$

[58] Robert M. Gagné, "Elementary Science: A New Scheme of Instruction," *Science,* 51 (January 1966), 49–53.

By definition, IQ is never an absolute measure of intellectual aptitude; it indicates only the rate at which the individual is achieving intelligence. Various studies suggest that intelligence, as measured by present tests, is not an innate and fixed quality. Other studies cast doubt on the assumption that behavioral organizations unfold more or less automatically as a function of physical growth and development. Tests of intellectual aptitude measure realized mental ability rather than intellectual capacity. While genetic inheritance does impose limits on one's potential for intellectual development, there is considerable evidence that a rich, stimulating environment enables a child to increase markedly his intellectual performance.

According to Piaget's ontogenetic theory of intellectual development, readiness for learning depends upon the development of central processes that are reflected in patterns of action used by the child in processing and organizing information. During each of four stages of intellectual development, through a process which Piaget calls *assimilation,* the child uses in new situations information or responses from previous situations. The child varies his response to achieve an *accommodation* to the new situation, and, in this process, action patterns or schemata for conceptualizing and processing information are modified and new ones are formed.

The crucial role of past experience in providing a readiness for learning in school is most clearly revealed in studies of the performance of children from culturally disadvantaged homes. It is in the area of language development that these children are likely to be most retarded. The syntax and grammar learned out of school by the slum child limits his development of conceptual thinking. Many programs initiated in an effort to overcome the experiential handicaps of culturally disadvantaged children have had only limited success. The effects of cultural deprivation are in part irreversible.

The task of preparing students for experiences in reading, mathematics, and science has made readiness a problem of particular interest to educators. Studies seem to show that when early reading by young children occurs naturally and without pressure, it not only does not interfere with subsequent reading experiences in school, but it contributes to increased learning and self-development as well. Studies of children's readiness for experiences in mathematics suggest that a pupil is ready to learn the concepts or skills at a given level of difficulty or complexity if he has mastered the concepts and skills in the learning sets of the hierarchy below that level. The current emphasis in science education is upon introducing young children to concepts which contribute to a scientific mode of thinking and build a readiness for later science experiences.

Study Questions

1. Focus on the grade or subject you expect to teach. How will you go about ascertaining the states of readiness of your pupils for learning? What kinds of data will you need and where will you obtain them?

2. Do our schools, in their promotion and grouping policies, act on the belief that one's intelligence can be increased or on the belief that one's intelligence remains fixed?

3. There has been a trend to introduce certain concepts, especially in mathematics and science, to students once thought too young to understand such concepts. How do you reconcile this with findings of studies of maturation and learning which indicate that practice and training are largely wasted if introduced prior to the time a child has gained the required physiological maturity?

4. What do you see as some of the implications of Piaget's theory of intellectual development for teachers in elementary school? How may an understanding of Piaget's theory be useful to teachers in junior and senior high school?

5. What factors discussed elsewhere in this book also have a bearing on the student's readiness for learning?

Suggested Readings

Lee J. Cronbach. *Educational Psychology*. Second Edition. New York: Harcourt, Brace & World, 1963. Chapter 4 defines readiness, presents and discusses four principles related to developing readiness, describes physical maturation, cultural pressures, and need satisfaction as these relate to readiness for learning. Chapters 5–8 examine differences in readiness, analysis of case examples, methods used in assessing readiness, and adapting schooling to individual differences.

J. McV.-Hunt. *Intelligence and Experience*. New York: Ronald Press, 1961. Examines the historical roots of the assumptions of fixed intelligence and predetermined development and documents the shift toward recognizing the crucial role of life experiences in the development of central processes of intelligence. Evidence of this shift from investigations of learning sets, programing of electronic computers, as well as Piaget's work investigating the development of intelligence and logical thinking in children is presented.

Frances L. Ilg and Louise D. Ames. *School Readiness: Behavior Tests Used at the Gesell Institute*. New York: Harper & Row, 1964. Contains a test battery developed to assess readiness for school entrance. The rationale for the selection of particular tests, directions for administration and scoring, norms, and estimates of reliability are discussed.

A. Harry Passow and Robert R. Leeper. Editors. *Intellectual Development: Another Look*. Washington: Association for Supervision and Curriculum Development, 1964. Contains papers on intellectual development, cognitive processes, curiosity and exploration, inquiry training, and the development of concepts by primary grade children in the areas of mathematics and science. The paper by Almy presents a very clear description of Piaget's theory of intellectual development.

Fred T. Tyler. "Issues Related to Readiness to Learn," in Ernest R. Hilgard. Editor. *Theories of Learning and Instruction.* Sixty-third Yearbook of the National Society for the Study of Education, Part I. Chicago: University of Chicago Press, 1964, pp. 210–239. Examines historical and theoretical issues relating to the concept of readiness. Considerable attention is given to the topic of maturation and some of the disagreements surrounding the use of this term. Presents a thorough analysis of the present status of the concept of readiness and its relation to learning.

Films

Portrait of a Disadvantaged Child: Tommy Knight, 16 mm , sound, black and white, 16 min. Bloomington, Indiana: Audio-Visual Center, Indiana University (rental fee, $4.65). By following the events in a day of the life of a slum child, Tommy Knight, the viewer is introduced to the special problems, needs, and strengths of the inner-city child, and the factors hindering his ability to learn. Contrasted are the home life and parental attitudes of disadvantaged children, showing that some homes are supportive while others are neglectful.

15

the outcomes of learning: cognitive

If all students are helped to the full utilization of their intellectual powers, we will have a better chance of surviving as a democracy in an age of enormous technological and social complexity.

≡ JEROME S. BRUNER

There are three major types of learning: *cognitive, psychomotor,* and *affective.* In this chapter we focus on cognitive learning and in the next on psychomotor and affective learning. Few if any behaviors, however, are purely cognitive, psychomotor, or affective, but one of these processes may predominate in a specific behavior pattern. Affective learning, in the form of likes and dislikes, tastes, and attitudes, accompanies all psychomotor and cognitive learning; psychomotor learning influences the development of cognitive structures; and perceptual and cognitive factors are involved in the learning of psychomotor skills.

Figure 15.1[1] portrays the hierarchies of learning outcomes, wherein successively more complex behavioral patterns are formed from combinations of simpler behavior patterns. For example, while patterns of problem solving and creative thinking (column 3) presumably require factual

[1] Modified from James M. Sawrey and Charles W. Telford, *Educational Psychology,* 2nd ed. (Boston: Allyn and Bacon, 1964), p. 95. Used by permission.

399

Dominant component	Relatively simple acquired patterns	More complex integrated patterns	Higher-level integrations of cognitive-psychomotor-affective outcomes	Still higher levels of integration
Cognitive	Preverbal percepts Factual information Meanings Percepts Concepts Principles	Problem solving Creative thinking Theories Systematized knowledge	Vocational and avocational competencies Personality traits Social traits Goals and aspirations Values	Personality Character Self-concept
Psychomotor	Locomotor habits Manual skills Manipulatory skills Facial expressions Verbal skills Graphic skills Habitual postures and gestures	More complex psychomotor skills (needed to become a musician, actor, artist, lecturer, technician, artisan, craftsman, etc.)		
Affective	Likes and dislikes Tastes and preferences	Attitudes Biases and prejudices		

Figure 15.1. A classification of the outcomes of learning (modified from Sawrey and Telford).

information, concepts, and principles, they may also require verbal and graphic skills (psychomotor patterns) and be influenced by likes and dislikes (affective patterns). Similarly, the higher-level integrations listed in column 4 and the still higher levels of integration in column 5 are formed from unique combinations of simpler patterns of cognitive, psychomotor, and affective learning.

Also listed in Figure 15.1 are a number of learning outcomes which appear to be only marginally influenced by formal educational experiences: facial expressions, habitual postures and gestures, acquired likes and dislikes, personality, character, values, and locomotor and manipulatory skills. Formal school learning does not focus directly on some of these outcomes, but many of the patterns learned incidentally in and out of school may be more important than some of the patterns the school does emphasize.

Another classification of learning outcomes particularly relevant for the school setting is a *Taxonomy of Educational Objectives*[2] which has been developed for the cognitive and affective domains. The cognitive domain of the taxonomy consists of six broad areas of cognitive learning arranged in order of increasing complexity: knowledge, comprehension, application, analysis, synthesis, and evaluation. For each of these broad areas of cognitive learning, the taxonomy identifies specific learning outcomes in behavioral terms and suggests ways whereby each of these educational objectives may be evaluated. Listed under the broad area of "knowledge," for example, are the following specific learning outcomes:

Knowledge of specifics
    knowledge of terminology
    knowledge of specific facts

Knowledge of ways and means of dealing with specifics
    knowledge of conventions
    knowledge of trends and sequences
    knowledge of classifications and categories
    knowledge of criteria
    knowledge of methodology

Knowledge of the universals and abstractions in a field
    knowledge of principles and generalizations
    knowledge of theories and structures

The taxonomy may assist the teacher in clarifying his educational objectives and modifying his teaching practices so that relevant, important outcomes of learning are identified and realized.

[2] Benjamin S. Bloom, *Taxonomy of Educational Objectives, Handbook I: Cognitive Domain* (New York: David McKay Co., 1956); David R. Krathwohl, Benjamin S. Bloom, and Bertram B. Masia, *Taxonomy of Educational Objectives, Handbook II: Affective Domain* (New York: David McKay Co., 1964).

Cognitive Processes

In our description of intellectual development in the preceding chapter, the learner was viewed as an information-processor, one who sorts and interprets sensory inputs in acquiring and organizing data. The processes through which one acquires, organizes, interrelates, and interprets the data of his experience are called *cognitive processes*. Cognitive processes include labeling, forming hypotheses, evaluating, and applying rules of transformation.[3]

The learner's initial cognitive task is to label the data acquired through sensory output. Piaget[4] and Bruner[5] have described how the very young child acquires labels through sensorimotor representations of external stimuli. When he learns to use spoken and written language, the child acquires symbolic labels. In accordance with these labels the child generates hypotheses. He then evaluates the meaning of the data suggested by the hypotheses he has made. Finally, he implements the hypothesis he has decided on, using an appropriate rule of transformation. The young child, for example, acquires a sensorimotor label (kinesthetic sensations, arm and leg movements) for having his snow suit put on. He hypothesizes that his mother is going to take him for a ride in the car. His positive evaluation of this anticipated experience is expressed in his smile. If his mother heads toward a neighbor's house, his initial hypothesis is replaced by a new one—that he is to be left with the neighbor while his mother goes shopping. His evaluative response to this new meaning is to start crying. The transformation rule which the child has learned and applied is "A change in clothing signals a change in activity."

Data acquired from experience, processed and transformed, become *cognitive outcomes* of increasing complexity—percepts, concepts, principles, hypotheses, theories. The developmental and hierarchical ordering of these cognitive outcomes is shown in Figure 15.2.[6] Preverbal percepts are formed as the infant gives labels to the sensorimotor data of his experience. The learning of language facilitates labeling and leads to an increase in factual information. Concepts are formed as objects or data are classified and grouped systematically. Generalizations and principles are formed by interrelating two or more concepts. The application of two or more principles to produce a new capability is called problem solving. Problem solving involves

[3] Jerome Kagan, "A Developmental Approach to Conceptual Growth," in Herbert J. Klausmeier and Chester W. Harris, *Analyses of Concept Learning* (New York: Academic Press, 1966), 97–116.

[4] Jean Piaget, *The Psychology of Intelligence,* trans. by M. Piercy and D. E. Berlyne (London: Routledge & Kegan Paul, 1947).

[5] Jerome S. Bruner, "The Course of Cognitive Growth," *American Psychologist,* 19 (January 1964), 1–15.

[6] Adapted from Herbert J. Klausmeier and William Goodwin, *Learning and Human Abilities,* 2nd ed. (New York: Harper & Row, 1966), p. 212. Used by permission.

forming and testing hypotheses and evaluating the results of tested hypotheses. Novel and original hypotheses and solutions to problems are evidence of creative (divergent) thinking. The products of either convergent thinking (common, conventional hypotheses and solutions) or divergent thinking become organized as theories—statements describing and explaining the nature of various phenomena. Finally, the aggregate of what one knows and believes about various phenomena constitutes his body of systematized knowledge.

The arrangement in Figure 15.2 should not be interpreted as meaning that only successively higher outcomes are learned at successively higher maturational levels. For example, we acquire percepts and factual information throughout our lives. Also, as one moves up the hierarchy from preverbal percepts to systematized knowledge, the cognitive outcomes at successively higher levels are more inclusive, general, and abstract. It is well to remember, however, that in organizing knowledge systematically, one moves

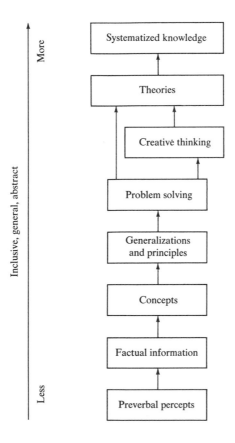

Figure 15.2. Developmental and hierarchical ordering of cognitive learning outcomes (from Klausmeier and Goodwin).

from the general to the specific as well as from the specific back to the general. We shall next discuss various aspects of cognitive learning: (1) concept formation, (2) generalizing, (3) problem solving, and (4) creativity.

Concept Formation

Before an individual can respond to the stimuli and events of his life, he must develop appropriate concepts. One is handicapped in solving problems in geometry, for instance, if he lacks the concepts of angle, point, or perpendicular; writing a story would be difficult without the concepts of sentence, plot, description, and characterization. Concepts influence all aspects of behavior. Moreover, the extension of knowledge depends upon the modification, refinement, or replacement of existing concepts. The development of space sciences, for example, had to await the refinement of old concepts and the development of new concepts relating to energy, mass, radiation, weightlessness, electronic computation, and data processing.

A major educational objective of the school, therefore, is to provide students with opportunities to develop and refine concepts needed to make adequate interpretations of and responses to life situations. A student, for example, will find that arithmetic concepts are inadequate for solving problems of change in acceleration and deceleration of automobiles, airplanes, or rockets; for this, concepts of differential calculus are needed. The teacher, by assisting the student to clarify, broaden, and test his present concepts and to develop new ones, helps him to make better provisional responses in new situations. The most significant learning experiences are those that afford opportunities for the formation or refinement of concepts required for making wiser provisional responses in new situations. This application of learned concepts and skills to new situations is known as *transfer* and is of central importance in learning.

Concepts are formed when an individual perceives that two objects or qualities can be placed in the same class. Thus, a young child with two different teddy bears learns to put both of them into the same class, labeled "teddy bears." Later, he may put teddy bears into more inclusive classes, such as "stuffed animals" or "toys." The ability to categorize and classify allows the individual to cope with the otherwise overwhelming mass of detail registered by his senses.

A concept, then, is a classification of stimuli that have common characteristics. In forming a concept, a student must first *discriminate* between relevant and irrelevant features of the data. In forming a concept of "natural resources," for example, he must distinguish between the water resources of a given region and the dams and artificial lakes constructed to conserve water and to generate electricity. Second, the student must *generalize* by correctly identifying the several instances or exemplars that belong to the conceptual category. In generalizing, the student extends such a category as, for instance, "assets indigenous to a geographical region" to include minerals, soil, stones, plants, animals, and climatic conditions. In short, he must include all essential features and omit all non-essential features.

Concepts and Experience

The concepts that children acquire depend upon the kinds and qualities of experiences they have had. Children acquire a great many concepts informally before they come to school. Indeed, most tests of reading readiness given in kindergarten and first grade measure the degree to which the child has grasped some of these concepts, such as "boy," "girl," "house," "tree," "largest," "smallest," "left," "right," "same," or "different." During successive years in school, students acquire, both formally and informally, a great many concepts of increasing complexity and abstractness. The following excerpts from the cases of Tab and David reveal the understanding of the concept of "gravity" which these intellectually able boys in the first and fourth grades, respectively, had acquired.

DECEMBER 5

A story about Santa's reindeer being stolen by the Man in the Moon was told. When it came to the part where Santa flew out of his chair aboard the rocket ship as the ship was going into the stratosphere, Tab said, "I know why that happens. It's the same as why they can jump through the air many feet up there. It's the pull of gravity. He ought to have a safety belt." At the end of the story he said, "That isn't a true story, but it's a good one anyway."

DECEMBER 14

In Science we were discussing "gravity." Someone asked why an astronaut is weightless if gravity is always acting.

"I can answer that, Mrs. D.," David said. "I read an article on that recently in one of my science magazines."

"All right, David, suppose you explain it to the class," I said.

David paused an instant as if trying to decide how to explain it in the simplest way. Then he said, "Well, you feel weight when something like the floor or ground resists the pull of gravity on you. When there is no resistance, as you fall, you are weightless. For instance, an astronaut becomes weightless when the rocket motors shut off because there is no force to resist the pull of gravity. He and the capsule are both weightless and falling freely together. He will remain weightless until some outside force acts on him."

"Like what?" asked Roy.

"Oh, like air resistance or rocket power," David replied.

This discussion, although fascinating to David, was completely beyond the comprehension of the class, so I steered it into channels which the group could understand.

Teachers sometimes ignore the importance of personal experience in the formation of concepts. Frequently, the development of concepts is limited to the teacher's definition and the material in a textbook. The teacher's failure to utilize illustrations of concepts drawn from students' experience often results in misunderstandings or incomplete learning on the parts of the students.

One teacher's use of children's out-of-school experiences is illustrated in the following account of a seventh-grade social science class's study of the poultry industry.

The class talked freely for several minutes in relating what they knew about chickens. Finally, Miss Jameson said, "Let's get some real facts down. I'll write them on the board. Now, where should we begin?"

Anne: My father works at Mangum's Hatchery. It is the largest hatchery in the world. The eggs are shipped there by trucks. When the eggs reach the hatchery, they are trayed.

Miss J.: I wonder if everyone knows what trayed means. I do not.

Vera: After a certain number of days, the eggs have to be turned.

Miss J.: Why is this so?

Carol: This is so the heat will be distributed evenly to every side. The temperature must remain at 97 degrees in the incubator.

Miss J.: What is meant by the term incubation?

Bobby: It is the period the young chick is in the egg before it is hatched.

Anne: But something more than time is needed. It is necessary to keep the eggs warm for the chicks to grow and hatch. I think we would have to say that incubation is a period when the proper conditions must be maintained for development and hatching.

David: We have referred to an unhatched chicken as a chick, but any unborn or unhatched animal in its early stages of development is really an embryo.

Miss J.: Good, David. We should be precise and accurate in our use of terms.

Two important principles emerge from this illustration. First, because of interaction with elements in his life space, a child may, through faulty generalization or lack of sufficient evidence, develop concepts which are partially or wholly untrue. This is shown in Bobby's limited understanding of the concept of incubation. Second, the teacher need not feel that she must know all the answers. Miss Jameson freely admitted that she could not answer some of her class's questions. She increased independence and motivation in the learners by encouraging them to seek answers themselves and to report their findings to the class.

The teacher, in helping students to crystallize, broaden, and refine concepts, also aids them to recognize and to modify stereotypes. A *stereotype* may be defined as "a tendency to attribute generalized and simplified characteristics to a group of people in the form of a verbal label."[7] Concepts based on partial or distorted data relating to peoples, groups, movements, or ideologies can be classed as stereotypes. Stereotypes, then, are the result of inadequate conceptualizations. Not all Italians are artistic and impulsive, nor are all Jews shrewd and mercenary, or all Americans industrious and materialistic. Concepts which ascribe common behaviors or characteristics to millions of individuals of a nationality or race are obviously inadequate, distorted, and overgeneralized.

Schools have a responsibility to encourage students to avoid stereotypes by helping them to develop adequate, valid concepts of people, places, and events. Teachers may help students to form more valid concepts by encouraging them (1) to examine their concepts, and, if necessary in the light of additional information, to revise them; and (2) by encouraging them to form more careful and accurate discriminations and generalizations from the total data available. How this may be achieved is described in the next section.

Strategies for Developing Concepts

To learn how people form concepts, one must find out what influences a person to attend to some features of an object or event and to ignore others. A common strategy in the formation of concepts is the use of examples or nonexamples. In helping students to form concepts, teachers should know whether examples, nonexamples, or examples and nonexamples combined are most effective.

Research shows that learners can acquire concepts through negative examples, but negative examples, which force the learner to memorize a multitude of things that a concept is not, are inefficient.[8] Braley[9] devised a learning task wherein subjects were required to use an exclusion strategy in learning the concept—that is, they were given reinforcement only for choosing nonexamples of the concept. Since only two of his subjects were able to

---

[7] W. E. Vinacke, "Explorations in the Dynamic Processes of Stereotyping," *Journal of Social Psychology*, 43 (1956), 105.

[8] H. E. Cahill and C. I. Hovland, "The Role of Memory in the Acquisition of Concepts," *Journal of Experimental Psychology*, 59 (1960), 137–144.

[9] Loy S. Braley, "Strategy Selections and Negative Instances in Concept Learning," *Journal of Educational Psychology*, 54 (June 1963), 154–159.

learn the concept, Braley concluded that attempting to remember all of the negative instances seldom leads to concept attainment.

Another common instructional strategy for facilitating concept attainment is reinforcement. Carpenter[10] studied the effects of partial reinforcement on students' learning of concepts. Four groups of students were studied. One group had correct responses reinforced 25 percent of the time; a second group had responses reinforced 50 percent of the time; a third group received 100 percent reinforcement of correct responses; and a fourth group had 100 percent of both correct and incorrect responses reinforced. The fourth group learned the concept in the fewest number of trials and in the shortest period of time. The superiority of immediate reinforcement is shown in a study by Sax.[11] In Sax's study, one group of students received only 50-percent feedback but received it immediately; another group was given 100-percent feedback but given it forty minutes after their response. The first group learned concepts in fewer trials.

Although the importance of reinforcement in the learning of concepts is underscored by these studies, reinforcement of every positive and negative instance may not be the most effective strategy for teaching every kind of concept. Some types of concepts may be mastered under different schedules of reinforcement, but further research is needed to test this hypothesis. Carpenter, however, urges teachers to focus on the intermediate steps and processes involved in learning a complex concept and to reinforce the learner's mastery of intermediate steps instead of rewarding only the final performance.[12]

Has a person really learned a concept if he is unable to verbalize it? Some contend that concepts may be learned at more than one level. Nonverbal learning may require a different set of responses than verbal learning. Because of possible differences in kinds and levels of learning, it may be unwarranted to expect 100-percent transfer of a concept between verbal and nonverbal levels. Carpenter, in the study cited above, found that 72 of his subjects responded in a manner that indicated they had learned the concept, although only 18 percent were able to verbalize the defining characteristics of the concept.

The relationships between learning concepts and learning to define concepts have been studied by several investigators. Johnson and O'Reilly[13] presented three groups of eleven- and twelve-year-old children with the task of learning the difference between two groups of birds. One group (pictorial) was asked to classify colored pictures of the birds, while a second group (verbal) was asked to classify verbal descriptions. After performing the classification task, each child was asked to define the difference between the two groups of birds and to sort ten cards containing pictures or verbal

[10] Finley Carpenter, "Conceptualization as a Function of Differential Reinforcement," *Science Education,* 38 (1954), 284–294.

[11] G. Sax, "Concept Acquisition as a Function of Differing Schedules and Delays of Reinforcement," *Journal of Educational Psychology,* 51 (1960), 32–36.

[12] Carpenter, p. 293.

[13] Donald M. Johnson and Charlene A. O'Reilly, "Concept Attainment in Children: Classifying and Defining," *Journal of Educational Psychology,* 55 (April 1964), 71–74.

descriptions of the two kinds of birds. A third group of children (pictorial-definition) received colored pictures to classify, but, after each five pictures, they were asked to define the difference between the two kinds of birds. They were given no evaluation of their answers. The verbal group learned the classification task most rapidly. Both the verbal and the pictorial-definition groups were superior to the pictorial group in the accuracy of their definitions of the difference between the groups of birds. The most important finding, however, was that the pictorial-definition group gave almost twice as many definitions judged "good" as did the pictorial group. Since both groups practiced classifying the same picture cards and reached the same criterion of mastery (ten consecutive correct identifications of birds), it appears that a small amount of practice in defining, even without knowledge of result, improves final defining performance.

It has been suggested that the difficulties students encounter in defining concepts may be related to their having to shift from one medium or symbol system to another in describing or explaining a concept. The problem is similar to that of an artist who has difficulty describing in words the idea or feeling he has sought to convey in a painting. Wilder and Green[14] have explored this problem. They had 88 fourth-grade pupils watch two coleus plants grow, one in the light and the other in the shade. After two weeks, the students were asked both to describe and to explain the differences between the two plants. Half of the pupils were asked to draw their descriptions and explanations; the other half were asked to write them. When this task had been completed, the two coleus plants were replaced by two begonia plants which had been treated similarly (one grown in the sun, the other in the shade) but had not been seen by the children. Again the children were asked to describe and explain the differences between the plants. However, half the children who had drawn the first set of plants were asked to write about the second set, and half the children who had written about the first set were asked to draw the second set. For the first set of plants, those children who *described* differences by drawing them did better than those who described differences by writing about them. For both sets of plants, those who *explained* differences by writing about them did better than those who explained differences by drawing them. In other words, children were better able to write about the cause of the stunting of the plants grown in the shade than to show that cause in a drawing. Wilder and Green suggest that their findings support the hypothesis that shifts from one medium to another—in this case, from words to pictures or from pictures to words—makes it more difficult to explain or describe a concept in words.

The strategies people use in acquiring concepts have been studied extensively by Bruner and his associates. Bruner and Olver[15] analyzed the

[14] Nancy E. Wilder and Donald R. Green, "Expression of Concepts through Writing and Drawing and Effects of Shifting Medium," *Journal of Educational Psychology,* 54 (August 1963), 202–207.

[15] Jerome S. Bruner and Rose R. Olver, "Development of Equivalence Transformations in Children" in John C. Wright and Jerome Kagan, "Basic Cognitive Processes in Children," *Monographs of the Society for Research in Child Development,* 28 (1963), 125–143.

rules of associative grouping which children in grades one, four, and six develop for processing data. They found that children used three major kinds of grouping strategies. In *superordinate grouping,* items are grouped on the basis of one or more attributes common to all; for example, a telephone, a radio, a painting, a book, and a newspaper are all classified as "things that communicate ideas." In *complex formations,* the subject uses selected attributes of the array of items without subordinating the entire array to any one attribute: "Newspaper, book, and painting tell stories; telephone and radio make sounds." In *thematic grouping,* the several items are linked together in a manner such as the following: "If you didn't get your morning newspaper, you could turn on your radio, go to the library for a book, study a painting in the art gallery, or telephone a friend." The grouping may tell a story, but the absence of any common attributes makes this essentially a "nogrouping" strategy. Superordinate groupings are generally more simple, inclusive, and efficient than the other grouping strategies.

Bruner and Olver found a developmental change between the first and sixth grades in the grouping strategies employed. Only 46 percent of the first graders used superordinate grouping strategies, whereas 86 percent of the sixth graders used this type of strategy. Children's skills in forming concepts increase as they use more efficient modes of grouping data.

The strategies that college students and adults use in learning a conjunctive concept have also been identified by Bruner and his associates. A conjunctive category (standing for a concept) is defined as the joint presence in exemplars of the appropriate values of one or more attributes. In Figure 15.3, an example of a conjunctive category is all houses with floor plan C (9 exemplars). Figure 15.3 presents a matrix that we may use to illustrate the learning of a conjunctive concept. Ardmore (shown in Figure 15.3) is a community of 27 homes, each of which is the same size, shape, and age, and made of the same materials. The homes differ as to street location (Elm, Maple, or Oak), color (white, green, or yellow), and floor plan (A, B, or C). In Ardmore, members of a secret political party live anonymously in houses which have in common one or more attributes. You are a party courier who has been ordered to deliver a secret message to each party member in the community. In reaching every party member, you are to make inquiries at a minimum number of houses so as not to arouse the suspicions of non-party members. Your contact tells you that one party member lives in the white house with floor-plan C on Maple Street. Information to assist you in identifying the category of houses of party members will consist of "Yes" or "No" answers to your question: "Does Henry live here?" In identifying the concept (houses where party members live), you will need to test six hypotheses: (1) all white houses, (2) all floor-plan C houses, (3) all houses on Maple Street, (4) all white houses with floor plan C, (5) all white houses on Maple Street, and (6) all floor-plan C houses on Maple Street. Given these conditions, what strategies would you employ for locating and delivering the message to all party members?

In analyzing the strategies that people use to identify a conjunctive

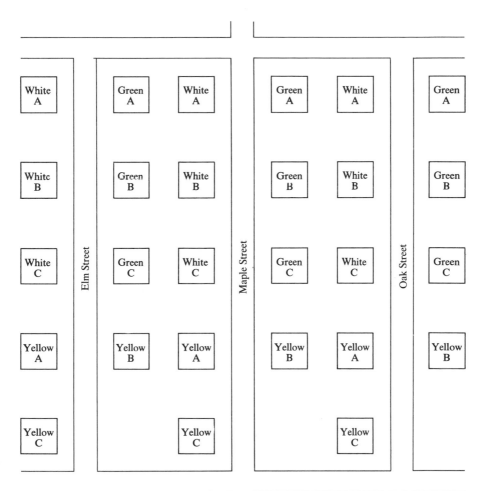

Figure 15.3. Matrix for the problem of identifying a conjunctive concept of "party members' houses" in a community of 27 houses which differ in three attributes: street, color (white, green, or yellow), and floor plan (A, B, or C).

concept, Bruner, Goodnow, and Austin[16] found that all persons can be classified as either *scanners* or *focusers*. Scanners tend to use information from each inquiry as an occasion for deducing which hypotheses are still

[16] Jerome S. Bruner, Jacqueline J. Goodnow, and George A. Austin, *A Study of Thinking* (New York: Science Editions, Inc., 1962), pp. 81–125.

tenable and which have been eliminated. If one attempts to check more than one hypothesis at a time, he is a *simultaneous scanner*. If one's strategy is to test a single hypothesis at a time, he is a *successive scanner*. A scanner would probably try to identify the concept by first ascertaining whether street is a relevant attribute, or, he might try to use information from a single inquiry to ascertain whether both street and house color are relevant attributes.

A focuser, on the other hand, starting with a positive instance (in this case, that one party member lives in the white house with floor-plan C on Maple Street) to use as a focus, proceeds to make a sequence of choices, each of which alters one or more attributes of the focus. If he alters only one attribute at a time, he is called a *conservative focuser*. If he alters more than one attribute at a time, he is called a *focus gambler*. A conservative focuser would probably check out the white houses, first on Maple Street and then on Oak Street. The focus gambler, however, would probably check white floor-plan C houses on Elm and Oak Streets.

Bruner found that the most efficient strategies are those that increase the likelihood that instances encountered will contain appropriate information, render less strainful the task of assimilating and keeping track of information, and regulate the amount of risk one will undergo in attaining a correct solution within a limited number of choices.

The reader may have surmised that focusing, especially conservative focusing, fulfills these criteria best and, hence, is the most efficient strategy. This conclusion is confirmed by Bruner, who found that scanners needed an average of 13 selections to acquire a concept, while focusers required an average of only 5. Scanners were more likely to make inquiries giving them information they already had.

Kates and Yudin[17] found that concepts are attained more quickly and efficiently when a learner making an inquiry has exposed in front of him all the results of all previous inquiries. When all previously encountered instances of a concept are available to the learner, memory load is reduced and efficiency of concept attainment is increased.

Ausubel[18] has proposed an instructional strategy for assisting students to learn and retain meaningful but unfamiliar concepts. He contends that an individual's existing cognitive structure—the organization, stability, and clarity of his knowledge at a given time—is the principal factor influencing his learning and retention of new material. He hypothesizes that a student will have difficulty learning unfamiliar concepts if he has not acquired the more general, inclusive, and overarching concepts under which these unfamiliar concepts can be grouped and related. In the study of biology, for example, it is important for students to know and understand the general concepts of energy, life processes, reproduction, fertilization, differentiation, growth, and enzyme before they are introduced to the more specific concepts

[17] Solis L. Kates and Lee Yudin, "Concept Attainment and Memory," *Journal of Educational Psychology*, 55 (April 1964), 103–109.

[18] David P. Ausubel, *The Psychology of Meaningful Verbal Learning* (New York: Grune and Stratton, 1963).

of gene, chromosome, DNA, mitosis, meiosis, and centriole. If the student does not already possess these more general, inclusive concepts (which Ausubel calls "advance organizers"), Ausubel recommends that he be given them before he is introduced to the new, more specific or more specialized concepts.

Ausubel devised a test of his hypothesis that the learning and retention of meaningful, but unfamiliar verbal material is facilitated by the advance introduction of relevant subsuming concepts.[19] Two groups of undergraduate students, equal in their ability to learn unfamiliar scientific material, were given an introductory passage of 500 words to study for five minutes forty-eight hours before and just before they were given learning material consisting of a 2500-word passage on the metallurgical properties of plain carbon steel. The introductory passage given the control group consisted of historically relevant background material on making steel. The passage given the experimental group contained background material at a higher level of abstraction and generality on the making of steel. After the second reading of the introductory passage, both groups studied the 250-word learning passage for thirty-five minutes. Three days later, they took a multiple-choice test covering this material. The significantly higher mean score made by the experimental group supports the conclusion that the introduction of relevant, more general and inclusive concepts does facilitate the learning and retention of unfamiliar specific concepts.

Generalizing

Generalizing is the act of deriving a general concept, principle, law, or theory from particular facts or observations. We noted that one forms a concept when he establishes a category with specified attributes; the concept becomes generalized as one finds and includes other examples in the category. The act of linking two or more concepts in meaningful combinations is a further example of generalizing. An interrelating of two or more concepts in the formula "If A, then B" results in the formation of a *principle*. Principles function to explain or to predict events and to control behavior. The use of concepts to form generalizations and principles and the use of these generalizations and principles to explain certain phenomena or events are illustrated in the following anecdotes from the case of David.

OCTOBER 15

I had been reading supplementary material to the class on the Lewis and Clark Expedition. In his diary, Lewis wrote, "I first tasted the water of the Great Columbia River." This entry was made soon after Lewis crossed the Continental Divide. The class did not understand what Lewis meant, since he was so far from the Columbia River at that time.

---

[19] David P. Ausubel, "The Use of Advance Organizers in the Learning and Retention of Meaningful Verbal Material," *Journal of Educational Psychology,* 51 (1960), 267–272.

David raised his hand and said, "I can explain that. Lewis was drinking from the Lemki River which is one of the small tributaries of the Columbia River system. Its waters eventually flow into the Columbia."

I asked if everyone understood now what Lewis meant. Several hands went up. They did not understand what David meant by tributaries or river system.

"David, can you make your explanation clearer?" I asked.

He thought a minute and said, "Yes, m'am, I think I can." He walked to the board and said, "A river system looks somewhat like the branches of a tree." He drew a picture of a tree. "Now here is the trunk, here are large branches, and from these grow small limbs; from them grow tiny twigs and from the twigs grow the leaves. In a river system the growth follows the opposite pattern. The leaves and tiny twigs represent very small streams and their sources which flow into larger streams or branches. These branches flow into larger streams and finally into the trunk or main river. The Lemki River begins just west of the Continental Divide and flows into the Salmon River. The Salmon flows into the Snake, which is a larger river. Then the Snake flows into the Columbia. So when Lewis drank from the Lemki River he was having his first drink from the Columbia."

After this explanation the class seemed to understand perfectly.

NOVEMBER 9

In a unit of study on Pioneer Life we read a story in which a little pioneer girl wanted to have her photograph made. She had to wait for a traveling photographer to come through.

I asked, "Why do you think she had to wait for a traveling photographer?"

Roy answered, "Because the pioneers were too poor to afford cameras."

Don offered, "There were very few cameras in those days."

David had sat quietly listening to the discussion without contributing to it, but at this point he raised his eyebrows in his own personal mannerism and drawled, "Well, pioneers lived before the time of mass production. Such items were scarce and expensive. Because of this the ordinary family did not have them. Mass production is the reason we have cameras and many other luxuries today at prices people can afford."

In the October 15 entry, David used the concepts of Continental Divide, river tributaries, river system, tree, trunk, branches, and twig to develop generalizations explaining a statement in Lewis's diary. By analogy, David used a familiar generalization, "Leaves, twigs, branches, and trunk form a tree," to derive another generalization, "Mountain streams and the successively larger rivers formed by the flow of water are the tributaries of a river system." David also used the generalization, "Water flows toward and collects in points of lowest elevation." The November 9 anecdote reveals that

David used concepts of pioneer life, photography, traveling photographer, camera, money, income, scarce, expensive, products, and mass production to form two generalizations: "Mass production permits cameras and other products to be manufactured at prices people can afford"; "The advantages of mass production were not available to pioneer families."

Often, a statement of relationships between two or more concepts is made without sufficient evidence to support it as a generalization. Such statements, called *hypotheses,* are useful tools in scientific inquiry. Hypotheses that are supported by subsequent empirical tests become generalizations. The statement "There is a greater incidence of lung cancer and heart disease among persons who have been heavy smokers than among nonsmokers" is a generalization supported by evidence. The statement "Smoking causes lung cancer" remains a hypothesis suggested by the above generalization. Statements of the stable or invariable relationships between certain concepts in mathematics and physics are called *laws.* The following are examples of laws: "The angle of incidence equals the angle of reflection"; "The pressure of a gas is inversely proportional to its volume if its temperature remains constant."

Generalizations may be acquired in either of two ways: by *deduction* from laws, premises, or other generalizations; or by *induction,* in which specific instances are combined. Both processes are indispensable tools in reasoning and problem solving. Because of the characteristics of their data, some disciplines, such as philosophy and mathematics, usually employ deductive methods in solving problems and extending knowledge; other disciplines, such as the natural and social sciences, more often employ inductive methods. Deductive and inductive methods are most effectively used in tandem, with conclusions reached using one method being verified and checked by the other method. Few conclusions can be drawn regarding the superiority of either method. There is some evidence that children taught by deductive methods perform better if tested on the kinds of materials they had used in learning the generalizations. Children taught by the inductive method, however, realize greater transfer benefits—that is, they are better able to utilize the generalization in learning new material.[20]

Thinking is another process or activity generally associated with cognitive functioning and development. Statements of educational objectives frequently include "the development of critical thinking." However, the term "thinking" has so many meanings (such as, "ponder," "reflect," "believe," "consider," "reason," "speculate," "deliberate") that it is not very useful as a description of cognitive processes unless it is clearly defined. For our purposes, we will define *thinking* as a generic term that refers to the mental activities of (1) organizing, manipulating, and interrelating facts and concepts, (2) forming and testing hypotheses, and (3) evaluating and interpreting evidence.

[20] W. H. Winch, *Inductive versus Deductive Methods of Teaching: An Experimental Research* (Baltimore: Warwick and York, 1913).

Many of our ideas concerning thinking as a process can be traced to the steps or phases of reflective thinking suggested by Dewey:[21]

1. Suggestions of a possible solution
2. Intellectualization of the difficulty or felt need
3. Use of one hypothesis after another to initiate and to guide observation and the collection of data
4. Mental elaboration of the idea or supposition
5. Testing of hypotheses by overt or imaginative action

These steps, or variations of them, describe the scientific method of problem solving and were introduced in Chapter 2.

Taba[22] has analyzed strategies used by teachers in promoting thinking in elementary school children. The following strategies are intended to evoke children's thinking in classroom discussion.

1. *Focusing* questions or remarks so as to establish both the content of the topic under consideration and the cognitive operations to be performed. Example: "What events and conditions favor the mobility of people in an underdeveloped country?"
2. *Extending* thought on the same level, which allows a sufficient amount of assimilation before thought is lifted to another level. This is essentially a strategy of inducing a number of students to respond to the same questions, rather than of pursuing a line of inquiry with the same student. Example: "What are some other reasons why people migrated westward?"
3. *Lifting* of the level of thought occurs when the teacher or child either gives or seeks information that shifts the thought to a higher level than a previously established one. Example: "What are some of the ways that the United States might be different today if it had been settled from west to east?"
4. *Controlling* thought, which occurs when the teacher does things for students that they should do for themselves. Example (a definition supplied by the teacher): "A homesteader is one who stakes out a land claim, erects buildings, and lives on the land."

From her analyses of these teacher strategies, Taba concludes that transformations of concrete operations into formal ones begin in the second grade and increase slowly through the third and fourth grades; finally, in the fifth and sixth grades, formal thought represents approximately one sixth of

[21] John Dewey, *How We Think* (New York: D. C. Heath & Co., 1933).
[22] Hilda Taba, *Thinking in Elementary School Children,* Cooperative Research Project No. 1574 (Washington, D.C.: U.S. Office of Education, Department of Health, Education, and Welfare, 1964).

all thought units offered. This suggests a somewhat earlier beginning of formal thought processes than has been postulated by Piaget. Taba views the development of thought as a continuous stream rather than as an accretion of specific skills. Taba concludes that the questions teachers ask are especially crucial in either limiting or enhancing the capacity of students to think.

The strategies that David's teacher used in encouraging thinking among her pupils are revealed in the following anecdote:

OCTOBER 26

We were discussing the Cuban blockade in class. The morning TV news had given the information that the U.S. knew the positions of some 25 Russian ships. Roy asked, "How is that possible?"

"By radar," David answered.

"I've seen radar screens on TV shows, but I don't understand how it works," remarked Roy.

David replied, "It's simple. Radio waves are sent out from a transmitter into space. When they strike an object they bounce back to their source, which has a receiver. We know the speed of radio waves so the time they take to go and return gives us the distance to the object."

"But how do we know the object they hit aren't our own ships at sea?" asked Roy.

"Because we know the location of our ships from their radio reports. There were none in the area where the Russian ships were," said David.

"Where were the radar stations that located the ships?" asked Carl.

"They were on our ships at sea. You see, radio waves can't follow the curvature of the earth, so ships at sea carry radar equipment and can locate objects if they are too far from our land-based radar stations," David explained.

Problem Solving

Problem solving is perhaps the most unique, complex, and significant of human abilities. Problem solving and creative behavior evidence a high level of cognitive development. The quality of problem-solving performance is dependent upon the availability of a broad range of concepts and generalizations and the development of thinking abilities. The full resources of one's development and learning are committed to solving the many kinds of problems he encounters in his daily life. The success one has in solving both mundane and challenging intellectual problems influences his concept of himself as a problem solver. A favorable image of self as problem solver is an impetus for continued problem-seeking, problem-solving behavior.

Problem-solving behavior occurs in response to a problem situation. One is confronted with a problem situation when he must choose and prepare for a vocation, when his income will not cover all of his expenses, or when his car will not start. The student at school may be confronted during any one day with a wide variety of problems: proving a theorem in geometry, diagramming a sentence, identifying the elements in a chemical solution, finding ways of improving the student body's school spirit, or getting elected to class office. Scientists are confronted with problems of overpopulation, finding a cure for cancer, and reaching planets in outer space. Problem situations, then, are unique to the individual, may be general or specific, vary in complexity and importance, and may be of short or long duration.[23]

A distinction may be made between problems whose solutions are known to someone and problems whose solutions are unknown and undiscovered. Solving a puzzle or an equation is an example of the first type, while achieving a permanent peace is an example of the second. "A problem situation exists, then, when there is a goal to be attained, but the individual sees no well-defined, well-established means of attaining it; or when the goal is so vaguely defined or unclear to the person that he cannot determine what are relevant means for attaining it."[24]

What are the steps in problem solving? We shall identify and discuss each step in relation to a concrete problem. Ed Richardson, an eighth grader, inherited an old grandfather's clock from his grandmother. After repairing, oiling, and refurbishing it, he found that it continuously lost time. The first step in problem solving is a recognition of a felt need, which is manifested in a *goal to be achieved*—in this case, developing a more reliable clock. Since Ed was uncertain whether the difficulty was in the clock mechanism or with the pendulum, it was necessary for him to *analyze the situation*. Ed tested the gear mechanisms and other moving parts and found that all moved freely. It soon became clear, in the *redefinition of the problem,* that restoring the accuracy of the clock would involve correcting the speed of the pendulum.

Ed's preliminary analysis of the situation led to his *making several hypotheses* for increasing the velocity of the pendulum. He could (1) lighten the weight, (2) shorten the pendulum arm, (3) release the pendulum weight from a higher point on the arc, (4) increase the force used in starting the pendulum swinging, or (5) use some combination of these variables. By *testing each hypothesis* while holding each of the other variables constant, Ed found that only changing the length of the pendulum arm influenced its velocity. Weight, height of the drop, and force of the push in starting it were excluded as influences on the velocity of the pendulum. The *generalization* emerging from the solution to this problem is that shortening the arm of a pendulum increases the velocity of the pendulum, while lengthening the arm decreases its velocity.

---

[23] See Frederick J. McDonald, *Educational Psychology,* 2nd ed. (Belmont, California: Wadsworth Publishing Co., 1965), p. 254.
[24] McDonald, p. 253.

Suchman[25] describes a procedure for helping elementary school children to improve their problem-solving performance through developing skills in inquiry. A sixth-grade class observes a film clip of a man holding a long metal blade with a wooden handle. When the blade is held over a flame, it bends downward. After heating, the blade is plunged into a tank of water and it straightens out again. When the blade is turned over and heated again, the blade bends upward. The children are asked to find out why the events in the filmed episode occurred. In order to gather the information they need, they must ask questions. Restricting them to questions which may be answered "yes" or "no" requires the children to think through and to structure their own questions.

Suchman found that children ask three types of questions about the filmed episode. Questions which seek information on temperature, pressure, shape of objects, or events in the episode are called *verification* questions (for example, "When heated, does the blade always bend in the same direction?"). In a second type of question, called *abstract-conceptual* questions, the child asks for a direct verification of his own hypothesis, thus avoiding having to gather data and make his own inferences (for example, "Does the bending of the blade have anything to do with the heat?"). A third type of question, called *concrete-inferential* questions, is much like an experiment in that the child manipulates a variable and then asks what the outcome of this manipulation would be (for example, "If we made the flame hotter, would the blade bend further?"). In this type of question, the child makes his own inference as to causality from the data he obtains. The object of inquiry training, according to Suchman, is to increase the amount of verification and experimentation undertaken by a child on his own, and to reduce the number of attempts he makes to pick the brains of the teacher with abstract-conceptual questions.

Suchman found that inquiry-trained groups asked significantly more verification questions than did control groups and significantly fewer abstract-conceptual questions. The two groups did not differ, however, in their use of experimentation; nor were there significant group differences on tests measuring knowledge of concepts. In spite of the negative nature of some of his results, Suchman concludes that inquiry training has a marked effect on the motivation, autonomy, and question-asking fluency of children: "They clearly enjoy having the freedom and power to gather their own data in their quest for assimilation."[26]

Numerous studies[27] suggest that young children are able to perform

---

[25] J. Richard Suchman, *The Elementary School Training Program in Scientific Inquiry* (Urbana, Illinois: University of Illinois Press, 1962).

[26] Suchman, p. 126.

[27] See, for example, David P. Ausubel and N. M. Schiff, "The Effect of Incidental and Experimentally Induced Experience in the Learning of Relevant and Irrelevant Causal Relationships by Children," *Journal of Genetic Psychology,* 84 (1954), 109–123; and Susan M. Ervin, "Training and a Logical Operation by Children," *Child Development* (September 1960), 555–563.

rather advanced problem-solving tasks, but that this ability tends to extinguish quickly, is subject to interference, and does not transfer to other tasks. These findings are seen by some as invalidating stimulus-response explanations of concept formation and supporting Piaget's theory that a child's performance of a given cognitive task must await his attainment of the requisite stage of intellectual development. Anderson,[28] however, hypothesizes that first-grade children who are given suitable training will acquire a rather advanced problem-solving skill. Anderson formed 60 first graders in the highest third of the mental age distribution into two groups, a training group and a control group. Three times a week, members of the training group were given individual twenty-minute training sessions in identifying a range of concepts (geometric figures, leaf facsimiles, cowboys with varying features, and a pegboard game). Following the training, both groups were tested on problems that required them to identify concepts similar to those presented earlier only to the training group. Anderson found that children receiving training solved more problems involving retention with fewer unnecessary trials; they also solved more transfer problems and solved them more efficiently than did the control group. Anderson interprets these findings as supporting a stimulus-response theory of concept development.

Many of the issues and variables that relate to learning in general may also be observed in problem solving. The reader will recall that puzzle boxes and problem-solving tasks are used by both cognitive field theorists (who favor an insight explanation of learning) and stimulus-response theorists (who favor a trial-and-confirmation explanation of problem solving). It appears that many puzzle-like problems lend themselves to a sudden solution, with few trials required once key concepts or relationships are grasped. "With six matches of equal length, make four and only four equilateral triangles" is a problem whose solution is dependent upon insight. Other problems lend themselves more readily to a trial and confirmation strategy—"Given: Three jars holding three, five, and eight quarts, respectively. The first two are empty, and the third is filled with water. Divide the liquid into two equal parts using only the three jars."

Success and failure appear to have a marked influence on problem-solving behavior.[29] Students who consistently fail in solving problems spend more time working on problems, evidence greater tension, have a stronger desire to give up and substitute a different goal, and, while working on the problem, engage in more fantasy and use less realistic problem-solving behavior. Schroder and Hunt[30] found that students who withdraw from a problem-solving situation prior to achieving a solution set higher goals originally, use fewer alternative solutions in attempting to solve the problem,

[28] Richard C. Anderson, "Can First Graders Learn an Advanced Problem-Solving Skill?" *Journal of Educational Psychology,* 56 (December 1965), 283–294.

[29] See B. Lantz, "Some Dynamic Aspects of Success and Failure," *Psychological Monographs,* 271 (1945).

[30] H. M. Schroder and D. E. Hunt, "Failure Avoidance in Situational Interpretation and Problem Solving," *Psychological Monographs,* 342 (1957).

and perform less effectively after failure than do those who achieve solutions. Klausmeier and Laughlin[31] found that differences in intelligence are related to success in problem solving, to problem-solving behavior, and to kinds of approaches to problems employed. Students with high IQs are more likely to note and correct mistakes, verify solutions, and use a logical approach in problem solving, while students with lower IQs offer incorrect solutions, make random approaches to the problem, and do not persist in their attempts to solve the problem.

Set

An individual's problem-solving performance is greatly influenced by his predisposition to perceive, to approach, and to respond to a given problem situation in a certain way. This predisposition is what psychologists call *set*. For most of us, a two-dimensional "set" will prevent, initially, our grasping the solution to the problem of forming four equilateral triangles with six matches of equal length. The influence of set is most evident when individuals taught to solve problems by one method persist in applying that method to problems even when it repeatedly fails to solve them. Thus, set promotes positive transfer to problems of the same class but produces negative transfer to problems of other classes. Negative transfer was demonstrated in a study by Birch and Rabinowitz[32] involving the problem of tying together two strings suspended from the ceiling and placed sufficiently far apart that they could not be held at the same time. The problem could have been solved by attaching a weight to one string, thus making it into a pendulum. Subjects had available to them an electrical switching relay they had used in a previous problem, but they were unable to see this object as a possible weight for making a pendulum.

The instructions a teacher gives a class for doing an assignment establishes a set that may significantly influence the learning of the class. Wittrock[33] found, for example, that students who were asked to remember "differences" or "similarities and differences" between Buddhism and the Judeo-Christian tradition learned and retained more information than did students who were asked to "understand and remember" material on these two topics. Similar results were obtained by Torrance and Harmon.[34] Each of three groups of students was given separate instructions either to apply creatively the content of assigned readings, or to evaluate the content of the readings critically, or to remember the content of the readings. Each group

---

[31] Herbert J. Klausmeier and L. J. Laughlin, "Behavior during Problem Solving among children of Low, Average, and High Intelligence," *Journal of Educational Psychology,* 52 (1961), 148–152.

[32] H. G. Birch and H. S. Rabinowitz, "The Negative Effect of Previous Experience in Productive Thinking," *Journal of Experimental Psychology,* 41 (1951), 121–125.

[33] M. C. Wittrock, "Effects of Certain Sets Upon Complex Learning Material," *Journal of Educational Psychology,* 54 (April 1963), 85–88.

[34] E. Paul Torrance and J. Harmon, "Effects of Memory, Evaluative, and Creative Reading Sets on Test Performance," *Journal of Educational Psychology,* 52 (1961), 207–214.

scored highest on the type of test (emphasizing creativity, evaluation, or memory) which conformed to the type of instructions received.

The set a student has prior to his beginning a learning activity is shaped by many factors. Later, in discussing creativity, we will note that some socialization patterns encourage convergent thinking while others encourage novelty, originality, and divergent thinking. Some persons may be open, flexible, and creative in dealing with some types of problems, but fixed, unyielding, and conventional in dealing with other types. A successful businessman, for example, may exhibit great flexibility and creativity in producing or marketing new products, but may remain very rigid in his approach to certain social and political problems. Most persons do feel more comfortable using patterns that have proven successful in the past. By the very nature of the task, however, problem solving calls for new, fresh, and original approaches.

The evidence indicates that a learner's set can be a strong deterrent to his solving of problems that require new approaches; but the evidence also shows that the teacher can help to modify the learner's set. The inhibiting effects of set can be reduced if teachers introduce students to problems that require different and varied approaches. Greater emphasis also should be given to the methods and processes involved in solving a problem and less stress should be given to problems that require "only one correct answer."

Transfer and Problem Solving

An important concern of the teacher in facilitating learning should be to assure that concepts and skills that students learn in one situation will be applied—in adapted form if necessary—in other situations. Do students who write, spell, and punctuate correctly on tests and exercises also spell and punctuate correctly in letters and themes? Do students who learn the Pythagorean theorem in geometry apply this theorem later in trigonometry? Evidences of *transfer* are often used as a measure of learning.

In no outcome of learning is transfer of greater importance than in problem solving. Solving a problem facing one at a particular moment may be of immediate practical value, but, since problem solving is a lifelong activity, the skills, methods, and insights gained in solving a particular problem have significance only as they may be transferred in the solving of other problems.

The advantages of knowing and applying generalizations in solving new but related problems were demonstrated in an early experiment by Judd.[35] Two groups of boys were given practice in throwing darts at a target submerged in a foot of water until both groups had developed approximately the same level of proficiency. At the beginning of the experiment, one group had been given an explanation of principles involved in the refraction of light.

---

[35] Charles H. Judd, "The Relation of Special Training to Special Intelligence," *Educational Review,* 36 (1908), 28–42. For a similar study, see G. Hendrickson and W. H. Schroeder, "Transfer of Training and Learning to Hit a Submerged Target," *Journal of Educational Psychology,* 32 (1941), 205–213.

Initially, this information appeared to have little influence on their performance in throwing darts. However, when the depth of the water was changed from 12 to 4 inches, the group which had been given the principle of refraction of light adjusted quickly to the new situation, while the group lacking the principle had difficulty adjusting.

Other studies show that transfer is increased when students derive principles for themselves. Haslerud and Meyers[36] gave a group of students two kinds of problems: (1) problems for which both the principles of solution and their application were explained, and (2) problems for which no directions relevant to solutions were given. On a test measuring transfer, following a practice test, students' scores increased significantly on those problems which required them to derive the principle in order to solve the problem. Haslerud and Meyers suggest that a specific explanation blocks transfer because it prevents the student from anticipating new applications of the principles.

Transfer in problem solving is facilitated when the student understands the principles involved in the solution of the original problem. The teacher has an important role in this process. The teacher may assist students in applying problem-solving learning to other situations by showing that a principle of solution is relevant to other problems, by having students apply a principle to a wide variety of problems, by preparing students to recognize problems similar to those on which they have worked, and by helping students to become aware of and to anticipate the usefulness of previously learned principles in solving new problems.[37]

Individual and Group Problem Solving

What evidence do we have concerning the relative superiority of groups or individuals in solving problems? In initial problem-solving learning, most studies have shown that the average small group outperforms the individual problem solver. There is some indication, however, that those who had solved problems initially as members of quads performed less well in a transfer situation when working alone. In a study by Klausmeier, Wiersma, and Harris,[38] 128 college students in an initial learning situation learned four concepts either individually, with a partner (pair), or as a member of a group of four (quad). Half of each group were given an immediate transfer task and the other half were given a delayed transfer task (presented after twelve minutes). The transfer task involved the attainment of concepts similar to those of the initial learning situation. The study found that the quads attained the concepts in the initial learning situation in the shortest

[36] George M. Haslerud and S. Meyers, "The Transfer Value of Given and Individually Derived Principles," *Journal of Educational Psychology,* 49 (1958), 293–298.

[37] McDonald, p. 282.

[38] Herbert J. Klausmeier, William Wiersma, and Chester W. Harris, "Efficiency of Initial Learning and Transfer by Individuals, Pairs, and Quads," *Journal of Educational Psychology,* 54 (June 1963), 160–164.

amount of time, but that those who had undertaken the initial learning task individually completed the immediate and the delayed transfer tasks more quickly than did those who had undertaken the initial task in pairs or quads. In interpreting their findings, Klausmeier and his associates suggest that in the initial learning situation, although the pairs and quads quickly secured a large amount of information, analyzed the information correctly, and deduced the correct concepts, not all members of the pairs and quads learned this problem-solving procedure equally well. When they worked alone on the transfer problem, some of them could not attain the concept quickly because they had depended on others in the initial learning. Individuals working alone on the initial task often made many mistakes, but they did learn how to go about solving the problem and were able to improve their performance in the transfer situation.

Hudgins and Smith[39] studied the relationship of group structure to productivity in problem solving. Among children in the fifth to eighth grades, group solutions to problems in arithmetic were not better than the individual solutions of the most able group member of high socioeconomic status. This finding suggests that when the most able member of a small problem-solving group is also a high-status member of the group, the productivity of the group is a function of the productivity of the high-ability member.

When the high-ability member of a problem-solving group was of low socioeconomic status, however, the group's productivity in solving problems was found to be higher than that of the high-ability student. This finding suggests that the low-status high-ability student is more closely examined by members of his group before they are willing to accept his solutions; because of this, the productivity of the group is likely to be enhanced. When a low-status member of a group played an important role in furnishing solutions to problems, and when the score of the group was similar to his own, the status of this member rose.

Creativity

There is no general agreement on what creativity is. Members of one symposium[40] variously defined creativity as life itself, as a way of life, as optimum growth in social interaction, and as a maximum of self-actualizing. McKinnon[41] has defined creativity as "a process extended in time and characterized by originality, adaptiveness, and realization." He elaborates:

[39] Bryce B. Hudgins and Louis M. Smith, "Group Structure and Productivity in Problem Solving," *Journal of Educational Psychology,* 57 (October 1966), 287–296.
[40] Harold H. Anderson, ed., *Creativity and Its Cultivation* (New York: Harper & Row, 1959).
[41] Donald W. McKinnon, "The Nature and Nurture of Creative Talent," *American Psychologist,* 16 (July 1962), 484–495.

If a response is to lay claim to being a part of the creative process, it must to some extent be adaptive to, or of, reality. It must serve to solve a problem, fit a situation, or accomplish some recognizable goal. And, thirdly, true creativity involves a sustaining of original insight, an evaluation and elaboration of it, a developing of it to the full.[42]

Some writers have found it useful to distinguish between creative behavior and original behavior. Original behavior is that behavior "which occurs relatively infrequently, is uncommon under given conditions, and is relevant to those conditions."[43] Originality, thus defined, may be more easily translated into behavioral terms and studied in relation to problem solving. Creative behavior, on the other hand, is behavior that *results* in products or achievements judged to be creative by relevant judges.[44]

Creativity and Intelligence

Since the term "gifted" has often been used to describe both creative individuals and those of high intelligence, it is not surprising that highly creative and highly intelligent persons have been pictured as sharing many of the same qualities. Independent researches have shown rather consistently, however, that while creative persons are generally above average in intelligence, the qualities associated with the highly creative person and the highly intelligent person are sufficiently different as to make each type independent and distinctive. Taylor[45] points out that traditional intelligence tests cover only a very few of the dimensions of the mind and suggests that IQ may be only one of several types of intellectual gifts.

Getzels and Jackson[46] identified a group of "high-creative" adolescents who scored at the 80th percentile in tests of creativity but below the 80th percentile in IQ. A group of "high-IQ" students from the same population scored at the 80th percentile or above in IQ but scored below the 80th percentile on tests of creativity. The mean IQ of the high-creative group was below the school mean and 23 points below the mean of the high-IQ group. McKinnon[47] found, in studies of creative mathematicians and architects, essentially a zero relationship between creativity and intelligence. He concluded that it is just not true that the more intelligent person is necessarily the more creative one.

Studies show that high-IQ students are generally preferred over average

---

[42] McKinnon, p. 485.
[43] I. Maltzman, "On the Training of Originality," *Psychological Review,* 67 (1960), 229.
[44] McDonald, p. 293.
[45] Calvin W. Taylor, "A Tentative Description of the Creative Individual," in Walter B. Waetjen, *Human Variability and Learning* (Washington: Association for Supervision and Curriculum Development, N.E.A., 1961), pp. 62–79.
[46] Jacob W. Getzels and Philip W. Jackson, *Creativity and Intelligence* (New York: John Wiley, 1962), pp. 13–76.
[47] McKinnon, pp. 487–488.

students by their teachers, while highly creative students tend to be less preferred. Nuss[48] found that creativity as measured by a creativity test is relatively independent of intelligence, but that creativity as measured by teachers' ratings is positively associated with intelligence. The same was true in the case of creativity and scholastic achievement. In the study of Getzels and Jackson (cited above), a close relationship was found between the qualities high-IQ students value in themselves and the qualities they believe lead to success, suggesting that high-IQ students are highly success oriented. The very low relationship found between the qualities high-creative students value in themselves and those they believe lead to success suggests that high-creative students are not highly success oriented, at least not by conventional adult standards.

Encouraging Creativity

Carl Rogers[49] has set forth a tentative theory of creativity relating to the nature of the creative act, the conditions under which it occurs, and the manner in which it may be constructively fostered. Rogers defines the creative process as "the emergence in action of a novel relational product, growing out of the uniqueness of the individual on the one hand, and the materials, events, people, or circumstances of his life on the other." The motivation for creativity is the directional trend which is evident in all organic life: the urge to expand, extend, develop, and mature. Rogers postulates that persons who possess an openness to experience, an internal locus of evaluation, and an ability to toy with elements will, in a climate of psychological freedom, form a greater number of creative products.

Hamby[50] tested parts of Rogers' theory in an investigation of the relationship between teacher behavior and change in children's creative performance. She hypothesized that fourth-grade children in art classes under a nondirective, nonevaluative teacher would show greater gains in creativity and self-concept than would fourth-grade students in art classes under a directive, evaluative teacher. With nondirective, nonevaluative structuring, the teacher was endeavoring to establish a climate of psychological safety and freedom and to encourage openness to experience and self-evaluation.

Children in art classes under nondirective, nonevaluative structuring made significantly higher scores than did children under directive, evaluative structuring on only two of twenty-one subtests of the Verbal Battery, Minnesota Tests of Creative Thinking. At the end of an eight-week period, children in nondirective, nonevaluative art classes received significantly

---

[48] Eugene M. Nuss, *"An Exploration of the Relationship between Creativity and Certain Personal-Social Variables,"* (unpublished doctor's dissertation, University of Maryland, 1961).

[49] Carl R. Rogers, "Toward a Theory of Creativity," in Anderson (see note 40), 69–82.

[50] Trudy M. Hamby, "An Investigation of the Relationship between Teacher Structuring and Change in Children's Creative Performance and Self-Ideal Self Reports" (unpublished doctor's dissertation, University of Maryland, 1966).

higher scores than children in directive, evaluative art classes on judges' evaluations of the creativity of their art products; at the end of sixteen weeks, however, the scores of the two groups were not significantly different.

Torrance[51] conducted a study of another teaching method designed to stimulate the flow of creative ideas among children in grades three through six. Each child was encouraged to have an "idea trap"—a small note pad on which he was to record his ideas any time they came to him. The children were urged to write down their ideas for poems, stories, jokes, songs, inventions, and cartoons. Every Friday, each pupil was asked to select from his idea trap one idea for possible use in a weekly magazine, *Ideas of the Week.* At the beginning and end of the six-week study, each pupil wrote an imaginary story. The stories were scored using scales developed for evaluating creativity.

Torrance found that children in grades three to six can be stimulated to do a great deal of creative work. The third graders were highest in productivity and showed significant growth in creative writing as measured by pre- and post-training stories. The fourth and sixth graders also showed growth on two of the three measures of creativity. The fifth graders, however, showed regressive trends. There was evidence in this study that the children had learned to value more highly their own ideas—indeed, they objected rather violently to the small amount of editing that was done on their creative writing. Torrance presents the following principles to guide teachers in encouraging and rewarding children's creative thinking.

1. Be respectful of children's questions.
2. Be respectful of imaginative and unusual ideas.
3. Show pupils their ideas have value.
4. Give opportunities for practice or experimentation without evaluation.
5. Encourage and evaluate self-initiated learning.
6. Evaluate in ways that foster the pupil's ability to see the causes and consequences of his behavior.[52]

Structure of the Intellect

An overview of the aspects and dimensions of cognitive functioning that have been discussed in this chapter is provided by Guilford's investigations into human intelligence. His model of the structure of the intellect (see Figure 15.4)[53] is organized in relation to three major aspects of cognitive functioning: *operations, products,* and *contents.* An *ability* is a combination

---

[51] E. Paul Torrance, *Rewarding Creative Behavior* (Englewood Cliffs, New Jersey: Prentice-Hall, 1965).

[52] Torrance, pp. 314–319.

[53] From J. P. Guilford, "Three Faces of Intellect," *American Psychologist,* 14 (1959), 470. Reproduced by permission.

OPERATIONS

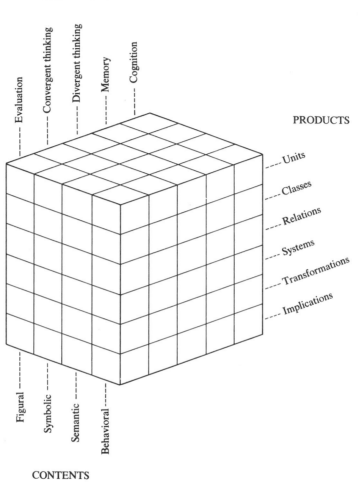

Figure 15.4. Model of the structure of the intellect (from Guilford).

of an operation, a content, and a product. In identifying five kinds of operations, four kinds of contents, and six kinds of products, Guilford hypothesizes that there are 120 possible abilities in the human cognitive domain. Guilford[54] describes each of the operations, contents, and products as follows:

[54] In J.P. Guilford and Ralph Hoepfner, *Structure-of-Intellect Factors and their Tests, 1966*, Reports from the Psychological Laboratory, University of Southern California, Los Angeles, California, Report No. 36, 1966, pp. 3–4. Used here by permission.

OPERATIONS	Major kinds of intellectual activities or processes; things that the organism does with the raw materials of information, information being defined as "that which the organism discriminates."
Cognition	Immediate discovery, awareness, rediscovery, or recognition of information in various forms; comprehension or understanding.
Memory	Retention of storage, with some degree of availability, of information in the same form it was committed to storage and in response to the same cues in connection with which it was learned.
Divergent production	Generation of information from given information, where emphasis is upon variety and quantity of output from the same source. Likely to involve what has been called transfer. This operation is most clearly involved in aptitudes of creative potential.
Convergent production	Generation of information from given information, where the emphasis is upon achieving unique or conventionally accepted best outcomes. It is likely the given (cue) information fully determines the response.
Evaluation	Reaching decisions or making judgments concerning criterion satisfaction (correctness, suitability, adequacy, desirability, etc.) of information.
CONTENTS	Broad classes or types of information discriminable by the organism.
Figural	Information in concrete form, as perceived or as recalled, possibly in the form of images. The term "figural" minimally implies figure-ground perceptual organization. Visual spatial information is figural. Different sense modalities may be involved, e.g., visual kinesthetic.
Symbolic	Information in the form of denotative signs, having no significance in and of themselves, such as letters, numbers, musical notations, codes, and words, when meanings and form are not considered.
Semantic	Information in the form of meanings to which words commonly become attached, hence most notable in verbal thinking and in verbal communication but not identical with words. Meaningful pictures also often convey semantic information.

Behavioral	Information, essentially nonverbal, involved in human interactions where the attitudes, needs, desires, moods, intentions, perception, thoughts, etc., of other people or ourselves are involved.
PRODUCTS	Forms that information takes in the organism's processing of it.
Units	Relatively segregated or circumscribed items of information having "thing" character. May be close to Gestalt psychology's "figure on a ground."
Classes	Conceptions underlying sets of items of information grouped by virtue of their common properties.
Relations	Connections between items of information based upon variables or points of contact that apply to them. Relational connections are more meaningful and definable than implications.
Systems	Organized or structured aggregates of items of information; complexes of interrelated or interacting parts.
Transformations	Changes of various kinds (redefinition, shifts, or modification) in existing information or in its function.
Implications	Extrapolations of information, in the form of expectancies, predictions, known or suspected antecedents, concomitants, or consequences. The connection between the given information and the extrapolated is more general and less definable than a relational connection.

Teachers may find this model useful for identifying and defining specific learning outcomes. Learning the multiplication table, for example, would be representative of the memory-symbolic-classes cell, while ascertaining the geographical position of Chicago by interpreting a map would be representative of the convergent-semantic-relations cell. Thus far, Guilford has identified 80 of the possible 120 abilities of his model.[55]

Guilford's model, especially those elements of it relating to convergent and divergent thinking, has stimulated considerable interest and investigation. Each kind of thinking appears to be associated with a distinctive personality pattern. Getzels and Jackson,[56] for example, found that adolescents high in divergent thinking and highly creative in their nonverbal productions are more stimulus-free (in that they tend to structure a task in their own

[55] J. P. Guilford, "Intelligence: 1965 Model," *American Psychologist*, 21 (January 1966), 20–26.

[56] Getzels and Jackson, pp. 50–52.

terms), more fanciful and humorous, and tend to express more aggression and violence. High-divergent, high-creative adolescents tend to produce new forms, to risk joining dissimilar articles, and to go off in new directions. High-IQ adolescents, on the other hand, tend to focus on the usual, the right answer or the socially acceptable answer, and to shy away from the risk and uncertainty of the unknown.

Gallagher,[57] using a system for classifying verbal statements developed from Guilford's model of the structure of the intellect, analyzed the productive thought processes displayed in the classroom by intellectually gifted adolescents and their teachers. Gallagher found that in nearly all class sessions, 50 percent or more of the questions teachers asked related to cognitive-memory operations. The second most frequently used category was that of convergent thinking, with a much smaller proportion of questions calling for divergent thinking or evaluation. The patterns of thought expressed by students were closely related to the kinds of questions they were asked. The findings of this study underscore the crucial role played by the teacher as the initiator and determiner of the kinds of thought processes expressed by children in the classroom.

Summary

The outcomes of learning may be organized into three major types or categories: *cognitive, psychomotor,* and *affective.* Although a given behavior pattern may be predominantly cognitive, psychomotor, or affective, the three types of outcomes and processes are interrelated. Learning outcomes become organized into hierarchies, wherein more complex behavior patterns and integrations are formed from simpler patterns.

The processes through which one acquires, organizes, interrelates, and interprets the data of his experience are called cognitive processes. The data acquired, processed, and transformed are cognitive outcomes of increasing complexity: preverbal percepts, factual information, concepts, generalizations and principles, problem solving, creative thinking, theories, and systematized knowledge.

A *concept* is a classification of stimuli that have common characteristics. In forming concepts, one must discriminate between relevant and irrelevant features of the data, and generalize by correctly identifying the several instances or exemplars which belong to this category of concept. The concepts that children and youth acquire depend upon the kinds and qualities of experiences they have. The teacher's failure to utilize illustrations of concepts drawn from students' experiences often results in misunderstanding and incomplete learning. Schools also have a responsibility to encourage

---

[57] James J. Gallagher, *Productive Thinking of Gifted Children,* Cooperative Research Project No. 965 (Washington, D. C.: U. S. Office of Education, Department of Health, Education, and Welfare, 1963).

pupils to avoid stereotypes by helping them to develop adequate, valid concepts of people, places, and events.

Studies of strategies used in concept attainment reveal that negative examples, because they place too heavy a load on the memory of the learner, are an inefficient means of learning. Other strategies are more successful. Students given 100-percent, immediate reinforcement learn concepts more quickly than students given partial or delayed reinforcement.

It appears that one may know and use a concept correctly without being able to verbalize it. There is also evidence that difficulties in forming concepts may arise when a shift occurs in the symbol system or medium used to describe or explain the concept.

Older children make more frequent use of *superordinate groupings* in forming concepts, while younger children make more frequent use of *complex formations*. Among older subjects, *conservative focusing,* involving the use of a positive instance to guide choices in altering the possible attributes of a concept one at a time, was found to be the most efficient strategy for identifying concepts. Students may be helped to learn and to retain unfamiliar concepts if they are introduced first to more general and inclusive concepts (*advance organizers*) under which the unfamiliar concepts can be grouped and related.

Generalizing is the act of deriving a general concept, principle, law, or theory from particular facts or observations. Generalizations may be acquired in either of two ways: by *deduction* from laws, premises, or other generalizations; or, by *induction,* in which specific instances are combined. In reasoning and problem solving, deductive and inductive methods are most effectively used in tandem, with conclusions reached using one method being verified and checked by the other method.

Problem solving—the most unique, complex, and significant of human abilities—is dependent upon the availability of a broad range of concepts and generalizations and the development of thinking abilities. The steps in problem solving include (1) identifying a goal to be achieved, (2) analyzing the situation, (3) redefining the problem, (4) making hypotheses, (5) testing each hypothesis, and (6) generalizing from the findings emerging from tests of hypotheses. The problem-solving abilities of elementary school children may be improved by improving their skills in inquiry. Through inquiry training, children are encouraged to undertake their own verification and experimentation instead of attempting to pick the brains of others in order to avoid gathering data and making independent inferences.

Problem-solving performance is greatly influenced by *set,* one's predisposition to perceive, to approach, and to respond to a given problem situation in a certain way. The learner's set is a strong deterrent to his solving of problems that require new approaches, but the limiting effects of set can be reduced if teachers give children practice with problems that require different and varied approaches. Studies show that *transfer* from one problem-solving situation to another is facilitated when the student understands the principles involved in the solution of the first problem. Studies also reveal that groups can attain a concept more quickly than individuals, but that individuals are likely to learn the procedures involved in attaining the concept more thoroughly.

Creativity often involves a high development of cognitive abilities. However, while creative persons are generally above average in intelligence, the qualities associated with highly intelligent persons and with highly creative persons are sufficiently different as to make each type independent and distinctive. The view that creativity is a quality that can, to some degree, be nurtured and developed in all students has prompted educators to develop programs which give greater emphasis and encouragement to creativity.

The major aspects and dimensions of cognitive functioning are represented in Guilford's model of the structure of the intellect. The various combinations of the components of the three major aspects of cognitive functioning—*operations, products,* and *contents*—indicate the abilities possible in the human cognitive domain.

Study Questions

1. The terms "knowledge," "comprehension," and "understanding" are frequently used in describing cognitive processes and outcomes. What distinctions would you make between these terms?

2. Identify one or more concepts you would expect your students to master. Describe the steps of the instructional strategies you would use in helping your students acquire these concepts. How would you provide in your selection of teaching strategies for individual differences among students?

3. What explanations can you offer as to why our schools in the past have seemed to fail to give strong emphasis and encouragement to the nurturing of creativity?

4. In view of the findings of Getzels and Jackson and others, do you think the schools can educate for both creativity and intellectual development, as measured by current intelligence tests, or are these two objectives incompatible with each other? Discuss.

Suggested Readings

Harold H. Anderson. Editor. *Creativity and Its Cultivation.* New York: Harper & Row, 1959. A collection of fifteen papers presented at the Interdisciplinary Symposia on Creativity. The writings emphasize the growing realization of the tremendous potentialities in the creativity of man, in the nature of human resources, and in respect for the individual.

Jerome S. Bruner. *The Process of Education*. Cambridge: Harvard University Press, 1960. An educational classic that emerged from a conference on educational methods. A major premise of Bruner's is that basic concepts in the sciences and humanities can be grasped by children at a much earlier age than was previously thought possible. Concepts of "structure" and "intuition" are examined in relation to intellectual development, teaching, and curriculum development.

Jerome S. Bruner, Jacqueline J. Goodnow, and George A. Austin. *A Study of Thinking*. New York: Science Editions, Inc., 1962. Describes and analyzes the strategies persons use to categorize sensory data in the development of concepts.

Jacob W. Getzels and Philip W. Jackson. *Creativity and Intelligence*. New York: John Wiley, 1962. Reports research which shows that highly creative persons and highly intelligent persons differ significantly with regard to personal values, imaginative productions, career goals, and family backgrounds. The implications of these findings for teaching and learning are discussed.

Barbel Inhelder and Jean Piaget. *The Growth of Logical Thinking from Childhood to Adolescence*. New York: Basic Books, Inc., 1958. Describes studies of the development of formal psychological structures which "mark the completion of the operational development of intelligence."

Frederick J. McDonald. *Educational Psychology*. Second Edition. Belmont, California: Wadsworth Publishing Co., 1965. Chapters 5, 6, and 7 provide a comprehensive treatment of cognitive processes and development, including concept formation, associative thinking, problem solving and creative behavior. Discussion is documented by research findings and supplemented by discussions of instructional strategies by which students may be helped to achieve relevant cognitive outcomes and goals.

Films

Focus on Behavior, 6. *No Two Alike*. 16 mm, sound, black and white, 30 min. Bloomington, Indiana: Audio-Visual Center, Indiana University (rental fee, $5.40). Examines some of the ways in which psychologists are developing new methods for measuring and increasing human capabilities. Dr. Lloyd Humphreys demonstrates the development of tests for choosing pilots in World War II, while Dr. James Gallagher shows the methods that are being used to develop productive or creative thinking in the modern day classroom.

16

the outcomes of learning: psychomotor and affective

There's only one corner of the universe you can be sure of improving and that's your own self.

≡   ALDOUS HUXLEY

Optimum self-development and psychological health depend upon the full development and integration of all of man's powers. This suggests that effective functioning as a person requires the harmonious blending of affective, cognitive, and psychomotor components of behavior. An individual's full development requires not only cognitive abilities, but also an adequate repertoire of psychomotor skills and affective responses.

Psychomotor Learning

The term *psychomotor* refers to a class of responses which involve the coordination of muscles in the movement of the body or any of its parts. We shall begin our study of psychomotor learning by identifying and discussing the characteristics of psychomotor skill.

Characteristics of Psychomotor Skill

Accurate conception of the task. The initial characteristic of an effective psychomotor performance is a clear conception of the goal to be achieved and of the general task and subtasks that must be executed in achieving it. Any skilled performance, even opening a door or writing one's name, involves hundreds of input-output sensation-nerve-muscle coordinations. The learner first visualizes the general task and consciously selects particular movements to be made. As he proceeds with the task, he plans the details and executes the steps with reference to the goal to be achieved. As the act is repeated, the subtasks may appear in different forms; eventually, as the learner integrates separate movements into a smoothly coordinated pattern, the subtasks drop out.[1]

These steps may be illustrated in the skill performance of driving a car. The beginning driver gives a great deal of his attention individually to the clutch, brake, accelerator, speedometer, steering wheel, where he is in relation to the edge of the road, the locations and presumed intentions of other cars around him, traffic lights, street signs, pedestrians, and countless other stimuli. So preoccupied is the beginner with these subtasks that he is unable to carry on a conversation with his passenger. Repetitions of the act of driving bring about a consolidation and habituation of the subtasks and responses. No longer does he have to consciously think about shifting, steering, or braking. As a result of habituation, the movements occur automatically. At this point, the maturing driver is likely to be carrying on an animated conversation with his passenger and is probably little aware of making the many individual movements and adjustments required in driving the car.

Use of cues. A skilled performer may be distinguished from one with less skill by his manner of utilizing cues. Cues are stimuli, originating both internally and externally, which guide an individual's responses in performing a skill. The beginner is more dependent than the expert on direct visual cues. The beginning typist or pianist must look at the keyboard to locate the correct letter or note, but his skilled counterpart is more likely to use only muscle cues in "feeling" the location on the keyboard of a letter or note. The experienced performer requires fewer cues and is able to take advantage of equivalent cues. The symphony orchestra violinist reads music in phrases rather than in separate notes. He also recognizes the equivalence of the term *Allegro* in the musical score to the quick tempo of the conductor's beat, to the "sound" in his mind of the music played at a quick tempo, and to the "feel" in his muscles of playing the music at an allegro tempo.

A skilled performer also makes finer and more precise cue discriminations than one who is less skilled. The fine musician can discriminate be-

---

[1] Howard L. Kingsley and Ralph Garry, *The Nature and Conditions of Learning* (Englewood Cliffs, New Jersey: Prentice-Hall, 1957), p. 299.

tween two tones that sound the same to most persons in the audience. The center fielder, anticipating the direction of a possible fly ball, responds to cues in the batter's movements even before the ball is hit.

As mastery of a skill increases, cue discriminations become more automatic and the number of cues required for performing the skill decreases. The many direct visual cues required by the beginning driver mentioned above drop out as his experience increases and his skill improves.

Feedback and correction. When he feels his car drifting to the left or right—perhaps because of road conditions, wind, or the condition of the tires or brakes –the driver moves the steering wheel slightly to compensate. The driver's sense that his car is drifting is an example of the process of *feedback;* his movement of the steering wheel is an example of *correction,* a response to feedback. Feedback and correction are interrelated processes that occur throughout a skilled performance. An experienced typist, pianist, high jumper, golfer, or lathe operator continuously evaluates his performance from feedback received through his sense of timing or the "feel" of his muscles and corrects his performance accordingly.

The phases of a skill performance thus correspond to the model of behavior proposed by Miller, Galanter, and Pribram.[2] They suggest that behavior may be described in terms of what they call TOTE units. TOTE is an acronym for Test-Operate-Test-Exit. The initial *test* consists of the learner's concept of the task or problem facing him. The task may involve a skilled performance (such as driving a car or shaping a piece of wood on a lathe) or it may involve a cognitive process (such as discovering the concept or principle needed to explain a phenomenon). *Operate* stands for the learner's response to the initial test—turning the steering wheel, guiding the lathe, or testing a hypothesis relative to a concept or principle. The next *test* involves a comparison of the results obtained by the operation process and the criteria of the goal of the process—arriving at a destination, making a table leg, explaining a phenomenon. This step involves the processes of feedback and correction described above. Often, many test-operate-test-operate-test units are required before the goal is achieved. When the criteria of the goal have been met, the test-operate sequence terminates, a step that is called *exit.*

The selection of particular TOTE units to be employed in the performance of a psychomotor skill implies the existence of a plan. *Plan* is a central construct of the theory of Miller and his associates and is defined as any hierarchical process in the organism that can control the order in which a sequence of operations is to be performed. A plan is for the organism essentially the same as a program is for a computer.

Coordination of movements. The performance of a skill usually requires a series of many simple movements involving the coordination of many muscles. In the early stages of learning a skill, each movement tends to

---

[2] George A. Miller, Eugene Galanter, and Karl H. Pribram, *Plans and the Structure of Behavior* (New York: Holt, Rinehart and Winston, 1960).

be performed as a separate act. The beginning driver is likely to focus in turn on releasing the brake, shifting the gear, letting out the clutch, and pressing lightly on the accelerator. The beginning typist concentrates on hitting the correct individual keys. The resulting performances are usually a series of jerky movements.

With practice, these separate movements become integrated into one smooth, rhythmic movement. This integration is what is meant by the term *motor coordination*. In such a coordination of movements, some responses are subordinated, others are blended together, and a few are emphasized. In a well-coordinated skill performance, these responses are carefully timed, each separate act occurring at the proper moment and in the proper sequence. The skilled typist and pianist respond not to separate letters or notes but to phrases or sequences of phrases. Coordination of responses permits the typist or pianist to incorporate longer or more complex sequences into the continuous rhythmical movements of a skilled performance.

Speed and accuracy. As a skilled performance comes to reflect more and more the operation of the processes described above, the performer's speed and accuracy usually increase. Indeed, speed and accuracy are the characteristics that most clearly distinguish the highly skilled performance from the less skilled performance. The typist, for example, with increased skill, is able to type more words per minute and make fewer errors doing it.

Acquiring and Improving Skill Performance

The quality of a skill performance is influenced by several kinds of variables. Frequent mention has been made of the wide differences that exist between learners with respect to such factors as strength, size, maturity, coordination, cultural background, and motivation. Considerable attention has been given to these *learner variables* in previous chapters. The performance of a given skill may also be analyzed in relation to the levels of strength, speed, reaction time, perceptual acuity, manual dexterity, and motor control required for the performance of that skill. These components may be referred to as *skill variables*. Guilford[3] has devised a matrix portraying the influence of variables of this kind (see Table 16.1). He has identified strength, impulsion, speed, static precision, dynamic precision, coordination, and flexibility as psychomotor factors. A psychomotor ability involves the movement or manipulation of some part of the body in relation to a psychomotor factor. Many psychomotor skills involve the integration of several psychomotor abilities. Weight lifting, for example, would require not only gross general strength, trunk strength, and limb strength, but also gross static balance and gross bodily coordination. Throwing a baseball would utilize limb thrust, arm aiming, arm speed, trunk and leg flexibility, and gross bodily coordination. Those who teach motor skills may find it useful to

---

[3] J. P. Guilford, "A System of Psychomotor Abilities," *American Journal of Psychology,* 71 (1958), 165. Table 16.1 is reproduced from this article by permission.

Table 16.1   Matrix of psychomotor abilities (from Guilford).

PART OF BODY INVOLVED	STRENGTH	IMPULSION	SPEED	STATIC PRECISION	DYNAMIC PRECISION	COORDINATION	FLEXIBILITY
Gross body	General strength	General reaction time		Static balance	Dynamic balance	Gross bodily coordination	
Trunk	Trunk strength						Trunk flexibility
Limbs	Limb strength	Limb thrust	Arm speed	Arm steadiness	Arm aiming		Leg flexibility
Hand					Hand aiming	Hand dexterity	
Finger		Tapping	Finger speed			Finger dexterity	

TYPE OF FACTOR

analyze specific skills (such as typing, operating a lathe, shooting a basketball) in relation to the matrix of psychomotor abilities shown in Table 16.1.

Instruction and guidance. The learning of a psychomotor skill does not necessarily depend upon receiving instruction from an outside source. Many simple motor skills may be mastered through practice undertaken on one's own. Some artists, musicians, and athletes possessing unusual aptitudes for skill performance may even develop their special abilities with little or no instruction. However, most skills are more quickly and efficiently learned with the help of external instructions.[4]

Guidance is a critical variable that can substantially influence the ease and speed with which a skill is learned. In early studies by Koch and Ludgate, an adequate amount of guidance provided early in the learning of a maze resulted in fewer errors than guidance introduced later in the training.[5] Cratty suggests that pre-task guidance should be mainly concerned with communicating knowledge of spatial relationships, of the speed of movement desired, or the force required for performance of the skill. Both visual demonstration and manual guidance may be helpful at this stage, but they should be appropriate to the student's level of comprehension.[6]

The teacher should guard against giving the student too much guidance or verbal instruction. Too much information at one time may make it difficult for the student to integrate new responses into patterns he has already learned. Too much focus on specific elements of a skill may impede the student's gaining a feeling for the whole skill. Cratty suggests that verbal instructions are most effective if given before the beginning of a skill performance or during its initial stages. Instructions given during the performance of the task should not interfere with the learner's movement patterns. At this point, visual demonstrations or a small amount of manual guidance may be superior to verbal instructions. Visual cues in the form of films or demonstrations tend to be superior to movement cues in learning such skills as golf, tennis, or baseball.

Speed versus accuracy. Although both speed and accuracy are characteristics of a skilled performance, it is obvious that for such skills as painting, sculpturing, ceramics, and woodworking, accuracy may be more important than speed. In other skills, such as handwriting, typewriting, or drafting, both speed and accuracy are important.

Solley[7] studied the effects of instructions emphasizing speed, accuracy, or both speed and accuracy on the performance of three groups trying to hit

[4] Bryant J. Cratty, *Movement Behavior and Motor Learning* (Philadelphia: Lea and Febiger, 1964), p. 252.
[5] H. L. Koch, "The Influence of Mechanical Guidance upon Maze Learning," *Psychological Monographs* 5 (1923); K. E. Ludgate, "The Effect of Manual Guidance Upon Maze Learning," *Psychological Monographs* 1 (1923).
[6] Cratty, pp. 252–264.
[7] W. H. Solley, "The Effects of Verbal Instruction of Speed and Accuracy upon the Learning of a Motor Skill," *Research Quarterly* 23 (1952), 231–240.

a target. During an initial training period, each group was given different instructions regarding speed and accuracy. Following that period, all three groups were instructed to place equal emphasis on accuracy and speed. It was found that the initial training period had a pronounced effect on later performance. Subjects whose training emphasized speed increased in accuracy while maintaining speed. Subjects whose training emphasized accuracy decreased in accuracy as soon as they increased their speed. Solley concluded that in motor skills where speed is a significant factor in ultimate performance, the initial emphasis should be on speed, with accuracy secondary. In skills where both speed and accuracy are required, the initial training should emphasize both.

Knowledge of results. Knowledge of a skill performance is a prerequisite for improving the performance. As we mentioned earlier, information relating to the adequacy or correctness of a performance is sometimes called *feedback*. Knowledge of results also functions as *reinforcement,* since those movements associated with correct performance tend to be repeated. Such knowledge may be communicated through the verbal comments of an instructor or observer, through the visual confirmation of accuracy, speed, or some other success criterion, or through the feel of a successfully completed movement. Knowledge of results will enable some learners to correct and improve performance through self-instruction; for other learners, further visual demonstrations, manual guidance, or verbal instruction may be needed.

The importance of knowledge of results in improving psychomotor skill performance has been demonstrated in several studies. The effectiveness of such feedback is improved when it is immediate rather than delayed.[8] The effectiveness of feedback is also improved if it is given continuously and frequently.[9] There is some evidence suggesting that students improve in their performance of a skill even when the feedback calling attention to correct performance is slightly disagreeable. Jones[10] asked two groups of adolescents to operate a punchboard maze. To learn the maze, the students had to make choices involving both correct and incorrect responses. For one group, an agreeable stimulus consisting of a pattern of lights was flashed on a board for every correct response; for the other group a disagreeable vibration in the stylus used to perform the task signaled a correct response. Jones found no differences in performance between the two groups and concluded that information relating to the correctness of a response may be reinforcing even if it is given in an unpleasant manner.

Effective practice. Practice of a skill should be conducted under conditions that approximate as closely as possible those under which the skill is to be performed. One learns what he does. Practicing typing actual sentences is

---

[8] Joel G. Greenspoon and Sally Foreman, "Effect of Delay of Knowledge of Results on Learning a Motor Task," *Journal of Experimental Psychology,* 51 (1956), 226–228.

[9] G. F. Arps, "Work with Knowledge of Results vs. Work without Knowledge of Results," *Psychological Monographs,* 28 (1920), 125.

[10] Harold E. Jones, "Trial and Error Learning with Differential Cues," *Journal of Experimental Psychology,* 35 (1945), 31–45.

more consistent with the criterion goal to be achieved than is practicing typing nonsense syllables. Similarly, studying English words is more efficacious in improving one's English vocabulary than studying Latin.

The superiority of practicing a skill under conditions approximating those of performance was demonstrated by Gates and Taylor.[11] One group of children traced letter forms on transparent paper placed over the forms, while another group practiced writing by copying a model. The tracing group improved their ability to trace letters, but when they were later tested for their ability to write, their writing was much poorer than those who practiced actual writing.

Massed versus spaced practice. Most studies show that the learning of psychomotor skills occurs more rapidly when practice sessions are well spaced. Spaced practice of motor skills is especially recommended for elementary school children, who vary considerably in physical maturity, energy levels, attention span, and interest. Many motor skills, such as handwriting, baseball, or playing a musical instrument, require the coordination and integration of both physical movements and cognitive processes. This suggests a further need for spaced practice.

Doré and Hilgard[12] showed that scores in pursuit rotor learning at the end of each successive minute within three-minute massed practice trials showed decreases that approximated progressive work decrements characteristic of work curves. Figure 16.1 shows that one group practiced pursuit rotor learning for one minute and rested for three minutes (*distributed practice*), while the other group practiced for three minutes and rested for one minute (*massed practice*). The gain from practice shows as recovery over the one-minute rests, but the massed practice group shows no performance advantage even though it had three times as much practice as the other group.

Appropriate practice units. For simple performances, such as stroking a golf ball or broad jumping—performances involving the integration of several responses into one continuous movement—practicing the skill as a whole is probably superior to practicing the skill in parts. However, in complex performances, such as playing the piano, swimming, playing tennis, or playing shortstop, breaking the total performance down into separate skills or components, each of which may logically constitute a whole, appears to be more advantageous. As the smaller wholes are mastered, practice should refocus on larger, more comprehensive units of the skill.

Instructional Strategies

The teacher may use verbal instructions, visual demonstrations, and manual guidance in introducing a psychomotor skill to students and in help-

[11] Arthur I. Gates and Grace A. Taylor, "The Acquisition of Motor Control in Writing by Preschool Children," *Teachers College Record,* 24 (1923), 459–468.

[12] L. R. Doré and E. R. Hilgard, "Spaced Practice and the Maturation Hypothesis," *Journal of Psychology,* 4 (1937), 245–259. Figure 16.1 is reproduced from this article by permission.

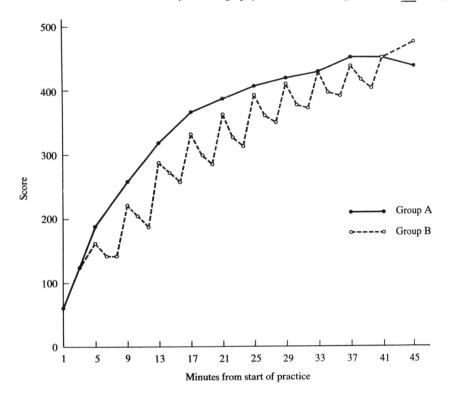

Figure 16.1. Distributed practice in pursuit learning. Group A practiced one minute and rested three minutes, while Group B practiced three minutes and rested one minute. Scores at each minute within the three-minute trials show progressive work decrement. (From Doré and Hilgard.)

ing students to improve their performances of this skill. By using knowledge of results, praise, encouragement, and evaluational procedures, the teacher may also influence students' progress in skill performance.

Although some teaching strategies may be expected to be superior to others, observations show that teachers using quite different approaches may obtain equally good results in helping students to improve their skill performances. It may be useful to analyze the strategies Mr. Haynes used in teaching his ninth-grade woodworking class to use the power jig saw:

Yesterday, in the last part of the period, I had introduced my ninth-grade class in wood shop to the proper way of operating the power jig saw and had demonstrated its use by cutting out a figure of a horse and rider. Today I reviewed briefly the steps required for inserting jig saw blades and in operating the machine. Then, while the class worked on their figures and designs for cutouts, I allowed two boys at a time to take turns inserting the correct blade and to get the feel of the saw by cutting spontaneous designs on scrap wood.

Later, during the latter half of the double period, several of the boys were ready to use the jig saw to cut out their figures and designs. Joe and Henry, two boys who have had previous experience with power tools, proceeded to cut out their designs on the jig saw with no need of correction or help from me. For these boys my verbal instructions appeared to be sufficient in enabling them to perform the skill. Ned Frost had not gotten very far with his cutting before the blade became bent. I recalled from working with Ned previously that he has difficulty conceptualizing in concrete terms verbal instructions which are given him. I showed him on the machine how the improper adjustment of the tension sleeve had caused the blade to bend. When some of the other boys encountered minor mishaps, my asking, "What do you think went wrong?" enabled them to find their error.

Later in the period, as I watched Ed Conroy start to cut out his design, I noticed that he was rather tense as he placed both hands on the face of his material and tried to wiggle it through. I went over to where he was working with the jig saw, asked him to grasp the ends of the board, placed my hands on his and guided the board as the blade cut along the line. I took my hand away, and he relaxed noticeably as he continued and completed his cutting.

Several points related to the strategies of teaching a psychomotor skill are revealed in this excerpt. Mr. Haynes provided both verbal instructions and visual demonstrations of how to insert blades and operate a jig saw. He also provided students with the opportunity to practice the skill that had been described and demonstrated. Each boy practiced inserting the blade and each had brief opportunities to get the feel of cutting with the jig saw using scrap material before cutting out the design for his project.

Mr. Haynes modified his teaching strategy to fit the needs and abilities of each boy. For some boys, verbal instructions were sufficient for preparing them to operate the jig saw; for Ned, however, a visual demonstration was needed, and for Ed, manual guidance was helpful. The boys gained knowledge of results through immediate feedback on the difficulties encountered operating the saw. When the machine was not working properly or the cut turned out to be imperfect, Mr. Haynes encouraged independent evaluation by asking the boy to analyze what he thought had gone wrong. Mr. Haynes was also quick to reinforce correct performance by praising a student not only for a good product but also for demonstrating good form in operating the saw and for finding the cause of any error himself.

Affective Learning

Affective learning consists of responses (expressed as positive or negative feelings) acquired as one evaluates the meaning of an idea, object, person, or event in terms of the maintenance and enhancement of his view of himself and the world. Affective learning is of particular interest to us because people are likely to respond to ideas, objects, persons, and events as much by what they think and feel about them as by what they know about them. Thus, affective learning—in the form of tastes, preferences, attitudes, and values—exerts a strong influence on behavior. Since attitudes and values are probably the most representative affective outcomes of learning, we shall focus our discussion on the nature and acquisition of attitudes and values.

Attitudes

An *attitude* is a predisposition to react favorably or unfavorably toward ideas, objects, persons, events, or situations. We may think of an attitude as a kind of mental *set* which leads one to respond to ideas, persons, and objects in terms of previously acquired feelings and thoughts. The object toward which one is thus predisposed to respond in a certain way is called an *attitude object*. It may be a physical object, a person, a group of people, an institution, an idea, or a particular characteristic of any of these.

Defining an attitude as a predisposition to respond favorably or unfavorably toward some object suggests that attitudes, like motives, provide *direction* to anticipated behavior. An attitude, however, is not the same as a motive. It may be recalled that a motive is an energy change and performs an energizing function in pushing the organism in the direction of the desired goal response. An attitude prepares an individual to be motivated in particular ways, but does not energize him.

It should be emphasized that attitudes, as well as feelings and emotions, are not innate but learned. Attitudes are the valuative meanings acquired and generalized from an individual's experiences with a particular idea, person, or object. The concepts upon which attitudes are based may, in varying degrees, be accurate or inaccurate, valid or invalid; and an individual's responses to those concepts may themselves be accurate or inaccurate, valid or invalid. One may have acquired a concept of the relationship between heavy cigarette smoking and the incidence of lung cancer yet maintain a favorable attitude toward smoking. This type of situation may point to a conflict in attitudes, a topic we shall discuss later.

Measurement of attitudes. We may gain information concerning a person's attitudes through inference from direct observation of his behavior. Observing that a student joins enthusiastically into all school activities, makes positive comments about his school, and expresses disappointment if forced to miss school because of illness, we may infer that the student's attitude toward school is positive. We may wish, however, to ascertain the student's predispositions to respond favorably or unfavorably to a much larger sample of phenomena. For this, direct observation alone is not enough, and we usually turn to the use of attitude scales.

Attitude scales seek to assess the degree of a subject's favorable or unfavorable response toward each of several items. Typically, an attitude scale samples a person's attitudes within a limited subject or area. Individual scales, for example, have been developed to elicit attitudes toward teaching, children, students' classroom behavior, child rearing practices, authority, conformity, and minority groups. Figure 16.2[13] presents part of an attitude questionnaire that seeks to elicit from college students or adults their attitudes toward children.

In order to be useful, an attitude scale, like any other measuring instrument, must give consistent results when administered on successive occasions and must measure the quality it claims to measure. It must, in other words, be reliable and valid. One who constructs an attitude scale seeks to eliminate ambiguous statements, so that each item in the scale will, as nearly as possible, convey the same meaning to all respondents. A test is considered reliable when an individual's responses to items in it do not change substantially when the test is administered to him on successive occasions. A test is considered valid if its results agree with other evidences of the individual's responses toward the attitude object. A positive response toward reading revealed in an attitude scale may be checked for validation against information concerning the proportion of the individual's leisure time spent in reading, the frequency of his trips to the library, and the amount of time he spends talking about books or articles he has read. We should remember, however, that inferences of an individual's attitudes, in order to be valid, must be drawn from a broad sampling of his behavior in a variety of situations.

Learning of attitudes. Allport[14] has identified four ways in which attitudes are formed. One way is through the *integration of numerous specific responses* of a similar type into a generalized response pattern. An attitude is seldom the result of a single experience; usually, an attitude is formed through an accretion of experience. Through such a process, an attitude becomes a "residuum of many repeated processes of sensation, perception, and feeling."[15] Attitude formation through the integration of experiences is exemplified in the strong positive feelings that one develops toward a tried and true friend through countless experiences of shared interests, concern, empathy, support, and affection, or, on the other hand, in the uniformly unpleasant, disappointing, or dissatisfying experiences one may have had in dealing with a particular business firm.

A second way attitudes are formed, according to Allport, is through the *differentiations* one makes in an original matrix of attitudes having a general positive or negative orientation. One acquires attitudes by differentiation, for example, when his feelings and actions toward a group reflect a growing awareness of individual differences among group members in place of general stereotyped attitudes toward the whole group.

The third way in which Allport believes attitudes are acquired is

---

[13] From Sandra Scarr, "Attitude Change in Human Development Students" (College Park, Maryland: Institute for Child Study, University of Maryland, 1966). Mimeographed. Used by permission.

[14] Gordon W. Allport, "Attitudes," in Carl Murchison, *Handbook of Social Psychology* (Worcester, Mass.: Clark University Press, 1935), pp. 810–812.

[15] Allport, p. 810.

Attitude Questionnaire

Listed below are a number of statements of opinion or of behavior that might or might not apply to you. You will probably find yourself agreeing with some items and disagreeing with others. We are interested in the extent to which you agree or disagree.

Mark each statement in the left margin according to how much you agree or disagree with it. Please mark every one. Write in 1, 2, 3, 4, 5, or 6 depending on how you feel in each case.

        1 - I disagree very much
        2 - I disagree pretty much
        3 - I disagree a little
        4 - I agree a little
        5 - I agree pretty much
        6 - I agree very much

There is no set of answers to these statements that is right for everyone: your answers will reflect your own point of view, which is the important thing.

_____Children should be seen and not heard.

_____Young people should be free to decide whether some mores and values of their parents are still relevant.

_____Self-discipline and respect for authority are essential in developing a well-integrated personality.

_____The authority of one's conscience is a more trustworthy guide to behavior than the authority of parents or teachers.

_____Children are usually the best judges of what is good for them.

_____Schools have no right to tell students how they should wear their hair.

_____Children should have enough respect for their teachers to sit quietly and do what they say.

_____Disobedience should be understood not punished.

_____Children ought to be allowed to study whatever interests them.

_____A child who is too obedient makes me uncomfortable.

Figure 16.2 Excerpts from a scale eliciting attitudes toward children (from Scarr).

447

through *dramatic experience or trauma*. An example of an attitude formed by a single traumatic experience would be an individual's aversion to a certain food that had once made him ill. Another example would be an attitude of distrust formed after abandonment or rejection by family or friends.

The fourth way in which attitudes are formed is through *imitation* of or *identification* with parents, teachers, or peers. Allport suggests that "even before he has an adequate background of appropriate experience, a child may form many intense and lasting attitudes toward races and professions, toward religions and marriage, toward foreigners and servants, and toward morality and sin."[16] The acquisition of ready-made attitudes through identification with others frequently occurs unconsciously. This unconscious acceptance of the attitudes of our parents, teachers, and peers is probably related to our needs to be loved and to belong—needs satisfied through interactions with parents, teachers, and peers.

The importance of identification in the learning of attitudes is clearly revealed in a study of prejudice among young children by Trager and Yarrow.[17] They concluded that prejudices are learned through adopting adult values and behavior patterns and conforming to adult expectations as part of the process of growing up. "Learning prejudices seems to be, to a great extent, a matter of learning 'the way things are.' " Parents, by placing restrictions on their children's friendships or encouraging friendships with particular children, create experiences which may influence their children's attitudes.

The influence of the teacher in shaping and reinforcing children's attitudes was revealed in Trager and Yarrow's study of two experimentally created teacher-led clubs. One club sought to demonstrate an acceptance of the values of cultural democracy; the second club sought to demonstrate a status-quo philosophy, reinforcing children's existing prejudices. The children involved in this experiment learned attitudes consistent with whichever club they were assigned to. In accepting the group situation and the leader, the child was disposed also to accept the values of the new culture—the club.

Conflicts in attitudes. An individual acquires some kind of valuative meaning from every experience, and, through time, becomes predisposed favorably or unfavorably toward a myriad of objects, persons, ideas, or events. Often, the meanings of his experiences produce in him two strongly held but incompatible attitudes. The child is in conflict, for instance, when events prevent him from maintaining positive attitudes toward parents and teachers and equally positive attitudes toward peers, justice, and fair play. An adult frequently faces conflicts in attitudes with respect to the demands and expectations of his sex role or his job. A bright, energetic woman with high achievement motivation may avoid competing with men for position and power out of fear of being viewed as unfeminine. The American may

[16] Allport, p. 811.
[17] Helen G. Trager and Marian R. Yarrow, *They Learn What They Live* (New York: Harper & Row, 1952), pp. 347–352.

find that his strong positive attitudes toward freedom and individuality conflict with his positive attitude toward conformity. His belief in competition and free enterprise may conflict with his equally strong belief in brotherly love and adherence to the golden rule. His positive attitude toward equality of opportunity for all people may conflict with his attitudes toward home and community.

In resolving such conflicts, the individual may seek to maintain those attitudes toward objects, people, or ideas that are most important to him, or he may seek to compromise his attitudes to make them compatible with one another. A politician frequently does this in order to satisfy the disparate elements of his constituency. He may come out in favor of a controversial law provided certain safeguards are built into the law to protect the interests of those of his constituents who oppose it.

Two theories have been advanced to explain and predict the behavior of persons in conflict. The first of these, proposed by Dollard and Miller,[18] is presented in Figure 16.3. In the figure, points of conflict are shown as the

[18] John Dollard and Neal E. Miller, *Personality and Psychotherapy* (New York: McGraw-Hill Book Co., 1950), pp. 350–360. Figure 16.3 is reproduced from this work by permission.

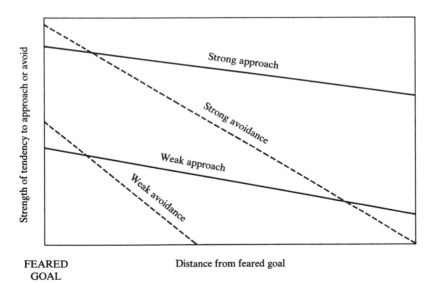

Figure 16.3. How increasing the strength of approach in an approach-avoidance conflict increases the amount of conflict. The subject will be expected to advance or retreat to the point where the gradients intersect—the point where the strengths of the competing tendencies are equal. Thus, as the strength of approach is increased, the subject will move nearer the goal. When he is nearer the goal, the strength of both tendencies will be increased and conflict will occur. (From Dollard and Miller.)

intersections of gradients representing tendencies to approach and to avoid a goal. As a person approaches a goal toward which he has conflicting attitudes, his feelings of avoidance become stronger. When these feelings are strong enough, the person is likely to terminate his approach and withdraw to a point where his feelings of approach and avoidance balance each other, the point in the figure where the gradients of approach and avoidance intersect. The person is likely to remain at this point of conflict until his attitudes change.

The second explanation of conflict is Festinger's[19] theory of *cognitive dissonance*. According to Festinger, a person experiences conflict when he perceives that alternative choices facing him are incompatible. Having to choose one alternative and reject the other produces cognitive dissonance. The amount of dissonance that exists after a decision has been made is a direct function of the number of things about the person's behavior, beliefs, or attitudes that a person knows are inconsistent with the choice he has made. In order to reduce this dissonance, according to Festinger's theory, the person reevaluates his attitudes, modifying them to fit the choice he has made. Perhaps a college student, after a careful analysis, has written a term paper very critical of a theory of motivation, not realizing that his professor identifies strongly and positively with the theory. After receiving a grade of *C* on the paper and reading the professor's critical comments, the student experiences dissonance. He may reduce this dissonance by adopting a more positive attitude toward the theory or by adopting a negative attitude toward the professor, whichever best enables him to maintain his self-concept.

Studies of attitudes. A number of studies have investigated the attitudes of children and youth. An early study by Horowitz[20] reported prejudice against Negroes expressed by children as young as five years old. In this study, the attitudes of Northern children toward Negroes were found to differ little from the attitudes expressed by Southern children. Horowitz concluded that children's attitudes toward Negroes are determined not by contact with Negroes, but by contact with the community's prevalent attitudes toward Negroes.

Trager and Yarrow,[21] in the study cited previously, also found that prejudice is often learned in early childhood, before and during the first years at school. While lack of longitudinal data made it impossible to judge whether children become more prejudiced as they grow older, the data available did show that stereotyping and expressions of hostility are more frequent among older children, and that attitudes are more crystallized. Neither age, sex, neighborhood, group membership, nor personality could be singled out as the determining factor in the prejudice of the children involved in this study.

[19] Leon Festinger, *Theory of Cognitive Dissonance* (Stanford, California: Stanford University Press, 1957).
[20] Eugene L. Horowitz, "Development of Attitudes toward Negroes," *Archives of Psychology*, 194 (1936).
[21] Trager and Yarrow, pp. 182, 346.

Remmers and Radler[22] found that teenagers from all parts of the United States present a fairly consistent picture in the attitudes they hold. Teenagers' strong need to be accepted by the peer group was reflected in a definite trend toward conformity found among teenagers of all social classes. More than half of Remmers and Radler's teenage respondents believed that censorship of books, magazines, newspapers, radio, and television is all right, that the F.B.I. and local police should be allowed to use wiretapping at will, and that most people are not capable of deciding what is best for themselves. A tendency among these teenagers to value others' opinions above their own was reflected in their stereotyped views on many national issues. A kind of anti-intellectualism was revealed in the belief, held by nearly 75 percent of the respondents, that development of a well-rounded personality is the main purpose of education and that personality counts for more than grades when it comes to finding a job.

A number of studies have investigated the influence of attendance at college on the formation of attitudes. A study[23] of the attitudes of girls at Bennington College sought to ascertain whether attendance at Bennington produced any substantial change in attitudes toward public affairs. It was found that the conservatism of the girls with respect to public issues decreased in each of the four years they spent at Bennington. On most public issues, juniors and seniors were significantly less conservative than freshmen. Comments of individual students revealed that those who identified with their families registered the least change in attitudes, while those who wished to break their family ties registered the greatest change in attitudes.

Jacob[24] also investigated the influence on attitudes and values of the college experience. In general, Jacob found that the college experience exerts little influence on students' standards of behavior, quality of judgment, sense of responsibility, keenness of understanding, or guiding beliefs. The values of American college students were found to be remarkably homogeneous, considering the variety of their backgrounds and their relatively unrestricted opportunities for thought and personal development. Students in this study appeared to be contented, were unabashedly self-centered, and aspired to material gratifications for themselves and their families.

In a study of one large midwestern university, Lehmann, Sinha, and Harnett[25] found that over the four-year period, students became less stereotyped and dogmatic in their beliefs and more "outer directed" in their value orientations. Women underwent a more marked change in their attitudes and values than did their male classmates. Students who withdrew from college before graduating in some instances manifested the same type of behavior as students who remained until graduation. Lehmann and his associates con-

22 H. H. Remmers and D. H. Radler, *The American Teenager* (Indianapolis: Bobbs-Merrill Co., 1957).
23 Theodore M. Newcomb, *Personality and Social Change* (New York: Dryden Press, 1943).
24 Philip E. Jacob, *Changing Values in College* (New York: Harper & Row, 1957).
25 Irvin J. Lehmann, Birenda K. Sinha, and Rodney T. Harnett, "Changes in Attitudes and Values Associated with College Attendance," *Journal of Educational Psychology,* 57 (April 1966), 89–98.

cluded that college acts as a catalyst to speed up changes that would occur anyway as the individual matures.

It would appear from the studies cited above that attendance at college has some effect in shaping students' attitudes and values, but that the effect is varied and in some cases indeterminate. Neither the quality of teaching nor the method of instruction appears to influence to any great extent the attitudes and values students form. For those students whose attitudes and values do change in college, the impetus does not seem to come from the formal educational process. Rather, it seems to come from the distinctive climate of a few institutions, from the influence and personal magnetism of a sensitive teacher, or from a student's significant personal experiences.

Values

A *value* is a preference for something cherished or desired; it is linked to one's satisfaction of needs, his realization of goals and purposes, and the maintenance and enhancement of his self-concept. A value tends to be marked by a degree of personal commitment, to emerge after a period of reflection, and to permeate the significant aspects of a person's life. Values are organized in a hierarchy and are manifested in a consistency of behavior. Values, like attitudes, orient and prepare the individual to respond to his environment in predetermined ways.

Some writers[26] make the distinction that values are preferences based on conceptions of what is desirable, while attitudes need not be based upon such conceptions. It appears, however, that tastes, attitudes, and values all connote preferences that are desired by the person registering the preference. The principal difference is the greater intensity characteristic of values, an intensity which leads to strong personal commitment and involvement.

The learning of values. Values are learned in the same ways that attitudes are learned. The most important way in which values are learned is through identification with significant others. The person comes to perceive situations in the same way the model, a parent, uncle, teacher, or athletic hero, perceives them. He experiences some of the same feelings in empathy with the model and adopts many of the same goals, attitudes, and values. It is natural to identify with persons who satisfy one's affectional and dependency needs. For many children and youth, parents, older siblings, aunt, uncle, coach or youth leader may serve as models for identification. For some students, a teacher or peer may serve as the identification object. Whoever the model may be, many of his values will be accepted ready-made by the student through the process of identification.

Values acquired through a strong emotional tie with another person may conflict with other values held by the individual or may be found invalid when tested against reality. In order to avoid adopting invalid or inconsis-

---

[26] See Frederick J. McDonald, *Educational Psychology,* 2nd ed. (Belmont, California: Wadsworth Publishing Co., 1965), p. 374.

tent values, one should check all values against his own experience and against objective criteria, if available. We are suggesting, therefore, that the development of a consistent system of values requires also the differentiation and reintegration of the meanings of one's experience. It is this need that confronts the late adolescent as he seeks to achieve the important developmental task of crystallizing a system of values and developing a philosophy of life. Many of the values he acquired prior to adolescence have been taken over by identification with parents, teachers, and peers. The events of his life in adolescence and his perceptions of these events frequently cause him to question some of his ready-made values. In this questioning and reexamination of values, we may observe the processes of differentiation and reintegration.

The following anecdotes from the case records of Tab, age six, Skippy, age ten, Doris, age fourteen, and Margaret Anne, age eighteen, contain expressions of these students' values. The processes of identification, differentiation, and integration—the processes through which values are learned and modified—are shown at each of these maturity levels.

MARCH 18

Tab was walking with the teacher. As we walked by the flag pole he stopped short and jerked the teacher's hand. "I've got a good idea," he said. "We're first ones out and while we wait for the others let's sing to the flag." The flags were beautiful flying against the blue sky and white clouds. The others agreed so they pledged allegiance to the flag and sang "America." "That was really fun," said Tab.

DECEMBER 2

We were making plans for a presentation of Christmas carols and songs to be given before the P.T.A. by the upper grades.

In the discussion, we listed three types of songs: the carols, songs dealing with Christmas customs, and songs of the Jewish Hanukkah. My class had presented the Hanukkah the previous year so I stated that I thought it was now some other class's turn to do that and that the eighth grade had volunteered to do it. In the voting I noticed that the Gentile children all voted to present a carol and the Jewish children didn't vote. I asked them what the trouble was.

Skippy: You didn't give us a chance to vote. You didn't mention Hanukkah.

Teacher: Yes, I did. I told you the eighth grade was doing it.

Skippy: But we want to.

Teacher: But you did it last year. Can't you see it would be fairer to give someone else the opportunity?

Skippy: Not if we want to do it more. There are more Jewish children in this room than in the eighth grade.

A Christian child: Yes, but if you have Hanukkah every year, when do we get a chance? Christmas belongs to us, not to you.

Skippy: Yeah, that's the way it always goes. You always get everything, and we always lose out.

Feeling that the discussion was too heated, the teacher dropped it here and changed the subject.

APRIL 8

Doris was supposed to bring me her report card during the sixth period. She came in smiling. Her hair was beautifully arranged in a long pageboy style. I complimented her on how nice it looked. She said, "I can't stand my hair if it is out of place. I like to work with it. I have five different shades of rinse I use on it. I like the bronze rinse best but it costs the most."

Doris discussed with the counselor something of her personal concerns. "There are three high school boys I like, one in particular, but none of them will look at me. I'll have a problem when it comes to finding a husband. I'll have to find one who is a member of the church. Mama wouldn't mind too much if he weren't a member, but it would break Daddy's heart if I married somebody outside the church."

DECEMBER 10

Margaret Anne was in my classroom this evening discussing things with other senior boys and girls. Margaret Anne said, "Well, Student Council is going to be respected, if I have to see to it myself. Most of the members sit at the meetings and never say anything. We had a boy up for going through the furnace room all the time, and they wouldn't say anything. Then I told him that we had told him several times not to go through, and I asked him why he continued. He said that he didn't see why he couldn't as the teachers did all the time. When I told him that there were only about twelve or thirteen teachers who did compared to three or four hundred pupils, he just looked at me."

One of the girls asked, "What did you do to him?"

Margaret Anne said, "I told him to write a two-hundred-word essay about 'Why I should not go through the furnace room.' "

Another student said, "And suppose he doesn't do it?"

Margaret Anne answered, "Then I'll write it myself and make him copy it. At least he'll know why he shouldn't and will learn to respect the Student Council."

Values in the classroom. Battle[27] investigated the influence of values on pupils and teachers in the determination of school marks in a public high school. An instrument containing value statements for ten classes of values was administered to a sample of high school teachers and their pupils. The study found that among pupils of similar aptitude, age, and sex, those who received high marks tended to have value patterns more closely related than the patterns of those who received low marks to patterns considered ideal by the teachers who determined the marks. Battle concludes that the degree of similarity between the teacher's ideal and the pupil's value pattern is directly related to the teacher's evaluation of the pupil's achievement.

The relationship of pupils' values to actual scholastic achievement was studied by Raths.[28] He hypothesized that underachievement is related in part to a student's failure to acquire and to clarify a set of values. Raths predicted that as attitudes and goals are clarified and values develop, under-achieving students will find new purpose in their school work and their achievement will increase. Several short individual conferences were held with a small experimental group of underachievers over the period of a semester for the purpose of helping these students to clarify their attitudes, beliefs, interests, purposes, aspirations, and values. In these conferences, the adult provided empathic support by listening and reacting to the student's discussions of topics of interest to him. After one semester, the experimental group registered a greater significant change toward higher rank-in-class and grade point average than did a matched control group which had no conferences.

Raths[29] and others have used the procedure described above to develop a strategy for helping students to clarify their values. Essential to such a strategy is the establishment of a permissive atmosphere. Students must feel psychologically safe to speak their minds without fear of harsh judgments or ridicule by peers or teachers. The teacher should be nonjudgmental, should be concerned with the ideas expressed by his students, and should provide opportunities in the classroom for students to express their opinions, purposes, feelings, beliefs, hunches, goals, and interests.

In helping students to clarify their ideas, a useful strategy is to ask probing questions. The questions should be ones to which only the student knows the answer, and they should be asked in a nonjudgmental manner:

[27] H. J. Battle, "Relation between Personal Values and Scholastic Achievement," *Journal of Experimental Education,* 20 (September 1957), 27–41.

[28] James D. Raths, "Underachievement and a Search for Values," *Journal of Educational Sociology,* 34 (May 1961), 423–424.

[29] James Raths, "A Strategy for Developing Values," *Educational Leadership,* 21 (May 1964), 509–514.

1. Reflect back what the student has said and add, "Is that what you mean?"
2. Reflect back what the student has said with distortions and add, "Is that what you mean?"
3. "How long have you felt that way?"
4. "Should everyone believe that?"
5. "Could you give me some examples of that?"

The teacher may also help students to clarify their beliefs and values by marking value statements in themes and other written work with symbols which really ask the student, "Do you believe this?" or "Do you want to change this?"

Values and behavior. The influence on behavior of a strong value orientation is strikingly shown in a study by Deutsch.[30] Deutsch studied the influence of varying types of orientation—cooperative, individualistic, and competitive—on individual behavior in an interpersonal conflict situation. In one study, a group of adolescents was invited to play "chicken" in the laboratory using a trucking game. In the laboratory game, each of two players was paid a fee for taking his truck from a starting point to a destination; from the fee was deducted the cost of the trip, which was determined by the amount of time it took to complete the trip. The players had to drive their trucks in opposite directions on the same road, and a large section of the road was only one lane in width. The players could see the position of both trucks at all times. If they arrived at the narrow section of the road at the same time, the players had to decide whether to go on or "chicken out." If he chose, each player could lock his truck in forward gear, committing himself irreversibly to an attempt to get through the narrow section. This commitment was immediately made known to the other player through a signaling device. If the trucks collided, the trial was ended and each player was charged money for the time spent since the beginning of the trial. The subjects played the game for twenty trials.

In one experiment, the subjects were divided into two groups and each group was given a different set of instructions—"chicken" instructions or "problem-solving" instructions. Under "chicken" instructions, subjects were told that the game separated people into two groups, "those who give in under pressure and those who do not." Under "problem-solving" instructions, subjects were told that the game separated people into two other groups, "those who can arrive at a solution to a problem that will bring maximum benefits to both players, and those who cannot work out the solution." Both groups were told, "It's important for you to earn as much money as you can and to lose as little as possible in the game." The subjects played for real money in amounts that were not insignificant to them.

The results of the study were striking. The "chicken" instructions re-

[30] Morton Deutsch, "Conflict and Its Resolution" (Paper presented at the meetings of the American Psychological Association, Chicago, September 5, 1965).

sulted in substantial mutual loss for nine of ten pairs of subjects, with the model pair having more than ten collisions in twenty trials. The "problem-solving" instructions, however, resulted in substantial mutual gain for all but three pairs of subjects, with the modal pair having less than four collisions in twenty trials. Deutsch concludes from this and other studies that both co-operative and competitive situations tend to be self-confirming and self-perpetuating; each tends to persist even if a change occurs in the originating conditions. The communication patterns, attitudes, perceptions, task orientations, and outcomes evoked by a given process tend to elicit the very same process that evoked them.

Summary

Optimum self-development and psychological health depend upon the full development and integration of all of man's powers. Thus, one's effective functioning as a person requires the blending of affective, cognitive, and psychomotor components of behavior into a harmonious, integrated whole.

The term *psychomotor* refers to a class of responses which involve the action and coordination of muscles in the movement of the body or any of its parts. A skilled psychomotor performance is characterized by (1) an accurate conception of the task, (2) efficient use of cues, (3) feedback and correction, (4) coordination of movements, and (5) speed and accuracy. Teachers may assist a student in acquiring and improving a skill with verbal instructions, visual demonstrations, and manual guidance. Verbal instructions appear to be most effective if given before skill performance or during the initial stages of performance. During later stages, visual demonstrations or minimal manual guidance may be superior to verbal instructions.

In the learning of psychomotor skills which require speed in performance, the initial emphasis should be on speed, with accuracy secondary. In the learning of skills which require both speed and accuracy, the initial emphasis should be on both.

Immediate knowledge of results, providing feedback and reinforcement, is important in helping a student to improve a skill performance. Effective practice is also important and should be conducted under conditions as close as possible to those under which the skill is to be performed. The learning of most psychomotor skills is more rapid when practice sessions are well spaced. In the case of a relatively simple skill, it is usually advantageous to practice the whole skill at once. In the case of a more complex skill, it is usually advantageous to divide the total performance into separate skills or components, each of which may be practiced by itself.

Affective learning, another important category of learning outcomes, is the acquisition of valuative meanings for ideas, objects, persons, or events. Affective learnings are manifested in tastes, preferences, attitudes, and values.

An *attitude* is a predisposition to react favorably or unfavorably toward an idea, object, person, event, or situation. The object toward which one is thus predisposed is called an *attitude object*. Information concerning a person's attitudes may be gained by making inferences from his behavior, but an attitude scale is more frequently used to sample a person's attitudes on a specific subject or topic.

Attitudes are learned (1) through the integration of numerous specific responses, (2) through differentiations made in an original matrix of attitudes, (3) through dramatic experience or trauma, and (4) through imitation and identification. The acquisition of ready-made attitudes through identification with parents, teachers, or peers contributes to the satisfaction of one's needs to be loved, to belong, to play roles, and to deal competently with the world. Research shows that young children learn prejudices by adopting adult values and behavior patterns and by conforming to adult expectations. An individual resolves conflicts in attitudes by maintaining those attitudes that are most important to him or by modifying his attitudes so as to make them compatible with each other. This second method is an illustration of Festinger's theory of *cognitive dissonance*.

Studies show that attitudes toward a minority group are determined not by contact with the group but by contact with the prevalent attitudes toward the group. Stereotyping and expressions of hostility toward minority groups are more frequent among older children than among younger children. One study revealed a general trend in teenage attitudes toward conformity and a kind of passive anti-intellectualism. College experience appears to produce a homogeneity of values among college students. The attitudes and values of college students are modified, if modified at all, not in formal classroom experiences, but in personally significant experiences with unusual professors or peers.

A *value* is a preference for something cherished or desired. A value is linked to one's satisfaction of needs, his realization of goals and purposes, and the maintenance and enhancement of his self-concept. The values a teacher holds influence his relationships with his students and his expectations of his students. The value patterns of students who receive high marks tend to be closely related to the value patterns considered ideal by the teachers who give the marks. A teacher who is emotionally accepted by his students may help those students to clarify their purposes, goals, attitudes, and beliefs.

Laboratory studies show that strong value orientations tend to persist even if changes occur in the situation from which they originated. Communication patterns, attitudes, perceptions, task orientations, and outcomes evoked by a given process tend to elicit the same process that evoked them.

Study Questions

1. You have been observing students performing a variety of psychomotor skills: writing a theme, playing the piano, and driving a golf ball. How would you ascertain in each case the degree to which a student's errors in performing are due to correctible factors, such as use of cues or feedback,

and the degree to which his errors are due to limitations of inherited body structure and coordination?

2. A student learning a psychomotor skill often becomes very dependent on the instructor for information, as to, for instance, what he should do to correct his mistakes. As an instructor, what steps would you take in trying to lessen the dependence of the student upon you?

3. Teachers frequently exhort students to make a greater effort with the familiar slogan, "Practice makes perfect." Comment on the validity and usefulness of this slogan as it pertains to the learning of a psychomotor skill.

4. What reasons can you suggest to account for the greater emphasis which schools appear to place on cognitive learning as compared to affective learning of attitudes and values? What dangers do you see in this trend?

5. Attitudes contributing to prejudice and discrimination are reflected in the racial conflicts and social unrest of the contemporary world. For the grade level and subject you expect to teach, what learning experiences would you plan that might encourage students to examine the attitudes they hold toward other peoples, cultures, religions, and political systems?

6. Values are a unique and deeply personal kind of learning. What responsibilities have parents for teaching children values? What responsibilities has the school? Discuss.

Suggested Readings

Association for Childhood Education, International. *Feelings and Learning.* Washington, D.C.: Association for Childhood Education, Inc., 1965. Contains photographs documenting the key experiences in the affective life of the young child and papers by Anna Freud, Lois Murphy, and others discussing the various aspects of the young child's emotional development and its relation to learning.

Bryant J. Cratty. *Movement Behavior and Motor Learning.* Philadelphia: Lea and Febiger, 1964. Presents fundamental concepts and principles of human movement and motor performance. Chapter 12 examines the problem of retention, whole versus part learning, and mass versus distributed practice. Chapter 13 discusses strategies teachers may employ to guide psychomotor learning.

Leon Festinger. *A Theory of Cognitive Dissonance.* Stanford, California: Stanford University Press, 1962. Proposes and discusses a theory of cognitive dissonance. Hypothesizes that the individual experiencing dissonance is motivated to reduce dissonance and achieve consonance and to avoid situations which might increase dissonance.

Helen G. Trager and Marian Radke Yarrow. *They Learn What They Live.* New York: Harper & Row, 1952. Reports a study of prejudice in young children. In general, a striking similarity was found between the child's values and the values of the adult social environment in which the child lives and learns.

facilitating development
and learning

17

organizing the classroom for learning

We must seek a different kind of education, an education that takes persons into account, that seeks, fosters, and builds on the universal human quest.

≡   HERBERT A. THELEN

In spite of man's long experience with the act of teaching and in spite of the considerable study given to teaching in recent years, we still do not have a clear understanding of what good teaching is or how to foster it. There appear to be as many approaches to effective teaching as there are good teachers. This lack of a precise definition of good teaching has caused some educators to deemphasize the teaching aspect and to emphasize the learner and the learning aspects of the teaching-learning activity. These educators contend that the important thing is not what the teacher does but what happens to the learner. A somewhat extreme statement of this view is made by Rogers:

> My experience has been that I cannot teach another person how to teach. . . . I have come to feel that the only learning which significantly influences behavior is self-discovered, self appropriated learning. Such self-discovered learning, truth that has been personally appropriated and assimilated in experience, cannot be directly communicated

to another. . . . Such experience would imply that we would do away with teaching. People would get together if they wished to learn.[1]

Many will sympathize with Rogers' concern for the learner. Nevertheless, it is clear that much of what students learn is greatly influenced by what teachers do in their efforts to foster learning: Learning in school is an interpersonal experience.

Teaching, as it is presently conceived, is not simply a matter of applying principles, procedures, or formulae to learning situations or problems. Teaching is still much more of an art than a science or technology. Teachers, however, as well as artists, utilize scientifically validated generalizations in the proper performance of their skills.

The milieu in which teaching takes place is continuously changing and is influenced by a great many variables, both known and unknown. In such a fluid and complex situation, the teacher must deal with many alternatives. He begins with a plan, but he cannot possibly foresee the modifications and redirections that may be required by the exigencies of the teaching situation. Hence, the tentative, spontaneous, and intuitive responses that teachers make in guiding learning are more like those of an artist than those of a technician. For teaching, "there is no complete catalog of recipes to combine certain ingredients under certain conditions to obtain certain effects. If there were, teaching would be a technology, and we could train teachers to apply purely technical skills to prearranged objectives."[2]

It would seem, then, that at the present time we cannot hope to provide a prescription detailing what a teacher should do to effect learning in students. On the other hand, fairly good agreement has been reached among educators on some of the criteria of good teaching and some of the characteristic flaws of poor teaching. Moreover, the increasing body of research into teaching methods, procedures, roles, and behavior contributes to our increased understanding of these complex activities and tasks. While we cannot specify precisely the effects of certain particular teaching methods, we can predict that certain methods are *more likely* to lead to certain outcomes than to certain other outcomes.

Teaching is here defined as *any interpersonal influence aimed at changing the ways in which persons can or will behave.*[3] This admittedly broad definition makes teachers of parents, ministers, peer-group members, youth leaders, psychotherapists, and friends. In this book, however, we are concerned only with the activities of the assigned teacher in the classroom.

[1] Carl R. Rogers, *On Becoming a Person* (Boston: Houghton Mifflin Co., 1961), pp. 276–277.

[2] Thomas E. Clayton, *Teaching and Learning* (Englewood Cliffs, New Jersey: Prentice-Hall, 1965), p. 6.

[3] N. L. Gage, "Paradigm for Research on Teaching," in N. L. Gage, *Handbook of Research on Teaching* (Chicago: Rand McNally and Co., 1963), p. 96.

Interpersonal Dynamics in the Classroom

In Chapter 3, we noted that human behavior has direction and purpose. Behavior is the organism's response to some inner disequilibrium, tension or need—a state of arousal we have called motivation. When motivated, the individual responds to need by directing energy toward a goal associated with satisfaction of the need. Of critical importance for improving individual and group performance in the teaching-learning situation is an analysis and understanding of the motivations of teacher and pupils.

A concept educators have found useful in analyzing the motivational dynamics of human behavior is the concept of needs. "Needs describe the relatively permanent tendencies in persons to be motivated in specific ways, and we infer them from the commonalities among the goals that the person appears to be seeking."[4] In analyzing any given teaching-learning situation, we focus upon the psychological needs, the deficiency or tension states which point to specific goals of teacher and pupils.

Pupil Needs

If a student is to utilize fully his capacities for learning, his *physiological needs* must be satisfied. A student who is hungry, thirsty, ill, fatigued, lacking in energy, or physically handicapped is less ready and able to learn than is a student whose physical needs have in large measure been satisfied. The school—through its health, safety, and physical education programs, and through teachers who provide children with opportunities to satisfy their unmet physical needs—shares responsibility with the home and community in this important area of development.

Of greater importance for most persons is the satisfaction of *psychological needs*. Foremost among these are the needs for *affection, belonging,* and *approval*. To win affection, belonging, and approval, the student must in some measure fulfill the expectations of his home, school, peers, and community. Failure to obey his parents or to conform to the standards of the peer group may result in a loss of affection, belonging, and approval.

Formal learning situations at school may also serve to promote or deny the satisfaction of a student's psychological needs. The affection and approval of the teacher, and often of parents and peers as well, are contingent upon the student's meeting successfully the expectations posed by the learning situation. Frequently, more potential threat, anxiety, and uncertainty is associated with learning situations than with situations outside of school. Since much of learning deals with the new, the different, and perhaps the difficult and unknown, there is a greater probability of error or failure in the

---

[4] Frederick J. McDonald, *Educational Psychology,* 2nd ed. (Belmont, California: Wadsworth Publishing Co., 1965), p. 114.

student's response in the classroom than in most situations outside the classroom. Any procedure for organizing the classroom for learning, therefore, should seek to provide students with unconditional emotional support. This support will make it easier for students to take the risks involved in the exploratory, tentative, intuitive, and divergent responses that are so vital to creativity and learning.

Another important set of human needs relates to the individual's ability to cope with his world. The individual satisfies these needs—needs for *achievement, competence, understanding, independence,* and *self-esteem*—by acquiring knowledge, skills, and interests; realizing goals and aspirations; and developing attitudes, values, and an adequate self-concept. When these fundamental needs are gratified, an individual may become one of those rare persons able to fulfill his highest need, the need for what Maslow[5] calls *self-actualization.*

Reciprocal Need Satisfactions

Teachers are motivated toward satisfying many of the same needs as students. We have already noted that the teacher's behavior, the kinds of relationships he establishes with students, and the ways he organizes the classroom serve to promote or deny the need satisfactions of his students. In addition, through the roles they play in the teaching-learning experience, teachers seek to satisfy their own needs for affection, belongingness, achievement, and self-esteem.

Some teachers satisfy their own need for affection in part through their relationships with pupils. The teacher's valuing responses toward pupils not only promote the gratification of students' affection and dependency needs but also elicit accepting and valuing responses from pupils toward the teacher, responses that contribute to the teacher's feeling of security. On the other hand, less secure teachers may be unable to maintain warm, affectionate relationships with students. Indeed, as we noted earlier, they may see such relationships as inappropriate or inconsistent with what they perceive to be the teacher's role. Some of these teachers may seek to gratify their own needs for self-esteem and at the same time gain a measure of "respect" in lieu of affection from pupils through controlling, dominative, punitive, and manipulative behavior. Such behavior thwarts the satisfactions of students' needs for affection and affiliation; as a result, the students may become hostile, unresponsive, and aggressive. Neither the pupils' nor the teacher's needs are satisfied in such a classroom environment.

The reciprocal relationship between teacher and pupil behavior and the effects of this on the need satisfactions of each are shown in a study by Anderson.[6] Anderson identified two contrasting types of teacher control,

[5] A. H. Maslow, *Motivation and Personality* (New York: Harper & Row, 1954).

[6] H. H. Anderson, "Domination and Socially Integrative Behavior," in R. G. Barker, J. S. Kounin, and H. F. Wright, *Child Behavior and Development* (New York: McGraw-Hill Book Co., 1943), pp. 459–483.

which he labeled "dominative" and "socially integrative" behavior. The teacher was considered dominative when the rigidity of his responses stifled differences in others, reduced the interplay of individual differences, and hence made understanding more difficult. The "dominating" teacher sets the goals of the learning experience and directs the activities of pupils toward reaching these goals. The "socially integrative" teacher is generally spontaneous and flexible, attempts to bring out differences in others and to find common purposes among these differences, and encourages self-direction of pupils toward achievement of goals. The principal findings of this study indicate that the teacher's classroom personality and pattern of behavior influence the behavior of the children under him. Kindergarten and primary grade teachers who used dominative techniques with children produced aggressive and antagonistic behavior in the children. Children expressed their aggression and antagonism not only toward the teacher but also toward peers, and a vicious circle of dominative behavior was created. In contrast, teachers who used socially integrative behaviors facilitated the adoption of integrative, cooperative, and self-directive behaviors by children. Thus, tendencies toward the dominative and uncooperative behavior so inimical to the need satisfactions of both teacher and pupils were minimized.

Davis[7] also points to the reciprocal relationship between teacher and pupil behavior. According to Davis, a system of circular reinforcement is established when the student conforms to the teacher's expectations. When he completes assignments, makes satisfactory academic progress, and maintains proper deportment, he is rewarded by praise and status privileges, his anxiety is reduced, and he repeats the rewarded behavior. In time, the teacher's smile and praises become secondary reinforcers of the approved behavior; they become goals in themselves. At the same time, the student's successful learning reinforces the teacher in continuing his acts of praise and reward. The teacher is rewarded by the behavior of good students because their scholastic performance and good deportment are evidence that he is a proficient teacher, and because through the children he is able to gain the approval of the parents. Davis emphasizes that this "circular reinforcement" is generally enjoyed only by upper-middle-class children and their teachers, since the social and learning behavior of the lower-class child less frequently earns him the praise and approval of the middle-class teacher.

The Learning Experience

The following description of the learning experience, based upon generalizations that have emerged from educational method and to a lesser extent from learning theory, presents characteristics and qualities which many educators hope or expect to see exemplified in classroom learning. Not all of

---

[7] Allison Davis and John Dollard, *Children of Bondage* (Washington: American Council on Education, 1940), pp. 279–290.

the characteristics are found in every learning experience, and some educators may hold somewhat different views of classroom learning. The description, then, is general and somewhat idealized but substantially accurate.

1. *Learning occurs when there is a change in the learner as the result of practice, training, or experience.* This is an oft-quoted definition of learning which points to the teacher's major goal—to bring about change in the learner. Implicit in this definition is the concept of learning as an active process. The learner must respond, either overtly or covertly, in exploring, relating, testing, and refining the concepts, skills, and feelings that emerge from his experience. Moreover, learning is an active response of the total organism—not just the brain, hands, or body. The learner therefore must be seen as an organized, unified whole. Learning must also be organized in relation to clearly defined objectives—objectives that reflect the needs of students as well as the needs of society. Learning experiences should provide for the uniqueness of each learner and allow him to be active in a variety of ways. Though pupils do learn by listening passively to a lecture or viewing a film, more active responses—discussing, searching, exploring, testing, evaluating, and synthesizing—bring out learning of greater depth and breadth.

2. *Learning is most likely to occur when pupils are ready and able to engage in activities and experiences that are relevant to that particular learning.* Chapter 14 described several dimensions of readiness—maturity, intelligence, intellectual development, and experience—and discussed the influence of each dimension on the learning process. When the learner's readiness is not assessed and taken into consideration, neither practice nor the efforts of the teacher are likely to be effectual. In addition to the dimensions of readiness already mentioned, an optimal learning experience would also be attuned to the pupil's psychological readiness for learning. Learning tends to take place more readily if the pupil perceives learning activities as useful and important to him. This implies that the teacher should know a great deal about individual pupils and should continuously explore with his pupils the relevance for their own lives of what they are learning.

3. *Objectives and goals define the behavioral changes to be sought and direct the activities of teacher and pupils in the learning experience.* Objectives and goals may be implicit or explicit. Although the teacher's objectives and goals frequently dominate classroom learning, the learner is likely to be more actively involved and his learning more significant if he shares in selecting and setting the goals of learning, in planning ways to achieve them, and in measuring his own progress toward them. Before he can share the goal-setting and plan-learning experiences cooperatively with students, the teacher may have to modify his perceptions of his own role and of his students' capacities for responsible self-direction. He must perceive that students need not depend on the teacher in order to learn, that talents and resources lie not only with the teacher but with the total group, and that students can, if given the chance, organize and pursue meaningful learning activities responsibly and independently. In organizing the classroom for learning, the

teacher should check periodically to make certain that pupils' choices and decisions are playing a part in goal setting, planning, and evaluation.

4. *The motivations of the learner influence his responses to learning situations and the kinds and qualities of behavior change that emerge from these situations.* The individual's motivations relate to the satisfaction or dissatisfaction of specific needs. For certain tasks, high motivation may be less effective than a moderate level of drive. Strong motivation, for example, can improve performance of relatively simple tasks involving few cues, but is likely to reduce lower performance of more complex tasks involving many cues. As noted earlier, motivation that arouses anxiety tends to distract the learner and to result in undesirable learning.

The emphasis that schools place on grades, examinations, and other rewards (incentives characteristic of extrinsic motivation) is lamented by many who feel that learning that increases one's capabilities and competence is its own reward (incentives characteristic of intrinsic motivation). Both intrinsic and extrinsic motives, however, influence all human behavior. Organizing the classroom so as to maximize intrinsic and minimize extrinsic motives in learning is seen by many as one of the most important tasks of the teacher.

5. *Self factors play a decisive role in learning.* The individual behaves according to the way he perceives himself and his world. Especially important in influencing his responses to the learning situation is his self-concept as a learner. Successful students reveal in their behavior the self-images "I am able to learn" and "I like school."

The learning experience is greatly influenced by the level of aspiration set by the learner in response to his self-concept. Pupils need help and practice in setting goals for themselves. By providing adequate feedback and evaluation, a teacher may help students to modify their aspirations, so that the goals are neither so low as to elicit little effort nor so high as to invite failure. In considering the many self factors that influence the learning experience, the sensitive teacher will be especially responsive to individual differences among learners and to the personal history of each learner.

6. *Knowledge of success promotes learning.* It has frequently been stated that behavior is purposeful. We have noted that the learner's responses in learning situations appear to relate to the satisfactions of his needs. Logic and empirical evidence suggest that the coping, striving, problem-solving behaviors characteristic of learning do not persist indefinitely in the absence of feedback. Knowledge of results, therefore, plays a significant role in all learning theories.

Learning is effective when the learner is able to see and to analyze the results of his own performance and to ascertain progress in the learning task. Thus, in organizing a classroom for learning, the teacher may aid the learner by describing and demonstrating good performance and by informing the learner of his mistakes, his degree of improvement, or his successful performance. It is especially important that the slow or retarded learner be made aware that he is able to spell correctly or to recognize two more words today than he was able to recognize yesterday.

7. *Failure may be used to build toward success in learning, but too many failures tend to discourage and to block learning.* Most of us have had some experience with intense or repeated failure and are well aware of the effects of repeated failure in diminishing motivation and level of performance. In pointing to the adverse effects of too much failure, we are not suggesting that children be protected from any experience of failure whatsoever. Such a situation would be unrealistic and would deny children the opportunity to learn from failure. Children need help and experience in analyzing their failures—in seeing what their mistakes are, why they are making them, and how they might avoid them in the future. Therefore, the social-emotional climate of the classroom should permit and encourage students to risk possible failure—although in a culture and an age that puts a high premium on getting the right answer, such a climate may not be easy to establish.

8. *Some learnings are enhanced through first-hand, concrete experiences, while others may be achieved as effectively through vicarious experiences.* Children learn most easily and readily those things that relate to their own concrete experiences and thus have personal meaning and significance for them: a visit to city hall, talks with a city official about problems of government, opportunities to make their own forecasts from weather maps and data from a classroom weather station. To depend on first-hand or concrete experience at all times, however, would be foolish or impossible. The accumulated wisdom of a culture is communicated to succeeding generations through established customs and traditions and through literature and art forms. Students are able to identify themselves with people, events, and ideas beyond face-to-face contacts, and eventually to show concern for problems larger than those they can solve at first hand, problems they can learn about only through second- and third-hand sources, such as books and mass media.

9. *Learning is enhanced when several rather than few sensory media are employed.* One acquires meanings from experience through each of the senses: sight, hearing, smell, taste, and touch. However, the great stress that is placed in school upon verbal, symbolic, and cognitive learning has resulted in a disproportionately high reliance on visual and auditory media. Children also need opportunities to experience and to learn through touching, tasting, and smelling.

Persons vary in their sensitivity to various kinds of sensory stimuli. Some children are tactually oriented; others are kinesthetically or spatially oriented. An individual student's preferred mode of experiencing is often revealed in his learning behavior. Some students may learn how a radio works by reading about it, others by seeing a film, others through learning to diagram circuits. Thus, many modes of experiencing and responding should be made available to students in their learning.

10. *Learning is facilitated when students acquire increased self-understanding and self-direction.* This generalization again emphasizes the very considerable contributions that pupils themselves make to their own learning. One of the purposes of education is to help pupils become independent, self-directive individuals, fully able to cope effectively with the life problems they encounter. Effective self-direction depends on a measure of self-understanding. Self-understanding is promoted in a climate of acceptance, wherein the individual is encouraged to accept himself and his feelings, to examine the meanings of his experience, to evaluate objectively and realistically his own behavior, and to plan courses of action that promote growth and self-enhancement.

A Model of Teacher Behavior

The model of teacher behavior presented here was proposed by Macdonald and Zaret[8] for studying the relative flexibility or rigidity of teacher behavior in verbal interactions with learners. Macdonald and Zaret use the terms "openness" and "closedness" to designate the end points of a continuum of teacher expectations and classroom behavior. The "open" teacher is one who exhibits maximum awareness and acceptance of the learner and his capabilities, needs, and aspirations. The "closed" teacher is characterized by perceptual rigidity, which limits his awareness and acceptance of the learner and the learner's capabilities, needs, and aspirations. Macdonald and Zaret hypothesize that the "open" teacher is more likely to make decisions that will encourage the student to explore and to consider a variety of responses in promoting his own development and learning.

Macdonald and Zaret's model of teacher behavior is shown in Figure 17.1. The *evaluation* or information-processing phase of that model encompasses the psychological, cognitive, and affective processes discussed in earlier chapters. Factors in the evaluation phase are the teacher's motivations, perceptions, beliefs, goals, attitudes, values, and self-concept. The teacher who is "open" perceives fewer conflicts and discrepancies between his observations of students and his expectations of what students should be like. He is more likely to accept students as they are, rather than to respond to them in terms of preconceived notions. The fewer discrepancies between his perceptions and his expectations mean that the "open" teacher is less threatened, and hence has less need to distort what he perceives. The teacher whose psychological-cognitive-affective system is more "closed" experiences many more conflicts and discrepancies between his perceptions and his expectations of students and the learning situation. He adjusts to the increase in threat produced by these discrepancies by distorting what he perceives so

8 James B. Macdonald and Esther Zaret, "Report of a Study of Openness in Classroom Interaction," Milwaukee, Wisconsin: College of Education, University of Wisconsin-Milwaukee, 1967). Mimeographed. Figure 17.1 is reproduced from this work by permission.

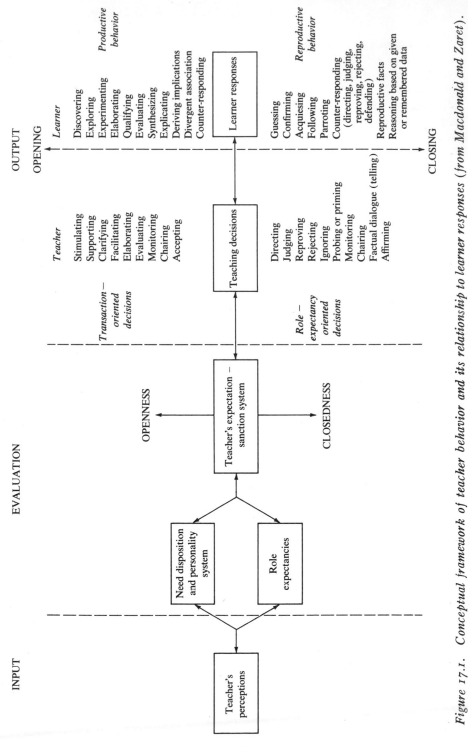

Figure 17.1. Conceptual framework of teacher behavior and its relationship to learner responses (from Macdonald and Zaret).

that it is more consistent with his expectations and beliefs about students and their learning.

The "open" or "closed" quality of a teacher's expectations and beliefs is reflected in his teaching output, his decisions and behaviors affecting students. "Open" teacher behaviors and decisions are *transaction oriented*—that is, they function to facilitate and to expand learning. They encourage students to respond with "open," *productive behavior* of their own, behavior that is manifested in efforts to explore, to extend, and to elaborate the concepts and skills acquired in the classroom. The "closed" teacher's behaviors and decisions, on the other hand, are *role-expectancy oriented*—that is, they function to direct, to judge, or to reprove in eliciting specific, prescribed, conforming, *reproductive behavior* from students (acquiescing, following, parroting what has been given them by teacher or textbook).

Organizing for Learning

We shall here examine studies of the teacher's role in (1) establishing a climate favorable for learning, (2) influencing behavior change, and (3) encouraging self-directive learning.

Establishing a Favorable Climate

There is some disagreement among educators regarding the kind of classroom atmosphere that is most conducive to learning. Some educators maintain that optimal learning will not occur if the pupil feels so safe and contented that he is not stimulated or challenged to seek new experiences and to change. This book has suggested, however, that optimal pupil development and learning will occur in social-emotional climates in which the pupil feels valued and accepted and has a sense of belonging.

One line of evidence favoring the establishment of a relatively non-threatening, psychologically safe climate for learning is to be found in the studies of anxiety and learning. The results of these studies are not unequivocal, but they do suggest that high anxiety is associated with low achievement. Among elementary school children, high-anxiety subjects make significantly more errors in a complex learning task than do low-anxiety subjects.[9] Anxiety is negatively correlated with intelligence and school achievement; that is, in general, children who register high anxiety tend to score lower on IQ and achievement tests.[10]

Further evidence of the relationship between climate and learning is

[9] A. Castaneda, B. McCandless, and D. Palermo, "The Relationship of Anxiety in Children to Performance in a Complex Learning Task," *Child Development,* 27 (1956), 333–337.
[10] S. B. Sarason, K. S. Davidson, F. F. Lighthall, R. R. Waite, and B. K. Ruebush, *Anxiety in Elementary School Children* (New York: John Wiley, 1960).

found in a classic study by Lewin, Lippitt, and White,[11] who investigated the effects of differing social climates and leadership roles on individual and group behavior. Four groups of eleven-year-old boys (with five boys in each group) were organized into clubs whose major activity was making papier-mâché masks and various club insignias. Each club met for six-week periods under a leader who employed either a democratic, an autocratic, or a laissez-faire leadership style. During successive six-week periods, each club had a different leader and each leadership style was carried out by each leader with different groups. The chief characteristics of each leadership style are described in Table 17.1.[12] Descriptions of group and individual behavior and interviews with children, parents, and teachers were analyzed to ascertain the effects of these varying leadership styles on the work and interpersonal behaviors of boys in each group.

A major finding of this study was that different styles of leadership produce differences in social climate and differing group and individual behavior. Under authoritarian leadership the boys became frustrated. They reacted with greater hostility, aggression, and a nearly unanimous disliking of their autocratic leader. More scapegoats emerged in authoritarian groups, and aggression increased when the autocratic leader left the room. Under democratic leadership, in contrast, the boys were responsive, spontaneous, friendly to each other, and more generous in their praise of each other's work. They continued working when the leader left the room and showed higher levels of frustration tolerance and less aggression and hostility.

An important implication of this study is that the teacher or leader is the single most significant variable influencing the social-emotional climate of the group or classroom. Leadership styles, not individual leaders themselves, are the primary factors to which children react. This clear demonstration of the influence of the leader on group life and the accomplishments and interpersonal relationships of the group has important consequences for education. As McDonald[13] has cautioned, however, we should not overgeneralize the results of this study. The terms *democracy* and *autocracy* mean different things to different people, and different children may give quite different interpretations to a teacher's behavior.

Lewin, Lippitt, and White's study helped to stimulate a series of further investigations of social-emotional climate. Withall[14] developed a "Climate Index," which was used to assess the social-emotional climate in the classroom by categorizing teacher statements contained in typescripts made from recordings of class sessions. The Climate Index contained six qualitative categories and one neutral category arranged on a continuum from

[11] K. Lewin, R. L. Lippitt, and R. K. White, "Patterns of Aggressive Behavior in Experimentally Created 'Social Climates,' " *Journal of Social Psychology*, 10 (1939), 271–299.

[12] From Lewin, Lippitt and White, "The 'Social Climates' of Children's Groups," in Roger G. Baker, Jacob S. Kounin, and Herbert F. Wright, *Child Behavior and Development* (New York: McGraw-Hill, 1943), p. 487. Used by permission.

[13] McDonald, p. 523.

[14] John G. Withall, "The Development of a Technique for the Measurement of Social-Emotional Climate in Classrooms," *Journal of Experimental Education*, 17 (1949), 347–361.

Table 17.1.   Leadership styles (from Lewin, Lippitt, and White).

AUTHORITARIAN	DEMOCRATIC	LAISSEZ-FAIRE
1. All determination of policy by the leader.	1. All policies a matter of group discussion and decision, encouraged and assisted by the leader.	1. Complete freedom for group or individual decision, with a minimum of leader participation.
2. Techniques and activity steps dictated by the authority, one at a time, so that future steps are always uncertain to a large degree.	2. Activity perspective gained during discussion period. General steps to group goal sketched, and where technical advice is needed the leader suggests two or more alternative procedures from which choice can be made.	2. Various materials supplied by the leader, who makes it clear that he will supply information when asked. He takes no other part in work discussion.
3. The leader usually dictates the particular work task and work companion of each member.	3. The members are free to work with whomever they choose, and the division of tasks is left up to the group.	3. Complete non-participation of the leader in determining tasks and companions.
4. The leader tends to be "personal" in his praise and criticism of the work of each member, but remains aloof from active group participation except when demonstrating.	4. The leader is "objective" or "fact-minded" in his praise and criticism, and he tries to be a regular group member in spirit without doing too much of the work.	4. Infrequent spontaneous comments on member activities unless questioned, and no attempt to appraise or regulate the course of events.

learner-supportive (if a high proportion of the teacher's statements are categorized as reassuring, clarifying, or problem-structuring) to *teacher-supportive* (if a high proportion of the teacher's statements are categorized as directing, reproving, or defending).

Withall's Index provided a reliable, valid measure of group climate and has been used by other researchers to study the effects of climate on the outcomes of different group contexts. Flanders,[15] in analyzing psychological and physiological data from a small group of students, found that demand-

[15] Ned A. Flanders, " Personal-Social Anxiety as a Function in Experimental Learning Situations," *Journal of Educational Research,* 45 (1951), 100–110.

ing, directive, and deprecating teacher behavior results in withdrawal, apathy toward achievement, aggressiveness, and hostility on the part of the pupils. On the other hand, problem-oriented, analytical, and learner-centered teacher behavior produces in students less interpersonal anxiety, more problem-solving behavior, and greater emotional integration.

Perkins,[16] in a study of in-service teacher-child study groups, also concluded that that climate under which learning occurs is a major factor influencing the quantity and quality of group learning. In group discussions, teachers in learner-centered (learner-supportive) groups revealed greater knowledge of child-development concepts, revealed warmer attitudes toward children, supported more frequently their interpretations of child behavior with facts or principles, and revealed more evidence of insight and sound reasoning than did teachers in leader-centered (teacher-supportive) groups.

Bush,[17] in a study of pupil-teacher relationships among 27 teachers and 650 students, found in general that both teachers and pupils express in ratings of each other a positive feeling toward each other. Pupils, on the whole, were more positive than were teachers, with almost 50 percent of the pupils giving their teachers the highest possible rating. Bush concludes on the basis of this finding that a teacher need not have a strong liking for his pupils, as educators have previously assumed. He suggests instead that the personal liking of a pupil for his teacher is a more powerful factor in bringing about an effective learning relationship. Bush also found that teachers who know most about their pupils and are aware of and sympathize with their individual needs and interests generally have effective relationships with a larger number of pupils than do the teachers whose major concern is knowledge of subject matter.

In a recent study, Schmuck[18] assessed classroom climate by analyzing sociometric structure. He studied the relationships between two kinds of group structure, diffuse and bimodal, and group cohesiveness. A *diffuse* peer-group structure is one in which almost every pupil is chosen as most liked or least liked by some other pupil. Schmuck identified this type of group structure with a more positive social climate. A *bimodal* group structure is one in which most pupils in the class choose a small number of pupils in the class as most liked and another small number as least liked. *Group cohesiveness* is evidenced by high scores on measures of positive attitudes toward peers, toward school in general, and toward self. Schmuck found that peer groups with diffuse structures are significantly more cohesive than groups with bimodal structures—that is, they express more positive attitudes toward classroom peers, school life, and themselves as pupils. They also share a more supportive perception of the teacher and of academic work. Schmuck also

[16] Hugh V. Perkins, "The Effects of Climate and Curriculum on Group Learning," *Journal of Educational Research*, 44 (December 1950), 269–286.

[17] Robert N. Bush, *The Teacher-Pupil Relationship* (Englewood Cliffs, New Jersey: Prentice-Hall, 1954), pp. 185–202.

[18] Richard Schmuck, "Some Aspects of Classroom Social Climate," *Psychology in the Schools*, 3 (January 1966), 59–65.

found that teachers in more positive social climates (more diffuse group structures) more frequently view teaching as facilitating both the academic learning and the personality growth and development of pupils.

The evidence presented in this section underscores the importance of the teacher's role and behavior in establishing a social-emotional climate conducive to learning. Climates that induce high anxiety generally produce lower academic performance. Studies of classroom groups reveal that the teacher is the most important variable in determining the climate of a learning situation. Positive, learner-centered climates are associated with greater productivity, increased learning, and warmer, more positive attitudes than are less positive, teacher-centered climates.

Teacher Influence and Behavior Change

Insights into the concept of teacher influence are provided by Hughes,[19] who developed a code for categorizing teachers' classroom behavior from an analysis of trained observers' written records of 41 elementary school teachers. This code consists of seven teacher-function categories relating to the concepts of teacher power (setting and applying standards and distributing rewards and punishment) and teacher responsiveness (accepting or rejecting what the student has said, approving or reproving the student). The categories are (1) control, (2) imposition, (3) facilitation, (4) content development, (5) personal response, (6) negative affectivity, and (7) positive affectivity. Under each of the seven teacher-function categories are listed specific teacher behaviors and roles. Hughes categorized the behavior of the teachers of her sample as controlling when the teachers sought to structure, to regulate, to set standards, or to judge. Support for the concept of teacher power is lent by Hughes' finding that nearly 50 percent of all teachers' behaviors in her sample were controlling.

In another major study, Flanders[20] developed an observation procedure to study how the spontaneous behavior of a teacher affects learning in the classroom. Using this procedure, a classroom observer classifies verbal statements into one of ten categories (see Table 17.2[21]). Seven categories apply to teacher statements, two to student statements, and one to silence or confusion. This system—the classifying of verbal behavior during a particular period of classroom activity—is called *interaction analysis*.[22] The procedure

[19] Marie M. Hughes, *Development of the Means for the Assessment of the Quality of Teaching in Elementary Schools,* Cooperative Research Project No. 353 (Washington, D.C.: U.S. Department of Health, Education and Welfare, Office of Education, 1960).

[20] Ned A. Flanders, *Teacher Influence, Pupil Attitudes, and Achievement,* Report of Cooperative Research Project No. 397 (Washington, D.C.: U.S. Department of Health, Education and Welfare, Office of Education, 1960).

[21] From Ned A. Flanders, "Interaction Analysis in the Classroom. A Manual for Observers" (Minneapolis, Minnesota: College of Education, University of Minnesota, 1959). Mimeographed. Used by permission.

[22] For a further explanation of interaction analysis procedure see Edmund J. Amidon and Peggy Amidon, *Interaction Analysis Training Kit—Level 1* (Minneapolis: Association for Productive Teaching, 1967).

Table 17.2. *Categories for interaction analysis (from Flanders).*

Teacher talk

1.* *Accepts feeling:* accepts and clarifies the feeling tone of the students in a nonthreatening manner. Feelings may be positive or negative. Predicting or recalling feelings included.

2. *Praises or encourages:* praises or encourages student action or behavior. Jokes that release tension, not at the expense of another individual, nodding head or saying "um hm?" or "go on" are included.

Indirect influence

3. *Accepts or uses ideas of student:* clarifying, building, or developing ideas suggested by a student. As teacher brings more of his own ideas into play, shift to category five.

4. *Asks questions:* asking a question about content or procedure with the intent that a student answer.

5. *Lecturing:* giving facts or opinions about content or procedure; expressing his own ideas, asking rhetorical questions.

6. *Giving directions:* directions, commands, or orders with which a student is expected to comply.

Direct influence

7. *Criticizing or justifying authority:* statements intended to change student behavior from nonacceptable to acceptable pattern; bawling someone out; stating why the teacher is doing what he is doing; extreme self-reference.

Student talk

8. *Response:* talk by students in response to teacher. Teacher initiates the contact or solicits student statement.

9. *Initiation:* talk by students which they initiate. If "calling on" student is only to indicate who may talk next, observer must decide whether student wanted to talk. If he did, use this category.

---

10. *Silence or confusion:* pauses, short periods of silence and periods of confusion in which communication cannot be understood by the observer.

---

* There is *no* scale implied by these numbers. Each number is classificatory; it designates a particular kind of communication event. To write these numbers down during observation is to enumerate, not to judge a position on a scale.

produces a series of numbers representing a sequence of teacher-student interactions. For example, in the categorization sequence 4–8, 3–5, the teacher asks a question, the student answers the teacher's question, and the teacher builds on the student's answer and then adds further facts or opinions of his own. Each pair of categorizations (4–8, 8–3, 3–5) is tallied on a cell matrix. By means of this matrix, statements that a teacher makes as an immediate response to students may be isolated and compared with statements that trigger student participation.

One of the outcomes of Flanders' research is "the rule of two thirds," which says that, generally, about two thirds of classroom time is spent in talking; that the chances are two out of three that the person talking is the teacher; and that the teacher spends two thirds of his "talking" time expressing facts or his own opinions, giving directions, or criticizing students. Flanders also found, however, that in classrooms where there is greater freedom for intellectual curiosity, more expression of ideas, more positive feelings, and higher achievement, the rule of two thirds becomes the rule of one half; in such classrooms, the teacher spends more time asking questions, clarifying, praising, encouraging, and developing student ideas and opinions.

Of particular interest in Flanders' research is his investigation of the ratio of a teacher's *indirect influence* (statements in categories 1–4 of Table 17.2) to his *direct influence* (statements in categories 5–7), which Flanders refers to as the *I/D ratio*. Although indirect patterns were found, on the whole, to stimulate more achievement regardless of student ability, direct teacher influence was found to increase learning when the student perceived clearly and accepted the learning goal.

Another variable used by Flanders to differentiate superior from less superior patterns of teacher influence was *teacher flexibility,* the teacher's tendency or ability to use a different pattern of influence in different phases of the instructional process. In superior classrooms, marked by greater teacher flexibility, pupils seem to depend less upon the teacher and to concentrate more energy on the learning task and less energy on finding out how to please the teacher.[23]

Another type of teacher influence is the linguistic patterns of classroom discussion. Bellack and Davitz[24] studied these patterns in relation to subsequent pupil learning and attitude change. Tape recordings were made of four sessions of fifteen high school classes. No effort was made to control methods of instruction; teachers were asked to prepare their lesson plans in any manner they believed appropriate. Transcripts of the four sessions of the fifteen classes served as the basis for analyzing the verbal interaction of teachers and pupils. Bellack and Davitz found that the linguistic activities of

[23] Ned A. Flanders, "Teacher and Classroom Influences on Individual Learning," in A. H. Passow, *Nurturing Individual Potential* (Washington: Association for Supervision and Curriculum Development, 1963), pp. 57–65.

[24] Arno A. Bellack and Joel R. Davitz, *The Language of the Classroom,* Report of Cooperative Research Project No. 1497 (Washington, D.C.: U.S. Department of Health, Education, and Welfare, Office of Education, 1963).

teacher and students constitute a kind of language game wherein verbal statements follow certain rules appropriate to the activities underway. Four kinds of verbal actions, called *pedagogical moves*, were identified: *structuring* moves, which serve to focus attention on subject matter or classroom procedure; *soliciting* moves, questions, commands, or requests; *responding* moves, responses to questions, commands, or requests; and *reacting* moves, which shape or mold classroom discussion by accepting, rejecting, modifying, or expanding what has been said previously.

The results of Bellack and Davitz's study show that the pedagogical roles of teachers and pupils are clearly delineated. Teachers are responsible for structuring the lesson, soliciting responses from pupils, and reacting to pupils' responses. Teachers are considerably more active than pupils in verbal activity, surpassing pupils by ratios of 3 to 1 in lines spoken and 3 to 2 in pedagogical moves. The pupil's primary task is to respond to the teacher's solicitations. Occasionally, pupils react to preceding statements, but these reactions are rarely evaluative. In general, pupils do not react evaluatively to teachers' statements, and they evaluate other pupils' responses only when the teacher asks them to do so. By far the largest proportion of classroom discourse involves empirical matters. Thus, most of the verbal interaction recorded by Bellack and Davitz was devoted to stating facts and explaining principles; considerably less was concerned either with defining terms or with expressing and justifying personal opinions.

Encouraging Self-Directed Learning

Two quite different teaching methodologies, each with its corresponding view of the learner, are described by Flanders' studies of teacher influence. One type of teacher, the "direct-influence" type, spends most of his class time lecturing, giving directions, and criticizing—in general treating the student as relatively passive. In contrast, teachers using the "indirect-influence" approach reflect a view of the learner as actively influencing the learning situation of which he is a part. Bruner[25] makes a similar distinction when he contrasts the *expository mode* of teaching with the *hypothetical mode*. In the expository mode, the decisions concerning the pace and style of exposition are determined principally by the teacher; the student is a listener. In the hypothetical mode, on the other hand, the pupil takes an active part in the formulation of decisions.

In recent years, considerable attention has been given to learning that involves the learner's active participation and the teacher's use of indirect influence or the hypothetical mode of teaching. The term *discovery learning* has been used to describe this process. Bruner suggests four advantages of learning by discovery:

1. Discovery learning increases the learner's ability to learn related material.

[25] Jerome S. Bruner, "The Act of Discovery," *Harvard Educational Review*, 31 (1961), 21–32.

2. It fosters an interest in the activity itself rather than in the rewards which may follow from the activity.

3. It develops one's ability to approach problems in a way more likely to lead to a solution.

4. It makes material that is learned easier to retrieve or to reconstruct.

Early studies demonstrated that learning through independent discovery is superior to learning by rote.[26] More recently, Kersh,[27] in a study cited in Chapter 3, sought to test the hypothesis that discovery learning is superior because it is more meaningful to the learner. It will be recalled that three groups of college students were given the task of learning the "odd-numbers" and the "constant-difference" rules of addition. The first group, called the "no-help" group, received no assistance from the experimenter. The second group, called the "directed-reference" group, received some direction, in the form of relevant data written on the board. Members of the third group, called the "rule-given " group, were told the rules for working the problems and were given practice in applying them without any reference to arithmetical or geometrical relationships. Thus, the experimental treatment called for two kinds of discovery learning (no-help and some-help) and one kind of rote or mechanical learning. The directed-reference treatment produced the greatest incidence of understanding; the no-help treatment produced less understanding than the directed-reference treatment but significantly more understanding than the rule-given treatment. Kersh noted, however, that the superiority of independent discovery may be better explained in terms of motivation than in terms of understanding. Subjects in the no-help group who failed to discover the rule during the practice sessions told of their efforts to learn the rule, some even going so far as to look up the algebraic formula in the library. In contrast, one subject in the rule-given group complained that not having been instructed to remember the rules, he had promptly forgotten them.

In a later study, Kersh[28] sought to explore further the role of motivation in discovery learning. Ninety high school geometry students were taught the two addition rules of the earlier study after having been divided into three groups: (1) A "guided-discovery" group, corresponding to the directed-reference group in the earlier study, was required to discover the rules with guidance from the experimenter; (2) a "rote-learning" group, corresponding to the rule-given group in the first experiment, was given rules without explanation; and (3) a "directed-learning" group was taught the rules and

[26] See, for instance, T. R. McConnell, "Discovery vs. Authoritative Identification in the Learning of Children," *University of Iowa Studies in Education,* 9 (1934), 11–62; and Esther Swenson, G. L. Anderson, and C. L. Stacey, *Learning Theory in School Situations* (Minneapolis: University of Minnesota Press, 1949).

[27] Bert Y. Kersh, "The Adequacy of 'Meaning' as an Explanation for the Superiority of Learning by Independent Discovery," *Journal of Educational Psychology,* 49 (1958), 282–292.

[28] Bert Y. Kersh, "The Motivating Effect of Learning by Directed Discovery," *Journal of Educational Psychology,* 53 (1962), 65–71. Table 17.3 is reproduced from this article by permission.

had the rules explained to them through a programmed-learning technique. After the learning period of the experiment, each of the three main groups was divided into three subgroups. Each subgroup was given a test of recall and transfer—the first subgroup after three days had elapsed since the learning period, the second subgroup after two weeks had elapsed, and the third subgroup after six weeeks had elapsed.

The results of Kersh's second study are presented in Table 17.3. The rote-learning and guided-discovery groups were found to be vastly superior to the directed-learning group in learning and retaining the rules. It would appear that the rote-learning group of this study was similar to the directed-reference group of the previous study; after having been given the rules, members of the rote-learning group still had to understand them, explain them, and learn how to use them—activities requiring discovery learning. Kersh suggested that the poorer performances of the guided-discovery and directed-learning groups, in contrast to the rote-learning group, could have been caused by the experimenter's explanation of the rules, which may have made it more difficult for the subjects to remember the rules. (This phenomenon is known as *retroactive inhibition.*)

Kersh concluded from the findings of his two experiments that attempts at relatively full explanation do not necessarily enhance retention or transfer of rules and procedures. Learning by self-discovery appears to be superior to learning with external direction only to the extent that it increases student motivation to pursue the learning task. If sufficiently motivated, the student may continue the learning process autonomously beyond the formal learning period. From the results of Kersh's second experiment, finally, it appears that highly formalized "lecture-drill" techniques, ordinarily considered sterile and meaningless, may, under certain conditions, produce better results than techniques which attempt to develop "understanding."[29]

Explanation, then, does not necessarily lead to understanding. Material that is meaningful, furthermore, may not necessarily be retained longer or transferred more readily than material that is less meaningful. Effective teaching, therefore, would seem to call for the teacher to provide explanation and self-direction in amounts appropriate to the capacity, background, learning mode or style, and self-concept of each student.

Summary

In spite of man's long experience with the act of teaching, we still do not have a clear understanding of what good teaching is or how to foster it. Teaching takes place in a milieu that is continuously changing and is influenced by a great many variables, both known and unknown. Teaching in a

---

[29] For another study, which produced results similar to Kersh's, see M. C. Wittrock, "Verbal Stimuli in Concept Formation: Learning by Discovery," *Journal of Educational Psychology,* 54 (August 1963), 183–190.

Table 17.3.   Number of subjects (of 10 in each cell) who used or stated learned rules correctly on a retest (from Kersh).

TREATMENT GROUPS	USED RULES		STATED RULES		
	ODD NUMBERS	CONSTANT DIFFERENCE	ODD NUMBERS	CONSTANT DIFFERENCE	TOTAL
	1	2	3	4	
Rote Learning					
3 days	7	7	7	9	
2 weeks	7	6	2	6	
6 weeks	4	4	0	3	
Total	18	17	9	18	62
Guided Discovery					
3 days	6	6	8	9	
2 weeks	3	5	3	4	
6 weeks	2	3	3	3	
Total	11	14	14	16	55
Directed Learning					
3 days	4	3	3	4	
2 weeks	4	3	1	3	
6 weeks	0	3	1	1	
Total	8	9	5	8	30

broad sense is *any interpersonal influence aimed at changing the ways in which persons can or will behave.*

Of critical importance for improving individual and group performance in the teaching-learning situation is an analysis and understanding of the motivations of teacher and pupils. Formal learning situations at school may serve to promote or to deny satisfaction of students' physical, interpersonal, and psychological needs. The teacher, by organizing the classroom in ways that maximize the achieving of a broad range of significant learnings, can help students to satisfy their interpersonal and psychological needs.

Teachers have many of the same needs as students. The teacher's valuing responses toward pupils not only promote the gratification of students' affection and dependency needs but elicit accepting and valuing responses from students toward the teacher, responses that contribute to the teacher's feeling of security.

Studies of teachers' classroom behavior reveal that what the teacher does in the classroom directly influences his pupils' responses in the teaching-learning situation. Teachers who use dominative techniques with children produce aggressive and antagonistic behavior in them. Children express this aggression and antagonism not only toward the teacher but also toward peers, and a vicious circle of dominative behavior is created. In contrast, teachers who use socially integrative techniques facilitate the adoption by children of integrative, cooperative, and self-directive behaviors.

A model of the learning experience may serve as a guide to organizing the classroom for learning. The descriptive model presented here emphasizes the view of learning as change involving the active response of the learner, the important role of readiness in facilitating learning, the need for objectives and goals for defining behavioral changes and guiding learning activities, and the central role of self factors, especially motivation, in learning. The model also stresses the importance of knowledge of success in promoting learning, the positive and negative effects of failure in promoting learning, the need for both concrete and vicarious experience, the facilitative effects of the use of many sensory media, and the contributions students can make in increasing their own learning.

A model of teacher behavior proposed by Macdonald and Zaret hypothesizes that the more "open" a teacher is to experience, the more likely he is to make effective spontaneous decisions in direct response to the learner. Such decisions will expand opportunities for variations in the learner's productive behavior.

A first step in organizing for learning is the establishment of a favorable climate for learning. Studies of anxiety and learning show that classroom climates that induce high anxiety in students are less facilitative of high academic performance than climates characterized by low anxiety. Studies reveal that the teacher is the most important variable in determining the climate in learning situations. Positive, *learner-centered* climates are more often associated with greater productivity and learning and warmer, more positive attitudes than are less positive, *teacher-centered* climates.

Studies also reveal that the teacher's use of open structure, flexibility, and indirect influence are associated with greater student participation in classroom discussion, increased achievement, and decreased student dependence on the teacher. Although teachers tend to dominate the verbal interaction of the classroom, classroom discourse may be viewed as a language game wherein pupils as well as teachers are able to influence the outcome by playing according to different but complementary sets of rules.

The findings of studies of self-directed *discovery learning* appear to have several implications for teaching. Learning by discovery is superior to learning with external direction only insofar as it increases student motivation to pursue the learning task ; meaningful learning acquired by discovery methods is not necessarily more readily retained or transferred. Effective teaching and learning would seem to call for the teacher to provide explanation and self-direction in amounts appropriate to the capacities, background, learning mode or style, and self-concept of each student.

Study Questions

1. Carl Rogers writes, "It seems to me that anything that can be taught to another is relatively inconsequential and has little or no significant influence on behavior." What do you believe Rogers means by this statement? Discuss.

2. Focus for a moment on the grade level or subject you teach. Describe some learning experiences through which your students might satisfy their needs for belongingness, independence, and self-esteem.

3. We see a great many students who make an active response in the learning situation only after the teacher asks, says, or assigns something. Some students, it will be observed, do not make any overt response at all. What kind of learning environment or teaching strategies do you think are needed to trigger continuous self-initiated learning activities and self-directed learning?

4. Why do you think much teacher behavior does not function to develop content, lacks flexibility, utilizes more direct influence than indirect influence, and does not help students build generalizations, look for alternatives, or look for consequences? What do these shortcomings reveal concerning teachers' perceptions of their own roles and the teaching-learning process?

5. How would you introduce and stimulate self-directed discovery learning in your class? Is the concept of discovery learning applicable more to some types of learning or subjects than to others? Discuss.

Suggested Readings

H. H. Anderson. "Domination and Socially Integrative Behavior," in R. G. Barker, J. S. Kounin, and H. F. Wright. Editors. *Child Behavior and Development*. New York: McGraw-Hill Book Co., 1943, pp. 459–483. Reports findings of classic studies investigating two contrasting types of teacher control, dominative and socially integrative. These studies found that kindergarten and primary grade teachers who used dominative techniques with children produced aggressive and antagonistic responses, whereas teachers who used socially integrative behaviors influenced their children to respond in ways that were cooperative, integrative, and self-directive.

Arno A. Bellack. Editor. *Theory and Research in Teaching*. New York: Bureau of Publications, Teachers College Press, Columbia University, 1963. A series of papers discussing theoretical problems of the classroom behavior of teachers and students. Problems and procedures involved in making systematic observations of classroom activities of students and teachers are described.

Arno A. Bellack, Herbert M. Kliebard, Ronald T. Hyman, and Frank L. Smith. *The Language of the Classroom*. New York: Teachers College Press, Columbia University, 1967. Discusses classroom teaching in terms of the verbal communication between teacher and pupil. The authors analyze the linguistic behavior of fifteen twelfth-grade classes. Through an analysis of the meanings of language "moves" used by teacher and pupils, the authors examine the different ways in which language is used in the classroom.

Ralph K. White and Ronald Lippitt. *Autocracy and Democracy*. New York: Harper & Row, 1960. Reports on the research design, data, and findings of the classic studies of experimentally created democratic, autocratic, and laissez-faire social-emotional climates conducted by Lewin, Lippitt, and White at the University of Iowa in 1938–1940. The influence of varying adult leadership styles on the group behavior of ten-year-old boys is analyzed and the implications of these findings for maintaining and strengthening democracy are discussed.

Films

Effective Learning in the Elementary School, 16 mm, sound, black and white, 20 min. Bloomington, Indiana: Audio-Visual Center, Indiana University (rental fee, $4.65). A fifth-grade teacher relates some of her own experiences in trying to make learning more effective. She relates that in her class teacher and pupil work together on reading, writing, arithmetic, social studies, and creative arts, but that motivation for work is strengthened through unit projects which provide opportunities for developing other important skills.

instructional methods and patterns of organization

We have yet to create the best school of which we are capable. To close the gap between reality and our best visions is a great task of human engineering, the mission that challenges every educator who wants to make good schools better.

≡   JOHN I. GOODLAD AND ROBERT H. ANDERSON

In the preceding chapter we described some of the ways in which the teacher may implement his models of the teaching-learning experience in order to establish a social and emotional climate conducive to learning. After such a climate has been established, further choices must be made of instructional methods and patterns of organization to be employed in carrying learning forward.

Instructional Methods

In this discussion we shall consider only the general instructional methods teachers use in facilitating classroom learning. Instructional methods in special subjects (such as typewriting, shorthand, industrial arts, home economics, music, art, physical education, speech, dramatics, foreign languages, and laboratory sciences) will not concern us here.

We shall focus instead on those methods and modes of instruction common to most subjects, with special emphasis on academic subjects.

Lecture versus Discussion Methods

The lecture method of teaching dates from antiquity and is based upon a conception of education in which a knowledgeable scholar or teacher communicates what he knows to less mature, less knowledgeable pupils. In institutions where the primary goal of education is perceived to be the transmitting of knowledge, the lecture method is still popular and widely used. One of the major propositions presented in the model of the learning experience in the preceding chapter, however, was that learning as a change in behavior is most likely to occur when it involves an active, overt response on the part of the learner. Since students usually have few opportunities to make active responses during lectures, they receive little feedback with which to test and to explore the meanings they perceive in the ideas presented by the lecturer. Lack of feedback does not appear to hinder the student in acquiring knowledge if he is motivated and if the material is not too difficult. Research evidence shows, however, that when the development of concepts or problem-solving skills is the major learning goal, active participation on the part of the learner is more effective than passive listening or observing.[1]

Many studies have compared the relative effectiveness of the lecture method with other methods of teaching. Most studies show few significant differences between comparable groups taught by lecture and discussion methods when knowledge of specific facts is the criterion used to assess effectiveness of instruction. However, discussion and problem-solving methods have proved to be superior in contributing to the understanding of concepts,[2] in promoting problem-solving skills and scientific attitudes,[3] and in increasing positive attitudes of teachers toward teaching and children.[4]

Many colleges and universities have endeavored to obtain the advantages of both the lecture and discussion methods by incorporating both into the same course. This pattern has been especially prevalent where lecture sections are quite large. Courses which combine lecture and discussion or recitation appear to elicit more favorable student attitudes than those in which lecturing predominates. When learning objectives include both the acquisition of information and the development of concepts, the combination

[1] W. J. McKeachie, "Research on Teaching at the College and University Level," in N. L. Gage, *Handbook of Research on Teaching* (Chicago: Rand McNally & Co., 1963), p. 1126.
[2] C. S. Hirschman, "An Investigation of the Small Group Discussion Classroom Method on Criteria of Understanding, Pleasantness and Self-Confidence Induced" (unpublished master's thesis, University of Pittsburgh, 1952).
[3] J. D. Barnard, "The Lecture-Demonstration versus the Problem-Solving Method of Teaching a College Science Course," *Science Education,* 26 (1942), 121–132.
[4] J. E. Casey and B. E. Weaver, "An Evaluation of Lecture Method and Small Group Method of Teaching in Terms of Knowledge of Content, Teacher Attitudes, and Social Status," *Journal of Colorado-Wyoming Academy of Science,* 4 (1956), 54.

of lecture and discussion methods offers important advantages. McKeachie[5] points out that the lecture can effectively present new research findings, whereas discussion can give students opportunities to analyze studies, discover relationships, and develop generalizations. Participating actively in discussion may assist students not only in learning generalizations but also in developing skill in critical thinking.

The superiority of discussion methods in changing behavior was early demonstrated by Lewin in studies of the effectiveness of methods used during World War II to persuade housewives to serve more sweetbreads and other less expensive meats and to give their children more milk, orange juice, and cod liver oil. In one study,[6] Lewin found that mothers who had twenty-five minutes of personal instruction in the use of cod liver oil for their babies were less likely to follow the recommendations of the expert than were mothers who participated in a twenty-five minute group discussion of the problem. Similarly, Levine and Butler[7] found discussion methods more effective than lecture methods in getting plant supervisors to use a new system of rating their employees.

There is evidence that group discussions promote more active thinking than lectures. Sound recordings of classes were used at the University of Chicago to stimulate students to recall their thoughts during class. As predicted, class discussion did stimulate more active thinking than did lectures.[8]

These studies show that the lecture is seldom the most effective method of promoting a broad range of learning. The lecture method appears to be most efficacious for communicating information to students, but it is not superior to discussion methods in this respect. Discussion methods appear to be clearly superior to the lecture for stimulating critical thinking and in enabling students to interpret data, draw inferences, and apply what they have learned to new situations. Discussion methods also appear to be superior in influencing long-term goals and subsequent behavior.

Group discussion, however, can be an effective method of learning only if the teacher and pupils learn needed group skills for playing the roles required for group problem solving. Often, the first task in the initial stages of group discussion is to examine and clarify the purposes of the meeting or the discussion. Even in a well-structured classroom learning activity, the purposes of the discussion may not be entirely clear. Basic to achieving an open, frank exchange of views is a feeling of mutual trust and personal regard between each member and the leader of the group. Each participant must feel sufficiently secure to state or accept disagreement or criticism without being unduly threatened.

5 McKeachie, p. 1127.
6 K. Lewin, "Group Decision and Social Change," in G. E. Swanson, T. M. Newcomb, and E. L. Hartley, *Readings in Social Psychology,* 2nd ed. (New York: Holt, Rinehart and Winston, 1952), pp. 330–344.
7 J. Levine and J. Butler, "Lecture vs. Group Decision in Changing Behavior," *Journal of Applied Psychology,* 36 (1952), 29–33.
8 B. S. Bloom, "Thought Processes in Lecture and Discussion," *Journal of General Education,* 7 (1953), 160–169.

If class discussions are to be productive, they must be kept relevant to the problem or topic. This is a responsibility of both the leader and the group members. Effective group discussion also requires the development of a high degree of sensitivity among group members to the feelings and ideas of others. It is important to "hear" not only what the other person is saying but what he is trying to say. Productive group discussions also require that group members distinguish between opinions and facts, between inferences and facts, and between judgments and facts.

In group discussion, the vital element of communication is often underrated or overlooked. If teachers view communication primarily as a process of transmitting information to students, then group interactions are likely to be limited to unilateral exchanges between teacher and individual students. If a group is viewed as made up of persons with information, talents, and skills to contribute to the group, however, then two-way communication among all members of the group, including the teacher or leader, will be encouraged. Various types of communication possible between teachers and students and the relative degrees of effectiveness of these types are shown in Figure 18.1.[9]

Learner-Centered versus Teacher-Centered Teaching

Because the discussion method involves student participation, we tend to associate this method with student-centered teaching. However, group discussions can be dominated by the teacher, and lectures may be so informal that student participation predominates. Therefore, it seems more useful and accurate to define the dimension of *learner-centeredness* versus *teacher-centeredness* in terms of the degree to which students and teacher share in the responsibility for identifying learning goals and for planning, carrying out, and evaluating learning activities. (Some of the variables which distinguish learner-centered classrooms from teacher-centered classrooms are shown in Table 18.1.[10])

Since the teacher is the designated authority figure in the classroom, the decision whether the class is to be learner-centered or teacher-centered would appear to lie with him. Students may be unable to influence the teacher not to decide to conduct the class in a teacher-centered manner, but their resistance to learning in such a class (characteristically expressed as disinterest, apathy, boredom, withdrawal, or failure to study or to complete assignments) may provide the teacher with feedback regarding their needs, interests, and concerns. On the other hand, the teacher may find it difficult to organize a learner-centered class if the students seek to remain dependent on him or if they fail to accept the teacher's invitation to share in the identification of goals and in the planning, carrying out, and evaluating of learning activities.

[9] From H. C. Lindgren, *Educational Psychology in the Classroom,* 3rd ed. (New York: John Wiley, 1967), p. 338. Used by permission.
[10] From McKeachie, p. 1134. Used by permission.

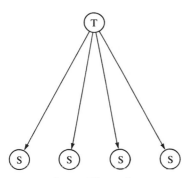

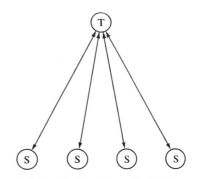

1. *Least effective.* The teacher attempts to maintain one-way communication with students in the class.

2. *More effective.* The teacher tries to develop two-way communication with students in the class.

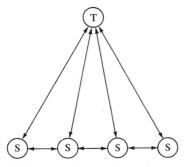

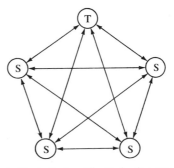

3. *Even more effective.* The teacher maintains two-way communication with students and also permits some communication among students on a rather formal basis.

4. *Most effective.* The teacher becomes a co-participant in the group and encourages two-way communication among all members of the group, including himself.

Figure 18.1. Various types of communicative relationships between teachers and students, in order of their effectiveness (Lindgren).

Several of the propositions that were part of the model of the learning experience presented in the preceding chapter provide support for student-centered approaches to learning. Those that refer to change in the learner, to the importance of his motivations and self-structure, and to the facilitation of learning through increased self-understanding and greater self-direction appear to be particularly relevant to the goals of student-centered learning.

McKeachie[11] points out that teaching methods described as "student-

11 McKeachie, p. 1134.

Table 18.1   *Characteristics of teacher-centered and learner-*
centered teaching (from McKeachie)

STUDENT-CENTERED	INSTRUCTOR-CENTERED
Goals	
Determined by group	Determined by instructor
Emphasis upon affective and attitudinal changes	Emphasis upon intellectual changes
Attempts to develop group cohesiveness	No attempt to develop group cohesiveness
Classroom activities	
Much student participation	Much instructor participation
Student-student interaction	Instructor-student interaction
Instructor accepts erroneous or irrelevant student contributions	Instructor corrects, criticizes, or rejects erroneous or irrelevant student contributions
Group decides upon own activities	Instructor determines activities
Discussion of students' personal experiences encouraged	Discussion kept on course materials
Deemphasis of tests and grades	Traditional use of tests and grades
Students share responsibility for evaluation	
Instructor interprets feelings and ideas of class member when necessary for class progress	Instructor avoids interpretation of feelings
Reaction reports	No reaction reports

centered," "nondirective," "group-centered," or "democratic" often vary widely, but that all have as their inspiration the desire to break away from the traditional instructor-dominated classroom and to encourage greater student participation and responsibility. The results of student-centered teaching may not be all positive, however. In its more extreme forms, student-centered teaching may result in lower achievement of such learning goals as knowledge of facts. Feedback and organization and structure are important to the learning process. If the teacher's role as information giver is reduced, his opportunities for providing feedback and for organizing and structuring content are sharply curtailed; thus, much of the burden for providing these functions falls on group members. In some groups, members may be capable of performing these functions; in other groups, however, they may not be capable of performing them.

If student-centered teaching reduces students' dependence on the instructor and thus diminishes his influence as a prestige figure, it could possibly also reduce his ability to effect attitudinal changes in students. McKeachie suggests, however, that this may be more than compensated for by increased recognition of group members as sources of influence. If, for example, a student's participation in group discussions earns him recognition and praise, his motivation should increase. This prediction was substantiated by Thistlethwaite,[12] who found that National Merit Scholars felt that one of the outstanding characteristics of teachers who contributed most to their desire to learn was "allowing time for classroom discussion." Other characteristics mentioned included "modifying course content to meet students' needs and interests," "treating students as colleagues," "taking a personal interest in students," and "providing evaluations reassuring the student of his creative or productive potentialities."

Many other studies have investigated the relative influences on learning of student-centered and teacher-centered methods of teaching. Several of the characteristics of student-centeredness listed in Table 18.1 were studied by Faw.[13] In Faw's study, a group of 102 students were together two hours per week for lecture and were divided into three groups of 34 students each for two hours of discussion per week. One discussion section was instructor-centered, another was student-centered, and the third alternated between the two methods. The student-centered class, unlike the instructor-centered class, was characterized by student participation, absence of correction by the instructor of inaccurate statements, absence of instructor direction, and a good deal of discussion of ideas related to personal experiences. The scores made by the student-centered class on an objective course examination based on the textbook were slightly higher than those made by students in the instructor-centered class. However, anonymous written comments by students in all sections seemed to indicate that students received greater social and emotional value from student-centered discussion groups than from the instructor-centered class.

In another study by Asch,[14] three sections of a course in psychology

[12] D. L. Thistlethwaite, *College Press and Changes in Study Plans of Talented Students* (Evanston, Illinois: National Merit Scholarship Corporation, 1960).

[13] V. D. Faw, "A Psychotherapeutic Method of Teaching Psychology," *American Psychologist,* 4 (1949), 104–109.

[14] M. J. Asch, "Nondirective Teaching in Psychology," *Psychological Monographs,* 65 (1951), No. 4. Whole No. 321.

were taught by methods similar to Faw's. In Asch's study, however, each student in the student-centered section evaluated his own performance and assigned his own grade and each student was told that his score on the final examination would in no way affect his grade in the course. On the final examination, students in the instructor-centered class scored significantly higher than members of the student-centered class on both the essay and the objective portions of the test. These results appear to be explained in part by the presumed higher motivation of instructor-centered classes to do well on the examination, since the examination would influence their final grade in the course. Haigh and Schmidt,[15] however, found no significant differences in a similar comparison.

As with many other problems in psychology and education, the evidence is not unequivocally in support of student-centered teaching. In a study comparing recitation, discussion, and group tutorial styles of teaching,[16] the more autocratic recitation method proved to be superior to the other two methods not only in improving performance on the final examination but also in stimulating interest in the subject matter of the course. The discussion and tutorial sections, however, were significantly more favorable than the recitation groups in their attitude toward the subject matter of the course—psychology. A follow-up of the students three years later revealed that seven men each from the tutorial and discussion groups majored in psychology but that none of those in the recitation sections did so. Bills[17] also found that members of a student-centered class were more favorable in their attitude toward the subject matter of the class, but he found no differences in achievement between classes taught by lecture-discussion and those taught by student-centered methods.

A number of other studies report no significant differences in achievement-test scores between student-centered and teacher-centered classes but have found that student-centered groups make greater gains in group cohesiveness and participation[18] and undergo greater changes in self-concept.[19] In addition, one study found higher morale among groups attending student-centered courses as compared with students taught by instructor-centered methods.[20]

Another important variable in group-centered classes is students' ac-

[15] G. V. Haigh and W. Schmidt, "The Learning of Subject Matter in Teacher-centered and Group-centered Classes," *Journal of Educational Psychology,* 47 (1956), 295–301.

[16] H. Guetzkow, E. L. Kelley, and W. J. McKeachie, "An Experimental Comparison of Recitation, Discussion and Tutorial Methods in College Teaching," *Journal of Educational Psychology,* 45 (1954), 193–209.

[17] R. E. Bills, "Investigation of Student-Centered Teaching," *Journal of Educational Research,* 46 (1952), 313–319.

[18] R. M. Maloney, "Group Learning through Group Discussion: A Group Discussion Implementation Analysis," *Journal of Social Psychology,* 43 (1956), 3–9.

[19] M. Slomowitz, "A Comparison of Personality Changes and Content Achievement Gains Occurring in Two Modes of Instruction" (unpublished doctor's dissertation, New York University, 1955).

[20] G. R. Rasmussen, "Evaluation of a Student-centered and Instructor-centered Method of Conducting a Graduate Course in Education," *Journal of Educational Psychology,* 47 (1956), 449–461.

ceptance of responsibility for learning. Patton[21] compared traditional psychology classes with two classes in which there were no examinations, no lectures and no assigned readings. Students in these experimental classes decided what reading they would do, what class procedure would be used, what they would hand in, and how they would be graded. As he had hypothesized, Patton found that students who took responsibility in the planning and operation of the course made greater gains in knowledge of psychology, developed greater ability to apply psychology, and rated higher the value of the course and their interest in psychology than students in classes that took less responsibility for planning and organizing the course. Thus, the effects of additional responsibility appear to depend upon students' readiness to accept that responsibility.

Nearly all of the investigations comparing student-centered and teacher-centered methods reported thus far have dealt with college populations. A study by Rehage,[22] however, compared pupil-teacher planning and teacher-directed procedures in eighth-grade social studies classes. In the experimental group, the pupils and teacher together worked out the particular objectives to be attained and the means to be used to attain them. Plans developed in the experimental group were used by the teacher also in the control group, but the latter group had no opportunity to participate in the formulation of the plans. Results of the year's experience revealed no significant differences between the two groups in amount of subject matter learned. Members of the pupil-teacher planning group, however, were markedly superior to members of the control group in their ability to discriminate between reasons that supported their choices of action in planning activities and those that did not. This seems to indicate that the experimental group gained greater insight into the process of group planning. Further research on student-centered versus teacher-centered learning in the lower grades is needed to determine whether the findings emerging from studies of college students obtain with younger students.

The research reported above indicates in general that members of student-centered classes do not score higher on achievement tests emphasizing facts and information than do students in teacher-centered classes. However, learners in student-centered classes do express greater satisfaction with the course, register more positive attitudes toward the subject field, make greater gains in personal adjustment, and select more frequently the subject field as their vocational choice.

Role Playing

Role playing is a valuable teaching technique, for it enables the player to become totally involved in the situation being enacted. A role-playing

[21] J. A. Patton, "A Study of the Effects of Student Acceptance of Responsibility and Motivation on Course Behavior" (unpublished doctor's dissertation, University of Michigan, 1955).

[22] Kenneth J. Rehage, "A Comparison of Pupil-Teacher Planning and Teacher Direction Procedures in Eighth Grade Social Studies Classes," *Journal of Educational Research,* 45 (1951), 111–115.

procedure called *sociodrama* has proved particularly useful for exploring feelings in an educational setting. Sociodrama is used to try out and evaluate several possible solutions to a problem facing a group. Consider the following problem:

> School boundaries have recently been changed in this district, and now about 200 students from lower-class homes have been reassigned to Jefferson High School, which heretofore has served predominantly middle-class communities. Fights, ugly words, and bad feelings have developed between lower-class and middle-class students. Feelings became intense this week when results of school-wide elections revealed that no lower-class student was elected as a cheer leader or class officer—even though several had campaigned and worked hard in the elections.

Students might be selected to play the parts of lower-class and middle-class students engaged in heated discussion in the homeroom after the announcement of the election results. The following[23] are steps that may be used for obtaining full benefit from such a role-playing experience.

1. First comes a general discussion about the situation. This is called the warm-up. Factors are brought out just enough to give the players a sense of knowing the problem. The stage is set with whatever props are necessary to make the playing easier and more definite—table, chair, books, etc.

2. Second is the enactment of the situation. The teacher watches this enactment and "cuts" the playing at any moment that seems productive for the purpose at hand.

3. The third step is interviewing the players to see how they felt as they were playing and what their interpretations are of what they were doing. This leads into group discussion of the consequences of the solution offered in the enactment.

4. Finally comes the re-enactment, with interviewing and discussion following. In role playing we are not seeking to establish an answer as the right one. We find that many satisfactory solutions are possible to nearly every situation involving people and that each solution carries with it negative and positive connotations. Our purpose is to examine these negative and positive elements in the light of our individual and group feelings to find solutions that are tolerable to us—ones which we wish to live.

Solutions are discussed not as abstract situations but rather in terms of their meaning for the persons concerned. Especially important are the opportunities to explore feelings and to look at the long-term consequences of each solution. Another use of role playing is in helping individuals to gain insight

[23] Condensed from Howard Lane and Mary Beauchamp, *Human Relations in Teaching: The Dynamics of Helping Children Grow,* copyright 1955, pp. 274, 276–278. Used by permission of Prentice-Hall, Inc., Englewood Cliffs, New Jersey.

into their own feelings, values, and motivations. It is essential that the actors be free to act out the situation as they really feel it, and the teacher is careful to give no judgments regarding the feelings or values expressed.

The teacher's function is to help the group members draw out of their role playing as many ideas and learnings as they are able to assimilate. Sociodrama enables one to bring out vividly the differences between the perceptions of persons involved in an event; it also permits the individual to gain added insight into his own motivations and values.

It is important in role playing that the teacher structure situations and remain in control so that no one is harmed. The teacher is cautioned not to ask persons with serious emotional problems to play roles which would arouse feelings or criticisms too difficult for them to handle. The following are examples of situations which may be played out in sociodrama.

1. Several members of Miss Brown's ninth-grade class were noisy and disrespectful during a school assembly. Mr. Abbott, the principal, commented over the public-address system about the poor behavior of some students. Miss Brown gave a heavy homework assignment that evening. The next day only three students handed in homework papers. Work out several solutions to the problem in structured sociodrama.

2. After recess I found Clara crying. She said, "The girls have started a good club and asked three boys to be in it. I want to be in it, but they won't let me." One girl answered, "Miss H., Clara is crying to be in our club, but we can't let her be in. She can't get along with anybody." Play the situation with Clara playing her own role and then reverse roles.

3. Ted Lawrence and Bob Brooks are shunned by most of their classmates. Their hair is extremely long, and they were ordered by the principal to have it cut. They refused and were suspended from school. Work out several solutions to the problem in structured sociodrama involving principal, guidance counselor, sympathetic teacher, and representative members of the student body. Reverse principal roles.

Patterns of Organization

Grouping for Learning

Whenever children have been assembled to be taught, their teachers have found it expedient to classify them in some manner for instruction. The traditional method of grouping has been by chronological age, with promotions to a higher grade contingent upon successful completion of work for a particular grade. The percentage of failures under this system has been high. In our large cities during the period from 1850 to 1891, the percentage of students who failed to be promoted ranged from 17 to 46 percent.[24]

---

[24] Douglas E. Lawson, "Analysis of Historic and Philosophic Considerations for Homogeneous Grouping," *Educational Administration and Supervision,* 43 (May 1957), 257–270.

After 1900, public school enrollment increased sharply and a need arose for multiple classes for the same grade or subject. The criterion most often applied to divide students into classes was some measure of actual or potential ability. In using such a criterion, it was assumed that grouping children into the able, the average, and the less able can be done accurately and easily, and that the ablest group, thus "set free," will rise to unprecedented heights.[25] Educational practices based on these assumptions led to widespread use of so-called homogeneous or ability grouping, which has persisted to the present time. Reading-ability or achievement-test scores have tended to replace IQ scores as the principal basis for grouping pupils homogeneously. Various other measures, however, such as physical maturity, social maturity, and organismic age, have also been used.

In recent years, studies of homogeneous grouping have brought the whole concept into question. Wilhelms and Westby-Gibson[26] have pointed out that if a group of children are divided into levels by any criterion or combination of criteria whatever, the total variability within each group is reduced only by about 20 percent. After these groups have been formed, they will still be markedly heterogeneous because of the tremendous range of individual differences which remain for all but the variable chosen as the basis for the division. The group cannot be homogeneous, because the individuals in it are not homogeneous within themselves. This suggests that any presumed homogeneity of instructional groups is an illusion, and that the concept itself is a misnomer.

There appears to be little support for other claims that have been made for ability grouping. After reviewing the research, Eash[27] concluded that ability grouping does not in itself produce improved achievement in children. Improved achievement appears to be related to more complex factors, such as curriculum adaptation, teaching methods, materials, and the ability of the teacher to relate to children. Miriam Goldberg and her associates,[28] for example, found that gains in achievement among fifth- and sixth-grade pupils were influenced more strongly by teachers and group differences in individual classrooms than by the presence or absence of gifted pupils, the range of ability in the class, or even the intellectual ability of the pupils.

Husen and Sevsen[29] found that under ability grouping, average and lower-ability students appear to suffer from the deprivation of intellectual stimulation that occurs when brighter children are removed from the class. On the other hand, the achievement of more able children appears not to be adversely affected when they remain in a class with average and lower-abil-

[25] Lawson.

[26] F. T. Wilhelms and D. Westby-Gibson, "Grouping: Research Offers Leads," *Educational Leadership,* 18 (April 1961), 410–413.

[27] Maurice J. Eash, "Grouping: What Have We Learned?" *Educational Leadership,* 18 (April 1961), 429–434.

[28] Miriam L. Goldberg, A. Harry Passow, and Joseph Justman, *The Effects of Ability Grouping* (New York: Teachers College Press, Columbia University, 1966).

[29] Tortsen Husen and Nils Eric Sevsen, "Pedagogic Milieu and Development of Intellectual Skills," *The School Review,* 68 (Spring 1960), 36–51.

ity students, at least through elementary school. It appears, too, that children from higher socioeconomic classes placed in higher-ability groups do not necessarily benefit from the increased emphasis upon academic work, at least through elementary and beginning junior high school.

Since teachers continue to teach students in groups, some type of grouping procedure will be used in organizing for instruction. Since evidence supporting any method of grouping is meager, tradition is likely to govern the choice of the method of grouping. However, a variety of grouping innovations have been proposed, and these apply not only to the classification of pupils but also to the assignment of teachers and the choice of instructional procedures. One such innovation has been suggested by Thelen,[30] who has proposed a concept of "teachable grouping" wherein students are assigned to a particular teacher's class because they possess the same or similar characteristics as students with whom (in the teacher's judgment) the teacher has been most successful in the past. Thelen investigated the concept of teachable grouping by comparing the achievement performance, attitudes toward learning, and personality characteristics of students who appeared to be "getting a great deal out of class" and students who seemed to be getting very little out of the same class. An intensive study of the classes of 13 teachers of academic subjects in grades eight to eleven revealed that "teachable" students gained no more on achievement tests and tended to like the teacher only slightly more than did control (less teachable) students. However, teachable students did tend to like each other better and to express a higher level of satisfaction with class activities and with the course as a whole than did the control group. "Teachable" students were also judged to be more psychologically mature—they were more work-oriented, freer in expressing emotion, more secure in the face of hostility, more autonomous, more cooperative, and better able to work with others in a group situation. Although the efficacy of "teachable groups" for increasing student achievement was not demonstrated by Thelen's research, the concept is an attractive one and should be tested by further research.

Horizontal and Vertical Organization

The appearance of many different types of grouping has made it necessary to distinguish between different meanings and uses of the term. Goodlad and Rehage[31] point out that schools exhibit both vertical and horizontal patterns of organization. The *vertical organization* of the school serves to classify students upwardly from admission to graduation. The division of students into grade levels (first, second, third) has been the traditional pattern of vertical organization. *Multigrading* and *nongrading* are alternative patterns. In a multigraded school, students in a classroom are permitted

[30] Herbert A. Thelen, *Classroom Grouping for Teachability* (New York: John Wiley, 1967).

[31] John I. Goodlad and Kenneth Rehage, "Unscrambling the Vocabulary of School Organization," *The NEA Journal,* 51 (November 1962), 34–36.

to work in several grades at once, depending on their progress in each subject. In a nongraded school, grade designations are entirely removed from some or all classes.

The *horizontal organization* of the school divides the student body among available teachers. Homogeneous and heterogeneous groupings of students into classes are the best-known examples of horizontal organization. Team teaching is a newer pattern of horizontal organization. Schools utilizing team teaching may be either graded or nongraded.

Nongraded programs. Nongrading is a pattern of vertical school organization which, its adherents believe, would give teachers more time to study the progress of individual pupils before making a decision on retention or promotion. A nongraded program, wherein a decision regarding promotion or retention is delayed two or three years, increases the probability that most children will complete the primary program in the normal period of time. The nongraded program seeks to increase the opportunities for each child to develop his capacities to the fullest, to provide for the continuous development of all children, and to reduce the incidence of the frustration that accompanies failure. Moreover, by increasing opportunities for success, the nongraded program reduces the feelings of frustration which accompany failure.

In most cases, only the primary grades are organized on a nongraded basis. A few schools, however, are experimenting with nongrading in the intermediate grades. Nongrading appears to have had its greatest influence on the program and patterns of grouping in reading. Characteristically, the reading experiences of the primary years are organized into eight to ten sequential steps or levels through which the child moves at his own rate. The number of reading levels in each classroom is limited, thereby reducing the range of reading abilities found in many classrooms. Overlapping levels between classes permit pupils to move up or down easily. A unique feature of the nongraded plan is the flexibility it allows in moving a child from group to group or from one classroom to another at any time his growth warrants such a change.[32]

Shapski[33] found that children in a nongraded program scored significantly greater gains than matched children in traditional graded schools. Children at all ability levels benefited from the individualized, flexible program, with those of superior intelligence making the greatest gains of all.

Halliwell[34] found that children in nongraded classrooms scored significantly higher in word knowledge and reading comprehension at the end of their first year of reading than did children in graded classrooms. At the end of the second year, however, pupils in nongraded classes were not signifi-

[32] See Hugh V. Perkins, "Nongraded Programs: What Progress?" *Educational Leadership,* 19 (December 1961), 166–169.
[33] Mary K. Shapski, "Ungraded Primary Reading Programs: An Objective Evaluation," *Elementary School Journal,* 61 (October 1960), 41–45.
[34] Joseph W. Halliwell, "A Comparison of Pupil Achievement in Graded and Nongraded Primary Classrooms," *Journal of Experimental Education,* 32 (1963), 59–64.

cantly superior in reading or in spelling; at the end of the third year, the nongraded pupils were superior in spelling only. Carbone[35] compared the achievement of 244 fourth-, fifth-, and sixth-grade pupils, 122 of whom had been taught during their primary years in a nongraded program, and 122 of whom had been taught in a graded program. The pupils from the graded primary classrooms were found significantly superior in all areas examined (vocabulary, reading comprehension, language, work-study skills, and arithmetic).

The philosophy of the nongraded program appears to be sound, but the great promise it holds for a markedly different and improved educational program has as yet not been realized. The organization of nongraded programs has so far tended to focus more attention on structured materials and techniques and less attention on the child's needs and interests. In many schools, attempts to introduce nongrading have merely resulted in the replacing of one graded program by another. When nongrading has been instituted, moreover, the change has been accompanied by few instructional innovations or curriculum reforms.

Team teaching. The term *team teaching* has been used to describe a number of different arrangements for the assigning of teachers and the grouping of pupils. Examples of team teaching vary from simple *coordinate teaching,* wherein two teachers are assigned to a large class and are equally responsible for instruction, to a hierarchy of teachers—for instance, team leader, senior teacher, auxiliary teacher, intern teacher, teacher aide, and clerk.

Implicit in the concept of team teaching is the belief that the wider range of competencies and skills provided by two or more teachers is superior to the narrower range provided by a single teacher. Today's tremendous increase in knowledge, the greater emphasis upon more mathematics, more science, more language, and the stress on the education of the gifted have caused educators to question whether one teacher can teach all subjects to all children with equal effectiveness and skill.

In team teaching, the strengths of several teachers are pooled so as to increase the quality of the instructional program. Team teaching is expected to redound to the benefit of the individual pupil, since a team of teachers and specialists conferring and planning together have opportunities to plan experiences in relation to the individual pupil's needs. Moreover, the flexibility of scheduling and grouping under team teaching permits a teacher to achieve closer contacts with individual pupils. Finally, advocates of team teaching note that by encouraging teachers to work together and to develop special competencies and leadership abilities, team teaching increases the professional status of teaching.

Team teaching is a major feature of Trump's[36] plan for the utilization

[35] Robert F. Carbone, "A Comparison of Graded and Nongraded Elementary Schools," *Elementary School Journal,* 42 (November 1961), 82–88.
[36] J. Lloyd Trump, *Images of the Future* (Washington D.C.: National Association of Secondary School Principals, National Education Association, 1959). Table 18.2 is reproduced from this work by permission.

of staff and the reorganization of the secondary school. This experimental plan, now being implemented in a number of secondary schools, is organized around three kinds of activities: (1) large-group instruction, (2) individual study, and (3) small-group discussion. The organization of instruction provided for by Trump's plan is shown in Table 18.2. Emphasis is upon flexibility, with the size of groups and length of class periods varying from day to day. Some aspects of learning are presented by specially qualified teachers to relatively large groups of students. This frees other teachers to work with other students individually or in small discussion groups. Under the plan, a student is expected to assume more individual responsibility for learning than he would be expected to assume in a traditional classroom.

Trump's plan calls for students to engage in individual study activities singly or in groups of two or three. Conferences between students and instructors are held whenever necessary to clarify goals, content, or personal problems. Students read, listen to records and tapes, gather data, analyze, think, and solve problems in projects which require them to assume increased responsibility for their own direction. The virtual absence of controlled studies evaluating team teaching has made it difficult to assess the effectiveness of this type of organization as compared to other types, such as the self-contained classroom. Drummond[37] reports that in general students do as well or perhaps a little better on standardized tests when taught by teaching teams; teachers generally are willing to continue the team approach, although not all teachers make good team members; and students and parents generally favor the approach. However, Drummond questions many of the educational advantages claimed for team teaching. Large group meetings, for example, by limiting the interactions between students and a superior teacher, may result in the individual student learning less than he would in a regular classroom. Moreover, some of the advantages of team teaching, such as increased flexibility of grouping and self-direction of learners, may also be obtained by other patterns of organization.

Grouping by sex. According to Waetjen and Grambs,[38] differences in sex roles make for differences in school learning. Girls, for instance, generally receive higher grades and fewer failures than boys, and achieve greater language development and verbal fluency. Boys, on the other hand, tend to score higher in quantitative skills and transfer.

Because boys and girls differ in the ways they learn, it has been hypothesized that the learning of each sex may be increased if boys and girls are segregated into classes adapted to the learning modes and patterns of each. In a test of this hypothesis, Fisher and Waetjen[39] conducted a study to

[37] Harold D. Drummond, "Team Teaching: An Assessment," *Educational Leadership,* 19 (December 1961), 160–165.

[38] Walter B. Waetjen and Jean D. Grambs, "Sex Differences: A Case of Educational Evasion?" *Teachers College Record,* 65 (December 1963), 261–271.

[39] John K. Fisher and Walter B. Waetjen, "An Investigation of the Relationship between Separation by Sex of Eighth Grade Boys and Girls and English Achievement and Self-Concept," *Journal of Educational Research,* 59 (May-June 1966), 409–412.

Table 18.2. Plan of organization of instruction under the Trump plan (from Trump).

	LARGE-GROUP INSTRUCTION	SMALL-GROUP DISCUSSION	INDIVIDUAL STUDY
Activity	Introduction Motivation Explanation Planning Group study Enrichment Generalization Evaluation	Group examination of terms and concepts and solutions of problems Reach areas of agreement and disagreement Improve interpersonal relations	Read Listen to records and tapes View, question, analyze, think Experiment, examine, investigate, consider evidence Write, create, memorize, record, make Visit Self-appraise
Place	Auditorium, little theater, cafeteria, study hall, classrooms joined via television or remodeling, other large room	Conference room, classroom	Library, laboratories, workshops, project and material centers, museums, inside and outside the school plant.
School Time	About 40 percent	About 20 percent	About 40 percent

ascertain whether boys and girls in eighth-grade sex-segregated classes achieve at higher levels in English and have more adequate self-concepts than pupils in mixed classes. The findings of this study, however, show that students in sex-segregated classes do not register greater gains in English achievement, nor do they report more adequate self-concepts than students in mixed classes. On the contrary, pupils in the mixed classes tested by Fisher and Waetjen scored higher on four comparisons of English achievement.

Sex is a variable which educators should take into consideration when organizing and planning for learning. Further research is needed to point the direction to ways to adapt classroom procedures to utilize more effectively the learning advantages related to the learner's sex.

Grouping within the Classroom

Grouping students within a classroom is a problem that faces nearly every teacher. Although the teacher may desire to teach the class as one group, the number of students and the individual differences among them suggest the desirability of organizing the class into smaller subgroups. Some kinds of learning, such as problem-solving, may be more effectively achieved in small-group study than in individual or large-group study. Small groups are more likely to elicit the active responses and involvement of learners than are large groups. Through this involvement, students learn to set goals, to plan, and to work cooperatively. In small groups, students have opportunities to acquire the social and work skills needed to become concerned, responsible citizens.

A variety of suggestions have been made for grouping students in specific subject fields. Schmid[40] found that fifth-grade children in groups they chose for themselves registered larger gains in arithmetic than did peers in groups formed by the teacher. In addition, children working in groups of their own choice were more responsive than children working in teacher-formed groups. Wilhelms and Westby-Gibson[41] suggest that in forming groups in social studies, it is advantageous to have a diversity of interests, points of view, and talents represented in each group. In free reading and recreational activities, however, it is probably best to encourage the formation of spontaneous, informal groups around shared interests or friendships.

Gordon[42] suggests the following principles to guide teachers in grouping students for learning.

1. The grouping should recognize the purposes of the individual child.
2. Heterogeneous groupings give children opportunities for learning to live and work with a variety of other people.
3. The number of children in the basic classroom group should be small enough for face-to-face encounters.
4. Children should remain in the same group long enough to develop a stake in each other's welfare and growth.
5. Each child should have the opportunity to share what he has with peers and to be challenged by peers.

40 John A. Schmid, "A Study of the Uses of Sociometric Techniques for Forming Instructional Groups for Number Work in the Fifth Grade" (unpublished doctor's dissertation, University of Maryland, 1960).

41 Wilhelms and Westby-Gibson, pp. 429–434.

42 Julia W. Gordon, "Grouping and Human Values," *School Life,* 45 (July 1963), 10–15.

Ideal or best ways for grouping students may be an illusion. In organizing for learning, each teacher should be guided by his understanding of individual students and by his and the class's educational objectives.

Summary

After a climate of learning has been established, further choices must be made of instructional methods and patterns of organization. While lecturing is a traditional and familiar method of instruction, most studies show few significant differences between comparable groups taught by lecture and discussion methods when knowledge of specific facts is the criterion used to assess effectiveness of instruction. Discussion methods appear to be superior to the lecture in stimulating critical thinking, in encouraging the interpretation of data and the drawing of inferences, and in influencing long-term goals and future behavior. If a group is viewed as made up of persons with information, talents, and skills to contribute to the group endeavor, then effective modes of communication will be seen as those that encourage two-way communication among all members of the group, including the teacher or leader.

A variable that differentiates learning experiences and teaching methods into two rather distinct types is the amount of direct influence and control which a teacher exerts on classroom activity. The dimensions of *learner-centeredness* and *teacher-centeredness* are reflected in the degree to which the student and the teacher share in the responsibility for identifying learning goals and for planning, carrying out, and evaluating learning activities.

Research investigating student-centered versus teacher-centered teaching reveals that members of student-centered classes generally do not score higher on achievement tests emphasizing facts and information than do students in teacher-centered classes. However, learners in student-centered classes do appear to show greater satisfaction with the course, more positive attitudes toward the subject field, and greater gains in personal adjustment. Students in these classes are also more likely to select the subject field as their vocational choice.

Since school learning is largely a group experience, one of the responsibilities of the school or teacher in organizing for learning is to determine the bases on which children are to be grouped for instruction. Although ability grouping is the pattern of most schools, there is little evidence that this method is the most satisfactory one.

Several innovations in grouping students have been tried. The nongraded program, which seeks to implement a continuous program of learning for children of varying abilities and rates of maturation, appears to be sound, but the great promise it holds has not yet been realized. The organization of nongraded programs has so far tended to focus more attention on structured materials and techniques and less attention on the child's needs and interests.

Team teaching, an innovation found in both elementary and secondary schools, seeks to make available to pupils the varied competencies and skills of two or more teachers. While pooling the strengths of several teachers may increase the quality of the instructional program, the emphasis team teaching places upon organization, scheduling, and team assignments may also cause the needs of the individual student to be overlooked.

There is considerable evidence that boys and girls differ in the ways they perceive and the ways they learn. Sex is yet another variable which educators should take into consideration when organizing for learning.

Grouping students within a classroom is a problem that faces nearly every teacher. Probably the most important criterion for effective learning is flexibility. There appears to be no best way of grouping students for learning. In organizing for learning, each teacher should be guided by his understanding of individual students and by his and the class's educational objectives.

Study Questions

1. What do you believe determines the teacher's choice of instructional methods—lecture versus discussion, teacher-centered versus learner-centered, role playing, etc.? What methods were used by the most effective teachers you have known?

2. Although the evidence is conflicting, there appears to be a greater range of pupil gains associated with student-centered than with teacher-centered teaching. How would one reconcile these results with the observation that most teachers are probably more teacher-centered than learner-centered? Discuss.

3. Identify problems or situations in your own teaching which might be meaningfully and profitably explored by your class through role playing or sociodrama.

4. Research findings appear to cast considerable doubt upon the efficacy of ability grouping in promoting learning, yet this pattern tends to be widely used in our public schools. How would you account for this seeming discrepancy between research and practice? Discuss.

5. What weight and consideration will you give to what variables in grouping students within your class? Describe the procedures you expect to use in grouping your students. How will you evaluate their effectiveness?

Suggested Readings

Nathaniel L. Gage. Editor. *Handbook of Research on Teaching.* Chicago: Rand McNally & Co., 1963. A series of comprehensive papers which report the findings of thousands of studies that have investigated the many facets and dimensions of teaching. Examines extensively the conceptual and methodological problems involved in conducting research on teaching.

John I. Goodlad and Robert H. Anderson. *The Nongraded Elementary School.* Revised Edition. New York: Harcourt, Brace & World, 1963. The authors challenge the efficacy of the graded school structure. Evidence is presented which suggests that the realities of child development require that schools break away from the rigorous ordering of children's abilities and achievements.

Maurie Hillson. *Change and Innovation in Elementary School Organization.* New York: Holt, Rinehart and Winston, 1965. A series of readings discussing new patterns of grouping and organization of the elementary school. The selections consider ability, homogeneous, departmentalized, and multigrade patterns of grouping, as well as team teaching and nongraded patterns of organization.

J. Lloyd Trump. *Images of the Future.* Washington, D.C.: National Association of Secondary School Principals, National Education Association, 1959. Describes an experimental program which features three major kinds of grouping: (1) large group instruction, (2) individual study, and (3) small group discussion. Emphasis is upon self-directed learning and flexibility.

Films

Experiment in Excellence, Part I, 16 mm, sound, black and white, 27 min. Part II, 16 mm, sound, black and white, 27 min. McGraw-Hill. Syracuse, New York: Film Library, Syracuse University (rental fees, Part I: $5.25; Part II: $5.25). Presents some of the modern educational techniques being adopted by schools throughout the country: speed reading, advanced placement programs, language laboratories, and team teaching. Particular emphasis is given to the role of the teacher in providing individual attention to each student.

Ways of Learning, 16 mm, sound, black and white, 11 min. Syracuse, New York: Film Library, Syracuse University (rental fee, $4.50). Describes the teaching procedures used in a beginning-level general education course taught at Antioch College. Shows the use of new teaching-learning procedures designed to develop self-directed learning.

19

evaluating development and learning

Evaluation is the process of making meaning out of experience. No one could learn from his experiences except by utilizing the feedback from these experiences and converting it into meaning for the future.

≡ RODNEY A. CLARK AND WALCOTT H. BEATTY

In this chapter we shall be concerned with the processes of measuring and evaluating the development and learning of students in school. In the larger perspective of human experience, however, we continuously evaluate ourselves and are evaluated by others without the use of formal tests. We are judged on how well we do our jobs and on the adequacy of our performances as husbands, wives, fathers, mothers, presidents of clubs, responsible citizens, and a host of other roles and activities. Thus, the processes of evaluation, like those of learning, appear to be coextensive with life itself.

Evaluation is a topic that arouses both positive and negative feelings in many of us. No matter how adequate we may be, someone's evaluation of our behavior in a given situation may find us lacking. On the other hand, evaluations wherein our performance is judged adequate, competent, and successful provide feedback that serves as a powerful stimulus for further successful behavior. Experiencing this ambivalence of feelings, a great many persons resignedly accept testing and evaluation as necessary evils. This is unfortunate, for evaluation processes are essential tools for making progress in achieving our most important goals. Without the use of reliable, valid measuring instruments and evaluation procedures, progress toward any of the outcomes of learning described in previous chapters would likely be haphazard and uncertain.

Evaluation is the process through which teacher and pupils judge the extent to which the goals of education are being achieved. Most educational goals relate to certain expected changes in student behavior, changes which are taken as evidence of the student's development and learning. Much class-room learning, therefore, is evaluated through the teacher's informal obser-vations. The first-grade teacher notes the children who recognize words that were introduced the day before and the children who are able to use cues in learning a new word. Similarly, learning is revealed in the history student's analysis of a current political crisis in relation to past events in history; in the science student's testing of alternative hypotheses before offering a tenta-tive conclusion; and in the typing student's improved rhythm, increase in speed, and decrease in errors.

These everyday observations reveal to the teacher which aspects of a performance need correction and improvement and which do not require further attention. Unplanned or casual evaluations, however, are often er-roneous or incomplete. Isolated behaviors of a student may not be typical, or they may constitute too small a sample to reflect accurately what the student has learned. Therefore, systematic, planned measurements of behavior change are needed if evaluation is to fulfill its role in promoting learning.

Evaluation is a process of judging performances in relation to given criteria. Evaluation has three aspects: "(1) a judgment of what, in general, constitutes a desirable behavior change; (2) a means of measuring whether the behavior change has occurred and, if so, to what degree; and (3) a judgment of the 'acceptability' of a particular behavior change."[1]

What it is that constitutes a desirable behavior change is specified by the learning objectives the teacher has chosen. A learning objective may be the correct spelling of a specified number of words of a particular level of difficulty, the solving of quadratic equations, a particular number of errorless words typed per minute, or the demonstration of correct procedure in the use of a power lathe in wood shop.

Measuring whether and to what degree a behavior has occurred involves the assigning of value to a student's performance in relation to some yard-stick or criterion. The means used for assessing change is frequently a test, but it may be a rating scale, a composition, a report, an interview, a con-ference, or observations of students' overt behaviors in various situations. Some of these means will yield more reliable data for evaluating student learning than others. The task of estimating the reliability and validity of evaluation devices will be discussed later in the chapter.

[1] Frederick J. McDonald, *Educational Psychology,* 2nd ed. (Belmont, California: Wads-worth Publishing Co., 1965), p. 581.

A judgment of the "acceptability" of a particular performance is made by the teacher or pupil with reference to the behavior criterion or standard whose achievement is a goal of the learning activity. The criterion or standard may be correctly spelling all words on the third-grade list or responding with correct answers to two-factor multiplication problems. More frequently, however, the standard is a percentage of correct responses, say 70 percent, which is designated as the passing grade or minimum level of acceptability.

To determine how "acceptable" the student's performance is, the teacher makes a judgment based on his criteria of acceptable degrees or amounts of change in student behavior. A fifth-grade student's score on a standardized achievement test in reading comprehension may meet the criterion of acceptability generally expected of a seventh-grade student, while the score of a classmate corresponds to the acceptable level or norm of the average fourth-grade student. Some learning tasks (such as recognizing printed words, doing simple number problems, or typing errorless words) may be evaluated in relation to a single inflexible standard. More frequently, however, a criterion of acceptable performance takes into consideration the maturity and capacity of the learner. It would be unrealistic to apply the same standards to first-grade children as to sixth-grade children, or to apply the same standards to mentally retarded children as to children of normal intelligence.

The reader may have noted the distinctions we have made in our use of the terms *measurement* and *evaluation*. A further clarification of these terms may be useful, since these concepts are frequently confused and misused. Evaluation is more inclusive than measurement; but in order for evaluation to be useful and effective, it should be based upon measurement of some sort. Measurement is concerned with the collection of data upon which evaluative judgments may be made. *Measurement* may be defined as the process of assigning numbers to the individual members of a set of objects or persons for the purpose of differentiating the degree to which they possess the characteristic being measured.[2] The task of measurement includes (1) the developing or obtaining of an instrument or device which adequately measures the behavior represented by the criterion, (2) the administration of such an instrument, and (3) the scoring of responses obtained by the instrument. Tests are the most familiar and most frequently used of measuring instruments; for evaluating some learning objectives, however, other measurement procedures may be more appropriate. Measurement, in essence, is the act of discriminating between the performances of two or more persons. Evaluation is the rendering of judgments about pupil progress in terms of a criterion of desirable behavior. According to Lindgren,[3] anything that a teacher does to determine how well an educational program is succeeding is evaluation.

The major purpose of evaluation is to promote the development and learning of students. Both student and teacher have a stake in ascertaining whether the desired behavior changes have occurred during or following the

[2] Robert E. Ebel, *Measuring Educational Achievement* (Englewood Cliffs, New Jersey: Prentice-Hall, 1965), pp. 454–455.

[3] Henry C. Lindgren, *Educational Psychology in the Classroom*, 3rd ed. (New York: John Wiley, 1967), p. 425.

learning activity. The student seeks some kind of confirmation that his responses and his understanding of concepts or content are appropriate, acceptable, or correct. Only through some kind of feedback in the form of confirmation or lack of confirmation will he have the evidence that he needs to judge whether he is more likely to achieve the desired behavior criterion by maintaining or by modifying his present behavior.

Evaluation also provides the teacher with feedback. The teacher wishes to ascertain whether his present methods, materials, and approaches are effective in influencing the desired behavior changes in his students. Since feedback concerning the student's progress in learning is of vital interest to both student and teacher, the learning goals of the class should be explicit and clearly understood by pupils as well as teacher.

In providing confirmation of the student's acceptable or correct responses, evaluation provides reinforcement to the learner in the form of reward or satisfaction. We recall from Chapter 13 that the learner tends to repeat those responses which were reinforced on previous occasions: These reinforced responses become strengthened and "learned." In the absence of evaluation and feedback, the learner is likely to become anxious and confused. Either he will give up and not respond in the learning situation, or he will modify his behavior in seeking a situation which will provide some kind of feedback.

Finally, systematic evaluation of a pupil's achievements enables the school to report the educational progress of students to parents and serves as a basis for making educational decisions. A student's school marks and achievement-test scores furnish one basis for determining whether he should be admitted to specific courses, programs, or curricula, or to a specific college or university; they may also determine in part his acceptability for certain kinds of employment. The most important kind of evaluation, however, is that which facilitates and improves learning performance. Good teaching and effective learning do not occur without careful evaluation. Thus, teaching, learning, and evaluation are interrelated parts of the total educational process.

Formulating Learning Objectives

The first step in evaluation is a question: What is to be evaluated? What kinds of changes in pupil behavior are we looking for? It is essential that learning objectives be identified and clarified in order that the behaviors and activities of teacher and pupils may have direction and purpose. All teaching is predicated on at least an implicit set of learning objectives. If objectives are unstated or vague or are not communicated to students, or if the objectives bear little relationship to learning activities, then learning outcomes may be quite different from those that were planned for, desired behavior changes may not occur, and educational purposes are likely to be thwarted.

Evaluation procedures should be consistent with the stated objectives of the learning activity. This principle implies that the method of measurement employed must assess the attainment of a stated behavioral objective and should yield data on the entire range of stated objectives.[4] A set of educational objectives for a school system, course, or unit of work is a matter of choice, and the educational objectives that are chosen reflect the value judgments of the community, school system, school, teacher, or some combination of these. Hopefully, too, a statement of objectives will reflect the developmental needs, interests, and concerns of students.

Statements of objectives may suffer from inadequacies and limitations in a number of ways. First, many teachers, in stating objectives, may not distinguish between *immediate* and *ultimate* objectives.[5] Such objectives as "educating pupils for good citizenship" or "educating for life adjustment" suggest behavior changes which can be assessed only at some future time, after schooling has been completed. Although immediate objectives should contribute to the later achievement of ultimate objectives, only immediate objectives are amenable to current assessment. We can evaluate a student's knowledge of the steps through which a bill becomes a law, but we cannot evaluate whether he will, as a good citizen, exercise his right to vote and be informed on national and local issues ten years from now.

Other shortcomings of many statements of objectives are that they focus on too narrow a range of behaviors or are too general and vague. Frequently, teachers will state that their objectives are to teach certain arithmetic concepts and skills or to communicate specific principles of science. The difficulty with such objectives is that they identify an area of subject-matter content to be presented but do not specify the behavior changes that students are expected to demonstrate.

A further shortcoming of many statements of objectives is the frequent discrepancy between their highly generalized but impressive goals and the virtual absence of classroom activities related to these goals. Developing in children the ability to think critically and stimulating their interest in science are laudable objectives, but they mean little if no specific behavior changes or planned learning experiences relate to them.

One evaluation procedure designed to state and to assess the achievement of learning objectives in terms of particular behavior changes and learning experiences has been developed by the Commission on Science Education of the American Association for the Advancement of Science[6] (see Figure 19.1). This procedure begins with the selection and definition of "action words," which denote observable activities. To "know," to "understand," and to "appreciate" seem to connote learning, but they are not as easily translated into observable performances as are the action words that follow:

[4] McDonald, p. 585.
[5] McDonald, p. 585.
[6] American Association for the Advancement of Science, Commission on Science Education, *An Evaluation Model and Its Application. Science—A Process Approach.* (Washington, D.C.: American Association for the Advancement of Science, 1965). Figure 19.1 is reproduced from this work by permission.

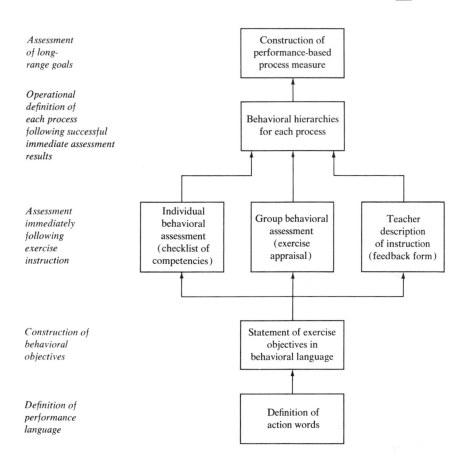

Figure 19.1.   Evaluation strategy used to assess achievement of learning objectives stated in terms of reliably observable behavior (from AAAS Commission on Science Education).

1. *Identifying.* The individual selects (by pointing to, touching, or picking up) the correct object of a class, in response to its class name. For example: Upon being asked, "Which animal is the frog?" when presented with a set of small animals, the child is expected to pick up, clearly point to, or touch the frog.

2. *Distinguishing.* Identifying objects or events which are potentially confusable (square, rectangle), or when two contrasting identifications (such as right and left) are involved.

3. *Constructing.* Generating a construction or drawing which identifies a designated object or set of conditions. Example: Beginning with a

line segment, the request is made, "Complete this figure so that it represents a triangle."

4. *Naming*. Supplying the correct name (orally or in written form) for a class of objects or events. Example: "What is this three-dimensional object called?" Response: "A cone."

5. *Ordering*. Arranging two or more objects or events in proper order in accordance with a stated category. For example: "Arrange these moving objects in order of their speeds."

6. *Describing*. Generating and naming all of the necessary categories of objects, object properties, or even properties that are relevant to the description of a designated situation. Example: "Describe this object." The child's description is considered sufficiently complete when there is a probability of approximately one that any other individual is able to use the description to identify the object or event.

7. *Stating a Rule*. Makes a verbal statement (not necessarily in technical terms) which conveys a rule or principle, including the names of the proper classes of objects or events in their correct order. Example: "What is the test for determining whether this surface is flat?" The acceptable response requires the mention of the application of a straightedge, in various directions, to determine if the surface touches all along the edge in each position.

8. *Applying a Rule*. Using a learned principle or rule to derive an answer to a question. The question is stated in such a way that the individual must employ a rational process to arrive at the answer. Such a process may be simple, as "Property A is true, property B is true, therefore property C must be true."

9. *Demonstrating*. Performing the operations necessary to the application of a rule or principle. Example: "Show how you would tell whether this surface is flat." The answer requires that the individual use a straightedge to determine if the surface touches the edge at all points and in various directions.

10. *Interpreting*. The child should be able to identify objects or events in terms of their consequences. There will be a set of rules or principles always connected with this behavior.[7]

Following the selection of action words, process exercises are developed for applying the action words. The third step is the field testing of process exercises through individual behavioral assessment, group behavioral assessment, and feedback in the form of teachers' descriptions of instruction.

The fourth step of the evaluation strategy is to identify the sequence of behaviors required to perform a given process. (The processes identified by the AAAS Commission on Science Education are *classifying, communicating, inferring, measuring, using numbers, observing, predicting,* and *using*

[7] American Association for the Advancement of Science, pp. 4–5.

space-time relations.) These sequences are behavioral hierarchies or learning sets, such as those developed by Gagné.[8] The behavioral hierarchy for the process of *observation* is shown in Figure 19.2. At the top of the figure are listed terminal behaviors which evidence observation (such as "identifying and describing objects"). The subordinate behaviors that precede the terminal behaviors are listed below them. Behavioral hierarchies have been developed for each of the processes used in scientific thinking and experimentation listed above.

The final step in the evaluation strategy is the construction of performance-based measures for assessing the student's progress in achieving the desired skills and competencies of each process. Items from such a measure are presented in Figure 19.3. Note that partially correct answers are not accepted for these items. The child is judged as having made either an acceptable response or an unacceptable response to a given item.[9]

The evaluation strategy of the AAAS Commission on Science Education demonstrates that learning goals can be stated in behavioral terms, that these behaviors can be arranged in a hierarchy for each process, and that each behavior may be assessed through observation and judgment of children's performances.

Since many persons, including educators, tend to view curriculum in terms of content (information, concepts, and skills to be taught and learned) it may be useful to show that a clearly formulated objective has two dimensions, a behavioral aspect and a content aspect. The interrelating of content and behavioral aspects in formulating objectives for a hypothetical high school course in biology is shown in Table 19.1. The headings of columns across the top list nine kinds of behavior aimed for in this particular course. In the left-hand column are listed topics or units of content with respect to which behavioral changes listed across the top are sought. An *X* marking the intersection of a behavioral column and a content row indicates that a behavioral aspect applies in this particular area of content. Thus, a student in this course is expected to develop an understanding of important facts and principles for every one of the content aspects, but he is expected to develop social attitudes only in connection with heredity and genetics, viruses and disease, vertebrates, biology of man, and ecological relationships.

Requirements of an Evaluation Procedure

Before an evaluative judgment can be made about a quality or level of performance, some kind of measurement must be carried out. The measurement process, as we noted earlier, enables us to ascertain whether the ex-

---

[8] Robert M. Gagné, *The Conditions of Learning* (New York: Holt, Rinehart and Winston, 1965), pp. 172–204.

[9] AAAS Commission on Science Education, *Science—A Process Approach. The Process Instrument* (Washington, D.C.: American Association for the Advancement of Science, 1965). Figures 19.2 and 19.3 reproduced from this work by permission.

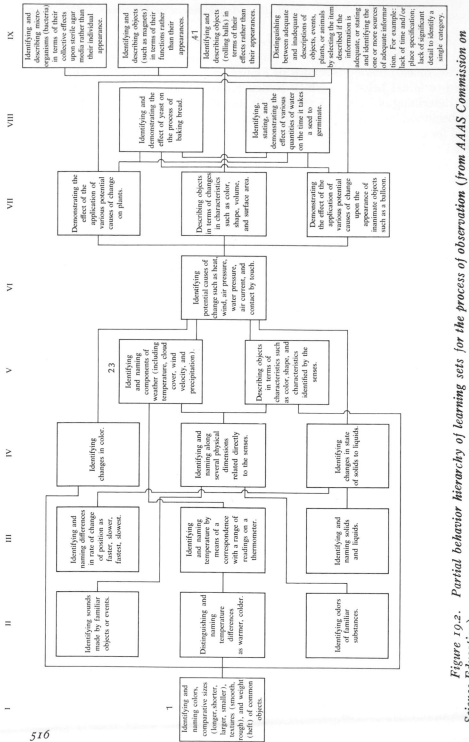

Figure 19.2. Partial behavior hierarchy of learning sets for the process of observation (from AAAS Commission on Science Education).

516

ITEM	PROCEDURE	INSTRUCTIONS TO THE CHILD	ACCEPTABLE RESPONSE
1	The tester places a card with red and green disks on the table in front of the child.	Put your finger on the object which is different from the other two. (Allow about 15 seconds for response.)	The child should point to the green disk.
23	The tester places a picture on the table in front of the child.	Tell me all that you can about the weather in this picture. (The child should be allowed two minutes to respond and after each response he should be asked if that is all.)	Mentions three of the following: (1) Wind speed (2) Temperature (3) Cloud cover (4) Precipitation
41	Take two wads of cotton of equal size. In front of the child fluff one out so it is twice as large as the first wad.	Watch these when I drop them. (Drop cotton wads simultaneously.) Tell me what happens. "Why did that happen?	a. Indicates the fluffy one dropped more slowly. b. More air resistance to fluffy one.

Figure 19.3.   Items from an observing-process measure (from AAAS Commission on Science Education).

pected behavior change has occurred and, if it has, to what extent. Some evidences of learning are revealed by direct observations of behavior. We might, for instance, ascertain a child's reading skill by hearing or watching him read; or we might determine a student's skill in tennis, typing, or playing the violin by watching him or listening to him perform. Other types of behavior may not relate directly to a given objective, but an inference may be drawn from a student's behavior which does relate to the objective. For instance, we may make inferences about a student's interest in science from his frequent selection of books on science and his frequent mention of scientific events, inventions, and discoveries.

Other evidences of learning are revealed most clearly on a test or other measuring device. Since a measuring device samples only a portion of the *population of behaviors* (all of the possible ways in which one might demonstrate behavior change) which constitute a body of content, the sample must be representative of the behaviors associated with that unit or course. In order for a measuring instrument to be representative, it must be comprehensive. A comprehensive test of American history would include items on colonial history as well as items on the Civil War and twentieth-century history. The test would seek to elicit student responses revealing an understanding of social history as well as political and economic history. While a

Table 19.1. *The interrelationships between behavioral objectives and content for a high school course in biology.**

CONTENT	Understands important facts and principles	Knowledge of classifications and categories	Ability to interpret data	Ability to apply principles	Ability to analyze relationships	Ability to plan and to carry out an experiment in solving a problem	Ability to interpret and to evaluate results of a scientific study	Development of broad and mature interests	Development of social attitudes
The nature of life									
Chemical basis of life, the cell	X		X	X	X	X	X	X	
The continuity of life									
Heredity and Genetics	X		X	X	X	X	X	X	X
Microbiology									
Viruses, bacteria, disease	X	X	X	X	X	X	X	X	X
Multicellular Plants									
Root, stem, leaf, structure and function	X	X	X	X	X	X	X	X	
Invertebrates									
Sponges, worms, mollusks, insects	X	X	X	X	X	X	X	X	

CONTENT	Understands important facts and principles	Knowledge of classifications and categories	Ability to interpret data	Ability to apply principles	Ability to analyze relationships	Ability to plan and to carry out an experiment in solving a problem	Ability to interpret and to evaluate results of a scientific study	Development of broad and mature interests	Development of social attitudes
Vertebrates									
Fishes, amphibians, reptiles, birds, mammals	X	X	X	X	X	X	X	X	X
Biology of man									
Body framework, nutrition, circulation	X		X	X	X		X	X	X
Ecological Relationships									
Environmental interrelationships in plant and animal life	X	X	X	X	X		X	X	X

* Content derived from J. H. Otto and Albert Towle, *Modern Biology* (New York: Holt, Rinehart and Winston, 1963). Objectives derived from B. S. Bloom, ed., *Taxonomy of Educational Objectives. Handbook I. Cognitive Domain* (New York: David McKay, 1956). Used by permission of David McKay Company, Inc.

test should be comprehensive, it should also seek to measure only those behavior changes which students have had the opportunity of learning in connection with a particular unit, course, or learning activity. One cannot construct a valid measuring instrument if he lacks detailed information about the learning activity he is seeking to evaluate. Finally, ease of administration and scoring are practical factors which influence the choice and use of a particular measuring instrument or procedure.

Reliability

Every measurement procedure must be reliable; that is, the results obtained by successive administrations of a test or procedure to the same subjects must be consistent. An educational achievement test can be considered reliable if the students of a particular class, without further study, place in about the same rank-order position on a second administration of the test as they did in the first administration. Thus, reliability is a measure of how accurately or how consistently a test or other procedure measures what it purports to measure.

No measuring instrument, not even a yardstick, is perfect—largely because of what we call *errors of measurement*. Errors of measurement can result from a faulty measuring instrument, or from the anxiety or fatigue of those being measured, or from less than optimal conditions of administration. A measuring instrument may be unreliable if some of the items in it are ambiguous or if the number of items it contains is not sufficient to provide an adequate assessment of the learning that has occurred in a given area. A test item is ambiguous if students consistently misinterpret what it asks for. A measuring instrument is also likely to have low reliability if it measures only a small proportion of the course content or expected learning outcomes. Thus, a student's performance on a hundred-item test of biological science is a more reliable measure of what he has learned than is his performance on a ten-item test over the same content. The longer test provides a more complete sampling of what the student has been expected to learn; hence, the reliability of a test may be increased by lengthening it. Again, it is essential that the additional items be representative of content area and relevant to the learning activity being evaluated.

Validity

In asking how valid a test is, we are asking whether the test measures what we want it to measure. Does this test really measure the student's knowledge and understanding of American history, or is it a test of how well he can memorize a body of facts? Is this other test a measure of arithmetic reasoning, or does it measure mental aptitude? The problem of validity is somewhat more elusive than that of reliability and is more difficult to demonstrate. Because of the difficulties of determining validity, many teachers assume that their tests and other measuring devices are valid without taking the effort to find out whether or not their assumption is tenable.

If one were able to show that the items of his test do match the course content and instructional objectives, he would then be able to claim that his test has *content* or *face validity*. This is essentially what a teacher does when he prepares a test blueprint, a detailed description of the learning objectives and of the course content relating to these objectives. Thus, a teacher's own test will probably have validity if he has made a wise and thoughtful analysis of course objectives and if he has exercised care, skill, and ingenuity in building test items to match the blueprint.

A biology teacher who finds that the scores of his students on a teacher-made biology examination have a correlation of .75 with the scores these same students made on a standardized biology test on similar material has demonstrated that his teacher-made test has *concurrent validity*. A demonstration of concurrent validity involves comparing or correlating the results of a new measuring instrument with an instrument whose validity has already been determined. Demonstrations of *construct* and *predictive validity* involve more extensive procedures and are undertaken when one is developing a standardized test or a measuring instrument for research purposes. An instrument has construct validity when those who score high on it also score high on traits or abilities related to the qualities being measured. A science test has construct validity if students who score high on it are observed to use an analytical approach in the solution of problems more frequently than students who score low on the test. A high school biology test has predictive validity if those who score high on it also do well in biology in college.

Construction of Classroom Tests

Most teachers do not give sufficient time and care to the construction of classroom tests. Developing a good test is something of an art. It is not something that happens as the result of the teacher's jotting down questions as he leafs through the textbook. Constructing a valid test is a deliberate and time-consuming process and requires thoughtful reflection. Stanley,[10] recognizing that a satisfactory test is extremely difficult to construct, suggests that several teachers might do well to work together on a test.

The primary function of a test, as of any evaluation procedure, is to ascertain to what extent pupils have achieved the objectives of instruction. If a test is to measure pupil achievement in all of the learning objectives, it must be carefully designed and planned to include items or questions relating to each objective. Particularly, the relative importance of an objective must be reflected in the number of items allotted to it or the number of points which may be earned on that part of the test. If a teacher writes objective test items as they occur to him without regard to course objectives or the scope of course content, the test is likely to be out of balance—overrepresenting some objectives or topics and underrepresenting others.

[10] Julian C. Stanley, *Measurement in Today's Schools* (Englewood Cliffs, New Jersey: Prentice-Hall, 1964), p. 171.

Lack of balance in a test often results because it is easier to write items that test recall and recognition of facts than it is to develop items that call for an understanding of generalizations or an application of principles. Moreover, it is easier to develop items or questions on some topics than it is on others. This is likely to lead to a preponderance of items or questions on the more testable topics or objectives. By failing to test some learning objectives or by testing others with disproportionate emphasis, a test falls short of its purpose. What students find emphasized on tests they will tend to emphasize in their study and preparation. Thus, the kind of test a teacher uses may cause students to emphasize in their study the recognition or recall of facts—learning objectives quite different from those the teacher may think he is emphasizing, namely, the evaluation of evidence and the application of principles.

As suggested, the first step in planning a test is to state and to define the learning objectives in terms of behavior. The second step is to outline the content to be covered by the test. (These two steps are incorporated into the chart in Table 19.2.) The third step is to relate the statement of objectives and the course content in developing a *test blueprint*.[11] In a test blueprint, test content is elaborated in detail. The blueprint contains only those objectives that can be measured either wholly or in part by paper-and-pencil test. In order to complete the blueprint, the test maker must decide on the relative emphasis to be given to each learning objective and content area. He may indicate relative emphasis by assigning a percentage to each objective. Each percentage serves as a guide to the number of items allotted that particular objective or topic on an objective test or the weight of the scoring of answers to essay questions. A test blueprint also contains the number of items on the test, the total time for the test, and the proportion of test items to be drawn from class lectures, discussion, laboratory sessions, and the textbook or other readings. A test blueprint for measuring the objectives of a high school course in biology in relation to course content is shown in Table 19.2. Objectives 8 and 9 on Table 19.1 (objectives relating to the development of interests and social attitudes) are not included in the blueprint in Table 19.2, since these are not readily measured by achievement tests.

Developing a test blueprint undoubtedly takes some time, but it does help to insure some kind of evaluation of each learning objective and area of course content. The analysis required by the test blueprint clarifies the objectives of the unit or course, guides in the preparation of a sound test, and aids in the teaching of the unit itself.

Developing Objective Tests

The two kinds of tests now in general use are the *essay* test and the *objective* test. An essay test requires the student to plan his own answer and

[11] For a further discussion of the test blueprint, see Robert L. Thorndike and Elizabeth Hagen, *Measurement and Evaluation in Psychology and Education,* 2nd ed. (New York: John Wiley, 1961), pp. 33–41.

Table 19.2. Test blueprint for evaluating achievement of objectives of a high school course in biology.

WEIGHT-ING	LEARNING OBJECTIVES IN TERMS OF BEHAVIOR	CONTENT
30%	1. Understands important facts and principles	protoplasm DNA pericardium Golgi body meiosis neuron homeostasis mutation myxedema photosynthesis cilia corpus luteum ATP epithelial tissue progesterone
10%	2. Knows and uses appropriate classification systems	Identifying, distinguishing between, and ordering exemplars of various forms of plant and animal life: phylum, division, class, order, genus, and species.
10%	3. Demonstrates ability to interpret data	Data are presented showing relationships among eight families in which feeble-mindedness appears. Student responds to statements with (1) true (2) insufficient evidence, or (3) false. Example: 1. Where both parents were feebleminded, all children who lived beyond infancy were feebleminded.
20%	4. Applies principles in solving problems	Examples: 1. If the DNA amino acid code consisted of two bases instead of three, how many amino acids could be coded? 2. Why is it easier to digest sour milk than fresh milk? 3. How would you design an experiment to prove whether or not the eye really sees an image upside down while the brain interprets it oppositely?
10%	5. Analyzes relationships between phenomena and events	Analyze the relationships between: 1. Different forms of energy 2. Plants and animals 3. Function and structure of organs 4. Systems of the human body 5. Climate, soil, water, forests, and wildlife
10%	6. Synthesizes various data in formulating hypotheses and deriving statements of relationships	Can derive and elaborate concepts and generalizations concerning fundamental life processes: reproduction, growth, differentiation, integration, metabolism, hierarchy of control and function, anabolism, catabolism.

WEIGHT-ING	LEARNING OBJECTIVES IN TERMS OF BEHAVIOR	CONTENT
10%	7. Interprets and evaluates critically results of a scientific study	Example: Two bean plants were planted in each of six three-inch pots. Three pots contained clay and were placed in a cupboard. Three pots containing sandy soil were placed in a window. All pots were watered regularly and uniformly. After three weeks the bean plants grown in the window had sturdy stalks and large green leaves. The bean plants grown in the cupboard had spindly stems and small yellow leaves. The investigator concluded that light is necessary for the normal growth of bean seedlings.

Total time for test —50 minutes
Total number of test items—50
40% of items to be drawn from textbook and readings
40% of items drawn from lectures and class discussions
20% of items drawn from laboratory work and demonstrations

express it in his own words. An objective test usually consists of many more items than an essay test, and each item requires the testee to choose from among several designated alternatives. As we shall see, both kinds of tests have advantages and disadvantages.

Historically, the earliest type of test was probably the oral examination, wherein questions were put by a teacher, an examiner, or a committee to the student, who was then marked on his ability to verbalize what he had learned. This method encouraged students to memorize facts verbatim—a sterile exercise, often performed without understanding. Performing under the scrutiny of peers as well as adults was usually an ordeal; and the amount of time required for an oral examination and the limited amount of content whose mastery could be evaluated for any one student made this a costly and inefficient method of examination. The oral examination is still used in special situations—for instance, in the evaluation of a single candidate seeking to qualify for honors at graduation, for professional certification, or for a master's or doctor's degree.

In time, written examinations took the place of oral examinations. Written examinations permit a much wider sampling of subject matter, and the student is freed from the scrutiny of teacher and pupils while he composes his answers. The chief criticism leveled at essay examinations is that teachers' marks on these examinations are unreliable. Starch and Elliott,[12]

[12] D. Starch and E. C. Elliott, "Reliability of the Grading of High School Work in English," *School Review,* 20 (1912), 442–457; "Reliability of Grading Work in Mathematics," *School Review,* 21 (1913), 254–259; "Reliability of Grading Work in History," *School Review,* 21 (1913), 676–681.

for instance, gave identical copies of an English examination paper to 142 English teachers, who were instructed to score it on the basis of 100 percent for a perfect paper. The scores assigned by the 142 teachers to the same paper ranged from 50 to 98 percent. Similar results were obtained with examination papers in geometry and in history. The unreliability of teachers' marks in scoring essay examinations led to the development of new objective examinations, consisting of a fairly large number of specific questions requiring only brief answers. The use of objective tests enables teachers to examine students over a broad area of content.

The objective test requires the individual taking the test to choose from among several designated alternatives. The principal kinds of objective examinations are (1) true-false, (2) multiple choice, (3) completion, and (4) matching.[13]

True-false items are limited to statements that are unequivocally true or demonstrably false. Because of this limitation, they measure the student's retention of specific, isolated, and often trivial facts. They appear to be best suited to test the student's recognition and definition of terms. *Completion* items ask the testee to recall and supply the best or correct answer from a limited number of possible answers. Completion tests are well suited to testing knowledge of vocabulary, names, or dates; identification of concepts; and ability to solve algebraic or numerical problems. Their chief disadvantage is that varied answers are likely to call for skill and discrimination in scoring and thus introduce subjectivity into the scoring procedure. Examples of true-false and completion items are shown in Figures 19.4[14] and 19.5.

A *multiple-choice* item consists of two parts: (1) the stem, which presents the problem; and (2) the list of possible answers. Multiple-choice items, the most flexible and most effective of all the objective items, are particularly useful for measuring information, vocabulary, understanding, application of principles, and the interpretation of data. For examples of multiple-choice items, see Figure 19.6.

A *matching* test, actually a type of multiple-choice test, measures the student's ability to recall relationships between pairs of items. Instead of a simple problem or stem, several problems are listed in one column, and a list of possible answers in another column. The testee must match items in the two columns. Matching items are often used in history tests, to measure the student's ability to relate names and events. Figure 19.7 shows that matching items may be adapted to test the student's ability to identify correctly a series of related organs, parts, or concepts in biology.

Scoring of objective tests consists of placing a key beside the answers marked by the student and counting the number of correct responses. Since (except for completion items) there is only one correct answer, error and

---

[13] For specific help in writing acceptable objective-test items see Thorndike and Hagen.

[14] Figures 19.4, 19.5, 19.6 and items 1, 2, and 3 of Figure 19.7 are reproduced from J. H. Otto, Sam S. Blanc, and E. H. Crider, *Series A, Tests in Biology* (New York: Holt, Rinehart and Winston, 1960). Used by permission. In Figure 19.7, items 4 and 5 are reproduced from B. S. Bloom, *Taxonomy of Learning Objectives. Handbook I. Cognitive Domain* (New York: David McKay Co., 1956). Used by permission.

Directions: If a statement is true, mark a T in the space in front of the number; if false, mark an F.

_____ 1. The fluid portion of the blood is called the plasma.

_____ 2. Red (oxygenated) blood flows through veins of the systemic circulation.

_____ 3. A person with normal blood volume and white-cell count but low red-cell count is suffering from hemophilia.

_____ 4. The muscular partition dividing the heart into a right and left side is called the ventricle.

_____ 5. A calorimeter is used for measuring blood pressure

_____ 6. The relaxed cycle of heart action is called diastole.

_____ 7. Stuffiness in a room is due largely to the low oxygen content of the air.

_____ 8. A tiny knoblike mass of capillaries surrounded by a kidney capsule is called a glomerulus.

_____ 9. The normal white-cell count per cubic millimeter is about 20,000.

_____10. Worn out red blood corpuscles are filtered out of the blood stream in the spleen.

Figure 19.4. A portion of a true-false test on respiration and circulation (from Otto, Blanc, and Crider).

bias on the part of the grader are eliminated. Moreover, the ease of scoring makes the objective test attractive to teachers. Although this kind of examination is relatively time-consuming and difficult to prepare, the items can be used again and again. And, as noted earlier, an objective test does permit a much broader sampling of content in a given subject. Students are able to respond to fifty multiple-choice items or a hundred true-false items during an hour's examination, whereas only six to eight essay questions could be answered in this period of time.

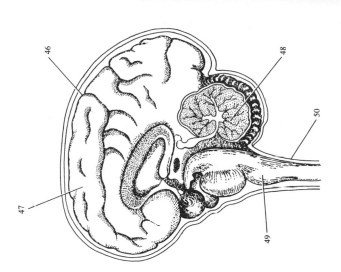

Directions: After each of the following statements,
write the word that completes the statement.

1. Chromosomes appear, shorten, and thicken
during the stage of mitosis known as _____

2. Another name for reduction division is _____

3. Characteristics which are present but
which do not appear in hybrids are
termed _____

4. Genes operate independently of other
genes. This fact illustrates Mendel's
Law of _____

Directions: This drawing is a cross section
of the human brain. Write the
names of the numbered parts in
the corresponding spaces below.

46._____

47._____

48._____

49._____

50._____

Figure 19.5. *Examples of completion items in tests in biology (from Otto, Blanc, and Crider).*

Directions: Match the terms on the left with
the definitions on the right, using
letter answers.

A. Amino acid   1. The roof of the mouth   _____

B. Colon   2. The large intestine   _____

C. Esophagus   3. Fingerlike projections
                     from the wall of the
D. Palate   small intestine   _____

E. Peristalsis   4. The sphincter valve at
                     the lower end of the
F. Pylorus   stomach   _____

G. Villi   5. The end product of
                     protein digestion   _____
H. Mesentery

6. A fanlike membrane which
anchors the loops of
intestine   _____

7. Rhythmic contractions of
the smooth muscle layers
of digestive organs   _____

8. The region of the alimentary
canal extending from pharynx
to stomach.   _____

Figure 19.6. A series of matching items on foods and digestion (from Otto, Blanc, and Crider).

A chief criticism of objective examinations is that they emphasize isolated, often trivial, bits of information and thus measure the student's ability to recognize the right answer but not his understanding of the material or his ability to recall or reproduce the right answer. In spite of this criticism, students who make high scores on objective tests also do well on essay examinations.[15] Thus, the two kinds of tests appear to measure the same kinds of competencies.

A further criticism of objective examinations is that they fail to measure the abilities of students to organize their ideas, to think through

[15] Lindgren, pp. 441–442.

Directions: Select the best choice to complete the
              following statements.   Write its letter
              in the space at the right.

1. The function of the sensory neurons is to carry impulses
   from the skin and sense organs to the
              A. muscles
              B. brain
              C. brain and spinal cord
              D. motor neurons   _____

2. Acetylcholine is a chemical substance which causes
              A. muscles to contract
              B. blindness
              C. deafness
              D. color blindness   _____

3. The cerebral cortex controls
              A. involuntary actions
              B. voluntary actions
              C. the sympathetic system
              D. the parasympathetic system   _____

    When on Thursday, February 8, 1951, a Chicagoan,
Mrs. Dorothy Mae Stevens, was found unconscious in a
passageway after a night of exposure to subzero weather,
"she was literally frozen stiff." Her temperature had
dropped to an unprecedented 64 degrees (Fahrenheit).
Twenty hours after her arrival at Michael Reese Hospital
her temperature had risen to 98.2 degrees. Early Friday
it was 101 and later 100.

4. At a body temperature of 64 degrees
   A. the blood carries more oxygen to the cells than
      normally because more gases dissolve in fluids at
      low temperatures rather than at high temperatures
   B. the blood vessels of the skin are dilated because
      the vasoconstrictor muscles are related
   C. the heart beats more rapidly because the cold
      stimulates the heart center in the medulla
   D. most activities slow down because all chemical
      activities decrease as the temperature falls _____

5. The immediate cause of Mrs. Stevens' unconsciousness
   was probably due to
   A. lack of a sufficient amount of oxygen to the
      brain cells
   B. lowering of the external temperature
   C. slow pulse rate
   D. decrease in muscle tone
   E. low breathing rate   _____

Figure 19.7.   Examples of multiple-choice items in tests in biology (from Otto, Blanc, and Crider and Bloom).

problems, to analyze relationships, and to apply principles. This criticism may be valid for true-false, completion, and matching items, but multiple-choice tests are flexible enough to test almost any objective that can be measured by a paper-and-pencil test.

There does appear to be some basis for the belief that a teacher communicates his objectives through the kinds of tests he gives and that students prepare for objective tests and for essay tests in different ways. Unless the teacher using objective tests includes items that measure such objectives as analysis of relationships, application of principles, and interpretation of data, his tests will reflect only informational goals. Students will focus on learning specific bits of information in that course. The limitations of strict information learning are all the more distressing when we recall the high incidence of forgetting of facts that occurs during six weeks following the completion of a course.

Essay Tests

As noted earlier, an essay examination asks the student to write extended answers to a relatively few questions. The essay examination has the following advantages: (1) It permits the student to organize his own answer and to express his individuality in the answers he writes on the test. (2) It requires the student to produce rather than merely to recognize the right answer. (3) If questions are well prepared, it can bring out the examinee's ability to select important facts and ideas, relate them to one another, and organize them into a coherent whole.

Thorndike and Hagen[16] offer several suggestions for the construction of good essay tests. Before starting to write an essay question, the teacher should have in mind the mental processes he wishes the students to use in answering the question. If the teacher is measuring pupils' abilities to comprehend, analyze, apply, interpret, evaluate, interrelate, contrast, or to think divergently, then he should begin an essay question with such words or phrases as *Compare, Contrast, Give reasons for, Present arguments for or against, Explain how or why,* or *What if.* Questions beginning with *What, Who, When,* and *List* should be avoided, since they generally elicit only specific bits of information. Imperatives such as *Discuss* also should be avoided because they do not pinpoint clearly and unambiguously the task the examinee is expected to carry out in answering the question.

The following essay questions seek to measure the attainment of learning objectives (presented earlier in the chapter) for a high school course in biology.

1. Self-preservation is a basic instinct of all vertebrates. Compare it with species preservation and give illustrations of each.

[16] Thorndike and Hagen, pp. 50–56.

2. Trace a nerve impulse through a reflex action starting with a nerve ending in the skin and ending with a muscle response. Explain how reflex actions are often safeguards against serious injury.

3. Distinguish between an *addiction* (such as occurs with the use of drugs and alcohol) and a *habit* (such as, for example, the tobacco habit).

4. Explain the changes in chromosome number which occur during meiosis and fertilization, and tell why these changes are necessary in preserving the proper number of chromosomes in the organism.[17]

Because of the potential low reliability of teachers' scoring of essay examinations, special care should be taken by the teacher to ensure that his evaluation of answers to essay questions are as objective as possible. The following suggestions[18] may help the scorer maintain some uniformity and consistency in his scoring of different answers to the same question.

First, the scorer should know exactly what factors are being measured by the test. If more than one quality is being measured, each should be evaluated separately. For example, a literature test might be given one score for the facts presented and another score for the organization and quality of written expression. Next, the scorer should prepare a model answer, showing the points that should be included in a satisfactory answer and specifying the maximum credit for each item or subitem. This model provides a common frame of reference for evaluating each paper. After the preliminary model has been prepared, it should be checked against a sample of student responses to the question to ascertain whether it is consistent with the students' interpretations of and answers to the question. The model and scoring scheme should then be modified so that it may serve as an adequate yardstick.

By reading all answers to one question before going on to the next question, the scorer can maintain a more uniform standard of evaluation, since he can compare one student's answer with another's. Moreover, this procedure lessens the contamination of the scorer's judgment with what the student wrote on a previous question.

Finally, the less the scorer knows about the person who wrote the answer, the more objectively he can grade what has been written.

Two types of procedures are generally used for scoring essay examinations. The first is to sort all answers to a single question into five piles on the basis of their quality (superior, good, fair, poor, inferior). Then, each paper is given a numerical score based on some type of equal-interval scale, such as 5, 4, 3, 2, 1 or 15, 12, 9, 6, 3. In this manner, each paper is scored for all questions, and an over-all score is computed. Another method is to construct a scale based on samples of responses representing degrees of correctness. Each pupil's answer to a question is then compared with the scale samples,

[17] Otto, Blanc, and Crider.
[18] From Thorndike and Hagen, p. 56.

and a scale value is assigned to the answer in terms of its degree of correctness as compared with the scale.

While both teachers and students will have their preferences for administering or taking an essay or an objective examination, we cannot state that one type is superior to the other. Each type has its strengths and weaknesses. Neither the essay test nor the objective test is satisfactory as a sole measure of academic achievement. Whether to administer an essay examination or an objective examination is likely to be determined by the particular learning objectives sought, the type of concept, skill, or content matter being assessed, and the characteristics and needs of the students being tested. If learning objectives direct learners to interpret and to interrelate ideas and to integrate a number of facts and concepts, such as might be required in the study of history or literature, then an essay examination would probably be the best vehicle for measuring the attainment of these objectives. If ability to organize one's ideas and to express them well in written English is not a goal of the particular learning activity, then an objective examination might be a more valid measure of what a class has learned in mathematics, science, business law, or electronics. Table 19.3[19] lists the strengths and weaknesses of essay and objective examinations.

Other Evaluation Procedures

Observation of Behavior

The teacher observes and describes pupil behavior in written anecdotes and case records primarily to increase his own understanding of the pupil's development and learning. He can use these same recorded behavioral data for evaluating a pupil's progress with respect to a range of learning objectives.

Although behavioral data on pupils are useful to educators in many ways, the difficulties of obtaining adequate, reliable samples of pupils' behavior have imposed limitations on their use. As noted in Chapter 2, anecdotal descriptions often contain opinions, generalizations, and interpretations instead of facts about the student's behavior. The following entry is illustrative.

> Tom is a large, overage boy in my sixth-grade class. He is loud and boisterous and frequently bothers others so that they cannot complete their work. He seldom completes his assignments, but instead wastes his time drawing racing cars and diagramming radio and television circuits. On the playground he is aggressive, plays roughly with other children, and is something of a bully.

[19] From *Making the Classroom Test: A Guide for Teachers,* Evaluation and Advisory Service Series, No. 4. © First edition, copyright 1959 by Educational Testing Service. Second edition, 1961. Reproduced by permission.

*Table 19.3.   Comparison of essay and objective examinations
(Educational Testing Service).*

	ESSAY	OBJECTIVE
Abilities measured	Requires the student to express himself in his own words, using information from his own background and knowledge.	Requires the student to select correct answers from given options, or to supply an answer limited to one word or phrase.
	Can tap high levels of reasoning such as required in inference, organization of ideas, comparison and contrast.	Can *also* tap high levels of reasoning such as required in inference, organization of ideas, comparison and contrast.
	Does not measure purely factual information efficiently.	Measures knowledge of facts efficiently.
Scope	Covers only a limited field of knowledge in any one test. Essay questions take so long to answer that relatively few can be answered in a given period of time. Also, the student who is especially fluent can often avoid discussing points of which he is unsure.	Covers a broad field of knowledge in one test. Since objective questions may be answered quickly, one test may contain many questions. A broad coverage helps provide reliable measurement.
Incentive to pupils	Encourages pupils to learn how to organize their own ideas and express them effectively.	Encourages pupils to build a broad background of knowledge and abilities.
Ease of preparation	Requires writing only a few questions for a test. Tasks must be clearly defined, general enough to offer some leeway, specific enough to set limits.	Requires writing many questions for a test. Wording must avoid ambiguities and "giveaways."
Scoring	Usually very time consuming to score.	Can be scored quickly.
	Permits teachers to comment directly on the reasoning processes of individual pupils. However, an answer may be scored differently by different teachers or by the same teacher at different times.	Answer generally scored only right or wrong, but scoring is very accurate and consistent.

This generalized description of Tom and his behavior is of only limited help in evaluating his development and learning. It tells us more about the values, biases, and expectations of the person who wrote the description than it tells us about Tom. In order for information obtained by observation to be valid, it must first of all be specific, factual, and descriptive. Second, a representative sample of a student's behavior must be obtained by observations of him in a variety of situations. We cannot assume that the way Tom behaves in arithmetic is the way he is all of the time. We need to observe Tom in reading, in the lunchroom, on the playground, and before and after school if we are to obtain a balanced picture of what he is really like.

In the following anecdotal descriptions of the behavior of Clare, a first grader, we note first that the teacher has described objectively and completely Clare's behavior during one period, the reading period, on a specific day. The second entry presents a more generalized description of Clare's behavior, based on observations and descriptions of Clare in many specific situations.

MARCH 6

Clare's reading group is the fastest one of four. This year I am giving the children many easy books before they are introduced to a hard-back book. The vocabularies are similar in most of the preprimers. Since we have been introducing the second and third of a series of preprimers, Clare has been more interested in reading.

This day, as usual, she brought her chair up to the circle and placed it next to the teacher. Their new preprimer, *My Little Red Story Book*, had been given to this class the day before to study. Clare just couldn't get the children into the circle fast enough. "Hurry up, Bunny. Sit here, Sally. Bring your chair over here. Don't sit too close. It's hot. Now, Miss J., everybody is ready. May I read?" She read four pages without a mistake.

MARCH 27

Clare is in the most mature reading group. The group has about ten children in it. This group has read ten preprimers from the Ginn and Scott-Foresman series. Clare frequently makes comments about the stories and helps others whether they need help or not. She often asks to be the first one to read. When given her turn, she reads with head cocked to one side. She reads well—smoothly, with understanding and humor, but methodically. She always tries to sit next to the teacher. When it is necessary to ask her to be quiet or to listen, she usually complies temporarily with a smile on her face.

Observations of classroom behavior frequently yield evidences of pupils' behavior change not revealed in paper-and-pencil tests. As indicated earlier, a teacher should continuously check his initial inferences of behavior change by further observations of the pupil. This is necessary to ensure that one's observations of pupil behavior are reliable and also to pick up changes in the pupil's behavior as soon as they occur. Table 19.4[20] presents a list of categories of student behaviors and learning activities which may assist one in observing pupils' classroom behavior.

Table 19.4. Observation categories of student behavior and learning activities (from Perkins).

STUDENT BEHAVIOR

LISWAT	Interested in ongoing work: listening and watching—passive.
REWR	Reading or Writing; working in assigned area—active.
HIAC	High activity or involvement: reciting or using large muscles—positive feeling.
WOA	Intent on work in another curricular area: school activity not assigned to be done right then.
WNA	Intent on work of nonacademic type: preparing for work assignment, cleaning out desk, etc.
SWP	Social, work-oriented—PEER: discussing some aspect of schoolwork with classmate.
SWT	Social, work-oriented—TEACHER: discussing some phase of work with teacher.
SF	Social, friendly: talking to peer on subject unrelated to schoolwork.
WDL	Withdrawal: detached, out of contact with people, ideas, classroom situation; daydreaming.

LEARNING ACTIVITIES

DISC	Large-group discussion: entire class discusses an issue or evaluates an oral report.
REC	Class recitation: teacher questions, student answers—entire class or portion of it participating.
IND	Individual work or project: student is working alone on task that is not a common assignment.
SEAT	Seat work, reading or writing, common assignment.
GRP	Small-group or committee work: student is part of group or committee working on assignment.
REP	Oral reports—individual or group: student is orally reporting on book, current events, or research.

---

[20] From Hugh V. Perkins, "A Procedure for Assessing the Classroom Behavior of Students and Teachers," *American Educational Research Journal,* 1 (November 1964), 251. Reproduced by permission.

Projects and Papers

Projects and papers give clear indications of a pupil's achievement of learning objectives. Through such activities, the student can demonstrate his individual abilities and talents, and he often acquires more knowledge and information than is called for on a test. The science fairs held in many junior and senior high schools provide ample opportunity for students to acquire a broad range of knowledge and skills by working on science projects.

Projects provide opportunities for students with limited reading and language skills to have a meaningful learning experience and to demonstrate some of the skills and concepts they have learned. Mature students and those with reading and language skills can demonstrate considerable ability in independent research papers if they are working on something that is interesting and important to them and if they are given freedom to choose and to develop their own subject. Thus, teachers would do well to involve students actively in the initiating, carrying out, and evaluating of projects and papers.

Standardized Achievement Tests

Standardized tests are tests that have been constructed to measure specific kinds and qualities of behavior for which available norms show the average or expected performance of persons at each age or grade level. The standardized tests most familiar to teachers and students are those that measure intelligence or intellectual aptitude and school achievement, but other standardized measures have been developed to assess interests, special aptitudes, personality, personal and social adjustment, and self-concept.[21]

Since qualities of behavior such as intelligence and scholastic achievement are multidimensional, a standardized test of intelligence or achievement frequently consists of a battery of several tests. An intelligence battery may have individual tests of vocabulary, analogies, spatial relationships, arithmetic reasoning, quantitative concepts, and nonverbal performance; an achievement battery may have separate scales for reading, language arts, and arithmetic, and possibly social studies, science, map reading, and study skills as well.

Most standardized tests appear in published form, but this is no guarantee of their quality. Judgments regarding the quality of a given test may be made by analyzing the information concerning its reliability and validity reported in the *Mental Measurements Yearbooks* edited by O. K. Buros (Gryphon Press, Highland Park, New Jersey). Unless one has had courses in educational measurements or statistics, he may wish to seek the assistance of a counselor or psychometrist in interpreting the information contained in the Buros reference.

---

[21] For a discussion of these tests, see L. J. Cronbach, *Essentials of Psychological Testing* (New York: Harper & Row, 1960); and A. Anastasi, *Psychological Testing* (New York: Macmillan Co., 1954).

The major value of a standardized test is that its results may be used to assess the performances of a specific individual, a class, a school, or a school district in relation to another comparable group. One may wish to compare the school achievement of a particular sixth-grade class or all the sixth-grade classes in a school district with that of sixth-grade children in classrooms or districts in other parts of the city, county, state, or country. Such data are useful in evaluating school programs, but they should be interpreted carefully, since groups that seem very similar may in fact be incomparable.

Characteristically, standardized tests have been administered to large samples of subjects, and performance *norms* have been developed through analyses of the scores obtained from these several samples. The samples of subjects selected constitute comparison groups. For example, the authors of a standardized achievement battery for a junior high school would have the battery administered to groups of seventh-, eighth-, and ninth-grade students in large and small schools; in middle-class and lower-class communities; in rural, urban, and suburban areas; and in different regions of the country. If these several samples of students collectively may be presumed to be representative of seventh-, eighth-, and ninth-grade students in the United States, then the average scores for each grade and each subscale of the battery would serve as the basis for deriving the *national norms* for this test.

Generally, the raw scores for each grade and subscale are converted to percentile scores ranging from 1 to 99. A percentile score indicates the percentage of students in the relative *comparison group* who scored above and below the student receiving that percentile score. Thus, an eighth-grade student whose performance on a subscale or a total test battery yields a percentile score of 75 has scored higher than 75 percent of the eighth graders in the comparison group on that measure and lower than 25 percent of the comparison group.

Achievement-test batteries developed for students in grades one to twelve often report norms in *grade equivalents*. A student whose score on a reading test yields a grade equivalent of 6 has performed as well as an average sixth-grade student.

A comparison between a student's achievement-test score and the norms for that test indicates this student's *relative performance* when matched against the performance of the comparison group. Educators should exercise caution in interpreting achievement-test scores. Norms do not represent ideal performances, nor do they represent what students ought to know. Moreover, norms that are based on the average performance (in arithmetic or language usage, for example) of a divers population in all parts of the United States are likely to be inadequate for judging the degree to which the learning objectives of a specific teacher and specific class have been achieved.

Standardized tests differ from teacher-made tests in that the former usually prescribe a set of specific controlled conditions under which they are to be administered. These conditions are generally set forth in the test manual which accompanies each test. Included in the manual is a statement of directions for taking the test that is read to examinees. If it is a timed test, the time limits for each part of the test are specified. Observance of these time limits by the test administrator ensures that all students have an equal opportunity to perform the tasks called for on the test. Directions read by the test administrator may urge persons taking the test to answer only when they are sure they are right, or may inform them that they will not be penalized for guessing. Thus, the prescribed set of conditions sought in the administration and scoring of a standardized test is a control to ensure comparable performances by all persons taking the test.

Standardized achievement-test batteries are generally administered at specified grade levels, together with a standardized group intelligence test, as part of the school's over-all testing program. No particular standardized achievement test will measure all of a teacher's learning objectives for his particular class; however, the results do provide information on the achievement of learning goals common to like classes or courses—at least in the elementary grades. As students progress up the educational ladder, there is less and less agreement concerning the skills, concepts, and information that should comprise a common core of learnings. Moreover, as students become older, the range of individual differences in their aptitudes and interests becomes wider and more varied. Consequently, achievement-test batteries appear to be less useful for evaluating the effectiveness of specific learning activities in secondary schools than they are in elementary schools.[22]

Reporting Pupil Progress

School Marks

After the task of measurement—whether by pupil recitation, teacher-made test, teacher observation, or standardized test—has been completed, the job of making and reporting judgments of pupils' performance in relation to a criterion performance still must be done. After evaluations of pupil behaviors have been made, some report of these evaluations should be given to the pupils themselves if the evaluations are to influence their subsequent performances in these learning activities.

Few would question the necessity of evaluation and feedback in improving learning, but that part of the evaluation process which involves the giving of a mark to stand for the student's achievement is frequently disturbing to teachers, parents, and pupils alike. Few issues in education have been so fraught with strong feelings, divergent points of view, and controversy as has been the problem of assigning school marks. Although school marks are only symbols of pupil achievement, often of low reliability at best, high marks are avidly sought and prized as evidence of one's intellectual attainments and as evidence predicting success in an achievement-oriented, highly competitive culture. Few will doubt that a high grade-point average is an important prerequisite for admission to a prestige college, university, gradu-

---

[22] Lindgren, pp. 450–451.

ate school, or professional school; for receiving a favorable job opportunity; and for winning approval from family and friends. In view of the continuing interest in and emphasis upon school marks, a further study of this aspect of the evaluation procedure is indicated.

After a test or other measuring device has been scored, it is necessary to evaluate the learner's status or change in behavior as represented by this score. This involves the classifying of scores made by the pupils into various levels or categories of acceptability or unacceptability of performance. Thus, each student's raw score is translated into a percentage score or placed in a category to indicate his position in relation to others in the group with whom he is being compared. The teacher might designate 70 percent as the minimum score for a passing grade, or he might categorize scores and distribute grades according to some kind of a frequency curve. He might decide that the three papers with the lowest scores will receive a grade of *F*, or he might decide to give no paper an *F* grade. In any case, the teacher should inform his students of the criteria he has used to arrive at grades and of the meaning of the grading symbols.

The teacher's labeling of categories of acceptable and unacceptable performance by assigning percent scores or letter marks is, of course, arbitrary. This arbitrariness is largely the result of a lack of clearly defined, generally accepted, and scrupulously observed definitions of what various marks should mean; and a lack of relevant, objective evidence to use as a basis for assigning marks.

Perhaps the most perplexing problem that confronts the teacher-evaluator is the question "What does a mark represent?" Presumably, it represents an estimate of the kinds of achievement or behavior change that have occurred in relation to the objectives of the unit, course, or learning activity. We use the term *estimate* because no test or other measuring device can be expected to measure everything a person knows about American history, English literature, or algebra.

First of all, the teacher-evaluator must decide, "Does this mark represent some level of absolute achievement (that is, my concept of what any student at this level of development should know or perform); or does it represent this student's achievement relative to achievements of other comparable students?" A school mark presumably represents the student's achievement relative to the achievements of comparable students; but the other criterion too frequently influences a teacher's marking practice. In addition, unless neatness, effort, the development of strong motivation, or positive attitudes and values is included among the learning objectives to be achieved, the assigning of a mark should not be influenced by these factors. Yet most teachers, either consciously or unconsciously, are probably influenced in some degree by these and other nonrelevant factors in their assignment of grades. Battle[23] found that students with the highest achievement as mea-

[23] H. J. Battle, "Relation between Personal Values and Scholastic Achievement," *Journal of Experimental Education,* 26 (1957), 27–41.

sured by school marks had attitudes and values more like the teachers award-
ing these marks than did the average student. Students with low achievement, on the other hand, had attitudes and values markedly unlike those of
their teachers.

Some studies show that the sex of the teacher and the sex and IQ of the
student influence the assigning of school marks. For example, in a class in
beginning algebra, Carter[24] found that teachers gave girls significantly
higher marks than boys, that women teachers in general gave higher marks
than did men teachers, and that teachers' marks reflected not only student
achievement but also student intelligence. This tendency for irrelevant
factors to influence grades helps to explain the low reliability of teachers'
marks.

Can the process of grading be made less arbitrary? It is possible to
assign school marks according to a normal curve which reflects the spread or
distribution of scores in a group. Figure 19.8[25] shows a normal curve of
distribution and the relations of various derived scores to the normal curve
and to each other. The *standard deviation* is a measure of variability, disper-
sion, or spread of a set of scores. In a normal distribution, 68.26 percent of
all the scores lie within one standard deviation of the mean. The *percentile
equivalent* is a number indicating the percentage of scores in the whole
distribution which fall below the point at which a particular given score lies.
A *quartile* is one of three points which divide a distribution of scores into
four parts of equal frequency. Q_1 refers to the first quartile and corresponds
to the 25th percentile; Md refers to the median or 50th percentile; and Q_3
refers to the third quartile or 75th percentile. The terms *z-scores* and *T-
scores* refer to two *standard scores* (scores, derived from raw scores, that can
be expressed on a uniform standard scale without seriously altering their
relationship to other scores in the distribution). *CEEB* and *AGCT* refer to
two standardized measures, the College Entrance Examination Board and
Army General Classification Test. The *stanine* scores, normally distributed
standard scores ranging from 1 to 9, may serve as a model for assigning
marks according to the normal curve of distribution. Here again, however,
the teacher must decide how wide each band should be for each grade. Should
a grade of *A* be assigned to stanine scores 8 and 9 and a grade of *F* to stanine
scores 1 and 2? How wide should the *B, C,* and *D* bands be?

In practice, the distribution curve of a teacher's grades for a class
seldom follows the normal symmetrical curve exactly, since most classes are
perceived to vary somewhat from the theoretically normal group. Indeed,
there is a tendency for teachers to assign overall a greater proportion of *A*
and *B* grades than *D* and *F* grades. Thus, the average grade on a five-point
scale is usually not a *C* but somewhere between a *B* and a *C*.

In spite of the limitations of school marks, they remain probably the

[24] R. S. Carter, "How Invalid Are Marks Assigned by Teachers?" *Journal of Educational Psychology,* 43 (April 1952), 218–228.
[25] Reproduced by permission of The Psychological Corporation, New York, New York.

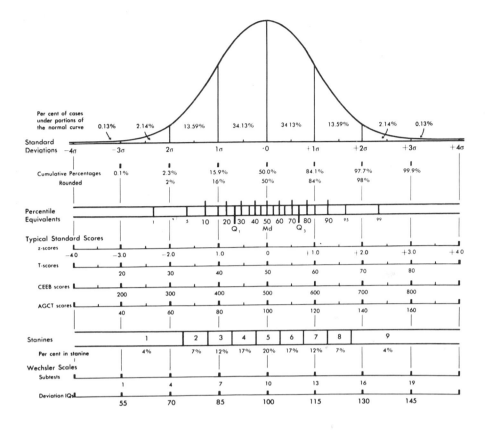

Figure 19.8. *The normal curve of distribution, percentiles, and standard scores.*

best single predictor of success in college, since the characteristics that enable a person to receive high grades at lower educational levels are presumed to contribute to academic achievement at higher levels.

Improving Marking Practices

There is strong dissatisfaction among some educators with current practices of marking and reporting student progress in academic achievement. The most frequent criticism is that no one really knows what a letter grade of *B* or *C* actually means. Compressing into a single letter mark an evaluation of a person's performance over several months or several years commits a gross injustice in failing to represent adequately the uniqueness, variability, and complexity of human behavior.

As evidence of the perplexity a letter grade may create, consider the following case:

Earl, Frank, and George each received a raw score of 147 on a standardized achievement test in American history. This score reflects accurately each boy's knowledge and understanding of this subject. Yet Earl is in a college-preparatory class where the teacher gives 40 percent of the class *A* or *B,* and Earl receives a *C.* Frank is in another college-preparatory section taught by a different teacher who gives 60 percent *A*s and *B*s, and Frank receives a *B.* George is in a history class which enrolls students in the general curriculum. George is one of the best students in the class and receives an *A.* Thus, in spite of equal performance in American history, Earl, Frank, and George receive *C, B,* and *A* grades, respectively, because they are in different classes.

One way of correcting such inequities is to obtain some common, relevant measure to which the performances by students in all sections of a course can be compared. Some schools administer a common final examination to all sections, but this practice is often resisted by both teachers and students, who contend that the learning objectives and experiences in the several sections are not comparable.

Another solution to the problem of determining what a grade means is to develop an institutional grading curve, wherein the percentages of students receiving *A, B, C, D,* and *F* grades are specified. Various flexible features are built into most such systems so that they may be used with honor classes as well as with classes of low-ability students. Frequently, such systems are tried and abandoned. Most teachers are unwilling to conform to an institutional straitjacket in assigning grades. Evaluating student progress and assigning marks is a jealously guarded teacher prerogative which need conform only to the general policy of the institution. Traditional marking systems persist despite their acknowledged limitations because of the failure of improved marking systems to gain acceptance.

In an effort to reduce the pressure on students for grades, some schools have experimented with the use of two grade classifications, "Pass" and "Fail," in place of the familiar five-mark grading system. Such a marking system does appear to reduce the pressure on students to strive for high grades, but it also reduces some students' motivation to perform as well as they might if recognition were given for superior performance. Moreover, the pass-fail system of marking provides even less information concerning the individual student's progress in learning than does the five-mark grading system. Recently, however, some colleges and universities have introduced the pass-fail system for one elective course each semester or year in an effort to encourage students to explore new fields of study without fear of receiving a poor grade.

More descriptive forms of reporting students' progress have been used for some years in many elementary schools. The chief advantages to be noted in the report form shown in Figure 19.9 are the identification and listing of the various individual competencies and skills under reading, language, social studies, science, and mathematics, and the spaces provided for the teacher to

FIRST REPORTING PERIOD

SECOND REPORTING PERIOD

THIRD REPORTING PERIOD

Parent's comments may be made on the reverse side of this form. If comments are written by parents, please detach this section and return in the child's envelope to the school.

Pupil Progress Report Grades 1, 2, & 3
Board of Education of Prince George's County, Maryland

KNOWLEDGE AND SKILLS

The following symbols indicate your child's progress in terms of his ability:
VG – Very Good   S – Satisfactory   NI – Needs to Improve   U – Unsatisfactory

	CONF.	REPORTING PERIODS		
		1	2	3

LANGUAGE ARTS

Reading
- Ready for reading
- Reads with understanding
- Retains basic vocabulary
- Works out new words
- Reads well to others
- Shows wide interest in reading

Language
- Hears and distinguishes differences in sounds
- Speaks distinctly
- Expresses ideas well orally
- Expresses ideas well in written work
- Uses correct English
- Writes creatively

Handwriting
- Forms letters correctly
- Spaces letters and words correctly
- Joins letters and slanting letters correctly in cursive writing

Spelling
- Spells assigned words correctly
- Uses correct spelling in written work

SOCIAL STUDIES AND SCIENCE
- Assumes responsibility
- Takes part in group discussions
- Helps the group to plan
- Helps carry out the plan
- Shows interest
- Shows growth in acquiring information
- Shows an understanding of science around us

MATHEMATICS
- Is developing an understanding of the number system
- Is learning and using number facts correctly
- Works accurately
- Uses reasoning in problem solving
- Shows understanding of numbers in everyday living

ART

MUSIC

PHYSICAL EDUCATION

WORK HABITS

SOCIAL ATTITUDES

PUPIL _____

SCHOOL _____ GRADE _____ TEACHER _____ YEAR _____

Aims and Purposes of Our School

In our school we strive to:
- understand the child as an individual
- provide the child with opportunities to learn basic skills
- help the child develop an incentive to learn
- develop self-discipline
- encourage individual intellectual growth and curiosity
- assist the child in his social and emotional adjustment
- promote the child's physical health
- help the child develop a sense of values

To bring about these aims and purposes, we provide developmental experiences in the following areas:

LANGUAGE ARTS   reading, oral language, written language, creative writing, handwriting, spelling literature, foreign language
MATHEMATICS   number facts, number language, processes, problem solving
SCIENCE   natural and physical phenomena
MUSIC   singing, rhythms, creative activities, listening
ARTS   fine dramatic, crafts
PHYSICAL EDUCATION   individual skills and games, health

ACHIEVEMENT

A check (✓) indicates your child's achievement in relation to Grade Level expectancies.

	READING			MATHEMATICS			SPELLING		
	1	2	3	1	2	3	1	2	3
Skill in using instructional materials									
Above Grade Level									
On Grade Level									
Below Grade Level									

ATTENDANCE RECORD

Days Tardy		
Days Absent		
Days Present		

CONFERENCE REPORT

Scheduled _____ Date _____
Held   Yes ☐   No ☐

PLACEMENT

End of Year

(To Be Completed at the End of the School Year)

Your child has been assigned to grade _____ for the coming school year.

TEACHER _____

PRINCIPAL _____

Figure 19.9. Report card containing a statement of school purposes and aims, individual competencies and skills covered by each academic subject, and space for the teacher to write descriptions of the student's progress.

write brief descriptions of the student's progress in school. Another type of report of student progress takes the form of a letter from the teacher to the parent, wherein the teacher is free to comment on many phases of the child's development and learning.

Another reporting practice used widely in the elementary school is the parent-teacher conference.[26] This and the teacher's visit to the home provide unusual opportunities for teacher and parent to communicate to each other information useful in assessing the child's development and learning. In conducting a teacher-parent conference the teacher should strive first to put the parent at ease and to develop a rapport with the parent. This may be facilitated by encouraging the parent to discuss the child. Although all of the information the teacher reports may not be positive, he should be positive in his acceptance of the child and his potentialities for growth. Information concerning the child's progress in learning should be presented frankly and should be accompanied by the teacher's ideas about how to help the child improve. The teacher may also wish to encourage the parent to offer suggestions for helping the child and to invite the parent to visit the classroom. It is desirable to conclude on a constructive, pleasant, or positive note—with a statement of encouragement or reassurance or a plan for cooperative action.

A new cooperative evaluation program is currently underway in the three junior high schools of one school district.[27] The ultimate purpose of this program, whose development is still in progress, is to replace course grades and report cards with measures of status and growth in the four, five, or six most widely recognized objectives of each field of study. These schools will continue to use report cards in their present form until parents, after receiving better and fuller information from the new reports, question the continued use of the traditional report card.

An evaluation committee serves as the coordinating body for administering this cooperative evaluation program in all three schools. The specific functions of this committee are to direct the program, to appoint advisers to small groups of twenty to thirty students, to receive reports of all "measures for the record" (newly developed evidences of achievement, such as reports and projects), to file these measures in the record folders of these students, and to transmit copies to parents at least three times a year, with interpretive comments whenever they are needed. Initially, the evaluation committee identified and accepted six learning goals: writing competence, independent reading, critical thinking, interests, work habits, and acceptance by peers.

Presently, advisers are usually members of teaching teams in which most of the new "measures of record" have been tried out. Later, students

26 A useful handbook on conducting parent-teacher conferences is Katherine E. D'Evelyn, *Individual Parent-Teacher Conferences* (New York: Bureau of Publications, Teachers College, Columbia University, 1945). Reproduced by permission of the Board of Education of Prince George's County, Maryland.

27 Frances R. Link and Paul B. Diederich, "A Cooperative Evaluation Program," in Fred T. Wilhelms, *Evaluation as Feedback and Guide* (Washington D.C.: Association for Supervision and Curriculum Development, N.E.A., 1967), pp. 121–180. Material taken from this reference is used by permission.

will be assigned advisers of their own choice. The plan is to involve all teachers as advisers. The principal function of the adviser is to know how each student in his advisory group is getting along in all courses and activities. His information comes from official detailed reports on each "measure for the record" prepared by each academic department. These are sent to the advisers of students concerned, not directly to the parents. Ultimately, only the adviser will report directly to parents and then only to the parents of the twenty to thirty students in his advisory group.

A "report for the record" is usually limited to a single page, so that it can be duplicated and copies made available to the teacher making the report, the student, the adviser, the parents, and the guidance counselor. These reports usually include a statement of the objectives measured, a description of the measuring device or procedure (sometimes with sample items), the reliability and standard error of the scores if these have been computed, distributions of the scores of the groups tested, and some indication of the position of the student in these distributions in the form of a numerical score or letter symbol referring to the quality of his performance in a particular area.

In order to achieve greater objectivity in teachers' scoring of papers, the pupils' names are withheld, and each paper is scored independently by two or more teachers.

This new cooperative evaluation program appears to offer an alternative to present methods of evaluation that fail to report student performance adequately. In comparison to a letter symbol, the "measure of record" offers more valid, complete, and useful information to student, parent, employer, and college admissions officer concerning the student's strengths and weaknesses in the various phases of a particular subject or field. Such a program appears to point the direction in which future effort to improve evaluation procedures should move.

Testing and Contemporary Culture

Many persons lament the increasing use of tests and the widespread emphasis placed on test results in our contemporary culture. So strong is the negative feeling toward tests in some that it has resulted in a kind of cultural bias toward testing in all of its forms. There is a feeling on the part of many that our present tests do not measure real growth and change in behavior. Rather than to reject test data altogether, however, a constructive course would be to improve the quality of tests and to develop a variety of procedures or instruments yielding data on the same learning objective, whose results can then be verified to obtain a more valid picture of student performance.

In a culture as complex as ours, judgments must continuously be made of people's potentialities or their competencies for playing needed roles in the culture. Many of those who decry the emphasis upon tests and testing have little to suggest in the way of alternative procedures. In the absence of alternatives, there is a tendency to fall back on subjective judgments, which are likely to be more subject to error than a mediocre test.

Our previous discussion has emphasized the shortcomings and limitations of tests. However, when interpreted cautiously and viewed in conjunction with other types of relevant data, test data can provide important information upon which to make judgments in assessing student achievement. One is less likely to make unwarranted interpretations of test results if he remembers that a test is composed of a limited number of samples selected from a large number of possible behaviors relating to a given learning objective. For a valid assessment of a student's achievement, the teacher must continue to obtain samples of the student's behavior on that learning dimension until a fairly consistent picture of his performance emerges.

Finally, measurement and evaluation are too often viewed as adjuncts to learning rather than integral parts of the teaching-learning process. An oft-quoted cardinal principle is that *evaluation should be continuous*. Plans for evaluating behavior change should be made at the same time that learning objectives are agreed upon and refined and curriculum content and materials are developed. Too often, evaluation procedures are developed hastily after the course is well underway. The improvement of learning and instruction depends on one's obtaining reliable, valid information on student behavior changes. We cannot teach well and students will not learn effectively if data on learning performance are faulty or lacking.

Summary

Testing and evaluation engender ambivalent feelings in many persons in contemporary society. Evaluation provides feedback that serves as a powerful stimulus for continuing adequate behavior or improving inadequate behavior. Without reliable, valid measuring instruments and evaluation procedures, progress toward achieving any of the outcomes of learning would likely be haphazard and uncertain.

Evaluation is a process of judging performances in relation to given criteria. It includes (1) a judgment of what, in general, constitutes a desirable behavior change; (2) a means of measuring whether the behavior change has occurred and, if so, to what degree; and (3) a judgment of the acceptability of a particular behavior change.

Evaluation is more inclusive than measurement, but in order for evaluation to be valid, it should be based upon measurement of some sort. *Measurement,* in essence, is the act of discriminating between the performances of two or more persons. Tests are familiar measuring instruments, but other kinds of devices for measuring specific kinds of performance or behavior change may also be used.

Identifying the goals to be achieved during a proposed learning activity is the teacher's first step in organizing for learning. Many learning objectives are difficult to measure and evaluate because of a failure to distinguish between *immediate* and *ultimate* objectives, because they focus on too narrow a range of behaviors, or because they are too general or vague. Learning objectives are of little effect if planned learning experiences have little or no relationship to these objectives.

If learning involves a change in behavior, it would seem to be appropriate to assess the achievement of learning objectives in terms of reliably observable behavior. In describing the instructional objectives of an elementary school science curriculum, "action words," such as *identifying, distinguishing, constructing, naming, ordering, describing, demonstrating,* and *interpreting* may be used. When curriculum is viewed in terms of content—information, concepts, and skills to be taught and learned—a clearly formulated objective is seen to have two aspects: a behavioral aspect and a content aspect.

The essential requirements of an evaluation procedure are that it be reliable and that it be valid. Reliability is a measure of how accurately or how consistently a test or other procedure measures what it is supposed to measure. In asking how valid a test is, we are asking whether the test measures what we want it to measure.

The primary function of a test, as of any evaluation procedure, is to ascertain to what extent pupils have achieved the objectives of instruction. If a test is to measure pupil achievement in all of the learning objectives, it must be carefully designed to include items or questions relating to each objective. An important step in planning a test is to relate the statement of objectives and course content in developing a *test blueprint*. In the test blueprint, the testmaker indicates the relative emphasis that is to be given in the test to each learning objective and content area.

The unreliability of teachers' marks in scoring essay examinations led to the development of new objective examinations consisting of a fairly large number of specific questions requiring only brief answers. The objective test requires the individual taking the test to choose from among designated alternatives. The principal kinds of objective examinations are: (1) *true-false,* (2) *multiple choice,* (3) *completion,* and (4) *matching.* Although choice-type objective examinations have been criticized for their failure to measure students' abilities to organize ideas, to think through problems, to analyze relationships, and to apply principles, proponents contend that multiple-choice tests may be used to test almost any objective that can be measured by a paper-and-pencil test.

The chief advantage of the essay examination is that it provides the student with an opportunity to organize his own answer. Because of the potential low reliability of teachers' scoring of essay examinations, special care should be taken to insure that his evaluation of answers to essay questions is as objective as possible. Both objective and essay tests have their strengths and weaknesses. The teacher's choice of which type to use should take into account the learning objectives to be evaluated, the nature of the course content, and the characteristics and abilities of the students being evaluated.

Other evaluation procedures include observations of students' behavior, projects and papers, and standardized tests. Observations of classroom behavior frequently yield evidence of pupil behavior change not revealed in paper-and-pencil tests, but, to be valid, the teacher's descriptions of observed classroom behavior must be objective and complete. Projects and papers have the potential of arousing strong student interest and involvement in an activity which permits the student to demonstrate his individual interests and talents. The major value of a standardized test is that its results may be used to assess the performances of a specific individual, class, school, or school district in relation to other, comparable groups of students.

After a test or other measuring device has been scored, it is necessary to evaluate the learner's status or change in behavior as represented by this score. This involves the classifying of scores made by pupils into various levels or categories of acceptability or unacceptability. This is essentially the task of assigning school marks.

Considerable dissatisfaction has been expressed with current practices of marking and reporting student progress. The chief criticism is that a single letter grade is grossly inadequate for representing the uniqueness, variability, and complexity of human behavior. Report cards which provide space for descriptive comments and identify important learning objectives in each curriculum area, parent-teacher conferences, and cooperative evaluation programs in which descriptive evaluations are made of each student with respect to important learning objectives are promising alternatives to traditional systems of grading.

Study Questions

1. What are some of the specific objectives, stated in terms of observable behavior, that you would develop for the subject and grade you will teach? Are some of these behaviors more fundamental than others? If so, arrange the behavioral objectives you have identified into a hierarchy.

2. Formulate test items which would enable you to evaluate the behavioral objectives you have listed for question 1.

3. What factors would you consider in deciding whether to administer an objective examination, an essay examination, or use some other form of evaluation?

4. In the subject or grade you teach, should one evaluate Frank Abell's performance in relation to the performances of the rest of the class, or should Frank be evaluated in relation to his capacities, aptitudes, and his level of knowledge and skill in the subject when he began this course? Defend your answer.

5. What distinctions, if any, would you make between the terms "evaluation" and "grading"?

6. We are reminded that evaluation should be an integral part of the planning and preparation of every learning activity. Also, for a very long time we

have been told that "evaluation should be continuous." What explanations would you offer for teachers' tendencies to treat evaluation as something apart from the learning activity (as evidenced by the fact that planning for evaluation often occurs long after the learning activity has gotten underway)?

Suggested Readings

Benjamin S. Bloom. Editor. *Taxonomy of Educational Objectives, Handbook I: Cognitive Domain.* New York: David McKay Co., 1956; David R. Krathwohl, Benjamin S. Bloom, and Bertram B. Masia. *Taxonomy of Educational Objectives, Handbook II: Affective Domain.* New York: David McKay Co., 1964. These references identify the range of educational objectives relative to the cognitive and affective domains of learning. Clear distinctions are made between various kinds and levels of cognitive and affective learning. Included are examples of statements of objectives in each domain together with test items designed to provide evidence of the achievement of each objective.

Robert L. Ebel. *Measuring Educational Achievement.* Englewood Cliffs, New Jersey: Prentice-Hall, 1965. Introduces and discusses concepts, principles, and procedures for assisting teachers to prepare better tests of educational achievement. Various types of tests and the methods teachers may use to evaluate their own tests are discussed.

Robert L. Thorndike and Elizabeth Hagen. *Measurement and Evaluation in Psychology and Education.* Second Edition. New York: John Wiley, 1961. A comprehensive and widely used text on educational measurement written primarily for persons who will use and interpret tests. Chapters 3 and 4 offer guidance to teachers in the planning, preparation, and evaluation of teacher-made tests.

Fred T. Wilhelms. Editor. *Evaluation as Feedback and Guide.* Washington, D.C.: Association for Supervision and Curriculum Development, 1967. Evaluation is seen as an important factor in curriculum improvement because it influences motivation and thus influences instructional programs. This yearbook suggests that current evaluation procedures fall far short of fulfilling their task of facilitating learning through the improvement of instruction. The plea is for evaluation that will enable the student not only to appraise himself validly, but will enable him to take greater responsibility for his own learning.

20

students who need special help

No matter how close to psychopathic our children may sometimes look, we haven't found one of them yet who didn't have lots of potential areas of value appeal lying within him.

≡   FRITZ REDL

Children with marked physical or intellectual handicaps which prevent them from making satisfactory progress in a regular school program have come to be referred to as exceptional children. In general, an *exceptional child* is one who deviates intellectually, physically, socially, or emotionally so markedly from what is considered to be normal that he requires a special class of instruction and services.[1] Exceptional children are both those with physical or intellectual handicaps and those with unusual physical or intellectual gifts. Table 20.1 presents estimates of the incidence in the United States of various types of handicapped exceptional children requiring special education services. In Table 20.1, the category *mentally retarded* includes "educable" children (IQs of 55 to 80) and "trainable" children (IQs below 55). The category *major learning disabilities* comprises children who have some type of cerebral dysfunction (such as brain damage).

[1] William M. Cruickshank and G. Orville Johnson, *Education of Exceptional Children and Youth* (Englewood Cliffs, New Jersey: Prentice-Hall, 1958), p. 3.

550

It is beyond the scope of this book to discuss every type of exceptional child in depth. In this chapter we shall focus on one type of exceptional child, the emotionally disturbed child, one or more examples of which nearly every teacher encounters in the regular classrooms. Later in the chapter we shall discuss the high ability underachiever, another category of exceptional child found in regular classrooms.

Table 20.1.   Estimated number of children needing special education services, 1968–1969. *

HANDICAP	NUMBER	PERCENTAGE OF TOTAL SCHOOL POPULATION*
Visually handicapped	51,000	.1
Deaf	38,250	.075
Hard of hearing	255,000	.5
Speech handicapped	1,785,000	3.5
Crippled and other health disorders	255,000	.5
Emotionally disturbed	1,020,000	2.0
Mentally retarded	1,173,000	2.3
Major learning disabilities	510,000	1.0
Total	5,087,250	9.975

* From *Projections of Educational Statistics to 1973–74* (Washington, D.C.: U.S. Department of Health, Education and Welfare, 1964). Based on an estimated 51,000,000 children in elementary and secondary schools in the United States in 1968–1969.

The Emotionally Disturbed Student

Symptoms of Emotional Disturbance

Of the many kinds of students who need special help, the emotionally disturbed child is one whom the teacher in a regular classroom frequently finds most difficult to understand. There are several reasons for this. First, emotional disturbance may be revealed in a variety of behaviors, many of which appear to be quite different from other symptoms of disturbance. For example, extreme submissiveness, withdrawal, and a compulsiveness for achieving perfection are frequently as much symptoms of emotional maladjustment as the more familiar evidences of antisocial behavior—persistent attention-seeking, aggression toward others or toward self, rigid or grossly distorted perceptions and delusions, bizarre behaviors, self-hate, and fantasy. Second, some types of emotional disturbance in students may go unrecognized because of unresolved emotional conflicts which the teacher still carries within himself. The teacher with a strong dependency tie to a parent, for example, may not recognize the student's strong dependence on the teacher as a symptom of potential maladjustment.

The teacher's task of identifying and helping the emotionally disturbed student is further complicated by the fact that *disturbing* behavior (such as disrupting and attention-seeking) does not in itself mean that the individual is emotionally disturbed. An aggressive or attention-seeking behavior may be a quite normal response to a stressful situation of limited duration or to changes in physical maturity. For example, the child who has a new sibling or who is not allowed by his peers to join in a game may respond with aggression, name-calling, or regression to an earlier pattern of behavior. Scornful remarks, teasing, and uncontrollable giggling are a few of the quite normal but disturbing behaviors characteristic of each sex's response to members of the opposite sex during preadolescence.

How then may one distinguish between emotionally disturbed and relatively healthy children, both of whom behave at times in similar ways? Several criteria have been suggested to assist teachers in spotting the child who may be emotionally disturbed. Single or infrequent instances of aggression, giggling, or impertinence may be dealt with by a frown, a disapproving comment, humor, or temporary isolation from the group—whatever teacher response has in the past proven efficacious for eliminating the disturbing behavior for this student or group of students. Most children engage in disturbing antics at one time or another, but if appropriate action by the teacher causes the disturbing behavior to subside, it is unlikely to be considered a serious problem.

More serious or more significant disturbing behaviors may manifest themselves in one or a combination of ways.[2] *Repetitious behavior* is a symptom of deeper underlying tensions. Continued aggressiveness, distractions, or daydreaming require further psychological study and understanding. A serious *single disturbance* may reflect a severe maladjustment in the child or deeper disorder within the group. A severe temper tantrum or sharp dropoff in academic performance indicates a need for further study. Finally, a child may engage in a *succession of different disturbances* which may appear to be unrelated. For example, a child may be very tense and hyperactive on one day, continuously hitting and pushing other children the next day, and moody and withdrawn the following day. Each of these disturbing behaviors mirrors the same complex problem or frustration. A clinically oriented teacher may be able to assist a child manifesting the first two types of emotional disturbance, but a child exhibiting the third type of disturbance should be referred for professional help to a psychological clinic or trained therapist.

In addition to the characteristics and symptoms already cited, nearly all emotionally disturbed persons experience a high degree of anxiety. The sources and manifestations of this anxiety vary with each type of emotional

[2] Charlotte Buhler, Faith Smitter, and Sybil Richardson, *Childhood Problems and the Teacher* (New York: Holt, Rinehart and Winston, 1952).

disturbance. The neurotic child's anxiety centers in his psychic fear of the disaster he feels will follow if he is forced to give up his neurotic behavior pattern. The anxiety of the psychotic child, on the other hand, frequently relates to his confusion of identity, perceptual distortions, inability to separate real and unreal, and fear of survival in the face of a wide assortment of dangers he perceives around him. Many emotionally disturbed children also experience difficulty in controlling their instinctual drives and impulses. The inability of these children to delay gratification, to tolerate frustration of immediate desires, or to hold back their urges in favor of long-term goals contributes to their difficulties in learning situations.

Because the emotionally disturbed person must expend energy in coping with anxiety and controlling his impulses, he experiences a moderate to marked reduction in behavioral freedom which in turn reduces his ability to function effectively in learning or in working with others. This loss of freedom affecting the child's educative and social experiences may be manifested in any one or more of five patterns of behavior:[3]

1. An inability to learn which cannot be adequately explained by intellectual, sensory, neurophysiological, or general health factors.
2. An inability to build or to maintain satisfactory interpersonal relationships with peers and teachers.
3. Inappropriate or immature types of behavior or feelings under normal conditions.
4. A general pervasive mood of unhappiness or depression.
5. A tendency to develop physical symptoms, such as speech problems, pains, or fears, associated with personal or school problems.

After the teacher has distinguished between children who are normal but disturbing and children who are emotionally disturbed, he is faced with the need to learn more about the emotionally disturbed student he wishes to help.

Studying the Emotionally Disturbed

Disturbed behavior, like normal behavior, has many causes; hence, many of the principles of behavior introduced in earlier chapters also apply to the emotionally disturbed student. A major difference between normal and disturbed behavior is that the latter often appears to be more irrational. For this reason, the causes of disturbed behavior are often more difficult to unravel.

When seeking to identify causes of behavior, the teacher is cautioned to avoid the assumption that one has explained behavior if he has given it a

---

[3] Eli M. Bower and Nadine M. Lambert, "In School Screening of Children with Emotional Handicaps," in Nicholas J. Long, William C. Morse, and Ruth G. Newman, *Conflict in the Classroom* (Belmont, California: Wadsworth Publishing Co., 1965), pp. 128–129.

label or described its symptoms. Subjective labels—"attention-seeking," "mischievousness," "laziness," "belligerence," or "boredom"—provide little insight into disturbed behavior and offer little help in explaining its causes. Instead of citing symptoms, we should ask, "What are the possible causes or reasons why this child behaves in this manner?" *By labelling a behavior, one does not explain it.*

Symptoms, however, do provide useful clues for understanding behavior. After the student's symptoms have been identified, teachers should evaluate the symptoms and test their relevance to assumed or known causes. By failing to evaluate symptoms, educators may, for instance, blame the home situation for chronic misbehavior that in fact is more closely related to the difficulty of academic work or to a lack of acceptance or understanding by teacher and peers. A key to interpreting and evaluating a behavioral symptom is the frequency and persistence with which a behavior pattern is used and its apparent effectiveness in enabling the individual to avoid or to cope with real or potential sources of threat.

Finally, prerequisite to understanding the emotionally disturbed child (as well as all human beings) is the accumulation, sifting, and analysis of a great deal of information about the child's past experiences and his present situation with respect to organic, interpersonal, cultural, and self factors. Because many of the real causes of behavior may be obscure, it is especially important that accurate, complete information be obtained. If one has adequate information, he is less likely to resort to oversimplified categorizations or labels. Collecting and having available valid information about an emotionally disturbed child is required if the teacher is to help him.

Helping the Emotionally Disturbed

Educators, parents, and community agencies have long recognized that existing psychological clinics, private therapists, and residential institutions can care for only a very small proportion of the severely maladjusted children and youth in this country. Since the school cannot depend upon clinics, professionals, and community agencies for treating the increasing number of emotionally disturbed children and youth, the school must develop its own programs and facilities for children who are unable to profit from learning activities in regular classrooms.

Cohen and LaVietes[4] suggest a number of ways of helping disturbed children through selective programing and modification of curriculum content. First of all, they point out, disturbed children have vague and distorted perceptions of time and often become anxious under pressure of time limits. Thus, the teacher's timing in the introduction and termination of activities, his use of time allotments and schedules, and his flexibility in adapting these to changing group needs influence the effectiveness of the learning situation

[4] Rosalyn S. Cohen and Ruth LaVietes, "Clinical Principles in Curriculum Selection," in Jerome Hellmuth, *Educational Therapy,* Vol. I (Seattle, Washington: Seattle Seguin School, Inc., 1966), pp. 139–154. Material describing curricula and programs for the emotionally disturbed is used with permission.

and the child's ability to function in the group. Because of the brief attention spans, intolerance of frustration, and extreme emotional patterns of emotionally handicapped children, pacing and sequencing of activities are essential for their effective learning. For example, introducing a quiet, structured activity such as handwriting after an active lunch period helps to reduce tension and anxiety in the classroom. Sudden or abrupt transitions from one activity to another is another source of tension for these children. Tension may arise from the child's inability to detach himself from what he is doing, his fear of the unfamiliar, or the effects of frequent changes in activity. Providing simple, nonchallenging, repetitive activities such as singing or coloring books and maintaining emotional contact with children prevents disorganization and makes the transitions between learning activities smoother.

The use of repetition and the maintenance of routines are especially important for stabilizing the world of the disturbed child. Routines, such as following a schedule or returning things to their assigned places, enable the child to order his world and provide him an opportunity to become comfortable with his environment.

High sensitivity to intense auditory or visual stimulation is characteristic of children who are emotionally disturbed. Thus, by endeavoring to control sensory input, the teacher is able to minimize distractions that could arouse impulsive behavior. At the same time, emotionally disturbed children tend to show strong preferences for specific sensory modalities and to distort many sensory experiences. By gradually exposing the child to other modalities, the teacher may help to minimize such a child's sensory distortions.

Some emotionally disturbed children cannot distinguish between fantasy and reality or become preoccupied with one particular fantasy for long periods of time. Curriculum materials which help such children to distinguish between fantasy and reality serve to minimize the limiting effects of perceptual distortion and inadequate cognitive functioning. Moreover, since the styles of thinking of disturbed children are either overly abstract or overly concrete, the teacher should become acquainted with each child's style of thinking and its limitations and help the child to acquire a more effective style.

Since emotionally disturbed children often lack a sense of curiosity, they sometimes have difficulty comprehending things unrelated to their past experience and distinguishing between the possible and the impossible. Science activities most likely to be stabilizing to the emotionally disturbed child are those related to the child's immediate life experience and containing constructive rather than destructive elements and ideas. The study of weather and the seasons, for example, may be more appropriate for the disturbed child than studies of lightning, earthquakes, and volcanoes. Art, music, dramatic play, and physical education also have potential for assisting seriously disturbed children to clarify their feelings, but, again, content and activities must be carefully planned to prevent overstimulation and anxiety-arousing associations.

The principles summarized above may appear to be most relevant to the task of working with groups or classes of emotionally disturbed students. Yet, for the teacher in a regular classroom who may have only one or two such students, these principles contain important suggestions. How might a regular classroom teacher work with a student whose emotional problems complicate his adjustment and hinder his learning in school? One approach is revealed in excerpts from the case of Herb Hendricks:

Herb Hendricks is fifteen and in the seventh grade. Herb's height is 63 inches and he weighs 100 pounds. He is of slight build and is exceedingly energetic. His eyes are dark brown and very expressive as is his entire countenance. He has an older sister and a younger brother. His father is a mechanic, but his mother does not work outside of the home.

At age six, Herb contracted polio and was hospitalized for several months. His record shows that during a medical examination he was irritable, nervous, talked all the time, and had no goal. Last year, the medical record stated that Herb has a typical behavior problem and recommended that he attend a mental hygiene clinic. This has been complied with. Last year, results on the Otis Mental Ability Test revealed Herb had an IQ of 104 and his achievement was at grade level for all subjects except reading and language, which were above grade level.

This description written by a former teacher is found in the cumulative record: "Herb has real ability, but he is careless and irresponsible. He contracted polio several years ago. There are no physical handicaps as a result, but he is terrifically spoiled and his mother is under the impression that it has left him with several nondescript ailments. He has had little discipline at home and this naturally shows up in his school life. He is easily led into mischief and is prone to carry even a casual joke too far."

Last year Herb encountered a great deal of difficulty in adjusting satisfactorily to junior high school. Finally, he became disturbed to the extent that it became advisable for him to discontinue his formal education. Previously, I taught Herb in the sixth grade and discovered his challenging and interesting individuality. My principal motive in selecting him for study is my sincere hope that by careful observation it will be possible to assist in enabling him to become a more intelligent and responsible citizen.

Herb returned to school this year and was placed in section 7C. It seems he formed several acquaintances in the group which were not too desirable. As a result of this, the progress of the entire section was retarded due to the personal attention which they required. At the conclusion of five weeks of school, his homeroom teacher suggested that he be transferred to 7A in hopes that he would react more favorably with new associates.

OCTOBER 21

This evening the 7A section was dismissed and several of the boys and girls remained after school to talk with me. After conversing with them for approximately fifteen minutes, I suddenly noticed that Herb was still sitting in his seat. No one was near him and his countenance was terribly dejected. I ventured no comment and finally he came up to my desk with measured steps. Very abruptly he stated, "Did you know that I missed my bus?"

"No, I didn't realize this," I responded. "Have you a reason for remaining?"

"Yes, I want to talk to you," he said. He then inquired, "Did you know they were getting up a petition to get me kicked out of this section?"

I had overheard some discussion regarding this. I asked, "Why do you think they are doing this? When you entered this room we decided that you were going to begin a new record."

Herb remained perfectly motionless and I saw tears creeping into his eyes. Suddenly he burst forth, "Well, I did make up my mind to do that, but I don't know, I went back to my classes and every teacher seemed to have her eyes on me. No matter what happened I was always blamed for it, so I decided that if they were looking for trouble, I would give it to them."

After a few moments silence I continued, "Do you think perhaps it would be a good idea for your mother to come to school and meet all of your teachers?"

His entire expression became pleasant and smiling as he replied, "Yes, tomorrow."

OCTOBER 23

The question was raised in our faculty meeting as to how profitable Herb's continuance in school was. The viewpoint of the specialized instructors was that the progress of the entire class was impeded by his insistence upon becoming the constant center of attention. They expressed the feeling that what he was acquiring was too minor to warrant the deducted time from the group. I suggested a conference in two weeks with Mrs. Hendricks and each of his instructors.

OCTOBER 27

Mrs. Hendricks came to school this aftenoon. Herb was enthusiastic as he ushered her into the room. He waited downstairs while we conversed. Mrs. Hendricks asked, "Don't you believe Herb is settling down better this year?"

I responded, "Yes, but more improvement is desirable."

Proceeding to tell me about his visit to the mental health clinic, she said, "Herb told me there wasn't anything wrong with him, but he thought someone should examine the doctor because he asked him such dumb questions." After this statement Mrs. Hendricks laughed heartily and continued, "You know, I wish Herb wouldn't mix with that awful gang over our way. It was just by luck that he wasn't with them when they broke into all those places." Just at this moment one of Herb's teachers came up the hall and I invited her in to confer with Mrs. Hendricks. The instructor related numerous incidents in which Herb had been exceedingly arrogant and defiant. Mrs. Hendricks said, "I know Herb is quite emotional and high-strung because he is that way at home."

Herb came back to the room and his mother inquired, "When shall I contact you again?"

"Every two weeks," Herb said. Then he put his arm around her and said, "Don't you think my Mom is cute? Dad sure is lucky!"

OCTOBER 28

We decided this morning to elect the person most suitable for our announcer in the Thanksgiving Assembly. Herb spoke to me several days ago and desired some part in the program. The class enumerated the necessary qualities for this position, and I particularly emphasized the requirement of a voice which would carry in the auditorium. This is definitely one of Herb's assets and the class recognized it by electing him with a great majority. When he was informed that he would be our announcer his eyes sparkled and he smiled broadly as he slid proudly into his seat.

NOVEMBER 12

Mrs. Hendricks came to school today. After exchanging casual greetings, she immediately inquired, "Have you heard any of those tales about Herb?"

I responded, "He spoke to me about an incident yesterday evening, but other than that I know nothing concerning it."

Quickly, she continued, "Well, I am going to speak to the principal about the matter. Everyone will think that I don't care what becomes of him. Whenever he isn't home by nine o'clock I begin calling about the neighborhood for him." Mrs. Hendricks proceeded down to the office and met me later in the cafeteria for lunch. She informed me that Herb was encountering special difficulty with several faculty members, so I suggested that she meet with them and discuss the problem. Approximately one half hour later, Mrs. Hendricks returned to my room practically in tears. She was so upset that she requested smoking privileges three times and was of course refused. Apparently Mrs. Hendricks did not use much psychology in conversing with the instructors. She informed one of them that Herb referred to her as his enemy number one. The expression which she used to describe the teacher's reaction to this statement was she "blew her top" and declared that "the feeling was mutual." I then said, "I will go down and take the math class so that you may meet with this faculty member also."

NOVEMBER 19

We had a practice this morning for our Thanksgiving Assembly. I was quite discouraged yesterday with Herb's performance, but before going home he had faithfully reassured me of vast improvement today. The curtains opened and all eyes were anxiously awaiting the arrival of Herb. Members of the chorus turned around and looked at me, but I ventured no comment. Finally, Herb came swaggering out on the stage swinging his arms and clicking his heels together. He continued to walk up to the very edge of the stage and as he spoke he balanced himself there like Humpty Dumpty. As he returned backstage, he waved gaily to one of his friends sitting down in the chorus. During the rehearsal of the play, I saw his mischievous eyes peering through the window curtains and his head ducking around the corner of the supposedly closed door.

When we returned to the classroom, one of the pupils raised his hand and said, "I think we should elect another announcer." Herb looked up and was obviously quite startled. I inquired, "All of those in favor of electing another announcer please raise your right hands." Practically the entire class affirmed this. We proceeded with our election. I particularly noticed that Herb cast his vote, but that his eyes were stormy and his lips were firmly compressed.

The patterns revealed in these excerpts continued throughout the year that Herb was studied by Miss Preston. Herb continued behaving in ways that brought him into conflict with teachers, principal, and peers. He disrupted play rehearsals and classes with his antics on numerous occasions and was suspended from school after he and two of his friends were truant and were picked up by the police hitchhiking to Baltimore. His mother continued to come to school periodically to confer with his teachers, but there is little evidence that her perceptions and attitudes or those of the teachers changed as the result of these conferences. Miss Preston made two visits to Herb's home, where she was warmly received by Herb and his parents. The parents were aware of Herb's difficulties, but took little positive action to help him to improve. Instead, they expressed the hope that he would outgrow his problems. Miss Preston maintained her calm, nonjudgmental acceptance of Herb while using every opportunity to help him examine his feelings and analyze the effects of his behavior on others. Her acceptance of Herb as a person resulted in a temporary reduction of antisocial behavior. Before long, however, the disturbing behavior recurred.

Yet, there are several positive factors which suggest a favorable prognosis for Herb. He has a normal IQ and his achievement is at grade level. He appears to feel secure in his family and with Miss Preston, and Miss Preston has made some progress in enlisting aid in helping him from other teachers.

One might expect that frequent conferences between Herb's mother and his teachers would lead to greater understanding of Herb and a positive change in his behavior. However, Mrs. Hendricks continued to indulge Herb and continued to be unable to comprehend the seriousness of his problem. By reason of this kind of lack of understanding, it is of the utmost importance that the parent receive professional counseling at the same time as the child.

It appears that a small special class under a teacher skilled in working with maladjusted students might permit Herb to make greater progress in development and learning than he would in a regular schedule of junior high school classes. Newman[5] describes an experimental program of reeducation for a group of six boys, ages eight to ten, who were far more seriously disturbed and hyperaggressive than Herb. This study sought to ascertain whether severely disturbed, hyperaggressive children of normal intelligence and with no perceptible organic damage can learn more effective patterns of psychological adjustment. The first task of the reeducation program was to help the boys unlearn the damaging experiences and responses of their past. The teachers, in attempting to be as accepting and permissive as possible, said to the boys, "This is not your old school; it is different. We like you here; we will help you if you will let us. No matter what you do, you will not be expelled." The activities of the experimental school program included block building, games, cutting out pictures, and puppetry, as well as reading, writing, and arithmetic. If a boy was unable to continue an activity during class, a new activity was started, and he was given individual help. He was not removed from the class so long as his disruptiveness did not break up the school activity. In order to satisfy the boys' needs for individual attention, their need for skills, and their need not to expose their scholastic inadequacies before peers, individual tutoring was used. Evaluations of the boys' daily classroom behavior revealed that during the two-year period of reeducation, five of the six boys developed more positive self-pictures, greater ability to cope with fears and to postpone gratification of infantile needs, and more positive relationships with adults and peers. Thus, the primary goal of teaching this type of severely disturbed, hyperaggressive student— that is, altering his perceptions of himself, his environment, and the people in his environment—was achieved.

Helping Teachers of the Emotionally Disturbed

A variety of programs have been developed to assist teachers in working with emotionally disturbed students and to promote mental health in the regular classroom. Newman and her associates[6] describe a comprehensive program of "technical assistance" which provides on-the-spot help for teachers who are baffled, frustrated, and discouraged in their efforts to help one or more emotionally disturbed children. Consultants providing technical assistance may be called into a school or classroom to help with a problem involving a specific child or group of children. For instance, a consultant was called in to help a teacher who lost her temper when Billy interrupted her lesson for the fourth time by bursting out with loud catcalls. Her loss of

[5] Ruth G. Newman, "Changes in Learning Patterns of Hyperaggressive Children," in Nicholas J. Long, William C. Morse, and Ruth G. Newman, *Conflict in the Classroom* (Belmont, California: Wadsworth Publishing Co., 1965), pp. 446–453; Ruth G. Newman, "A Study of the Difficulties of Hyperaggressive, Emotionally-Disturbed Children in Adjusting to School and in Deriving Satisfying Learning Experiences from School" (unpublished doctor's dissertation, University of Maryland, 1957).

[6] Ruth G. Newman, Claire Bloomberg, Ruth Emerson, Marjorie Keith, Howard Kitchener, and Fritz Redl, "Technical Assistance." Report of the Washington School of Psychiatry, Washington, D.C., 1964. Summary used by permission.

control was unbecoming and she felt that she had alienated other students in the class. She was filled with chagrin and self-loathing. The consultant, after breaking through the teacher's defensiveness, communicated to her the following facts:

1. Losing one's temper might have been a mistake in that instance, but it was a very human mistake.
2. Nothing was gained for Billy or herself in doing so and something might have been temporarily lost in her relationship with the class.
3. Billy needs limits.
4. The time to tackle Billy was the second catcall not the fourth, before Billy got out of bounds completely and before the teacher had reached her level of frustration.
5. Records and reports of Billy's behavior with other teachers point to the possibility that Billy did this because he wanted attention and because he was conveying a message that the work was too hard for him at that given moment. Rather than be called on and appear dumb to his classmates, he was breaking up the class.

The teacher gave the consultant important information about Billy. The consultant, in turn, supported the teacher's observations and efforts to deal with the situation and helped the teacher gain insight concerning other methods and materials that could be used to influence Billy's behavior and improve his opportunities for achievement. After a careful review of the situation, teacher and consultant together planned ways the teacher could help Billy and reestablish rapport with the class.

Morse[7] offers another plan for helping teachers who have emotionally disturbed children in their classrooms. He suggests that each school include on its staff a "crisis teacher" who would work with pupils whose behavior exhausts the teacher and prevents other students from learning. Thus, the crisis teacher is a resource immediately available when a deterioration in classroom deportment and learning occurs. He is available not only to teachers but also to individual pupils. His work with individual pupils may involve tutoring, an informal talk, a diversionary activity, or an intensive life-space interview. What the crisis teacher does is what any teacher would want to do were it possible to act on the basis of the needs of the individual child rather than the large-group learning process. Morse emphasizes that the crisis teacher can be effective only to the degree that the entire staff of the school is concerned about understanding and helping the deviant child.

Programs whose goal is improving the general mental health of all students and teachers also offer help to teachers of emotionally disturbed children. Many of these programs emphasize preventive mental health and seek, through training or educational experiences, to provide participants

[7] William C. Morse, " 'The Crisis Teacher,' Public School Provision for the Disturbed Pupil," *The University of Michigan School of Education Bulletin*, 37 (April 1962), 101–104.

with new insights into the causes of human behavior. One of the oldest of such programs is the child-study program for teachers sponsored by participating school systems and the Institute for Child Study of the University of Maryland.[8] In this program, teachers are organized into groups of six to twelve persons. Each teacher selects a student in his classroom for study and, over a period of a year, writes an objective case record on this student. These records are read and analyzed during biweekly group meetings.

During each of two years devoted to the study of an individual student, teachers gain skills in observing and writing full, objective case records, develop a functional knowledge of behavioral principles, and learn to use the scientific method to arrive at sound, valid judgments about children and youth. Especially useful in achieving these ends is a six-area framework used to organize and interrelate case-record facts about the student and scientific data and principles which assist in explaining his behavior. The six areas used are the physical, the affectional, the cultural, the peer group, the self-developmental, and the self-adjustive. Especially pertinent to understanding the disturbed child are the analytic steps taken by teachers during the latter part of the program in making inferences concerning the child's self-concept and his concept of the world. Important also is the shift that usually occurs in the attitudes of participating teachers toward accepting and valuing students, regardless of their behavior.

Ojemann[9] has developed another program for improving mental health in the classroom. His program is designed to help teachers gain a deeper understanding of the underlying causes of behavior. He has developed materials and procedures for use in the classroom that are designed to help students gain increased skill in using the causal approach in understanding behavior. This goal—the development of causally oriented children—involves educating teachers in the teaching of causally oriented content materials and the practice of the causal approach in daily relations with pupils. Efforts are also made to encourage use of the causal approach in the home and the community.

This causal approach was incorporated into a human-relations program introduced into classrooms as part of a social studies curriculum. Actual learning experiences at the primary level involved demonstrations furnished by the teacher's behavior, use of narratives, and use of expositions designed to enable the child to understand and appreciate the work of the teacher and other persons with whom the child interacts directly. For example, the teacher might have read a narrative about a boy who gets into so many fights that something has to be done. The teacher in the story is about to deal with

[8] See Daniel A. Prescott, *The Child in the Educative Process* (New York: McGraw-Hill Book Co., 1957); Richard M. Brandt and Hugh V. Perkins, "Research Evaluating a Child Study Program," *Monographs of the Society for Research in Child Development* 21 (1956), Serial No. 62; Bernard Peck and Daniel A. Prescott, "The Program at the Institute for Child Study, The University of Maryland," *Personnel and Guidance Journal,* 37 (October 1958), 114–122.

[9] Ralph H. Ojemann, "Basic Approaches to Mental Health: The Human Relations Program at the State University of Iowa," *Personnel and Guidance Journal,* 37 (1958), 198–206.

this in the usual way when he recalls that such things do not happen of their own accord. After a little probing, the teacher learns that this boy has been teased a great deal about having to help take care of his baby sister and not having time to play with other children. When the teacher learns this, he takes measures to work out the problem. Each narrative was preceded by a short introduction by the teacher and followed by a discussion. The emphasis of this program was on learning more about the behavior of people and what the effects of that behavior are on others. Evaluations of the program revealed that a significant shift toward greater use of causal explanations of behavior took place in the fifth-grade pupils taught under the program.

The Underachiever

The problem of high-ability students who do not achieve at levels commensurate with their potential has been for many years the focus of considerable concern on the part of educators. For more than half a century, periodic assessments of intellectual aptitude and school achievement by standardized measures of large populations of students have provided data useful in effecting improvements in individual and group learning and in modifying educational programs. These assessments have often shown, however, a wide disparity between intelligence scores and achievement measures for a great number of students, students who have become known as underachievers. In general, an *underachiever* may be defined as a student whose academic performance, judged either by grades or achievement test scores, is markedly below his measured or demonstrated aptitude for academic achievement.[10]

The phenomenon of underachievement, especially among high-ability students, is particularly baffling to teachers and parents because it seems so illogical that students with high measured ability should not necessarily perform at least moderately well in school. The finding that many students do not perform academically in a manner commensurate with their mental abilities lends further support to the proposition that academic performance, like human behavior in general, is the product of many varied and complex forces. This conclusion was expressed by Bowman: "The characteristics that distinguish the underachiever are not superficial ones; they involve the deepest roots of a personality."[11]

Incidence of Underachievement

The incidence of underachievement is distressingly high. Wolfle[12] reports that of American high school students who rank in the top third in

[10] Leonard M. Miller (ed.), *Guidance for the Underachiever with Superior Ability,* OE-25021 (Washington D.C.: Office of Education, U.S. Department of Health, Education and Welfare, 1961), p. 15.

[11] Paul H. Bowman, "Factors Related to Scholastic Underachievement" (Quincy, Illinois: Quincy Youth Development Project, undated). Mimeographed.

[12] Dael L. Wolfle, *America's Resources of Specialized Talent* (New York: Harper & Row, 1954).

intellectual ability, 40 percent do not enter college. Of those who do enter, 60 percent do not finish college. Another study [13] shows that 15 to 25 percent of the gifted children in most school systems become classified as under-achievers. Gowan[14] reports that in one California high school, 7 percent of the students were identified as gifted, but that 42 percent of these were regarded as underachievers. In one New York City high school, approxi-mately 50 percent of the high-ability (IQs of 130 or above) ninth-grade students were not functioning at expected levels in their school work.[15]

No comparable data are available for the incidence of underachievement in the elementary school. Shaw and McCuen[16] found, however, that under-achievement may begin in the early elementary years and increase with age. Underachieving boys begin to receive lower grades than achieving boys in grade one, with the differences between the two groups becoming significant in grade three and increasing in significance from grade three to grade ten. Among girls, underachievers actually exceed achievers in grade point average for grades one to five, but begin to drop sharply below achievers in grade six, with differences becoming significant in grade nine. These statistics appear to confirm the observations of most educators that there is much underachieve-ment at all educational levels.

Family Backgrounds of Achievers and Underachievers

The importance of family and cultural factors in behavior and develop-ment noted in earlier chapters leads one to expect that unfavorable family and cultural factors are related to underachievement. Research tends to con-firm this. Families of underachieving students are generally lower in socio-economic status than are families of achievers. Fathers of underachievers have lower-ranked occupations and less education than fathers of achieving students.[17] High-achieving students, more frequently than low-achieving students, name their fathers as having been an important influence in their lives. The high achiever, in contrast to the underachiever, is more frequently the first-born or an only child.[18]

[13] National Education Association, Educational Policies Commission, *The Identification and Education of the Academically Talented Student in the American Secondary School* (Washington: National Education Association, 1958).

[14] J. C. Gowan, "The Underachieving Child—A Problem for Everyone," *Exceptional Children*, 21 (1955), 247–249.

[15] New York City Board of Education, "The New York City Talent Preservation Proj-ect," *Annual Report* (June 1959).

[16] Merville C. Shaw and J. T. McCuen, "The Onset of Academic Underachievement in Bright Children," *Journal of Educational Psychology*, 51 (1960), 103–108.

[17] E. Frankel, "A Comparative Study of Achieving and Underachieving High School Boys of High Intellectual Ability," *Journal of Educational Research*, 53 (1960), 172–180; H. E. Roberts, "Factors Affecting the Academic Underachievement of Bright High School Students," *Journal of Educational Research*, 56 (1962), 175–183.

[18] J. V. Pierce, *Educational Motivation Patterns of Superior Students Who Do and Do Not Achieve in High School*, Cooperative Research Project No. 208 (Washington, D.C.: Office of Education, U.S. Department of Health, Education and Welfare, 1960).

Parents of achieving and underachieving students also differ in their attitudes and their child-rearing practices. One study[19] found that parents of underachievers have more negative attitudes toward their children, greater anxiety with respect to sexual matters, and greater dissatisfaction with the parental role. Mothers of high achievers, in contrast to mothers of low achievers, place a higher value on imagination, hold higher educational expectations for their children, and perceive their children as more independent and responsible. Mothers of high-achieving boys are more democratic in their relationships with their sons; mothers of high-achieving girls, however, are authoritarian in their relationships with their daughters.[20] Parents of underachievers reveal greater confusion over how to handle problems of discipline and are less firm in insisting that children conform to parental expectations and standards.[21]

Social, ethnic, and religious family differences are also related to differences in children's achievement motivation and academic performance. These differences are clearly revealed in a study by Strodtbeck,[22] who investigated the influence of family interaction and values on the achievement, motivations, and self-perceptions of Jewish and Italian adolescent boys. Strodtbeck hypothesized that Jewish beliefs emphasizing hard work, achievement, success, and a rational mastery of the world would be reflected in patterns of family influence encouraging high achievement motivation and high academic performance. He predicted that Italian beliefs emphasizing loyalty to family, filial obedience to parental authority, and man's inability to control his own fate would be reflected in patterns of family influence placing less stress on achievement and personal success. A sample of 48 adolescent boys, ages fourteen to seventeen, in New Haven, Connecticut, was selected. The sample included 12 overachieving and 12 underachieving Italian boys, and 12 overachieving and 12 underachieving Jewish boys. Each group of 12 contained 4 upper-class, 4 middle-class, and 4 lower-class boys.

An attitude scale (*V scale*) was developed to measure the degree to which a respondent believes that achievement and success depend more upon personal efforts and abilities than upon fate. Adolescents and parents of relatively high socioeconomic status, overachievers and their fathers, and Jewish mothers made higher V scores than did adolescents and parents of lower socioeconomic status, underachievers and their fathers, and Italian mothers. In general, results obtained by the V scale tended to confirm Strodtbeck's hypothesis that the Jewish family's values encourage higher achievement than do the Italian family's values.

[19] M. C. Shaw and B. E. Dutton, "The Use of the Parent Attitude Research Inventory with Parents of Bright Academic Underachievers," *Journal of Educational Psychology,* 53 (1962), 203–208.

[20] Pierce.

[21] B. B. Williams, "Identifying Factors Relating to Success in School" (Rochester, New York: West Irondequoit Central School, April 20, 1962). Mimeographed.

[22] Fred L. Strodtbeck, "Family Interaction, Values, and Achievement," in D. C. McClelland, A. L. Baldwin, U. Bronfenbrenner, and F. L. Strodtbeck, *Talent and Society* (Princeton, New Jersey: D. Van Nostrand Co., 1958), pp. 135–195.

In the second part of this same study, questionnaires requiring the respondent to take a position regarding typical family problems were completed separately by the boy participating in the study, his father, and his mother. After completing the questionnaire, mother, father and son were asked to discuss each family problem presented in the questionnaire and to reach a family decision regarding each problem. The relative power of father, mother, and son in influencing the family decision was revealed in the amount of the verbal interaction of each, the amount of support each received from the others, and the number of decisions each won (family decisions that confirmed his initial response to the questionnaire item).

Results of this phase of the study revealed few differences between Italian and Jewish families in patterns of family interaction. The power of the father (reflected in the number of decisions won), regardless of social class or ethnic identity, was significantly greater than the mother's power, while the mother's power was only slightly greater than the adolescent son's power. The higher the socioeconomic status of the family, the less power the son had and the greater power the father had in influencing decisions—a reality keenly felt by the adolescent son. Strodtbeck concludes that the power balance in the family influences the adolescent's feeling that he is or is not able to influence the course of events, and this, in turn, has a bearing on his future success or failure. In families where a strong father dominates the son, the son may feel that he faces forces beyond his control. He may give up and not try to achieve. The findings of Strodtbeck's study suggest that subcultures exert a very strong influence on students' motivations and achievement.

Achievers' and Underachievers' Perceptions of Parents

One might expect that achieving students would perceive themselves as more accepted and valued by parents, while underachieving students would perceive themselves as less valued, but the evidence on this point is neither consistent nor conclusive. In a study by Haggard,[23] higher achievers perceived their parents as somewhat overprotective, pressuring for achievement, and lacking in emotional warmth. High achievers in spelling and language perceived their parents and other authority figures as omnipotent, rejecting, and generally punitive. Although these children were dependent upon their parents, they seemed unable to show any real affection for or to establish warm emotional relationships with them. Morrow and Wilson,[24] on the other hand, found that high achievers more often than underachievers described their parents as approving, trusting, affectionate, and encouraging (but not pressuring), and described themselves as accepting their parents'

[23] Ernest A. Haggard, "Socialization, Personality, and Academic Achievement in Gifted Children," *The School Review*, 65 (1957), 388–414.

[24] William R. Morrow and Robert C. Wilson, "Family Relations of Bright High Achieving and Underachieving High School Boys," *Child Development*, 32 (September 1961), 501–509.

standards. Both achievers and underachievers in Morrow and Wilson's study, however, expressed considerable respect and affection for their parents, described their parents' relationships as relatively harmonious, and stated that they were neither seriously overprotected nor excessively pressured to achieve.

A somewhat different view of parents was expressed by students in the study by Williams[25] cited earlier. High achievers reported that their parents exerted strong pressures on them to perform well academically, to maintain strict standards, and to obtain needed help from parents and siblings. Although parents did punish them by withholding privileges, these children felt that their parents trusted and had faith in them and encouraged them to be independent and responsible. In contrast, underachievers perceived in their relationships with their parents a lack of firmness and strictness and reported unfavorable parental comparisons with successful siblings. Underachievers also reported conflict with parents over school matters, a feeling of a lack of praise and support from parents, and little feeling of independence.

Sex Differences in Achievement

Underachievement in one's sex group is a very different phenomenon for boys than for girls. Haggard,[26] in a study of the achievement of children in grades three to seven, found that three fourths of the boys performed better on reading tests and three fourths of the girls performed better on spelling and language tests. These findings suggest that boys develop greater proficiency in abstract reasoning and using linguistic symbol systems, while girls seem to develop greater facility in use of the tangible, rule-bound skills associated with spelling and language. Research on problem solving, however, shows that while, in general, males are superior to females in problem solving, the more appropriate the problem is to the subject's sex role, the more the sex differences are diminished.[27] Thus, if the problem-solving abilities of girls were tested by asking them to solve problems of cooking or dress design, their problem-solving abilities would be found to equal those of boys.

The general superiority of girls over boys in academic achievement during elementary school and high school, especially in language, has been attributed to a variety of reasons. It has been suggested that girls' earlier physical maturation is one advantage. Pierce[28] suggests, however, that differing cultural expectations for boys and girls may provide a more comprehensive explanation for sex differences in achievement. In middle-class culture, girls are required to be more conforming than boys, and, by conforming in social behavior and school tasks, girls achieve earlier and more readily. Furthermore, the fact that most teachers are women, especially in

[25] Williams, pp. 14–15.
[26] Haggard, pp. 396–398.
[27] G. A. Milton, "Sex Differences in Problem Solving as a Function of Role Appropriateness in the Problem Content," *Psychological Reports*, 5 (1959), 705–708.
[28] Pierce.

the elementary school, means that girls can identify more readily than boys with the teacher and her values.

Differences in Motivation and Cognitive Style

Some studies have found a close relationship between achievement motivation and scholastic achievement, while other studies have found low correlations between these variables. In interviews with students, Williams[29] found that high achievers held high internalized standards and goals for school success and tremendous inner pressure to compete and to succeed coupled with strong feelings of guilt when they did not do their homework. All of the students interviewed agreed that the inner pressure stemmed from their parents. Underachievers, on the other hand, reported difficulty in accepting increased responsibility for their own learning, a loss of closeness to the teacher when changing teachers, and a lack of inner goal, occupation orientation, and serious intention of going to college. Many enjoyed reading, but not school-assigned reading. Other studies have found that high-achieving and overachieving boys express a greater need for the value of achievement than do high and overachieving girls and underachieving boys and girls. Another study found that high achievers in high school regard college as preparation for graduate school and a professional career, while underachievers view college as direct vocational preparation.[30]

Overachievers and underachievers also differ in their cognitive styles and their approaches to learning tasks. Overachievers, in contrast to underachievers, are more empirical and excel in tasks where rote memory is useful or required. The relationships they see between objects and events are based on frequency of occurrence rather than on common attributes. Instead of formal analysis, they rely on past experiences in approaching new problems. Underachievers, on the other hand, are more analytic and more abstract in their cognitive activity, more prone to dig under the surface of a problem, and more likely to organize events in terms of formal characteristics.[31]

Differences in Self-Perceptions and Adjustment

Achievers and underachievers reveal markedly different perceptions of themselves and the school situation. Underachievers report that they are unable to do well in the classroom if their teacher does not organize well, dislikes them, ignores them, or if the teacher himself is disinterested in the subject. They are embarrassed in front of teachers, concerned about their reputations, and anxious whenever new material is not covered in class and they have to learn it for themselves at home. Achievers, on the other hand,

29 Williams, p. 16; J. V. Pierce, *Sex Differences in Achievement Motivation,* Cooperative Research Report No. 1097 (Washington, D.C.: Office of Education, U.S. Department of Health, Education and Welfare, 1962); J. S. Bruner and A. J. Caron, "Cognition, Anxiety, and Achievement in the Preadolescent." (Paper read at American Psychological Convention, 1959.)
30 Frankel, pp. 179–180.
31 Bruner and Caron.

report that they keep studying and trying even though the teacher is boring, has discipline problems, or is disinterested in his subject. They report that getting good grades is not always related to what is learned.[32] Achievers are somewhat more stable and confident than underachievers, and they score higher on tests of creativity.[33]

Studies of self-concept and achievement reported in Chapter 8 reveal that underachievers generally have less adequate self-concepts than do achievers. Underachieving boys, in particular, view themselves as inadequate, passive, reckless, mischievous, restless, and powerless to improve or change the situation. Raph, Goldberg, and Passow[34] found that high and low achievers do not differ significantly in self-estimates with respect to personal and social abilities and characteristics. They do, however, differ significantly on school-related or task-oriented items—suggesting that underachieving youths appraise realistically the discrepancy between their ability and their performance. There is also a tendency for high school underachievers to evaluate themselves as "pretty average" or "about like others." Seeing themselves as having higher ability holds little attraction, for this seems to promise only the dubious reward of higher expectations, which they feel themselves unable to fulfill, regardless of the effort they expend.

These studies also show that underachievers repeatedly identify a particular teacher as the cause of their failure. In addition to blaming teachers, however, underachievers also blame themselves. They say, for example, "If I just studied more . . . if I weren't so lazy . . . if I applied myself, I could do it." When asked for their reasons for not applying themselves, underachievers seem to be at a loss: "I keep on telling myself I'm going to try to do my best. But when the time comes, well, I get in trouble, and I can't help it. I don't know." It appears that irrational factors are operative and that some underachievers are unable to function effectively even when they try.

The prediction that underachievers have poorer personal adjustment than achievers is in large measure substantiated by research. Achievers have fewer antisocial tendencies, fewer social skills, and better family relations,[35] while underachievers complain, express dissatisfaction mixed with self-pity, and report a strong urge to escape from the pressures of school.[36] One study reported that hostility is more pronounced in bright male underachievers than in bright male achievers, but that achieving and underachieving girls do not differ significantly in expressions of hostility.[37] Haggard,[38] however,

[32] Williams, p. 15.

[33] Department of Special Services Staff, Champaign, Illinois, "Factors Associated with Underachievement and Overachievement of Intellectually Gifted Children," *Exceptional Children,* 28 (1961), 167–175.

[34] Jane B. Raph, Miriam L. Goldberg, and A. Harry Passow, *Bright Underachievers* (New York: Teachers College Press, Columbia University, 1966), pp. 181–183.

[35] J. C. Easton, "Some Personality Traits of Underachieving and Achieving High School Students of Superior Ability," *Bulletin of the Maritime Psychological Association,* 8 (1959), 34–39.

[36] Williams, p. 15.

[37] M. C. Shaw and J. Grubb, "Hostility and Able High School Underachievers," *Journal of Counseling Psychology,* 5 (1958), 263–266.

[38] Haggard, p. 394.

found more evidence of poor personal adjustment among high achievers than among low achievers. High achievers relieve their anxieties by intellectualizing and mastering new knowledge; however, they are also aggressive, persistent, hard driving and competitive. Some high achievers withdraw into themselves, while others are markedly passive and dependent upon outside sources for direction of their thoughts and actions.

The studies reviewed above present a highly generalized and incomplete picture of the underachiever. What is an underachiever really like? Consider the case of Jeff, as seen through the eyes of his teacher:

Jeff is eleven years old and is repeating the fifth grade. His IQ in the second grade on the California Test of Mental Maturity was 105 and on another form of the same test in the fourth grade his IQ was 99. Results of the California and Stanford Achievement tests show him to be from one to two grade levels below fifth grade in most subjects. His father is a polisher in a local industrial plant and his mother is a paint sprayer. Both of his parents have a high school education. He has two older sisters, one entering eighth grade and the other a sophomore in high school.

Last year's teacher made the following entry in Jeff's permanent record: "Jeff is an extremely nervous boy. He cannot force himself to be still and always has his mind elsewhere than on his studies. Though he always appears cheerful, I feel that he is extremely unhappy. He has often indicated that the other children do not like him, yet he goes out of his way to be a good sport. He has an exceptional sense of humor for his age and has a good mind. He daydreams frequently, at which times he appears sad. His feelings are easily hurt and he cries easily. Both parents are extremely concerned, and both work, and Jeff, seeking companionship, has gotten into several theft and vandalism problems after school."

SEPTEMBER 30

In my month's observation I have found him looking out of the window much of the time, even though his seat was on the opposite side of the room from the windows. I have had to remind him to watch his book when we are checking spelling or reading workbooks. Oftentimes I ask his opinion on a subject being discussed, then see him search his books to find what we are talking about. He has several times been kept after school because of disobeying one rule or another, usually for talking boisterously or not finishing work. He chews gum whenever he can get by with it.

OCTOBER 12

I was giving the individualized oral reading test furnished by the *Weekly Reader* magazine to all class members. When Jeff read to me, he read fairly well. When I questioned him about the main ideas he remembered all that he had read. I praised him for his performance and he just sat still in his seat, with slightly flushed face showing that he had heard me.

NOVEMBER 2

Today we were studying our *Weekly Reader* and one of the news items was about water skiing. Jeff paid close attention to this item although he had been looking out of the window up to this time. He volunteered the information that his father was an expert water skier. He said he goes to Cherokee Lake and can really do a lot of tricks on his skis. I remembered now how his first grade teacher had told of how much he talked about his father and of how proud he seemed to be of his father.

NOVEMBER 21

10:30 a.m. I mentioned to Jeff that tonight was P.T.A. and the night for the conference with his parents. He quickly said, "Miss Terrell, they won't come. They never come to P.T.A." I suggested that he remind them of the date anyway.

7:15 p.m. Jeff's parents came, even arriving ten minutes early for their conference. I showed them his achievement record and told them I was sure he knew more than the achievement scores reflected, but I thought it possible that Jeff had not kept his mind on the test when taking it. I pointed out that in his oral reading to me and consequent answering of questions he registered very good understanding and had a good memory for facts. His mother said she had asked him to read to her at home and he had little trouble with the words, and she, too, thought he understood what he was reading. We discussed his dreaminess, and the parents said that had been his trouble in other years.

His mother said Jeff was much interested in science and liked to read about that. She said he seemed to like our changing classes as we do in the subject block system this year. She said that practice would get the youngsters ready for later years in junior high. Both parents thanked me for letting them come in the evening as they said last year they had taken off work to come in the daytime and it was more convenient this way. They did not remain for P.T.A. meeting.

DECEMBER 1

In English we were studying outlining to give good reports orally. We had the beginning of an outline in our books which was to be finished. As I checked around the room, I noticed that Jeff was including items not in the story in the book. I asked him where he got those items. He said, "Well, they show in the picture!" I checked and found that he was quite right.

DECEMBER 5

Jeff's grades for the past six weeks in my room were as follows: Reading *D*, Writing *C⁻*, Spelling *C*, English *D⁺*. The social studies teacher gave me grades for him of *C* in geography and *D* in history. The math-science teacher has not yet reported. In the last six weeks he dropped one letter in reading, spelling, and almost two grades in English. He remained the same in writing and geography and came up one letter in history. English grade was low because of his not learning a poem, making a book report, or correcting wrong assignments. The requirements were heavier than last time.

DECEMBER 9

When Jeff received his grade card he asked me why he had gotten a *D* in reading. I had already explained his grades to him before, but he must not have remembered about the *D*. I got out my grade book and showed him that all of his *Weekly Reader* quizzes had been *F*, his workbook was unsatisfactory, and his seatwork exercise totals had given him an average score of 56 percent. Then I explained that I had raised the grade, really, because I knew that his oral work was better than *F* and I had given him the benefit of what he knew generally. He had a serious expression on his face all of the time I was talking. When I finished, he nodded, but turned away very slowly. He did not question his English grade, but I had also explained that to him earlier in the week.

I asked him to keep at his work steadily, not letting himself get lost in thought. I told him it was my belief that he forgot to keep at his work then realized he was not getting done and would hurry through his workbook pages just to get done and did not really try hard. He nodded slightly and went out of the room.

MARCH 16

Lately I have had a struggle with Jeff when I have insisted that he keep his desk free of notes to girls. Mrs. R., a sixth-grade teacher, related that some of the mothers of girls in our rooms are taking them by car to the theater and leaving them there, not realizing that inside the girls meet several boys who sit with them, hold hands, kiss them, cuddle up to them, etc. These boys are from their school class and Jeff is one of them.

By accident, someone on Jeff's telephone line lifted the receiver and heard a conversation Jeff had with Genevieve, one of his girl friends.

Jeff: Do you love me?

Genevieve: Yes.

Jeff: Do you love me a whole lot?

Genevieve: Yes, sure.

Jeff: Tonight my folks are going away and I want you to come over. Then you can really show me if you love me or not.

Jeff went on to say, "Oh, the things we can do!" Mrs. R. said the whole conversation was very suggestive.

These excerpts describe an underachiever who probably does not have high ability. It appears that Jeff has a long history of daydreaming and not completing his work. His parents appear cooperative, but not deeply concerned. We may make hypotheses concerning Jeff's poor school performance, but the record reveals few clues pointing to the likely causes for Jeff's low achievement.

Helping the Underachiever

Unfortunately, little research has been devoted to the development and evaluation of programs designed to help underachievers increase their scholastic performance. One of the few extensive programs for underachievers was carried out in one New York City high school and is reported by Raph, Goldberg, and Passow.[39] Initially, one tenth-grade class of gifted underachieving boys was assigned to the same teacher for homeroom and for social studies. It was hypothesized that if these students could share each other's problems and could at the same time become closely identified with and receive support from a teacher, their general school attitudes and performances would improve. Although some students did improve, the average marks earned by underachievers in this class were not significantly different from the average marks earned by matched underachievers in the regular school program.

In the eleventh grade, this special class was assigned to a social studies teacher who had been successful in working with honor students. This teacher, expecting high-quality performance, was unable to accept the erratic, tardy, and often slipshod work of these students. School marks dropped precipitously and resistance to the teacher was expressed in poor work and disturbing class behavior. The special class was placed with a different teacher in the second semester, a teacher who allowed more leeway in performance standards, showed interest in individual problems of students, and taught much-needed study skills. Although individual students showed improvements in school marks, at the end of two years the average marks received by members of this special group did not differ significantly from those of the underachieving control group. This experience seems to suggest that grouping underachievers together in a class may not be wise, since underachieving classmates tend to give each other negative support.

Placing other groups of underachievers in a special geometry class and in group-guidance and study-skill classes also resulted in no significant improvement in school marks. It appears that for many underachieving students underachievement becomes a deeply rooted way of life, unamenable to change through school efforts. If this is so, then perhaps preventive pro-

[39] Raph, Goldberg, and Passow, pp. 136–179.

grams, administered early in elementary school, would be more efficacious than curative programs, administered in later grades.

A similar approach to helping underachieving gifted pupils was used by Smith.[40] An eighth-grade class in arithmetic was organized so that three class sessions a week were devoted to subject matter and two class sessions a week were conducted as seminars. Through seminar discussions, efforts were made to help the students develop more adequate self-concepts. By the end of the year, 11 of the 16 students had shown some academic improvement, with 7 of these maintaining their level of progress through the ninth grade. Those improving in achievement were found to have replaced negative self-attitudes with positive ones.

The influence of a supportive adult in reducing underachievement by listening and reacting to a student's discussions of topics of personal interest was demonstrated by Raths[41] in a study cited in Chapter 16. In face-to-face conferences, a nonteaching adult, by providing empathic support, endeavored to help an underachiever clarify his attitudes, beliefs, interests, purposes, and aspirations. After one semester, the group of underachievers receiving this treatment registered a significant change toward higher rank-in-class and grade point average than did a control group of underachievers who had not received this treatment.

Can group counseling improve the mental health and academic performances of gifted underachieving students? In a study reported by Broedel and his associates,[42] four groups of 6 to 8 underachieving boys and girls met twice a week for eight weeks in group-counseling sessions. Following this group-counseling experience, students in experimental groups registered a significantly greater mean gain in acceptance of self and others than did students in control groups. However, the school grades and achievement-test scores of students in the experimental groups dropped, while those of students in the control groups improved or remained the same. Broedel concluded that group counseling does not result in increased school performance by underachievers unless closer cooperation between counselors and teachers leads to greater awareness of and provision for the needs of underachieving students. Greater success was obtained by Harris and Trotta,[43] who used group therapy with a group of 8 underachieving seventh-grade students in helping them to explore their attitudes toward school and to identify future goals. Six of the 8 made some improvement in school grades. Trotta and Smith, as well as Broedel, found that including disturbed or hostile students in a group with other underachievers impedes the therapeutic process and the progress of the total group.

[40] M. C. Smith, "Motivating the Underachieving Gifted Pupil in Junior High School," *Journal of Secondary Education*, 36 (1961), 79–82.

[41] James D. Raths, "Underachievement and a Search for Values," *Journal of Educational Sociology*, 34 (May 1961), 423–424.

[42] J. Broedel, M. Ohlsen, and F. Proff, "The Effects of Group Counseling on Gifted Underachievers." (Paper read at the American Psychological Association Convention, 1958.) Mimeographed.

[43] P. Harris and F. Trotta, "An Experiment with Underachievers," *Education*, 82 (1962), 347–349.

Will underachievers make greater progress if placed in a class of equally bright but achieving students (homogeneous grouping), or will they make greater progress in a classroom where there are varying levels of achievement (heterogeneous grouping)? Karnes and her associates,[44] in studying this problem in grades two to five, hypothesized that gifted underachievers placed in homogeneous classes with high achievers would be stimulated to raise their level of achievement, would become more creative, and would perceive their peers and parents as being more accepting of them than would underachieving intellectually gifted children in heterogeneous classes. Karnes and her associates found that underachievers in homogeneous classes make greater gains in achievement, score higher on a test of creativity, and express a greater acceptance and valuing of their parents than do underachieving gifted children placed in heterogeneous classes.

Summary

Nearly every teacher has seen in his classroom some students with physical, emotional, or mental handicaps that cause them to make little progress in school. These children have come to be referred to as exceptional children. An *exceptional child* is one who deviates intellectually, physically, socially, or emotionally so markedly from what is considered to be normal growth and development that he requires a special class or supplementary instruction and services. Two types of exceptional children which nearly every teacher encounters in the regular classroom are the emotionally disturbed child and the underachiever.

Of all the many kinds of students who need special help, the emotionally disturbed child is one whom the teacher in a regular classroom frequently finds most difficult to understand and to help. Disturbing behavior may be repetitious behavior, such as continual aggressiveness, distractions, or daydreaming; a serious single disturbance, such as a severe temper tantrum or sharp decline in academic performance; or a succession of different disturbances that may appear to be unrelated.

Many of the principles of behavior that increase our understanding of normal students are also useful in the study of the emotionally disturbed. When seeking to identify causes of behavior, the teacher is cautioned to avoid the assumption that one has explained behavior if he has given it a label or described its symptoms. Teachers are advised to weigh symptoms and to consider their relations to their assumed or known causes. Collecting reliable information about an emotionally disturbed student is a necessary first step toward helping him.

Characteristic of nearly all categories of emotional disturbance is high anxiety. Since a child's anxiety must be reduced before the child can make

[44] M. B. Karnes, G. McCoy, R. R. Zehrback, J. P. Wollersheim, and H. F. Clarizio, "The Efficacy of Two Organizational Plans for Underachieving Intellectually Gifted Children," *Exceptional Children,* 30 (May 1963), 438–446.

progress in mastering academic skills, the teacher must recognize manifestations of anxiety and modify the situation so as to reduce that anxiety. The anxieties of emotionally disturbed children may be reduced through selective programing and modification of curriculum content. A therapeutic curriculum for emotionally disturbed children should emphasize meaningful emotional content useful in explaining human action, should clarify emotional distortions, should define and classify emotions in terms of appropriateness or inappropriateness, and should teach the meaning of facial expressions and gestures.

Among the programs that have been developed to assist teachers in working with emotionally disturbed students are those that provide on-the-spot help to teachers of emotionally disturbed children or provide a "crisis teacher" in a school to work directly with these children when problems arise. Other approaches include a program of direct study of children involving the writing and analysis of case records and a program which helps teachers and their students, through a human relations approach, to gain insight into the underlying causes of behavior.

The problem of why many high-ability students do not achieve at levels commensurate with their potential has been for many years the focus of considerable concern on the part of educators. In general, an *underachiever* may be defined as a student whose academic performance, judged either by grades or achievement test scores, is markedly below his measured or demonstrated aptitude for academic achievement.

Studies of underachievement reveal that parents of underachievers are more authoritarian and less accepting of their children. There is greater confusion in the underachiever's home regarding the parental role, discipline, and parental expectations and standards of school success. Underachievers report that their parents lack firmness and seldom praise or support them. Underachievers experience little feeling of independence and are unfavorably compared with siblings. Social class, and ethnic, religious, and cultural identity appear to influence the student's achievement motivation and vocational aspiration.

Sex differences affect achievement. Underachievement among males appears to be a distinctly different phenomenon from underachievement among females. Underachieving boys are similar to overachieving girls in placing less value on achievement and showing less concern or anxiety over lack of achievement.

In cognitive activity, the underachiever tends to be more analytic, more abstract, and more likely to dig under the surface of a problem, while overachievers are more empirical and excel in tasks that require good memory. The self-concepts of male underachievers reveal that they see themselves as inadequate, mischievous, argumentative, and restless. Often, they feel alienated from society and family and do not accept the ideals, goals, and values of the dominant culture. Underachieving girls tend to be ambivalent in their feelings toward themselves. The poorer personal adjustment of underachievers is reflected in their antisocial tendencies, their poorer family relations, their complaining, their hostility, their dissatisfaction, and their strong urge to escape the pressures of school.

Few researchers have focused on helping the underachiever to improve his academic performance. Helping underachievers to clarify their attitudes, beliefs, and aspirations through empathic support appears to hold considerable promise for helping the underachiever to improve his academic performance. Placing gifted underachievers in classes with high achievers seems to result in the underachievers raising their academic performance. Several studies have noted, however, that placing underachievers together in one class or group may not be wise, since underachieving classmates tend to give each other negative support and block the progress of the group.

Study Questions

1. Describe the range of behaviors revealed by emotionally disturbed students at the maturity level you teach. What are some of the ways in which you would try to help these students?

2. Should a socially maladjusted student be placed in a regular or a special classroom? Defend your answer.

3. Which of the special programs for helping teachers understand and work with emotionally disturbed students that you have learned about appear best suited for helping you and the emotionally disturbed students whom you teach? Discuss.

4. What explanations would you offer for the seemingly limited understanding of the causes of underachievement that research studies have provided? What hypotheses would you offer to explain this phenomenon?

5. How would you account for the meager gains in achievement registered by groups of underachievers placed in special classroom and counseling groups? What approaches for helping underachievers would you suggest?

6. Should a student have a right to be an underachiever if he chooses, or should we deny him that right? Discuss.

Suggested Readings

Charlotte Buhler, Faith Smitter, and Sybil Richardson. *Childhood Problems and the Teacher*. New York: Holt, Rinehart and Winston, 1952. A book designed to give teachers an understanding of the dynamics of behavior problems. Case examples are presented to help the teacher ascertain what he may achieve in various circumstances and to identify the types of problems for which the teacher needs special assistance.

William M. Cruickshank and G. Orville Johnson. Editors. *Education of Exceptional Children and Youth*. Englewood Cliffs, New Jersey: Prentice-Hall, 1958. A book of readings presenting basic information on the education of the major groups of exceptional children. The first three chapters identify the major types of exceptionality, trace the historical development of special education, and describe current practices in special education. Chapter 13 discusses the education of socially maladjusted and emotionally disturbed children.

Nicholas J. Long, William C. Morse, and Ruth G. Newman. Editors. *Conflict in the Classroom*. Belmont, California: Wadsworth Publishing Co., 1965. A book of readings discussing methods of identifying, helping, teaching, and treating emotionally disturbed children in the classroom. Chapters 4 and 5 describe several types of school programs being used to help these students.

Jane B. Raph, Miriam L. Goldberg, and A. Harry Passow. *Bright Under-achievers*. New York: Teachers College Press, Columbia University, 1966. Reviews studies of underachievement and reports the findings of two extensive studies of underachievement conducted by the Horace Mann-Lincoln Institute of Teachers College, Columbia University.

Films

The Exceptional Child: The Socially Maladjusted Child, 16 mm, sound, black and white, 29 min. Bloomington, Indiana: Audio-Visual Center, Indiana University (rental fee, $5.40). Discusses the problems of the socially maladjusted child and explains the causes and factors related to the development of maladjustment. Interviews with a delinquent boy and the parent of a socially maladjusted youngster are shown.

Problem of Pupil Adjustment: The Drop-Out, 16 mm, sound, black and white, 20 min. Bloomington, Indiana: Audio-Visual Center, Indiana University (rental fee, $4.15). Examines the reasons why the school failed to meet the needs of Steve Martin, who dropped out of school as soon as the law permitted. Emphasizes the importance of a life-adjustment program in the school and of relating class subjects to the interests of the students.

Problem of Pupil Adjustment: The Stay-in, 16 mm, sound, black and white, 19 min. Bloomington, Indiana: Audio-Visual Center, Indiana University (rental fee $4.15). Shows how a school which concentrates on meeting the needs of students may reduce the number of dropouts.

21

teaching and the educative process

The degree to which I can create relationships which facilitate the growth of others as separate persons is a measure of the growth I have achieved in myself.

≡ CARL R. ROGERS

Creating the conditions that facilitate optimum development and learning calls for effective teaching. There is little agreement, however, on the criteria that should be used for judging effective teaching or on how the effectiveness of teaching can be measured. By examining briefly some of the approaches that have been used to define and measure teaching effectiveness, we may be able to gain a clearer understanding of the problem.

If the goal of the educative process is to bring about certain desired changes in pupils, an obvious way of assessing a teacher's effectiveness is to measure the extent to which these changes actually occur under the teacher's tutelage. Judging teacher effectiveness in this manner is not as simple as it appears; difficulties arise in measuring pupil growth and in determining precisely how much of the change can be directly attributed to the teacher. It is difficult to obtain comparable measures of pupil growth for pupils who differ in aptitudes, initial level of learning, and rate of intellectual development. The difficulty of determining precisely what changes can be attributed to the teacher relates to our inability to distinguish between what the present learning situation and what past learning situations have each contributed to a student's present performance.

Another approach to the problem of judging teacher effectiveness has been to identify, according to some external criterion, a group of "effective" teachers and a contrasting group of "ineffective" teachers. The external criterion chosen might be the gain students have made on a standardized achievement test or the independence and flexibility students demonstrate in solving problems. A large number of teacher-characteristics studies have been conducted for the purpose of discovering which traits or combinations of traits are closely associated with the chosen criterion of teacher effectiveness. Finding that certain traits are highly correlated with the criterion would permit one to predict that an individual possessing these traits would become an effective teacher. However, the results of most of these studies have been disappointing. For a host of variables (including intelligence, mastery of subject matter, age, experience, cultural background, socioeconomic status, sex, marital status, teaching attitude, teaching aptitude, job interest, voice quality, and special abilities), little or no relationship has·been found with teaching effectiveness.

The view that effective teaching is a matter of acquiring certain competencies is also open to question. Combs[1] points out that we can seldom prescribe what a beginner should do by examining what an expert does. Some methods used by the expert can only be used because he is an expert. An experienced teacher, for example, may have learned to deal with classroom disturbances by ignoring them, but the beginning teacher dare not ignore them. Moreover, the development of long lists of competencies has the discouraging effect of setting impossible goals of excellence. The fallacy of using particular competencies as a measure of good teaching, irrespective of personalities, situations, or purposes, is evident when we realize that by such a criterion some of the people who taught us most would be classified as poor teachers! The difficulties in defining and assessing effective teaching have been summarized by Ellena, Stevenson, and Webb:

> There appears to be no such single person as the universally effective teacher. Teaching is a complex of professions, each widely differing in requirements and activities. Teaching is as complex as the educational process in the modern world.[2]

The relatively fruitless efforts that have been expended in attempts to identify characteristics of effective teaching have led to a new and quite

[1] Arthur W. Combs, *The Professional Education of Teachers* (Boston: Allyn and Bacon, 1965), pp. 4–6.

[2] William J. Ellena, Margaret Stevenson, and Harold V. Webb, *Who's a Good Teacher?* (Washington, D.C.: American Association of School Administrators, Department of Classroom Teachers of the N.E.A., National School Board Association, 1961), p. 36.

different conception of teaching. This new conception of teaching centers in *what the teacher is,* his personal sense of being and becoming, rather than in what the teacher does. This does not reflect a view of the teacher as passive. Rather, it reflects a view of the teacher's activity as a response to the personal meanings that emerge from his analysis and understanding of his students' needs, perceptions, and self-concepts, as well as his own needs, perceptions, and self-concept. According to this view, what the teacher does in the teaching-learning encounter is done in response not to some prescription of effective teaching but to the personal meanings of the encounter with students.

A Model of Effective Teaching

Our model of effective teaching consists of a series of propositions presented as guidelines for facilitating optimum development and learning. The model of effective teaching is admittedly global and utopian. In our view, effective teaching should not be judged by the number of students who achieved a given criterion score on an achievement test. Our concern is with broader and more fundamental changes in behavior. In our view, teaching should be judged effective to the degree that both students and teacher are observed during and following a learning experience to be self-involved and actively engaged in the search for the meaning and relevance of ideas and problems that perplex them. In short, learning is effective to the degree that it stimulates students and teacher to engage in self-initiated searches for increased understanding. This type of behavior is most characteristic of what has been variously described as the self-actualizing person,[3] the fully-functioning person,[4] or the adequate personality.[5] This is an individual who is experiencing self-fulfillment, who is becoming that which he is capable of being.

1. The effective teacher is involved and concerned with people. Involvement with and concern for others is the hallmark of a real human being in the full meaning of the term. The teacher's involvement and concern is centered in his students and in their development and learning. What a teacher is and does must, of necessity, relate to those whom he seeks to guide and help. Too many teachers view their task as teaching subjects or skills rather than as helping people to grow and to learn. While effective teaching certainly calls for much more than being involved and concerned, optimum learning of students is unlikely to occur when these qualities are lacking in the teacher-pupil relationship.

Kelley describes the stake which the fully functioning person has in

[3] A. H. Maslow, *Motivation and Personality* (New York: Harper & Row, 1954).

[4] Carl R. Rogers, *On Becoming a Person* (Boston: Houghton Mifflin Co., 1961).

[5] Arthur W. Combs and Donald Snygg, *Individual Behavior* (New York: Harper & Row, 1959).

others: "He has a selfish interest in those around him and has responsibility in some degree for that quality."[6] The concepts of involvement and concern are expressed in a question by Rogers: "How can I promote a relationship which this person may use for his own personal growth?"[7] Combs describes the adequate personality as having a strong identification with others: "Warmth and humanity come easily to these people as a logical outgrowth of their feeling of oneness with their fellows."[8]

The introductions to two case records reveal something of the involvement and concern which two teachers felt for two students:

> When John was given written assignments to do in school, he would write only one or two sentences. They were so poorly written that they were not legible compared to the work of his peer group. This peer group did not accept him. I thought this would be a good opportunity to try to help John to overcome his writing difficulty and also help him to be accepted by his peer group.

> I selected the child designated in this study by his nickname Skippy as the most normal child in my room. I also had a personal desire to attain a more sympathetic understanding of children of the Jewish faith, who now form about 50 percent of my class membership.

2. *The effective teacher is accepting and empathic in relating to others.* A teacher can hardly be involved with and concerned about his students without at the same time experiencing an acceptance of and empathy for them. Indeed, the teacher's involvement and concern are expressed in his acceptance of students as worthwhile, valued individuals, each possessing potentialities for growth and fulfillment.

The focus of the teaching-learning experience is upon what happens to people. Of primary interest and concern are the changes in pupils' development and learning that emerge from the teaching-learning activity. Effective teaching, however, also enhances the growth of the teacher. Few would doubt that teachers learn much from their students, but this learning does not occur automatically. Learning from students is most likely to occur when the teacher is open, perceptive, and sensitive to the feelings as well as the words of students. Involvement, concern, acceptance, and empathy between teacher and pupils are realized only when there is free, open communication between them.

The learning of the teacher from his pupils may take many forms. Frequently, teaching provides opportunities to achieve insights into how people learn or fail to learn. Students' comments, questions, and illustrations

---

[6] Earl C. Kelley, "The Fully Functioning Self," in Arthur W. Combs, *Perceiving, Behaving, Becoming* (Washington: Association for Supervision and Curriculum Development, 1962), p. 18.

[7] Rogers, p. 32.

[8] Combs, *Perceiving, Behaving, Becoming,* pp. 54–55.

will often illuminate meaning and significance in concepts the teacher may not have thought of or considered. If given freedom, encouragement, and opportunities to interact, students will raise significant issues that may never have occurred to the teacher.

The qualities of acceptance and empathy are discussed by Rogers:

> . . . When I can accept another person, which means specifically accepting the feelings and attitudes and beliefs that are a real and vital part of him, then I am assisting him to become a person. . . . If I can provide a certain type of relationship, the other person will discover within himself the capacity to use that relationship for growth, and change and personal development will occur.[9]

A teacher's acceptance and empathy toward children may be revealed in a variety of ways, as the following excerpts show.

FEBRUARY 9

During our sharing periods the past two weeks the children have shared their hobbies with other members of the class. When John's turn came, he went up in front of the room and said, "Class, I want you to see my new dinosaur model. It is a trachodon, and it was a vegetarian. Trachodon means 'rough-toothed.' They spent most of their time in water. They had about two thousand teeth. Their worst and greatest enemy was tyrannosaurus rex. These creatures died out by the end of the crustacean period." John pranced back and forth in front of the class as he talked on for more than twenty minutes about the trachodon.

Finally, Beth cut in, "Don't you know about anything else? I'm sick of hearing about dinosaurs."

John's smile faded; he stuck out his lip and said, "Well, they're important to me."

Mrs. W. volunteered, "Most of us have hobbies or activities which seem almost as important to us as eating. Frank likes baseball, Frances is thrilled with every new addition to her collection of foreign dolls, and for John it is dinosaurs. We have learned a lot today from John about dinosaurs and we will be counting on John to give us more information about dinosaurs when we begin to study about them in two weeks." John's face broke into a smile as he took his seat.

FEBRUARY 23

Barbara came to me this morning and said, "Mrs. C., I'm in the best group in arithmetic. Don't you think I'm doing all right?" I told her I thought she was doing very well with our new work in fractions. "Why,

9 Rogers, pp. 21, 33.

then," she asked, "did you call my father and tell him I was failing and would have to do a lot of practicing?" (I was caught!)

I said, "Barbara, some practicing is good for all of us, but I'm afraid your father misunderstood. I'll arrange a conference with him and we'll talk it over." (I have not even talked to the father. I get no response to requests for conferences.)

FEBRUARY 17

Ben is a thirteen-year-old slow learner attending a rural school in a mining community. A photographer's representative gave me a sample package of six small photos and one enlargement of a girl with braided hair. Ben said, "Please, Mrs. K., give me one of them."

I said, "Ben, you don't know this girl."

He said, "That doesn't make any difference."

Davy said, "I bet Ben wants it because she looks something like Carol." He turned around and said, "Ben, is that the reason?"

Ben said, "Yes, she has pretty braids like Carol has." I asked what he would do with it. He said he wanted it to put in his room to make it pretty.

Davy said, "Don't give them to Ben. Give them to Stover, Lynn, Barry, and me." (Davy is always trying to strive for recognition from these boys. He rejected Ben on choice of work partners in the sociometric test.)

Ben looked at me with a hurt look. I said, "Ben, whom would you like me to give them to?"

He said, "I don't care, but I would like to have just one."

I said, "All right, you make your choice since I have six small ones and one large one."

He gave a big grin and said, "Gee, thanks, I'll take the big one and tack it on the wall in my room where I sleep." I gave the smaller pictures to Davy and the boys he had chosen.

3. *The effective teacher accepts and understands himself.* The involvement, concern, acceptance, and empathy of the teacher for others, especially his students, are dependent upon the continuing personal growth of the teacher himself. Acceptance of others is not a quality that suddenly appears fully developed. A number of studies have shown that acceptance of others is achieved to the degree that one accepts himself. In analyzing client statements made during therapy, Sheerer[10] found that there was a substantial and significant positive relationship between expressed attitudes of acceptance of self and expressed acceptance of others.

Self-acceptance and self-understanding are of primary importance in the individual's full development of his potentialities. Fromm points out that concern for others and concern for self are neither alternatives nor opposites.

[10] Elizabeth T. Sheerer, "An Analysis of the Relationship between Acceptance for Self and Acceptance and Respect for Others," *Journal of Consulting Psychology,* 13 (June 1949), 169–175.

Self-love does not imply selfishness. The ability to love productively springs from a love of self. If one can love only others, he cannot love at all. Fromm concludes, "Just as one has to know another person and his real needs in order to love him, one has to know one's own self in order to understand what the interests of the self are and how they can be served."[11]

Rogers,[12] in his description of a growth-facilitating therapeutic relationship, states that when the therapist is open, genuine, warm, positive, acceptant, and empathic in his relationship with his client, then the client, finding someone else listening acceptantly to his feelings, little by little becomes able to listen to himself. As he expresses more and more hidden and shameful aspects of self, the therapist shows a consistent and unconditional positive regard for him and his feelings. Gradually, the client begins to take the same attitude toward himself; he begins to accept himself as he is and is therefore ready to move forward in the process of becoming. The quality of reciprocal self-acceptance achieved in such a therapeutic relationship holds considerable promise for interpersonal relationships in the classroom. As teachers genuinely come to accept themselves, they have a greater readiness to accept students. Self-acceptance in the one has the effect of encouraging reciprocal self-acceptance in the other.

The emphasis that Combs places on self-acceptance in the development of the adequate personality also has implications for effective teaching. The primary quality of the adequate personality is a positive view of self. An individual with an adequate personality sees himself as liked, wanted, accepted, able, and as having dignity, integrity, worth, and importance. It is important that a student preparing to become a teacher feel that "It is all right to be me," and that "This self with which I begin can become a good teacher."[13]

Rogers[14] has indicated that self-acceptance tends to free the individual from guilt and anxiety, which distort his feelings about and perceptions of himself. When one accepts himself, he is able to view himself and his world with increased openness and objectivity, qualities essential to self-understanding.

In the following excerpts the teachers of John and Skippy each demonstrate qualities of self-acceptance and self-understanding:

OCTOBER 31

On Saturday evening, October 29, I helped seat people at the church supper. Today, before school started, John said, "Mrs. W., you sure seated a lot of people Saturday night. You must have enjoyed doing it because you kept on smiling."

[11] Erich Fromm, *Man for Himself* (New York: Holt, Rinehart and Winston, 1947), p. 134.
[12] Rogers, pp. 61–63.
[13] Combs, *The Professional Education of Teachers,* p. 100.
[14] Rogers, pp. 183–198.

I said, "Yes, I did enjoy seeing a lot of people that I hadn't seen for a long time."

He said with a big grin, "I sure had fun."

NOVEMBER 15

Skippy was lingering around my desk, obviously with something to say. So finally I asked, "What is it, Skippy? The thing to do is to say it and get it over with and it won't trouble you."

Skippy blurted out, "Miss Denham, you weren't fair this morning." (He looked as if it had been an effort to say it.)

Teacher: "In what way?"

Skippy: "You don't like Jackie, and this morning you let it show. You were meaner to him than you are to any of the rest of us."

Teacher: "How, Skippy? I simply told him to stay in his seat."

Skippy: "Oh, it wasn't what you said. It was the way you said it. You weren't friends."

(This is an embarrassingly accurate observation. The child in question is the whiney, immature type I find difficult to sympathize with.)

Because of his marked progress in reading during the fall semester Skippy was transferred to the higher, A section of fifth grade. On February 17, Miss Denham saw Skippy and asked him how he liked the A section.

Skippy: "Not so well. I can do the work so far and the kids are nice, but I liked the B section better. You know those kids have it tough."

Teacher: "How?"

Skippy: "Well, A kids are brighter and can do more. No matter how hard they try the B kids can't 'cause they're dumber. Why are some kids dumber than others?"

Teacher: "Lots of reasons. Environment, homes, heredity, opportunity, illness, handicaps."

Skippy: "Why didn't God make everyone equal?"

Teacher: "Probably because he realized it would be uninteresting if we were all alike, don't you think?"

Skippy: "That isn't what I meant. Why are some kids dumb and why are you deaf?"

Teacher: "I don't know that exact answer, but I do know I'm not deaf because God wanted it that way. I had an ear disease that medical men didn't know enough to prevent or control. As they learn more about it, that form of deafness will disappear and that is the reason it is so important to be eager to learn. Sometimes we help scientists by money contributions to have freedom to learn, and their knowledge removes our inequalities. Make sense?"

Skippy: "Un-huh, but it's tough on the guys who have the inequalities."

4. An effective teacher is knowledgeable and well informed.   Doing an effective job of teaching is a demanding and difficult task. To be effective, a teacher needs to acquire both depth and breadth of knowledge about the subject, content, and skills he is communicating, the learners whom he is helping and guiding, and the learning process.

Many would agree that learning involves much more than merely acquiring information. In an earlier discussion of perception, we noted that knowledge does not exist in its own right before learning begins. Rather, knowledge is unique to the individual, is subjectively held, and is a product of experience. Kelley points out that "we can of course learn from others, but we can only learn those parts of what others can offer which we can fit into our experience and purposes."[15]

Learning, as Combs has suggested, is the acquisition of personal meanings from the data of one's experience: "Any piece of information will have its effect upon behavior in the degree to which an individual discovers its personal meaning."[16] Content, then, must be meaningful to the teacher as well as his students, but a fact, concept, or principle may be expected to mean something quite different for each. Instead of collecting facts, teachers need skills for discovering meaning in facts and for helping students to discover their own meanings in facts.[17]

The teacher may help students to discover personal meanings in facts, concepts, and experiences by helping them to accept and clarify their feelings about events and concepts they encounter. If this is done, learning is likely to be related to the fulfillment of students' purposes rather than the teacher's purposes.

It is probably more difficult now than ever before for the teacher or any professional person to remain knowledgeable and well informed. We are witnessing an explosion of knowledge of awesome proportions. The consequences of this knowledge explosion are profound. One of the most significant of these is the growing tendency to view the human being as an *infor-*

[15] Earl C. Kelley, *Education for What Is Real* (New York: Harper & Row, 1947), p. 62.
[16] Arthur W. Combs, "Personality Theory and Its Implications for Curriculum Development," in Alexander Frazier, *Learning More About Learning* (Washington, D.C.: Association for Supervision and Curriculum Development, N.E.A., 1959), pp. 5–20.
[17] Combs, *The Professional Education of Teachers,* pp. 44–47.

mation processor rather than as a collector or storer of knowledge. In a world in which it is becoming virtually impossible to know everything, even in one's limited field of interest, the importance of education in helping learners to clarify personal meanings and to become skilled processors of data is clearly evident. Knowledge in the form of facts and information is no longer the mark of an educated man. Rather, the educated person is now one who is continuously developing new processing skills required to cope with the problems posed by an increasingly complex world.

As a second implication of the knowledge explosion, if teachers and others are to continue to be knowledgeable and well informed, they must become *lifelong learners*. A teacher may be fairly well informed in his major field when he completes an undergraduate or graduate program, but he will not remain well informed unless he continues to study and to grow. It is imperative that the teacher keep abreast of developments in the subject fields he teaches and in the field of education.

One of the ways in which teachers may further their knowledge of their profession is through participation in such projects as child-study programs. Evaluations of one child-study program have revealed that teachers participating in this type of professional study increase their knowledge of children and youth and that they utilize classroom practices that are more frequently associated with better rather than poorer teaching.[18] Lehman[19] found that among the teachers of one school system who participated in a child- and youth-study program, 73 percent of those teaching in junior high school and 63 percent of those teaching in elementary school were rated higher by their principals in the spring than they had been in the fall. Other factors undoubtedly contributed to these gains, but it can be presumed that participation in child and youth study was a contributing factor.

Greene[20] found from analyses of their case records on children that teachers participating in a three-year child-study program became increasingly more positive in their ways of handling children and showed steady and significant decreases in their use of negative methods of handling children. Teachers who used more positive methods stimulated positive responses from children, whereas teachers who used more negative methods stimulated negative responses. Other studies have shown that during three years of participation in a program of child study, teachers increased in their ability to analyze and to draw sound conclusions from case-study data and revealed greater sensitivity to and use of human-development principles.[21]

5. *The effective teacher is one who gives of himself in helping others to grow, to learn, and to become.* This proposition seems to express the

---

[18] Richard M. Brandt and Hugh V. Perkins, "Research Evaluating a Child Study Program," *Monographs of the Society for Research in Child Development*, 21 (1956), 62.

[19] Inez W. Lehman, "Evaluation of the Individual Child Study Groups in Long Beach, California" (unpublished master's thesis, Stanford University, 1952).

[20] John D. Greene, "Changes in Curriculum Practices of Teachers Who Participated in Child Study" (unpublished doctor's dissertation, University of Maryland, 1952).

[21] Brandt and Perkins, 35–38, 68–76.

essence of what it means to be a teacher. Rogers[22] offers several clues as to how a teacher may help a learner to grow, to learn, and to become. Rogers specifies the attributes of a true "helper": genuineness and transparency on the part of the "helper," warm acceptance and personal valuing of the one being helped, and an ability to see the world and the self of the other person as the other sees them. A person experiencing a relationship based on these qualities may be expected to become more integrated and more effective, more similar to the person he would like to be, more self-directing and self-confident, more understanding and acceptant of others, and better able to cope with problems of life in a more adequate and comfortable manner.

A helping relationship between a teacher and students may manifest itself through many different responses and activities. The following[23] are some general patterns of helping relationships:

1. Children are free to express what they feel and seem secure in their knowledge that the teacher likes them as they are.
2. Goals are clearly defined; structure is understood and accepted by the group.
3. Within appropriate limits, children are given responsibility and freedom to work.
4. Less teacher domination; more faith that children can find answers satisfying to them.
5. Less teacher talk; more listening to children, allowing them to use the teacher and the group as a sounding board when ideas are explored.
6. Less questioning for the right answer, more open-ended questions with room for differences and exploration of many answers.
7. More acceptance of mistakes. The very process of becoming involves the challenge of new experiences, of trying the unknown, all of which necessarily results in some mistakes being made.
8. The teacher communicates clearly to children that learning is self-learning. Faith is demonstrated that all children want to become and pupils show satisfaction as they become aware of their growth.

A teacher who possesses a fair measure of the qualities which we have enumerated has numerous opportunities for helping a student to develop, to learn, and to become. One teacher with the qualities necessary to establish a helping relationship is Mrs. W., who is portrayed in the following excerpts.

DECEMBER 5

The class was in line to get dressed for physical education period. John was sitting at his desk and his P.E. clothes were in his hands. I asked, "John, aren't you going to dress for P.E. today?"

[22] Rogers, pp. 37–38.
[23] From Combs, *Perceiving, Behaving, Becoming*, p. 237.

He put his head down and said in a low, defeated-like voice, "I don't want to dress for P.E. I can't do the things the other pupils can do anyway. Could I please be excused from dressing?"

I said in a kindly and encouraging voice, "John, you may be excused but *please try* to do what the class does. *You can if you try.* Nearly everyone has some things in life that are hard for them to do. I had trouble learning to roller skate when I was a little girl. I always say, 'Practice makes perfect.' " The class said, "Come on, John. We will help you."

He lifted his head and said with a big smile, "I'll try real hard." The rest of the children dressed and all went to P.E. class.

DECEMBER 16

We were writing stories about our pets. The results and participation were very good. Each child had his story ready to correct by the middle of the period. John brought his story on "Dinosaurs" to me, smiled, and said, "When I show effort I can really accomplish things that I want to do and have it ready on time." His story was good and no corrections had to be made.

I patted him on the back and said, "John, I am real proud of the job you have done. Please keep that effort 'alive'!"

He smiled and said, "OK."

MARCH 6

After school we were talking about the short unit we had planned on dinosaurs. I said, "John, since your hobby is the study of dinosaurs, I would like for you to take charge. We have planned and formed our questions. But you don't always complete your other assignments."

He jumped up like a Jack-in-the-box and in a very loud voice said, "Completing the assignments is no problem—I'll get them done! If I take charge, will you call me 'Professor'? I am so excited!"

The following excerpt illustrates the helping relationship of Miss Denham with Skippy, one of her fifth-grade students:

JANUARY 24

Skippy asked me for a conference to discuss the poor test grades he had received recently. Skippy asked me to write a note to his parents explaining the situation, as Skippy's father has been very critical of his low marks. In the note, I explained Skippy's request for the note, that I felt that he did not need a tutor because he was very capable of doing the work and a tutor might make him weaker because he would rely on outside help, that his low grades were due to a phase of poor conduct which I felt was already past, that Skippy had made nearly a year's progress in reading in a half year by standard measurements and I thought that should be considered good.

Skippy read the note and asked, "Will you please change that to Mr. Roth? Dad gets mad because teachers always send everything to Mom."

I changed my greeting from Dear Mrs. Roth to Dear Mr. and Mrs. Roth.

Skippy: "You see Dad always shows up when things go wrong, gets the wrong idea, and raises Cain. I go to Maine to camp every year and it's grand there. The very day Mom and Dad came to see me one of the kids hit me in the face with a hard ball and I had a couple of teeth out and some stitches in my lip when Dad saw me. He nearly had a fit and wanted to bring me right home. I had an awful hard time showing him it was just an accident and the camp does take care of us."

Teacher: "He wants you to be just about perfect, doesn't he?"

Skippy: "I guess that's it."

Teacher: "I wonder if you can realize that that might be one of your troubles, Skippy. You are trying so hard to please your Dad on tests that maybe you guess rather than think. I really thought you could read better than your reading score indicated because you tried to read too fast and made too many mistakes."

Skippy: "Maybe, I'm always scared."

Teacher: "Couldn't you face the fact that you are trying to do your best on tests and let it go at that?"

Skippy: "I can try. There's one thing more. Could you please let me take that spelling test over and not tell Dad?"

Teacher (At this point wisdom deserted me and I decided in favor of the golden rule): "Yes."

Skippy: "Gee, thanks. You're a pal."

The model of the effective teacher presented above has focused more on what the teacher is than upon specific characteristics of what he does. We do not wish to leave the impression that our effective teacher is a superman or superwoman. Effective teachers may be found in nearly every school. Many, indeed, are superior persons, and most have developed capacities for continuous self-growth. As one studies the chapters of this book in seeking an understanding of the ways in which the processes of human development and learning influence the becoming of children and youth, the sensitive, growing teacher cannot help reflecting on how these same processes, motivational, physical, cultural, and psychological, have shaped his own life. It is true that our personalities have been formed by many influences, both favorable and unfavorable, and that over some of these influences we had little control.

Summary

The relatively fruitless efforts that have been made to identify the characteristics of effective teaching have led to the development of a conception of teaching centering in what a teacher *is,* his personal sense of being and becoming, rather than on what a teacher *does.* This concept of effective teaching is expressed in the teacher's unique responses to the personal meanings of his encounter with students.

We propose a model of effective teaching consisting of five propositions that define dimensions of the process of facilitating optimum development and learning. The guidelines or criteria embodied in the propositions of the model define the effective teacher's role in the teaching-learning activity. The five propositions of the model are as follows:

1. The effective teacher is involved and concerned with people.
2. The effective teacher is accepting and empathic in relating to others.
3. The effective teacher accepts and understands himself.
4. The effective teacher is knowledgeable and well informed.
5. The effective teacher is one who gives of himself in helping others to grow, to learn, and to become.

Education is predicated on the belief that people can change. An understanding of human development and learning offers a key to the continual growth and becoming of both students and teacher.

Study Questions

1. Some educators have suggested that a major task of preservice teacher education is to help prospective teachers develop a view of teaching that is not confined to the view they acquired as students. What are some of the reasons why students' attitudes toward teaching are often more strongly influenced by what they have experienced as students than by what has been communicated in professional courses in teacher education?
2. Write out a brief description of one of the best teachers you have ever had. In what ways are the qualities of your best teacher similar to or different from those of the effective teacher presented in this chapter?
3. What kinds of experiences should prospective teachers have to enable them to develop the qualities suggested by the model of effective teaching? Discuss.

4. Are all persons capable of achieving a measure of self-understanding? What factors or experiences would likely contribute to self-understanding and what ones might be expected to limit one's understanding of himself? Discuss.

Suggested Readings

Nathaniel Cantor. *The Teaching-Learning Process*. New York: Holt, Rinehart and Winston, 1953. Presents an analysis of the teaching-learning process. The meaning of the ideas presented are explored by the author and a seminar group of teachers. Emphasized are the importance of the learner wanting to learn, a classroom atmosphere that is accepting and reality-centered, and concern both for the needs of the child and the needs of society.

Arthur W. Combs. Chairman. *Perceiving, Behaving, Becoming*. Washington, D.C.: Association for Supervision and Curriculum Development, 1962. Contains papers by Kelley, Maslow, Rogers, and Combs describing the qualities of the fully functioning, self-actualizing, truly adequate personality. The implications of the concept of the adequate personality for teaching and learning are discussed.

Arthur W. Combs. *The Professional Education of Teachers*. Boston: Allyn and Bacon, 1965. Discusses the implications for teaching of perceptual psychology—which is deeply concerned with people, values, perceptions, and man's eternal search for being and becoming—and the problem of improving teacher education.

Clark E. Moustakas. *The Alive and Growing Teacher*. New York: Philosophical Library, 1959. Describes the emotional atmosphere, the conditions, and the processes of learning of a group of teachers and principals meeting regularly in a group experience led by the author. Group members examine openly in a climate of support and acceptance their experiences with children and fellow teachers and gain new insights into the feeling and thinking of the problems they have discussed.

Marie I. Rasey. *This Is Teaching*. New York: Harper & Row, 1950. Translates into concrete terms the abstractions of the holistic approach to personality growth as these relate to teaching and learning. Presents the dialogue of members of a university seminar in which the holistic approach to personality growth was implemented by teacher and students.

Carl R. Rogers. *On Becoming a Person*. Boston: Houghton Mifflin Co., 1961. Contains a series of lectures and papers by the author in which he describes the meanings that have emerged from theory and research in client-centered therapy. Discusses the implications of these concepts for facilitating the becoming of people in general. Chapters which discuss the helping relationship, the facilitation of personal growth, and the fully functioning person are particularly relevant to the role of teaching.

Films

Guiding the Growth of Children, 16 mm, sound, black and white, 18 min. Bloomington, Indiana: Audio-Visual Center, Indiana University (rental fee, $4.65). Shows through the personal experiences of a fifth-grade teacher that guiding the growth of the student, as an individual, is the most important part of the teacher's job.

If These Were Your Children, Part I, 16 mm, sound, black and white, 28 min.; Part II, 16 mm, sound, black and white, 21 min. New York: Metropolitan Life Insurance Co., 1 Madison Avenue (no charge). Shows how a concerned, accepting, and knowledgeable second-grade teacher provides a stimulating, growth-facilitating environment enhancing the development and learning of a second-grade class. Specific problems of development and individual differences among children are highlighted.

author index

case index

subject index

Discriminated operant, 352
Displacement:
 and acquired motives, 55
 as an adjustment pattern, 237
 in Freudian psychology, 200
DNA (deoxyribonucleic acid), 80,
 337
Drives:
 curiosity, 57–58
 exploratory, 57
 as motives, 45
 primary, 50–51
 secondary, 50, 350–351
Dynamic organization, 79

Early adolescence:
 characteristics, 305–310
 emotional development, 311–313
 physical development, 310–311
 psychological development, 314–
 315
 social development, 311–313
Early adulthood:
 characteristics, 315–319
 personal development, 323–325
 physical development, 319–320
 psychological development, 323–
 325
 social development, 320–323
Early elementary childhood:
 characteristics, 273–277
 mental development, 279–280
 physical development, 277–278
 social development, 278–279
Educational Testing Service, 532–533
Ego, 200
Electra complex, 115
Emotion (*see also* Affect, Self-adjustment):
 disabling effects, 226–228
 physiological basis, 225–226
 and self-adjustment, 224–225
Emotional climate, 112–114
Emotional response patterns, 231–232
Emotional stress, 226–228
Emotionally disturbed student:
 characteristics, 551–553

Emotionally disturbed student (continued)
 helping teachers understand, 560–
 563
 methods for helping, 554–560
 studying, 553–554
Energy:
 and behavior, 81–88
 body's uses, 81–82
 conservation, 75
 cycle, 76–77
 expended in mental activity, 82
 expended in muscular activity, 81
Energy change, 45
Energy levels:
 differences by age, 85–86
 differences by sex, 87–88
 effects of dietary deficiency, 82–83
 effects of emotional factors, 84
 effects of fatigue, 84
 effects of physical defects, 83–84
 effects of poor health, 83
 individual differences, 86–87
Entropy, 75
Enzymes, 78
Errors of measurement, 520
Evaluation (*see also* Measurement):
 as a process, 508–509
 defined, 508
 in learning, 510–511
 strategies in instruction, 511–515
Evaluation methods:
 observation of behavior, 532, 534–
 535
 projects and papers, 536
 reliability, 520
 requirements, 515–520
 standardized achievement tests,
 536–538
 teacher-made tests, 521–532
 validity, 520–521
Exceptional child, 550–551
Excitatory potential, 349

Family:
 as a cultural institution, 136
 declining influence, 3–4
 influence of ordinal position on se-